LIBERTY, EQUALITY, POWER

A History of the American People
Volume II: Since 1863

SEVENTH EDITION

John M. Murrin
Princeton University, Emeritus

Pekka Hämäläinen
University of Oxford

Paul E. Johnson
University of South Carolina, Emeritus

Denver Brunsman
George Washington University

James M. McPherson
Princeton University, Emeritus

Alice Fahs
University of California, Irvine

Gary Gerstle
University of Cambridge

Emily S. Rosenberg
University of California, Irvine

Norman L. Rosenberg
Macalester College, Emeritus

CENGAGE
Learning·

Australia • Brazil • Mexico • Singapore • United Kingdom • United States

CENGAGE
Learning·

Liberty, Equality, Power:
A History of the American
People, Volume II: Since 1863,
Seventh Edition

John M. Murrin, Pekka
Hämäläinen, Paul E. Johnson,
Denver Brunsman, James M.
McPherson, Alice Fahs, Gary
Gerstle, Emily S. Rosenberg,
and Norman L. Rosenberg

Product Director: Suzanne Jeans

Product Manager: Clint
Attebery

Content Developer: Alison Levy

Product Assistant: Andrew
Newton

Marketing Brand Manager: Kyle
Zimmerman

IP Analyst: Alexandra Ricciardi

IP Project Manager: Amber
Hosea

Manufacturing Planner: Sandee
Milewski

Art and Design Direction,
Production Management, and
Composition: Lumina
Datamatics, Inc.

Cover Image: *Towards the Light
Times Square*, 1998 (oil on canvas),
Bill Jacklin (contemporary artist).
Private Collection. The
Bridgeman Art Library

For product information and
technology assistance, contact us at **Cengage Learning
Customer & Sales Support, 1-800-354-9706**

For permission to use material from this text or product, submit
all requests online at **www.cengage.com/permissions.**
Further permissions questions can be emailed to
permissionrequest@cengage.com.

Library of Congress Control Number: 2015930695

Student Edition:
ISBN: 978-1-305-49289-9

Cengage Learning
20 Channel Center Street
Boston, MA 02210
USA

Cengage Learning is a leading provider of customized learning
solutions with office locations around the globe, including
Singapore, the United Kingdom, Australia, Mexico, Brazil, and
Japan. Locate your local office at **www.cengage.com/global**.

Cengage Learning products are represented in Canada by
Nelson Education, Ltd.

To learn more about Cengage Learning Solutions, visit
www.cengage.com.

Purchase any of our products at your local college store or at our
preferred online store **www.cengagebrain.com**.

Printed in the United States of America
Print Number: 01   Print Year: 2015

About the Authors

JOHN M. MURRIN
Princeton University, Emeritus

John M. Murrin studies American colonial and revolutionary history and the early republic. He has edited one multivolume series and five books, including two essay collections, *Colonial America: Essays in Politics and Social Development*, Sixth Edition (2011), and *Saints and Revolutionaries: Essays in Early American History* (1984). His own essay topics range from ethnic tensions, the early history of trial by jury, the emergence of the legal profession, the Salem witch trials, and the political culture of the colonies and the new nation to the rise of professional baseball and college football in the 19th century. He served as president of the Society for Historians of the Early American Republic in 1998–1999.

PEKKA HÄMÄLÄINEN
University of Oxford

Pekka Hämäläinen is the Rhodes Professor of American History at the University of Oxford. A specialist in early American, Native American, borderlands, and environmental history, he is the author of *The Comanche Empire* (2008), which won multiple awards, including the Bancroft Prize, the Merle Curti Award, the Norris and Hundley Award, the William P. Clements Prize, and the Caughey Western History Association Prize. His writings have appeared in the *American Historical Review*; the *Journal of American History; History and Theory*; the *William and Mary Quarterly*; and the *Western Historical Quarterly*. He is currently working on a project on nomadic empires in world history, which is funded by the European Research Council.

PAUL E. JOHNSON
University of South Carolina, Distinguished Professor Emeritus

A specialist in early national social and cultural history, Paul E. Johnson is the author of *The Early American Republic, 1789–1829* (2006); *Sam Patch, the Famous Jumper* (2003); and *A Shopkeeper's Millennium: Society and Revivals in Rochester, New York, 1815–1837*, 25th Anniversary Edition (2004). He is coauthor (with Sean Wilentz) of *The Kingdom of Matthias: Sex and Salvation in 19th-Century America* (1994) and editor of *African-American Christianity: Essays in History* (1994). He has been awarded the Merle Curti Prize of the Organization of American Historians (1980), the Richard P. McCormick Prize of the New Jersey Historical Association (1989), and fellowships from the National Endowment for the Humanities (1985–1986), the John Simon Guggenheim Foundation (1995), the Gilder Lehrman Institute (2001), and the National Endowment for the Humanities (2006–2007).

DENVER BRUNSMAN
George Washington University

Denver Brunsman writes on the politics and social history of the American Revolution, the early American republic, and the British Atlantic world. His book, *The Evil*

Necessity: British Naval Impressment in the Eighteenth-Century Atlantic World (2013), received the Walker Cowen Memorial Prize for outstanding work in 18th-century studies in the Americas and Atlantic world. He is also an editor of *The American Revolution Reader* (2013) and *Colonial America: Essays in Politics and Social Development*, Sixth Edition (2011), among other works. His honors include yearlong research fellowships from the National Endowment for the Humanities at the Newberry Library, Chicago; the Eisenberg Institute for Historical Studies, University of Michigan; and the McNeil Center for Early American Studies, University of Pennsylvania. He teaches an annual course on "George Washington and His World," which meets at Washington's Mount Vernon estate.

JAMES M. McPHERSON
Princeton University, Emeritus

James M. McPherson is a distinguished Civil War historian and was president of the American Historical Association in 2003. He won the 1989 Pulitzer Prize for his book *Battle Cry of Freedom: The Civil War Era*. His other publications include *Marching Toward Freedom: Blacks in the Civil War*, Second Edition (1991); *Ordeal by Fire: The Civil War and Reconstruction*, Third Edition (2001); *Abraham Lincoln and the Second American Revolution* (1991); *For Cause and Comrades: Why Men Fought in the Civil War*, which won the Lincoln Prize in 1998; *Crossroads of Freedom: Antietam* (2002); and *Tried by War: Abraham Lincoln as Commander in Chief* (2008), which won the Lincoln Prize for 2009.

ALICE FAHS
University of California, Irvine

Alice Fahs is a specialist in American cultural history of the 19th and 20th centuries. Her 2001 *The Imagined Civil War: Popular Literature of the North and South, 1861–1865* was a finalist in 2002 for the Lincoln Prize. Together with Joan Waugh, she published the edited collection *The Memory of the Civil War in American Culture* in 2004; she also edited Louisa May Alcott's *Hospital Sketches* (2004), an account of Alcott's nursing experiences during the Civil War first published in 1863. Her most recent book is *Out on Assignment: Newspaper Women and the Making of Modern Public Space* (2011). Her honors include an American Council of Learned Societies Fellowship and a Gilder Lehrman Fellowship, as well as fellowships from the American Antiquarian Society, the Newberry Library, and the Huntington Library.

GARY GERSTLE
University of Cambridge

Gary Gerstle is the Paul Mellon Professor of American History at the University of Cambridge. He previously taught at Princeton University, the Catholic University of America, the University of Maryland, and Vanderbilt University. A historian of the 20th-century United States, he is the author, coauthor, and coeditor of six books and the author of nearly 35 articles. His books include *Working-Class Americanism: The Politics of Labor in a Textile City, 1914–1960* (1989); *American Crucible: Race and Nation in the Twentieth Century* (2001), winner of the Saloutos Prize for the best work in immigration and ethnic history; *The Rise and Fall of the New Deal Order, 1930–1980* (1989); and *Ruling America: Wealth and Power in a Democracy* (2005). A new book on the principles underlying the use of public power in America from the Revolution to the present will soon be published by Princeton University Press. He has served on the board of editors of the *Journal of American History* and the *American*

Historical Review. His honors include a National Endowment for the Humanities Fellowship, a John Simon Guggenheim Memorial Fellowship, the Harmsworth Visiting Professorship of American History at the University of Oxford, membership in the Society of American Historians, and the 2013 Jeffrey Nordhaus Award for Excellence in Undergraduate Teaching at Vanderbilt University.

EMILY S. ROSENBERG
University of California, Irvine

Emily S. Rosenberg specializes in U.S. foreign relations in the 20th century and is the author of *Spreading the American Dream: American Economic and Cultural Expansion, 1890–1945* (1982); *Financial Missionaries to the World: The Politics and Culture of Dollar Diplomacy* (1999), which won the Ferrell Book Award; *A Date Which Will Live: Pearl Harbor in American Memory* (2004); and *Transnational Currents in a Shrinking World, 1870–1945* (2014). Her other publications include (with Norman L. Rosenberg) *In Our Times: America Since 1945*, Seventh Edition (2003), and numerous articles dealing with foreign relations in the context of international finance, American culture, and gender ideology. She has served on the board of the Organization of American Historians, on the board of editors of the *American Historical Review*, and as president of the Society for Historians of American Foreign Relations.

NORMAN L. ROSENBERG
Macalester College

Norman L. Rosenberg specializes in legal history with a particular interest in legal culture and First Amendment issues. His books include *Protecting the "Best Men": An Interpretive History of the Law of Libel* (1990) and (with Emily S. Rosenberg) *In Our Times: America Since 1945*, Seventh Edition (2003). He has published articles in the *Rutgers Law Review, UCLA Law Review, Constitutional Commentary, Law & History Review*, and many other journals and law-related anthologies.

Brief Contents

Contents

Maps

To the Student

WHY STUDY HISTORY?

Why take a course in American history? This is a question that many college and university students ask. In many respects, students today are like the generations of Americans who have gone before them: optimistic and forward looking, far more eager to imagine where we as a nation might be going than to reflect on where we have been. If anything, this tendency has become more pronounced in recent years, as the Internet revolution has accelerated the pace and excitement of change and made even the recent past seem at best quaint, at worst uninteresting and irrelevant.

But it is precisely in these moments of change that a sense of the past can be indispensable in terms of guiding our actions in the present and future. We can find in other periods of American history moments, like our own, of dizzying technological change, rapid alterations in the concentration of wealth and power, and basic changes in patterns of work, residence, and play. How did Americans at those times create, embrace, and resist these changes? In earlier periods of American history, the United States was home, as it is today, to a broad array of ethnic and racial groups. How did earlier generations of Americans respond to the cultural conflicts and misunderstandings that often arise from conditions of diversity? How did immigrants of the early 1900s perceive their new land? How and when did they integrate themselves into American society? To study how ordinary Americans of the past struggled with these issues is to gain perspective on the opportunities and problems that we face today.

History also provides an important guide to affairs of state. What role should America assume in world affairs? Should we participate in international bodies such as the United Nations, or insist on our ability to act autonomously and without the consent of other nations? What is the proper role of government in economic and social life? Should the government regulate the economy? To what extent should the government promote morality regarding religion, sexual practices, drinking and drugs, movies, TV, and other forms of mass culture? And what are our responsibilities as citizens to each other and to the nation? Americans of past generations have debated these issues with verve and conviction. Learning about these debates and how they were resolved will enrich our understanding of the policy possibilities for today and tomorrow.

History, finally, is about stories—stories that we all tell about ourselves; our families; our communities; our ethnicity, race, region, and religion; and our nation. They are stories of triumph and tragedy, of engagement and flight, and of high ideals and high comedy. When we tell these stories, "American history" may be the furthest thing from our minds. But, often, an implicit sense of the past informs what we say about grandparents who immigrated many years ago; the suburb in which we live; the church, synagogue, or mosque at which we worship; or the ethnic or racial group to which we belong. How well, we might ask, do we really understand these individuals, institutions, and groups? Do our stories about them capture their history and complexity? Or do our stories wittingly or unwittingly simplify or alter what these individuals and groups experienced? A study of American history helps us first to ask these questions and then to answer them. In the process, we can embark on a journey of intellectual and personal discovery and situate ourselves more firmly than we had thought possible in relation to those who came before us. We can gain a firmer self-knowledge and a greater appreciation for the richness of our nation and, indeed, of all humanity.

Preface

We are pleased to present the seventh edition of *Liberty, Equality, Power*. Like the previous six editions, this one captures the drama and excitement of America's past, from the pre-Columbian era through our own time. It integrates social and cultural history into a political story that is organized around the themes of liberty, equality, and power, and synthesizes the finest historical scholarship to create a narrative that is balanced, lively, and accessible to a broad range of students.

THE *LIBERTY, EQUALITY, POWER* APPROACH

In this book, we tell many small stories, and one large one: how America transformed itself, in a relatively brief period of world history, from a land inhabited by hunter-gatherer and agricultural Native American societies into the most powerful industrial nation on earth. This story has been told many times before, and those who have told it in the past have usually emphasized the political experiment in liberty and equality that took root here in the 18th century.

We, too, stress the extraordinary and transformative impact that the ideals of liberty and equality exerted on American politics, society, and economics during the American Revolution and after. We show how the creation of a free economic environment—one in which entrepreneurial spirit, technological innovation, and manufacturing have flourished—underpinned American industrial might. We have also emphasized the successful struggles for freedom that, over the course of the country's 240 years of existence, have brought—first to all white men, then to men of color, and finally to women—rights and opportunities that they had not previously known.

But we have also identified a third factor in this pantheon of American ideals—that of power. We examine power in many forms: the accumulation of vast economic fortunes and their influence on the economy and on politics; the dispossession of American Indians from land that they regarded as their home; the enslavement of millions of Africans and their African American descendants for a period of almost 250 years; the relegation of women and of racial, ethnic, and religious minorities to subordinate places in American society; and the extension of American control over foreign peoples, such as Latin Americans and Filipinos, who would have preferred to have been free and self-governing. We do not mean to suggest that American power has always been turned to these negative purposes. Subordinate groups have also marshaled power to combat oppression, as in the abolitionist and civil rights crusades, the campaign for woman suffrage, and the labor movement. The government has at times used its power to moderate poverty and to manage the economy in the interests of general prosperity. And it has used its military power to defeat Nazi Germany, World War II Japan, the cold war Soviet Union, and other enemies of freedom.

The invocation of power as a variable in American history impels us to widen the lens through which we look at the past and to enrich the stories we tell. Ours has been a history of freedom and domination; of progress toward realizing a broadly democratic polity and of delays and reverses; of abundance and poverty; of wars for freedom and justice and for control of foreign markets. In complicating our master narrative in this way, we think we have rendered American history more exciting and intriguing. Progress has not been automatic, but the product of ongoing struggles.

In this book, we have tried to capture the diversity of the American past, both in terms of outcomes and in terms of the variety of groups who have participated in America's making. American Indians are not presented simply as the victims of European aggression but as peoples diverse in their own ranks, with a variety of systems of social organization and cultural expression. We give equal treatment to the industrial titans of American history—the likes of Andrew Carnegie and John D. Rockefeller—and to those, such as small farmers and poor workers, who resisted the corporate reorganization of economic life. We celebrate the great moments of 1863, when African Americans were freed from slavery, and of 1868, when they were made full citizens of the United States. But we also note how a majority of African Americans had to wait another 100 years, until the civil rights movement of the 1960s, to gain full access to American freedoms. We tell similarly complex stories about women, Latinos, and other groups of ethnic Americans.

Political issues are only part of America's story. Americans have always loved their leisure and have created the world's most vibrant popular culture. They have embraced technological innovations, especially those promising to make their lives easier and more fun. We have, therefore, devoted considerable space to a discussion of American popular culture, from the founding of the first newspapers in the 18th century and the rise of movies, jazz, and the comics in the early 20th century to the cable television and Internet revolutions in recent years. We have also analyzed how American industry has periodically altered home and personal life by making new products—such as clothing, cars, refrigerators, and computers—available to consumers. In such ways, we hope to give our readers a rich portrait of how Americans lived at various points in our history.

New to the Seventh Edition

Two major changes mark the seventh edition: the addition of two new authors, Pekka Hämäläinen and Denver Brunsman, and an expansion of our primary source program. We brought Pekka and Denver on board to revise the sections originally authored by John Murrin and Paul Johnson, who are retiring. Pekka is an expert on the history of Indians, the borderlands, and the West from the 17th through 19th centuries; his presence on the team will allow us to maintain the textbook's extraordinary coverage of indigenous populations while expanding the continental sweep of the textbook's chapters on early America. Denver is an expert on British-American relations of the late 18th and early 19th centuries and thus brings to the textbook's already strong North Atlantic focus the latest and best scholarship on the topic. The contributions of our two new authors have enabled us to preserve our textbook's robust history of British America while also enhancing its coverage of Spanish America, French America, and Native America. Pekka and Denver worked very closely with our retiring authors both to introduce new material and perspectives and to maintain the great strengths of earlier editions. We are delighted that they have joined the *Liberty, Equality, Power* team.

We also chose this edition to undertake the most significant overhaul of our primary source program in a decade. The most important change is a new feature, **What They Said**, which appears in several chapters in this Advantage edition. Each

What They Said feature focuses on a controversial issue pertinent to the time period covered in that chapter, and presents two or more sides of that issue in the words of individuals who were actual participants in the debates. We have put a great deal of care into choosing feature themes and into editing the primary documents into a form suitable for university and Advanced Placement high school students. The primary source excerpts themselves are longer than any we have previously used in the textbook; we undertook this expansion deliberately in order to allow students to grapple with issues in depth, and to grasp what was at stake in key historical controversies. Our hope is that these features can be used in multiple ways: as brief modules that professors can insert directly into lectures; as materials that can be read and discussed in weekly sections; and as documents that can form the basis for weekly assignments.

To facilitate their use, the primary source excerpts in each feature are prefaced with an introductory note that places them in their appropriate historical context. We also conclude each feature with a question or two that can guide student users and teachers in their thinking, discussions, and assignments. Instructors might want to think about using these features to stage debates in their classrooms; in our own teaching, we have found such debates to be a very successful pedagogical device. Most of all, we hope that instructors will share our enthusiasm regarding the utility of this feature for encouraging students to explore primary documents and to use them to engage productively with past controversies.

Finally, the textbook's much admired *History Through Film* series remains a prize feature of this textbook. These essays asks students to think critically about what they see on screen and allow instructors to stimulate students' historical interest through a medium they enjoy. For the seventh edition, we are pleased to introduce three new films: *John Adams* (the miniseries), *Master and Commander: The Far Side of the World,* and *12 Years a Slave.*

As in past editions, we have continued to make sure that the textbook's last chapter (Chapter 32) is up to date and gives adequate attention to the important developments in politics, economics, and culture of the 21st century. George W. Bush's victories in 2000 and 2004; the destruction of the World Trade Center towers on September 11, 2001; the resulting wars on terrorism and on Saddam Hussein in Iraq and the Taliban in Afghanistan; Barack Obama's victories in 2008 and 2012; the financial crash of 2008–2009; the passage of the Affordable Care Act and the rise of the Tea Party: all receive substantial treatment in this edition.

In preparing for this revision, we solicited feedback from professors and scholars throughout the country, many of whom have used the sixth edition of *Liberty, Equality, Power* in their classrooms. Their comments proved most helpful, and many of their suggestions have been incorporated into the seventh edition. Thus, for example, at the prompting of reviewers, we have shortened the overall word length of the textbook by 5 percent and strengthened our primary source program. We have also undertaken for this edition a major reorganization and overhaul of Chapters 2 and 3 so as to encompass more of a continental perspective to supplement the textbook's already strong Atlantic focus. The textbook now offers, as a result, considerably more than did previous editions on the early history of North American territory that would become California, New Mexico, and Texas. Throughout the early American chapters, we have also expanded significantly the attention to environmental history. Chapters 4–10 have also been substantially revised to situate America in both a larger continental and global context while bringing the latest scholarship to bear on these subjects: the role of women in 18th-century transatlantic consumer society; loyalists in the American revolutionary era; slavery and the Atlantic slave trade; the international threats faced by the United States in the early decades of the 19th century; and the relations among European empires, Native Americans, and the United States in the first half of the 19th century.

We have carried over and, in some cases, enhanced pedagogical changes that we made to earlier editions and that have proved popular with professors and students. **Chapter outlines** and **chronology boxes** continue to appear at the beginning of each chapter. Each map in our outstanding map program comes equipped with a brief caption instructing students about how to interpret the geographical and topographical data it contains.

Finally, we have scrutinized each page of this textbook, making sure our prose is clear, the historical issues well presented, and the scholarship up to date and accurate.

SPECIFIC REVISIONS TO CONTENT AND COVERAGE

Chapter 1 (MAJOR REVISION) Streamlined and reorganized the chapter material to focus the narrative and clarify the chronology; new chapter title; added two new subsections, "Agricultural Take-off in North America" and "North America in 1491."

Chapter 2 (MAJOR REVISION) New chapter title; expanded coverage of Native Americans throughout; condensed material on English explorers; added new subsection, "The Collapse of Tsenacommacah"; revised and moved into this chapter from Chapter 3 the subsection on "Puritan Indian Missions"; condensed and streamlined "The Chesapeake and West Indian Colonies," "The New England Colonies," "From Civil War to the First Restoration Colonies," and "Brotherly Love: The Quakers and America" sections and moved material on late 17th- and early 18th-century developments into Chapter 3 to highlight change over time; new *What They Said* feature, "English Colonists and Huron Indians Enter New Worlds"; expanded conclusion to cover continental developments.

Chapter 3 (MAJOR REVISION) Substantively revised and reorganized. Now titled "Empires, Indians, and the Struggle for Power in North America, 1670–1720," it expands coverage beyond English America by adopting a continental approach and by incorporating material from the sixth edition's Chapters 2 and 4; new opening section, "Indians, Settlers, Upheaval: The Cataclysmic 1670s and 1680s," and subsection, "New France Besieged"; added section, "Converging Empires: Spain and France in North America," which includes new material on Spanish North America, French North America, and Native Americans; added section, "The Rise of England's Atlantic Empire"; expanded "An Empire of Settlement: The Growth of British America" to include two new subsections, "Spanish and French Counterpoints" and "The Colonial Rim and the Indigenous Interior"; revised table, "The Spectrum of Settlement: Demography, Ethnicity, Economy, 1650–1700"; reworked Conclusion.

Chapter 4 Expanded coverage and updated figures on the Atlantic slave trade; revised figures on early German immigration to North America; revised section on "The Enlightenment in America"; new section on "Women and the Consumer Revolution"; new *What They Said* feature, "The Controversy over Religious Revivals"; revised section on "Political Culture in the Colonies"; added material on British naval impressment in the colonial era; condensed discussion of Spain's entry into the Seven Years' War; moved material on the Cherokee War of 1759–1761 to Chapter 5.

Chapter 5   New section on "Impetus for Reform"; condensed treatment of the Townshend Acts crisis; new *History Through Film* feature, *John Adams*; new section on "Divided Loyalties"; consolidated treatment of the feudal revival and the regulator movement in the Carolinas in a new section on "Urban and Rural Discontent"; expanded coverage of Dunmore's Proclamation and its influence on the southern colonies' support for independence; expanded discussion of the social and intellectual influences on the Declaration of Independence.

Chapter 6   Added material on the global and continental contexts of the Revolutionary War, including the role of Spain and its North American territories; new section on "Loyalists, Black and White"; new section on "Britain's Southern Strategy"; revised material on state constitutions and the Articles of Confederation in a new section, "American Constitutionalism"; expanded treatment of the Constitutional Convention.

Chapter 7   Expanded section on "The American Republic in a Changing World," which considers the relations between the early United States and its Spanish and Indian neighbors in North America as well as the republic's struggle to maintain its sovereignty during the wars of the French Revolution; added section, "New Spain and the Bourbon Reforms"; streamlined discussion of the Jeffersonians and the courts; revised treatment of the causes and fighting in the War of 1812; new *History Through Film* feature, *Master and Commander: The Far Side of the World*.

Chapter 8   Streamlined discussion of internal improvements and other economic and cultural changes in the North due to the Market Revolution; expanded treatment of early American manufacturing, including the role of gender.

Chapter 9   Revised discussions of slavery, black culture, and the interstate slave trade based on the latest scholarship; new *History Through Film* feature, *12 Years a Slave*.

Chapter 10   Revised treatment of religion in antebellum America, including expanded coverage of the Second Great Awakening; new section on "The Emergence of Mormonism."

Chapter 11   Streamlined and condensed discussion throughout; expanded coverage of Indian removal.

Chapter 12   Streamlined and condensed discussion throughout; new *What They Said* feature, "Making Fun of Women's Rights."

Chapter 14   New *What They Said* feature, "Reactions to John Brown."

Chapter 18   New *What They Said* feature, "Differing Visions of Black Progress: Booker T. Washington and W. E. B. Du Bois."

Chapter 22   New *What They Said* feature, "Should America Become an Imperial Nation?"

Chapter 26   As with all the remaining chapters, the prose has been streamlined in search of the best possible, most clear discussions. Every section and virtually every paragraph has undergone revision.

Chapter 27   Entire chapter revised for greater clarity and representation of recent scholarship; new *What They Said* feature, "Civil Rights Divide the Democratic Party, 1948."

Chapter 28   (MAJOR REVISION) Entire chapter reorganized, reframed, and refocused in response to suggestions by our colleague Gary Gerstle and several outside reviewers; recent scholarship was integrated into the discussion.

Chapter 29   (MAJOR REVISION) Entire chapter reorganized, reframed, retitled, and updated in light of most recent scholarship.

Chapter 30   Streamlined prose and updated scholarship for a chapter that had undergone a major overhaul in the previous edition.

Chapter 31   (MAJOR REVISION) Refocused and streamlined chapter in light of suggestions from reviewers; new *What They Said* feature, "The Sports Construction Boom: Who Pays, Who Gains?"

Chapter 32   (MAJOR REVISION) Revised and updated entire chapter, especially on economic issues and on post-2010 politics; new *What They Said* feature, "Debating Torture."

Supplements

INSTRUCTOR RESOURCES

MindTap™   MindTap for *Liberty, Equality, Power: A History of the American People*, Seventh Edition, is a personalized, online digital learning platform providing students with an immersive learning experience that builds critical thinking skills. Through a carefully designed chapter-based learning path, MindTap allows students to easily identify the chapter's learning objectives, complete readings that are organized into short, manageable blocks, and test their content knowledge with Aplia™ Critical Thinking Activities developed for the most important concepts in each chapter (see Aplia description below).

- *Activator:* Each chapter of the MindTap begins with a brief video that introduces the chapter's major themes in a compelling, visual way that encourages students to think critically about the subject matter.

- *Aplia:* The Aplia Critical Thinking assignments will include at least one map-based exercise, one primary source–based exercise, and an exercise summarizing the content and themes of the chapter.

- *Reflection Activity:* Every chapter ends with an assignable, gradable writing assignment, either an essay or discussion board, through which students can apply a theme or idea they've just studied.

MindTap also provides a set of Web applications known as MindApps to help you create the most engaging course for your students. The MindApps range from Read-Speaker (which reads the text out loud to students) to Kaltura (allowing you to insert inline video and audio into your curriculum) to ConnectYard (allowing you to create digital "yards" through social media—all without "friending" your students). MindTap for *Liberty, Equality, Power* goes well beyond an eBook, a homework solution/digital supplement, a resource center Web site, or a Learning Management System. It is truly a personal learning experience that allows you to synchronize the text reading and engaging assignments. To learn more, ask your Cengage Learning sales representative to demo it for you—or go to www.Cengage.com/MindTap.

Aplia™   Aplia is an online interactive learning solution that improves comprehension and outcomes by increasing student effort and engagement. Founded by a professor to enhance his own courses, Aplia provides automatically graded assignments with detailed, immediate explanations on every question. The interactive assignments have been developed to address the major concepts covered in *Liberty, Equality, Power* and are designed to promote critical thinking and engage students more fully in learning. Question types include questions built around animated maps, primary sources such as newspaper extracts, or imagined scenarios, like engaging in a conversation with a historical figure or finding a diary and being asked to fill in some blanks; more in-depth primary source question sets address a major topic with a number of related primary sources and questions that promote deeper analysis of historical evidence. Many of the questions incorporate images, video clips, or audio clips. Students get immediate feedback on their work (not only what they got right or wrong, but why), and they can choose to see another set of related questions if they want more practice. A searchable eBook is available inside the course as well so that students can easily reference it as they work. Map-reading and writing tutorials are also available to get students off to a good start.

Aplia's simple-to-use course management interface allows instructors to post announcements, upload course materials, host student discussions, e-mail students, and manage the gradebook. A knowledgeable and friendly support team offers assistance and personalized support in customizing assignments to the instructor's course schedule. To learn more and view a demo for this book, visit www.aplia.com.

Instructor Companion Web Site   This Web site is an all-in-one resource for class preparation, presentation, and testing for instructors. Accessible through Cengage.com/login with your faculty account, you will find an Instructor's Manual, PowerPoint presentations (descriptions below), and test bank files (please see Cognero description).

Instructor's Manual This manual contains for each chapter: a chapter outline, chronology, topics for class discussion, essay suggestions, lecture outlines, and additional teaching resources.

PowerPoint® Lecture Tools These presentations are ready-to-use, visual outlines of each chapter. They are easily customized for your lectures. There are presentations of only lecture or only images, as well as combined lecture and image presentations. Also available is a per chapter JPEG library of images and maps.

Cengage Learning Testing, powered by Cognero® for *Liberty, Equality, Power* is accessible through Cengage.com/login with your faculty account. This test bank contains multiple-choice and essay questions for each chapter. Cognero® is a flexible, online system that allows you to author, edit, and manage test bank content for *Liberty, Equality, Power: A History of the American People*, Seventh Edition. Create multiple test versions instantly and deliver them through your LMS from your classroom, or wherever you may be, with no special installs or downloads required.

The following format types are available for download from the Instructor Companion site: Blackboard, Angel, Moodle, Canvas, Desire2Learn. You can import these files directly into your LMS to edit, manage questions, and create tests. The test bank is also available in PDF format from the Instructor Companion Web site.

MindTap Reader for *Liberty, Equality, Power: A History of the American People,* **Seventh Edition**   is an eBook specifically designed to address the ways students assimilate content and media assets. MindTap Reader combines thoughtful navigation ergonomics, advanced student annotation, note-taking, and search tools, and embedded media assets such as video and MP3 chapter summaries, primary source documents with critical thinking questions, and interactive (zoomable) maps. Students can use the eBook as their primary text or as a multimedia companion to their printed book. The MindTap Reader eBook is available within the MindTap platform and can be found at www.cengagebrain.com.

CourseReader   is an online collection of primary and secondary sources that lets you create a customized electronic reader in minutes. With an easy-to-use interface and assessment tool, you can choose exactly what your students will be assigned—simply search or browse Cengage Learning's extensive document database to preview and select your customized collection of readings. In addition to print sources of all types (letters, diary entries, speeches, newspaper accounts, etc.), the collection includes a growing number of images and video and audio clips. Each primary source document includes a descriptive headnote that puts the reading into context and is further supported by both critical thinking and multiple-choice questions designed to reinforce key points. For more information, visit www.cengage.com/coursereader.

Reader Program   Cengage Learning publishes a number of readers, some containing exclusively primary sources, others a combination of primary and secondary sources, and some designed to guide students through the process of historical inquiry. Visit Cengage.com/history for a complete list of readers.

Cengagebrain.com   Save your students time and money. Direct them to www.cengagebrain.com for choice in formats and savings and a better chance to succeed in your class. Cengagebrain.com, Cengage Learning's online store, is a single destination for more than 10,000 new textbooks, eTextbooks, eChapters, study tools, and audio supplements. Students have the freedom to purchase à la carte exactly what they need when they need it. Students can save 50 percent on the electronic textbook and can pay as little as $1.99 for an individual eChapter.

Custom Options   Nobody knows your students like you, so why not give them a text that is tailored to their needs? Cengage Learning offers custom solutions for your course—whether it's making a small modification to *Liberty, Equality, Power* to match your syllabus or combining multiple sources to create something truly unique. You can pick and choose chapters, include your own material, and add additional map exercises along with the Rand McNally Atlas to create a text that fits the way you teach. Ensure that your students get the most out of their textbook dollar by giving them exactly what they need. Contact your Cengage Learning representative to explore custom solutions for your course.

STUDENT RESOURCES

MindTap Reader   MindTap Reader is an eBook specifically designed to address the ways students assimilate content and media assets. MindTap Reader combines thoughtful navigation ergonomics, advanced student annotation, note-taking, and search tools, and embedded media assets such as video and MP3 chapter summaries, primary source documents with critical thinking questions, and interactive (zoomable) maps. Students can use the eBook as their primary text or as a multimedia companion to their printed book. The MindTap Reader eBook is available within the MindTap platform found at www.cengagebrain.com.

Reader Program   Cengage Learning publishes a number of readers, some containing exclusively primary sources, others a combination of primary and secondary sources, and some designed to guide students through the process of historical inquiry. Visit Cengage.com/history for a complete list of readers.

Cengagebrain.com   Save time and money! Go to www.cengagebrain.com for choice in formats and savings and a better chance to succeed in your class. Cengagebrain.com, Cengage Learning's online store, is a single destination for more than 10,000 new textbooks, eTextbooks, eChapters, study tools, and audio supplements. Students have the freedom to purchase à la carte exactly what they need when they need it. Students can save 50 percent on the electronic textbook and can pay as little as $1.99 for an individual eChapter.

Writing for College History, 1e [ISBN: 9780618306039]   Prepared by Robert M. Frakes, Clarion University. This brief handbook for survey courses in American history, Western Civilization/European history, and world civilization guides students through the various types of writing assignments they encounter in a history class. Providing examples of student writing and candid assessments of student work, this text focuses on the rules and conventions of writing for the college history course.

The History Handbook, 2e [ISBN: 9780495906766]   Prepared by Carol Berkin of Baruch College, City University of New York, and Betty Anderson of Boston University. This book teaches students both basic and history-specific study skills such as how to read primary sources, research historical topics, and correctly cite sources. Substantially less expensive than comparable skill-building texts, *The History Handbook* also offers tips for Internet research and evaluating online sources.

Doing History: Research and Writing in the Digital Age, 2e [ISBN: 9781133587880]   Prepared by Michael J. Galgano, J. Chris Arndt, and Raymond M. Hyser of James Madison University. Whether you're starting down the path as a history major, or simply looking for a straightforward and systematic guide to writing a successful paper, you'll find this text to be an indispensable handbook to historical research. This text's "soup to nuts" approach to researching and writing about history addresses every step of the process, from locating your sources and gathering information, to writing clearly and making proper use of various citation styles to avoid plagiarism. You'll also learn how to make the most of every tool available to you—especially the technology that helps you conduct the process efficiently and effectively.

The Modern Researcher, 6e [ISBN: 9780495318705]   Prepared by Jacques Barzun and Henry F. Graff of Columbia University. This classic introduction to the techniques of research and the art of expression is used widely in history courses but is also appropriate for writing and research methods courses in other departments. Barzun and Graff thoroughly cover every aspect of research, from the selection of a topic through the gathering, analysis, writing, revision, and publication of findings, presenting the process not as a set of rules but through actual cases that put the subtleties of research in a useful context. Part One covers the principles and methods of research; Part Two covers writing, speaking, and getting one's work published.

Rand McNally Historical Atlas of the World, 2e [ISBN: 9780618841912]   This valuable resource features more than 70 maps that portray the rich panoply of the world's history from preliterate times to the present. They show how cultures and civilization were linked and how they interacted. The maps make it clear that history is not static. Rather, it is about change and movement across time. The maps show change by presenting the dynamics of expansion, cooperation, and conflict. This atlas includes maps that display the world from the beginning of civilization; the political development of all major areas of the world; expanded coverage of Africa, Latin America, and the Middle East; the current Islamic world; and the world population changes in 1900 and 2000.

ACKNOWLEDGMENTS

We recognize the contributions of reviewers who read portions of the manuscript in various stages:

Sam Abrams, *The Beacon School*
William Allison, *Weber State University*
Angie Anderson, *Southeastern Louisiana University*
Kenneth G. Anthony, *University of North Carolina, Greensboro*
Rick Ascheman, *Rochester Community and Technical College*
Paul R. Beezley, *Texas Tech University*
David Bernstein, *California State University at Long Beach*
Sue Blanchette, *Hillcrest High School*
Jeff Bloodworth, *Ohio University*
Michael R. Bradley, *Motlow College*
Betty Brandon, *University of South Alabama*
Daniel Patrick Brown, *Moorpark College*
Ronald G. Brown, *College of Southern Maryland*
Susan Burch, *Gallaudet University*
Thomas M. Cangiano, *The Lawrenceville School*
Jeffrey W. Coker, *Belmont University*
Phil Crow, *North Harris College*
Lorenzo M. Crowell, *Mississippi State University*
Amy E. N. Darty, *University of Central Florida*
Thomas M. Deaton, *Dalton State College*
Norman C. Delaney, *Del Mar College*
Ted Delaney, *Washington and Lee University*
Andrew J. DeRoche, *Front Range Community College*
Rebecca de Schweinitz, *Brigham Young University*
Bruce Dierenfield, *Canisius College*
Brian R. Dirck, *Anderson University*
Maura Doherty, *Illinois State University*
R. Blake Dunnavent, *Lubbock Christian University*
Eileen Eagan, *University of Southern Maine*
Derek Elliott, *Tennessee State University*
B. Jane England, *North Central Texas College*
William B. Feis, *Buena Vista University*
David J. Fitzpatrick, *Washtenaw Community College*
Van Forsyth, *Clark College*
Michael P. Gabriel, *Kutztown University of Pennsylvania*
Gary Gallagher, *Pennsylvania State University*
Kevin M. Gannon, *Grand View University*
Gerald Ghelfi, *Santa Ana College*
Michael Goldberg, *University of Washington, Bothell*
Kathleen Gorman, *Minnesota State University, Mankato*
David E. Hamilton, *University of Kentucky*
Michael J. Haridopolos, *Brevard Community College*
Mark Harvey, *North Dakota State University*
Brenda Hasterok, *Spain Park High School*
Kurt Hohenstein, *Hampden Sydney College*
Mark Huddle, *University of Georgia*
Samuel C. Hyde Jr., *Southeastern Louisiana University*

Thomas N. Ingersoll, *Ohio State University*
J. Michael Jeffries, *Northeastern Technical College*
Frank Karpiel, *Ramapo College of New Jersey*
Anthony E. Kaye, *Pennsylvania State University*
Michael Kazin, *Georgetown University*
Michael King, *Moraine Valley Community College*
Greg Kiser, *Northwest Arkansas Community College*
Michael Krenn, *Appalachian State*
Donna Kumler, *Grayson College*
Frank Lambert, *Purdue University*
Pat Ledbetter, *North Central Texas College*
Michelle LeMaster, *Eastern Illinois University*
Jan Leone, *Middle Tennessee State University*
Craig Livingston, *Montgomery College*
Robert F. Marcom, *San Antonio College*
Suzanne Marshall, *Jacksonville State University*
Brenda Taylor Matthews, *Texas Wesleyan University*
Joanne Maypole, *Front Range Community College*
Christopher McColm, *Aims Community College*
Jimmie McGee, *South Plains College*
Nora E. McMillan, *San Antonio College*
Jerry Mills, *Midland College*
Charlene Mires, *Villanova University*
Brock Mislan, *Watchung Hills Regional High School*
Rick Moniz, *Chabot College*
Caryn Neumann, *Miami University of Ohio*
James Nichols, *Queensborough Community College*
Michael R. Nichols, *Tarrant County College, Northwest*
Linda Noel, *Morgan State University*
Christy Olsen, *Skyline High School*
Richard B. Partain, *Bakersfield College*
William Pencak, *Pennsylvania State University*
Teresa Thomas Perrin, *Austin Community College*
David Poteet, *New River Community College*
Howard Reed, *University of Bridgeport*
Jonathan Rees, *Colorado State University–Pueblo*
Thomas S. Reid, *Valencia Community College*
Anne Richardson, *Texas Christian University*
Lelia M. Roeckell, *Molloy College*
Thomas J. Rowland, *University of Wisconsin, Oshkosh*
Mark Sattler, *Rockingham Community College*
Roy Scott, *Mississippi State University*
Reynolds J. Scott-Childress, *State University of New York at New Paltz*
Katherine A. S. Sibley, *St. Joseph's University*
Herb Sloan, *Barnard College*
M. Todd Smallwood, *Manatee Community College*
John Smolenski, *University of California, Davis*
Steve Stein, *University of Memphis*
Michael J. Steiner, *Northwest Missouri State University*
Jennifer Stollman, *University of Mississippi*
Siegfried H. Sutterlin, *Indian Hills Community College*

Richard O. Swanson, *Duxbury High School*
John Wood Sweet, *The University of North Carolina at Chapel Hill*
Teresa Fava Thomas, *Fitchburg State College*
Xiansheng Tian, *Metro State College of Denver*
Jamie Underwood, *Montana State University Northern*
Juan Valenzuela, *Kennesaw State University*
Vincent Vinikas, *University of Arkansas, Little Rock*
Vernon Volpe, *University of Nebraska*
Harry L. Watson, *The University of North Carolina at Chapel Hill*
Thomas Weyant, *University of Akron*
William Benton Whisenhunt, *College of DuPage*
David K. White, *McHenry County College*
Laura Matysek Wood, *Tarrant County College, Northwest*

We wish to thank the members of the Cengage staff, many of them new to the project, for embracing our textbook wholeheartedly and for expertly guiding the production of this seventh edition. We are indebted to Ann West, our former Senior Sponsoring Editor of the last five years, for her savvy, inspiration, and commitment. She is one of the best editors we have worked with and has contributed mightily to this edition. Carol Newman, Senior Content Project Manager, has done a superb job supervising work on the seventh edition while Michelle Dellinger, Managing Editor at Integra-Chicago, has expeditiously coordinated the numerous tasks required to bring this book to press. We thank Reba Frederics, photo Permissions Project Manager at PreMediaGlobal, for collecting many of the beautiful photographs and illustrations that grace these pages. Suzanne Jeans, Product Director, has kept on a sharp eye on this project, stepping in when needed to guide this ocean liner of a project to its pier.

We owe a great debt, yet again, to our longtime developmental editor, Margaret McAndrew Beasley, who has worked with us on six editions and, by now, knows the book as well as we do. Margaret's editing skills, organizational expertise, wisdom, good cheer, and belief in this book and its authors keep us going. We needed those skills and dedication in even greater abundance this edition in order to educate our new authors as to the LEP way of doing things, and to manage the transition in the last months of production from Ann West to our new Product Manager Clint Attebery. Margaret, we really can't thank you enough.

A big thanks, finally, to Cengage's marketing department and to the sales representatives who have worked hard and creatively to generate interest in our book among university, college, and high school teachers across America.

No project of this scope is completely error free. If you find any errors, please let us know what they are. Feel free as well to send queries and suggestions our way. The book will be enriched by such feedback. Please send comments to our product manager, Clint Attebery at **clint.attebery@cengage.com**.

Finally, each of us would like to offer particular thanks to those historians, friends, and family members who helped to bring this project to a successful conclusion.

PERSONAL ACKNOWLEDGMENTS

JOHN M. MURRIN Mary R. Murrin has provided the kind of moral and personal support that made completion of this project possible. James Axtell and Gregory Evans Dowd saved me from many mistakes, mostly about Indians. John E. Selby and Eugene R. Sheridan were particularly helpful on the Revolution. Fred Anderson and Virginia DeJohns Anderson offered acute suggestions. Several former colleagues and graduate students have also contributed in various ways, especially Stephen Aron, Andrew Isenberg, Ignacio Gallup-Diaz, Evan P. Haefeli, Beth Lewis-Pardoe, Geoffrey Plank, Nathaniel J. Sheidley, and Jeremy Stern.

PEKKA HÄMÄLÄINEN   I would like to thank Gary Gerstle and the other authors for welcoming me so warmly to the team. Gary was an inexhaustible source of knowledge and guidance, and Denver Brunsman was an absolute delight to work with. I also want to express my gratitude to John Murrin and Paul Johnson for the opportunity to continue and build on their work. I am grateful to Margaret Beasley for her remarkable proficiency, support, and patience.

PAUL E. JOHNSON   My greatest debt is to the community of scholars who write about the United States between the Revolution and the Civil War. Closer to home, I owe thanks to the other writers of this book, particularly to John Murrin. The Department of History at the University of South Carolina provided time to work, while my wife, Kasey Grier, and stray dogs named Lucy, Bill, Buddy, and Patty provided the right kinds of interruptions.

DENVER BRUNSMAN   I thank Gary Gerstle and the other authors for inviting me to write for *Liberty, Equality, Power*, a textbook that I have long admired. Gary has provided generous support and served as a model leader of our team. John Murrin helped to create this book and continues to inspire us and countless other scholars. I am indebted to him and Paul Johnson for so graciously allowing me and Pekka Hämäläinen to revise their chapters. I could not have had a better partner in this enterprise than Pekka. His wit and good cheer made working on the book a joy. Although she is not credited as an author, our extraordinary editor, Margaret Beasley, has left her distinguished mark on every page. I am also grateful to our reviewers and my students at George Washington University for providing thoughtful feedback on the book. Finally, the boundless support and affection of my wife, Taryn, and our children, Gavin and Sanne, have made this project particularly rewarding.

JAMES M. McPHERSON   My family provided an environment of affection and stability that contributed immeasurably to the writing of my chapters, while undergraduate students at Princeton University who have taken my courses over the years provided feedback, questions, and insights that helped me to understand what students know and don't know, and what they need to know.

ALICE FAHS   Thanks are due to Gary Gerstle, whose keen editorial eye and judgment helped greatly with revisions of Chapter 19. Our "team leader" among the authors, Gary has given generously of his time to the rest of us, providing constant support. Margaret Beasley continues to be a crucial resource of intelligence and good cheer as our development editor; we all know we are very lucky. I am grateful as well to Ann West, our former editor at Cengage, for her exceptional leadership and commitment to excellence; and to James M. McPherson for the initial invitation to become part of *Liberty, Equality, Power*. At the University of California, Irvine, David Igler was an important resource for past revisions of Chapter 18. My students, both undergraduate and graduate, have continued to be a source of inspiration to me in conceptualizing this textbook. Finally, my family continues to listen patiently to history anecdotes over breakfasts, lunches, and dinners—whether in California or Texas. To Charlie and to Mimi, many thanks.

GARY GERSTLE   A long time ago, Jerald Podair, Thomas Knock, and the late Roy Rosenzweig gave me exceptionally thorough, thoughtful, and insightful critiques on early drafts of my chapters. This textbook still benefits from their good and generous work. Former graduate students Kathleen Trainor, Reynolds Scott-Childress, Linda Noel, Kelly Ryan, Robert Chase, Marcy Wilson, Thomas Castillo, and Katarina Keane offered skillful research assistance on earlier editions. At Vanderbilt, research assistants Monte Holman and William Bishop made many indispensable and timely contributions to the sixth and seventh editions. My undergraduate students at the University of Maryland and at Vanderbilt University have kept me young, and on my toes. Teaching American history to them has been a great joy and has repeatedly replenished my enthusiasm for this textbook. A special thanks both to my original coauthors for their intelligence, wit, and deep commitment to this project, and to my new coauthors, who have already helped me to imagine what a textbook for this new American century ought to look like. Ann West carried us on her shoulders during a trying time. Margaret Beasley is the best textbook editor on the planet and a dear friend.

EMILY AND NORMAN ROSENBERG would like to thank our children—Sarah, Molly, Ruth, and Joe—for all of the wisdom and good cheer they provided while the six of us were moving through the period of history related in the final chapters of this book. Successive generations of students at Macalester College, some now academics themselves, offered pointed critiques of our classes, and these inspired (and provoked) us continually to revise our approach toward teaching and writing about the recent past. Our former colleagues at Macalester merit a similar kind of thanks. (Here, we note, with deep sadness and fond memories, the recent passing of one them, Jerry K. Fisher, a keen, inside observer of electronic and digital media as well as a professor who excelled in moving student learning beyond the classroom.) More recently, Emily Rosenberg's graduate students at the University of California, Irvine, helped clarify how our chapters might better reach out to students who may be using this seventh edition. We also thank the historians who offered both supportive and helpfully critical comments on earlier versions of *Liberty, Equality, Power*. We have not always followed their advice, but this seventh edition is much the better for their assistance. Finally, our deepest thanks go to Margaret Beasley for her personal friendship, expert guidance, and close oversight. We shudder to contemplate how Chapters 26–32 might have looked had Margaret not been on the case.

John M. Murrin, Pekka Hämäläinen, Paul E. Johnson,
Denver Brunsman, James M. McPherson, Alice Fahs, Gary Gerstle,
Emily S. Rosenberg, Norman L. Rosenberg

17

RECONSTRUCTION, 1863–1877

FROM THE BEGINNING of the Civil War, the North fought to "reconstruct" the Union. Lincoln at first attempted to restore the Union as it had existed before 1861, but once the abolition of slavery became a northern war aim, the Union could never be reconstructed on its old foundations. Instead, it must experience a "new birth of freedom," as Lincoln had said at the dedication of the military cemetery at Gettysburg.

But precisely what did "a new birth of freedom" mean? At the very least, it meant the end of slavery. The slave states would be reconstructed on a free-labor basis. But what would liberty look like for the 4 million freed slaves? Would they become citizens equal to their former masters in the eyes of the law? Would they have the right to vote? Should Confederate leaders and soldiers be punished for treason? On what terms should the Confederate states return to the Union? What would be the powers of the states and of the national government in a reconstructed Union?

WARTIME RECONSTRUCTION

Lincoln pondered these problems long and hard. At first he feared that whites in the South would never extend equal rights to the freed slaves. After all, even most northern states were denying full civil equality to the few black people within their borders. In 1862, Lincoln encouraged freedpeople to emigrate to all-black countries such as Haiti, where they would have a chance to get ahead without having to face the racism of whites. Black leaders, abolitionists, and many Republicans objected to that policy. Blacks were Americans. Why should they not have the rights of American citizens instead of being urged to leave the country?

Lincoln eventually embraced the logic and justice of that view. But in beginning the process of reconstruction, he first reached out to southern whites whose

CHRONOLOGY

1863	Lincoln issues Proclamation of Amnesty and Reconstruction
1864	Congress passes Wade-Davis bill; Lincoln kills it by pocket veto
1865	Congress establishes Freedmen's Bureau
	Andrew Johnson becomes president, announces his reconstruction plan
	Southern states enact Black Codes
	Congress refuses to seat southern congressmen elected under Johnson's plan
1866	Congress passes civil rights bill and expands Freedmen's Bureau over Johnson's vetoes
	Race riots in Memphis and New Orleans
	Congress approves Fourteenth Amendment
	Republicans increase congressional majority in fall elections
1867	Congress passes Reconstruction Acts over Johnson's vetoes
	Congress passes Tenure of Office Act over Johnson's veto
1868	Most southern senators and representatives readmitted to Congress under congressional plan of Reconstruction
	Andrew Johnson impeached but not convicted
	Ulysses S. Grant elected president
	Fourteenth Amendment is ratified
1870	Fifteenth Amendment is ratified
1871	Congress passes Ku Klux Klan Act
1872	Liberal Republicans defect from party
	Grant wins reelection
1873	Economic depression begins with the Panic of 1873
1874	Democrats win control of House of Representatives
1875	Democrats implement Mississippi Plan
	Congress passes Civil Rights Act
1876	Centennial celebration in Philadelphia
	Disputed presidential election causes constitutional crisis
1877	Compromise of 1877 installs Rutherford B. Hayes as president
	Hayes withdraws troops from South
1883	Supreme Court declares Civil Rights Act of 1875 unconstitutional

allegiance to the Confederacy was lukewarm. On December 8, 1863, Lincoln issued his Proclamation of Amnesty and Reconstruction, which offered a presidential pardon to southern whites who took an oath of allegiance to the United States and accepted the abolition of slavery. In any state where the number of white males aged 21 or older who took this oath equaled 10 percent of the number of voters in 1860, that nucleus could reestablish a state government to which Lincoln promised presidential recognition.

Because the war was still raging, this policy could be carried out only where Union troops controlled substantial portions of a Confederate state: Louisiana, Arkansas, and Tennessee in early 1864. Nevertheless, Lincoln hoped that once the process had begun in those areas, it might snowball as Union military victories convinced more and more Confederates that their cause was hopeless. But those military victories were long delayed, and in most parts of the South, reconstruction did not begin until 1865.

Radical Republicans and Recons-truction	Growing opposition within Lincoln's own party slowed the process as well. Many Republicans believed that white men who had fought against the Union should not be rewarded with restoration of their political rights while black men who had fought for the Union were denied those rights.

Radical Republicans, led by Thaddeus Stevens in the House and Charles Sumner in the Senate, distrusted oaths of allegiance sworn by ex-Confederates. Rather than simply restoring the old ruling class to power, asked Sumner, why not give freed slaves the vote, to provide a genuinely loyal nucleus of supporters in the South? If the freedpeople were landless, some Radical Republicans said, provide them with land by confiscating the plantations of leading Confederates as punishment for treason.

These radical positions did not command a majority of Congress in 1864. Yet the experience of Louisiana, the first state to reorganize under Lincoln's more moderate policy, convinced even non-Radical Republicans to block Lincoln's program. Enough white men in the occupied portion of the state took the oath of allegiance to satisfy Lincoln's conditions. They adopted a new state constitution and formed a government that abolished slavery and provided a school system for blacks. But despite Lincoln's private appeal to the new government to grant literate blacks and black Union soldiers the right to vote, the reconstructed Louisiana legislature chose not to do so. It also authorized planters to enforce restrictive labor policies on black plantation workers. Louisiana's actions alienated a majority of congressional Republicans, who refused to admit representatives and senators from the "reconstructed" state.

At the same time, though, Congress failed to enact a reconstruction policy of its own. This was not for lack of trying. In fact, both houses passed the Wade-Davis reconstruction bill (named for Senator Benjamin Wade of Ohio and Representative Henry Winter Davis of Maryland) in July 1864. That bill did not **enfranchise** blacks, but it did impose such stringent loyalty requirements on southern whites that few of them could take the required oath. Lincoln therefore vetoed it.

Lincoln's action infuriated many Republicans, and the bitter squabble threatened for a time to destroy Lincoln's chances of being reelected. Union military success in fall 1864, however, reunited the Republicans behind Lincoln. The collapse of Confederate military resistance the following spring set the stage for compromise between the president and Congress on a policy for the postwar South. Two days after Appomattox, Lincoln promised that he would soon announce such a policy, which probably would have included voting rights for some blacks and stronger measures to protect their civil rights. But three days later, Lincoln was assassinated.

ANDREW JOHNSON AND RECONSTRUCTION

In 1864, Republicans had adopted the name Union Party to attract the votes of War Democrats and border-state Unionists who could not bring themselves to vote Republican. For the same reason, they also nominated Andrew Johnson of Tennessee as Lincoln's running mate.

Of "poor white" heritage, Johnson had clawed his way up in the rough-and-tumble politics of east Tennessee. This region of small farms and few slaves held little love for the planters who controlled the state. Andrew Johnson denounced the planters as "stuck-up aristocrats" who had no empathy with the southern yeomen for whom Johnson became a self-appointed spokesman. Johnson, although a Democrat, was the only senator from a seceding state who refused to support the Confederacy. For this stance, the Republicans rewarded him with the vice presidential nomination, hoping to attract the votes of pro-war Democrats and upper-South Unionists.

Booth's bullet therefore elevated to the presidency a man who still thought of himself as primarily a Democrat and a southerner. The trouble this might cause in a party that was mostly Republican and northern was not immediately apparent, however. In fact, Johnson's enmity toward the "stuck-up aristocrats" whom he blamed for leading the South into secession prompted him to utter dire threats. "Traitors must be impoverished …. They must not only be punished, but their social power must be destroyed."

Radical Republicans liked the sound of this. Johnson seemed to promise the type of reconstruction they favored—one that would deny political power to ex-Confederates and would enfranchise blacks. They envisioned a coalition between these new black voters and the small minority of southern whites who had never supported the Confederacy. These men could be expected to vote Republican. Republican governments in southern states would guarantee freedom and would pass laws to provide civil rights and economic opportunity for freed slaves. They would also strengthen the Republican Party nationally.

Johnson's Policy   From a combination of pragmatic, partisan, and idealistic motives, therefore, Radical Republicans prepared to implement a progressive reconstruction policy. But Johnson unexpectedly refused to cooperate. Instead of calling Congress into special session, he moved ahead on his own. On May 29, 1865, Johnson issued two proclamations. The first provided a blanket **amnesty** for all but the highest-ranking Confederate officials and military officers, and those ex-Confederates with taxable property

Andrew Johnson and Frederick Douglass. *By 1866, the president and the leading black advocate for equal rights represented opposite poles in the debate about reconstruction. Johnson wanted to bring the South back into the Union on the basis of white suffrage; Douglass wanted black men to be granted the right to vote. Johnson's resistance to this policy as Republicans tried to enact it was a factor in his impeachment two years later.*

worth $20,000 or more—the "stuck-up aristocrats." The second named a provisional governor for North Carolina and directed him to call an election of delegates to frame a new state constitution. Only white men who had received amnesty and taken an oath of allegiance could vote. Similar proclamations soon followed for other former Confederate states. Johnson's policy was clear: He would exclude both blacks and upper-class whites from the reconstruction process.

Although at first many Republicans supported Johnson's policy, the radicals were dismayed. They feared that restricting the vote to whites would lead to oppression of the newly freed slaves and restoration of the old power structure in the South. They began to sense that Johnson (who had owned slaves) was as dedicated to white supremacy as any Confederate. "White men alone must govern the South," he told a Democratic senator. After a tense confrontation with a group of black men led by Frederick Douglass, who had visited the White House to urge black suffrage, Johnson told his private secretary: "I know that damned Douglass; he's just like any nigger, and he would sooner cut a white man's throat than not."

Moderate Republicans believed that black men should participate to some degree in the reconstruction process, but in 1865 they were not yet prepared to break with the president. They regarded his policy as an "experiment" that would be modified as time went on.

Southern Defiance

As it happened, none of the state conventions enfranchised a single black. Some of them even balked at ratifying the Thirteenth Amendment (which abolished slavery). Reports from the South told of neo-Confederate violence against blacks and their white sympathizers. Johnson seemed to encourage such activities by allowing the organization of white militia units.

Then there was the matter of presidential pardons. After talking fiercely about punishing traitors, and after excluding several classes of them from his amnesty proclamation, Johnson began to issue special pardons to many ex-Confederates, restoring to them all property and political rights. Under the new state constitutions, southern voters were electing hundreds of ex-Confederates to state offices. Even more alarming to northerners, who thought they had won the war, was the election to Congress of no fewer than nine ex-Confederate congressmen, seven ex-Confederate state officials, four generals, four colonels, and even the former Confederate vice president, Alexander H. Stephens.

Somehow the aristocrats and traitors Johnson had denounced in April had taken over the reconstruction process. They did so by flattering the presidential ego. Thousands of prominent ex-Confederates applied for pardons, confessing the error of their ways and appealing for presidential mercy. Johnson reveled in his power over these once-haughty aristocrats. Johnson also received praise and support from leading northern Democrats. Although the Republicans had placed him on their presidential ticket in 1864, Johnson was after all a Democrat. That party's leaders enticed Johnson with visions of reelection as a Democrat in 1868 if he could manage to reconstruct the South in a manner that would preserve a Democratic majority there.

The Black Codes

That was just what the Republicans feared. In the fall of 1865, their concern that state governments devoted to white supremacy would reduce the freedpeople to a condition close to slavery was confirmed when some of those governments enacted "**Black Codes**."

One of the first tasks of the legislatures of the reconstructed states was to define the rights of 4 million former slaves. The option of treating them exactly like white citizens was scarcely considered. Instead, the states excluded black people from juries and the ballot box, did not permit them to testify against whites in court, banned interracial marriage, and punished blacks more severely than whites for certain crimes. Some states defined any unemployed black person as a vagrant and hired him out to a planter, forbade blacks to lease land, and provided for the apprenticing to whites of black youths.

These Black Codes aroused anger among northern Republicans, who saw them as a brazen attempt to reinstate a **quasi-slavery**. "We tell the white men of Mississippi," declared the *Chicago Tribune,* "that the men of the North will convert the State of Mississippi into a frog pond before they will allow such laws to disgrace one foot of the soil in which the bones of our soldiers sleep and over which the flag of freedom waves." And in fact, the Union army's occupation forces did suspend the implementation of Black Codes that discriminated on racial grounds.

Land and Labor in the Postwar South   The Black Codes, although discriminatory, were designed to address a genuine problem. The end of the war had left black-white relations in the South in a state of limbo. The South's economy was in a shambles. Burned-out plantations, fields growing up in weeds, and railroads without tracks, bridges, or rolling stock marked the trail of war. Nearly half of the livestock in the former Confederacy and most other tangible assets except the land had been destroyed. Law and order broke down in many areas. The war had ended early enough in the spring to allow the planting of at least some food crops. But who would cultivate them? One-quarter of the South's white farmers had been killed in the war; the slaves were slaves no more. "We have nothing left to begin anew with," lamented a South Carolina planter. "I never did a day's work in my life, and I don't know how to begin."

Despite all of this trouble, life went on. Soldiers' widows and their children plowed and planted. Slaveless planters and their wives calloused their hands for the first time. Confederate veterans drifted home and went to work. Former slave owners asked their former slaves to work the land for wages or shares of the crop, and many did so. Others refused, because for them an essential part of freedom was leaving the place where they had been in bondage.

Thus, the roads were alive with freedpeople who were on the move in summer 1865. Many of them signed on to work at farms just a few miles from their old homes. Others moved into town. Some looked for relatives who had been sold away during slavery or from whom they had been separated during the war. Some wandered aimlessly. Crime increased as people, both blacks and whites, stole food to survive, and as whites organized vigilante groups to discipline blacks and force them to work.

The Freedmen's Bureau   Into this vacuum stepped the U.S. Army and the **Freedmen's Bureau**. Tens of thousands of troops remained in the South as an occupation force until civil government could be restored. The Freedmen's Bureau (its official title was Bureau of Refugees, Freedmen, and Abandoned Lands), created by Congress in March 1865, became the principal agency for overseeing relations between former slaves and owners. Headed by the antislavery general Oliver O. Howard and staffed by army officers, the bureau established posts throughout the South to supervise free-labor wage contracts between landowners and freedpeople. The Freedmen's Bureau also issued food rations to 150,000 people daily during 1865, one-third of them to whites. Southern whites viewed the Freedmen's Bureau with hostility. Without it, however, the postwar chaos and devastation in the South would have been much greater—as some whites privately admitted. Bureau agents used their influence with freedpeople to encourage them to sign free-labor contracts and return to work.

In negotiating labor contracts, the bureau tried to establish minimum wages. Lack of money in the South, however, caused many contracts to call for **share wages**—that is, paying workers with shares of the crop. At first, landowners worked their laborers in large groups (called gangs). But many black workers resented this arrangement as reminiscent of slavery. Thus, a new system evolved, called **sharecropping**, whereby a black family worked a specific piece of land in return for a share of the crop produced on it.

Land for the Landless

Freedpeople, of course, would have preferred to own the land they farmed. Some black farmers did manage to save up enough money to buy small plots of land. Demobilized black soldiers purchased land with their bounty payments, sometimes pooling their money to buy an entire plantation on which several black families settled. Northern philanthropists helped some freedmen buy land. But most ex-slaves found the purchase of land impossible. Few of them had money, and even if they did, whites often refused to sell their land because it would mean losing a source of cheap labor and encouraging notions of black independence.

Several northern radicals proposed legislation to confiscate ex-Confederate land and redistribute it to freedpeople, but those proposals went nowhere. The most promising effort to put thousands of slaves on land of their own also failed. In January 1865, after his march through Georgia, General William T. Sherman had issued a military order setting aside thousands of acres of abandoned plantation land in the Georgia and South Carolina lowcountry for settlement by freed slaves. The army even turned over some of its surplus mules to black farmers. The expectation of **40 acres and a mule** excited freedpeople in 1865, but President Johnson's Amnesty Proclamation and his wholesale issuance of pardons restored most of this

Library of Congress, Prints and Photographs Division

A Black School during Reconstruction. *In the antebellum South, teaching slaves to read and write was forbidden. Thus about 90 percent of the freedpeople were illiterate in 1865. One of their top priorities was education. At first, most of the teachers in the freedmen's schools established by northern missionary societies were northern white women, but as black teachers were trained, they took over the elementary schools, such as this one, photographed in the 1870s.*

property to pardoned ex-Confederates. The same thing happened to white-owned land elsewhere in the South. Placed under the temporary care of the Freedmen's Bureau for subsequent possible distribution to freedpeople, by 1866 nearly all of this land had been restored to its former owners by order of President Johnson.

Education   Abolitionists were more successful in helping freedpeople obtain an education. During the war, freedmen's aid societies and missionary societies founded by abolitionists had sent teachers to Union-occupied areas of the South to set up schools for freed slaves. After the war, this effort was expanded with the aid of the Freedmen's Bureau. Two thousand northern teachers, three-quarters of them women, fanned out into every part of the South. There they trained black teachers to staff first the mission schools and later the public schools established by Reconstruction state governments. After 1870, the missionary societies concentrated more heavily on making higher education available to African Americans. Many of the traditionally black colleges in the South today were founded and supported by their efforts. This education crusade, which the black leader W. E. B. Du Bois described as "the most wonderful peace-battle of the nineteenth century," reduced the southern black illiteracy rate to 70 percent by 1880 and to 48 percent by 1900.

THE ADVENT OF CONGRESSIONAL RECONSTRUCTION

Political reconstruction shaped the civil and political rights of freedpeople. By the time Congress met in December 1865, the Republican majority was determined to control the process by which former Confederate states would regain full representation. Congress refused to admit the representatives and senators elected by the former Confederate states under Johnson's reconstruction policy and set up a special committee to formulate new terms. The committee held hearings at which southern Unionists, freedpeople, and U.S. Army officers testified to abuse and terrorism in the South. Their testimony convinced Republicans of the need for stronger federal intervention to define and protect the civil rights of freedpeople. Many radicals wanted to go further and grant the ballot to black men.

Most Republicans realized that northern voters would not support such a radical policy, however. Racism was still strong in the North, where most states denied the right to vote to the few blacks living within their borders. Moderate Republicans feared that Democrats would exploit northern racism in the congressional elections of 1866 if Congress made black suffrage a cornerstone of Reconstruction. Instead, the special committee decided to draft a constitutional amendment that would encourage southern states to enfranchise blacks but would not require them to do so.

Schism between President and Congress   Meanwhile, Congress passed two laws to protect the economic and civil rights of freedpeople. The first extended the life of the Freedmen's Bureau and expanded its powers. The second defined freedpeople as citizens with equal legal rights and gave federal courts appellate jurisdiction to enforce those rights. To the dismay of moderates who were trying to heal the widening breach between the president and Congress, Johnson vetoed both measures. He followed this action with a speech to Democratic supporters in which he denounced Republican leaders as traitors who did not want to restore the Union except on terms that would degrade white southerners. Democratic newspapers applauded the president for vetoing bills that would "compound our race with niggers, gypsies, and baboons."

The Fourteenth Amendment   Johnson had thrown down the gauntlet to congressional Republicans, and they did not hesitate to take it up. With more than a two-thirds majority in both houses, they passed the Freedmen's Bureau and Civil Rights bills over the president's vetoes. Then on April 30, 1866, the special committee submitted to Congress its proposed Fourteenth Amendment to the Constitution. After lengthy debate, the amendment received the required two-thirds majority in Congress on June 13 and went to the states for ratification. Section 1 defined all native-born or naturalized persons, including blacks, as American citizens and prohibited the states from abridging the "privileges and immunities" of citizens, from depriving "any person of life, liberty, or property without due process of law," and from denying to any person "the equal protection of the laws." Section 2 gave states the option of either enfranchising black males or losing a proportionate number of congressional seats and electoral votes. Section 3 disqualified a significant number of ex-Confederates from holding federal or state office. Section 4 guaranteed the national debt and repudiated the Confederate debt. Section 5 empowered Congress to enforce the Fourteenth Amendment by "appropriate legislation." The Fourteenth Amendment had far-reaching consequences. Section 1 has become the most important provision in the Constitution for defining and enforcing civil rights.

The 1866 Elections   Republicans entered the 1866 congressional elections campaign with the Fourteenth Amendment as their platform. They made clear that any ex-Confederate state that ratified the amendment would be declared "reconstructed" and that its representatives and senators would be seated in Congress. Tennessee ratified the amendment, but Johnson counseled other southern legislatures to reject the amendment, which they did. Johnson then prepared for an all-out campaign to gain a friendly northern majority in the congressional elections.

Johnson began his campaign by creating a National Union Party made up of a few conservative Republicans who disagreed with their party, some border-state Unionists who supported the president, and Democrats. But many northern Democrats still carried the taint of having opposed the war effort, and most northern voters did not trust them. Further, race riots in Memphis and New Orleans, with white mobs attacking blacks, bolstered Republican arguments that national power was necessary to protect "the fruits of victory" in the South. Perhaps the biggest liability of the National Union Party was Johnson. In a whistle-stop tour through the North, he traded insults with hecklers and embarrassed his supporters by comparing himself to Christ and his Republican adversaries to Judas.

"PARDON, Columbia—'Shall I Trust These Men'?"

"FRANCHISE—'And Not This Man'?"

Cartoons for Freedom. *One of the best political cartoonists in American history, Thomas Nast drew scores of cartoons for* Harper's Weekly *in the 1860s and 1870s advocating the use of federal power to guarantee the liberty and enforce the equal rights of freed slaves. This illustration (1865) is an eloquent graphic expression of a powerful argument for giving freedmen the right to vote: Black men who fought for the Union were more deserving of this privilege than white men who fought against it. Several of the kneeling figures are recognizable Confederate leaders: Alexander Stephens and Robert E. Lee in the foreground, Jefferson Davis to Lee's left, and John C. Breckinridge, Joseph E. Johnston, and Robert Toombs behind and to Davis's left.*

Republicans swept the election: They gained a three-to-one majority in the next Congress. Having rejected the Reconstruction terms embodied in the Fourteenth Amendment, southern Democrats now faced far more stringent terms. "They would not cooperate in rebuilding what they destroyed," wrote an exasperated moderate Republican, so "we must remove the rubbish and rebuild from the bottom. Whether they are willing or not, we must compel obedience to the Union and demand protection for its humblest citizen."

The Reconstruction Acts of 1867

In March 1867, the new Congress enacted over Johnson's vetoes two laws prescribing new procedures for the full restoration of the former Confederate states to the Union. The Reconstruction Acts of 1867 divided the 10 southern states into five military districts, directed army officers to register voters for the election of delegates to new constitutional conventions, and enfranchised males aged 21 and older (including blacks) to vote in those elections. When a state had adopted a new constitution that granted equal civil and political rights regardless of race and had ratified the Fourteenth Amendment, it would be declared reconstructed, and its newly elected congressmen would be seated.

These measures embodied a true revolution. Just a few years earlier, southern whites had been masters of 4 million slaves and part of an independent Confederate nation. Now they were shorn of political power, with their former slaves not only free but also politically empowered. In 1867, the emancipation and enfranchisement of black Americans seemed, as a sympathetic French journalist described it, "one of the most radical revolutions known in history."

Like most revolutions, the reconstruction process did not go smoothly. Many Southern Democrats breathed defiance and refused to cooperate. The presence of the army minimized anti black violence, but thousands of white southerners who were eligible to vote refused to do so, hoping that their nonparticipation would

NEW YORK, SATURDAY, MAY 26, 1866.

according to Act of Congress, in the Year 1866, by Harper & Brothers, in the Clerk's Office of the District Court for the Southern District of New

Library of Congress, Prints and Photographs Division

The Burning of a Freedmen's School. *Because freedpeople's education symbolized black progress, whites who resented and resisted this progress sometimes attacked and burned freedmen's schools. This dramatic illustration shows a white mob burning a school during antiblack riots in Memphis in May 1866.*

delay the process long enough for northern voters to come to their senses and elect Democrats to Congress.

Blacks and their white allies organized **Union leagues** to inform and mobilize the new black voters into the Republican Party. Democrats branded southern white Republicans as "**scalawags**" and northern settlers as "**carpetbaggers.**" By September 1867, the 10 states had 735,000 black voters and only 635,000 white voters registered. At least one-third of the registered white voters were Republicans.

President Johnson did everything he could to block Reconstruction. He replaced several Republican generals in command of southern military districts with Democrats. He had his attorney general issue a ruling that interpreted the Reconstruction acts narrowly, thereby forcing a special session of Congress to pass a supplementary act in July 1867. He encouraged southern whites to obstruct the registration of voters and the election of convention delegates.

Johnson's purpose was to slow the process until 1868 in the hope that northern voters would repudiate Reconstruction in the presidential election of that year, when Johnson planned to run as the Democratic candidate. Off-year state elections in fall 1867 encouraged that hope. Republicans suffered setbacks in several northern states, especially where they endorsed referendum measures to enfranchise black men.

THE IMPEACHMENT OF ANDREW JOHNSON

Johnson struck even more boldly against Reconstruction after the 1867 elections. "What does Johnson mean to do?" an exasperated Republican asked another. "I am afraid his doings will make us all favor impeachment." In February 1868, Johnson removed from office Secretary of War Edwin M. Stanton, who had administered the War Department in support of the congressional Reconstruction policy. This appeared to violate the Tenure of Office Act, passed the year before over Johnson's veto, which required Senate consent for such removals. By a vote of 126 to 47 along party lines, the House impeached Johnson on February 24. The official reason for **impeachment** was that he had violated the Tenure of Office Act (which Johnson considered unconstitutional). The real reason was Johnson's stubborn defiance of Congress on Reconstruction.

Under the U.S. Constitution, impeachment by the House does not remove an official from office. It is more like a grand jury indictment that must be tried by a petit jury—in this case, the Senate, which sat as a court to try Johnson on the impeachment charges brought by the House. If convicted by a two-thirds majority of the Senate, he would be removed from office.

The impeachment trial proved long and complicated, which worked in Johnson's favor by allowing passions to cool. The Constitution specifies the grounds on which a president can be impeached and removed: "Treason, Bribery, or other high Crimes and Misdemeanors." The issue was whether Johnson was guilty of any of these acts. His able defense counsel exposed technical ambiguities in the Tenure of Office Act that raised doubts about whether Johnson had actually violated it. Several moderate Republicans feared that the precedent of impeachment might upset the delicate balance of powers between the executive branch, Congress, and the judiciary that was an essential element of the Constitution. Behind the scenes, Johnson strengthened his case by promising to appoint the respected general John M. Schofield as secretary of war and to stop obstructing the Reconstruction acts. In the end, seven Republican senators plus all Democrats voted for acquittal on May 16, and the final tally fell one vote short of the necessary two-thirds majority.

The Completion of Formal Reconstruction   The impeachment trial's end cleared the poisonous air in Washington, and Johnson quietly served out his term. Constitutional conventions met in the South during the 1867–1868 winter and the following spring. Hostile whites described them as "Bones and Banjoes Conventions" and the Republican delegates as "ragamuffins and jailbirds." In sober fact, however, the delegates were earnest advocates of a new order, and the constitutions they wrote were among the most progressive in the nation. Three-quarters of the delegates to the 10 conventions were Republicans. About 25 percent of those Republicans were northern whites who had relocated to the South after the war; 45 percent were native southern whites who braved the social ostracism of the white majority to cast their lot with the despised Republicans; and 30 percent were blacks. Only in the South Carolina convention were blacks in the majority.

The new state constitutions enacted **universal male suffrage**, putting them ahead of most northern states on that score. Some of the constitutions disfranchised certain classes of ex-Confederates for several years, but by 1872, all such disqualifications had been removed. The constitutions mandated statewide public schools for both races for the first time in the South. Most states permitted segregated schools, but schools of any kind for blacks represented a great step forward. Most of the constitutions increased the state's responsibility for social welfare beyond anything previously known in the South.

Violence in some parts of the South marred the voting on ratification of these state constitutions. The **Ku Klux Klan**, a night-riding white terrorist organization, made its first appearance during the elections. Nevertheless, voters in seven states ratified their constitutions and elected new legislatures that ratified the Fourteenth Amendment in spring 1868. That amendment became part of the U.S. Constitution the following summer, and the newly elected representatives and senators from those seven states, nearly all Republicans, took their seats in the House and Senate.

The Fifteenth Amendment   The remaining three southern states completed the reconstruction process in 1869 and 1870. Congress required them to ratify the Fifteenth as well as the Fourteenth Amendment. The Fifteenth Amendment prohibited states from denying the right to vote on grounds of race, color, or previous condition of servitude. Its purpose was not only to prevent the reconstructed states from any future revocation of black suffrage, but also to extend equal suffrage to the border states and to the North. With final ratification of the Fifteenth Amendment in 1870, the Constitution became truly color blind for the first time in U.S. history.

But the Fifteenth Amendment still left half of the population disfranchised. Many supporters of woman suffrage were embittered by its failure to ban discrimination on the grounds of gender as well as race. The radical wing of the suffragists, led by Elizabeth Cady Stanton and Susan B. Anthony, therefore opposed the Fifteenth Amendment, causing a split in the woman suffrage movement.

This movement had shared the ideological egalitarianism of abolitionism since the Seneca Falls Convention of 1848. In 1866, male and female abolitionists formed the American Equal Rights Association (AERA) to work for both black and woman suffrage. Although some Republicans sympathized with the suffragists, they knew that no strong constituency among male voters favored granting the vote to women. Most members of the AERA thought that black enfranchisement should come first.

Stanton and Anthony refused to accept this reasoning. Why should illiterate southern blacks have the right to vote, they asked, when educated northern women remained shut out from the polls? The Fifteenth Amendment would establish "the most odious form of aristocracy the world has ever seen: an aristocracy of sex." When a majority of delegates at the 1869 convention of the AERA voted to endorse the Fifteenth Amendment, several women led by Stanton and Anthony walked out and founded the National Woman Suffrage Association. The remaining delegates reorganized as the American Woman Suffrage Association. For the next two decades, these rival organizations, working for the same cause, remained at odds with each other.

The Election of 1868

Just as the presidential election of 1864 was a referendum on Lincoln's war policies, so the election of 1868 was a referendum on the Reconstruction policy of the Republicans. The Republican nominee was General **Ulysses S. Grant**. Although he had no political experience, Grant commanded greater authority and prestige than anyone else in the country. As general-in-chief of the army, he had opposed Johnson's Reconstruction policy in 1866 and had broken openly with the president in January 1868. That spring, Grant agreed to run for the presidency in order to preserve in peace the victory he had won in war.

The Democrats turned away from Andrew Johnson, who carried too many political liabilities. They nominated Horatio Seymour, the wartime governor of New York, bestowing on him the dubious privilege of running against Grant. Hoping to put together a majority consisting of the South plus New York and two or three other northern states, the Democrats adopted a militant platform denouncing the Reconstruction acts as "a flagrant usurpation of power ... unconstitutional, revolutionary, and void." The platform also demanded "the abolition of the Freedmen's Bureau, and all political instrumentalities designed to secure negro supremacy."

The vice presidential candidate, Frank Blair of Missouri, proclaimed that Democrats sought to "allow the white people to reorganize their own governments." The only way to achieve this bold counterrevolutionary goal was to suppress Republican voters in the South. This the Ku Klux Klan tried its best to do. In Louisiana, Georgia, Arkansas, and Tennessee, the Klan or Klan-like groups committed dozens of murders and intimidated thousands of black voters. The violence helped the Democratic cause in the South, but probably hurt it in the North, where many voters perceived the Klan as an organization of neo-Confederate paramilitary guerrillas. In fact, many Klansmen were former soldiers, and such famous Confederate generals as Nathan Bedford Forrest and John B. Gordon held high positions in the Klan.

Seymour did well in the South, carrying five former slave states and coming close in others, despite the solid Republican vote of the newly enfranchised blacks. Grant, however, swept the electoral vote 214 to 80. Seymour actually won a slight majority of the white voters nationally; without black enfranchisement, Grant would have had a minority of the popular vote.

THE GRANT ADMINISTRATION

Grant is usually considered a failure as president. That indictment is only partly correct. Grant's inexperience and poor judgment betrayed him into several unwise appointments of officials, who were later convicted of corruption, and scandals that plagued his back-to-back administrations (1869–1877). His secretary of war was impeached for selling appointments to army posts and Indian reservations, and his attorney general and secretary of the interior resigned under suspicion of malfeasance in 1875.

Although he was an honest man, Grant was too trusting of subordinates. He appointed many former members of his military family, as well as several of his wife's relatives, to offices for which they were scarcely qualified. In an era notorious for corruption at all levels of government, many of the scandals were not Grant's fault. The Tammany Hall "Ring" of "Boss" William Marcy Tweed in New York City may have stolen more money from taxpayers than all of the federal agencies combined. It was said that the only thing the Standard Oil Company could not do with the Ohio legislature was to refine it. In Washington, one of the most widely publicized scandals, the **Credit Mobilier Affair**, concerned Congress rather than the Grant administration. Several congressmen had accepted stock in the Credit Mobilier, a construction company for the Union Pacific Railroad, which received loans and land grants from the government. In return, the company expected lax congressional supervision, thereby permitting its financial manipulations.

What accounted for this explosion of corruption in the postwar decade? During the war, expansion of government contracts and the bureaucracy had created new opportunities for the unscrupulous. Following the intense sacrifices of the war years came a relaxation of tensions and standards. Rapid postwar economic growth, led by an extraordinary rush of railroad construction, further encouraged greed and get-rich-quick schemes of the kind satirized by Mark Twain and Charles Dudley Warner in their 1873 novel *The Gilded Age,* which gave its name to the era.

Civil Service Reform

Some of the apparent increase in corruption during the Gilded Age was more a matter of perception. Reformers focused a harsh light into the dark corners of corruption, hitherto unilluminated because of the nation's preoccupation with war and reconstruction. Thus, reformers' publicity may have exaggerated the actual extent of corruption. In reality, during the Grant administration, several government agencies made real progress in eliminating abuses that had flourished in earlier administrations.

The chief target of civil service reform was the "**spoils system.**" With the slogan "To the victor belongs the spoils," the victorious party in an election rewarded party workers with appointments as postmasters, customs collectors, and the like. The spoils system politicized the bureaucracy and staffed it with unqualified personnel who spent more time working for their party than for the government. It also plagued every incoming president (and other elected officials) with the "swarm of office seekers" that loom so large in contemporary accounts (including those of the humorist Orpheus C. Kerr, whose nom de plume was pronounced "Office Seeker").

Civil service reformers wanted to separate the bureaucracy from politics by requiring competitive examinations for the appointment of civil servants. This movement gathered steam during the 1870s and finally achieved success in 1883 with the passage of the Pendleton Civil Service Reform Act, which established the modern structure of the civil service. When Grant took office, he seemed to share the sentiments of civil service reformers; several of his cabinet officers inaugurated examinations for certain appointments and promotions in their departments. Grant also named a civil service commission headed by George William Curtis, a leading reformer and editor of *Harper's Weekly.* But many congressmen, senators, and other politicians resisted civil service reform because **patronage** greased the political machines that kept them in office. They managed to subvert reform, sometimes using Grant as an unwitting ally and thus turning many reformers against the president.

Foreign Policy Issues

A foreign policy controversy added to Grant's woes. The irregular procedures by which his private secretary had negotiated a treaty to annex Santo Domingo (now the Dominican Republic) alienated leading Republican senators, who defeated ratification of the treaty. Politically inexperienced, Grant acted like a general who needed only to give orders, rather than as a president who must cultivate supporters. The fallout from the Santo Domingo affair widened the fissure in the Republican Party between "spoilsmen" and "reformers."

But, the Grant administration had some solid foreign policy achievements to its credit. Hamilton Fish, the able secretary of state, negotiated the Treaty of

Washington in 1871 to settle the vexing *Alabama* claims. These were damage claims against Britain for the destruction of American shipping by the C.S.S. *Alabama* and other Confederate commerce raiders built in British shipyards. The treaty established an international tribunal to arbitrate the U.S. claims, resulting in the award of $15.5 million in damages to U.S. ship owners and a British expression of regret.

Reconstruction in the South   During Grant's two administrations, the "Southern Question" was the most intractable issue. A phrase in Grant's acceptance of the presidential nomination in 1868 had struck a responsive chord in the North: "Let us have peace." With the ratification of the Fifteenth Amendment, many people breathed a sigh of relief at the apparent resolution of "the last great point that remained to be settled of the issues of the war." It was time to deal with other matters that had been long neglected. Ever since the annexation of Texas a quarter-century earlier, the nation had known scarcely a moment's respite from sectional strife. "Let us have done with Reconstruction," pleaded the *New York Tribune* in 1870. "LET US HAVE PEACE." But there was no peace. Reconstruction was not over; it had hardly begun. State governments elected by black and white voters were in place in the South, but Democratic violence against Reconstruction and the instability of the Republican coalition that sustained it portended trouble.

Blacks in Office   Because the Republican Party had no antebellum roots in the South, most southern whites perceived it as a symbol of conquest and humiliation. In the North, the Republican Party represented the most prosperous, educated, and influential elements of the population, but in the South, most of its adherents were poor, illiterate, and landless.

About 80 percent of southern Republican voters were black. Although most black leaders were educated and many had been free before the war, most black voters were illiterate ex-slaves. Neither the leaders nor their constituents, however, were as ignorant or as venal as stereotypes portrayed them. Of 14 black representatives and two black senators elected in the South between 1868 and 1876, all but three had attended secondary school and four had attended college. Several of the blacks elected to state offices were among the best-educated men of their day. Jonathan Gibbs, secretary of state in Florida from 1868 to 1872 and state superintendent of education from 1872 to 1874, was a graduate of Dartmouth College and Princeton Theological Seminary. Francis L. Cardozo, secretary of state in South Carolina for four years and treasurer for another four, was educated at the University of Glasgow and at theological schools in Edinburgh and London.

It is true that some lower-level black officeholders, as well as their constituents, could not read or write, but the fault for that situation lay not with them but with the slave regime that had denied them an education. Illiteracy did not preclude an understanding of political issues for them any more than it did for Irish American voters in the North, some of whom were also illiterate. Southern blacks thirsted for education. Participation in the Union League and the

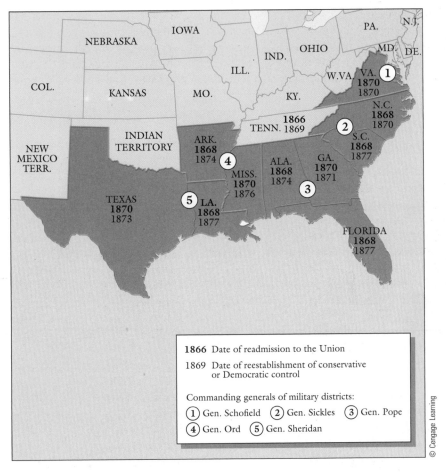

MAP 17.1 Reconstruction in the South

The dates for each state listed on this map show how short-lived "Radical Reconstruction" was in most Southern states.

experience of voting were forms of education. Black churches and fraternal organizations proliferated during Reconstruction and tutored African Americans in their rights and responsibilities.

Linked to the myth of black incompetence was the legend of the "Africanization" of southern governments during Reconstruction. The theme of "Negro rule" was a staple of Democratic propaganda. It was enshrined in folk memory and in generations of textbooks. In fact, blacks held only 15 to 20 percent of public offices, even at the height of Reconstruction in the early 1870s. No states had black governors (although the black lieutenant governor of Louisiana acted as governor for a month), and only one black man became a state supreme court justice. Nowhere except in South Carolina did blacks hold office in numbers anywhere near their proportion of the population; in that state, they constituted 52 percent of all state and federal elected officials from 1868 to 1876.

Three African American Members of Congress during Reconstruction.
Pictured clockwise from upper left are Blance K. Bruce, Robert Smalls, and Robert B. Elliott. Born into slavery, Bruce and Smalls became the two most prominent blacks in Congress during the 1870s. Bruce was elected to the United States Senate from Mississippi in 1875 and served his full six-year term despite the takeover of Mississippi by white-supremacist Democrats later in 1875. Smalls gained fame when he delivered the Confederate dispatch steamer Planter to the Union blockade fleet outside Charleston in 1862. After working as a pilot for the navy, Smalls emerged as a leader of the South Carolina Republican Party during Reconstruction and served several terms in the House. Of West Indian descent, Elliott was born in England and immigrated to South Carolina in 1867. He was elected to the House for two terms and became an eloquent spokesman for civil rights.

"Carpetbaggers"   Next to "Negro rule," carpetbagger corruption and scalawag rascality have been the prevailing myths of Reconstruction. Carpetbaggers did hold a disproportionate number of high political offices in southern state governments during Reconstruction. More than half of the Republican governors and nearly half of the congressmen and senators were northerners. A few did resemble the proverbial adventurer who came south with nothing but a carpetbag in which to stow the loot plundered from a helpless people. But most of the northerners were Union army officers who stayed on after the war as Freedmen's Bureau agents, teachers in black schools, or business investors. They hoped to rebuild southern society in the image of the free-labor North. Many were college graduates at a time when fewer than 2 percent of Americans had attended college. Most brought not empty carpetbags but considerable capital, which they invested in what they hoped would become a new South. They also invested human capital—themselves—in a drive to modernize the region's social structure and democratize its politics. But they underestimated the hostility of southern whites, most of whom regarded them as agents of an alien culture and leaders of an enemy army—as indeed they had been—in a war that for many southerners was not yet over.

"Scalawags"   Most of the native-born whites who joined the southern Republican Party came from the upcountry Unionist areas of western North Carolina and Virginia, eastern Tennessee, and elsewhere. Others were former Whigs who saw an opportunity to rebuild the South's economy in partnership with northern Republicans. Republicans, said a North Carolina scalawag, were the "party of progress, of education, of development .... Yankees and Yankee notions are just what we want in this country. We want their capital to build factories and work shops, and railroads."

But Yankees and Yankee notions were just what most southern whites did not want. Democrats saw that the southern Republican Party they abhorred was a fragile coalition of blacks and whites, Yankees and southerners, hill-country yeomen and lowcountry entrepreneurs, illiterates and college graduates. The party was weakest along the seams where these disparate elements joined, especially the racial seam. Democrats attacked that weakness with every weapon at their command, from social ostracism of white Republicans to economic intimidation of black employees and sharecroppers. The most potent Democratic weapon was violence.

The Ku Klux Klan   The generic name for the secret groups that terrorized the southern countryside was the Ku Klux Klan, but some went by other names (the Knights of the White Camelia in Louisiana, for example). Part of the Klan's purpose was social control of the black population. Sharecroppers who tried to extract better terms from landowners, or black people who were considered too "uppity," were likely to receive a midnight whipping—or worse—from white-sheeted Klansmen. Scores of black schools, perceived as a particular threat to white supremacy, went up in flames.

The Klan's main purpose was political: to destroy the Republican Party by terrorizing its voters and, if necessary, by murdering its leaders. No one knows how many politically motivated killings took place—certainly hundreds, probably thousands. Nearly all of the victims were Republicans; most of them were black. In one notorious incident, the Colfax Massacre in Louisiana (April 18, 1873), a clash between black militia and armed whites left three whites and nearly 100 blacks dead. Half of the blacks were killed in cold blood after they had surrendered. In some places, notably Tennessee and Arkansas, Republican militias formed to suppress and disarm the Klan, but in most areas the militias were outgunned and outmaneuvered by ex-Confederate veteran Klansmen. Some Republican governors were reluctant to use black militia against white guerrillas for fear of sparking a racial bloodbath—as happened at Colfax.

The answer seemed to be federal troops. In 1870 and 1871, Congress enacted three laws intended to enforce the Fourteenth and Fifteenth Amendments. Interference with voting rights became a federal offense, and any attempt to deprive another person of civil or political rights became a felony. The third law, passed on April 20, 1871, and popularly called the Ku Klux Klan Act, gave the president power to suspend the writ of **habeas corpus** and send in federal troops to suppress armed resistance to federal law.

Armed with these laws, the Grant administration moved against the Klan. Because Grant was sensitive to charges of "military despotism," he used his powers with restraint. He suspended the writ of habeas corpus in only nine South Carolina counties. Nevertheless, there and elsewhere federal marshals backed by troops arrested thousands of suspected Klansmen. Federal grand juries indicted more than 3,000, and several hundred defendants pleaded guilty in return for suspended sentences. To clear clogged court dockets so that the worst offenders could be tried quickly, the Justice Department dropped charges against nearly 2,000 others. About 600 Klansmen were convicted; most of them received fines or light jail sentences, but 65 went to a federal penitentiary for terms of up to five years.

The Election of 1872

These measures broke the back of the Klan in time for the 1872 presidential election. A group of dissident Republicans had emerged to challenge Grant's reelection. They believed that conciliation of southern whites rather than continued military intervention was the only way to achieve peace in the South. Calling themselves Liberal Republicans, these dissidents nominated Horace Greeley, the famous editor of the *New York Tribune*. Under the slogan "Anything to beat Grant," the Democratic Party also endorsed Greeley's nomination, although he had long been their antagonist. On a platform denouncing "bayonet rule" in the South, Greeley urged his fellow northerners to put the issues of the Civil War behind them and to "clasp hands across the bloody chasm which has too long divided" North and South.

This phrase would come back to haunt Greeley. Most voters in the North were still not prepared to trust Democrats or southern whites. Powerful anti-Greeley cartoons by political cartoonist Thomas Nast showed Greeley shaking the hand of a Klansman dripping with the blood of a murdered black Republican. Nast's most famous cartoon portrayed Greeley as a pirate captain bringing his craft alongside the ship of state, while Confederate leaders, armed to the teeth, hid below waiting to board it.

Grant swamped Greeley on Election Day. Republicans carried every northern state and 10 of the 16 southern and border states. Blacks in the South enjoyed more freedom in voting than they would again for a century. But this apparent triumph of Republicanism and Reconstruction would soon unravel.

The Panic of 1873   The U.S. economy had grown at an unprecedented pace since recovering from a mild postwar recession. The first transcontinental railroad had been completed on May 10, 1869, when a golden spike was driven at Promontory Summit, Utah Territory, linking the Union Pacific and the Central Pacific. But the building of a second transcontinental line, the Northern Pacific, precipitated a Wall Street panic in 1873 and plunged the economy into a five-year depression.

Jay Cooke's banking firm, fresh from its triumphant marketing of Union war bonds, took over the Northern Pacific in 1869. Cooke pyramided every conceivable kind of equity and loan financing to raise the money to begin laying rails west from Duluth, Minnesota. Other investment firms did the same as a fever of speculative financing gripped the country. In September 1873, the pyramid of paper collapsed. Cooke's firm was the first to go bankrupt. Like dominoes, thousands of banks and businesses also collapsed. Unemployment rose to 14 percent, and hard times set in.

THE RETREAT FROM RECONSTRUCTION

It is an axiom of American politics that the voters will punish the party in power in times of economic depression. That axiom held true in the 1870s. Democrats made large gains in the congressional elections of 1874, winning a majority in the House for the first time in 18 years.

Public opinion also began to turn against Republican policies in the South. The campaign by Liberal Republicans and Democrats against "bayonet rule" and "carpetbag corruption" that left most northern voters unmoved in 1872 found a growing audience in subsequent years. Intraparty battles among Republicans in southern states enabled Democrats to regain control of several state governments. Well-publicized corruption scandals also discredited Republican leaders. Although corruption was probably no worse in southern states than in many parts of the North, southern postwar poverty made waste and extravagance seem worse. White Democrats scored propaganda points by claiming that corruption proved the incompetence of "Negro-carpetbag" regimes.

Northerners grew increasingly weary of what seemed to be the endless turmoil of southern politics. Most of them had never had a strong commitment to racial equality, and they were growing more and more willing to let white supremacy regain sway in the South. "The truth is," confessed a northern Republican, "our people are tired out with this worn out cry of 'Southern outrages'!!! Hard times & heavy taxes make them wish the 'nigger,' 'everlasting nigger,' were in hell or Africa."

By 1875, only four southern states remained under Republican control: South Carolina, Florida, Mississippi, and Louisiana. In those states, white Democrats had revived paramilitary organizations under various names: White Leagues

HISTORY THROUGH FILM

The Birth of a Nation (1915)

Directed by D.W.Griffith. Starring Lillian Gish (Elsie Stoneman), Henry B. Walthall (Ben Cameron), Ralph Lewis (Austin Stoneman), George Siegmann (Silas Lynch).

Few if any films have had such a pernicious impact on historical understanding and race relations as *Birth of a Nation*. This movie popularized a version of Reconstruction that portrayed predatory carpetbaggers and stupid, brutish blacks plundering a prostrate South and lusting after white women. It perpetuated vicious stereotypes of rapacious black males. It glorified the Ku Klux Klan of the Reconstruction era, inspiring the founding of the "second Klan" in 1915, which became a powerful force in the 1920s.

The first half of the film offers a conventional Victorian romance of the Civil War. The two sons and daughter of Austin Stoneman (a malevolent Radical Republican who is a thinly disguised Thaddeus Stevens) become friends with the three sons and two daughters of the Cameron family of "Piedmont," South Carolina, through the friendship of Ben Cameron and Phil Stoneman at college. The Civil War tragically separates the families. The Stoneman and Cameron boys enlist in the Union and Confederate armies and—predictably—face each other on the battlefield. Two Camerons and one Stoneman are killed in the war, and Ben Cameron is badly wounded and captured, to be nursed back to health by—you guessed it—Elsie Stoneman. After the war, the younger Camerons and Stonemans renew their friendship.

During the Stonemans' visit to South Carolina, Ben Cameron and Elsie Stoneman, and Phil Stoneman and Flora Cameron fall in love. If the story had stopped there, *Birth of a Nation* would have been just another Hollywood romance. But Austin Stoneman brings south with him Silas Lynch, an ambitious, leering mulatto demagogue who stirs up the animal passions of the ignorant black majority to demand "Equal Rights, Equal Politics, Equal Marriage." A "renegade Negro," Gus, stalks the youngest Cameron daughter, who saves herself from rape by jumping from a cliff to her death. Silas Lynch tries to force Elsie to marry him. "I will build a Black Empire," he tells the beautiful, virginal Elsie (Lillian Gish was the Hollywood beauty queen of silent films), "and you as my queen shall rule by my side."

Finally, provoked beyond endurance, white South Carolinians led by Ben Cameron organize the Ku Klux Klan to save "the Aryan race." Riding to the rescue of embattled whites in stirring scenes that anticipated the heroic actions of the cavalry against Indians in later Hollywood Westerns, the Klan executes Gus, saves Elsie, disperses black soldiers and mobs, and carries the next election for white rule by intimidating black voters. The film ends with a double marriage that unites the Camerons and Stonemans in a symbolic rebirth of a nation that joins whites of the North and South in a new union rightfully based on the supremacy of "the Aryan race."

The son of a Confederate lieutenant colonel, David Wark (D. W.) Griffith was the foremost director of the silent movie

Bettmann/Corbis

Ben Cameron (Henry B. Walthall) kissing the hand of Elsie Stoneman (Lillian Gish) in Birth of a Nation.

era. He pioneered many precedent-setting cinematic techniques and profoundly influenced filmmaking throughout the world. *Birth of a Nation* was the first real full-length feature film, technically and artistically superior to anything before it. Apart from its place in the history of cinema, though, why should anyone today watch a movie that perpetuates such wrong-headed history and noxious racist stereotypes? Precisely because it reflects and amplifies an interpretation of Reconstruction that prevailed from the 1890s to the 1950s, and thereby shaped not only historical understanding but also contemporary behavior (as in its inspiration for the Klan of the 1920s). Although *Birth of a Nation* aroused controversy in parts of the North and was picketed by the NAACP, some 200 million people saw the film in the United States and abroad from 1915 to 1946. The story, and director Griffith, demonstrated in dramatic fashion how the South, having lost the Civil War, won the battle for how the war and especially Reconstruction would be remembered for more than half a century.

(Louisiana), Rifle Clubs (Mississippi), and Red Shirts (South Carolina). Unlike the Klan, these groups operated openly. In Louisiana, they fought pitched battles with Republican militias in which scores were killed. When the Grant administration sent large numbers of federal troops to Louisiana, people in both North and South cried out against military rule. The protests grew even louder when soldiers marched onto the floor of the Louisiana legislature in January 1875 and expelled several Democratic legislators after a contested election. Was this America? Republican senator Carl Schurz asked in a widely publicized speech: "If this can be done in Louisiana, how long will it be before it can be done in Massachusetts and Ohio? How long before a soldier may stalk into the national House of Representatives, and, pointing to the Speaker's mace, say 'Take away that bauble!'"

The Mississippi Election of 1875   The backlash against the Grant administration affected the Mississippi state election of 1875. Democrats there devised a strategy called the Mississippi Plan. The first step was to "persuade" the 10 to 15 percent of white voters still calling themselves Republicans to switch to the Democrats. Only a handful of carpetbaggers could resist the economic pressures, social ostracism, and threats that made it "too damned hot for [us] to stay out," wrote one white Republican who changed parties.

The second step in the Mississippi Plan was to intimidate black voters because, even with all whites voting Democratic, the party could still be defeated by the 55 percent black majority. Economic coercion against black sharecroppers and workers kept some of them away from the polls, but violence was the most effective method. Democratic "rifle clubs" showed up at Republican rallies, provoked riots, and shot down dozens of blacks in the ensuing melees. Governor Adelbert Ames—a native of Maine, a Union general who had won a medal of honor in the war, and one of the ablest of southern Republicans—called for federal troops to control the violence. Grant intended to comply, but Ohio Republicans warned him that if he sent troops to Mississippi, the Democrats would exploit the issue of "bayonet rule" to carry Ohio in that year's state elections. Grant yielded—in effect giving up Mississippi for Ohio. The U.S. attorney general replied to Ames's request for troops:

> The whole public are tired out with these annual autumnal outbreaks in the South, and the great majority are now ready to condemn any interference on the part of the government .... Preserve the peace by the forces in your own state, and let the country see that the citizens of Mississippi, who are ... largely Republican, have the courage to fight for their rights.

Governor Ames did try to organize a loyal state militia, but that proved difficult—and in any case, he was reluctant to use a black militia for fear of provoking a race war. "No matter if they are going to carry the State," said Ames with weary resignation, "let them carry it, and let us be at peace and have no more killing." The Mississippi Plan worked like a charm. In five of the state's counties with large black majorities, the Republicans polled 12, 7, 4, 2, and 0 votes, respectively. What had been a Republican majority of 30,000 in 1874 became a Democratic majority of 30,000 in 1875.

The Supreme Court and Reconstruction

Even if Grant had been willing to continue intervening in southern state elections, Congress and the courts would have constricted such efforts. The new Democratic majority in the House threatened to cut any appropriations for the Justice Department and the army intended for use in the South. In 1876, the U.S. Supreme Court handed down two decisions that declared parts of the 1870 and 1871 laws for enforcement of the Fourteenth and Fifteenth Amendments unconstitutional. In *U.S. v. Cruikshank* and *U.S. v. Reese,* the Court ruled on cases from Louisiana and Kentucky. Both cases grew out of provisions in these laws authorizing federal officials to prosecute *individuals* (not states) for violations of the civil and voting rights of blacks. But, the Court pointed out, the Fourteenth and Fifteenth Amendments apply to actions by *states:* "No State ... deprive any person of life, liberty, or property ... nor deny to any person ... equal protection of the laws" and the right to vote "shall not be denied ... by any State." Therefore, the

Bettmann/Corbis

How the Mississippi Plan Worked. *This cartoon shows how black counties could report large Democratic majorities in the Mississippi state election of 1875. The black voter holds a Democratic ticket while one of the men, described in the caption as a "Democratic reformer," holds a revolver to his head and says: "You're as free as air, ain't you? Say you are, or I'll blow your black head off!"*

portions of these laws that empowered the federal government to prosecute individuals were declared unconstitutional.

The Court did not say what could be done when states were controlled by white-supremacy Democrats who had no intention of enforcing equal rights. Meanwhile, in another ruling, *Civil Rights Cases* (1883), the Court declared unconstitutional a civil rights law passed by Congress in 1875. That law banned racial discrimination in all forms of public transportation and public accommodations. If enforced, it would have effected a sweeping transformation of race relations—in the North as well as in the South. Even some of the congressmen who voted for the bill doubted its constitutionality, however, and the Justice Department had made little effort to enforce it. Several cases made their way to the Supreme Court, which in 1883 ruled the law unconstitutional —again on grounds that the Fourteenth Amendment applied only to states, not to individuals. Several states—all in the North—passed their own civil rights laws in the 1870s and 1880s, but less than 10 percent of the black population resided in those states. The mass of African Americans lived a segregated existence.

The Election of 1876   In 1876, the remaining southern Republican state governments fell victim to the passion for "reform." The mounting revelations of corruption at all levels of government ensured that reform would be the leading issue in the presidential election. In this centennial year of the birth of the United States, marked by a great exposition in Philadelphia, Americans wanted to put their best foot forward. Both major parties gave their presidential nominations to governors who had earned reform reputations in their states: Democrat Samuel J. Tilden of New York and Republican Rutherford B. Hayes of Ohio.

Democrats entered the campaign as favorites for the first time in two decades. It seemed likely that they would be able to put together an electoral majority from a "solid South" plus New York and two or three other northern states. To ensure a solid South, they looked to the lessons of the Mississippi Plan. In 1876, a new word came into use to describe Democratic techniques of intimidation: *bulldozing*. To bulldoze black voters meant to trample them down or keep them away from the polls. In South Carolina and Louisiana, the Red Shirts and the White Leagues mobilized for an all-out bulldozing effort.

The most notorious incident, the Hamburg Massacre, occurred in the village of Hamburg, South Carolina, where a battle between a black militia unit and 200 Red Shirts resulted in the capture of several militiamen, five of whom were shot "while attempting to escape." This time Grant did send in federal troops. He pronounced the Hamburg Massacre "cruel, blood-thirsty, wanton, unprovoked ... a repetition of the course that has been pursued in other Southern States."

The federal government also put several thousand deputy marshals and election supervisors on duty in the South. Although they kept an uneasy peace at the polls, they could do little to prevent assaults, threats, and economic coercion in backcountry districts, which reduced the potential Republican tally in the former Confederate states by at least 250,000 votes.

Disputed Results   When the results were in, Tilden had carried four northern states, including New York with its 35 electoral votes, and all of the former slave states except—apparently—Louisiana, South Carolina, and Florida, which produced disputed returns. Because Tilden needed only one of them to win the presidency, while Hayes needed all three,

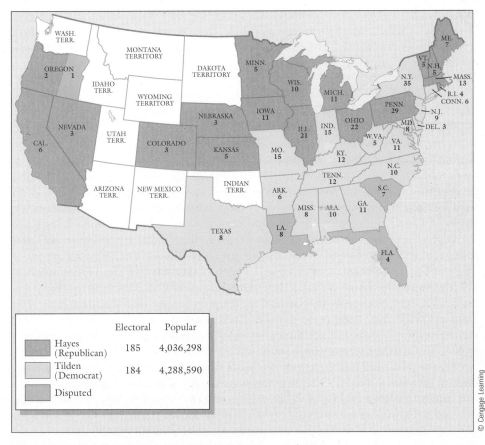

	Electoral	Popular
Hayes (Republican)	185	4,036,298
Tilden (Democrat)	184	4,288,590
Disputed		

© Cengage Learning

MAP 17.2 Hayes-Tilden Disputed Election of 1876

A comparison of this map with Map 17.1 shows the persistence of geographical voting patterns once Southern Democrats had overthrown most Republican state governments and effectively disfranchised many black voters.

and because Tilden seemed to have carried Louisiana and Florida, it appeared initially that he had won the presidency. But frauds and irregularities reported from several bulldozed districts in the three states clouded the issue. For example, a Louisiana parish that had recorded 1,688 Republican votes in 1874 reported only 1 in 1876. Many other similar discrepancies appeared. The official returns ultimately sent to Washington gave all three states—and therefore the presidency—to Hayes, but the Democrats refused to recognize the results, and they controlled the House.

The country now faced a serious constitutional crisis. Armed Democrats threatened to march on Washington. Many people feared another civil war. The Constitution offered no clear guidance on how to deal with the matter. A count of the state electoral votes required the concurrence of both houses of Congress, but with a Democratic House and a Republican Senate, such concurrence was not forthcoming. To break the deadlock, Congress created a special electoral commission consisting of five representatives, five senators, and five Supreme Court justices split evenly between the two parties, with one member, a Supreme Court justice, supposedly an independent—but in fact a Republican.

Tilden had won a national majority of 252,000 popular votes, and the raw returns gave him a majority in the three disputed states. But an estimated 250,000 southern Republicans had been bulldozed away from the polls. In a genuinely fair and free election, the Republicans might have carried Mississippi and North Carolina as well as the three disputed states.

The Compromise of 1877   In February 1877, three months after voters had gone to the polls, the electoral commission issued its ruling. By a partisan vote of 8 to 7—with the "independent" justice voting with the Republicans—the commission awarded all of the disputed states to Hayes. The Democrats cried foul and began a **filibuster** in the House to delay the final electoral count beyond the inauguration date of March 4, to throw the election to the House of Representatives, an eventuality that threatened to bring total anarchy. But, behind the scenes, a compromise began to take shape. Both northern Republicans and Southern Democrats of Whig heritage had similar interests in liquidating the sectional rancor and in getting on with the business of economic recovery and development. To wean southern Whiggish Democrats away from a House filibuster, Hayes promised his support as president for federal appropriations to rebuild war-destroyed **levees** on the lower Mississippi and federal aid for a southern transcontinental railroad. Hayes's lieutenants also hinted at the appointment of a southerner as postmaster general, who would have a considerable amount of patronage at his disposal—the appointment of thousands of local postmasters.

Most important, southerners wanted to know what Hayes would do about Louisiana and South Carolina. Hayes signaled his intention to end "bayonet rule," which he had for some time considered a bankrupt policy. He believed that the goodwill and influence of southern moderates would offer better protection for black rights than federal troops could provide. In return for his commitment to withdraw the troops, Hayes asked for—and received—promises of fair treatment of freedpeople and respect for their constitutional rights.

The End of   Such promises were easier to make than to keep, as future
Reconstruction   years would reveal. In any case, the Democratic filibuster col-
                        lapsed, and Hayes was inaugurated on March 4. He soon
fulfilled his part of the Compromise of 1877: Ex-Confederate Democrat David Key of Tennessee became postmaster general; in 1878, the South received more federal money for internal improvements than ever before; and federal troops left the capitals of Louisiana and South Carolina. The last two Republican state governments collapsed. The old abolitionist and Radical Republican warhorses denounced Hayes's actions as a sellout of southern blacks.

But voices of protest could scarcely be heard above the sighs of relief that the crisis was over. Most Americans, including even most Republicans, wanted no more military intervention in state affairs.

CONCLUSION

Before the Civil War, most Americans had viewed a powerful government as a threat to individual liberties. That is why the first 10 amendments to the Constitution (the Bill of Rights) imposed strict limits on the powers of the federal government. During the Civil War and especially during Reconstruction, however, the national government had to exert an unprecedented amount of power to free the slaves and guarantee their equal rights as free citizens. That is why the Thirteenth, Fourteenth, and Fifteenth Amendments to the Constitution contained clauses stating that "Congress shall have power" to enforce these provisions for liberty and equal rights.

During the post–Civil War decade, Congress passed civil rights laws and enforcement legislation to accomplish this purpose. Federal marshals and troops patrolled the polls to protect black voters, arrested thousands of Klansmen and other violators of black civil rights, and even occupied state capitals to prevent Democratic paramilitary groups from overthrowing legitimately elected Republican state governments.

By 1875, many northerners had grown tired of or alarmed by this continued use of military power to intervene in the internal affairs of states. The Supreme Court stripped the federal government of much of its authority to enforce certain provisions of the Fourteenth and Fifteenth Amendments. Traditional fears of military power as a threat to individual liberties came to the fore again.

The withdrawal of federal troops from the South in 1877 constituted both a symbolic and a substantive end of the 12-year postwar era known as Reconstruction. Reconstruction had achieved the two great objectives inherited from the Civil

War: (1) to reincorporate the former Confederate states into the Union, and (2) to accomplish a transition from slavery to freedom in the South.

That transition was marred by the economic inequity of sharecropping and the social injustice of white supremacy. A third goal of Reconstruction, enforcement of the equal civil and political rights promised in the Fourteenth and Fifteenth Amendments, was betrayed by the Compromise of 1877. In subsequent decades, the freed slaves and their descendants suffered repression into segregated, second-class citizenship.

18

A Transformed Nation: The West and the New South, 1865–1900

CHAPTER OUTLINE

• An Industrializing West • Conquest and Resistance: American Indians in the Trans-Mississippi West • Industrialization and the New South • The Politics of Stalemate

---

"How I do wish you could all come out here," the new Kansas homesteader Mary Abell wrote to her family back east in 1871. "It is such a beautiful country—I did not know there was any thing so beautiful in the whole world as the country we passed over in coming here." Just arrived from New York with her husband, Abell was excited about the prospect of a new life in the West: "Robert has got a piece of land that suits him," she told her sister. "It seems so fortunate." She knew there was much to do in the days ahead—"There is a house to be built fences to make—a well to be dug and a cow to be got." But Abell didn't seem to mind: "I should never be content to live East now," she said. "Things there would look very little."

Abell was part of a great wave of settlement in the post–Civil War era that would transform the West. From 1865 to 1890, the white population in the trans-Mississippi West increased some 400 percent to 8,628,000—a figure that includes both native-born and white immigrants. The dream of western lands also inspired many African Americans, whose cherished hopes for liberty led hundreds of thousands to leave the South for points west from 1880 to 1910. At the same time, immigrants from China, Mexico, and other countries were drawn to the economic opportunities of the West as part of a global movement of peoples in this period.

All of these men and women were driven by desires for a better life, but this motivation often conflicted with the rights and desires of the diverse peoples who already inhabited the West, including, among others, a variety of Indian cultures and societies; borderlands villages of Spanish-speaking peoples; settlements of Chinese miners and laborers; and Mexicans in California. Settlement set in motion

CHRONOLOGY

1862	Sioux uprising in Minnesota; 38 Sioux executed
1864	Colorado militia massacres Cheyenne in village at Sand Creek, Colorado
1866	Cowboys conduct first cattle drive north from Texas
1869	President Grant announces his "peace policy" toward Indians
1876	Sioux and Cheyenne defeat Custer at Little Big Horn
1880	James A. Garfield elected president
1881	Garfield assassinated; Chester A. Arthur becomes president
1883	Pendleton Act begins reform of civil service
1884	Grover Cleveland elected president
1887	Dawes Severalty Act dissolves Indian tribal units and implements individual ownership of tribal lands
1888	Benjamin Harrison elected president
1889	Government opens Indian Territory (Oklahoma) to white settlement
1890	Wounded Knee massacre
	New Mississippi constitution pioneers black disfranchisement in South
	Republicans try but fail to enact federal elections bill to protect black voting rights
	Congress enacts McKinley Tariff
1892	Grover Cleveland again elected president
1895	Booker T. Washington makes his Atlanta Compromise address
1896	*Plessy v. Ferguson* legalizes "separate but equal" state racial segregation laws
1898	*Williams v. Mississippi* condones use of literacy tests and similar measures to restrict voting rights

conflict and resistance in numerous locations. Who would gain power over western lands? Whose liberty would be respected? What efforts would be made to achieve equality—or deny equality—to all of these peoples?

AN INDUSTRIALIZING WEST

Industrialization in the West had many linked components: settlement, including the creation of farms, communities, and western cities; production of commodities such as cattle and timber that could be shipped east; creation of western consumers and thus the demand for manufactured goods; extraction of resources through mining and logging; and the shipment of commodities using a national transportation network. These western processes of resource extraction may have looked different from the factory-centered industrialization that developed in the

East and Midwest at this time, but they still involved the transformation of an agrarian economy into an industrial society. Like eastern industrialization, western industrialization also had global reach, pulling immigrants from China, Peru, Chile, Hawaii, Europe, and Mexico to the already diverse West.

The Homestead Act   Many migrants to the West were able to become homesteaders because of legislation that took effect on January 1, 1863—the same day that the Emancipation Proclamation became law. Meant to provide free land for western settlers, the **Homestead Act** embodied a cherished American ideal that stretched back to the Jeffersonian era: the belief that individual ownership of land by farmers was at the heart of a virtuous citizenry and a sound democratic republic.

In the 1850s, many people believed that a western "safety valve" was necessary to ward off the potential evils of industrialization, urbanization, and capitalist expansion. Free land in the West would allow individual farmers to support themselves and ultimately help preserve American values of democratic individualism. Yet, settlement of the West was not so much an escape from industrialization as an important factor in the ongoing industrialization of the West.

The provisions of the Homestead Act were remarkably egalitarian for their day—up to a point. Both men and unmarried women were eligible to file for up to 160 acres of surveyed land in the public domain, as long as they were over the age of 21. (Married women were assumed to be dependents of their homesteading husbands.) Immigrants who affirmed their intention to become citizens were also eligible. As long as homesteaders lived on the land for five years, not only cultivating it but also "improving" it by building a house or barn, they could receive full title for a fee of only $10. Utilizing these provisions, white homesteaders ultimately claimed some 285 million acres of land.

Despite this surface egalitarianism, the Homestead Act privileged white farmers over African Americans and Hispanics, who rarely had the resources necessary to homestead. Even free land required tools and seed, plus costly transportation. The act also denied access to Chinese laborers, who could not become U.S. citizens and had few property rights. It made no provisions for the truly poor.

Furthermore, the Homestead Act was part of a larger process of conquest, driven by the twin pressures of industrialization and white settlement, through which Indians were irrevocably stripped of their lands. A final problem with the act was corruption in its implementation. Those who agitated for a homestead act in the antebellum period had been fueled by a sense of idealism. Ironically, however, through chicanery, outright fraud, and government giveaways, more public land actually fell into the hands of railroads, other corporations, and speculators than into the hands of individual farmers.

Railroads   Nothing was more important to the industrialization of the West than the railroad. Just as free land for homesteaders was a long-held dream for many Americans, so, too, was the creation of a transcontinental railroad that would link East and West. The two dreams were connected: The settlement of the West would be greatly facilitated by the extension of the railroad into far-flung territory. Thus, it was no accident that in 1862, the year the government passed the Homestead Act, it also passed the Pacific Railroad Bill, which provided large loans and extremely generous subsidies of land to two railroad companies, the Union Pacific (working west) and the Central Pacific (working east), in order to enable them to build a transcontinental line stretching from Omaha, Nebraska, to Sacramento, California. (Railroad lines already existed from Omaha to the East.) Two years later, the government also provided a substantial monetary subsidy for each mile of track laid in the West. Ultimately, the government would give away 131 million acres of land to support transcontinental railroads.

These lavish subsidies set off a frenzy of railroad building; they also made a few individuals very rich, including the "Big Four" of the Central Pacific: Leland Stanford, Collis P. Huntington, Mark Hopkins, and Charles Crocker. Big in every way (they collectively weighed 860 pounds), the four men had come to California during the gold rush and had shrewdly sized up its entrepreneurial opportunities. They now avidly seized the historic opportunity at hand and formed a partnership that split up the work necessary in such a giant task, including the work of influencing lawmakers. Like so many others involved in the notoriously corrupt postwar railway boom, they were not shy about using bribery or graft to achieve their aims.

Having provided generous subsidies, the government expected the railroads to obtain their own financing. Various railroads sold millions of dollars of stocks or bonds, often selling as much stock as the market would bear without much relationship to the actual value of the railroads. This "watered" stock was part of the runaway corruption that surrounded financing railroads. The Big Four participated wholeheartedly in this corruption, creating construction contracts, for instance, that paid them $90 million for work that only cost them $32.2 million.

Once financing had been arranged for this complex venture, the Union Pacific and Central Pacific embarked on a daunting task that would engage some 20,000 workers at a time. From 1865 on, the two railroads raced against one another, as whoever laid the most track stood to gain in government subsidies as well as later commerce. The Union Pacific employed primarily Irish laborers, while the Central Pacific employed a workforce that was by 1867 almost 90 percent Chinese.

Chinese Laborers and the Railroads   A global economy had drawn thousands of Chinese laborers to California during the gold rush, beginning in 1849. Mostly peasants emigrating from the Pearl River delta of Guangdong Province in southeast China, they were pushed from home by poverty and unstable political conditions related to China's defeat in the British Opium Wars. While only a few hundred men emigrated in 1849 and 1850, by the mid-1850s, thousands of Chinese immigrants arrived annually. By 1870, there were some 63,000 Chinese in the United States, with over three-quarters settled in California.

Almost entirely men, Chinese immigrants intended to be sojourners, not permanent settlers: They planned to take their hard-earned savings home to the wives and families they had left behind. At first they worked as independent prospectors panning for gold, but as gold profits dwindled, they moved into other areas of work. In the 1860s, labor contractors in China actively recruited young men to come to America to build the transcontinental railroad, as well as to work as agricultural laborers, to develop fisheries and vineyards, and to help reclaim California swamplands. Some 12,000 Chinese laborers ultimately built the Central Pacific Railroad, often under exceptionally harsh conditions, and with substantially less pay than white laborers.

Even before they began working on the railroads, Chinese miners and laborers faced prejudice from white nativists. In 1850, the California State legislature responded to anti-foreigner agitation with a Foreign Miners' Tax aimed at all foreigners; two years later, the legislature specifically targeted Chinese immigrants. Western labor leaders, particularly Dennis Kearney of the Workingman's Party of California, inflamed nativist crowds of white workers with anti-Chinese rhetoric: In 1877, during the national Great Railway Strike, mobs of white workers rioted against Chinese workers in San Francisco's Chinatown. Violence against Chinese workers occurred in numerous places in the West during the 1870s and 1880s, including a massacre in Rock Springs, Colorado, after the Union Pacific Railroad decided to hire Chinese workers. Twenty-eight Chinese died in an attack that included burning down Chinese homes; similar attacks soon occurred throughout the West.

At the local level, Chinese immigrants faced a host of discriminatory ordinances specifically targeting them, from queue ordinances regulating the length of men's hair (forbidding the distinctive braid worn by Chinese men) to sidewalk ordinances preventing the carrying of baskets on shoulders. At the state level, California laws denied Chinese the right to own land, to testify in court, to intermarry with whites, and to immigrate. Under these conditions, Chinese workers created communities of their own against stiff odds. By 1850, a thriving Chinatown had emerged in San Francisco, and Chinese sections emerged in numerous communities throughout the West.

In 1882, the federal government weighed in with its first discriminatory law targeting a specific immigrant group. The **Chinese Exclusion Act** suspended Chinese immigration for 10 years with the exception of a few job categories. Wealthy Chinese businessmen and merchants were allowed entry because of the U.S. government's interest in trade with China. But, the law forbade Chinese laborers, who were said to endanger "the good order of certain localities." Renewed in 1892, the Chinese Exclusion Act achieved its aim: The population of Chinese declined from 105,465 in 1880 to 89,863 in 1900, during a period in which immigration swelled for other groups.

The Golden Spike   By the early spring of 1869, what one commentator called the "irrepressible railroad" was almost an accomplished fact. The only question was where East and West would meet. In the final stages of track-laying, the two railroads—which would receive money, after all, based on miles of track built—actually built some track parallel to one another before finally being instructed by no less than President Grant to determine a meeting point.

The result, on May 10, 1869, was the historic driving of a "golden spike" in Promontory, Utah, to mark the merging of the two lines. Present that day, we know from the historical record, were "men of every color, creed, and nationality," including the Chinese laborers who had built the railroad and laid the very last track. But official photographs of the event leave them out—a silence that speaks volumes about racial prejudice at the time.

By 1893, a total of five transcontinental railroads were in service, and track mileage west of the Mississippi had increased from 3,272 miles at the end of the Civil War to 72,473 miles. No single factor was as important to the industrialization of the West as the building of railroads, which provided an infrastructure for the western economy as well as connection to eastern markets.

Railroads and Borderlands Communities

The arrival of the railroads, as well as the Anglo settlers who followed swiftly in their wake, dramatically changed the borderlands communities of northern New Mexico and southern Colorado. In the 1870s, Hispanic villagers lived communally in this area, grazing sheep and cattle on the open range.

But the coming of the railroads in the 1880s put new pressure on Hispanic village life. In places like Rio Arriba County, New Mexico, Hispanic villagers who had done a thriving trade freighting—hauling goods by wagons—found themselves replaced by the railroads. Even worse, in a pattern repeated throughout the West, Hispanic villagers found that Anglo settlement and fencing of once-open lands reduced the available range for grazing their sheep.

As Anglo-owned livestock companies moved in, bringing in better breeds and buying up grazing land, they began to squeeze out the Hispanic farmers. By the 1890s villagers began to depend on credit for the first time; in the turbulent economy of that decade, many of them were unable to pay their debts. The end result was the loss of their sheep—and livelihood—to Anglo businessmen who had extended credit to them. Many ended up working for livestock companies, sometimes caring for herds they had once owned themselves. Eventually others ended up as miners, forced to become wage laborers.

Resentment became active resistance in the 1880s, when a secret organization, *Las Gorras Blancas* (The White Caps), rode mostly at night to cut fences, tear up railroad track, and burn bridges. "Our purpose is to protect the rights of the people in general and especially those of the helpless classes," the group declared in its platform. But, the group had only limited success in achieving these goals.

Mining

A similar process held true in mining. The California Gold Rush of 1849 and the early 1850s had drawn miners from across the United States—and from Mexico, Europe, China, Chile, and other countries, as well—to pan for gold. But by the 1870s the majority of miners had become wage laborers who worked for corporations, not for themselves. Mining was big business, with groups of investors consolidating holdings in some of the richest mines. George Hearst began by investing in 1859 in the legendary Comstock Lode in Nevada—the richest vein of silver in America. "If you're ever inclined to think that there's no such thing as luck," Hearst remarked, "just think of me." In 1877, Hearst and business partners bought the Homestake Mine in the Black Hills, and then enriched their holdings still further by buying up the claims of surrounding miners. Other financiers invested in the industries related to mining, including railroads, lumber companies, and smelters.

Gold rush prospectors had worked the surface of the earth with picks, shovels, and tin pans. But soon miners and mining companies developed new technologies to extract ore, whether on the surface of the earth or underground. Hydraulic mining, used as early as the 1850s, employed high-pressure jets of water to wash away banks of earth and even mountains in order to extract gold. By the 1880s, hydraulic mining produced 90 percent of California's gold, but it also ravaged the environment, tearing away indiscriminately at earth, boulders, and trees, and leaving desolate landscapes in its wake. The debris (tailings) from hydraulic mining clogged rivers and caused floods, ruining farms with muddy waste. Other types of mining destroyed landscapes as well: Copper mining in particular created strip-mining moonscapes.

Railroads played a central role in the development of industrial mining, not only providing access to mines but also enabling a new kind of mining late in the century. Gold discoveries had propelled the first waves of western settlement, but by the 1870s, silver eclipsed gold in volume and, some years, even in value. Copper mining became profitable because the railroads allowed the transportation of huge quantities of ore. In Butte, Montana, the 1881 arrival of the railroad made possible the extraction of a copper lode known as the "richest hill on earth." The railroad also catalyzed copper mining in southern Arizona in the 1880s. Large-scale resource extraction was at the heart of western industrialization.

Working conditions in these heavily mechanized hard-rock mines grew steadily worse. Miners sometimes worked in mines with temperatures of well over 100 degrees—sometimes as much as 150 degrees deep underground. Miners died of the heat, of poor ventilation, of the release of toxic gases, and of accidents with mining equipment. Accidents disabled one out of every 30 miners in the 1870s. By the end of the 19th century, mining was the most dangerous industry in the country.

Unions gained only a limited foothold in the 1870s and 1880s. But wage cuts in the early 1890s inspired a new burst of labor radicalism and resistance. After a violent confrontation in 1892 between miners and the National Guard at Coeur d'Alene, Idaho, mining unions met at Butte, Montana, in 1893 to form the **Western Federation of Miners (WFM)**, whose radical politics included a call to transform the American economic system. That year, a violent strike at Cripple Creek, Colorado, broke out over mine owners' attempts to move from an eight-hour to a ten-hour day. These strikes were part of nationwide labor activism and resistance in the 1890s. Ultimately the WFM would help to found the 20th-century Industrial Workers of the World (IWW). The IWW's leader, William "Big Bill" Haywood, later remembered being approached by a WFM organizer as a young man in Idaho. "I had never heard of the need of workingmen organizing for mutual protection," Haywood said, but he soon became a leader of the WFM himself. The industrialization of the West became a radicalizing political experience for many.

Cattle Drives and the Open Range

A postwar boom in the range cattle industry had its beginnings in southern Texas. The Spaniards had introduced longhorn cattle there in the 18th century. This hardy breed multiplied rapidly: By the 1850s, millions of them roamed freely on the Texas plains. The market for them was limited in this sparsely settled region—the nearest railhead was usually too far distant to make shipping them north and east economically feasible.

The Civil War changed all that. With beef supplies depleted in the older states, prices rose to the unheard-of sum of $40 per head. The postwar explosion of population and railroads westward brought markets and railheads ever closer to western cattle that were free to anyone who rounded them up and branded them.

Astute Texans quickly saw that the longhorns represented a fortune on the hoof—if they could be driven northward the 800 miles to the railhead at Sedalia, Missouri. In spring 1866, cowboys hit the trail with 260,000 cattle in the first of the great drives. Disease, stampedes, bad weather, Indians, and irate farmers in Missouri (who were afraid that the Texas fever carried by some of the longhorns would infect their own stock) killed or ran off most of the cattle.

Only a few thousand head made it to Sedalia, but the prices they fetched convinced ranchers that the system would work, if only they could find a better route. By 1867, the rails of the Kansas Pacific had reached Abilene, Kansas, 150 miles closer to Texas, making it possible to drive the herds through a sparsely occupied portion of Indian Territory. About 35,000 longhorns reached Abilene that summer, where they were loaded onto cattle cars for the trip to Kansas City or Chicago. This success resulted in the interlocking institutions of the cattle drive and the Chicago stockyards. The development of refrigerated rail cars in the 1870s enabled Chicago to ship dressed beef all over the country. Abilene mushroomed overnight from a sleepy village where one bartender spent his spare time catching prairie dogs into a boomtown where 25 saloons stayed open all night.

More than a million longhorns bellowed their way north on the **Chisholm Trail** to Abilene over the next four years, while the railhead crept westward to other Kansas towns, chiefly Dodge City, which became the most wide-open and famous of the cow towns. As buffalo and Indians disappeared from the grasslands north of Texas, ranches moved northward to take their place. Cattle drives grew shorter as railroads inched forward. Ranchers grazed their cattle for free on millions of acres of open, unfenced government land. But clashes with "grangers" (the ranchers' contemptuous term for farmers), on the one hand, and with a growing army of sheep ranchers on the other—not to mention rustlers—led to several "range wars." Most notable was the Johnson County War in Wyoming in 1892. Grangers and small ranchers there (who had sometimes gotten their start by rustling) defeated the hired guns of the Stock Growers' Association, which represented larger ranchers.

By that time, open-range grazing was already in decline. The boom years of the early 1880s had overstocked the range and driven down prices. Then came record cold and blizzards on the southern range in the winter of 1884 and 1885, followed by even worse weather on the northern plains two years later. Hundreds of thousands of cattle froze or starved to death. These catastrophes spurred reforms that ended open-range grazing. The ranchers who survived turned to growing hay and supplemental feed for the winter. They reduced the size of their herds, started buying or leasing land and fencing in their cattle, and invested in scientific breeding that crossed longhorns with higher-quality stock to produce a better grade of beef.

The Industrialization of Ranching   As open-range grazing declined, industrialized ranching expanded. By 1900, the California corporation Miller & Lux was one of the largest industrial enterprises in the country, having integrated raising cattle on vast landholdings together with meatpacking in San Francisco. Its two founding partners were German immigrants who had started out working as butchers in San Francisco but soon owned their own shops. Mobilizing large amounts of capital, they employed over a thousand laborers in extensive operations that tightly connected ranchlands with the city.

Industrial Cowboys

Some of their employees were cowboys who rode the extensive Miller & Lux landholdings. Before the 1870s, the most valuable of the firm's cowboys were **vaqueros**, Mexican cowboys who rounded up cattle, branded them, and drove them to San Francisco. The tradition of the vaqueros had arrived in the New World with the Spanish, who introduced herding by men on horseback. By the late 19th century, the raising of cattle herds by *vaqueros* had been practiced for centuries in California. But the

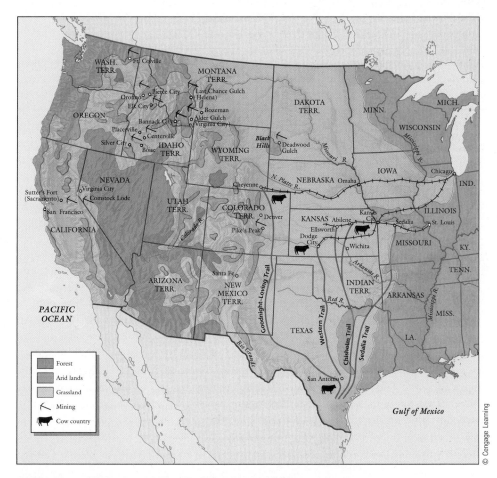

© Cengage Learning

MAP 18.1 Mining and Cattle Frontiers, 1870s

Most of the mines shown on this map produced gold and silver. The next generation would begin to exploit the copper to be found in Montana and Arizona, and later generations would extract oil from Texas and Oklahoma and coal and oil from Wyoming.

arrival of railroads took a toll on the positions of *vaqueros*: After the 1870s, cattle were shipped to market by rail.

Mexican Americans

The *vaqueros* at Miller & Lux received less pay than their white coworkers, reflecting prevalent discrimination against Mexicans. Throughout the late 19th century, Mexican Americans, many of whom had owned their land for generations, lost both property and political influence to incoming Anglo-American settlers. Many elite *Californios*, who were ranchers in southern California, had to sell their lands to pay outstanding debts after devastating droughts in the 1860s virtually destroyed the ranching industry. But even as early as 1849 in the northern California goldfields, resentment of "foreigners" provoked violence against Mexican American miners—and the Foreign Miners' Tax of 1850 effectively forced Mexican Americans out of the goldfields (even though they were not "foreigners"). As the 19th century progressed, hordes of Anglo-American "squatters" invaded the expansive holdings of *Californios*, who were forced to seek relief in the courts. Although their claims were generally upheld, legal proceedings often stretched on for years. After exorbitant legal fees and other expenses were taken into account, a legal triumph was often a Pyrrhic victory. In the end, most Mexican American landholders in northern California, like those in southern California, had to sell the very lands they had fought to keep in order to pay their mounting debts.

The migration of Anglos into eastern Texas had played a role in fomenting the war for Texas independence and in bringing about the war with Mexico. By the latter half of the 19th century, eastern Texas was overwhelmingly Anglo; most *Tejanos* (people of Mexican origin or descent) were concentrated in the Rio Grande Valley of southern Texas. As in California, Anglos in Texas used force and intimidation, coupled with exploitative legal maneuvering, to disenfranchise the *Tejanos*. The Texas Rangers often acted as an Anglo vigilante force that exacted retribution for the real or imagined crimes of Mexican Americans.

Similar patterns prevailed in New Mexico, but the effects were mitigated somewhat because New Mexicans continued to outnumber Anglo-American settlers. Throughout the Southwest, Spanish-speaking peoples maintained their cultural traditions in the face of Anglo settlement, with the Roman Catholic Church serving as an important center of community life. An influx of immigrants from Mexico toward the end of the century created a new basis for community as well.

Itinerant Laborers

For many workers in the West, itinerancy was the norm; a virtual army of workers and wanderers traveled the western countryside. Most low-level jobs in ranching were seasonal, meaning that workers were forced to move from place to place periodically in search of work. And as western industrialization uprooted many workers from their traditional lives, more and more people took to the road. As Henry George said in his best-selling 1879 book, *Progress and Poverty,* a scathing indictment of the current economic system, "the 'tramp' comes with the locomotive." For George, who had been a prospector before becoming a newspaper editor in California, the fault lay in a system of "land monopoly" that allowed control of land and resources by the few at the expense of the many.

Erwin E. Smith Collection/Library of Congress Prints and Photographs Division

Black Cowboys. *Some studies of cowboys estimate that one-quarter of them were black. That estimate is probably too high for all cowboys, but it might be correct for Texas, where this photograph was taken.*

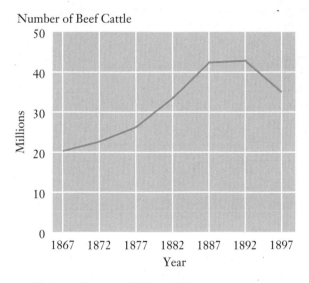

Number of Beef Cattle

Beef Cattle in the United States, 1867–1897

At Miller & Lux, itinerant laborers were Chinese, Portuguese, Italian, Mexican, and Mexican American, in addition to white, native-born Americans. One itinerant laborer on an irrigation crew, Joseph Warren Matthews, was a farmer who had heavy debts. To pay his debts he had taken on a series of grueling temporary jobs, including wage labor for a lumber company in the Pacific Northwest, work in the Alaskan goldfields, pipe laying for a water company, ore smelting, and ditch digging. His situation underlined the precariousness of many lives in the industrializing West.

Homesteading and Farming   Homesteaders and farmers shared that precariousness. Not only were 49 percent of all homesteaders unable to "prove up" their claims, but many were ultimately forced off their homesteads by the unforgiving climate of the Great Plains.

A great wave of settlement of the Great Plains occurred during the late 1870s to the mid-1880s, when rainfall was relatively abundant, but years of drought

Kansas State Historical Society/Topeka/Kansas

Destruction of the Buffalo. *Historians estimate that as many as 30 million bison (popularly called buffalo) once roamed the grasslands of North America. By the mid-19th century, however, expansion of the European American settlement, the demand for buffalo robes in the European and eastern U.S. markets, and competition from Indian horses for grazing lands had reduced the herds by many millions. Such pressures intensified after the Civil War—as railroads penetrated the West and new technology enabled tanners to process buffalo hides for leather. Professional hunters flocked to the range and systematically killed the bison. By the 1880s, the buffalo were almost extinct, leaving behind millions of bones, which were gathered in piles, as in this photograph of buffalo skulls, and shipped to plants that ground them into fertilizer.*

inevitably followed. The truth was that the average normal rainfall on the Great Plains was scarcely enough to support farming except in certain river valleys. Homesteaders and farmers in Minnesota, Iowa, and parts of Kansas and Nebraska were relatively lucky—those areas had rich soil and adequate rainfall. In Iowa, for instance, farmers had great success with a "corn and hog" farm economy. But other land was arid and unproductive, producing heartbreak for homesteaders and farmers. Between 1888 and 1892, half the population of Kansas and Nebraska was forced to give up and move back east to Illinois or Iowa.

The Experience of Homesteading	Homesteading families on the Great Plains literally built their houses from the ground up: In an environment without trees, they cut the dense prairie sod into blocks and stacked them up to form walls, providing a small window and a door in a

"soddy" of around 18 by 24 feet. **Soddies** were a practical solution to a difficult problem on the plains, but they were also dark, dank, and claustrophobic.

As Kansas homesteader Mary Abell explained to her sister: "Imagine living in a place dug out of the side of a hill (one side to the weather with door and window—top covered with dirt and you have our place of abode). No one east would think of putting pigs in such a place." Abell's letters from 1871 to 1875 make clear the hard labor involved in homesteading: In addition to caring for five children, in the fall of 1873, she had been her husband's "sole help in getting up and stacking at least 25 tons of hay and oats." Less than a week later, "one of those dreadful prairie fires" swept through the Abells' land, and they lost not only their hay and oats but also chickens and farm equipment. In 1874, she faced both drought and grasshoppers, and wrote to her family that "none of you have the least conception" of "actual want, destitution." In 1875, Abell died at the age of 29.

Not all homesteaders faced dire straits. Of the 4 million immigrants who came from Germany, the Czech region of the Austro-Hungarian Empire, and the Scandinavian countries from 1865 to 1890, many settled in the upper Midwest and northern plains and became successful farmers. The northern plains region had the highest proportion of foreign-born residents in the nation during the last quarter of the century. These European immigrants formed homogenous ethnic enclaves that maintained the distinctive culture and traditions of their homelands. Swedish immigrants in Minnesota spoke Swedish with one another and centered their lives around the Swedish Lutheran church; their children attended Swedish schools and learned to read the Swedish bible, sing Swedish songs, and recite Swedish history; and both men and women wore traditional Swedish dress on holidays. By the end of the century, there were also homogenous ethnic communities of Germans, Czechs, Poles, Hungarians, and Norwegians dotting the northern landscape.

Gender and Western Settlement	The Homestead Act was unusual in allowing unmarried women to make claims; between 5 and 15 percent of homestead entries in different locales went to women in the late 19th century. Many of these women probably "proved up" only to immedi-

ately sell their land, rather than farm it themselves. Still, the existence of women homesteaders suggests just one way gender roles were different in the West than other regions.

Another difference was the overwhelmingly masculine makeup of mining camps and towns. During the gold rush, California was up to 93 percent male, and many ranches, including Miller & Lux holdings, were exclusively male as well. Mining towns were known as violent places, and many observers were anxious to establish a more respectable family life there.

Prostitutes from all over the world were drawn to mining towns throughout the late 19th century, but nowhere except in San Francisco were women systematically forced into sexual slavery. There, the situation of Chinese laborers encouraged an exploitative world trade in women. Although by the last decades of the century Chinese merchants were allowed to bring their wives and daughters to America, laborers had no such rights. Furthermore, respectable single women were expected to stay home. The number of Chinese women in America never rose above 5,000 during the 19th century.

The absence of Chinese women encouraged a brutal international trade in prostitution. Chinese women who were kidnapped or purchased from poor parents were sold into indentured servitude or slavery and shipped to America to become prostitutes. In San Francisco, an estimated 85 to 97 percent of Chinese women were prostitutes in 1860; around 72 percent in 1870; and between 21 and 50 percent in 1880. They faced a harsh existence. However, a number of women managed to escape prostitution. Some married men who had saved up enough money to

Library of Congress, Prints and Photographs Division

A Nebraska Soddy. *This young family stands proudly in front of their Nebraska soddy in 1884 or 1885, during a time when rainfall was abundant on the Great Plains. A long-term drought began in 1886, however, making us wonder whether this family was able to hang on to its homestead through the coming difficult times.*

purchase the contracts that bound them; Protestant missionaries worked to rescue prostitutes, as well.

As these few examples show, settlement patterns of the West produced—at least for a short period of time—societies with unequal numbers of men and women, with different results in different places. The impact of these disparities continues to intrigue historians, who still puzzle, for instance, over the reasons why several western states were the first to grant woman suffrage.

CONQUEST AND RESISTANCE: AMERICAN INDIANS IN THE TRANS-MISSISSIPPI WEST

The westward expansion of ranching and farming after 1865 doomed the free range of the Plains Indians and the buffalo. In the 1830s, eastern tribes had been forcibly moved to preserves west of the Mississippi so as permanently to separate whites and Indians. Yet in scarcely a decade, white settlers had penetrated these lands via the overland trails to the Pacific coast. In the 1850s, when the Kansas and Nebraska territories opened to white settlement, the government forced a dozen tribes living there to cede 15 million acres, leaving them on reservations totaling less than 1.5 million acres. Thus began what one historian has called the "policy of concentration": No longer were Indians to be pushed ever westward. Instead, they were to be concentrated onto reservations a fraction of the size of where they had formerly hunted freely.

Even before the Civil War, the nomadic Plains Indians, whose culture and economy were based on the buffalo, faced pressure not only from the advancing tide of white settlement but also from the forced migration of eastern tribes into their domain. In the aftermath of the Civil War, the process of concentrating Indian tribes on reservations accelerated. Chiefs of the five "Civilized Tribes"—Cherokees, Creeks, Choctaws, Chickasaws, and Seminoles—had signed treaties of alliance with the Confederacy. At that time, they were living in Indian Territory (most of present-day Oklahoma), where their economy was linked to the South. Many of them, especially members of the mixed-blood upper class, were slaveholders. Bitter toward the United States, the tribal leaders cast their lot with the Confederacy on the principle that "the enemy of my enemy is my friend." The Cherokee leader Stand Watie rose to brigadier general in the Confederate army and was the last Confederate commander to surrender, on June 23, 1865.

But siding with the Confederacy proved to be a costly mistake for these tribes. The U.S. government "reconstructed" Indian Territory more quickly and with less contention than it reconstructed the former Confederate states. Treaties with the five tribes in 1866 required them to grant tribal citizenship to their freed slaves and reduced tribal lands by half. The government then settled Indians who had been dispossessed from other areas on the land it had taken from these tribes.

Conflict with the Sioux   The Civil War set in motion a generation of Indian warfare that was more violent and widespread than anything since the 17th century. Herded onto reservations along the Minnesota River by the Treaty of Traverse des Sioux in 1851, the Santee Sioux

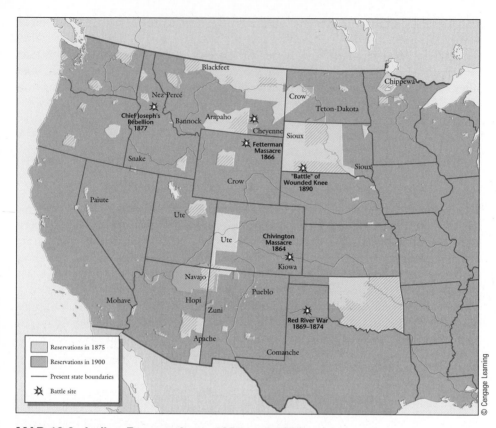

Reservations in 1875
Reservations in 1900
Present state boundaries
Battle site

MAP 18.2 Indian Reservations, 1875 and 1900

Before the Civil War, Indians had hunted and trapped over most of this vast region. The shrinking areas on which they were confined by the reservation policy vividly illustrate that for the first Americans, the story was not "the expansion of America" but "the contraction of America."

were angry in the summer of 1862 that annuity payments did not arrive, threatening starvation. Warriors began to speak openly of reclaiming ancestral hunting grounds. Then, on August 17, a robbery in which five white settlers were murdered seemed to open the floodgates. The warriors persuaded Chief Little Crow to take them on the warpath, and over the next few weeks, at least 500 white Minnesotans were massacred.

Hastily mobilized militia and army units finally suppressed the uprising. A military court convicted 319 Indians of murder and atrocities and sentenced 303 of them to death. Appalled by this ferocious retaliation, Lincoln personally reviewed the trial transcripts and reduced the number of executions to 38—the largest act of executive clemency in American history. Even so, the hanging of 38 Sioux on December 26, 1862, was the largest mass execution the country has ever witnessed. The government evicted the remaining Sioux from Minnesota to Dakota Territory.

In the meantime, the army's pursuit of fleeing Santee Sioux provoked other Sioux tribes farther west. By 1864, and for a decade afterward, fighting flared between the army and the Sioux across the northern plains. It reached a climax in 1874 and 1875 after gold-seekers poured into the Black Hills of western Dakota, a sacred place to the Sioux. At the **Battle of Little Bighorn** in Montana Territory on June 25, 1876, Sioux warriors led by **Sitting Bull** and Crazy Horse, along with their Cheyenne allies, wiped out George A. Custer and the 225 men with him in the Seventh Cavalry. In retaliation, General Philip Sheridan carried out a winter campaign in which the Sioux and Cheyenne were crushed.

The largest and most warlike of the Plains tribes, the Sioux were confined to a reservation in Dakota Territory where poverty, disease, and alcoholism reduced them to a desperate condition.

Suppression of Other Plains Indians   Just as the Sioux uprising in Minnesota had triggered war on the northern plains in 1862, a massacre of Cheyenne in Colorado in 1864 sparked a decade of conflict on the southern plains. The discovery of gold near Pike's Peak set off a rush to Colorado in 1858–1859. The government responded by calling several Cheyenne and Arapaho chiefs to a council, and with a combination of threats and promises, persuaded the chiefs to sign a treaty giving up all claims to land in this region (guaranteed by an earlier treaty of 1851) in exchange for a reservation at Sand Creek in southeast Colorado.

In 1864, hunger and resentment on the reservation prompted many warriors to return to their old hunting grounds and to raid white settlements. Skirmishes soon erupted into open warfare. In the fall, Cheyenne chief Black Kettle, believing that he had concluded peace with the Colorado settlers, returned to the reservation. There, at dawn on November 29, militia commanded by Colonel John Chivington surrounded and attacked Black Kettle's unsuspecting camp, killing 200 Indians, half of them women and children.

The notorious **Sand Creek massacre** set a pattern for several similar attacks on Indian villages in subsequent years. Ever since the earliest battles between colonists and Indians in the 17th century, whites had followed the strategy of burning Indian crops and villages as a means of destroying or driving off the Indians. Sherman and Sheridan had adopted a similar strategy against the Confederates and followed it again as military commanders responsible for subduing the Plains Indians. Their purpose was to corral the Indians onto the reservations that were being created throughout the West. In addition to trying to defeat the Indians in battle, which proved to be difficult against the mounted Plains Indians, the army encouraged the extermination of the buffalo herds. Professional hunters slaughtered the large, clumsy animals by the millions for their hides, thus depriving Plains Indians of both physical and spiritual sustenance. When the buffalo became nearly extinct in 1883, the Plains Indians understood that their old way of life was gone forever. "Nothing happened after that," recalled one Crow warrior. "We just lived. There were no more war parties, no capturing horses from the Piegan and the Sioux, no buffalo to hunt. There is nothing more to tell."

The Indians were left with no alternative but to come into the reservations, and by the 1880s, nearly all of them had done so. Chief Joseph of the Nez Percé pronounced the epitaph for their way of life when federal troops blocked the escape of his band from Montana to Canada in 1877:

> I am tired of fighting. Our chiefs are killed. The old men are all dead. It is cold and we have no blankets ... no food .... The little children are freezing to death .... Hear me, my chiefs; I am tired; my heart is sick and sad. From where the sun now stands, I will fight no more forever.

The "Peace Policy"

Many eastern reformers condemned America's suppression of the Indians. The most prominent was Helen Hunt Jackson, whose *A Century of Dishonor* (1881) was an outraged indictment of anti-Indian violence, exploitation, and broken treaties. Yet, as sympathetic as Jackson was to the Indians' plight, she was not sympathetic to Indian culture; like other white Protestant reformers of her day, she believed that Indians must be stripped of their culture in order to assimilate to American society.

In this she was in alignment with the government. In 1869 President Grant had announced a new "peace policy" toward Indians, urging "their civilization and ultimate citizenship." "Civilization" meant acceptance of white culture, including the English language, Christianity, and individual ownership of property. It also meant allegiance to the United States rather than to a tribe. In 1869, Grant established a Board of Indian Commissioners and staffed it with humanitarian reformers. In 1871, the century-long policy of negotiating treaties with Indian "nations" came to an end. From then on, Indians became "wards of the nation," to be "civilized" and prepared for citizenship, first on reservations and eventually on individually owned parcels of land that were carved out of the reservations. Most Indians acquiesced in the "reconstruction" that offered them citizenship by the 1880s—they had little choice.

The Dawes Severalty Act and Indian Boarding Schools

In order to further the goal of Indian ownership of private property, Protestant reformers in the 1880s found themselves in a strange alliance with land-hungry westerners, who greedily eyed the 155 million acres of land tied up in reservations. If part of that land could be allotted directly for individual ownership by Indian families, the remainder would become available for purchase by whites. The 1887 **Dawes Severalty Act** combined these impulses toward greed and reform. This landmark legislation called for the dissolution of Indian tribes as legal entities, offered Indians the opportunity to become citizens, and allotted heads of families 160 acres of farmland or 320 acres of grazing land, as long as they were "severed" from their tribe.

For whites who were eager to seize reservation land, the Dawes Act brought a bonanza. At noon on April 22, 1889, the government threw open specified parts of the Indian Territory to "Boomers," who descended on the region like locusts and by nightfall had staked claim to nearly 2 million acres. Indians did not just lose the lands legally opened for white settlement: Many Indians who received individual land titles through the Dawes Act also lost these lands to unscrupulous whites through fraud and misrepresentation. Eventually, whites gained title to 108 million acres of former reservation land.

For Indians, the Dawes Severalty Act was a disaster. Private ownership of land was an alien concept to most tribes. Indians received little training for a transition to farming, much less the appropriate tools and supplies. Moreover, the poor quality of their land allotments made farming difficult, if not impossible. In an attempt to strip Indians of their culture, the Dawes Act forbade Indian religions and the telling of Indian myths and legends, as well as the practices of medicine men.

Indian boarding schools, established beginning in the late 1870s, were another attempt to deny Indians their culture. Children were taken from their families to the Hampton Institute in Virginia and the Carlisle Institute in Pennsylvania, among other schools. There they were forbidden to speak Indian languages or wear Indian clothing. As one 1890 set of instructions from the U.S. Bureau of Indian Affairs put it: "Pupils must be compelled to converse with each other in English, and should be properly rebuked or punished for persistent violation of this rule." The writer Zitkala-Sa, a Yankton Sioux, later remembered her life in an Indian school: "The melancholy of those black days has left so long a shadow that it darkens the path of years that have since gone by."

After graduation from an Indian boarding school, Zitkala-Sa taught at the Carlisle School and became a much-praised writer in New York. But later she would undergo a spiritual crisis: She compared herself to a "slender tree" that had been "uprooted from my mother, nature, and God," and lamented that she had "forgotten the healing in trees and brooks." Eventually she left New York, married a Sioux, and became an activist for Native American rights.

The Ghost Dance

At a time of despair for many Indians, a new visionary religious movement swept through Indian peoples in 1890, offering a different kind of resistance to white domination. The **Ghost Dance** began with the visions of the Paiute shaman Wovoka, who counseled Indians that if they gave up alcohol, lived a simple life, and devoted themselves to prayer, white men would disappear from the earth, Indian lands would be restored, and dead Indians would rejoin the living. This message of hope was embodied in the Ghost Dance ritual, involving days of worship expressed in part through dance.

When the Ghost Dance religion spread to those Sioux led by Sitting Bull, and they began days of ecstatic dancing, Indian agents grew alarmed: As one agent telegraphed authorities, "Indians are dancing in the snow and are wild and crazy. *We need protection and we need it now.*" The results of the ensuing confrontations between Indians and authorities were tragic. First Sitting Bull and his grandson were killed in a skirmish with reservation authorities. A few days later, trigger-happy members of the Seventh Cavalry—Custer's old regiment—opened fire on Sioux men, women, and children at **Wounded Knee** in the Pine Ridge Reservation, killing 146 Indians, including 44 women and 18 children. Twenty-five soldiers also died. For many, the massacre at Wounded Knee symbolized the death of 19th-century Plains Indian culture.

The Granger Collection, NYC

The Ghost Dance. *This photograph shows a Sioux performing the Ghost Dance with a sacred whistle in 1890. This religious dance became part of a movement of resistance to white domination that ended tragically in the Wounded Knee Massacre of 1890.*

Sitting Bull and Buffalo Bill: Popular Myths of the West   Only a few years before he was killed, Sitting Bull had been one of the prime attractions in the entertainment extravaganza known as Buffalo Bill Cody's Wild West Show. Sitting Bull had been a canny negotiator of fees for his appearances in 1885; he required an interpreter, several attendants, and a salary that came to half the annual salary of the typical Indian agent. He also used press interviews while on the Wild West tour to ask the U.S. government to live up to its promises to Indians. If Cody was using Sitting Bull, Sitting Bull was certainly using Cody right back.

Having "real" Indians in his show was of vital importance to Cody, who capitalized on the public's hunger for "authentic" spectacular entertainments in his popular Wild West shows. Cody was an extraordinary mix of the new industrializing West, the frontier West, and an emerging culture of mass entertainment. Having begun his career as a soldier in the Civil War, Cody then worked for one of the transcontinental railroad lines (where he gained the nickname "Buffalo Bill" for slaughtering buffalo) before becoming a scout for the Fifth Cavalry. When he became the subject of a popular dime Western novel, the most improbable turn in Cody's career occurred: He decided to dramatize his own life in a series of theatrical entertainments. By the year Sitting Bull joined Buffalo Bill's Wild West Show with its band of trick riders and sharpshooters, it required 18 railroad cars to transport performers (including a number of Indians), work crews, animals, and equipment.

The Wild West Show celebrated the white conquest of the West in a series of acts called "The Drama of Civilization," which showed scenes of an emigrant train crossing the prairie, Buffalo Bill rescuing a pioneer family from Indians, and a mining camp. Billed as "America's National Entertainment," these shows revealed just how tightly linked industrialization and conquest were in Americans' thinking—and even in their entertainment.

INDUSTRIALIZATION AND THE NEW SOUTH

Like the West, the South underwent a surge of industrialization in the last decades of the 19th century. Boosters like the energetic and influential Henry Grady, editor of the Atlanta *Constitution,* proclaimed that a New South had emerged, one hospitable to industry and to northern investment.

Some people scoffed at such promotional talk in a world that was still decidedly rural, but in fact the pace of industrialization quickened in the last decades of the century, with textiles leading the way. In 1880, the South had only 5 percent of the country's textile-producing capacity; by 1900, it had 23 percent and was well on its way to surpassing New England a generation later. Tobacco industrialized as well, with James B. Duke of North Carolina transforming the industry.

Railroads and iron also saw a surge in growth. Between 1877 and 1900 the South built railroads faster than any other region in the country. In 1880, the former slave states produced only 9 percent of the nation's pig iron; by 1890, after a decade of extraordinary expansion for the industry nationwide, that proportion had doubled. Most of the growth was concentrated in northern Alabama, where the proximity of coal, limestone, and ore made the new city of Birmingham the "Pittsburgh of the South."

But there were limits to southern industrialization. It was difficult to catch up with well-established northern industries. Thus, southerners competed in the few areas in which they could find markets for local crops and resources: textiles produced from their own cotton; cigarettes manufactured from southern tobacco; as well as lumber, sugar, and iron.

Not all of the wealth from the new industries went into the pockets of southerners, though. Over the late 19th century, southern industry attracted more and more northern capital in a pattern that held true across industries. At first, for instance, southerners supplied most of the capital in the expansion of the textile industry. But after 1893, an increasing amount came from the North, as New England mill owners began to recognize the benefits of relocating to the low-wage, nonunion South. In the tobacco industry, too, initial southern capital gave way to northern financing, especially after James Duke moved to New York in the 1880s. But most dependent on northern capital were the railroads and iron industries. When in 1886 southern railroads switched their tracks from the regional gauge to the national standard, the symbolic domination of the North seemed complete.

Heavy northern investment in southern industry meant that the South had less control over economic decisions that affected its welfare. Some historians have referred to the South's "colonial" relationship to the North in the late 19th century. One result was that the low wages prevailing in the South made for inequitable distribution of the economic benefits of industrial growth. Average southern per capita income remained only two-fifths of the average in the rest of the country well into the 20th century.

Race and   Even those low wages were unequally distributed, as the pol-
Industrialization itics of race influenced the structuring of industrial jobs.
                  Along the piedmont from Virginia to Alabama, new cotton
mills sprang up for a white labor force drawn from farm families on the worn-out
red clay soil of this region. About 40 percent of the workers were women, and
25 percent were children aged 16 and younger. Living in company towns, workers
labored long hours for wages about half the level prevailing in New England's
mills, with their cheap labor giving mill owners a competitive advantage.

At first, African Americans assumed that there would be jobs for them in this
new textile industry. And why not? Blacks had worked in mills before the Civil
War, and they continued to work in tobacco factories in the postwar era, albeit in
the lowest-paid jobs and performing the dirtiest work. There seemed no reason why
such a large and inexpensive workforce might not become a mainstay of the mills.

But industrialization did not mean progress for blacks. Instead, it went hand in
hand with segregation in the increasingly white supremacist world of the 1880s and
1890s. To attract white workers, mill owners promised them segregated environments. The bargain offered was this: Mill workers might not earn very much, but
they would gain what one historian has called the "wages of whiteness," a sense of
racial superiority that could serve as compensation for their low economic status.
Thus, the emerging industrial economy of the New South was built around the politics of race. For most African Americans, agricultural work was thus the only option.

Southern   A major success story, however, was increasing black owner-
Agriculture   ship of land in the post-Reconstruction period, with almost
                   200,000 farmers achieving that cherished goal. Most black
landowners in the South were in the upper South or coastal areas; others were in
the trans-Mississippi West.

Still, most blacks were tenants rather than landowners, and many blacks and
whites faced lives of grinding rural poverty. Those who owned land risked sliding
into tenantry; those who did not own land found it impossible to make the leap to
landownership. One-crop specialization, overproduction, declining prices, and an
exploitative credit system all contributed to the problem. The basic institution of
the southern rural economy was the crop lien system, which came into being
because of the shortage of money and credit in the war-ravaged South. Few banks
had survived the war, and land values had plummeted, which left farmers unable to
secure a bank loan with their land as collateral. Instead, merchants in the crossroads country stores that sprang up across the South provided farmers with supplies and groceries in return for a lien on their next crop.

This system might have worked well if the merchants had charged reasonable
interest rates and if cotton and tobacco prices had remained high enough for the
farmer to pay off his debts after harvest with a little left over. But the country store-
keeper charged a credit price 50 or 60 percent above the cash price, and crop prices,
especially for cotton, were dropping steadily. Cotton prices declined from an average
of 12 cents per pound in the 1870s to 6 cents in the 1890s. As prices fell, many farmers went deeper and deeper into debt to the merchants. **Sharecroppers** and tenants
incurred a double indebtedness: (1) to the landowner whose land they sharecropped

or rented, and (2) to the merchant who furnished them supplies on credit. Because many landowners became merchants, and vice versa, that indebtedness was often to the same man.

One reason cotton prices fell was overproduction. Britain had encouraged the expansion of cotton growing in Egypt and India during the Civil War to make up for the loss of American cotton. After the war, southern growers had to face international competition. By 1878, the southern crop had reached the output of the best antebellum year, and during the next 20 years, output doubled. This overproduction drove prices ever lower. To obtain credit, farmers had to plant every acre with the most marketable cash crop—cotton. This practice exhausted the soil and required ever-increasing amounts of expensive fertilizer, which fed the cycle of overproduction and declining prices.

It also reduced the amount of land that could be used to grow food crops. Farmers who might otherwise have produced their own cornmeal and raised their own hogs for bacon became dependent on merchants for these supplies. Before the Civil War, the cotton states had been nearly self-sufficient in food; by the 1890s, they had to import nearly half their food at a price 50 percent higher than it would have cost to grow their own. Many southerners recognized that only diversification could break this dependency, but the crop lien system locked them into dependency.

Exodusters and Emigrationists   Many rural African Americans dreamed of escaping these difficulties by leaving the South entirely. In the late 1870s, a movement called Exodus gained momentum among African Americans who believed that they might have to "repeat the history of the Israelites" and "seek new homes beyond the reign and rule of Pharaoh." Most pinned their hopes on internal emigration to the West, although some explored the possibility of emigration to Liberia as well. In 1875, Benjamin Singleton, a former Tennessee slave, helped a group of African Americans establish new lives in an agrarian colony in western Kansas; three years later, he circulated an advertisement picturing prairie abundance in the hopes of enticing a few hundred more settlers. Instead, in the spring of 1879, some 20,000 African Americans began an exodus to Kansas from all over the Southwest—drawn not just by the advertisement but also by rumors that there was free land available for settlers as well as free supplies from the government. The rumors were false, but many of these **Exodusters** stayed on in Kansas anyway, although not as homesteaders amidst the prairie abundance but as domestics and laborers in Kansan towns, including some they founded, such as Nicodemus.

Race Relations in the New South   The desire to emigrate for better jobs, autonomy, and a place where African Americans could be truly free did not end with the Exodusters. "The disposition among the colored people to migrate now is strong, and is increasing," commented a white southerner in 1889. There was a net loss of 537,000 African Americans in the South between 1880 and 1910. Economic reasons were important, but so too was the worsening world of white supremacy that arose in that period.

Adherence to the industrial ideology behind the New South, with its emphasis on racial cooperation, was shallow at best among broad classes of whites. Many refused to let go of the legacy of the defeated plantation South. They celebrated the Lost Cause by organizing fraternal and sororal organizations such as the United Daughters of the Confederacy (UDC). The UDC, like the Daughters of the American Revolution (DAR) on which it was modeled, was open only to white women who could prove their relation to the "first families" of the South. Its members decorated the graves of Confederate soldiers, funded public statues of Confederate heroes, and sought to preserve a romanticized history of the slavery era. Several white southern authors became famous writing stories about this fabled South. Thomas Nelson Page's racist sentimental story "Marse Chan" created a national craze for southern literature in the 1880s. Published in a northern magazine, the story was written in what Page claimed to be authentic black dialect, with an aging freedman telling of the glorious days before the war when slaves supposedly had little work to do. Such stories romanticized the southern plantation, cleansing it of the horrors of slavery.

The national appeal of such stories made it clear that antiblack racism was not just a southern phenomenon. Certainly, there was shockingly little northern reaction to the wave of lynchings of black men in the South in the 1890s. Lynchings rose to an all-time high, averaging 188 per year, while the viciousness of racist propaganda reached an all-time low. At a time when many middle-class blacks were steadily gaining economically even as a downward spiral in the rural economy frustrated whites, lynchings of black men were not just extraordinarily violent acts. They were also clear symbolic messages to entire black communities to keep their "place" in a white-dominated society. Ritualized expressions of white power, lynchings were not secret or furtive events, but often well-orchestrated community affairs advertised in advance and sometimes even including men, women, and children as spectators.

In 1892, three respected African American businessmen who owned a grocery store in Memphis, Tennessee, were taken from the jail where they awaited trial and lynched by a white mob. Their ostensible crime was attempted murder—firing on three white intruders who had burst into their store—but their real offense was successfully challenging the dominance of a white grocery store in their area.

In response to the lynching, the African American journalist **Ida B. Wells** embarked on an extensive anti-lynching campaign involving an economic boycott as well as a series of fiery editorials in her newspaper, *Free Speech,* that called into question the usual white rationale for lynching: the supposed rape or molestation of a white woman. Exposing this common trumped-up charge as "the old racket," Wells ignited the wrath of white Memphis residents and was forced to flee for her life to the North. But there her anti-lynching campaign met with indifference from northerners until Wells traveled to England on a speaking tour. She received widespread publicity as she called into question how civilized America could be if it tolerated a barbaric practice like lynching; she also touched a nerve back home. Upper-class white northerners indifferent to the murder of blacks but sensitive to English opinion finally sat up and began to notice her campaign. Her English travels were a brilliant strategy to shake up northern complacency and challenge northern complicity in lynching.

Everett Collection/Newscom

Ida B. Wells. *A passionate crusader for justice, the renowned journalist Ida B. Wells received death threats after she began a campaign against lynching in her Memphis, Tennessee, newspaper,* Free Speech, *in 1892. Forced to leave Memphis, Wells moved to Chicago and continued her anti-lynching crusade in pamphlets, newspaper columns, and public lectures delivered both in the United States and in England. Together with Booker T. Washington, Wells was one of the most prominent African American leaders of the 1890s.*

The Emergence of an African American Middle Class

Wells was part of an extensive African American middle class that came of age in the 1880s and 1890s. These men and women, educated in the emerging black colleges, became teachers, doctors, lawyers, ministers, and business owners. They formed numerous civic organizations, such as the 1896 National Association of Colored Women, which was part of the women's club movement of the late 19th century. Echoing the moral reform activities of white middle-class women, its president, Mary Church Terrell, called on middle-class black women to work with "the masses of our women" and to "uplift and claim them."

Differing Visions of Black Progress: Booker T. Washington and W. E. B. Du Bois

The most prominent black leader at the turn of the century, Booker T. Washington was not without critics. Compare the two selections below. The first is a passage from Washington's famous 1895 Atlanta Exposition Address, delivered to a primarily white audience but widely read by blacks. The second selection is a discussion of Washington's philosophy by the emerging African American leader **W. E. B. Du Bois**. The passage is taken from his masterpiece *The Souls of Black Folk,* a set of essays written between 1897 and 1903.

Booker T. Washington

Our greatest danger is that in the great leap from slavery to freedom we may overlook the fact that the masses of us are to live by the productions of our hands, and fail to keep in mind that we shall prosper in proportion as we learn to dignify and glorify common labour, and put brains and skill into the common occupations of life; shall prosper in proportion as we learn to draw the line between the superficial and the substantial, the ornamental gewgaws of life and the useful. No race can prosper till it learns that there is as much dignity in tilling a field as in writing a poem. It is

at the bottom of life we must begin, and not at the top. Nor should we permit our grievances to overshadow our opportunities.

To those of the white race who look to the incoming of those of foreign birth and strange tongue and habits for the prosperity of the South, were I permitted I would repeat what I say to my own race, "Cast down your bucket where you are." Cast it down among the eight millions of Negroes whose habits you know, whose fidelity and love you have tested in days when to have proved treacherous meant the ruin of your firesides. Cast down your bucket among these people who have, without strikes and labour wars, tilled your fields, cleared your forests, builded your railroads and cities, and brought forth treasures from the bowels of the earth, and helped make possible this magnificent representation of the progress of the South. Casting down your bucket among my people, helping and encouraging them as you are doing on these grounds, and to education of head, hand, and heart, you will find that they will buy your surplus land, make blossom the waste places in your fields, and run your factories. While doing this, you can be sure in the future, as in the past,

Such institution building, combined with increasing prosperity, gave middle-class blacks great optimism that "racial uplift" might reduce or even eliminate racism in American society. "We as a race are enjoying the brightest rays of Christian civilization," wrote one bishop in the African Methodist Episcopal (AME) Church. Middle-class blacks believed that through education and self-improvement, they could become "best men" and "best women," seen as equals by middle-class whites. These were not naïve hopes as black entry into the middle class surged in the 1880s and early 1890s.

that you and your families will be surrounded by the most patient, faithful, law-abiding, and unresentful people that the world has seen. As we have proved our loyalty to you in the past, in nursing your children, watching by the sick-bed of your mothers and fathers, and often following them with tear-dimmed eyes to their graves, so in the future, in our humble way, we shall stand by you with a devotion that no foreigner can approach, ready to lay down our lives, if need be, in defense of yours, interlacing our industrial, commercial, civil, and religious life with yours in a way that shall make the interests of both races one. In all things that are purely social we can be as separate as the fingers, yet one as the hand in all things essential to mutual progress.

W. E. B. Du Bois

Mr. Washington represents in Negro thought the old attitude of adjustment and submission; but adjustment at such a peculiar time as to make his programme unique. This is an age of unusual economic development, and Mr. Washington's programme naturally takes an economic cast, becoming a gospel of Work and Money to such an extent as apparently almost completely to overshadow the higher aims of life. Moreover, this is an age when the more advanced races are coming in closer contact with the less developed races,

and the race-feeling is therefore intensified; and Mr. Washington's programme practically accepts the alleged inferiority of the Negro races. Again, in our own land, the reaction from the sentiment of war time has given impetus to race-prejudice against Negroes, and Mr. Washington withdraws many of the high demands of Negroes as men and American citizens .... But so far as Mr. Washington apologizes for injustice, North or South, does not rightly value the privilege and duty of voting, belittles the emasculating effects of caste distinctions, and opposes the higher training and ambition of our brighter minds,— so far as he, the South, or the Nation, does this,—we must unceasingly and firmly oppose them.

Q *How do Washington and Du Bois differ in their vision of the place of blacks in American life? Are their aims fundamentally different, or can you find similarities in their two philosophies?*

Sources: (first) Booker T. Washington's famous *1895 Atlanta Exposition Address.* Accessed at: http://historymatters.gmu.edu/d/39/; (second) W. E. B. Du Bois's *The Souls of Black Folk,* 3rd. ed., (Chicago: A. C. McClurg & Co., 1903), pp. 50 & 59. Accessed at: http://books.google.com/books? id=7psUAAAAYAAJ&printsec=frontcover&dq=the +souls+of+black+folk&hl=en&sa=X&ei=Lf8VU_yz O8uE2AXd14CIBw&ved=0CCkQ6AEwAA#v=one page&q=the%20souls%20of%20black%20folk&f =false.

The Rise of Jim Crow   But these visible successes of middle-class African Americans enraged white supremacists, who denied any possibility of class solidarity across racial lines. Serious antiblack riots broke out in Wilmington, North Carolina, in 1898 and in Atlanta in 1906. Several states adopted new constitutions that disfranchised most black voters by means of literacy or property qualifications (or both), poll taxes, and other clauses implicitly aimed at black voters. The new constitutions contained "understanding clauses" or "grandfather clauses" that enabled registrars to register white voters who were unable to meet the new requirements. In *Williams v. Mississippi* (1898), the U.S. Supreme Court upheld these disfranchisement clauses on the grounds that they did not discriminate "on their face" against blacks. State Democratic parties then established primary elections in which only whites could vote.

During these same years, most southern states passed **Jim Crow laws** mandating racial segregation in public facilities of all kinds. Many African Americans resisted: In 1884, Ida B. Wells, at the time a young schoolteacher, refused to give up her seat in a railway "ladies' car." The conductor "tried to drag me out of the seat," she remembered, "but the moment he caught hold of my arm I fastened my teeth in the back of his hand. I had braced my feet against the seat in front and was holding to the back, and as he had already been badly bitten he didn't try it again by himself. He went forward and got the baggageman and another man to help him and of course they succeeded in dragging me out." Wells sued the railroad, winning her case in a lower court before losing it on appeal.

In 1896 came a tremendous setback for American equality. In the landmark case of **Plessy v. Ferguson**, the Supreme Court sanctioned Jim Crow laws so long as the separate facilities for blacks were equal to those for whites—which, in practice, they never were. At this "nadir" of the black experience in freedom, as one historian has called the 1890s, a new black leader emerged as successor of the abolitionists and Reconstruction politicians who were fading from the scene. **Booker T. Washington**, a 39-year-old educator who had founded Tuskegee Institute in Alabama, gave a speech at the 1895 Atlanta Exposition that made him famous—and has been controversial ever since.

Speaking to a white audience at this celebration of southern industry and progress, Washington was introduced as "a representative of Negro enterprise and civilization." Assuring his audience that he wanted to "cement the friendship of the races," Washington talked of the "new era of industrial progress" and told the industrialists before him that they should hire African Americans rather than immigrants. "Cast down your bucket where you are," he told them, "among the eight million of Negroes whose habits you know." If they did so, Washington said, they would not only find people to "run your factories," but could also be assured that they would be surrounded by a "faithful, law-abiding, and unresentful" people. In the most famous sentence of the speech, Washington then promised that "in all things that are purely social we can be as separate as the fingers, yet one as the hand in all things essential to mutual progress." In effect, Washington accepted segregation as a temporary accommodation between the races in return for white support of black efforts for education, social uplift, and economic progress.

It was a complex, canny speech, much like the man himself, and Washington's listeners came away with very different impressions. Many African Americans applauded his appeal for black inclusion in the new industrial order; many white audience members simply took away the idea that Washington approved of segregation, vocational training for blacks, and a permanent, second-class status.

THE POLITICS OF STALEMATE

During the 20 years between the Panic of 1873 and the Panic of 1893, serious economic and social issues beset the American polity. The strains of rapid industrialization, an inadequate monetary system, agricultural distress, and labor protest built up to a potentially explosive force. The two mainstream political parties, however, seemed indifferent to these problems. Partisan memories of the Civil War mired Americans in the politics of the past. Paralysis gripped the national government.

Knife-Edge Electoral Balance

The five presidential elections from 1876 through 1892, taken together, were the most closely contested elections in American history. No more than 1 percent separated the popular vote of the two major candidates in any of these contests except 1892, when the margin was 3 percent. The Democratic candidate won twice (Grover Cleveland in 1884 and 1892), and in two other elections carried a tiny plurality of popular votes (Tilden in 1876 and Cleveland in 1888) but lost narrowly in the Electoral College. During the 20 years covered by these five administrations, the Democrats controlled the House of Representatives in seven Congresses to the Republicans' three, while the Republicans controlled the Senate in eight Congresses to the Democrats' two. During only six of those 20 years did the same party control the presidency and both houses, and then by only razor-thin margins.

Divided government and the even balance between the two major parties made for political stalemate. Neither party had the power to enact a bold legislative program; both parties avoided taking firm stands on controversial issues. At election time, Republican candidates "waved the bloody shirt" to keep alive the memory of the Civil War. They castigated Democrats as former rebels or Copperheads who could not be trusted with the nation's destiny. Democrats, in turn, especially in the South, denounced racial equality and branded Republicans as the party of "Negro rule." From 1876 almost into the 20th century, scarcely anyone but a Confederate veteran could be elected governor or senator in the South.

The solid Democratic South and the rather less solid Republican North gave each party a firm bloc of electoral votes in every election. But in three large northern states—New York, Ohio, and Indiana—the two parties were so closely balanced that the shift of a few thousand votes would determine the margin of victory for one or the other party in the state's electoral votes. These three states alone represented 74 electoral votes, fully one-third of the total necessary for victory. Of 20 nominees for president and vice president by the two parties in five elections, 16 were from these three states. Only once did each party nominate a presidential candidate from outside these three states—both lost.

Civil Service Reform

The most salient issue of national politics in the early 1880s was civil service reform. Old-guard factions in both parties opposed it. Republicans split into three factions known in the colorful parlance of the time as Mugwumps (the reformers), Stalwarts (who opposed reform), and Half-Breeds (who supported halfway reforms). Mugwumps and Half-Breeds combined to nominate James A. Garfield for president in 1880. Stalwarts received a consolation prize with the nomination of Chester A. Arthur for vice president. Four months after Garfield took office, a man named Charles Guiteau approached the president at the railroad station in Washington and shot him. Garfield lingered for two months before dying on September 19, 1881.

Described by psychiatrists as a paranoid schizophrenic, Guiteau was viewed by the public as a symbol of the spoils system at its worst. He had been a government clerk and a supporter of the Stalwart faction of the Republican Party but had lost his job under the new administration. As he shot Garfield, he shouted, "I am a Stalwart and Arthur is president now!" This tragedy gave a final impetus to civil service reform. If the spoils system could cause the assassination of a president, it was time to get rid of it.

In 1883, Congress passed the Pendleton Act, which established a category of civil service jobs that were to be filled by competitive examinations. At first, only one-tenth of government positions fell within that category, but a succession of presidential orders gradually expanded the list to about half by 1897. State and local governments began to emulate federal civil service reform in the 1880s and 1890s.

Like the other vice presidents who had succeeded presidents who had died in office (John Tyler, Millard Fillmore, and Andrew Johnson), Arthur failed to achieve nomination for president in his own right. The Republicans turned in 1884 instead to their most charismatic figure, James G. Blaine of Maine. His 18 years in the House and Senate had included six years (1869–1875) as Speaker of the House. He had made enemies over the years, however, especially among Mugwumps, who believed that his cozy relationship with railroad lobbyists while Speaker and rumors of other shady dealings disqualified him for the presidency.

The Mugwumps were small in number but large in influence. Many were editors, authors, lawyers, college professors, or clergymen. Concentrated in the Northeast, particularly in New York, they admired the Democratic governor of that state, Grover Cleveland, who had gained a reputation as an advocate of reform and "good government." When Blaine won the Republican nomination, the Mugwumps defected to Cleveland.

In such a closely balanced state as New York, that shift could make a decisive difference. Cleveland carried New York State by 1,149 votes (a margin of one-tenth of 1 percent) and thus became the first Democrat to be elected president in 28 years.

The Tariff Issue   Ignoring a rising tide of farmer and labor discontent, Cleveland decided to make or break his presidency on the tariff issue. He devoted his annual State of the Union message in December 1887 entirely to the tariff, maintaining that lower duties would help all Americans by reducing the cost of consumer goods and by expanding American exports through reciprocal agreements with other nations. Republicans responded that low tariffs would flood the country with products from low-wage industries abroad, forcing American factories to close and throwing American workers out on the streets. The following year, the Republican nominee for president, Benjamin Harrison, pledged to retain the protective tariff. To reduce the budget surplus that had built up during the 1880s, the Republicans also promised more generous pensions for Union veterans.

The voters' response was ambiguous. Cleveland's popular-vote plurality actually increased from 29,000 in 1884 to 90,000 in 1888 (out of more than 10 million votes cast). Even so, a shift of six-tenths of 1 percent put New York in the Republican column and Harrison in the White House. Republicans also gained control of both houses of Congress. They promptly made good on their campaign pledges by passing legislation that almost doubled Union pensions and by enacting the McKinley Tariff of 1890. Named for Congressman William McKinley of Ohio, this law raised duties on a large range of products to an average of almost 50 percent.

The voters reacted convincingly—and negatively. They handed the Republicans a decisive defeat in midterm congressional elections, converting a House Republican majority of 6 to a Democratic majority of 147, and a Senate Republican majority of 8 to a Democratic majority of 6. Nominated for a third time in 1892, Cleveland built on this momentum to win the presidency by the largest margin in 20 years, but this outcome was deceptive. On March 4, 1893, when Cleveland took the oath of office for the second time, he stood atop a social and economic volcano that would soon erupt.

Conclusion

In 1890, the superintendent of the U.S. Census made a sober announcement of dramatic import: "Up to and including 1880 the country had a frontier of settlement, but at present the unsettled area has been so broken into by isolated bodies of settlement that there can hardly be said to be a frontier line ... any longer."

This statement prompted a young historian at the University of Wisconsin, Frederick Jackson Turner, to deliver a paper in 1893 that became the single most influential essay ever published by an American historian. For nearly 300 years, said Turner, the existence of a frontier of European American settlement advancing relentlessly westward had shaped American character. To the frontier Americans owed their upward mobility, their high standard of living, and the rough equality of opportunity that made liberty and democracy possible. "American social development has been continually beginning over again on the frontier," declared Turner. He continued:

> This perennial rebirth, this fluidity of American life, this expansion westward with its new opportunities ... furnish the forces dominating American character .... Frontier individualism has from the beginning promoted democracy [and] that restless, nervous energy, that dominant individualism ... and withal that buoyancy and exuberance which comes with freedom—these are traits of the frontier, or traits called out elsewhere because of the existence of the frontier.

For many decades, Turner's insight dominated Americans' perceptions of themselves and their history. Today, however, the Turner thesis is largely discredited as failing to explain the experiences of the great majority of people throughout most of American history who lived and worked in older cities and towns or on farms or plantations hundreds of miles from any frontier, and whose culture and institutions were molded more by their place of origin than by a frontier. The whole concept of a frontier as a line beyond which lay empty, uninhabited land has also been discredited.

The Turner thesis also ignored the environmental consequences of the westward movement. The virtual destruction of the bison, the hunting almost to extinction of other forms of wildlife, the ravaging of virgin forests by indiscriminate logging, and the plowing of semi-arid grasslands on the plains drastically changed the ecological balance in the West. These ecological changes stored up trouble for the future in the form of soil erosion, dust bowls, and diminished biodiversity. Thoughtful Americans began to express concern about these problems in the 1890s, foreshadowing the launching of a conservation movement in the following decade.

For most Americans, however, the exploitation of the West was a matter of pride, not concern. The positive claims of the Turner thesis reflected beliefs shared widely among whites. They *believed* that liberty and equality were both at least partly the product of the frontier, of the chance to go west and start a new life. And now that opportunity seemed to be ending. In fact, to many Americans it seemed that a new and worrisome power had overtaken American life, threatening American liberty: the power of the corporation.

19

THE RISE OF CORPORATE AMERICA, 1865–1914

IN THE SUMMER OF 1877, the same year that President Rutherford B. Hayes withdrew federal troops from the South and effectively ended Reconstruction, he called out the military to suppress the most serious labor uprising in the nation's history. The Great Railroad Strike was a national event that ultimately involved hundreds of thousands of people across America; claimed at least 100 lives; resulted in injuries to hundreds more; and caused the destruction of millions of dollars of property. It also caught many onlookers by surprise: "Sudden as a thunderburst from a clear sky," one journalist wrote, "the crisis came upon the country. It seemed as if the whole social and political structure was on the very brink of ruin."

But the strike was not so sudden as it seemed to shocked middle-class observers: Tensions between capital and labor had been building for years. The end of the Civil War had inaugurated an era of rapid economic expansion, but industrialization left many workers as permanent wage earners, with little hope of the independence that had been a cherished part of antebellum free-labor ideology. As a roller-coaster economy also subjected employers to boom-and-bust cycles, many resorted to periodic price-cutting and wage-cutting, even while demanding longer hours. The result was that capital and labor had never been more at odds with one another.

The Great Railroad Strike raised troubling questions that would continue to haunt Americans over the next few decades: Who held power in the emerging corporate order? How was liberty now defined, and whose liberty would the government uphold? Had America become a permanently unequal society?

CHRONOLOGY

1869	Knights of Labor founded
1873	Financial panic begins economic depression
1877	Railroad strikes cost 100 lives and millions of dollars in damage
1883	Railroads establish four standard time zones
1886	Knights of Labor membership crests at 700,000
	Haymarket triggers antilabor backlash
	American Federation of Labor founded
1888	Edward Bellamy publishes *Looking Backward*
1890	Congress passes Sherman Antitrust Act
1892	Homestead Strike fails
	Populists organize the People's Party
1893	Financial panic begins economic depression
1894	"Coxey's army" of the unemployed marches on Washington
	Pullman Strike paralyzes the railroads and provokes federal intervention
1896	William McKinley defeats William Jennings Bryan for the presidency
1897	Depression ends; prosperity returns
1899	Theodore Roosevelt urges Americans to live the "strenuous life"
1901	U.S. Steel is formed from 200 separate companies
	Andrew Carnegie devotes himself to philanthropic pursuits
	One of every 400 railroad workers dies on the job
1909	Henry Ford unveils his Model T

A DYNAMIC CORPORATE ECONOMY

The decades following the Civil War saw an unprecedented surge of growth in the economy. The gross national product was $9 billion for the five-year period from 1869 to 1873; it was $37 billion for the period from 1897 to 1901. In the 1880s, manufacturing began to outstrip agriculture as a source of new value added to the economy, underlining America's ongoing transformation to an industrial society. America moved from fourth in the world in production in 1865 to first in 1900.

But this tremendous economic growth was accompanied by spectacular volatility. Cycles of overexpansion and overproduction were followed by inevitable contraction. Significant labor uprisings correlated with economic downturns, as employers and businesses sought to cut their losses by cutting wages or laying workers off. The **Great Railroad Strike of 1877** occurred during an extended depression; 1886, another depression year, saw 1,400 strikes involving half a million workers. The great Homestead Strike of 1892 followed the announcement of a wage cut of 18 percent. Another extended depression stretched from 1893 to 1897.

Still, the enormous growth of the economy in this period meant great opportunity and increased prosperity for many Americans. Titans of industry piled up previously unimaginable fortunes. A flourishing middle class achieved new power. But the working class shared unequally in this rising prosperity.

Engines of Economic Growth   The railroads were the largest single employer of labor in this period. An important spur to economic growth, railroads increased in miles of track from 30,000 in 1860 to some 200,000 in 1900. Railroad expansion meant a greater need for coal and iron, and later steel, to build railroad cars and lay track: Steel production soared from 732,000 tons in 1878 to 10,188,000 tons by 1900. The steel industry in turn was a catalyst for a host of other industries, in a pattern repeated across the American industrial landscape.

As a result, manufacturing expanded dramatically in this period. In 1859, the value of American manufactured goods was $1.9 billion, but by 1899 it had risen to $13 billion.

Just before the Civil War, there were 140,000 factories and manufacturing shops across the country; by 1899, this figure had risen to 512,000 and included the rise of industrial giants such as Carnegie Steel.

Growth after 1900 was also dramatic. Employment in Chicago's International Harvester factory, where agricultural implements were built, nearly quadrupled from 4,000 in 1900 to 15,000 in 1916. Delaware's DuPont Corporation, a munitions and chemical manufacturer, employed 1,500 workers in 1902 and 31,000 workers in 1920.

Technological Innovation   Growth in manufacturing spurred technological innovation, while invention in turn spurred increased and more efficient manufacturing. Railroads, for instance, ran on a promise of reliability and efficiency, but poorly constructed tracks and rails were a significant hindrance to delivering on that promise. Technological advances like automatic signals and air brakes not only improved railroad efficiency, but aided railroad growth; similarly, the switch from iron to steel tracks aided the efficient production of railroad tracks and promoted the growth of the new steel industry.

No one understood the link between technological innovation and manufacturing growth better than **Thomas Alva Edison**, who invented an astonishing array of devices in this period, from a patented vote-recording machine before he was 21, to the phonograph, the incandescent light bulb, and the kinetoscope (or movie camera). "The Wizard of Menlo Park" was a savvy businessman and self-promoter who kept a sharp eye on the market. "I have always kept," he once told a reporter, "strictly within the lines of commercially useful inventions." In 1876, Edison moved a group of workers to Menlo Park, New Jersey, to set up an "invention factory" that deliberately mimicked the world of manufacturing.

An inventor-entrepreneur, Edison incorporated the Edison Electric Light Company in 1878.

Scientists had long been fascinated by electricity, but only in the late 19th century did they find ways to make it practically useful. The work of Edison, George Westinghouse, and Nikola Tesla not only produced the incandescent bulb that brought electric lighting into homes and offices but also the alternating current (AC) that made electric transmission possible over long distances. From 1890 to 1920, the proportion of American industry powered by electricity rose from virtually nil to almost one-third. A host of other inventions in this period spurred economic growth as well: gasoline engines, Kodak cameras, the Otis elevator, and Alexander Graham Bell's telephone.

The Rise of Big Business

But technological breakthroughs alone do not fully explain the nation's spectacular economic boom. New corporate structures and new management techniques created the conditions that powered economic growth. Before the Civil War, most American businesses were local, family-run affairs that received little or no aid from the

The Great Railway Strike. *On August 11, 1877, the national magazine Harper's Weekly printed this illustration with the caption, "The Great Strike—the Sixth Maryland Regiment Fighting Its Way Through Baltimore." At first glance the illustration seems sympathetic to the strikers being fired upon in the foreground. The article accompanying this illustration, however, talked of the "reign of terror inaugurated by the railroad strikers" and "scenes of riot and bloodshed," such as "we have never before witnessed in the uprising of labor against capital."*

Value Added by Economic Sector, 1869–1899 (in 1879 prices)

government and did not sell stock to raise capital. But railroad companies inaugurated a new era of big business that had profound effects on business practice. Many businesses after the Civil War organized as corporations rather than single proprietorships: Corporations could raise capital through selling shares in a company directly to the public. They also used boards of directors as a management tool, allowing for shared responsibility and a new scale and complexity of enterprise.

Railroads were big business in every way, requiring huge tracts of land as well as enormous amounts of capital. In order to encourage railroad building, between 1862 and 1871 the government stepped in with extremely generous land and monetary subsidies, signaling the beginning of a close relationship between government and business in the postwar period. Indeed, throughout the late 19th century and into the 20th century, government supported the rights of corporations rather than the rights of workers in a series of legal cases as well as major strikes.

Railroad companies needed often-staggering sums of money in order to build. Financiers, bankers, and a wealthy elite seized this golden opportunity to obtain power in the new industrial order. The savvy young banker **J.P. Morgan** helped finance the Albany & Susquehanna Railroad in upstate New York and joined its board in 1870. Morgan would become the most celebrated and powerful banker of the late 19th century, in large part through his shrewd investing in a variety of industries, including Edison's first electric power plant in 1882. Numerous other bankers would also gain new power through providing the finance capital needed by industry.

But there were financial losers as well as winners in the railroad-building frenzy of the post–Civil War era. The most spectacular and far-reaching downfall of the postwar years was that of Jay Cooke, the legendary financial genius behind the sale of Union bonds during the Civil War. Cooke was undone by his attempts to finance the Northern Pacific Railroad: He ran out of capital in 1873 after selling risky bonds and mortgaging government property. When the Northern Pacific went into receivership, Cooke was forced to close his powerful Philadelphia banking house. Within hours, his closure triggered the crash of the New York Stock Exchange, which in turn began the Panic of 1873. In the severe depression that followed, 18,000 businesses went under. Ordinary investors who hoped to make their fortunes by investing in the railroads often lost their shirts instead.

Corporate Consolidation   Corporations began looking for ways to insulate themselves from harrowing downturns in the business cycle. The railroads led the way in tackling this problem. Rather than engaging in ruinous rate wars, railroads took to sharing information on costs and profits, establishing standardized rates, and allocating discrete portions of the freight business among themselves. These cooperative arrangements rarely succeeded for long because they depended heavily on voluntary compliance. During difficult economic times, the temptation to lower rates and exceed one's market share could become too strong to resist.

Corporate efforts to restrain competition and inject order into the economic environment continued unabated, however. A number of corporate titans innovated with corporate organization, including **Andrew Carnegie**, the industrial leader who built giant Carnegie Steel after the Civil War. Carnegie steadily took control of all parts of the steelmaking process, starting with the mining of the raw material of iron ore and ending with the transportation and marketing of the final product. This vertical integration was a powerful new form of business organization that allowed for unprecedented consolidation and the building of business on a previously unimagined scale.

Another titan, the ruthless **John D. Rockefeller** of Standard Oil, either bought out or ruined his rivals through practices such as "predatory pricing" (selling below cost until he bankrupted a competitor) and demanding secret rebates from railroads that wanted his business. In the 1880s, he pioneered a new form of corporate structure, the trust. A vehicle for the creation of a monopoly, a trust was initially used by Rockefeller to gain control over the oil-refining industry and create the horizontal integration of one aspect of his business. Soon, he engaged in vertical integration as well in order to gain control over every aspect of the oil industry, from extraction of crude oil to marketing. By the 1890s, Rockefeller controlled 90 percent of the oil business, with Standard Oil a major force on the world stage.

Mergers also emerged as an important instrument of corporate expansion and consolidation. Smoking tobacco manufacturer James Buchanan Duke led the way in 1890 when he and four competitors merged to form the American Tobacco Company. Over the next eight years, the quantity of cigarettes produced by Duke-controlled companies quadrupled, from 1 billion to almost

Andrew Carnegie.

*An industrialist and business magnate, Carnegie (1835–1919) was an immigrant from Scotland who created a vast fortune in steel, often using ruthless methods to achieve his goals. A classic rags-to-riches story, Carnegie later disavowed the pursuit of money for its own sake, arguing in his famous 1889 "Gospel of Wealth" that the rich should act as "trustees" of their wealth for the public good. One of several **"robber barons"** who later became philanthropists, Carnegie was famous in his own day for providing free public library buildings around the nation.*

4 billion per year. American Tobacco used its powerful position in cigarette manufacture to achieve dominance in pipe tobacco, chewing tobacco, and snuff manufacture as well.

The **merger movement** intensified as the depression of the 1890s lifted. Many of the corporations that would dominate American business throughout most of the 20th century acquired their modern form: Armour and Swift in meatpacking, Standard Oil in petroleum, General Electric and Westinghouse in electrical manufacture, American Telephone and Telegraph (AT&T) in communications, International Harvester in the manufacture of agricultural implements, and DuPont in munitions and chemical processing. The largest merger occurred in steel in 1901, when Andrew Carnegie and J.P. Morgan together fashioned the U.S. Steel Corporation from 200 separate iron and steel companies. U.S. Steel controlled 60 percent of the country's steelmaking capacity. Moreover, its 78 iron-ore boats and 1,000 miles of railroad gave it substantial control over procuring raw materials and distributing finished steel products.

A weak federal government and a conservative Supreme Court set few limits on corporations in this period, despite significant antitrust agitation in the 1880s and 1890s. By then, many Americans feared the power wielded by tycoons who had established monopolies or monopoly market shares not only in oil and steel, but also in sugar, tobacco, and transportation, among other industries. The **Sherman Antitrust Act of 1890** was an attempt to declare any form of "restraint of trade" illegal, but it was so vague as to be almost useless in the actual prosecution of corporations. In 1895, the Supreme Court dealt a crippling blow to the already weak Sherman Antitrust Act when it ruled in *U.S. v. E.C. Knight Company* that the federal government did not have authority over manufacturing because it was not commerce—a form of semantic hair-splitting that revealed the conservative Court's unwillingness to curtail the power of big business.

Mass Production and Distribution

In 1900, Henry Ford was an eccentric 37-year-old mechanic who built race cars in Michigan. In 1909, Ford unveiled his Model T: an unadorned, even homely car, but reliable enough to travel hundreds of miles without servicing and cheap enough to be affordable to most working Americans.

Ford dreamed of creating an automobile civilization with his Model T, and by the 1920s Americans were buying his car by the millions. The stimulus this insatiable demand gave to the economy can scarcely be exaggerated. Millions of cars required millions of pounds of steel alloys, glass, rubber, petroleum, and other material. Millions of jobs in coal and iron-ore mining, oil refining and rubber manufacturing, steelmaking and machine tooling, road construction, and service stations came to depend on automobile manufacturing.

Ford innovated with **mass-production** techniques that increased production speed and lowered unit costs. Mass production often meant replacing skilled workers with machines that were coordinated to permit high-speed, uninterrupted production at every stage of the manufacturing process. But such production techniques were profitable only if large quantities of output could be sold. Although a burgeoning domestic market offered a vast potential for sales, manufacturers often found distribution systems inadequate. This was the case with James Buchanan Duke, who almost single-handedly transformed the cigarette into one of the best-selling commodities in American history. In 1885, at a time when relatively few Americans smoked, Duke invested in several Bonsack cigarette machines, each of which manufactured 120,000 cigarettes per day. To create a market for the millions of cigarettes he was producing, Duke advertised his product aggressively throughout the country. He also established regional sales offices so that his sales representatives could keep in touch with local jobbers and retailers. As cigarette sales skyrocketed, more corporations sought to emulate Duke's techniques. Over the course of the next 20 years, those corporations that integrated mass production and mass distribution, as Duke did in the 1880s and 1890s, came to define American "big business."

Revolution in Management

The growth in the number and size of corporations revolutionized corporate management. The ranks of managers mushroomed. Increasingly, senior managers took over from owners the responsibility for long-term planning. Day-to-day operations fell to middle managers who oversaw particular departments (e.g., purchasing, research, production, labor) in corporate headquarters or who supervised regional sales offices or directed particular factories. Middle managers also managed the people—accountants, clerks, foremen, engineers, salesmen—in these departments, offices, or factories. The rapid expansion within corporate managerial ranks created a new middle class, whose members were intensely loyal to their employers but at odds both with blue-collar workers and with the older middle class of shopkeepers, small businessmen, and independent craftsmen.

As management techniques grew in importance, companies tried to make them more scientific. Firms introduced cost-accounting methods. Many corporations began requiring college or university training in science, engineering, or accounting for entry into middle management. Corporations that had built their success on a profitable invention or discovery created research departments and hired professional scientists—those with doctorates from American or European universities—to come up with new technological and scientific breakthroughs. Such departments were modeled on Thomas Edison's industrial research laboratory.

CORPORATIONS AND AMERICAN CULTURE

New technological innovations reshaped almost all Americans' lives. Electricity, streetcars, and elevators were just a few of the industrial innovations that changed urban dwellers' everyday relationship to physical space. Even people's relationship to time changed. The world of mass-produced consumer goods provided a new standardization of experience and created a new national consumer culture.

Standardized Time   Before the post–Civil War boom in railroads, there was no such thing as "standard" time; instead, many localities and cities kept their own time, derived from the sun's meridian in each locality. If the clock read noon in Chicago, for instance, it read 11:50 in St. Louis, 11:38 in St. Paul, and 11:27 in Omaha, with many other local times in between. This situation played havoc with railroad timetables.

In a sign of corporations' power over American life, in 1883 a consortium of railroad companies agreed to standardize North American time with the creation of four different time zones—much as they exist today—in which all clocks would be set to exactly the same time. Some grumbling followed about the arrogance of railroad presidents changing "God's time." But "railroad time" was quickly adopted by people everywhere, although Congress did not officially sanction standard time zones until 1918.

A National Consumer Culture   Consumer goods also standardized American experience as manufacturers produced national brands such as Ivory soap, Quaker oats, and Jell-O. Advertising firms began working hand in hand with manufacturers to create national marketing campaigns. Expenditures on advertising increased enormously: from some $50 million in 1867 to $500 million by 1900.

Advertisements became part of a shared visual culture, as technological improvements in lithography and the half-tone process in the 1880s and 1890s allowed advertisers to create bright, colorful images that were distributed nationally. Multicolor advertising trade cards (including baseball cards from cigarette companies) became a national fad. Technological breakthroughs in printing allowed new popular magazines and mass-circulation newspapers to reach hundreds of thousands of readers nationally, as well. The *Ladies' Home Journal,* founded in 1893, soon reached over 500,000 readers. Newspapers responded to the demands of a growing population with the first color comics, women's pages, Sunday sections, society pages, and sports pages.

Advertising revenues from department stores fueled the growth of newspapers in large cities around the country. These "palaces of consumption" dramatically changed the urban experience of buying consumer goods. In a major retailing innovation, stores such as Marshall Field & Co. in Chicago (1865) and R. H. Macy's in New York (1866) sold a wide variety of items—from perfume to shoes to hats to clothing to household goods—all under one roof in different departments, instead of in different stores. Customers strolled down carpeted aisles—arranged to mimic city streets—and gazed at a dazzling array of goods in glass cases. Ornate interiors with mirrors and lights added to a sensory experience of profusion, color, and excitement.

Outside of cities, men and women could participate in the new national culture of consumption through mail order. Mail-order catalogs were the brilliant idea of A. Montgomery Ward, who had worked at Marshall Field's firm in Chicago. Starting with a single price sheet of items in 1872, by 1884 Ward was producing a thick, 240-page catalog that listed close to 1,000 items for sale—everything from women's underclothing to entire houses.

Ideas of Wealth and Society   A profusion of consumer goods reached a wide national audience in this period. But among the wealthy, some also practiced what the economist Thorstein Veblen described in *The Theory of the Leisure Class* (1899) as "conspicuous consumption." They sent agents to Europe to buy paintings and tapestries from impoverished aristocrats. In their mansions on Fifth Avenue and their summer homes at Newport, Rhode Island, they entertained lavishly. At one famous costume ball in New York in 1897, guests in satin gowns sewn with jewels impersonated aristocrats. Such aristocratic pretensions extended to marriage: Between 1874 and 1911, 72 American heiresses married British peers. The extravagant habits of a wealthy elite gave substance to Mark Twain's labeling of this era as the Gilded Age. The estimated number of *millionaires* (a word that came into use during this era) in 1860 was 300; by 1892, the number was 4,000. While this was not a large proportion of the population, it was nevertheless a highly visible group.

Many among the wealthy, and eventually among a broader middle class as well, justified their right to wealth with an emerging post–Civil War vocabulary of **Social Darwinism**. "The growth of a large business," wrote John D. Rockefeller, "is merely a survival of the fittest, the working out of a law of nature and a law of God." In assuming that market forces were in fact laws of nature, Rockefeller and other industrial titans such as Andrew Carnegie drew upon the influential work of the English author Herbert Spencer, who had coined the phrase "survival of the fittest" in applying the evolutionary theories of Charles Darwin to human society. According to the tenets of Social Darwinism, human history could be understood in terms of an ongoing struggle among races, with the strongest and fittest invariably triumphing. The wealth and power of the Anglo-Saxon race were ample testimony, in this view, to its superior fitness.

At first popular mostly among intellectuals (the social sciences took shape during these years), Social Darwinism was quickly adopted by a broader public, with "survival of the fittest" becoming a popular catchphrase. Social Darwinism provided a comfortable way of understanding the glaring social inequality of the era: Workers were doomed to be permanent wage laborers not because of some fault in the emerging corporate system, but because they were not "fit." The rich, meanwhile, were entitled to every dollar that came their way.

Sharpened Class Distinctions

The well-publicized activities of the wealthy sharpened a growing sense of class distinction in this era. Throughout the late 19th century, many Americans worried over the class distinctions they saw emerging around them as part of the corporate reordering of American life. Was this sharpened sense of class distinctions acceptable in a republican society that promised equality for all? A source of uneasiness at first, class distinctions became a source of alarm among numerous observers in the 1880s and especially the 1890s, when widespread labor activism challenged the existing social order.

The rise of corporations produced a need for salaried managers, engineers, office workers, and retail clerks—"white-collar" workers (a reference to detachable, starched white collars for shirts). Agricultural labor dropped from 53 percent of the gainfully employed in 1870, to 35 percent in 1900, and to 21 percent in 1930; clerical work in the same period rose from less than 1 percent to over 8 percent. The profession of engineer, directly related to the expansion of manufacturing, leapt by an astonishing 586 percent between 1870 and 1900.

Many members of this new corporate middle class sought to distinguish themselves from the "lower classes." The post–Civil War suburbanization movement was one important spatial realization of this drive for distinction. As early as 1873, *Scribner's* magazine noted that "the middle class, who cannot live among the rich, and will not live among the poor ... go out of the city to find their houses." By the end of the 19th century, suburban communities of detached houses, surrounded by lawns, were markers of the middle-class status of businessmen and professionals who worked by day in cities and traveled back and forth by train or streetcar to their homes.

Theater, literature, and art were also arenas of class distinction. Before the Civil War, performances of Shakespeare had often been rowdy, participatory, cross-class events. By the end of the century, however, the middle class not only claimed Shakespeare as an icon of "high" culture, but also imposed new expectations of "genteel" silence during performances. In literary magazines, middle-class critics decried the vulgarity of "low" literature such as dime novels and westerns. *Century* and *Harper's New Monthly* published "tasteful" fiction, including literature of nostalgia for slavery with virulently racist portrayals of blacks. This white nostalgia for black subordination paralleled growing middle-class alarm over the "insubordination" of the working class in late-19th-century labor strife. A new art movement, American Impressionism, also expressed a middle-class desire for gentility. Influenced by French Impressionism, artists such as William Merrit Chase and Childe Hassam painted light-flecked landscapes or flower-filled urban parks, recording middle-class pleasures in cities strikingly devoid of workers.

Yet, increasingly over the late 19th century, mere gentility began to seem arid to some middle-class artists and writers. Painters such as Thomas Eakins and Thomas Anshutz pioneered a style that would develop into the "realism" of the early 20th century, with its grittier view of city life and less idealized vision of the human form. The dean of American letters, William Dean Howells, wrote novels exploring issues that had rarely been touched by American authors, including divorce, the moral bankruptcy of capitalism, and interracial marriage.

Alarmed by the widening gulf between the classes, Edward Bellamy, in his 1888 utopian novel, *Looking Backward,* imagined a world in the year 2000 in which "labor troubles" and social inequities had been eradicated through a form of socialism called Nationalism. Bellamy's powerful fictional indictment of Gilded Age society resonated with half a million readers, making his novel one of the most popular of the 19th century.

Obsession with Physical and Racial Fitness   The fractious events of the 1890s induced many middle-class and wealthy Americans to engage in what Theodore Roosevelt dubbed **"the strenuous life."** In an 1899 essay with that title, Roosevelt exhorted Americans to live vigorously, to test their physical strength and endurance in competitive athletics, and to experience nature through hiking, hunting, and mountain climbing. Other writers, too, argued that through sport and vigorous activity, men could find and express their virility.

The 1890s were a time of heightened enthusiasm for competitive sports, physical fitness, and outdoor recreation. Millions of Americans, both women and men, began riding bicycles and eating healthier foods. Young women began to engage in organized sports and other athletic activities. A passion for athletic competition also gripped American universities. The power and violence of football helped make it the sport of choice at the nation's elite campuses, and, for 20 years, Ivy League schools were the nation's football powerhouses.

In the country at large, the new enthusiasm for athletics and the outdoor life reflected a widespread dissatisfaction with the growing regimentation of industrial society. Among middle-class and wealthy Americans, the quest for physical superiority reflected a deeper and more ambiguous anxiety: their *racial* fitness. Most of them were native-born Americans whose families had lived in the United States for several generations and whose ancestors had come from the British Isles, the Netherlands, or some other region of northwestern Europe. Having embraced the principles of Social Darwinism, they liked to attribute their success and good fortune to their "racial superiority." They saw themselves as "natural" leaders, members of a noble Anglo-Saxon race endowed with uncommon intelligence, imagination, and discipline. But events of the 1890s challenged the legitimacy of the elite's wealth and authority, and the ensuing depression mocked their ability to exert economic leadership. The immigrant masses laboring in factories, despite their poverty and alleged racial inferiority, seemed to possess a vitality that the "superior" Anglo-Saxons lacked.

CHANGES IN MIDDLE-CLASS WOMEN'S LIVES

After the Civil War, many middle-class women continued to adhere to the ideology of domesticity, assuming that their place was in the home. Yet, an increasing number of women entered a wider sphere of life.

Middle-Class Women and Work

By 1900, 21 percent of all women—middle class and working class—were in the workforce, as opposed to 9.7 percent of women in 1860. After the Civil War, women moved into nursing and office work, while continuing to be a mainstay in teaching. By the end of the 19th century, middle-class women were also becoming editors, literary agents, and journalists in larger numbers, while also entering the professions of medicine and law in small numbers. Many college women moved to cities to take up work, living in apartments on their own as "bachelor girls."

The increased interest in work was reflected in literature of the period. Louisa May Alcott's 1873 novel *Work* imagined an ideal cross-class, cross-race world of supportive female workers. Elizabeth Stuart Phelps spoke for many discontented middle-class women in her 1877 novel *The Story of Avis,* in which the despairing heroine ultimately gave up being an artist for her marriage. Writer and economist Charlotte Perkins Gilman's 1892 biting novella *The Yellow Wallpaper* spoke powerfully of a new domestic claustrophobia. In that brief work, the unnamed heroine desires to write after the birth of a child but is told by her husband and doctor that she must rest instead and is virtually imprisoned in her home.

Few middle-class observers—men or women—were able to imagine women combining work with family. And yet many women had to do so: The nationally known journalist Jane Croly, for instance, who wrote columns under the name "Jenny June," supported her sick husband and four children as an editor and author during the 1880s before becoming the first female professor of journalism at Rutgers University.

The Women's Club Movement   In 1868, the New York Press Club decided to bar women journalists from a celebratory dinner for the great novelist Charles Dickens, who was touring the United States. Croly was insulted and furious, but turned that fury toward a positive purpose: forming the women's club Sorosis (the name was chosen to suggest sisterhood). Composed primarily of professional women writers, Sorosis met regularly to discuss topics of the day and to exchange professional advice.

Sorosis inaugurated a movement of women's clubs among working and non-working middle-class women in communities across the nation. Distinct from antebellum moral reform societies, the new women's clubs were secular and had a variety of different purposes, from intellectual discussion to civic reform. They also provided a bridge to middle-class women's activism during the Progressive era. By the turn of the 20th century, the women's club movement was an important source of support for the revived suffrage movement. What's more, by 1900, women had used the women's club movement to move into and even take over a variety of civic organizations—a way of practicing politics by other means in an era before women had the vote.

This was especially important in the Jim Crow South, where black men were disfranchised in the 1890s. Middle-class black women drew on their extensive experiences in church organizations and Republican aid societies to create effective new networks of public civic organizations. African American women also joined the largest women's social organization of the late 19th century, the Woman's Christian Temperance Union (WCTU). Under the leadership of Frances Willard beginning in 1879, the WCTU engaged in a variety of social reform activities nationally and endorsed woman suffrage in 1884.

The "New Woman"   The "**New Woman**" became a dominant figure of American popular culture in the 1890s. In cartoons, illustrations, paintings, short stories, and essays, the New Woman was a public figure who was athletic, self-confident, young, and independent: She wore the new, less confining fashion of shirtwaists and skirts; rode a bicycle; and even smoked in some images.

But to some observers, the New Woman threatened the sanctity of the home and traditional gender roles. A backlash against middle-class women's new roles took different shapes but was often rooted in new "scientific" expertise. Arguing against women's higher education, for instance, the Harvard Medical School professor Edward H. Clarke asserted in 1873 that intellectual work damaged women's reproductive organs. "A girl could study and learn," he warned, "but she could not do all this and retain uninjured health, and a future secure from neuralgia, uterine disease, hysteria, and other derangements of the nervous system."

The Comstock Law (1872) made it illegal to send reproductive literature or devices through the mails on the grounds that they were "obscene," eroding women's already-limited control of reproduction. During the bicycle craze of the 1890s, experts warned that it would be unhealthy for women to expend so much strength in physical activity. Women actively resisted these attacks in articles, lectures, and through their own actions, both large and small. Frances Willard of the WCTU, for instance, took up bicycling at age 53 in part, she said, because she knew her example would "help women to a wider world."

Higher Education and Professional Organizations   Women moved into higher education in large numbers in the late 19th century. In the Midwest and the West, public universities as well as land-grant universities (a result of the 1862 Morrill Act) expanded and began to admit women in the 1860s. In the East there were fewer coeducational institutions, but the founding of women's colleges—with Vassar leading the way in 1865—meant that by 1890, women were approximately 40 percent of all college graduates nationally.

This move into higher education did not translate into greater ease of access to professional education. Women had broken into medical training in 1849 with the admission of Elizabeth Blackwell to Geneva Medical College in upstate New York. But as separate medical colleges gave way to medical schools within universities in the late 19th century, women lost ground. Professional organizations often excluded women as well; at the turn of the 20th century, the American Medical Association, a gatekeeper to the profession, was an all-white, all-male organization, as were the American Bar Association, the American Historical Association, and the American Economic Association. While new professional organizations established much-needed uniform standards and training in a variety of professions and disciplines, they also closed ranks against women and minorities.

WORKERS' RESISTANCE TO CORPORATIONS

A national culture of consumption had grown up in the last decades of the 19th century, but not everyone had equal access to it. Wages that did not keep pace with the booming economy meant less money to spend, not to mention a struggle to put food on the table.

Although the average per capita income of all Americans increased by 35 percent from 1878 to 1893, real wages advanced only 20 percent. That advance masked sharp inequalities of wages by skill, region, race, and gender. Many unskilled and semiskilled workers made barely enough to support themselves, much less a family; many families, especially recent immigrants (who formed a large part of the blue-collar workforce), needed two or three wage earners to survive.

"Eight hours for work, eight hours for rest, eight hours for what we will" was a famous slogan of the labor movement in the post–Civil War era. In the demand for "eight hours for what we will," workers voiced their belief that they had a right to leisure time under their own control. As one worker told a Senate committee in 1883, "A workingman wants something besides food and clothes in this country .... He wants recreation. Why should not a workingman have it as well as other people?"

Why not indeed? While some alarmed middle-class observers believed that all workers were revolutionaries who wanted to overturn the American government, only a small percentage were political radicals, much less revolutionaries. The truth was more prosaic: Workers wanted fair wages and fair conditions in the workplace. They wanted equality in a system in which power had been systematically stripped from them, and liberty seemed to accrue more to corporations than to individuals. Broad-based workers' movements throughout the late 19th century attempted to rectify a situation in which equal opportunities no longer seemed to be available to all.

Industrial Conditions

One source of the rising tide of worker discontent was the dangerous conditions in the industrial workplace. The drive for even greater speed and productivity on railroads and in factories gave the United States the unhappy distinction of having the world's highest rate of industrial accidents. The railroads were particularly hazardous, with over 72,000 deaths of employees on the tracks between 1890 and 1917. What one historian has called "mechanized violence" characterized other industries as well: Coal mines threatened underground collapses, explosions, and the release of toxic gases; iron mills and steel mills required work with molten metals at open hearths; textile mills threatened mutilation and dismemberment. Yet there was little government regulation of industrial safety, and workmen's compensation did not appear until the 1930s. As a result, many families were impoverished by workplace accidents that killed or maimed their chief breadwinner.

Another source of discontent was the erosion of worker autonomy in factories, where new machinery took over tasks once performed by skilled workers and where managers made decisions about the procedures and pace of operations once made by workers. Many crafts that had once been a source of pride to those who practiced them became just a job that could be performed by anyone. Labor increasingly became a commodity bartered for wages rather than a craft whereby the worker sold the product of his labor rather than the labor itself. For the first time in American history, the census of 1870 reported that a majority of employed persons worked for wages paid by others rather than working for themselves.

Skilled artisans considered this loss of independence an alarming trend. In 1866, the leaders of several craft unions had formed the National Labor Union, which advocated for an eight-hour day at a time when many industries required workers to work for 10 or even 12 hours daily. Labor parties sprang up in several states; the Labor Reform candidate for governor of Massachusetts in 1870 won 13 percent of the vote.

The Great Railroad Strike of 1877

Yet the National Labor Union withered away in the depression of the 1870s, and industrial violence escalated. The worst labor violence in U.S. history up to that time, the Great Railroad Strike of 1877 underscored the deep discontent of workers nationwide. In July, the Baltimore and Ohio Railroad cut wages by 10 percent—its third recent wage reduction. When workers in Martinsburg, West Virginia, walked out in protest, workers up and down the B & O line joined them.

The strike touched a nerve nationally and spread rapidly; within a few days, what had begun as a local protest had traveled to Baltimore, Philadelphia, Pittsburgh, New York, Louisville, Chicago, St. Louis, Kansas City, and San Francisco. Women as well as men joined angry crowds in the streets; workers from a variety of industries walked out in sympathy. Strikers and militia in a number of cities fired on each other, and workers set fire to railroad cars and depots. Alarmed at the possibility of a "national insurrection," President Hayes called in the army. The strike finally ended in early August—"The strikers have been put down *by force,*" Hayes noted in his diary.

But this spontaneous, unorganized labor upheaval did not produce solutions to workers' dilemmas. On the contrary, fears of a workers' "insurrection" led to a new cohesion in the middle class, which began to talk of a "war" between capital and labor. Not only did the middle class strongly support military intervention in the wake of 1877, but it also supported the construction of armories in the nation's largest cities.

The Knights of Labor

Many workers in the wake of 1877 looked to a new labor organization for inspiration. The **Knights of Labor** had been founded in 1869 in Philadelphia as a secret fraternal organization, one of many such artisan societies in eastern cities. Under the leadership of Terence Powderly, a machinist by trade, it became public in 1879 and then expanded rapidly in the wake of the Great Railroad Strike, finally achieving hundreds of thousands of members nationally in the 1880s.

The Knights of Labor offered workers an inspiring vision of an alternative to competitive corporate society. Rooted in the artisan republicanism of the antebellum era, with even its name suggesting a nostalgic look backward, the Knights opposed the wage labor system, declaring "an inevitable and irresistible conflict between the wage-system of labor and republican system of government." Instead it offered an inclusive vision of a "cooperative commonwealth" that would include both men and women and would not discriminate by race. In its platform it called for an eight-hour day, equal pay for women, public ownership of railroads, abolition of child labor, and a graduated income tax.

By the late 1870s, the Knights were a potent national federation of unions— or "assemblies," as they were officially known—and departed in several respects from the norm of labor organization at that time. Most of its assemblies were organized by industry rather than by craft, giving many unskilled and semi-skilled workers union representation for the first time. It was also a more inclusive labor organization than most, although in local practice the Knights did not live up to its lofty ideals. Only some assemblies admitted women or blacks. Tendencies toward exclusivity of craft, gender, and race divided and weakened many assemblies.

A paradox of purpose also plagued the Knights. Most members wanted to improve their lot within the existing system through higher wages, shorter hours, better working conditions—the bread-and-butter goals of working people. This meant collective bargaining with employers; it also meant strikes. The assemblies won some strikes. Powderly and the Knights' national leadership discouraged strikes, however, partly out of practicality: A losing strike often destroyed an assembly, as employers replaced strikes with strikebreakers, or "scabs."

Another reason for Powderly's antistrike stance was philosophical. Strikes constituted a tacit recognition of the legitimacy of the wage system. In Powderly's view, wages siphoned off to capital a part of the wealth created by labor. The Knights, he said, intended "to secure to the workers the full enjoyment of the wealth they create." This was a goal grounded both in the past independence of skilled workers and in a radical vision of the future, in which workers' cooperatives would own the means of production. "There is no reason," said Powderly, "why labor cannot, through cooperation, own and operate mines, factories, and railroads."

The Knights did sponsor several modest workers' cooperatives. Their success was limited, though, partly from lack of capital and of management experience and partly because even the most skilled craftsmen found it difficult to compete with machines in a mass-production economy. Ironically, the Knights gained their greatest triumphs through strikes. In 1884 and 1885, successful strikes against the Union Pacific and Missouri Pacific railroads won prestige and a rush of new members, which by 1886 totaled 700,000. Expectations ran high, but defeat in a second strike against the Missouri Pacific in spring 1886 was a serious blow. Then came the **Haymarket** bombing in Chicago.

Haymarket

Chicago was a center of labor activism and radicalism. In 1878, the newly formed Socialist Labor Party won 14 percent of the vote in the city, electing five aldermen and four members of the Illinois legislature. With recovery from the depression after 1878, the Socialist Labor Party fell onto lean times. Four-fifths of its members were foreign-born, mostly Germans. Internal squabbles generated several offshoots of the party in the 1880s. One of these embraced anarchism and called for the violent destruction of the capitalist system so that a new socialist order could be built on its ashes. Anarchists infiltrated some trade unions in Chicago and leaped aboard the bandwagon of a national movement centered in that city for a general strike on May 1, 1886, to achieve the eight-hour workday. Chicago police were notoriously hostile to labor organizers and strikers, so the scene was set for a violent confrontation.

The May 1 showdown coincided with a strike at the McCormick farm machinery plant in Chicago. A fight outside the gates on May 3 brought a police attack on the strikers in which four people were killed. Anarchists then organized a protest meeting at Haymarket Square on May 4. Toward the end of the meeting, when the rain-soaked crowd was already dispersing, the police suddenly arrived in force. When someone threw a bomb into their midst, the police opened fire. When the wild melee was over, 50 people lay wounded and 10 dead, 6 of them policemen.

Haymarket set off a wave of hysteria against labor radicals. Police in Chicago rounded up hundreds of labor leaders. Eight anarchists (seven of them German-born) went on trial for conspiracy to commit murder, although no evidence turned up to prove that any of them had thrown the bomb. All eight were convicted; seven were sentenced to hang. One of the men committed suicide; the governor commuted the sentences of two others to life imprisonment; the remaining four were hanged on November 11, 1887. The case became a cause célèbre that bitterly divided the country. Many workers, civil libertarians, and middle-class citizens who were troubled by the events branded the verdicts judicial murder, but most Americans applauded the summary repression of radicalism they regarded as un-American.

The Knights of Labor were caught in this antilabor backlash. Although the Knights had nothing to do with the Haymarket affair and Powderly had repeatedly denounced anarchism, his opposition to the wage system sounded to many Americans suspiciously like socialism, perhaps even anarchism. Membership in the Knights plummeted from 700,000 in spring 1886 to fewer than 100,000 by 1890.

The American Federation of Labor (AFL)   As the Knights of Labor waned, a new national labor organization waxed. Founded in 1886, the American Federation of Labor (AFL) was a loosely affiliated association of unions organized by trade or craft: cigar makers, machinists, carpenters, typographers, plumbers, painters, and so on. Most AFL members were skilled workers. The leader of the AFL, **Samuel F. Gompers**, was a onetime Marxist and cigar maker who was reelected to the AFL presidency every year from 1896 until his death in 1924.

Many workers understood that the only hope for economic improvement lay in organizing unions powerful enough to wrest wage concessions from reluctant employers. But this was no easy task. Federal and state governments had shown themselves ready to use military force to break strikes. The courts, following the lead of the U.S. Supreme Court, repeatedly found unions in violation of the Sherman Antitrust Act, even though that act had been intended to control corporations, not unions. Judges in most states usually granted employer requests for injunctions—court orders that barred striking workers from picketing their place of employment (and thus from obstructing employer efforts to hire replacement workers). Before 1916, no federal laws protected workers' right to organize or required employers to bargain with the unions to which their workers belonged.

This hostile legal environment retarded the growth of unions from the 1890s through the 1920s. It also made the AFL, the major labor organization of those years, more timid and conservative than it had been before the depression of the 1890s. Few AFL members were women and blacks. The AFL accepted capitalism and the wage system. Instead of agitating for governmental regulation of the economy and the workplace, it concentrated on the bread-and-butter issues of better conditions, higher wages, shorter hours, and occupational safety within the system—"pure and simple unionism," as Gompers called it.

The AFL had concluded that labor's powerful opponents in the legislatures and the courts would find ways to undermine whatever governmental gains organized labor managed to achieve. That conclusion was reinforced by a 1905 ruling, *Lochner v. New York,* in which the U.S. Supreme Court declared unconstitutional a seemingly innocent New York state law that limited bakery employees to a 10-hour day.

Yet, in its early years the AFL showed considerable vitality under the leadership of Gompers, with its membership quadrupling from less than a half million in 1897 to more than 2 million in 1904. Craft unions negotiated contracts, or trade agreements, with employers that stipulated the wages workers were to be paid, the hours they were to work, and the rules under which new workers would be accepted into the trade. These agreements were accorded the same legal protection that American law bestowed on other commercial contracts.

Still, the AFL had limited success. Its 2 million members represented only a small portion of the industrial workforce. Its concentration among craft workers, moreover, distanced it from most workers, who were not skilled. Unskilled

Pennsylvania Militia at Carnegie's Homestead Steel Mill, 1892. *After the shootout between striking workers and Pinkerton guards, the Pennsylvania militia reopened the mills and protected strikebreakers from striking workers. This photograph shows the militia using steel beams manufactured by the mill as a makeshift barricade.*

North Wind/North Wind Picture Archives

and semiskilled workers could only be organized into an industrial union that offered membership to all workers in a particular industry. Gompers understood the importance of such unions and allowed several of them, including the United Mine Workers (UMW) and the International Ladies Garment Workers Union (ILGWU), to participate in the AFL. But AFL ranks remained dominated by skilled workers who looked down upon the unskilled, especially immigrants. AFL members demonstrated even worse prejudice toward black workers, with more than 10 AFL unions excluding African Americans from membership in the early 20th century.

The Homestead Strike   During the 1890s, strikes occurred with a frequency and a fierceness that made 1877 and 1886 look like mere preludes to the main event. The most dramatic confrontation took place in 1892 at the **Homestead** plant (near Pittsburgh) of the Carnegie Steel Company. Carnegie and his plant manager, Henry Clay Frick, were determined to break the power of the country's strongest union, the Amalgamated Association of Iron, Steel, and Tin Workers. Frick used a dispute over wages and work rules as an opportunity to close the plant (a "lockout"), preparatory to reopening it with nonunion workers. When the union called a strike and refused to leave the plant, Frick called in 300 Pinkerton guards to oust them. (The Pinkerton detective agency had evolved since the Civil War era into a private security force that specialized in anti-union activities.) A full-scale gun battle between strikers and Pinkertons erupted on July 6, leaving nine strikers and seven Pinkertons dead and scores wounded. Frick persuaded the governor to send in 8,000 militia to protect the strikebreakers, and the plant reopened. Public sympathy, much of it pro-union at first, shifted when an anarchist tried to murder Frick on July 23. The failed Homestead Strike crippled the Amalgamated Association; another strike against U.S. Steel (successor of Carnegie Steel) in 1901 destroyed it.

The Depression of 1893–1897   By the 1890s, the use of state militias to protect strikebreakers had become common. Events after 1893 brought an escalation of conflict. The most serious economic crisis since the 1873–1878 depression was triggered by the Panic of 1893, a collapse of the stock market that plunged the economy into a severe four-year depression. The bankruptcy of the Reading Railroad and the National Cordage Company in early 1893 set off a process that by the end of the year had caused 491 banks and 15,000 other businesses to fail. By mid-1894, the unemployment rate had risen to more than 15 percent.

An Ohio reformer named Jacob Coxey conceived the idea of sending Congress a "living petition" of unemployed workers to press for appropriations to put them to work on road building and other public works. "Coxey's army," as the press dubbed it, inspired other groups to hit the road and ride the rails to Washington during 1894. This descent of the unemployed on the capital provoked arrests by federal marshals and troops, and ended in anticlimax when Coxey and others were arrested for trespassing on the Capitol grounds. Coxey's idea for using public works to relieve unemployment turned out to be 40 years ahead of its time.

The Pullman Strike

The explosive tensions between capital and labor fueled the **Pullman Strike** of 1894. George M. Pullman had made a fortune in the manufacture of sleeping cars and other rolling stock for railroads. Workers in his large factory complex lived in the company town of Pullman just south of Chicago, with paved streets, clean parks, and decent houses rented from the company. But Pullman controlled many aspects of their lives, including banning liquor from the town and punishing workers whose behavior did not suit his ideas of decorum. When the Panic of 1893 caused a sharp drop in orders for Pullman cars, the company laid off one-third of its workforce and cut wages for the rest by 30 percent, but did not reduce company house rents or company store prices. Pullman refused to negotiate with a workers' committee, which called a strike and appealed to the American Railway Union (ARU) for help.

The ARU had been founded the year before by Eugene V. Debs. A native of Indiana, Debs had been elected secretary of the Brotherhood of Locomotive Firemen in 1875 at the age of 20. By 1893, he had become convinced that the conservative stance of the various craft unions in railroading (firemen, engineers, brakemen, and so forth) was divisive and contrary to the best interests of labor. He formed the ARU to include all railroad workers in one union. With 150,000 members, the union won a strike against the Great Northern Railroad in spring 1894. When George Pullman refused the ARU's offer to arbitrate the strike of Pullman workers, Debs launched a boycott by which ARU members would refuse to run any trains that included Pullman cars. When the railroads attempted to fire the ARU sympathizers, whole train crews went on strike and quickly paralyzed rail traffic.

Over the protests of Illinois governor John P. Altgeld, who sympathized with the strikers, President Grover Cleveland sent in federal troops. That action inflamed violence instead of containing it. The U.S. attorney general (a former railroad lawyer) obtained a federal injunction against Debs under the Sherman Antitrust Act on grounds that the boycott and the strike were a conspiracy in restraint of trade. This creative use of the Sherman Act was upheld by the Supreme Court in 1895 and became a powerful weapon against labor unions in the hands of conservative judges.

For a week in July 1894, the Chicago railroad yards resembled a war zone. Millions of dollars of equipment went up in smoke. Thirty-four people, mostly workers, were killed. Finally, 14,000 state militia and federal troops restored order and broke the strike. Debs went to jail (for violation of the federal injunction) for six months. He emerged from prison a socialist.

To many Americans, 1894 was the worst year of crisis since the Civil War. The Pullman Strike was only the most dramatic event of a year in which

750,000 workers went on strike and another 3 million were unemployed. But it was a surge of discontent from farmers that wrenched American politics off its foundations in the 1890s.

FARMERS' MOVEMENTS

Between 1870 and 1890, America's soaring grain production increased three times as fast as the American population. Only rising exports could sustain such expansion in farm production. But by the 1880s, the improved efficiency of large farms in eastern Europe brought intensifying competition and consequent price declines, especially for wheat, just as competition from Egypt and India had eroded prices for American cotton. Prices on the world market for these two staples of American agriculture—wheat and cotton—fell about 60 percent from 1870 to 1895, while the wholesale price index for all commodities (including other farm products) declined by 45 percent during the same period. Not surprisingly, distress was greatest and protest loudest in the wheat-producing West and the cotton-producing South.

Victims of a world market largely beyond their control, farmers lashed out at targets nearer home: railroads, banks, commission merchants, and the monetary system. In truth, these institutions did victimize farmers, although not always intentionally.

Resistance to Railroads   The power wielded by the railroad companies inevitably aroused hostility. Companies often charged less for long hauls than for short hauls in areas with little or no competition. The rapid proliferation of tracks produced overcapacity in some areas, which led to rate-cutting wars that benefited some shippers at the expense of others—usually large shippers at the expense of small ones. To avoid "ruinous competition" (as the railroads viewed it), companies formed "pools" by which they divided traffic and fixed their rates. Some of these practices made sound economic sense, but others appeared discriminatory and exploitative. Railroads gave credence to farmers' charges of monopoly exploitation by keeping rates higher in areas with no competition (most farmers lived in areas served by only one line) than in regions with competition. Grain elevators, many of which were owned by railroad companies, came under attack for cheating farmers by rigging the classification of their grain.

Farmers responded by organizing cooperatives to sell crops and buy supplies. The umbrella organization for many of these cooperatives was the Patrons of Husbandry, known as the Grange, founded in 1867. But because farmers could not build their own railroads, they organized "antimonopoly" parties and elected state legislators who enacted "Granger laws" in several states. These laws established railroad commissions that fixed maximum freight rates and warehouse charges. Railroads challenged the laws in court. Eight challenges made their way to the U.S. Supreme Court, which in *Munn v. Illinois* (1877) ruled that states could regulate businesses clothed with a "public interest"—railroads and other common carriers, millers, innkeepers, and the like. It was a landmark decision.

The welter of different and sometimes conflicting state laws, plus rulings by the U.S. Supreme Court in the 1880s that states could not regulate interstate railroad traffic, brought a drive for federal regulation. After years of discussion, Congress passed the Interstate Commerce Act in 1887. This law, like most such laws, reflected compromise between the varying viewpoints of shippers, railroads, and other pressure groups. It outlawed pools, discriminatory rates, long-haul versus short-haul differentials, and rebates to favored shippers. It required that freight and passenger rates must be "reasonable and just." What that meant was not entirely clear, but the law created the Interstate Commerce Commission (ICC) to define the requirement on a case-by-case basis. Because the ICC had minimal enforcement powers, however, federal courts frequently refused to issue the orders the ICC requested. Staffed by men who were knowledgeable about railroading, the ICC often sympathized with the viewpoint of the industry it was supposed to regulate. Nevertheless, its powers of publicity had some effect on railroad practices, and freight rates continued to decline during this period as railroad operating efficiency improved.

The Greenback and Silver Movements   The long period of price deflation from 1865 to 1897, unique in American history, made credit even more costly for farmers. When the price of wheat or cotton declined, farmers earned even less money with which to pay back loans from country store merchants. Thus, it was not surprising that angry farmers who denounced banks or country store merchants for gouging them also attacked a monetary system that brought deflation.

The federal government's monetary policies worsened deflation problems. The 1862 emergency wartime issuance of treasury "greenback" notes had created a dual currency—gold and greenbacks—with the greenback dollar's value relative to gold rising and falling according to Union military fortunes. After the war, the U.S. Treasury moved to bring the greenback dollar to par with gold by reducing the amount of greenbacks in circulation. This limitation of the money supply produced deflationary pressures, with the South and West suffering from downward pressures on prices they received for their crops. Western farmers were particularly vociferous in their protests against this situation, which introduced a new sectional conflict into politics—not North against South, but East against West.

Many farmers in 1876 and 1880 supported the Greenback Party, whose platform called for the issuance of more U.S. Treasury notes (greenbacks). Even more popular was the movement for **"free silver."** Until 1873, government mints had coined both silver and gold dollars at a ratio of 16 to 1—that is, 16 ounces of silver were equal in value to 1 ounce of gold. However, when new discoveries of gold in the West after 1848 placed more gold in circulation relative to silver, that ratio undervalued silver, so that little was being sold for coinage.

Silver miners joined with farmers to demand a return to silver dollars. In 1878, Congress responded by passing, over President Hayes's veto, the Bland-Allison Act requiring the Treasury to purchase and coin no less than $2 million and no more than $4 million of silver monthly. Once again, silver dollars flowed from the mint. But with increased production of new silver mines, the market price of silver actually dropped to a ratio of 20 to 1.

Pressure for "free silver"—that is, for government purchase of all silver offered for sale at a price of 16 to 1 and its coinage into silver dollars—continued during the 1880s. The admission of five new western states in 1889 and 1890 contributed to the passage of the Sherman Silver Purchase Act in 1890. That act increased the amount of silver coinage, but not at the 16-to-1 ratio. Even so, it went too far to suit "gold bugs," who wanted to keep the United States on the international gold standard.

President Cleveland blamed the Panic of 1893 on the Sherman Silver Purchase Act, which caused a run on the Treasury's gold reserves triggered by uncertainty over the future of the gold standard. Cleveland called a special session of Congress in 1893 and persuaded it to repeal the Sherman Silver Purchase Act, setting the stage for the most bitter political contest in a generation.

Grangers and the Farmers' Alliance   Agrarian reformers supported the free silver movement, but many had additional grievances concerning problems of credit, railroad rates, and the exploitation of workers and farmers by the "money power." Both the Grange and the Farmers' Alliance, a new farmers' organization that expanded rapidly in the 1880s, addressed these political concerns. Both also addressed farm families' social and cultural needs, providing them with a sense of community that helped reduce rural isolation. The Grange sponsored picnics and cultural events, actively encouraging the participation of women. Local chapters were required to have female members, and women took up positions of leadership at the local level and also attended national meetings. The Grangers were not anti-consumption, but they desired to avoid middlemen; this made them a good audience for the new mail-order catalogs. Indeed, the innovative retailer Montgomery Ward first gained a foothold in the mail-order business by styling himself the official supply house for the Grange.

Like the Grange, the Farmers' Alliance also provided a sense of community for farmers. Starting in Texas as the Southern Farmers' Alliance, it expanded into other southern states and the North. By 1890, the movement had evolved into the National Farmers' Alliance and Industrial Union, which was affiliated with the Knights of Labor. It was also affiliated with a separate Colored Farmers' Alliance, formed by African Americans who recognized the utility of the Farmers' Alliance but were not welcome in the larger whites-only organization. Reaching out to 2 million farm families, the Farmers' Alliance set up marketing cooperatives to eliminate the middlemen who profited as "parasites" on the backs of farmers. Like the Grange, the Alliance served the social needs of farm families as well as their economic needs, organizing picnics and educational institutes in addition to camp meetings. Appealing to women as well as men, the Alliance helped farmers to overcome their isolation, especially in the sparsely settled regions of the West. The Alliance also gave farmers a sense of pride and solidarity to counter the image of "hick" and "hayseed" being purveyed by an increasingly urban American culture.

The Farmers' Alliance developed a comprehensive political agenda. At a national convention in Ocala, Florida, in December 1890, it set forth these objectives: (1) a graduated income tax; (2) direct election of U.S. senators (instead of election by state legislatures); (3) free and unlimited coinage of silver at a ratio of 16 to 1; (4) effective government control and, if necessary, ownership of railroad, telegraph, and telephone companies; and (5) the establishment of "subtreasuries" (federal warehouses) for the storage of crops, with government loans at 2 percent interest on those crops. The most important of these goals, especially for southern farmers, was the subtreasuries. Government storage would allow farmers to hold their crops until market prices were more favorable. Low-interest government loans on the value of these crops would enable farmers to pay their annual debts and thus escape the ruinous interest rates of the crop lien system in the South and bank mortgages in the West.

These were radical demands for the time. Nevertheless, most of them eventually became law: the income tax and the direct election of senators by constitutional amendments in 1913; government control of transportation and communications by various laws in the 20th century; and the subtreasuries in the form of the Commodity Credit Corporation in the 1930s.

Anticipating that the Republicans and the Democrats would resist these demands, many Alliancemen were eager to form a third party. In Kansas they had already done so, launching the People's Party, whose members were known as Populists, in summer 1890. White southerners, mostly Democrats, opposed the idea of a third party for fear that it might open the way for the return of the Republican Party, and African Americans, to power.

In 1890, farmers helped elect numerous state legislators and congressmen who pledged to support their cause, but the legislative results were thin. By 1892, many Alliance members were ready to take the third-party plunge. The two-party system seemed fossilized and unable to respond to the explosive problems of the 1890s.

THE RISE AND FALL OF THE PEOPLE'S PARTY

Enthusiasm for a third party was particularly strong in the plains and mountain states, five of which had been admitted since the last presidential election: North and South Dakota, Montana, Wyoming, and Idaho. The most prominent leader of the Farmers' Alliance was Leonidas L. Polk of North Carolina. A Confederate veteran, Polk commanded support in the West as well as in the South. He undoubtedly would have been nominated for president by the newly organized People's Party had not death cut short his career at the age of 55 in June 1892.

The first nominating convention of the People's Party met at Omaha a month later. The preamble of their platform expressed the grim mood of delegates. "We meet in the midst of a nation brought to the verge of moral, political, and material ruin," it declared. "The fruits of the toil of millions are boldly stolen to build up colossal fortunes for a few.... From the same prolific womb of governmental injustice we breed the two great classes—tramps and millionaires." The platform called for unlimited coinage of silver at 16 to 1; creation of the subtreasury program for crop storage and farm loans; government ownership of railroad, telegraph, and telephone companies; a graduated income tax; direct election of senators; and laws to protect labor unions against prosecution for strikes and boycotts. To ease the lingering tension between southern and western farmers, the party nominated Union veteran James B. Weaver of Iowa for president and Confederate veteran James G. Field of Virginia for vice president.

Despite winning 9 percent of the popular vote and 22 electoral votes, Populist leaders were shaken by the outcome. In the South, most of the black farmers who were allowed to vote stayed with the Republicans. Democratic bosses in several southern states dusted off the racial demagoguery and intimidation machinery of Reconstruction days to keep white farmers in line for the party of white supremacy. Only in Alabama and Texas, among southern states, did the Populists get more than 20 percent of the vote. They did even worse in the older agricultural states of the Midwest, where their share of the vote ranged from 11 percent in Minnesota down to 2 percent in Ohio. Only in distressed wheat states such as Kansas, Nebraska, and the Dakotas and in the silver states of the West did the Populists do well, carrying Kansas, Colorado, Idaho, and Nevada.

The party remained alive, however, and the anguish caused by the Panic of 1893 seemed to boost its prospects. In several western states, Populists or a Populist-Democratic coalition controlled state governments for a time, and a Populist-Republican coalition won the state elections of 1894 in North Carolina. Women as well as men campaigned for the Populists: Mary Lease, one of the few women practicing law in Kansas, became famous for her impassioned speeches against corporate power.

In 1893, President Cleveland's success in getting the Sherman Silver Purchase Act repealed drove a wedge into the Democratic Party. Southern and western Democrats turned against Cleveland. In what was surely the most abusive attack on a president ever delivered by a member of his own party, Senator Benjamin Tillman of South Carolina told his constituents in 1894: "When Judas betrayed Christ, his heart was not blacker than this scoundrel, Cleveland, in deceiving the Democracy. He is an old bag of beef and I am going to Washington with a pitchfork and prod him in his fat ribs."

The Silver Issue   Clearly the silver issue stirred deep emotions. For many people silver meant far more than a mere change in monetary policy: It also represented a widespread yearning for a more equitable society in which corporations and banks held less power. Thus when Democratic dissidents stood poised to take over the party in 1896, they adopted free silver as the centerpiece of their program. This stand raised possibilities for a fusion with the Populists, who hoped the Democrats would adopt other features of

An Anti-Bryan Cartoon, 1896. *This cartoon in Judge magazine, entitled "The Sacrilegious Candidate," charged William Jennings Bryan with blasphemy in his "Cross of Gold" speech at the Democratic National Convention. Bryan grinds his Bible into the dust with his boot while waving a crown of thorns and holding a cross of gold. In the background, a bearded caricature of an anarchist dances amid the ruins of a church and other buildings.*

The Granger Collection, NYC

their platform as well. Meanwhile, out of the West came a new and charismatic figure, a silver-tongued orator named **William Jennings Bryan**, whose shadow would loom large across the political landscape for the next generation. A one-term congressman from Nebraska, Bryan had taken up the cause of free silver. He came to the Democratic convention in 1896 as a young delegate—only 36 years old. Given the opportunity to make the closing speech in the debate on the silver plank in the party's platform, Bryan brought the house to its feet in a frenzy of cheering with his peroration: "You shall not press down upon the brow of labor this crown of thorns, you shall not crucify mankind upon a cross of gold."

This speech catapulted Bryan into the presidential nomination. He ran on a platform that not only endorsed free silver but also embraced the idea of an income tax, condemned trusts, and opposed the use of injunctions against labor. Bryan's nomination created turmoil in the People's Party. Although some Populists wanted to continue as a third party, most of them saw fusion with silver Democrats as the road to victory. At the Populist convention, the fusionists got their way and endorsed Bryan's nomination. In effect, the Democratic whale swallowed the Populist fish in 1896.

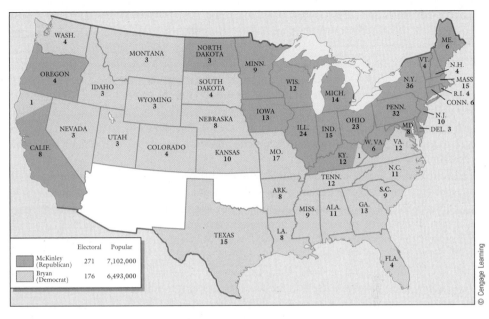

MAP 19.1   Presidential Election of 1896

Note the continuity of voting patterns over the two generations from the 1850s to the 1890s by comparing this map with the election maps in previous chapters.

The Election of 1896

The Republicans nominated William McKinley, who would have preferred to campaign on his specialty, the tariff. Bryan made that impossible. Crisscrossing the country in an unprecedented whistle-stop campaign covering 18,000 miles, Bryan gave as many as 30 speeches a day, focusing almost exclusively on the free silver issue. Republicans responded by denouncing the Democrats as irresponsible inflationists. Free silver, they said, would mean a 57-cent dollar and would demolish the workingman's gains in real wages achieved over the preceding 30 years.

Under the skillful leadership of Ohio businessman Mark Hanna, chairman of the Republican National Committee, McKinley waged a "front-porch campaign" in which various delegations visited his home in Canton, Ohio, to hear carefully crafted speeches that were widely publicized in the mostly Republican press. Hanna sent out an army of speakers and printed pamphlets in more than a dozen languages to reach immigrant voters. His propaganda portrayed Bryan as a wild man from the prairie whose monetary schemes would further wreck an economy that had been plunged into depression during a Democratic administration. McKinley's election, by contrast, would maintain the gold standard, revive business confidence, and end the depression.

The 1896 election was the most impassioned and exciting in a generation. Many Americans believed that the fate of the nation hinged on the outcome. The number of voters jumped by 15 percent over the 1892 election. The sectional pattern of South and West versus Northeast and North Central was almost as pronounced as the North–South split of 1860. Republicans won a substantial share of the urban, immigrant, and labor vote by arousing fear about the Democratic 57-cent dollar and by inspiring hope with the slogan of McKinley as "the advance agent of prosperity." McKinley rode to a convincing victory by carrying every state in the northeast quadrant of the country. Bryan carried most of the rest. Republicans won decisive control of Congress as well as the presidency. They would maintain control for the next 14 years. The election of 1896 marked a crucial turning point in American political history away from the stalemate of the preceding two decades.

Whether by luck or by design, McKinley did prove to be the advance agent of prosperity. The economy pulled out of the depression during his first year in office and entered into a long period of growth—not because of anything the new administration did (except perhaps to encourage a revival of confidence) but because of the mysterious workings of the business cycle. With the discovery of rich new goldfields in the Yukon, in Alaska, and in South Africa, the silver issue lost potency, and a cascade of gold poured into the world economy. The long deflationary trend since 1865 reversed itself in 1897. Farmers entered a new—and unfamiliar—era of prosperity. Bryan ran against McKinley again in 1900 but lost even more emphatically. The nation seemed embarked on a placid sea of plenty. But below the surface, the currents of protest and reform that had boiled up in the 1890s still ran strong.

"ROBBER BARONS" NO MORE

The depression of the 1890s—along with the Populist movement and labor protests such as the Homestead and Pullman strikes—shook the confidence of members of the industrial elite. Industrialists were terrified when in 1892 anarchist Alexander Berkman marched into the office of Henry Clay Frick, Andrew Carnegie's right-hand man, and shot him at point-blank range (Frick survived). Although such physical assaults were rare, anger over ill-gotten and ill-spent wealth was widespread. In the 1890s, popular rage forced Mrs. Bradley Martin and her husband to flee to England after she spent $370,000 (roughly $3.5 million in 2007 dollars) on one evening of entertainment for her friends in New York's high society.

Industrial titans were often called "robber barons." Seeking a more favorable image, some industrialists began to restrain their displays of wealth and use their private fortunes to advance the public welfare. As early as 1889, Andrew Carnegie had advocated a "gospel of wealth." The wealthy, he believed, should consider all income in excess of their needs as a "trust fund" for their communities. In 1901, the year in which he formed U.S. Steel, Carnegie withdrew from industry and devoted himself to philanthropic pursuits, especially in art and education. By the time he died in 1919, he had given away or entrusted to several Carnegie foundations 90 percent of his fortune. Among the projects he funded were New York's Carnegie Hall, Pittsburgh's Carnegie Institute (now Carnegie-Mellon University), and 2,500 public libraries throughout the country.

Other industrialists, including John D. Rockefeller, soon followed Carnegie's lead. A devout Baptist with an ascetic bent, Rockefeller had never flaunted his wealth, but his ruthless business methods in assembling the Standard Oil Company and in crushing his competition made him one of the most reviled of the robber barons. In the wake of journalist Ida Tarbell's stinging 1904 exposé of Standard Oil's business practices, and of the federal government's subsequent prosecution of Standard Oil for monopolistic practices in 1906, Rockefeller transformed himself into a public-spirited philanthropist. Between 1913 and 1919, his Rockefeller Foundation dispersed an estimated $500 million. His most significant gifts included money to establish the University of Chicago and the Rockefeller Institute for Medical Research (later renamed Rockefeller University). His charitable efforts did not escape criticism, however; many Americans interpreted them as an attempt to establish control over American universities, scientific research, and public policy. Still, Rockefeller's largesse helped build for the Rockefeller family a reputation for public-spiritedness and good works, one that grew even stronger in the 1920s and 1930s. Many other business leaders, such as Julius Rosenwald of Sears Roebuck and Daniel and Simon Guggenheim of the American Smelting and Refining Company, also dedicated themselves to philanthropy during this time.

CONCLUSION

For many Americans, the strikes and violence and third-party protests of the 1890s were a wake-up call. They realized that wrenching economic change threatened the liberty and equality they had long taken for granted as part of the American dream. Many middle-class Americans began to support greater government power to carry out progressive reforms that might cure the ills of an industrializing society.

The rise of corporate America created a fundamental paradox: On the one hand, the new industrial landscape denied workers independence and subjected them to harsh conditions, which they resisted as best they could in a series of strikes in the late 19th and early 20th centuries. Yet that same corporate world provided significant opportunities for a better life—opportunities that were especially embraced by the millions of immigrants who settled in American cities at the turn of the century. There, immigrants often found greater liberties than they had known before. But opportunity did not necessarily translate into equality: The search for a more equal society was far from finished.

20

CITIES, PEOPLES, CULTURES, 1890–1920

AMERICA'S CITIES GREW RAPIDLY in the late 19th and early 20th centuries, both to accommodate expanded production and trade and to house masses of workers who labored on the wharves, streets, and factories. Growth called forth technological advance: running water, electric lighting and trolley lines, steel suspension bridges, skyscrapers, and elevators. Immigration soared to remedy severe labor shortfalls in manufacturing and construction; foreign languages and cultures, as a result, became a more prominent feature of American urban life.

New economic elites sought to impart to their cities an architectural elegance and cultural *gravitas* that, in their minds, rivaled those of the greatest cities in history—London, Paris, Rome, Athens, Berlin. Their plans transformed cities but also brought the rich into conflict with the poor, whose presence could not be ignored. A vigorous commercial culture had taken root in working-class and ethnic districts of the city, appearing in dance halls, **nickelodeons**, and amusement parks. Exuberance rather than refinement, adventure rather than education defined these working-class leisure pursuits. Young, working-class women pioneered a sexual revolution, and immigrants energized cities with the diversity of their communities and cultures. The interactions among the different ethnic communities, as well as between rich and poor, made American cities sites of innovation, transformation, and conflict. In them, a new America was taking shape.

CHRONOLOGY

1893	Columbia Exposition opens
1900	Chicago joins New York City and Philadelphia as the only U.S. cities with populations exceeding 1 million
1900–1914	Immigration averages more than 1 million per year
1907	Congress establishes Dillingham Commission to study immigration problems
1907–1911	An average of 73 of every 100 Italian immigrants return to Italy
1908	Israel Zangwill's play, *The Melting-Pot*, debuts
1909	Immigrants and their children constitute more than 96 percent of labor force building and maintaining railroads
1910	Black skilled tradesmen in northern cities reduced to 10 percent of total skilled trades workforce
	Roughly 20,000 nickelodeons dot northern cities
1911	Triangle Shirtwaist Company fire kills 146 workers
1914	Theda Bara, movies' first sex symbol, debuts
	The Masses, a radical journal, begins publication
1916	Randolph Bourne publishes "Trans-National America"
1919	Japanese farmers in California sell $67 million in agricultural goods, 10 percent of state's total
1920	Nation's urban population outstrips rural population for first time

THE RISE OF THE CITY

By the late 19th century, cities were changing the face of America. Their populations, their physical size, and their capacity to transform the landscapes they inhabited dwarfed those of cities a mere 50 years earlier. The rate of urban growth was staggering. Chicago, for example, grew from 30,000 residents in 1850 to 500,000 in 1880 to 1,700,000 by 1900. The number of cities with more than 100,000 residents soared from 18 in 1870 to 38 in 1900. Chicago, along with New York and Philadelphia, surpassed 1 million.

A new kind of building, the skyscraper, symbolized the aspirations taking shape in these expanding urban milieux. These modern towers were made possible by the use of steel rather than stone in the framework and by the invention of electric-powered elevators. Impelled upward by rising real estate values, they were intended to evoke the same sense of grandeur as Europe's Gothic cathedrals. But these monuments celebrated man, not God; material wealth, not spiritual riches; science, not faith. Reaching into the sky, dwarfing Europe's cathedrals, they were convincing embodiments of America's urban might.

If advances in construction made possible the vertical reach of America's urban areas, technological advances encouraged horizontal expansion. Most important in this regard was the application of electricity to urban transportation systems. Between 1890 and 1920, virtually every major city built electric-powered transit systems to replace horse-drawn trolleys and carriages. By 1912, some 40,000 miles of electrical railway and trolley track had been laid. In Boston, electricity made possible the construction of the first subways in 1897, and New York and Philadelphia soon followed suit.

As a result of these transportation improvements, it now became possible for urban dwellers to live miles away from where they worked. As recently as the 1870s, many of America's urban centers had been **walking cities**. They were compact entities, with residential areas abutting work districts, and different income and ethnic groups living in close proximity to each other. By the 1890s, these walking cities had given way to metropolitan entities, with core areas of work and commerce—"downtowns"—now surrounded by expanding rings of residential areas offering inhabitants their own homes and gardens and the promise of tree-lined streets. The intensifying congestion, dirt, poor air, and poverty of urban cores impelled the more affluent residents of these areas to seek homes in the quiet and healthy neighborhoods taking shape on the periphery. In some cases, these areas were jurisdictionally separate from cities, becoming prototypes of the independent 20th-century suburb: Brookline, Massachusetts, a town southwest of Boston, and Evanston, Illinois, a town north of Chicago, were two early examples of this phenomenon. In other urban centers, the new residential districts arose as part of the cities themselves. The old cores, meanwhile, increasingly became home to the poor, to immigrants, and to racial minorities.

Changes in cities below ground matched those going on above. None were more important than water and sewage systems. By 1900, Chicago was pumping 500 million gallons per day to its inhabitants through 1,900 miles of water pipes. Another 1,500 miles of sewage pipe carried used water and other waste products away from Chicagoan households. The 139 gallons that Chicago and other American cities were pumping a day for each inhabitant dwarfed the 20 to 40 gallons per capita that British and German cities were distributing to their residents. The scale and power of these water systems made flush toilets and bathtubs standard equipment in every American middle-class urban home by 1900. Such improvements came more slowly to the urban poor. In cities such as Pittsburgh, for example, water supplies and water pressure were much steadier in prosperous than in poor neighborhoods. As late as the First World War, a significant percentage of working-class families still lacked running water in their homes. Still, America's urban poor had better access to running water than did their counterparts in Europe.

These water systems were impressive engineering feats. In New York City, a network of aqueducts that one historian has described as "the greatest project in water engineering since the Roman Empire" carried water in tunnels that were more than 13 feet in diameter a distance of 30 miles from upstate reservoirs. If measured by their ability to procure, pump, and carry away huge volumes of water, these American systems were unrivalled in the world.

If measured by efforts to control costs, to ensure the safety of workers building tunnels and aqueducts, and to enhance public health, these waterworks were less impressive. The construction and administration of these projects occurred within political systems that were often corrupt. City and state officials expected to receive kickbacks for awarding contracts. Some regarded the size of the kickback as a more important consideration in choosing a contractor than the firm's competence or the prudent use of taxpayer monies. Those in charge of designing and building this infrastructure often did not do enough to protect laborers from the hazards of working underground, to ensure that consumers used the water efficiently, or to protect local lakes, rivers, and oceans against contamination from sewage. In Chicago in 1882, the city's polluted water gave rise to a typhoid fever outbreak that killed more than 20,000 people. In some cities, nonbacterial contaminants compromised water quality, limiting its use for drinking. One Philadelphia newspaper reported in 1895 that the local water tasted "like a solution of gum boots and coal tar."

By 1900, the problems caused by contaminated water had begun to recede. Urban governments were installing water filtration systems and developing safer processes for sewage disposal and treatment. Newly paved roads reduced the amount of dirt, mud, and stagnant pools of water on city streets and thus further curtailed the spread of disease. As a result, urban mortality rates began to fall.

Advances in water systems, in transportation, and in housing reflected a growing commitment in America's urban centers to improving the lives of urban dwellers. This commitment extended well beyond questions of physical well-being to those of education and morals. In the late 19th century, urban elites launched major campaigns for cultural improvement. Symphonies, opera companies, museums, and libraries sprouted in countless cities, often housed in imposing buildings that transformed the urban landscape. In cities such as New York, Cleveland, and Philadelphia these institutions, interwoven with newly designed urban parks, anchored ambitiously conceived urban districts meant to be places where city dwellers might escape the struggles of daily life and cultivate their higher sensibilities. Thus in New York City, the Metropolitan Museum of Art and the American Museum of Natural History appeared in the 1870s alongside Central Park, the first landscaped public park in the United States. The park's principal designer, **Frederick Law Olmsted**, imagined his 50-block-long masterpiece, with its 5 million plantings, as a refuge from the city, a place where people "may stroll for an hour, seeing, hearing, and feeling nothing of the bustle and jar of the streets." If these same people took another hour to contemplate the artistic masterpieces of the Metropolitan Museum or marvel at the holdings of the American Museum of Natural History, so much the better. Olmsted's success with parks in New York gave him an opportunity to replicate it in numerous other cities, including Atlanta, Boston, Brooklyn, Hartford, Detroit, Chicago, Louisville, and Washington, D.C. No other single individual exercised as large an influence on American urban landscapes.

Urban elites of the late 19th century were drawn to Beaux-Arts architecture, a Paris-based style that merged neoclassical size and scale with Italian Renaissance and Baroque decorative influences. By 1902, the Metropolitan Museum had acquired its signature Beaux-Arts façade, which defines the exterior look of the museum to this day. A few years earlier, the Boston Public Library, then the finest public library in the world, moved into magnificent new quarters, whose features included a massive reading room resembling a Roman basilica and a central court-yard modeled on a 16th-century Italian Renaissance cloister. Free and open to the public, the library was celebrated by local newspapers as a "palace of the people" and as "feeding the most careless or unconscious eye with the food of high artistic loveliness."

The scale and ornateness of these buildings revealed the ambitions of the urban elites who founded them. These elites believed that the structures they were building would stand as permanent monuments to their civic vision and influence. They were, at the same time, making a deep investment in their cities, proclaiming their concern for the well-being of the urban masses. Founders of the Metropolitan expressed this sentiment in 1880, when they talked about diffusing "knowledge of art in its higher forms of beauty" so as to "educate and refine a practical and laborious people."

The energy that they poured into these institutions, however, also revealed anxieties about their own social status. For the newly wealthy in their ranks, museums, symphonies, operas, and the like offered a form of alchemy that converted their riches into cultural prestige and authority: As one museum leader said, these institutions would "convert pork into porcelain, grain and produce into priceless pottery, the rude ores of commerce into sculptured marble, and railroad shares and mining stocks … into the glorified canvas of the world's masters."

Elites worried, too, about plebeian resistance to their civilizing projects. What if the masses ignored these institutions? Or misused them? Both the New York museums and Central Park were sites of conflict in the late 19th century between administrators and the people: the former laying down fastidious sets of rules about dress and comportment when using these institutions, the latter repeatedly declaring their intention to be left alone or demanding a role in shaping park and museum rules. In the 1880s, 100 labor organizations, representing 50,000 workers, presented petitions to the Metropolitan and Natural History museums asking that these institutions open their doors to the public on Sunday, the only day that was free of work for most of New York City's inhabitants. Religious groups and pious members of the boards of trustees brought intense pressure on these museums to keep their doors closed on the Sabbath. By 1892, however, both institutions decided to open on Sundays, handing a victory to the city's labor movement. Privately, at least, the more visionary museum leaders had to be pleased that the demand among the city's poor for access had become so strong.

The conflicts of urban life were acutely felt in Chicago. As the fastest-growing American city, it was also one of the hardest to control. Rapid growth spurred innovation but also generated a great gulf between the rich and the poor, violent labor-capital conflict, and widespread corruption. The city had also suffered from disasters such as the typhoid epidemic of 1882 and the Chicago Fire of 1871, which destroyed the homes of 100,000 residents across a stretch of land four miles long. The massive destruction caused by the fire actually accelerated urban creativity and innovation. One of the most interesting groups of American architects, the so-called Chicago School, coalesced in the city a decade after the fire. It included men such as Louis Sullivan and John Wellborn Root and a young draftsman by the name of Frank Lloyd Wright. America's most daring skyscraper designs emerged from their ranks, as did buildings (mostly Sullivan's creations) that merged crisp modern lines, functionality, and wondrous ornamentation. At a later time, Wright would take what he learned as Root's and Sullivan's assistant and develop a distinctive American form of modernist architecture that made his buildings in Chicago and elsewhere among the most original and admired in 20th-century America.

Chicago's remarkable ascent as a center for manufacturing, trade, and architectural innovation made it the choice for hosting the Columbia Exposition of 1893, a world's fair to celebrate the 400th anniversary of Columbus's discovery of America. The fair's two square miles of area made it three times as large as the fair in Paris four years before, and the giant Ferris wheel unveiled by exposition planners was meant to rival the Eiffel Tower as an architectural marvel wrought of iron and steel.

At the heart of this enterprise was a monumental set of gleaming buildings called the **"White City,"** meant to evoke the classical grandeur of Greece and Rome and to trumpet the maturation of American civilization. One set of buildings—Agriculture, Transportation, Manufacturing, among them—devoted itself to inventorying America's achievements in various economic sectors. Other buildings celebrated American women; the histories, cultures, and peoples of the individual states; and the contributions of foreign nations to the story of human progress. The Transportation Building, designed by Sullivan, was the most innovative of the fair's structures, while the Manufactures Building was the largest, covering more

Union Station, Washington D.C. 1928 (color litho), American School (20th century)/Private Collection/
Peter Newark American Pictures/The Bridgeman Art Library

Union Station, Washington, D.C. *The capital city's train station, which opened in 1908 and is still being used today, is an exemplary piece of City Beautiful architecture. Its lines and landscaping reveal how much it was influenced by Chicago's White City. Indeed, the two projects shared an architect, Daniel Burnham. This color lithograph dates from 1928.*

than twice as much area as the Great Pyramid of Egypt and requiring 120,000 incandescent lamps to keep it lit. Steel skeletons held the buildings up; they were sheathed in perishable stucco, unlikely to survive even one Chicago winter. The stucco was easy to work with, however, and thus allowed architects to unleash their decorative instincts in their building designs.

The individual buildings were carefully laid out around a man-made lagoon created by landscape master Olmsted himself, who imparted a neoclassical unity to the entire enterprise. Broad, open courts studded with statuary and interspersed with fountains and parks connected the buildings to each other. It is remarkable that exposition planners invested so much effort in a "city" meant to exist only for a few months.

The planners nevertheless hoped that their work would endure in terms of influencing urban design, if not as an actual urban space. Indeed, the White City, an exemplar of Beaux-Art principles, gave rise to a movement of urban architectural renovation that would become known as the **City Beautiful movement**. Its carefully composed vision of urban order, it was hoped, would offer city planners an inspiration for imposing a similar kind of order on the actual urban environments in which they lived. Metaphorically, the rise of this White City out of the swamps of Jackson Park south of Chicago symbolized the city's and the nation's capacity for rebirth. A utopian dream of an ordered city and a triumphant industrial civilization, the White City embodied America's quest for and belief in perfection.

With paid admissions exceeding 21 million people in a nation with a population of 63 million, the Columbia Exposition was by far the most successful fair in American history. Americans from all over the country came to marvel at this reincarnation of ancient Rome and to record their impressions in special printed books that thoughtfully guided them through the fair, beginning with the page, "My first day in the 'White City.'" The White City did fill many fairgoers with pride and inspiration, much as the planners of the fair hoped it would. Visitors, however, also found their attention drawn to another part of the fair, one that focused on amusement rather than education, and on the dissonances of modern life rather than its symmetry. The **Midway Plaisance** was a long strip located at some distance from the White City, full of concessions where one could buy food and drink, engage in games, line up for rides including the Ferris wheel, and gaze upon the curiosities that countless small entrepreneurs had gathered into their traveling dime museums and freak shows. This, Daniel Burnham, the fair's head designer understood, was "the lighter and more fantastic side of the Fair." The chaotic variety of its sights and smells proved irresistible to tourists.

Part of Midway's variety was deliberately ethnographic, as numerous pavilions displayed life in areas of Africa and Asia. The accent was on the primitive and exotic: The pavilions did not emphasize the modernizing elites of these far-away places, or their achievements in manufacture or transportation, but rather native peoples supposedly barely touched by civilization. It was hard to miss the implication that civilization occurred in America and Europe, as represented in the White City, while primitivism belonged to people of color from Africa, the Middle East, and Asia.

The very structure of the fair thus embodied and reinforced a racial hierarchy that posited the superiority of white, middle-class civilization. African Americans understood how much this hierarchy organized not only America's relationship with much of the world but also life within the United States itself. The anti-lynching crusader Ida B. Wells published a pamphlet, with contributions from several black leaders, titled "The Reason Why the Colored American Is Not in the World's Columbian Exposition." Exploring the intertwined histories of American slavery and racism, this pamphlet offered a detailed accounting of the refusal of fair organizers to include African Americans in their plans. "Theoretically open to all Americans, the Exposition practically is, literally and figuratively, a 'White City,'" the pamphlet asserted. Wells boycotted the fair on "Colored American Day," but former abolitionist Frederick Douglass attended in order to give a stirring speech. "Men talk of the Negro problem," he said. "There is no Negro problem. The problem is whether the American people have honesty enough, loyalty enough, honor enough, patriotism enough to live up to their own Constitution." Try as it might, the Columbia Exposition could not erase the question of race; nor could all the striving for unity and placidity in the White City erase the presence in Chicago and every other major American city of polyglot populations of diverse ethnic origins. International populations were present in virtually all American cities of the North and West, and they would stake a claim to define them as much as the elites who built the palatial museums, opera houses, and White Cities.

IMMIGRATION

The United States had always been a nation of immigrants, but never had so many come in so short a time. Between 1880 and 1920, some 23 million immigrants came to a country that numbered only 76 million in 1900. From 1900 to 1914, an average of 1 million immigrants arrived each year. In many cities of the Northeast and Midwest, immigrants and their children constituted a majority of the population. In 1920s Boston, New York City, Chicago, and Milwaukee, immigrants accounted for more than 70 percent of the total population; in Buffalo, Detroit, and Minneapolis, more than 60 percent; and in Philadelphia, Pittsburgh, and Seattle, more than 50 percent. Everywhere in the country, except in the South, the working class was overwhelmingly ethnic.

European immigration accounted for approximately three-fourths of the total. Some states received significant numbers of non-European immigrants—Chinese, Japanese, and Filipinos in California; Mexicans in California and the Southwest; and French Canadians in New England. Although their presence profoundly affected regional economies, politics, and culture, their numbers, relative to the number of European immigrants, were small. Immigrants from Latin America were free to enter the United States throughout this period, but few did until 1910, when the social disorder caused by the Mexican Revolution propelled a stream of refugees to southwestern parts of the United States. Half a million French Canadians had migrated to New England and the upper Midwest between 1867 and 1901. After that, the rate slowed as the pace of industrialization in Quebec quickened.

European Immigration

Most of the European immigrants who arrived between 1880 and 1914 came from eastern and southern Europe. Among them were 3 to 4 million Italians, 2 million Russian and Polish Jews, 2 million Hungarians, and an estimated 5 million Slavs and other peoples from eastern and southeastern Europe (Poles, Bohemians, Slovaks, Russians, Ukrainians, Lithuanians, Serbians, Croatians, Slovenians, Montenegrins, Bulgarians, Macedonians, and Greeks). Hundreds of thousands came as well from Turkey, Armenia, Lebanon, Syria, and other Near Eastern lands abutting the European continent.

These post-1880 arrivals were called "new immigrants" to underscore the cultural gap separating them from the "old immigrants," who had come from northwestern Europe—Great Britain, Scandinavia, and Germany. Old immigrants were regarded by many native-born Americans as racially fit, culturally sophisticated, and politically mature. The new immigrants, by contrast, were often regarded as racially inferior, culturally impoverished, and incapable of assimilating American values and traditions. This negative view of the new immigrants reflected in part a fear of their alien languages, religions, and economic backgrounds. Few spoke English, and most adhered to Catholicism, Orthodoxy, or Judaism rather than Protestantism. Most, with the exception of Jewish immigrants, were peasants, unaccustomed to urban industrial life, but they were not as different from the old immigrants as the label implied. For example, many of the earlier-arriving Catholic peasants from Ireland and Germany had had no more familiarity with American values and traditions than did the Italians and Slavs who arrived later.

Most mass immigration was propelled by economic hardship. Europe's rural population was growing faster than what the land could support. An individual's or family's decision to emigrate often depended on having a contact—a family member, relative, or fellow villager—already established in an American city. These people provided immigrants with a destination, inspiration (they were examples of success in America), advice about jobs, and financial aid. Sometimes

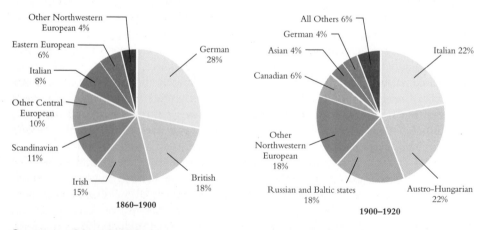

Sources of Immigration

Source: Data from *Historical Statistics of the United States, Colonial Times to 1970* (White Plains, NY: Kraus International, 1989), pp. 105–109.

whole villages in southern Italy or western Russia—or at least all of the young men there—seemed to disappear, only to reappear in a certain section of Chicago, Pittsburgh, or New York. Villages without contacts in the United States were relatively unaffected by the emigration mania.

Most immigrants viewed their trip to the United States as a temporary sojourn. They came not in search of permanent settlement but in search of high wages that would enable them to improve their economic standing in their homeland. For them, America was a land of economic opportunity, not a land to call home. This attitude explains why men vastly outnumbered women and children in the migration stream. From 1899 to 1910, three-fourths of the immigrants from southern and eastern Europe were adult men. Some had left wives and children behind; more were single. Most wanted merely to make enough money to buy a farm in their native land. True to their dream, many did return home. For every 100 Italian immigrants who arrived in the United States between 1907 and 1911, for example, 73 returned to Italy. Before the First World War, an estimated 60 to 80 percent of all Slavic immigrants eventually returned to the land of their birth. Most immigrants looked forward to returning to Europe. Not until the First World War shut down transatlantic travel did most immigrants begin to regard their presence in the United States as permanent.

Chinese and Japanese Immigration

The relatively small numbers of Chinese and Japanese immigrants who came to the United States in the late 19th and early 20th centuries reflected the efforts of native-born Americans and their allies to keep them out. As many as 300,000 Chinese immigrants arrived in the United States between 1851 and 1882, and more than 200,000 Japanese immigrants journeyed to Hawaii and the western continental United States between 1891 and 1907. They contributed in major ways to the development of two of the West's major industries: railroad building and commercial agriculture. These two immigrant groups might have formed two of America's largest, each numbering in the millions, but the U.S. government began to exclude Chinese immigrant laborers in 1882 (via the Chinese Exclusion Act) and Japanese immigrant laborers in 1907. The government also interpreted a 1790 law to mean that Chinese, Japanese, and other East Asian immigrants were ineligible for citizenship. These exclusions remained in force until the 1940s and 1950s. They expressed the racial prejudice felt by most native-born white Americans toward nonwhite Asian immigrants, and they also revealed how determined America was to remain a nation of European immigrants and their descendants.

The early streams of Chinese and Japanese migration to the United States were overwhelmingly composed of men looking for work. Similar to the European immigrants, the Chinese and Japanese sojourners tended to follow precise migratory paths—from one region or village in China or Japan to one city or region in the United States. Conditions in China were more desperate than those in Japan, where industrialization had begun to generate new wealth and absorb some of the rural population. Chinese immigrants, as a result, often suffered greater hardship than did their Japanese counterparts. In the 19th century, many were forced to sign contracts with suppliers of overseas laborers that subjected them to slavelike conditions: They were herded onto boats for the transpacific voyage, bound to particular employers for years on end, thrust into dangerous working conditions, and paid paltry wages.

Significant numbers of Chinese and Japanese immigrants continued to try to enter the United States during the period of Asian immigrant exclusion—after 1882 in the case of the Chinese and after 1907 in the case of the Japanese. Some were desperate to reunite with family members already living in the United States, while others were driven to escape deteriorating economic circumstances in their homeland. Many attempted to enter the United States with forged papers declaring them to be merchants (a permitted class of Chinese and Japanese immigrants) when they were not, or stating that they had been resident in the United States before the exclusion laws had gone into effect (and were thus entitled to return). San Francisco was their principal port of entry, and Angel Island, in San Francisco Harbor, became the counterpart of Ellis Island in New York Harbor: the place where inspectors for the U.S. Bureau of Immigration interrogated them and scrutinized their documents and often sent them back to Asia.

Bettmann/Corbis

Immigrant Japanese Children Arrive at Angel Island, San Francisco Harbor, 1905. *Beginning in 1907, as a result of the "gentlemen's agreement" between the United States and Japanese governments, it would no longer be possible for Japanese immigrants such as these children to come to the United States.*

Other East Asian immigrants attempted to enter the United States through Canada or Mexico, hoping to find a nonpatrolled part of the land border and to cross into the United States undetected. They became, in effect, America's first illegal aliens. That a certain percentage of East Asian immigrants had entered the country illegally, and was subject to deportation, generated considerable fear among the Asian immigrant populations resident in the United States, deepening tendencies within these communities to secrecy and to separation from mainstream American culture and society. Despite these considerable hardships, Asian immigrants would prove to be resourceful and would find ways to build homes and livelihoods in America.

Immigrant Labor   In the first decade of the 20th century, immigrant men and their male children constituted 70 percent of the workforce in 15 of the 19 leading U.S. industries. They concentrated in industries where work was the most backbreaking. Immigrants built the nation's railroads and tunnels; mined its coal, iron ore, and other minerals; stoked its hot and sometimes deadly steel furnaces; and slaughtered and packed its meat in Chicago's putrid packinghouses. In 1909, first- and second-generation immigrants—especially Greeks, Italians, Japanese, and Mexicans—constituted more than 96 percent of the labor force that built and maintained the nation's railroads. Of the 750,000 Slovaks who arrived in America before 1913, at least 600,000 headed for the coal mines and steel mills of western Pennsylvania. The steel mills of Pittsburgh, Buffalo, Cleveland, and Chicago also attracted disproportionately large numbers of Poles and other Slavs.

Immigrants also performed "lighter" but no less arduous work. Jews and Italians predominated in the garment manufacturing shops of New York City, Chicago, Philadelphia, Baltimore, and Boston. In 1900, French Canadian immigrants and their children held one of every two jobs in New England's cotton textile industry. By 1920, the prosperity of California's rapidly growing agricultural industry depended primarily on Mexican and Filipino labor. In these industries, immigrant women and children, who worked for lower wages than men, formed a large part of the labor force. Few states restricted child labor. More than 25 percent of boys and 10 percent of girls aged 10 to 15 were "gainfully employed."

Those who worked in heavy industry, mining, or railroading were especially vulnerable to accident and injury. In 1901, for instance, 1 in every 400 railroad workers died on the job and 1 in every 26 suffered injury. Between the years 1906 and 1911, almost one-quarter of the recent immigrants employed at the U.S. Steel Corporation's South Works (Pittsburgh) were injured or killed on the job. Lax attention to safety rendered even light industry hazardous and sometimes fatal. In 1911, a fire broke out on an upper floor of the **Triangle Shirtwaist Company**, a New York City garment factory. The building had no fire escapes. The owners of the factory, moreover, had locked the entrances to each floor as a way of keeping their employees at work. A total of 146 workers, mostly young Jewish and Italian women, perished in the fire or from desperate nine-story leaps to the pavement below.

Chronic fatigue and inadequate nourishment increased the risk of accident and injury. Workweeks averaged 60 hours—10 hours every day except Sunday. Workers who were granted Saturday afternoons off, thus reducing their workweek to 55 hours, considered themselves fortunate. Steelworkers were not so lucky. They labored from 72 to 89 hours per week and were required to work one 24-hour shift every two weeks.

Most workers had to labor long hours simply to eke out a meager living. In 1900, the annual earnings of American manufacturing workers averaged only $400 to $500 per year. Skilled jobs offered immigrants far more (as much as $1,500 to $2,000 per year), but most of these jobs were held by Yankees and by Germans, Irish, Welsh, and other "old immigrant" Europeans. Through their unions, workers of northern European extraction also controlled access to new jobs that opened up and usually managed to fill them with a son, relative, or fellow countryman. Consequently, relatively few of the new immigrants rose into the prosperous ranks of skilled labor. In any case, employers were replacing many skilled workers with machines operated by cheaply paid operatives.

Most working families required two or three wage earners to survive. If a mother could not go out to work because she had small children at home, she might rent rooms to some of the many single men who had recently immigrated. But economic security was difficult to attain. In his 1904 book, *Poverty*, social investigator Robert Hunter conservatively estimated that 20 percent of the industrial population of the North lived in poverty.

Living Conditions   Strained economic circumstances confined many working-class families to cramped and dilapidated living quarters. Many of them lived in two- or three-room apartments, with several people sleeping in each room. To make ends meet, one immigrant New York City family of eight living in a two-room apartment took in six boarders. Some boarders considered themselves lucky to have their own bed. That luxury was denied the 14 Slovaks who shared eight beds in a small Pittsburgh apartment and the New York City printer who slept on a door he unhinged every night and balanced across two chairs. The lack of windows in city tenements allowed little light or air into these apartments. Crowding was endemic. The population density of New York City's Lower East Side—where most of the city's Jewish immigrants settled—reached 700 per acre in 1900, a density matching or exceeding that of the world's poorest cities. Overcrowding and poor sanitation resulted in high rates of infectious diseases, especially diphtheria, typhoid fever, and pneumonia. In the early years of the 20th century, improvements in the quality of housing and public health finally began to ease the dangers of urban life.

BUILDING ETHNIC COMMUNITIES

The immigrants may have been poor, but they were not helpless. Migration had required a good deal of resourcefulness, self-help, and mutual aid—assets that survived in the new surroundings of American cities.

A Network of Institutions   Each ethnic group quickly established a network of institutions that supplied a sense of community and multiplied sources of communal assistance. Some immigrants simply reproduced those institutions that had been important to them in the Old Country. The devout established churches and synagogues. Lithuanian, Jewish, and Italian radicals reestablished Old World socialist and anarchist organizations. Irish nationalists set up clandestine chapters of the Clan Na Gael to keep alive the struggle to free Ireland from the English. Germans felt at home in their traditional *Turnevereins* (athletic clubs) and musical societies.

Immigrants developed new institutions as well. In the larger cities, foreign-language newspapers disseminated news, advice, and culture. Each ethnic group created fraternal societies to bring together immigrants who had known each other in the Old Country, or who shared the same craft, or who had come from the same town or region. Most of these societies provided members with a death benefit (ranging from a few hundred to a thousand dollars) that guaranteed the deceased a decent burial and the family a bit of cash. Some fraternal societies made small loans as well. Among those ethnic groups that prized home-ownership, especially the Slavic groups, the fraternal societies also provided mortgage money. And all of them served as centers of sociability—places to have a drink, play cards, or simply relax with fellow countrymen. The joy, solace, and solidarity these groups generated helped countless immigrants adjust to American life.

The Emergence of an Ethnic Middle Class

Within each ethnic group, a sizable minority directed their talents and ambitions toward economic gain. Some of these entrepreneurs addressed their communities' needs for basic goods and services. Immigrants preferred to buy from fellow countrymen with whom they shared a language, a history, and presumably a bond of trust. Enterprising individuals responded by opening dry-goods stores, food shops, butcher shops, and saloons in their ethnic neighborhoods. Those who could not afford to rent a store hawked their fruit, clothing, or dry goods from portable stands, wagons, or sacks carried on their backs. The work was endless and the competition tough. Men often enlisted the entire family—wife, older children, younger children—in their undertakings. Few family members were ever paid for their labor, no matter how long or hard they worked. Although many of these small businesses failed, enough survived to give some immigrants and their children a toe-hold in the middle class.

Other immigrants turned to small industry, particularly garment manufacture, truck farming, and construction. A clothing manufacturer needed only a few sewing machines to become competitive. Many Jewish immigrants, having been tailors in Russia and Poland, opened such facilities. If a rented space proved beyond their means, they set up shop in their own apartments. Competition among these small manufacturers was fierce, and critics condemned the work environments as "sweatshops." Workers suffered from inadequate lighting, heat, and ventilation; 12-hour workdays and 70-hour workweeks during peak seasons, with every hour spent bent over a sewing machine; and poor pay and no employment security, especially for the women and children who made up a large part of this labor force. Even at this level of exploitation, many small manufacturers failed; but over time, significant numbers of them managed to firm up their position as manufacturers and to evolve into stable, responsible employers. Their success contributed to the emergence of a Jewish middle class.

The story was much the same in urban construction, where Italians who had established themselves as labor contractors, or *padroni,* went into business for themselves to take advantage of the rapid expansion of American cities. Although few became general contractors on major downtown projects, many of them did well building family residences or serving as subcontractors on larger buildings.

In southern California, Japanese immigrants chose agriculture as their route to the middle class. Working as agricultural laborers in the 1890s, they began to acquire their own land in the early years of the 20th century. Their specialization in fresh vegetables and fruits (particularly strawberries), combined with their family-labor-intensive agricultural methods, was yielding $67 million in annual revenues by 1919—one-tenth of the total California agriculture revenue that year. Japanese farmers sold their produce to Japanese fruit and vegetable whole-salers in Los Angeles, who had chosen a mercantile route to middle-class status. The success of Japanese farmers was all the more impressive given that the state of California had passed the Alien Land Law in 1913, prohibiting Japanese and other Asian aliens from owning property in the state. Japanese immigrant farmers thus depended on their native-born children or friendly whites to acquire land for them, arrangements that made them more vulnerable to losing the land—or con-trol of it—than if they had been able to own it outright themselves.

Each ethnic group created its own history of economic success and social mobility. From the emerging middle classes came leaders who would provide their ethnic groups with identity, legitimacy, and power and would lead the way toward Americanization and assimilation. Their children tended to do better in school than the children of working-class ethnics, and academic success served as a ticket to upward social mobility in a society that increasingly depended on university-trained engineers, managers, lawyers, doctors, and other professionals.

Political Machines and Organized Crime

The underside of this success story was the rise of govern-ment corruption and organized crime. Many ethnic entre-preneurs operated on the margins of economic failure and bankruptcy, and some accepted the help of those who promised financial assistance. Sometimes the help came from honest unions and upright government officials, but other times it did not. Unions were generally weak, and some government officials, lacking experience and economic security, were susceptible to bribery. Economic necessity became a breeding ground for government corruption and greed. A contractor who was eager to win a city contract—to build a trolley system, a sewer line, or a new city hall, for example—would find it necessary to pay off government officials who could throw the contract his way. By 1900, such payments, referred to as "graft," had become essential to the day-to-day operation of government in most large cities. Graft, in turn, made local office holding a source of economic gain. Politicians began building political organizations called machines to guarantee their success in municipal elections. The machine "bosses" used a variety of legal and illegal means to bring victory on Election Day. They won the loyalty of urban voters—especially immigrants—by providing poor neighborhoods with paved roads and sewer systems. They helped newly arrived immigrants find jobs (often on city payrolls) and occasionally provided food, fuel, or clothing to families in need. Many of their clients were grateful for these services in an age when government provided little public assistance.

The bosses who ran the **political machines**—including "King Richard" Croker in New York, James Michael Curley in Boston, Tom Pendergast in Kansas City, Martin Behrman in New Orleans, and Abe Ruef in San Francisco—served their own needs first. They saw to it that construction contracts went to those who offered the most graft, not to those who were likely to do the best job. They protected gamblers, pimps, and other purveyors of urban vice who contributed large amounts to their machine coffers. They often required city employees to contribute to their campaign chests, to solicit political contributions, and to get out the vote on Election Day. And they engaged in widespread election fraud by rounding up truckloads of newly arrived immigrants and paying them to vote a certain way; having their supporters vote two or three times; and stuffing ballot boxes with the votes of phantom citizens who had died, moved away, or never been born.

Big-city machines, then, were both positive and negative forces in urban life. Reformers despised them for disregarding election laws and encouraging vice, but many immigrants valued them for providing social welfare services and for creating opportunities for upward mobility.

Underworld figures, too, influenced urban life. In the early years of the 20th century, gangsterism was a scourge of Italian neighborhoods, where Sicilian immigrants had established outposts of the notorious Mafia, and in Irish, Jewish, Chinese, and other ethnic communities as well. Favorite targets of these gangsters were small-scale manufacturers and contractors, who were threatened with violence and economic ruin if they did not pay a gang for "protection." Gangsters imposed their demands with physical force, beating up or killing those who failed to abide by the "rules." In Chinese communities, secret societies originating in China, or *tongs,* and initially set up in America to strengthen communal life among the immigrants, occasionally crossed the line into crime. Sometimes this transition resulted from good intentions—for example, tong members might smuggle into the United States the wife and children of an immigrant Chinese man who had no legal way of reuniting his family—but other times, tongs became enmeshed in far more damaging criminal activities, such as the opium trade, prostitution, and gambling.

Greedy for money, power, and fame and willing to use any means necessary, many immigrant and ethnic criminals considered themselves authentic entrepreneurs cut from the American mold. By the 1920s, petty extortion had escalated in urban areas, and underworld crime had become big business. **Al Capone**, the ruthless Chicago mobster who made a fortune from gambling, prostitution, and bootleg liquor during Prohibition, once quipped: "Prohibition is a business. All I do is to supply a public demand. I do it in the best and least harmful way I can." New York City's Arnold Rothstein, whose financial sophistication won him a gambling

Der Schuhputzer Tammany's.

"Keeping Tammany's Boots Shined." *This 1880s cartoon by Joseph Keppler declares that the real boss of New York City was not its elected mayor, Hugh Graham, here depicted as a lowly shoe-shiner, but the Tammany Hall political machine. The loose strap underneath the boot, used to control both City Hall and Tammany, belongs to Richard Croker, Tammany's leader from 1886 to 1901.*

empire and the power to fix the 1919 World Series, nurtured his reputation as "the J. P. Morgan of the underworld." Mobsters like Rothstein and Capone were charismatic figures, both in their ethnic communities and in the nation at large. Few immigrants, however, followed their criminal path to economic success.

African American Labor and Community

Unlike immigrants, African Americans remained a predominantly rural and southern people in the early 20th century. Most blacks were sharecroppers and tenant farmers. The markets for cotton and other southern crops had stabilized in the early 20th century, but black farmers remained vulnerable to exploitation. Landowners, most of them white, often forced sharecroppers to accept artificially low prices for their crops. At the same time, they charged high prices for seed, tools, and groceries at the local stores they controlled. Few rural areas generated enough business to support more than one store or to create a competitive climate that might force prices down. Those sharecroppers who traveled elsewhere to sell their crops or purchase their necessities risked retaliation—either physical assaults by white vigilantes or eviction from their land. Thus, most remained beholden to their landowners, mired in poverty and debt.

Some African Americans sought a better life by migrating to industrial areas of the South and the North. In the South, they worked in iron and coal mines, in furniture and cigarette manufacture, as railroad tracklayers and longshoremen, and as laborers in the steel mills of Birmingham, Alabama. By the early 20th century, their presence was growing in the urban North as well, where they worked on the fringes of industry as janitors, elevator operators, teamsters, and servants of various kinds.

In southern industries, blacks were subjected to hardships and indignities that even the newest immigrants were not expected to endure. Railroad contractors in the South, for example, treated their black tracklayers like prisoners. Armed guards marched them to work in the morning and back at night. Tracklayers were paid only once a month and forced to purchase food at the company commissary, where the high prices claimed most of what they earned. Their belongings were locked up to discourage them from running away. Although other southern employers of black workers did not engage in labor practices as harsh as those of the railroad contractors, they still confined blacks to the dirtiest and most grueling jobs. The Jim Crow laws passed by every southern state legislature in the 1890s legalized this rigid separation of the black and white races.

The nation's worsening racial climate adversely affected the southern blacks who moved north, even though these migrants had moved to states that generally did not have Jim Crow laws. Northern industrialists generally refused to hire black migrants for manufacturing jobs, preferring the labor of European immigrants. Only when those immigrants went on strike did employers turn to African Americans.

African Americans who had long resided in northern urban areas also experienced intensifying discrimination in the late 19th and early 20th centuries. In 1870, about one-third of the black men in many northern cities had been skilled tradesmen: blacksmiths, painters, shoemakers, and carpenters. Serving both black and white clients, these men enjoyed steady work and good pay, but by 1910 only 10 percent of black men made a living in this way. In many cities, the number of barbershops and food catering businesses owned by blacks also went into sharp decline, as did black representation in the ranks of restaurant and hotel waiters.

These barbers, food caterers, and waiters had formed a black middle class whose livelihood depended on the patronage of white clients. By the early 20th century, this middle class was in decline, the victim of growing racism. Whites were no longer willing to engage the services of blacks, preferring to have their hair cut, beards shaved, and food prepared and served by European immigrants. The residential segregation of northern blacks also rose in these years, as whites excluded them from growing numbers of urban neighborhoods.

African Americans did not lack for resourcefulness. In urban areas of settlement, they laced their communities with the same array of institutions—churches, fraternal insurance societies, political organizations—that solidified ethnic neighborhoods. A new black middle class arose consisting of ministers, professionals, and businesspeople who serviced the needs of their racial group. Black-owned real estate agencies, funeral homes, doctors' offices, newspapers, groceries, restaurants, and bars opened for business on the commercial thoroughfares of African American neighborhoods. Many businessmen had been inspired by the words of black educator Booker T. Washington, and specifically by his argument that blacks should devote themselves to self-help and self-sufficiency. **Madame C.J. Walker** offers one example of a black woman who built a lucrative business from the hair and skin lotions she devised and sold to black customers throughout the country. In many cities, African American real estate agents achieved significant wealth and power.

Nevertheless, entrepreneurial success remained a tougher task among African Americans than among immigrants. Black communities were often smaller and poorer than white ethnic ones; economic opportunities were fewer, and black businessmen found it more difficult than their white ethnic counterparts to cultivate customers outside of their core community. Racial prejudice stood as an obstacle to black business success. Meanwhile, blacks were so marginalized in politics that they had little opportunity to gain power or wealth through holding political office or controlling a political machine. Thus the African American middle class remained smaller and more precarious than did its counterpart in ethnic communities, less able to lead the way toward affluence and assimilation.

WORKING-CLASS AND COMMERCIAL CULTURE

As much as the white elites and their middle-class allies attempted to impose a genteel order on city life, the city's vitality escaped such bounds. Most workers shared in a new culture of commercial entertainment that included dance halls, music halls, vaudeville theaters, nickelodeons (early storefront movie theaters), amusement parks, and ballparks. Storefront vaudeville theaters, for instance, began to advertise "cheap amusements" to a broad working public in the 1880s. With roots in such antebellum entertainments as minstrelsy, circuses, and dime museums, vaudeville shows offered a variety of miscellaneous short acts for only a dime: A typical show might include sentimental ballads, acrobats, soft-shoe dances, magicians, mind readers, one-act plays, blackface minstrelsy, sports stars from baseball or boxing, puppeteers, jugglers, and dancing bears. Not considered respectable middle-class fare at first, vaudeville became increasingly popular and eventually became a cross-class, national phenomenon.

Amusement parks such as Steeplechase Park at Coney Island, built in 1895, attracted a large working-class audience of men and women while soon also appealing to middle-class youth. Older middle-class commentators found the unchaperoned mingling of young men and women in an urban public space troubling, even shocking, but that loosening of restraint was what made Coney Island so pleasurable and exciting. A new kind of institution in American life, Coney Island was a structured world promoting gaiety and play, with dozens of rides and titillating attractions such as the "Blowhole Theater," whose jets of air blew women's skirts up. "Will she throw her arms around your neck and yell?" asked a sign for the "Cannon Coaster," providing its own answer: "Well, I guess, yes!"

The rides at Coney Island offered young men and women a temporary escape from their industrial working lives, yet ironically enough many of the rides themselves imitated the industrial workplace. The 1884 Switchback Railroad, for instance, an early precursor to the roller coaster, was directly inspired by the operation of gravity-powered coal cars in the shafts of coal mines. New innovations in technology and transportation found a pleasurable mirror at Coney Island and at the other amusement parks around the country that quickly sprang up in imitation.

While vaudeville theaters and amusement parks at first attracted a primarily working-class crowd of pleasure-seekers, they appealed to growing middle-class audiences as well. These cross-class populations were the ones drawn in such large numbers to the sights and sounds of the Midway at the 1893 Columbia Exposition, their attraction to commercial entertainment on that strip subverting the work of those elites who were attempting to impose "White City" notions of order and demeanor on America's city dwellers.

Popular Literature

Just as in the antebellum period, urban workers read a wide variety of dime novels (paperbacks that sold for a dime); and newspapers. Beginning in the 1860s and 1870s, a flourishing cheap literature reflected the presence of working women in the new industrial order. The popular 1871 story, "Bertha the Sewing Machine Girl; or, Death at the Wheel," inspired many imitators and was staged as a popular play in New York City. Its author, Laura Jane Libbey, published more than 60 novels in the 1880s appealing to a working-class audience. Working women read a variety of romances as well, purchasing dime novels from newsstands and pushcarts in large cities. Featuring wealthy heroines or working women who discovered that by birth they were actually aristocrats, these romantic tales offered fantasies that—in imagination, at least—closed the gulf between the classes. Dime novels appealing to working-class men often told heroic stories of working-class manhood in which men overcame numerous obstacles to become the foremen or owners of factories. Such stories allowed a form of imagined compensation for the loss of independence men actually experienced as permanent wage earners.

NICKELODEONS IN MAJOR AMERICAN CITIES, 1910

Cities	Population	Nickelodeons (estimate)	Seating Capacity	Population per Seat
New York	4,338,322	450	150,000	29
Chicago	2,000,000	310	93,000	22
Philadelphia	1,491,082	160	57,000	26
St. Louis	824,000	142	50,410	16
Cleveland	600,000	75	22,500	27
Baltimore	600,000	83	24,900	24
San Francisco	400,000	68	32,400	12
Cincinnati	350,000	75	22,500	16
New Orleans	325,000	28	5,600	58

Source: Garth Jowett, *Film: The Democratic Art* (Boston: Little, Brown, 1976), p. 46.

If literature gestured toward the past, another form of commercial entertainment, the movies, pointed toward the future. Movies were well suited to poor city dwellers with little money, little free time, and little command of the English language. Initially, the movies cost only a nickel. The "nickelodeons" where they were shown were usually converted storefronts in working-class neighborhoods. Movies required little leisure time because at first they lasted only 15 minutes on average. Viewers with more time on their hands could stay for a cycle of two or three films (or for several cycles). And even non-English-speakers could understand what was happening on the "silent screen." By 1910, approximately 20,000 nickelodeons dotted northern cities.

These early "moving pictures" were primitive by today's standards, but they were thrilling just the same. The figures appearing on the screen were "larger than life." Moviegoers could transport themselves to parts of the world they would otherwise never see, encounter people they would otherwise never meet, and watch boxing matches they could otherwise not afford to attend. The darkened theater provided a setting in which secret desires, especially sexual ones, could be explored. As one newspaper breathlessly commented in 1899: "For the first time in the history of the world it is possible to see what a kiss looks like."

No easy generalizations are possible about the content of these early films, more than half of which came from France, Germany, and Italy. American-made films tended toward slapstick comedies, adventure stories, and romances such as those generated by Buster Keaton and Fatty Arbuckle, two silent screen stars. Producers did not yet shy away, as they soon would, from the lustier or seedier sides of American life. The Hollywood formula of happy endings had yet to be worked out. In fact, the industry, centered in New York City and Fort Lee, New Jersey, had yet to locate itself in sunny southern California. In 1914, the movies' first sex symbol,

Theda Bara, debuted in a movie that showed her tempting an upstanding American ambassador into infidelity and ruin. She would be the first of the big screen's vamps, so-called because the characters they portrayed, like vampires, thrived on the blood (and death) of men.

THE NEW SEXUALITY AND THE RISE OF FEMINISM

The appearance of the vamp was one sign that popular culture had become an arena in which Americans were beginning to experiment with more open expressions of sexuality. Another sign was the growing number of women who began insisting that they be accorded the same sexual freedom long enjoyed by men. This impulse was strongest among young, single, working-class women who were entering the workforce in large numbers and mixing at workplaces, in loosely supervised ways, with men their own age. The associations between young men and women that sprang up at work carried over into their leisure. Young people of both sexes flocked to the dance halls that were opening in every major city. They rejected the stiff formality of earlier ballroom dances such as the cotillion or the waltz for the freedom and intimacy of newer forms, such as the foxtrot, tango, and bunny-hug. They went to movies and to amusement parks together, and they engaged, far more than their parents had, in premarital sex. It is estimated that the proportion of women having sex before marriage rose from 10 to 25 percent in the generation that was coming of age between 1910 and 1920.

This movement toward sexual freedom was one expression of women's dissatisfaction with the restrictions that had been imposed on them by earlier generations. By the second decade of the 20th century, eloquent spokeswomen had emerged to make the case for full female freedom and equality. The author Charlotte Perkins Gilman called for the release of women from domestic chores through the collectivization of housekeeping. Social activist Margaret Sanger insisted in her lectures on birth control that women should be free to enjoy sexual relations without having to worry about unwanted motherhood. The anarchist Emma Goldman denounced marriage as a kind of prostitution and embraced the ideal of "free love"—love unburdened by contractual commitment. Alice Paul, founder of the National Women's Party, brought a new militancy to the campaign for woman suffrage.

These women were among the first to use the term **feminism** to describe their desire for complete equality with men. Some of them came together in Greenwich Village, a community of radical artists and writers in lower Manhattan, where they found a supportive environment in which to express and live by their feminist ideals. Crystal Eastman, a leader of the feminist **Greenwich Village** group called Heterodoxy, defined the feminist challenge as "how to arrange the world so that women can be human beings, with a chance to exercise their infinitely varied gifts in infinitely varied ways, instead of being destined by the accident of their sex to one field of activity."

The movement for sexual and gender equality aroused considerable anxiety. Parents worried about the promiscuity of their children. Conservatives were certain

HISTORY THROUGH FILM

Coney Island (1917)

Directed by Roscoe "Fatty" Arbuckle (uncredited).
Starring Roscoe "Fatty" Arbuckle (Fatty), Buster Keaton (Rival), Alice Mann (Love Interest), Agnes Neilson (Fatty's Wife), and Al St. John (Old Friend).

Coney Island was one of the first silent films to feature a classic comedy duo: Roscoe "Fatty" Arbuckle and Buster Keaton. The two met through a mutual friend in New York City in 1917 and quickly struck up a silver-screen partnership. Arbuckle, already a silent movie star, and Keaton, a veteran of the vaudeville circuit, crafted a crude, slapstick tour de force of pratfalls, gags, and fights. It was the beginning of a popular style of comedy on film, the fat/skinny buddy pic, which would be recast in famous teams like Abbot and Costello, Laurel and Hardy, and to an extent, the Three Stooges.

Coney Island opens to images of Luna Park at night: brightly lit towers, luminescent avenues, mechanized roller coasters. Highlighting these modern inventions, the film showcases the technological innovations of the late 19th and early 20th centuries. Coney Island itself—its state-of-the-art rides (The Witching Waves, Chutes), its street vendors hawking ice cream and candy, its carnival-like, consumer-driven atmosphere—is one of the most prominent "characters" in the film. It is cast as having irresistible allure. Like the Midway Plaisance and in contrast to the White City, Coney Island sought to fill urban dwellers' leisure time with adventure and fun rather than with moral improvement.

At the beginning of the film, Buster Keaton's character watches a parade with his girlfriend (Alice Mann) before the two decide to enter Luna Park. When Keaton comes up short on the entry fee, his lady friend drops him for a man who has the admission cash (Al St. John). Meanwhile, Fatty sits, bored, on the beach with his dowdy wife, but he eventually sneaks away from her after burying himself in the sand to hide. For the rest of the film, Keaton, Arbuckle, and St. John vie for Mann's attention, punching and pranking each other in the process. Keaton eventually wins back Mann's affection, and Fatty and St. John swear off women altogether, until they spy another young lady and run after her.

The raucous style of physical comedy that dominates this film offers us a glimpse of the values then coursing their way through working-class commercial culture. The cinematic displays of informal association between men and women, of adventure and sexuality, had been inspired by behaviors that many young urban dwellers, including sizable numbers of immigrants, had themselves embraced. The film is notable, too, for the breadth of its attack on social conventions and authority figures. In the movie, no relationship is sacred (the primary narrative follows Fatty's attempts to cheat on his wife), no authority figure powerful (the inadequate and often thickly mustachioed Keystone Kops end up locked in jail, knocked out cold), and no gender line firm (Fatty cross-dresses to disguise himself from his wife). While the assault on authority in the movie is presented in a hilarious style, it carries a more serious message; namely, that working-class individuals were going to make their own way in the world. It is precisely these declarations of cultural independence that made urban elites and their middle-class allies so anxious about their ability to impose their own sense of order and morality on city life.

By the 1920s, executives in the movie industry had taken steps to expunge Arbuckle-style antics from their films, and to make these art forms more suitable for refined middle-class audiences. Once decorum in the movies became the rule of the day, lords of cinematic anarchy, like Arbuckle, lost their footing.

In fact, Arbuckle's career crashed in the twenties. In 1921, actress Virginia Rappe died four days after attending a bootleg liquor party at Fatty's San Francisco apartment. Arbuckle was accused of rape and was tried three times for manslaughter. Though eventually acquitted, his career as an actor never recovered. He died in 1933 of a heart attack at age 46. Buster Keaton, however, went on to become a successful actor, sharing the Hollywood limelight with the likes of Charlie Chaplin.

Courtesy of Everett Collection

Fatty Arbuckle (center) getting clobbered by Buster Keaton (right) in a scene from Coney Island. Their love interest, played by Alice Mann, looks on.

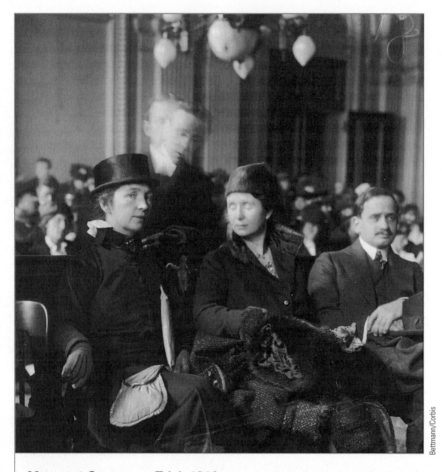

Bettmann/Corbis

Margaret Sanger on Trial, 1916. *Feminist Margaret Sanger, left, was put on trial for using the U.S. mail service to circulate her book,* The Woman Rebel, *which advocated birth control. A federal law barred the use of the mail system to spread birth control advice or techniques.*

that sexual assertiveness among women would transform American cities into dens of iniquity. Vice commissions sprang up in every major city to clamp down on prostitution, drunkenness, and pornography. The campaign for prohibition—a ban on the sale of alcoholic beverages—gathered steam. Movie theater owners were pressured into excluding "indecent" films from their screens. Many believed lurid tales of international vice lords scouring foreign lands for innocent girls who could be delivered to American brothel owners. This "white slave trade" inspired passage of the 1910 Mann Act, which made the transportation of women across state lines for immoral purposes a federal crime.

Nor did it escape the attention of conservatives that Greenwich Village was home not only to the exponents of "free love" but also to advocates of class warfare. William "Big Bill" Haywood, leader of a newly formed radical labor organization, the Industrial Workers of the World (IWW), frequented Greenwich Village.

So, too, did IWW organizer and Heterodoxy member Elizabeth Gurley Flynn. Flynn's lover, Carlo Tresca, was an IWW theoretician. When Greenwich Village radicals began publishing an avant-garde artistic journal in 1914, they called it *The Masses;* its editor was Max Eastman, the brother of Crystal. This convergence of labor and feminist militancy intensified conservative feeling that the nation had strayed too far from its roots.

REIMAGINING AMERICAN NATIONALITY

The large presence of immigrants in America also alarmed conservatives. Among the native-born middle and upper classes, the prevailing view was that immigrants should shed their ethnic backgrounds and become thoroughly American in speech, dress, and culture and in their commitment to the principles of liberty and democracy. A refusal or inability to do so was increasingly interpreted by these conservative sectors of the population as marking the inferiority of the immigrant group in question or its unfitness for life in America. Such interpretations of immigrant behavior generated support for coercive Americanization campaigns and for legislation that would extend the ban on "undesirable" immigrant groups from East Asians to eastern and southern Europeans, West Asians, and Africans. In 1907, Congress established the Dillingham Commission to collect information on every immigrant group in America with an eye toward making a factual case for closing America's immigrant gates.

As these pressures mounted, others began to fight back, some insisting that all immigrants had the capacity to become fully American, others declaring that America would be a better place if it made room for at least some of the diversity that immigrants had brought to American culture. In 1908, Israel Zangwill, an Anglo-Jewish writer, debuted his play, *The Melting-Pot,* on Broadway. The play's theme was that all immigrants, even those originating from eastern Europe, could become the most successful and best of Americans. The play's protagonist, David Quixano, belongs to a Russian Jewish family that has been killed in Russian anti-Jewish riots. David alone survives and flees to New York City, where he is taken in by his uncle and his uncle's mother, both older souls who will never successfully adapt their lives to the rhythms of America. But David himself has the youth, drive, and desire to succeed. A talented musician, he seizes the opportunity that America gives him, writes a successful American symphony, marries the Gentile girl of his dreams, and becomes a proud American.

It mattered greatly to Zangwill, the playwright, that David's success grew out of his willingness to abandon his ethnic and religious past and to embrace America. Zangwill imagined an America in which all immigrants, or at least all immigrants from Europe, would succeed in similar ways, leaving behind their Old World cultures (and grievances) and melting together to form a new and vigorous nationality. The climactic moment in the play comes when Zangwill puts these words in David's mouth: "America is God's Crucible, the great Melting-Pot where all the races of Europe are melting and re-forming!"

Zangwill attracted prominent individuals to his point of view. President Theodore Roosevelt wrote Zangwill in 1908, after watching a performance of *The Melting-Pot:* "I do not know when I have seen a play that stirred me as much."

And President Woodrow Wilson declared in 1915 that America was "the only country in the world" that experiences a "constant and repeated rebirth." Wilson credited this rebirth to immigrants and to the contributions they had made to the "glory and majesty of a great country." In such ways did Zangwill's views about the **melting pot** resonate with prominent political figures who were beginning to identify themselves with reform.

Other thinkers were discomfited by the kind of melting pot that Zangwill had advocated. One of them was the native-born intellectual Randolph Bourne. Bourne located America's uniqueness in the encounters that occurred between immigrant cultures on the one hand and the nation's atmosphere of freedom and democracy on the other. This atmosphere permitted individuals from all kinds of groups, immigrant and native-born, both to preserve their own cultures and to partake of others. Bourne believed that immigrants delighted in the process of cultural exchange that America's environment of freedom encouraged. He celebrated such exchanges, and the variety of identities that arose from them, as essential to the American ideal. Through this process of exchange, Bourne argued, individuals would share more and more of their cultures with each other and would, as a result, become more cooperative with others. These exchanges, too, would make immigrants patriotic, able to believe that they "may have a hand in the destiny of America." Such integration, cooperation, and patriotism would create a nationality superior, Bourne wrote, to any emerging from a "narrow 'Americanism' or forced chauvinism."

Bourne specifically rejected the melting pot as an appropriate metaphor for the American nationality that he saw emerging around him. Unlike Zangwill, Bourne did not look forward to an America in which everyone had been melted into one shape. Bourne celebrated variety, and believed that America's atmosphere of freedom and commitment to democracy would allow such variety to flourish here as it had in few other places. **Cosmopolitanism** was the word he used to describe his vision of American nationality.

Zangwill and Bourne both failed to grapple sufficiently with race and with the discrimination that America imposed on groups marked as racially different, especially African Americans. Their writings did not address the perniciousness of Jim Crow, nor did they acknowledge the reality of Chinese and Japanese exclusion. Nevertheless, these thinkers' reckoning with the immigrant presence in America was innovative. They were among the first to articulate in public forums arguments that the immigrants could be a positive and dynamic force in American culture. And Bourne was one of the first to celebrate diversity and cosmopolitanism as values to be promoted in American life.

Like feminism, cosmopolitanism generated anxiety in large stretches of America, especially in farming communities and small towns, and in the South, where industrialization and urbanization were proceeding at a slower rate than elsewhere. To these Americans, it seemed as though the cultures that immigrants were creating in cities were taking the nation too far from its Anglo-Saxon roots.

The urban elites who exercised considerable cultural power in America were also troubled by the immigrant masses and the urban cultures they were creating. Many of their members, long frustrated by the apparent immigrant preference for movies, amusement parks, and saloons over the "civilizing forces" of museums, libraries, and lectures, were not predisposed to find virtue in immigrant cultures. Nevertheless, change was beginning to occur in these elite circles, as the positive reactions of Presidents Roosevelt and Wilson to Zangwill's ideas of the melting pot indicate. Both Roosevelt and Wilson had begun to understand that American nationality might be strengthened by the infusion into it of new peoples and new cultures, and that the resulting hybridity might be superior to an imagined Anglo-Saxon purity. Jane Addams, an important urban reformer who increasingly traveled in Roosevelt's and Wilson's political circles, ventured beyond where these two presidents were willing to go by acknowledging the importance of "immigrant gifts"—aspects of immigrant cultures that should be preserved even as immigrants assimilated into an American nationality. Addams's concession to diversity was a small one, and she would continue to insist, across several decades of work with immigrants, on the importance of immigrant assimilation to American middle-class values and norms. Nevertheless, Addams's gesture was evidence that the peoples and cultures of the cities had begun to influence the ways in which broader circles of Americans thought about their nation.

CONCLUSION

By 1920, America's urban population outstripped its rural population for the first time in the country's history. Despite a political system that was chronically vulnerable to corruption, urban leaders found ways to build housing and infrastructure that enabled cities to address the demands placed on them by rapid growth. Through the invention of skyscrapers, elevators, electrified railroad and trolley lines, and sophisticated water systems, cities became centers of technological innovation. Urban elites wanted to make their cities centers of culture, too, and embarked on grand projects of architectural and landscape renovation to spread culture, civilization, and refinement through urban populations.

The gap between the elites and their cultural projects on the one hand and the lives of the urban masses on the other remained large, however. The number of new workers, many of them foreign born, arriving in cities was enormous. Their working and living conditions were often poor. Groups defined as racially different—African Americans, Chinese and Japanese immigrants, and even groups of southern and eastern European immigrants—suffered from prejudice as well. Every group could point to examples of economic success among its ranks, and, by the second decade of the 20th century, solid middle classes had emerged within them. Yet, majorities remained working class, coming up short in their quest for equality and opportunity in America.

If economic success remained elusive, the new urban masses nevertheless demonstrated a spirit of creativity and independence that profoundly shaped urban culture. The culture emerging out of dance halls, amusement parks, and nickelodeons prized adventure rather than refinement, liberty rather than order, and diversity rather than conformity. Many urban dwellers thrived in this new environment. Working-class women discovered liberties in dress, employment, dating, and sex that they had not known and propelled feminism into being. Social critics began to imagine forms of American nationality that not only put immigrants on the same footing as the native born, but also praised diversity as a central part of the American experience. Cities, meanwhile, acquired reputations for being innovative and being places for forward-looking and independently minded Americans to settle.

This association of the cities with newness and difference only increased the cultural distance between them and the countryside. Within the cities, the popular culture of the immigrant masses also troubled urban elites and their middle-class allies. These cultural tensions had already begun to spill over into politics, shaping a new and important movement called progressivism.

21

PROGRESSIVISM, 1900–1917

PROGRESSIVISM was a reform movement that took its name from individuals who left the Republican Party in 1912 to join Theodore Roosevelt's new party, the Progressive Party. The term *progressive*, however, refers to a much larger and more varied group of reformers than those who gathered around Roosevelt in 1912.

As early as 1900, these reformers had set out to cleanse and reinvigorate an America whose politics and society they considered in decline. Progressives wanted to rid politics of corruption, tame the power of the "trusts," and in the process inject more liberty into American life. They fought against prostitution, gambling, drinking, and other forms of vice. They first appeared in municipal politics, organizing movements to oust crooked mayors and to break up local gas or streetcar monopolies. They carried their fights to the states and finally to the nation. Two presidents, Theodore Roosevelt and Woodrow Wilson, placed themselves at the head of this movement.

Progressivism was popular among a variety of groups who brought to the movement distinct, and often conflicting, aims. On one issue, however, most progressives agreed: the need for an activist government to right political, economic, and social wrongs. Some progressives wanted government to become active only long enough to clean up the political process, root out vice, upgrade the electorate, and break up trusts. These problems were so difficult to solve that many other progressives endorsed the notion of a permanently active government—with the power to tax income, regulate industry, protect consumers from fraud, empower workers, safeguard the environment, and provide social welfare. Many progressives, in other words, came to see the federal government as the institution best equipped to solve social problems.

CHRONOLOGY

1889	Hull House established
1890–1904	All ex-Confederate states pass laws designed to disfranchise black voters
	Virtually all states adopt the Australian (secret) ballot
1900	La Follette elected governor of Wisconsin
	City commission plan introduced in Galveston, Texas
1901–1914	More than 1,000 African Americans lynched
1901	Johnson elected reform mayor of Cleveland
	McKinley assassinated; Roosevelt becomes president
1902	Direct primary introduced in Mississippi
	Initiative and referendum introduced in Oregon
	Roosevelt sides with workers in coal strike
1903	*McClure's Magazine* publishes Standard Oil exposé
	Federal court dissolves Northern Securities Company
1904	Roosevelt defeats Alton B. Parker for presidency
1905	National Forest Service established
1906	La Follette elected to U.S. Senate
	Congress passes Hepburn Act
	Upton Sinclair publishes *The Jungle*
	Congress passes Pure Food and Drug Act and Meat Inspection Act
1908	Taft defeats Bryan for presidency
1909	Congress passes Payne-Aldrich Tariff Act
1910	Ballinger-Pinchot controversy
	NAACP founded
	Wilson elected governor of New Jersey
1911	National Urban League founded
	City manager plan introduced in Sumter, South Carolina
	Wisconsin Industrial Commission established
	Frederick Winslow Taylor publishes *The Principles of Scientific Management*
1912	Roosevelt forms Progressive Party
	Wilson defeats Roosevelt, Taft, and Debs for presidency
1913	Sixteenth (federal income tax) and Seventeenth (direct election of U.S. senators) Amendments ratified
	Congress passes Underwood-Simmons Tariff
	Congress establishes Federal Reserve

1914	Congress establishes Federal Trade Commission
	Congress passes Clayton Antitrust Act
1916	Louis Brandeis appointed to Supreme Court
	Kern-McGillicuddy Act, Keating-Owen Act, and Adamson Act passed
	National Park Service formed
	National Women's Party founded
1919	Eighteenth Amendment (prohibition) ratified
1920	Nineteenth Amendment (woman suffrage) ratified

Such positive attitudes toward government power marked an important change in American politics. Americans had long been suspicious of centralized government, viewing it as the enemy of liberty. The Populists had broken with that view, but they had been defeated. The progressives had to build a new case for strong government as the protector of liberty and equality.

WHERE REFORM INCUBATED

Progressivism emerged in the early years of the 20th century from the activities of multiple groups. Four such groups were of particular importance: young, alienated middle-class Protestants; journalists who took the name "muckrakers"; women active in the settlement house movement; and an assortment of socialists.

**Young
Protestants**

Progressivism emerged first and most strongly among young, mainly Protestant, middle-class Americans who felt alienated from their society. Many had been raised in Protestant homes in which religious conviction had often been a spur to social action. They were expected to become ministers or missionaries or to serve their church in some other way. They had abandoned this path, but they never lost their zeal for righting moral wrongs and for uplifting the human spirit. They were distressed by the immorality and corruption in American politics and by the gap that separated rich from poor.

Other Protestant reformers retained their faith. This was true of William Jennings Bryan, the former Populist leader who became an ardent progressive and evangelical. Throughout his political career, Bryan insisted that Christian piety and American democracy were integrally related. Billy Sunday, a former major league baseball player who became the most theatrical evangelical preacher of his day, elevated opposition to saloons and the "liquor trust" into a righteous crusade. And Walter Rauschenbusch led a movement known as the Social Gospel, which emphasized the duty of Christians to work for the social good.

Muckrakers

Many disaffected Protestants found a focus for their alienation in the work of investigative journalists known as **"muckrakers,"** so-called because of their determination to dredge up the "muck" permeating important institutions of American life. Ida Tarbell revealed the shady practices by which John D. Rockefeller had transformed his Standard Oil Company into a monopoly. Lincoln Steffens unraveled the webs of bribery and corruption that were strangling local governments in the nation's cities. George Kibbe Turner documented the extent of prostitution and family disintegration in the ethnic ghettos of those cities. These muckrakers wanted to shock the public into recognizing the shameful state of political, economic, and social affairs and to prompt "the people" to take action.

The muckrakers were riding a wave of expanded magazine circulation. Cheap, 10-cent periodicals such as *McClure's Magazine* and *Ladies' Home Journal*, with circulations of 400,000 to 1 million, were displacing genteel and relatively expensive 35-cent publications such as *Harper's* and *The Atlantic Monthly*. The expanded readership brought journalists considerably more money and prestige and attracted many talented and ambitious men and women to the profession. Wider circulation also made magazine publishers more receptive to stories that might appeal to their expanded readership.

A large middle class, uneasy about the state of American society, applauded the muckrakers for telling stories exposing America's problems and began trumpeting the virtues of reform. Members of this class pressured city and state governments to send crooked government officials to jail and to stamp out the sources of corruption and vice. Between 1902 and 1916, more than 100 cities launched investigations of the prostitution trade. The federal government, meanwhile, began to raise questions about "the trusts"—large corporations that had amassed overwhelming economic power. Progressivism began to crystallize into a political movement centered on the abuses the muckrakers had exposed.

Settlement Houses and Clubwomen   Progressivism also began to take shape in settlement houses, urban institutions set up by middle-class, largely Protestant women to help the urban poor cope with the harsh conditions of city life. Jane Addams and Ellen Gates Starr established the nation's first settlement house in Chicago in 1889 when they bought a decaying mansion that had once been the country home of a prominent Chicagoan, Charles J. Hull. By 1889, **"Hull House"** stood amidst factories, churches, saloons, and tenements inhabited by poor, largely foreign-born working-class families.

Addams moved into the building and demanded that all who worked there do the same. She, and the women such as Florence Kelley and Julia Lathrop who assisted her, set up a nursery for the children of working mothers, a penny savings bank, an employment bureau, a baby clinic, a neighborhood playground, and social clubs. Determined to minister to cultural as well as economic needs, Hull House sponsored an orchestra, reading groups, and a lecture series. Members of Chicago's widening circle of reform-minded intellectuals, artists, and politicians contributed their energies to the enterprise. John Dewey taught philosophy, and Frank Lloyd Wright lectured on architecture. Clarence Darrow, the workingman's lawyer, and Henry Demarest Lloyd, Chicago's radical muckraker, spent considerable time at Hull House. In 1893, Illinois governor John P. Altgeld named Hull House's Florence Kelley as the state's chief factory inspector. Her investigations led to Illinois's first factory law, which prohibited child labor, limited the employment of women to eight hours a day, and authorized the state to hire inspectors to enforce the law.

Jane Addams. *The founder of the settlement house movement, Addams was the most famous female reformer of the Progressive Era. This photograph depicts her late in her career, sitting with a girl in the Hull House nursery school.*

Wallace Kirkland//Time Life Pictures/Getty Images

Julia Lathrop used her appointment to the State Board of Charities to agitate for improvements in the care of the poor, the handicapped, and the delinquent. With Edith Abbott and Sophonisba Breckinridge, she established the Department of Social Research at the University of Chicago (which would evolve into the nation's first school of social work). Alice Hamilton, who had overcome gender discrimination to become a doctor, pioneered in the field of public health.

Thousands of women across the country were inspired to build their own settlement houses on the Hull House model (eventually more than 400 settlement houses would open nationwide). By 1910, Jane Addams had become one of the nation's most famous women. She and other settlement house workers played a critical role in fashioning the progressive agenda and in drafting pieces of progressive legislation.

Settlement house workers were more sympathetic toward the poor, the illiterate, and the downtrodden than the muckrakers were. Although she disapproved of machine politics, Jane Addams saw firsthand the benefits that machine politicians delivered to their constituents. She respected the cultural inheritance of the immigrants and admired their resourcefulness. Although she wanted them to become Americans, she encouraged them to integrate their "immigrant gifts" into their new identities. Those attitudes were more liberal than those of other reformers, who considered many immigrants to be culturally, even racially, inferior.

But there were limits even to Addams's sympathy for the immigrants. She disapproved of the new working-class entertainments that gave adolescents extensive and unregulated opportunities for intimate association. She was troubled by the emerging sexual revolution, which she worried would lead many more poor women into prostitution. And she critiqued male working-class drinking habits, which she saw as encouraging alcoholism, draining away meager family resources, and increasing tensions between these men and their wives. Addams and other settlement house workers joined hands with the Women's Christian Temperance Union (245,000 members strong by 1911) and the Anti-Saloon League to push for legislation to shut down the saloons. By 1916, this anti-drinking coalition had won prohibition of the sale and manufacture of alcoholic beverages in 16 states. In 1919, its crowning achievement was the Eighteenth Amendment to the U.S. Constitution, making prohibition the law of the land.

In depicting alcohol and saloons as unmitigated evils, the prohibition movement ignored the larger role that saloons played in ethnic, working-class communities. On Chicago's South Side, for example, saloons provided food, meeting space for fraternal organizations, and camaraderie to men longing to speak in their native tongue. Saloonkeepers sometimes functioned as informal bankers, cashing checks and making small loans. Not surprisingly, many immigrants shunned the prohibition movement.

Settlement house workers comprised one part of a vast network of female reformers. Hundreds of thousands of women belonged to local women's clubs that sought to improve schools, build libraries and playgrounds, expand educational and vocational opportunities for girls, and secure fire and sanitation codes for tenement houses. In so doing, they made traditional female concerns—the nurturing and education of children, the care of the home—questions of public policy.

WOMEN ENROLLED IN INSTITUTIONS OF HIGHER EDUCATION, 1870–1930

Year	Women's Colleges (thousands of students)	Coed Institutions (thousands of students)	Total (thousands of students)	Percentage of All Students Enrolled
1870	6.5	4.6	11.1	21.0%
1880	15.7	23.9	39.6	33.4%
1890	16.8	39.5	56.3	35.9%
1900	24.4	61.0	85.4	36.8%
1910	34.1	106.5	140.6	39.6%
1920	52.9	230.0	282.9	47.3%
1930	82.1	398.7	480.8	43.7%

Source: From Mabel Newcomer, *A Century of Higher Education for American Women* (New York: Harper and Row, 1959), p. 46.

Clubwomen rose to prominence in black communities, too, and addressed similar sorts of issues; on matters of sexuality and alcohol, they often shared the conservative sentiments of white clubwomen. Some groups of black clubwomen ventured into community affairs more boldly than their white counterparts, especially in southern states, where black men were being stripped of the right to vote, to serve on juries, and to hold political office.

Socialists   In the early 20th century, **socialism** stood for the transfer of control over big businesses from the capitalists who owned them to the laboring masses who worked in them. Socialists believed that such a transfer, usually defined in terms of government ownership and operation of corporations, would make it impossible for wealthy elites to control society.

The Socialist Party of America, founded in 1901, became a political force during the first 20 years of the century, and socialist ideas influenced progressivism. In 1912, at the peak of its influence, the Socialist Party enrolled more than 115,000 members. Its presidential candidate, the charismatic **Eugene Victor Debs** of Terre Haute, Indiana, attracted almost a million votes—6 percent of the total votes cast that year. In that same year, 1,200 Socialists held elective office in 340 different municipalities. Of these, 79 were mayors of cities as geographically and demographically diverse as Schenectady, New York; Milwaukee, Wisconsin; Butte, Montana; and Berkeley, California. More than 300 newspapers and periodicals, with a combined circulation exceeding 2 million, spread the socialist gospel. The most important socialist publication was *Appeal to Reason*, published by Julius Wayland from Kansas and sent out each week to 750,000 subscribers. In 1905, Wayland published, in serial form, a novel by a muckraker named Upton Sinclair, which depicted the scandalous working conditions in Chicago's meatpacking industry. When it was later published in book form, in 1906, *The Jungle* created such an outcry that the federal government was forced to regulate the meat industry.

Socialists came in many varieties. In Milwaukee, they consisted of predominantly German working-class immigrants and their descendants; in New York City, their numbers were strongest among Jewish immigrants from eastern Europe. In the Southwest, tens of thousands of disgruntled native-born farmers who had been Populists in the 1890s now flocked to the socialist banner. In the West, socialism was popular among miners, timber cutters, and others who labored in isolated areas where industrialists possessed extraordinary power over work, politics, and community life. These westerners gravitated to the militant labor union, the Industrial Workers of the World (IWW), which found a home in the Socialist Party from 1905 to 1913.

Although the IWW's membership at any one time rarely exceeded 20,000, it acquired a national reputation by organizing the poorest and most isolated workers and leading them in strikes against employers who were unaccustomed to having their authority challenged. Violence lurked beneath the surface of these strikes and occasionally erupted in bloody skirmishes between strikers and police, National Guardsmen, or the private security forces hired by employers.

Mainstream socialists, led by Debs, shared the IWW's desire to end capitalism but believed that socialism could be achieved democratically, by electing socialists to office and ultimately to the presidency itself. Progressives often worked hand-in-hand with socialists to win economic and political reforms. Many intellectuals and reformers—including John Dewey, Richard Ely, Thorstein Veblen, and Helen Keller, the leading spokesperson for the disabled—moved back and forth between socialism and progressivism. But Debs's radicalism also scared progressives, as did his efforts to organize a working-class political movement independent of middle-class involvement or control. Although progressives wanted to tame capitalism, they stopped short of wanting to eliminate it. They wanted to improve working and living conditions for the masses but not cede political control to them. The progressives hoped to offer a political program with enough reform elements to counter the appeal of Debs's more radical movement. In this, they would be successful.

REFORM OF CITY GOVERNMENTS

Progressive Era reform battles first erupted over control of municipal transportation networks and utilities. Private corporations typically owned and operated street railways and electrical and gas systems. Many of these corporations used their monopoly power to charge exorbitant fares and rates, and they often won that power by bribing city officials who belonged to one of the political machines. Corporations achieved generous reductions in real estate taxes in the same way.

The attack on private utilities and their protectors in city government gained momentum in the mid-1890s. Occasionally, a reform politician would rise to power through one of the regular political parties. But this path to power was a difficult one, especially in cities where the political parties were controlled by political machines. Consequently, progressives worked to strip the parties of their power. Two of their favorite reforms were the city commission and the city manager forms of government.

First introduced in Galveston, Texas, in 1900, in the wake of a devastating tidal wave, city commissions shifted municipal power from the mayor and his aldermen to five city commissioners, each responsible for a different department of city government. In Galveston and elsewhere, the impetus for this reform came from civic-minded businessmen who were determined to rebuild government on the principles of efficient and scientific management that had energized the private sector. The results were often impressive. The Galveston commissioners restored the city's credit after a brush with bankruptcy, improved the city's harbor, and built a massive seawall to protect the city from future floods. They accomplished all of this on budgets that had been cut by one-third. By 1913, more than 300 cities, most of them small to middling in size, had adopted the city commission plan.

The city commission system did not always work to perfection, however. Sometimes the commissioners used their position to reward electoral supporters with jobs and contracts; other times, they pursued power and prestige for their respective departments. The city manager plan was meant to overcome such problems. Under this plan, the commissioners continued to set policy, but policy implementation now rested with a "chief executive." This official, who was not elected but appointed by the commissioners, would curtail rivalries among commissioners and ensure that no outside influences interfered with the impartial, businesslike management of the city. The job of city manager was modeled after that of a corporation

Helen Keller, Labor Activist. *Best known for her work in calling attention to the rights and needs of disabled Americans, Keller also agitated on behalf of America's workers. Here she stiffens the resolve of actors on strike against a New York City opera house. Her companion, Anne Sullivan Macy, stands to her right, serving as Keller's interpreter.*

Bettmann/Corbis

executive. First introduced in Sumter, South Carolina, in 1911 and then in Dayton, Ohio, in 1913, by 1919 the city manager plan had spread to 130 cities.

Although these reforms limited corruption and improved services, they were not universally popular. Poor and minority voters, in particular, saw their influence in local affairs weakened by them. Previously, candidates for municipal office (other than the mayor) competed in ward elections rather than in citywide elections. Voters in working-class wards commonly elected workingmen to represent them, and voters in immigrant wards made sure that fellow ethnics represented their interests on city councils. Citywide elections diluted the strength of these constituencies. Candidates from poor districts often lacked the money needed to mount a citywide campaign, and they were further hampered by the nonpartisan nature of such elections. Denied the support of a political party or platform, they had to make themselves personally known to voters throughout the city. That was a much easier task for the city's "leading citizens"—manufacturers, merchants, and lawyers—than it was for workingmen. In Dayton, the percentage of citizens voting Socialist rose from 25 to 44 percent in the years following the introduction of the commission manager system, but the number of Socialists elected to office declined from five to zero. Progressive political reforms thus sometimes reduced the influence of radicals, minorities, and the poor in elections.

REFORM IN THE STATES

As at the local level, political parties at the state level were often dominated by corrupt politicians who did the bidding of powerful private lobbies. In New Jersey in 1903, for example, industrial and financial interests, working through the Republican Party machine, controlled numerous appointments to state government, including the chief justice of the state supreme court, the attorney general, and the commissioner of banking and insurance. Such webs of influence ensured that New Jersey would provide large corporations such as the railroads with favorable political and economic legislation.

Overhauling Election Laws and the Electorate   Progressives introduced reforms designed to undermine the power of party bosses, restore sovereignty to "the people," and encourage honest, talented individuals to enter politics. One such reform was the direct primary, a mechanism that enabled voters, rather than party bosses, to choose party candidates. Mississippi introduced this reform in 1902 and Wisconsin in 1903. By 1916, all but three states had adopted the direct primary. Closely related was a movement to strip state legislatures of their power to choose U.S. senators. State after state enacted legislation that permitted voters to choose Senate candidates in primary elections. In 1912, a reluctant U.S. Senate was obliged to approve the Seventeenth Amendment to the Constitution, mandating the direct election of senators. The state legislatures ratified this amendment in 1913.

Populists had first proposed direct election of U.S. senators in the 1890s; they also proposed the **initiative** and the **referendum,** both of which were adopted first by Oregon in 1902 and then by 18 other states between 1902 and 1915. The initiative allowed reformers to put legislative proposals before voters in general elections without having to wait for state legislatures to act. The referendum gave voters the right in general elections to repeal an unpopular act that a state legislature had passed. Less widely adopted but important nevertheless was the **recall,** a device that allowed voters to remove from office public servants who had betrayed their trust. As a further control over the behavior of elected officials, numerous states enacted laws that regulated corporate campaign contributions and restricted lobbying activities in state legislatures. These laws neither eliminated corporate privilege nor destroyed the power of machine politicians. Nevertheless, they made politics more honest and strengthened the influence of ordinary voters.

Progressive reformers focused as well on creating a responsible electorate that understood the importance of the vote and that resisted efforts to manipulate elections. To create this ideal electorate, reformers had to see to it that all of those citizens who were deemed virtuous could cast their votes free of coercion and intimidation. At the same time, reformers sought to disfranchise citizens who were considered irresponsible and corruptible. In pursuing these goals, progressives substantially altered the composition of the electorate and strengthened government regulation of voting. Progressives enlarged the electorate by extending the right to vote to women; but they also either initiated or tolerated laws that barred large numbers of minority and poor voters from the polls.

Government regulation of voting had begun in the 1890s, when virtually every state adopted the **Australian ballot (secret ballot)**. This reform required voters to vote in private rather than in public. It also required the government, rather than political parties, to print the ballots and supervise the voting. Before this time, each political party had printed its own ballot with only its candidates listed. At election time, each party mobilized its loyal supporters. Party workers offered liquor, free meals, and other bribes to entice voters to the polls and to "persuade" them to cast the party ballot. Because the ballots were cast in public, few voters who had accepted gifts of liquor and food dared to cross watchful party officials. Critics argued that the system corrupted the electoral process. They also pointed out that it made "ticket splitting"—dividing one's vote between candidates of two or more parties—virtually impossible.

The Australian ballot solved these problems. Although it predated progressivism, it embodied the progressives' determination to use government power to encourage citizens to cast their votes responsibly and wisely.

That same determination was apparent in the progressives' support for the personal registration laws that virtually every state passed between 1890 and 1920. These laws allowed prospective voters to register to vote only if they appeared at a designated government office with proper identification. Frequently, these laws also mandated a certain period of residence in the state before registration and a certain interval between registration and actual voting.

Personal registration laws were meant to disfranchise citizens who showed no interest in voting until Election Day, when a party worker arrived with a few dollars and offered a free ride to the polls. However, they also excluded many hardworking, responsible, poor people who wanted to vote but had failed to register, either because their work schedules made it impossible or because they were intimidated by the complex regulations. The laws were particularly frustrating for immigrants with limited knowledge of English.

Progressives also promoted election laws expressly designed to keep noncitizen immigrants from voting. In the 1880s, 18 states had passed laws allowing immigrants to vote without first becoming citizens. Progressives reversed this trend. At the same time, the newly formed Bureau of Immigration and Naturalization (1906) made it more difficult to become a citizen. Most progressives defended the added rigor of the naturalization process. U.S. citizenship, they believed, carried responsibilities; it was not to be bestowed lightly. Yet, in cities and towns where immigrants dominated the workforce, the numbers of registered voters fell steeply.

Laws excluding voters from the electorate affected the South more than any other region. Between 1890 and 1904, every ex-Confederate state passed laws designed to strip blacks of their right to vote. Because laws explicitly barring blacks from voting would have violated the Fifteenth Amendment, this exclusion had to be accomplished indirectly—through literacy tests, property qualifications, and poll taxes mandated by the legislatures of the ex-Confederate states. Any citizen who failed a reading test, or who could not sign his name, or who did not own a minimum amount of property, or who could not pay a poll tax, lost his right to vote. The citizens who failed these tests most frequently were blacks—who formed the poorest and least educated segment of the southern population—but a large segment of the region's poor whites also failed the tests. The effects of **disfranchisement** were stark. In 1900, only 1,300 blacks voted in Mississippi elections, down from 130,000 in the 1870s. Virginia's voter turn-out dropped from 60 percent of adult men (white and black) in 1900 to 28 percent in 1904.

Many progressives in the North, such as Governor Robert La Follette of Wisconsin, criticized southern disfranchisement. Some, including Jane Addams and John Dewey, joined in 1910 with W. E. B. Du Bois and other black reformers to found the **National Association for the Advancement of Colored People (NAACP)**, an interracial political organization that made black equality its primary goal. In the South, however, white progressives rarely challenged disfranchisement.

In the process of identifying particular groups as "unfit" to hold the franchise, some progressives soured on the electoral process altogether. The more they looked for rational and virtuous voters, the fewer they found. The growing disillusionment with the electorate, in combination with intensifying restrictions on the franchise, created an environment in which fewer and fewer Americans actually went to the polls. Voter participation rates fell from 79 percent in 1896 to only 49 percent in 1920.

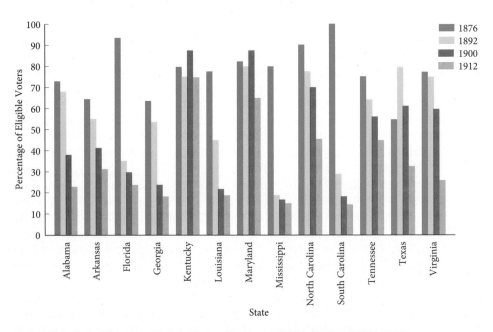

Voter Participation in 13 Southern States, 1876, 1892, 1900, 1912

Source: Data from *Historical Statistics of the United States, Colonial Times to 1970* (White Plains, NY: Kraus International, 1989).

Woman Suffrage

The major exception to this trend was the enfranchisement of women. This momentous reform was adopted by several states during the 1890s and the first two decades of the 20th century and became federal law with the ratification of the Nineteenth Amendment to the Constitution in 1920.

Wyoming, which attained statehood in 1890, became the first state to grant women the right to vote, followed in 1893 by Colorado and in 1896 by Idaho and Utah. The main reason for success in these sparsely populated western states was not egalitarianism but rather the conviction that women's supposedly gentler and more nurturing nature would tame and civilize the men who had populated the frontier.

In the mid-19th century, supporters of women's suffrage (those who wanted to give women the vote) had insisted that women were fundamentally equal to men. In the Progressive Era, however, many suffragists did not base their argument for enfranchisement on male-female equality. Women, they stressed, were different than men, possessing a moral sense and a nurturing quality that men lacked. Consequently, they could be trusted to vote virtuously and thereby advance the progressive aim of cleansing politics of corruption. Their experience as mothers and household managers, moreover, would enable them to guide local and state governments in efforts to improve education, sanitation, family wholesomeness, and the condition of women and children in the workforce. In other words, the enfranchisement of women would enhance the quality of both public and private life without obligating anyone to think that members of the female sex were the equals of men in all respects.

Suffragists were slow to ally themselves with blacks, Asians, and other disfranchised groups. In fact, many suffragists, especially those in the South and West, opposed the franchise for Americans of color. They, like their male counterparts, believed that members of these groups lacked moral strength and thus did not deserve the right to vote. Unlike the suffrage pioneers of the 1840s and 1850s, many Progressive Era suffragists were little troubled by racial discrimination and injustice.

Washington, California, Kansas, Oregon, and Arizona followed the lead of the other western states by enfranchising women between 1910 and 1912. After a series of setbacks in eastern and midwestern states, the movement regained momentum under the leadership of the strategically astute Carrie Chapman Catt, who became president of the **National American Woman Suffrage Association (NAWSA)** in 1915 and successfully coordinated myriad grassroots campaigns. Equally important was Alice Paul, a radical who founded the Congressional Union in 1913 and later renamed it the National Woman's Party. Paul and her supporters focused their attention on the White House, picketing President Wilson's home 24 hours a day, brandishing large posters that chastised him for abandoning his democratic principles, and daring the police to arrest them. When several suffrage demonstrators were jailed, they continued their protests by going on hunger strikes (refusing to eat). Aided by a heightened enthusiasm for democracy generated by America's participation in the First World War, which generated a more positive popular

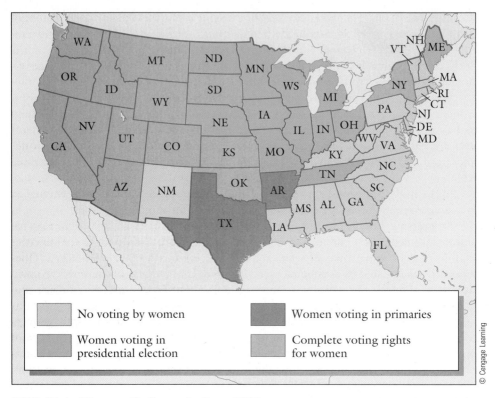

No voting by women

Women voting in presidential election

Women voting in primaries

Complete voting rights for women

© Cengage Learning

MAP 21.1 Woman Suffrage before 1920

This map illustrates how woman suffrage prior to 1920 had advanced furthest in the West.

response to Paul's tactics than might otherwise have been the case, the suffragists achieved their goal of universal woman suffrage in 1920.

Predictions that suffrage for women would radically alter politics turned out to be false. The political system was neither cleansed of corruption, nor did the government rush headlong to address the private needs of women and their families. Although the numbers of voters increased after 1920, voter participation rates continued to decline. Still, the extension of the vote to women, 144 years after the founding of the nation, was a major political achievement.

Wisconsin and New York: State Laboratories of Reform

In some states, progressives extended reform efforts well beyond election law and the electorate. Progressives also fought to limit corporate power, strengthen organized labor, and offer social welfare protection to the weak. Many state governments were pressured into passing such legislation by progressive alliances of middle-class and working-class reformers and by dynamic state governors.

Nowhere did the progressives' campaign for social reform flourish as it did in Wisconsin. The movement arose first in the 1890s, in hundreds of Wisconsin cities and towns, as citizens began to mobilize against the state's corrupt Republican Party and the special privileges the party had granted to private utilities and railroads. In 1897, Robert La Follette assumed leadership of this movement.

La Follette was born into a prosperous farming family in 1855. Elected governor in 1900, he secured for Wisconsin both a direct primary and a tax law that stripped the railroad corporations of tax exemptions they had long enjoyed.

A tireless campaigner and a spellbinding speaker, "Fighting Bob" won election to the U.S. Senate in 1906. Meanwhile, Wisconsin's labor and socialist movements impelled progressive reformers to focus their legislative efforts on issues of shrinking corporate profits and expanding social welfare. By 1910, reformers had passed state laws that regulated railroad and utility rates, instituted the nation's first state income tax, and provided workers with compensation for injuries, limitations on work hours, restrictions on child labor, and minimum wages for women.

Many of these laws were written by social scientists at the University of Wisconsin. In the first decade of the 20th century, John R. Commons, University of Wisconsin economist, drafted Wisconsin's civil service and public utilities laws. In 1911, Commons designed and won legislative approval for the Wisconsin Industrial Commission, which brought together employers, trade unionists, and professionals and gave them broad powers to investigate and regulate relations between industry and labor throughout the state. For the first time, a state government had put the rights of labor on par with those of industry. Equally important was the responsibility the commission delegated to nonelected professionals: social scientists, lawyers, engineers, and others. These professionals on the commission, Wisconsin reformers believed, would resolve disputes between capital and labor with their expertise, impartiality, and good judgment.

Ohio, Indiana, New York, and Colorado quickly adopted this "**Wisconsin Idea.**" In 1913, the federal government established its own Industrial Relations Commission and hired Commons to direct its investigative staff. In other areas, too, reformers began urging state and federal governments to shift the policy-making initiative away from political parties and toward administrative agencies staffed by professionals.

New York was second only to Wisconsin in the vigor and breadth of its progressive movement. As in Wisconsin, New York progressives focused first on fighting political corruption, establishing several public service commissions to regulate railroads and utility companies. Also as in Wisconsin, the labor movement exercised its influence. New York City garment workers struck and forced state legislators to regulate working conditions. With the establishment of the Factory Investigating Committee, New York, like Wisconsin, became a pioneer in labor and social welfare policy.

New York's state legislators faced pressure from middle-class reformers—settlement house workers such as Lillian Wald of the Henry Street Settlement and lawyers such as Louis Brandeis—who had become convinced of the need for new laws to protect the disadvantaged. This combined pressure from working-class and middle-class constituencies persuaded some state Democrats, including Assemblyman Alfred E. Smith and Senator Robert F. Wagner, to convert from machine to reform politics. Their appearance in the progressive ranks represented the arrival of a new reform sensibility. Wagner and Smith were both ethnic Catholics (Wagner was born in Germany, and Smith was the grandchild of Irish immigrants). Though they opposed city commissions, voter registration laws, and other reforms whose intent seemed anti-immigrant or anti-Catholic, they supported reforms meant to improve the working and living conditions of New York's urban poor. They agitated for a minimum wage, factory safety, workmen's compensation, the right of workers to join unions, and the regulation of excessively powerful corporations. Their participation in progressivism accelerated the movement's national shift away from a preoccupation with political parties and electorates and toward questions of economic justice and social welfare.

Scientific Management and the Reform of Work

Progressivism drew support, too, from businessmen who saw in it an opportunity to introduce efficiency, science, and harmony into industrial relations. Just as business-oriented progressives in Galveston and elsewhere drew on the principles of scientific management to reform local government, so, too, some businessmen attempted to use those principles to create more productive and cohesive workplaces.

Scientific management had developed in the last two decades of the 19th century among managers and engineers who were looking to develop arrangements of machines and workers that would achieve the highest speed in production with the fewest human or mechanical interruptions. Their leader was **Frederick Winslow Taylor**, who, as chief engineer at Philadelphia's Midvale Steel Company in the 1880s, had examined every human task and mechanical movement involved in his company's production process. Taylor pioneered the "time-and-motion study," the technique through which managers recorded every distinct movement a worker made in performing his or her job, how long it took, and how often it was performed. Taylor hoped thereby to identify and eliminate wasted human energy. His goal was to make human labor emulate the smooth and apparently effortless operation of an automatic, perfectly calibrated piece of machinery.

Taylor's program of "scientific management" fired the imagination of the business-and-efficiency-oriented sectors of the progressive movement. By the time he published in 1911 his popular treatise, *The Principles of Scientific Management*, Taylor himself had been influenced by the spirit of progressive reform. He now offered his program as a way of achieving industrial peace. Scientific management, Taylor claimed, would allow each worker to be matched with a job well suited to his abilities. Efficiency and wages would rise; so, too, would worker satisfaction. Most, if not all, workplace antagonisms would then dissolve.

Henry Ford, the pioneer in automobile manufacturing, was a Taylor disciple. By 1910, Ford's engineers had broken down the production of its main car, the "Model T," into a series of simple, sequential tasks. Each worker performed only one task: adding a carburetor to an engine, inserting a windshield, mounting tires onto wheels. Then, in 1913, Ford's engineers introduced the first moving assembly line, a continuously moving conveyor belt that carried cars in production through each workstation. This innovation eliminated precious time previously wasted in transporting car parts (or partially built cars) by crane or truck from one work area to another. It also limited the time available to workers to perform their assigned tasks. Only the foreman, not the workers, could stop the line or change its speed.

By 1913, the continuous assembly line made Ford Motor Company's new Highland Park plant the most tightly integrated and continuously moving production system in American industry. The pace of car production at Ford exceeded all expectations. Between 1910 and 1914, production time on Model Ts dropped by 90 percent, from an average of more than 12 hours per car to 1.5 hours. This striking increase in the rate of production enabled Ford to slash the price of a Model T from $950 in 1909 to only $295 in 1923, a reduction of 70 percent. The number of Model Ts purchased by Americans increased sixteenfold between 1912 and 1921, from 79,000 to 1,250,000. The assembly line quickly became the most admired—and most feared—symbol of American mass production.

Problems immediately beset the system, however. Repeating a single motion all day long induced mental stupor, and managerial efforts to speed up the line produced physical exhaustion—both of which increased the incidence of error and injury. Some workers tried to organize a union to gain a voice in production matters, but most Ford workers expressed their dissatisfaction simply by quitting. By 1913, employee turnover at Highland Park had reached the astounding rate of 370 percent per year. At that rate, Ford had to hire 51,800 workers every year just to keep his factory fully staffed at 14,000.

A problem of that magnitude demanded a dramatic solution. Ford provided it in 1914 by raising the wage he paid his assembly-line workers to $5 per day, double the average manufacturing wage then prevalent in American industry. The result: Workers, especially young and single men, flocked to Detroit. The high productivity rates of Ford's factories permitted him to absorb the wage increase without cutting substantially into profits.

Taylor had believed that improved efficiency would lead to dramatic wage gains. Ford's ability to double his wage payout, in this respect, proved Taylor right. But Taylor's theory of human psychology remained primitive, inadequate to the task of comprehending the range of emotions that employees brought to the workplace and the multiple sources of employee–employer conflict. Ford recognized that workers were more complex than Taylor had allowed, which is why his innovations went well beyond what Taylor himself had contemplated. Thus, Ford set up a sociology department, forerunner of the personnel department, to collect job, family, and other information about his employees. He sent social workers into workers' homes to inquire into their personal lives. For the foreign-born, he instituted Americanization classes. He offered his employees housing subsidies, medical care, and other benefits. Ford's success was widely admired; nevertheless, it would take another generation or two for significant sectors of the corporate world to follow his lead. And thus throughout the first two decades of the 20th century, American industry remained more the target than the ally of progressive reform.

A NEW CAMPAIGN FOR RACIAL EQUALITY

The reform energy unleashed by the progressives inspired a new generation of African American activists to insist that the nation grapple again with issues of racial inequality. Indeed, the modern civil rights movement can be said to have started in the early years of the 20th century.

Booker T. Washington's message—that blacks should accept segregation and disfranchisement as unavoidable and focus their energies instead on self-help and self-improvement—faced increasing criticism from young black activists such as **W. E. B. Du Bois**, Ida B. Wells, Monroe Trotter, and others. Washington's accommodationist leadership, in their eyes, brought southern blacks no reprieve from racism. More than 100 blacks had been lynched in 1900 alone; between 1901 and 1914, at least 1,000 others would be hanged.

Increasingly, unsubstantiated rumors of black assaults on whites became occasions for white mobs to rampage through black neighborhoods and destroy life and property. In 1908, a mob in Springfield, Illinois, attacked black businesses and individuals; a force of 5,000 state militia was required to restore order. The troops were too late, however, to stop the lynching of two innocent black men, one a successful barber and the other an 84-year-old man who had been married to a white woman for more than 30 years.

Booker T. Washington had long believed that blacks who educated themselves or who succeeded in business would be accepted as equals by whites. As Du Bois and other black militants observed, however, white rioters made no distinction between rich blacks and poor, or between solid citizens and petty criminals. All that had seemed to matter was the color of one's skin. Similarly, many black militants knew from personal experience that individual accomplishment was not enough to overcome racial prejudice. Du Bois was a brilliant scholar who became,

Lynching. *This grim photo records the deaths of five of the approximately 1,000 African Americans who were lynched between 1901 and 1914. The increase in lynching was one measure of the virulence of white racism in the early years of the 20th century.*

The Granger Collection, NYC

in 1899, the first African American to receive a doctorate from Harvard University. Had he been white, Du Bois would have been asked to teach at Harvard or another elite academic institution, but no prestigious white university made him an offer.

Seeing no future in accommodation, Du Bois and other young black activists came together at Niagara Falls in 1905 to fashion a new political agenda. They demanded that African Americans regain the right to vote in states that had taken it away, that segregation be abolished, and that the many discriminatory barriers to black advancement be removed. They declared their commitment to freedom of speech, the brotherhood of all men, and respect for the workingman. Although their numbers were small, the members of the so-called Niagara movement were inspired by the example of the antebellum abolitionists. Meeting in Boston, Oberlin, and Harpers Ferry—all places of special significance to the abolitionist cause—they hoped to rekindle the militant, uncompromising spirit of that earlier crusade.

The 1908 Springfield riot had shaken many whites. Some, especially those already working for social and economic reform, now joined in common cause with the Niagara movement. Together, black and white activists planned a conference for Lincoln's birthday in 1909 to revive, in the words of author William English Walling, "the spirit of the abolitionists" and to "treat the Negro on a plane of absolute political and social equality." The conference brought together distinguished progressives, white and black, including Mary White Ovington, Jane Addams, Oswald Garrison Villard, John Dewey, William Dean Howells, Ida B. Wells, and W. E. B. Du Bois. They drew up plans to establish an organization dedicated to fighting racial discrimination and prejudice. In May 1910, the National Association for the Advancement of Colored People (NAACP) was launched, with Moorfield Storey of Boston as president, Walling as chairman of the executive committee, and Du Bois as the director of publicity and research.

The formation of the NAACP marked the beginning of the modern civil rights movement. The organization launched a magazine, *The Crisis,* edited by Du Bois, to publicize and protest the lynchings, riots, and other abuses directed against black citizens. Equally important was the Legal Redress Committee, which initiated lawsuits against city and state governments for violating the constitutional rights of African Americans. The committee scored its first major success in 1915, when the U.S. Supreme Court ruled that the so-called grandfather clauses of the Oklahoma and Maryland constitutions violated the Fifteenth Amendment. (These clauses extended the right to vote to whites who had failed to pay their state's poll tax or to pass its literacy test while denying the same right to blacks.) NAACP lawyers won again in 1917 when the Supreme Court declared unconstitutional a Louisville, Kentucky, law that required all blacks to reside in predetermined parts of the city.

By 1914, the NAACP had enrolled thousands of members in scores of branches throughout the United States. The organization's success generated other civil rights groups. The National Urban League, founded in 1911, worked to improve the economic and social conditions of blacks in cities.

Progress toward racial equality remained slow. Attacking segregation and discrimination through lawsuits was, by its nature, a strategy that would take decades to complete. The growing membership of the NAACP, although impressive, was not large enough to qualify it as a mass movement, and its interracial character made the organization seem dangerously radical to millions of whites. White NAACP leaders responded to this hostility by limiting the number and power of African Americans who worked for the organization. This policy, in turn, angered black militants who argued that no civil rights organization should be in the business of appeasing white racists.

Despite its limitations, the NAACP made significant strides. It gave Du Bois the security and visibility he needed to carry on his fight against Booker T. Washington's accommodationist philosophy. The NAACP, more than any other organization, helped resurrect the issue of racial equality at a time when many white Americans had accepted as normal the practices of racial segregation and discrimination.

THE ROOSEVELT PRESIDENCY

Progressives increasingly sought to increase their influence in national politics. State regulations seemed inadequate to the task of curtailing the power of the trusts, protecting workers, or monitoring the quality of consumer goods. The courts repeatedly struck down as unconstitutional state laws regulating working hours or setting minimum wages, on the grounds that they impinged on the freedom of contract and trade. A national progressive movement could force passage of federal laws that were less vulnerable to judicial veto or elect a president who could overhaul the federal judiciary with progressive-minded judges.

National leadership was slow to emerge from Congress. The Populist challenge of the 1890s had left the Democratic Party divided between radical Bryanites and the conservative followers of Grover Cleveland. An "Old Guard" controlled the Republican Party in Congress. The impetus for innovation and reform thus shifted from the legislative to the executive branch, and to one chief executive in particular, Theodore Roosevelt.

When the Republican bosses chose Theodore Roosevelt as William McKinley's running mate in 1900, their purpose was more to remove this headstrong, unpredictable character from New York State politics than to groom him for national leadership. As governor of New York, Roosevelt had been a moderate reformer, but even his modest efforts to rid the state's Republican Party of corruption and patronage were too much for the state party machine. Consigning Roosevelt to the vice presidency seemed a safe solution. McKinley was a young, vigorous politician, fully in control of his party and his presidency. Less than a year into his second term, in September 1901, McKinley was shot by an anarchist assassin. The president clung to life for nine days, and then died. Upon succeeding McKinley, Theodore Roosevelt, age 42, became the youngest chief executive in the nation's history.

Although born to an aristocratic New York City family, Roosevelt developed an uncommon affection for "the people." Asthmatic, sickly, and nearsighted as a boy, he remade himself into a vigorous adult. With an insatiable appetite for high-risk adventure—everything from "dude ranching" in the Dakota Territory, to big-game hunting in Africa, to wartime combat—he was also a voracious reader and an accomplished writer. Aggressive and swaggering in his public rhetoric, he was in private a skilled, patient negotiator. A believer in the superiority of the English-speaking

Theodore Roosevelt. *The youthful and animated president addresses a crowd in Evanston, Illinois (a suburb of Chicago), in 1903.*

The Granger Collection, NYC

peoples, he nevertheless assembled an administration that was diverse by the standards of the time. Rarely has a president's personality so enthralled the American public. He is the only 20th-century president immortalized on Mount Rushmore.

Regulating the Economy

Roosevelt quickly revealed his flair for the dramatic. In 1902, he ordered the Justice Department to prosecute the Northern Securities Company, a $400 million monopoly that controlled all railroad lines and traffic in the Northwest from Chicago to Washington State. Never before had an American president sought to use the Sherman Antitrust Act to break up a business monopoly. The news shocked the banker J. P. Morgan, who had brokered the deal that had created Northern Securities. Morgan rushed to the White House, where he is said to have told Roosevelt: "If we have done anything wrong, send your man to my man and they can fix it up." Roosevelt would have none of this "fixing." In 1903, a federal court ordered Northern Securities dissolved, and the U.S. Supreme Court upheld the decision the next year. Roosevelt was hailed as the nation's "trust-buster."

Roosevelt, however, did not believe in breaking up all, or even most, large corporations. Industrial concentration, he believed, brought the United States wealth, productivity, and a rising standard of living. Rather than bust them up, Roosevelt argued, government should regulate the industrial giants and punish those that used their power improperly. This new role would require the federal government to expand its powers. A newly fortified government—the centerpiece of a political program that Roosevelt would later call the **New Nationalism**—was to be led by a forceful president, who was willing to use his power to achieve prosperity and justice.

Roosevelt displayed his willingness to use government power to protect the economically weak in a 1902 coal miners' strike. Miners in the anthracite fields of eastern Pennsylvania wanted recognition for their union, the United Mine Workers (UMW). They also wanted a 10 to 20 percent increase in wages and an eight-hour day. When their employers, led by George F. Baer of the Reading Railroad, refused to negotiate, they went on strike. In October, the fifth month of the strike, Roosevelt summoned the mine owners and John Mitchell, the UMW president, to the White House. Baer expected Roosevelt to threaten the striking workers with arrest by federal troops if they failed to return to work. Instead, Roosevelt supported Mitchell's request for arbitration and warned the mine owners that if they refused to go along, 10,000 federal troops would seize their property. Stunned, the mine owners agreed to submit the dispute to arbitrators, who awarded the unionists a 10 percent wage increase and a nine-hour day.

The mere fact that the federal government had ordered employers to compromise with their workers carried great symbolic weight. Roosevelt enjoyed a surge of support from Americans convinced that he shared their dislike for ill-gotten wealth and privilege. He also raised the hopes of African Americans when, only a month into his presidency, he dined with Booker T. Washington at the White House and then shrugged off the protests of white southerners.

In his 1904 election campaign, Roosevelt promised that, if reelected, he would offer every American a "square deal." The slogan resonated with voters and helped carry Roosevelt to a victory (57 percent of the popular vote) over the conservative Democrat Alton B. Parker. To the surprise of many, Roosevelt had aligned the Republican Party with the cause of reform.

Emboldened by his victory, the president intensified his efforts to extend government regulation of economic affairs. In 1906, he persuaded Congress to pass the Hepburn Act, which significantly increased the Interstate Commerce Commission's ability to set railroad shipping rates and thereby to eliminate the industry's discriminatory marketing practices. Roosevelt supported the Pure Food and Drug Act, passed by Congress that same year, which protected the public from fraudulently marketed and dangerous foods and medications. He also campaigned for the Meat Inspection Act (1906), which obligated the government to monitor the quality and safety of meat being sold to American consumers.

Conserving the Environment   Roosevelt also did more than any previous president to extend federal control over the nation's physical environment. He was not a "preservationist" in the manner of John Muir, founder of the Sierra Club, who insisted that the beauty of the land and the well-being of its wildlife should be protected from all human interference. Instead, Roosevelt viewed the wilderness as a place to live strenuously, to test oneself against the rough outdoors, and to match wits against strong and clever game. He further believed that in the West—that land of ancient forests, lofty mountain peaks, and magnificent canyons—Americans could learn something important about their nation's roots and destiny. To preserve this West, Roosevelt oversaw the creation of 5 new national parks, 16 national monuments, and 53 wildlife reserves. The work of his administration led directly to the formation of the National Park Service in 1916.

Roosevelt also emerged a strong supporter of the "**conservationist**" movement. Conservationists cared little for national parks or grand canyons. They wanted to manage the environment scientifically so as to ensure that the nation's resources were put to the most efficient economic use. Roosevelt shared the conservationists' belief that the plundering of western timberlands, grazing areas, water resources, and minerals had reached crisis proportions. They sought to deploy in environmental policy a version of the scientific management model then being applied both to city government and private industry.

Roosevelt therefore appointed a Public Lands Commission in 1903 to survey public lands, inventory them, and establish permit systems to regulate the kinds and numbers of users. Soon after, the Departments of the Interior and Agriculture placed certain western lands rich in natural resources and waterpower off-limits to agricultural users. Government officials also limited waterpower development by requiring companies to acquire permits and pay fees for the right to generate electricity on public land. When political favoritism and corruption within the Departments of the Interior and Agriculture threatened these efforts at regulation, Roosevelt authorized the hiring of university-trained experts to replace state and local politicians. Scientific expertise, rather than political connections, would now determine the distribution and use of western territory.

Gifford Pinchot, a specialist in forestry management, and Roosevelt's close friend, led the drive for scientific management of natural resources. In 1905, he persuaded Roosevelt to relocate jurisdiction for the national forests from the Department of the Interior to the Department of Agriculture, which, Pinchot argued, was the most appropriate department to oversee the efficient "harvest" of the nation's forest crop. The newly created National Forest Service, under Pinchot's control, quickly instituted a system of competitive bidding for the right to harvest timber on national forest lands. Pinchot and his expanding staff of college-educated foresters also exacted user fees from livestock ranchers who had previously used national forest grazing lands for free. Armed with new legislation and authority, Pinchot and fellow conservationists in the Roosevelt administration declared vast stretches of federal land in the West off-limits to mining and dam construction.

The Republican Old Guard disliked these initiatives. When Roosevelt recommended prosecution of cattlemen and lumbermen who were illegally using federal land for private gain, congressional conservatives struck back with legislation (in 1907) that curtailed the president's power to create new government land reserves. Roosevelt responded by seizing another 17 million acres for national forest reserves before the new law went into effect. To his conservative opponents, excluding commercial activity from public land was bad enough, but flouting the will of Congress with a 17-million-acre land grab violated constitutional principles governing the separation of powers. Yet, among millions of American voters, Roosevelt's willingness to defy western cattle barons, mining tycoons, and other "malefactors of great wealth" increased his popularity.

Progressivism: A Movement for the People? Historians have long debated how much Roosevelt's economic and environmental reforms altered the balance of power between the "interests" and the people. Some have argued that many corporations were eager for federal government regulation—that railroad corporations wanted relief from the rate wars that were driving them into bankruptcy, for example, and that the larger meat packers believed that the costs of government food inspections would drive smaller meat packers out of business. So, too, historians have shown that agribusinesses, timber companies, and mining corporations in the West believed that government regulation would aid them and hurt smaller competitors. According to this view, government regulation benefited sectors of corporate America more than it benefited workers, consumers, and small businessmen.

Indeed, these early reforms often curtailed corporate power only to a limited extent. But in 1907, the progressive program was still evolving. Popular anger over corporate power and political corruption remained a driving force of progressivism. The presence in the Senate of La Follette, Albert Beveridge of Indiana, and other anticorporate Republicans gave that anger an influential national voice. Whether the corporations or the people would benefit most from progressive reforms had yet to be determined.

THE TAFT PRESIDENCY: PROGRESSIVE DISAPPOINTMENT AND RESURGENCE

Deepening fissures between Roosevelt and Old Guard conservatives in the Republican Party influenced Roosevelt's decision not to seek reelection in 1908. Sensing that he might fail to win his party's nomination, and mindful of a rash promise he had made in 1904 not to run again in 1908, Roosevelt announced his retirement from politics. It was a decision he would soon regret. Barely 50 years old, he was too young and energetic to end his political career.

Roosevelt thought he had found in William Howard Taft, his secretary of war, an ideal successor. But Taft was very different from Roosevelt. He had held only one elected office, and a minor one. He was by nature a cautious and conservative man. Taft easily won the election of 1908, defeating Democrat William Jennings Bryan with 52 percent of the vote. His conservatism soon revealed itself in his choice of corporation lawyers, rather than reformers, for cabinet positions.

Battling Progressives Taft's troubles began when he appeared to side against progressives in an acrimonious congressional battle over tariff legislation. The Payne-Aldrich Tariff Act that Taft signed into law in 1909 did little to effect the tariff reductions that progressives had deemed so important as a way of reducing an average workingman's cost of living.

A bruising fight over Taft's conservation policies brought relations between Taft and the insurgent Republicans to the breaking point.

Secretary of the Interior Richard A. Ballinger had aroused progressives' suspicions by reopening for private commercial use 1 million acres of land that the Roosevelt administration had previously brought under federal protection. Gifford Pinchot, still head of the National Forest Service, accused Ballinger of bowing to corporate interests and of profiting personally from the leases of this land. When Taft defended Ballinger, Pinchot went public with his charges. Whatever hope Taft may have had of escaping political damage disappeared when Roosevelt, returning from an African hunting trip by way of Europe in spring 1910, staged a publicized rendezvous with Pinchot in England. In so doing, Roosevelt signaled his continuing support for his old friend Pinchot and his displeasure with Taft.

Roosevelt's Return

Roosevelt had barely returned to the United States in summer 1910 when he dove back into politics. In September, Roosevelt embarked on a speaking tour, the high point of which was his elaboration at Osawatomie, Kansas, of his New Nationalism, an ambitious reform program that called for the federal government to stabilize the economy, protect the weak, and restore social harmony.

The 1910 congressional elections confirmed the popularity of Roosevelt's positions. Insurgent Republicans trounced conservative Republicans in primary after primary, and the Democrats' embrace of reform brought them a majority in the House of Representatives for the first time since 1894. When Robert La Follette, who was challenging Taft for the Republican presidential nomination, seemed to suffer a nervous breakdown in February 1912, Roosevelt announced his own candidacy. In the 13 states sponsoring preferential primaries, Roosevelt won nearly 75 percent of the delegates, but the party's national leadership remained in the hands of the Old Guard, and they were determined to deny Roosevelt the Republican nomination. At the Republican convention in Chicago, Taft won renomination on the first ballot.

Roosevelt had expected this outcome. The night before the convention opened, he had told an assembly of 5,000 supporters that the party leaders would not succeed in derailing their movement. "We stand at Armageddon," he declared, and "we battle for the Lord." The next day, Roosevelt and his supporters withdrew from the convention and from the Republican Party. In August, the reformers reassembled as the new **Progressive Party**, nominated Roosevelt for president and California governor Hiram W. Johnson for vice president, and hammered out the reform platform they had long envisioned: sweeping regulation of the corporations, extensive protections for workers, a sharply graduated income tax, and woman suffrage. "I am as strong as a bull moose," Roosevelt roared as he readied for combat; his proud followers took to calling themselves "Bull Moosers."

Some of them, however, probably including Roosevelt, knew that their mission was likely futile. Not enough Republicans had subscribed to Roosevelt's third-party cause to force Taft out of the race. A split in Republican votes between Roosevelt

Woodrow Wilson. *The Democratic presidential candidate campaigning from the back of a train in 1912, pledging to fulfill progressivism's promise.*

Historical/Corbis

and Taft would likely open the door to a Democratic challenger, a rising star from New Jersey, Woodrow Wilson.

The Rise of Woodrow Wilson and the Election of 1912   Few would have predicted in 1908 that the distinguished president of Princeton University, Woodrow Wilson, would be the 1912 Democratic nominee for president of the United States. Before 1910, Wilson had never run for elective office, nor had he ever held an appointed post in a local, state, or federal administration. The son of a Presbyterian minister from Virginia, Wilson had practiced law for a short time after graduating from Princeton (then the College of New Jersey) in 1879 before settling on an academic career. Earning his doctorate in political science from Johns Hopkins in 1886, he taught history and political science at Bryn Mawr and Wesleyan (Connecticut) before returning to Princeton in 1890. He became president of Princeton in 1902, a post he held until he successfully ran for the governorship of New Jersey in 1910.

Identifying himself with the anti-Bryan wing of the Democratic Party, Wilson attracted the attention of wealthy conservatives, who saw him as a potential presidential candidate. They convinced the bosses of the New Jersey Democratic machine to nominate Wilson for governor in 1910. Wilson accepted the nomination

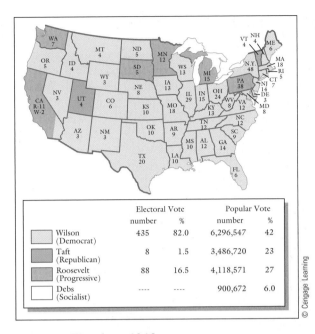

	Electoral Vote		Popular Vote	
	number	%	number	%
Wilson (Democrat)	435	82.0	6,296,547	42
Taft (Republican)	8	1.5	3,486,720	23
Roosevelt (Progressive)	88	16.5	4,118,571	27
Debs (Socialist)	----	----	900,672	6.0

© Cengage Learning

MAP 21.2 Presidential Election, 1912

Taft and Roosevelt split the Republican vote, allowing Wilson to win with a plurality of the popular vote (42 percent) and a big majority (82 percent) of the electoral vote.

and won the governorship handily. He then shocked his conservative backers by declaring his independence from the state's Democratic machine and moving New Jersey into the forefront of reform.

At the Democratic convention of 1912, Wilson was something of a dark horse, running a distant second to House Speaker Champ Clark of Missouri. When the New York delegation gave Clark a simple majority of delegates, virtually everyone assumed that Clark would soon command the two-thirds majority needed to win the nomination. But Wilson's managers held on to Wilson's delegates and began chipping away at Clark's lead. On the fourth day, on the 46th ballot, Wilson won the nomination.

Given the split in Republican ranks, Democrats had their best chance in 20 years of regaining the White House. A Wilson victory, moreover, would give the country its first southern-born president in almost 50 years. Finally, whatever its outcome, the election promised to deliver a vote for reform. Both Roosevelt and Wilson were running on reform platforms, and the Socialist Party candidate, Eugene V. Debs, was attracting larger crowds and generating greater enthusiasm than had been expected. Taft was so certain of defeat that he barely campaigned.

Debate among the candidates focused on the trusts. All three reform candidates— Roosevelt, Wilson, and Debs—agreed that corporations had acquired too much economic power. Debs argued that the only way to ensure popular control of that power was for the federal government to take ownership of the trusts. Roosevelt called for the establishment of a strong government that would regulate and, if necessary, curb the power of the trusts. This was the essence of his New Nationalism, the program he had been advocating since 1910.

Rather than regulate the trusts, Wilson declared his intention to break them up. He wanted to reverse the tendency toward economic concentration and thus restore opportunity to the people. This philosophy, which Wilson labeled the **New Freedom**, called for a temporary concentration of governmental power in order to dismantle the trusts. But once that was accomplished, Wilson promised, the government would relinquish its power.

Wilson won the November election with 42 percent of the popular vote to Roosevelt's 27 percent and Taft's 23 percent; Debs made a strong showing with 6 percent, the largest in his party's history.

THE WILSON PRESIDENCY

Wilson quickly assembled a cabinet of talented men who could be counted on for wise counsel, loyalty, and influence over vital Democratic constituencies. He cultivated a public image of himself as a president firmly in charge of his party and as a faithful tribune of the people. Wilson first turned his attention to tariff reform. The House passed a tariff-reduction bill within a month, and Wilson used his leadership skills to push the bill through a reluctant Senate. The resulting Underwood-Simmons Tariff Act of 1913 reduced tariff barriers from approximately 40 to 25 percent. To make up for revenue lost to tariff reductions, Congress then passed an income tax law. The Sixteenth Amendment to the Constitution, ratified by the states in 1913, had already given the government the right to impose an income tax. The law passed by Congress made good on the progressive pledge to reduce the power and privileges of wealthy Americans by requiring them to pay taxes on a greater percentage of their income than the poor.

The Rise and Fall of the New Freedom   Wilson then asked Congress to overhaul the nation's financial system. The banking interests and their congressional supporters wanted the government to give the authority to regulate credit and currency flows either to a single bank or to several regional banks. Progressives opposed the vesting of so much financial power in private hands and insisted that any reformed financial system must be publicly controlled. Wilson worked out a compromise plan that included both private and public controls, and he marshaled the votes to push it through both the House and the Senate. By the end of 1913, Wilson had signed the **Federal Reserve Act**, the most important law passed in his first administration.

The Federal Reserve Act established 12 regional banks, each controlled by the private banks in its region. Every private bank in the country was required to deposit an average of 6 percent of its assets into its regional Federal Reserve bank. The reserve would be used to make loans to member banks and to issue paper currency (Federal Reserve notes) to facilitate financial transactions. The regional banks were also instructed to use their funds to shore up member banks in distress and to respond to sudden changes in credit demands by easing or tightening the flow of credit. A Federal Reserve Board appointed by the president and responsible to the public rather than to private bankers would set policy and oversee activities within the 12 reserve banks.

The Federal Reserve system strengthened the nation's financial structure and was in most respects an impressive political achievement for Wilson. In its final form, however, it revealed that Wilson was retreating from his New Freedom pledge. The Federal Reserve Board was a less powerful and less centralized federal authority than a national bank would have been, but it nevertheless represented a substantial increase in the central government's control of banking. Moreover, the bill authorizing the system made no attempt to break up private financial institutions that had grown too powerful or to prohibit the interlocking directorates that large banks used to augment their power. Because it sought to work with large banks rather than to break them up, the Federal Reserve system seemed more consonant with the principles of Roosevelt's New Nationalism than with those of Wilson's New Freedom.

Wilson's failure to mount a vigorous antitrust campaign confirmed his drift toward the New Nationalism. For example, in 1914, Wilson supported the Federal Trade Commission Act, which created a government agency by that name to regulate business practices. The Federal Trade Commission (FTC) had wide powers to collect information on corporate pricing policies and on cooperation and competition among businesses. The FTC might have attacked trusts for "unfair trade practices," but the Senate stripped the FTC Act's companion legislation, the Clayton Antitrust Act, of most provisions that would have allowed the government to prosecute the trusts. Wilson supported this weakening of the Clayton Act, having decided that the breakup of large-scale industry was no longer practical or preferable. The FTC, in Wilson's eyes, would help businesses, large and small, to regulate themselves in ways that contributed to national well-being. In accepting giant industry as an inescapable feature of modern life and in seeking to regulate industrial behavior by means of government agencies such as the FTC, Wilson had become, in effect, a New Nationalist.

At first, Wilson's shift to New Nationalist policies led him to support business interests. His nominations to the Federal Reserve Board, for example, were generally men who had worked for Wall Street firms and large industrial corporations. At the same time, he usually refused to use government powers to aid organized groups of workers and farmers. Court rulings had made worker and farmer organizations vulnerable to prosecution under the terms of the Sherman Antitrust Act of 1890. AFL president Samuel Gompers and other labor leaders tried but failed to convince Wilson to insert into the Clayton Antitrust Act a clause that would unambiguously grant labor and farmer organizations immunity from further antitrust prosecutions.

Nor did Wilson, at this time, view with any greater sympathy the campaign for African American political equality. He supported efforts by white southerners in his cabinet, such as Postmaster General Albert Burleson and Treasury Secretary William McAdoo, to segregate their government departments, and he largely ignored pleas from the NAACP to involve the federal government in a campaign against lynching.

Progressivism for the People   In late 1915, however, Wilson moved to the left, in part because he feared losing his reelection in 1916. The Bull Moosers of 1912 were retreating back to the Republican Party. Wilson remembered how much his 1912 victory, based on only 42 percent of the popular vote, had depended on the Republican split. To halt the progressives' rapprochement with the GOP, he made a bid for their support. In January 1916, he nominated Louis Brandeis to the Supreme Court. Not only was Brandeis one of the country's most respected progressives, but he was also the first Jew nominated to serve on the country's highest court. Congressional conservatives did everything they could to block the confirmation of a man they regarded as dangerously radical, but Wilson, as usual, was better organized, and by June his forces in the Senate had emerged victorious.

Wilson followed up this victory by pushing through Congress the first federal workmen's compensation law (the Kern-McGillicuddy Act, which covered federal employees), the first federal law outlawing child labor (the Keating-Owen Act), and the first federal law guaranteeing workers an eight-hour day (the Adamson Act, which covered the nation's 400,000 railway workers). The number of Americans affected by these acts was relatively small. Nevertheless, Wilson had reoriented the Democratic Party to a New Nationalism that cared as much about the interests of the powerless as the interests of the powerful.

Trade unionists flocked to Wilson, as did most of the prominent progressives who had followed the Bull Moose in 1912. Meanwhile, Wilson had appealed to the supporters of William Jennings Bryan by supporting legislation that made federal credit available to farmers in need. He had put together a reform coalition capable of winning a majority at the polls. In the process, he had transformed the Democratic Party. From 1916 on, the Democrats, rather than the Republicans, became the chief guardians of the American reform tradition.

That Wilson did so underscores the strength of the reform and radical forces in American society. By 1916, the ranks of middle-class progressives had grown broad and deep. Working-class protest had also accelerated in scope and intensity. In Lawrence, Massachusetts, in 1912, and in Paterson, New Jersey, in 1913, for example, the IWW organized strikes of textile workers that drew national attention, as did a 1914 strike by Colorado mine workers. These protests reflected the mobilization of those working-class constituencies—immigrants, women, the unskilled—long considered inconsequential both by mainstream labor leaders and party politicians. Assisted by radicals, these groups had begun to fashion a more inclusive and politically ambitious labor movement. Wilson and other Democrats understood the potential strength of this new labor insurgency, and the president's pro-labor legislative agenda in 1916 can be understood, in part, as an effort to channel labor's new constituents into the Democratic Party. It was a successful strategy that contributed to Wilson's reelection in 1916.

CONCLUSION

By 1916, the progressives had accomplished a great deal. They demonstrated that traditional American concerns with democracy and liberty could be adapted to an industrial age. They exposed and curbed some of the worst abuses of the American political system. They enfranchised women and took steps to protect the environment. They broke the hold of laissez-faire economic policies on national politics and replaced it with the idea of a strong federal government committed to economic regulation and social justice. They transformed the presidency into a post of legislative and popular leadership. They enlarged the executive branch by establishing new commissions and agencies charged with administering government policies.

The progressives, in short, had begun to create a strong national government, one in which power increasingly flowed away from municipalities and states and toward Washington. This reorientation followed a compelling logic: A national government stood a better chance of solving the problems of growing economic inequality, mismanagement of natural resources, and consumer fraud than did local and state governments. This emphasis on involving the federal government in economic and social affairs became progressivism's most enduring legacy. It made the movement a forerunner of the liberalism and "New Deal" that emerged under Franklin Roosevelt's leadership in the 1930s.

The rise of progressivism had also revealed, however, that powerful economic interests could themselves become quite comfortable with government regulation, believing that they would be able to turn it to their own advantage. Another danger lurked in the claims by new government regulators to a special authority deriving from their expertise in science and management. Would they truly be disinterested civil servants, capable of discerning and implementing democratic wishes? In 1916, progressivism remained a work in progress, its accomplishments still partial, its character not yet fully formed.

22

BECOMING A WORLD POWER, 1898–1917

FOR MUCH OF THE 19TH CENTURY, most Americans were preoccupied by continental expansion. Elections rarely turned on international events, and presidents rarely made their reputations as statesmen in the world arena. The diplomatic corps, like most agencies of the federal government, was small and inexperienced. The government projected its limited military power westward and possessed virtually no capacity or desire for involvement overseas.

The nation's rapid industrial growth in the late 19th century forced a turn away from such continentalism. Technological advances, especially the laying of transoceanic cables and the introduction of steamship travel, diminished America's physical isolation. The babble of languages one could hear in American cities testified to how much the Old World had penetrated the New. Then, too, Americans watched anxiously as England, Germany, Russia, Japan, and other industrial powers intensified their competition for overseas markets and colonies. Some believed America also needed to enter this contest.

A war with Spain in 1898 gave the United States an opportunity to upgrade its military and acquire colonies and influence in the Western Hemisphere and Asia. Under Presidents William McKinley and Theodore Roosevelt, the United States pursued these initiatives and established a small but strategically important empire. Not all Americans supported this imperial project, and many protested the subjugation of the peoples of Cuba, Puerto Rico, and the Philippines that imperial expansion seemed to entail. In the eyes of anti-imperialists, the United States seemed to be

CHRONOLOGY

1893	Frederick Jackson Turner publishes an essay announcing the end of the frontier
1898	Spanish-American War (April 14–August 12)
	Treaty of Paris signed (December 10), giving United States control of Philippines, Guam, and Puerto Rico
	United States annexes Hawaii
1900	United States annexes Puerto Rico
	United States and other imperial powers put down Chinese Boxer Rebellion
1899–1902	American-Filipino War
1901	United States forces Cuba to adopt constitution favorable to U.S. interests
1903	Hay–Bunau-Varilla Treaty signed, giving United States control of Panama Canal Zone
1904	"Roosevelt Corollary" to Monroe Doctrine proclaimed
1905	Roosevelt negotiates end to Russo-Japanese War
1906–1917	United States intervenes in Cuba, Nicaragua, Haiti, Dominican Republic, and Mexico
1907	Roosevelt and Japanese government reach a "gentlemen's agreement" restricting Japanese immigration and ending the segregation of Japanese schoolchildren in California
1907–1909	Great White Fleet circles the world
1909–1913	Taft conducts "dollar diplomacy"
1910	Mexican Revolution
1914	Panama Canal opens
1914–1917	Wilson struggles to develop a policy toward Mexico
1917	United States purchases Virgin Islands from Denmark

becoming the kind of nation that many Americans had long despised—one that valued power more than liberty.

Roosevelt brushed aside these objections and set about creating an international system in which a handful of industrial nations pursued their global economic interests, dominated world trade, and kept the world at peace. Woodrow Wilson, however, was more troubled by America's imperial turn. His doubts became apparent in his efforts to devise a policy toward post-revolutionary Mexico that restrained American might and respected Mexican desires for liberty. It was a worthy ambition but one that proved difficult to achieve.

THE UNITED STATES LOOKS ABROAD

By the late 19th century, sizable numbers of Americans had become interested in extending their country's influence abroad. The most important groups were Protestant missionaries, businessmen, and imperialists.

Protestant Missionaries
Protestant missionaries were among the most active promoters of American interests abroad. Overseas missionary activity grew quickly between 1870 and 1900, most of it directed toward China. Between 1880 and 1900, the number of women's missionary societies doubled, from 20 to 40; by 1915, these societies enrolled 3 million women. Convinced of the superiority of the Anglo-Saxon race, Protestant missionaries considered it their Christian duty to teach the Gospel to the "ignorant" Asian masses and save their souls. Missionaries also believed that their conversion efforts would free those masses from their racial destiny, enabling them to become "civilized."

Businessmen
Industrialists, traders, and investors also began to look overseas, sensing that they could make fortunes in foreign lands. Exports of American manufactured goods rose substantially after 1880. By 1914, American foreign investment equaled a sizable 7 percent of the nation's gross national product. Companies such as Eastman Kodak (film and cameras), Singer Sewing Machine, Standard Oil, American Tobacco, and International Harvester had become multinational corporations with overseas branch offices.

Some industrialists became entranced by the prospect of clothing, feeding, housing, and transporting the 400 million people of China. James B. Duke, who headed American Tobacco, was selling 1 billion cigarettes per year in East Asian markets. Looking for ways to fill empty boxcars heading west from Minnesota to Tacoma, Washington, the railroad tycoon James J. Hill imagined stuffing them with wheat and steel destined for China and Japan. He actually distributed wheat cookbooks throughout East Asia to convince Asians to shift from a rice-based to a bread-based diet (so that there would be a market there for U.S. flour exports). Although export trade with East Asia during this period never fulfilled the expectations of Hill and other industrialists, their talk about the "wealth of the Orient" impressed on politicians its importance to American economic health.

Events of the 1890s only intensified the appeal of foreign markets. First, the 1890 U.S. census announced that the frontier had disappeared and that America had completed the task of westward expansion. Then, in 1893, a young historian named Frederick Jackson Turner published an essay, "The Significance of the Frontier in American History," articulating what many Americans feared: that the frontier had been essential to the growth of the economy and to the cultivation of democracy.

Living in the wilderness, Turner argued, had transformed the Europeans who settled the New World into Americans. They shed their European clothing styles, social customs, and political beliefs, and acquired distinctively American characteristics—rugged individualism, egalitarianism, and a democratic faith. How, Turner wondered, could the nation continue to prosper now that the frontier had gone?

In recent years, historians of the American West have criticized **Turner's "frontier thesis."** They have argued that the very idea of the frontier as uninhabited wilderness overlooked the tens of thousands of Indians who occupied the region and that much else of what Americans believed about the West was based more on myth than on reality. They have also pointed out that it makes little sense to view the 1890s as a decade in which opportunities for economic gain disappeared in the West. Yet, Turner's essay is still relevant for the way in which it expressed a fear that America had lost its way. As the deep depression of the 1890s settled on the nation, Americans began to ask what the republic could do to regain its economic prosperity and political stability. Where would it find its new frontiers? One answer to these questions focused on the pursuit of overseas expansion.

Imperialists   Eager to assist in the drive for overseas expansion was a group of politicians, intellectuals, and military strategists who viewed such expansion as essential to the pursuit of world power. They

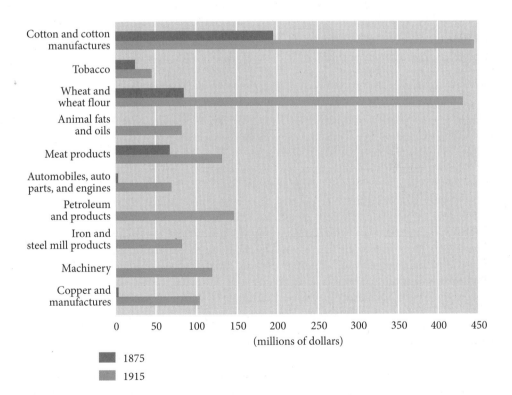

Leading U.S. Exports, 1875 and 1915

Source: Data from *Historical Statistics of the United States, Colonial Times to 1970* (White Plains, NY: Kraus International, 1989).

wanted the United States to join Britain, France, Germany, and Russia as a great imperial nation. They believed that the United States should build a strong navy, solidify a sphere of influence in the Caribbean, and extend markets into Asia. Their desire to control ports and territories beyond the continental borders of their own country made them **imperialists**.

One of the best-known imperialists of the period was **Alfred Thayer Mahan**. In an influential book, *The Influence of Sea Power upon History, 1660–1783* (1890), Mahan argued that past empires, beginning with Rome, had relied on their capacity to control the seas. Mahan called for the construction of a U.S. navy with enough ships and firepower to make its presence felt across the world. To be effective, that global fleet would require a canal across Central America through which U.S. warships could pass swiftly from the Atlantic to the Pacific oceans. It would also require a string of far-flung service bases from the Caribbean to the southwestern Pacific. Mahan recommended that the U.S. government take possession of Hawaii and other strategically located Pacific islands with superior harbor facilities.

Presidents William McKinley and Theodore Roosevelt would eventually make almost the whole of Mahan's vision a reality, but in the early 1890s, Mahan doubted that Americans would accept the responsibility and costs of empire. Many Americans still insisted that the United States should not acquire overseas bases and colonize foreign peoples.

Mahan underestimated, however, the government's alarm over the scramble of Europeans to extend their imperial control. Every U.S. administration from the 1880s on committed to a "big navy" policy. By 1898, the U.S. Navy ranked fifth in the world, and by 1900, it ranked third. Already in 1878, the United States had secured rights to Pago Pago, a superb deep-water harbor in Samoa (a collection of islands in the southwest Pacific inhabited by Polynesians), and in 1885, it had leased Pearl Harbor from the Hawaiians. Both harbors were expected to serve as fueling stations for the growing U.S. fleet.

These attempts to project U.S. power overseas had already deepened the government's involvement in the affairs of distant lands. In 1889, the United States established a protectorate over part of Samoa, a move meant to forestall German and British efforts to weaken American influence on the islands. In the early 1890s, President Grover Cleveland's administration was increasingly drawn into Hawaiian affairs, as tensions between American sugar plantation owners there and native Hawaiians upset the islands' economic and political stability. In 1891, U.S. plantation owners succeeded in deposing the Hawaiian king and putting into power Queen Liliuokalani. But when Liliuokalani strove to establish her independence from American interests, the planters, assisted by U.S. sailors, overthrew her regime, too. Cleveland declared Hawaii a protectorate in 1893, but he resisted the imperialists in Congress who wanted to annex the islands.

Still, imperialist sentiment in Congress and across the nation continued to grow, fueled by "jingoism." Jingoists were nationalists who thought that a swaggering foreign policy and a willingness to go to war would enhance their nation's glory. The anti-imperialist editor of *The Nation*, E. L. Godkin, exclaimed in 1894: "The number of men and officials of this country who are now mad to fight somebody is appalling." Recent feminist scholarship has emphasized the degree to which men of the 1890s saw war as an opportunity to revive frontierlike notions of masculinity—of men as warriors and conquerors—that were proving difficult to sustain in industrializing and bureaucratizing America. Spain's behavior in Cuba in the 1890s gave those men the war they sought.

THE SPANISH-AMERICAN WAR

Relations between the Cubans and their Spanish rulers had long been deteriorating. The Spanish had taken 10 years to subdue a revolt begun in 1868. In 1895, the Cubans staged another revolt, sparked by their continuing resentment of Spanish control and by a depressed economy. The fighting was brutal. Cuban forces destroyed large areas of the island to make it uninhabitable by the Spanish. The Spanish army, led by General Valeriano Weyler, responded in kind, forcing large numbers of Cubans into concentration camps. Denied adequate food, shelter, and sanitation, an estimated 200,000 Cubans—one-eighth of the island's population—died of starvation and disease.

Such tactics, especially those ascribed to "Butcher" Weyler (as he was known in much of the U.S. press), inflamed American opinion. Many Americans sympathized with the Cubans, who seemed to be fighting the kind of anticolonial war Americans had waged more than 100 years earlier. Americans stayed informed about Cuban-Spanish struggles by reading the *New York Journal,* owned by William Randolph Hearst, and the *New York World,* owned by Joseph Pulitzer. Hearst and Pulitzer were transforming newspaper publishing in much the same way that *McClure's Magazine* and *Ladies' Home Journal* had revolutionized the magazine business. To boost circulation, Hearst and Pulitzer sought out sensational and shocking stories and described them in lurid detail. They were accused

THE U.S. NAVY, 1890–1914: EXPENDITURES AND BATTLESHIP SIZE

Fiscal Year	Total Federal Expenditures	Naval Expenditures	Naval Expenditures as Percentage of Total Federal Expenditures	Size of Battleships (average tons displaced)
1890	$318,040,711	$22,006,206	6.9%	11,000
1900	520,860,847	55,953,078	10.7	12,000
1901	524,616,925	60,506,978	11.5	16,000
1905	657,278,914	117,550,308	20.7	16,000
1909	693,743,885	115,546,011	16.7	27,000 (1910)
1914	735,081,431	139,682,186	19.0	32,000

Source: (for expenditures) E. B. Potter, *Sea Power: A Naval History* (Annapolis: Naval Institute Press, 1982), p. 187; (for size of ships) Harold Sprout, *Toward a New Order of Sea Power* (New York: Greenwood Press, 1976), p. 52.

of engaging in **"yellow journalism"**—embellishing stories with titillating details when the true reports did not seem dramatic enough.

The sensationalism of the yellow press and its frequently jingoistic accounts failed to bring about American intervention in Cuba, however. In the final days of his administration, President Cleveland resisted mounting pressure to intervene. William McKinley, who succeeded him in 1897, denounced the Spanish even more harshly, with the aim of forcing Spain into concessions that would satisfy the Cuban rebels and end the conflict. Initially, this strategy seemed to work: Spain relieved "Butcher" Weyler of his command, released some incarcerated Cubans from concentration camps, and granted Cuba limited autonomy. But these concessions did not satisfy Cuban rebels, who were demanding full independence. Late in 1897, when riots broke out in Havana, McKinley ordered the battleship *Maine* into Havana Harbor to protect U.S. citizens and their property. Then, two unexpected events set off a war.

The first was the February 9, 1898, publication in Hearst's *New York Journal* of a letter stolen from Enrique Dupuy de Lôme, the Spanish minister to

Uncle Sam Gives Spain More Than It Can Handle. *By going to war in 1898, this poster suggests, the United States would topple Spain and the remnants of its empire.*

The Granger Collection, NYC

Washington, in which he described McKinley as "a cheap politician" and a "bidder for the admiration of the crowd." The de Lôme letter also implied that the Spanish cared little about resolving the Cuban crisis through negotiation and reform. The news embarrassed Spanish officials and outraged many in the United States. Then, only six days later, the *Maine* exploded in Havana Harbor, killing 260 American sailors. Although subsequent investigations revealed that the most probable cause of the explosion was a malfunctioning boiler, Americans were certain that it had been the work of Spanish agents. "Remember the *Maine!*" screamed the headlines in the yellow press. On March 8, Congress responded to the clamor for war by authorizing $50 million to mobilize U.S. forces. In the meantime, McKinley notified Spain of his conditions for avoiding war: Spain would pay an indemnity for the *Maine,* abandon its concentration camps, end the fighting with the rebels, and commit to Cuban independence. On April 9, Spain accepted all the demands but the last. Nevertheless, on April 11, McKinley asked Congress for authority to go to war. Three days later, Congress approved a war resolution, which included a declaration (spelled out in the Teller Amendment) that the United States would not use the war as an opportunity to acquire territory in Cuba. On April 24, Spain responded with a formal declaration of war against the United States.

"A Splendid Little War"   Secretary of State John Hay called the fight with Spain "a splendid little war." Begun in April, it ended in August. More than 1 million men volunteered to fight, and fewer than 500 were killed or wounded in combat. The American victory over Spain was complete, not just in Cuba but in the neighboring island of Puerto Rico and in the Philippines, Spain's strategic possession in the Pacific.

Actually, the war was more complicated than it seemed. The main reason for the easy victory was U.S. naval superiority. In the war's first major battle, a naval engagement in Manila's harbor in the Philippines on May 1, a U.S. fleet commanded by Commodore George Dewey destroyed an entire Spanish fleet and lost only one sailor (to heat stroke). On land, the story was different. On the eve of war, the U.S. Army consisted of only 26,000 troops. These soldiers were skilled at skirmishing with Indians but ill-prepared and ill-equipped for all-out war. A force of 80,000 Spanish regulars awaited them in Cuba, with another 50,000 in reserve in Spain. Congress immediately increased the army to 62,000 and called for an additional 125,000 volunteers. The response to this call was astounding, but outfitting, training, and transporting the new recruits overwhelmed the army's capacities. Its standard-issue, blue flannel uniforms proved too heavy for fighting in tropical Cuba. Rations were so poor that soldiers referred to one common item as "embalmed beef." Most of the volunteers had to make do with ancient Civil War rifles that still used black, rather than smokeless, powder. The army as a whole was unprepared for the effects of malaria and other tropical diseases.

That the Cuban revolutionaries were predominantly black also came as a shock to the U.S. forces. In their attempts to arouse support for the Cuban cause, U.S. newspapers had portrayed Cuban rebels as similar to white Americans. They were described as intelligent, civilized, and democratic, possessing an

"Anglo-Saxon tenacity of purpose." And they were "fully nine-tenths" white, according to one report. The Spanish oppressors, by contrast, were depicted as dark-complexioned—"dark cruel eyes, dark swaggering men" wrote author Sherwood Anderson—and as possessing the characteristics of their "dark race": barbarism, cruelty, and indolence. The U.S. troops' first encounters with Cuban and Spanish forces challenged these stereotypes. Their Cuban allies appeared poorly outfitted, rough mannered, and largely black. The Spanish soldiers appeared well disciplined, tough in battle, and light-complexioned.

The Cuban rebels were skilled guerrilla fighters, but racial prejudice prevented most U.S. soldiers and reporters from crediting their military expertise. Instead, they judged the Cubans harshly—as primitive, savage, and incapable of self-control or self-government. White U.S. troops preferred not to fight alongside the Cubans; increasingly, they refused to coordinate strategy with them.

At first, the U.S. Army's logistical unpreparedness and its racial misconceptions did little to diminish the soldiers' hunger for a good fight. No one was more eager for battle than Theodore Roosevelt, who, along with Colonel Leonard Wood, led a volunteer cavalry unit composed of Ivy League gentlemen, western cowboys, sheriffs, prospectors, Indians, and small numbers of Hispanics and ethnic European Americans. Roosevelt's **Rough Riders**, as the unit came to be known, landed with the invasion force and played an active role in the three battles fought in the hills surrounding Santiago. Their most famous action, the one on which Roosevelt would build his lifelong reputation as a military hero, was a furious charge up Kettle Hill into the teeth of Spanish defenses. Roosevelt's bravery was stunning, although his judgment was faulty. Nearly 100 men were killed or wounded. Reports of Roosevelt's bravery overshadowed the equally brave performance of other troops, notably the **Ninth and Tenth Negro Cavalries**, which played a pivotal role in clearing away Spanish fortifications on Kettle Hill and allowing Roosevelt's Rough Riders to make their charge. One Rough Rider commented: "If it had not been for the Negro cavalry, the Rough Riders would have been exterminated." The Twenty-fourth and Twenty-fifth Negro Infantry Regiments performed equally vital tasks in the U.S. Army's conquest of the adjacent San Juan Hill.

Theodore Roosevelt saw the Rough Rider regiment that he commanded in the Spanish-American War as a melting pot of different groups of white Americans. Combat, he further believed, would forge these many groups into one, as war had always done in the American past. African Americans were the group most conspicuously absent from the Rough Rider mix. Yet the fury of the fighting on Kettle Hill and San Juan Hill so scrambled the white and black regiments that by the time the troops reached the San Juan summit, they were racially intermixed. Combat had brought blacks into the great American melting pot. The black troops, Roosevelt declared, were "an excellent breed of Yankee," and no "Rough Rider will ever forget," he added, "the tie that binds us to the Ninth and Tenth Cavalry."

But Roosevelt did not truly believe that blacks were the equals of whites or that they could be absorbed into the American nation. So, a few months after returning home, he began downplaying the role of black troops and questioned their ability to fight. The attack on black fighting abilities would become so widespread that by the start of the First World War, the U.S. military had largely excluded black troops from combat roles. Thus, an episode that had first demonstrated the possibility of interracial cooperation in America ended in the hardening of racial boundaries.

The taking of Kettle Hill, San Juan Hill, and other high ground surrounding Santiago gave the U.S. forces a substantial advantage over the Spanish defenders in Santiago. Nevertheless, the troops were short of food, ammunition, and medical facilities. Their ranks were devastated by malaria, typhoid, and dysentery, and more than 5,000 soldiers died from disease. Fortunately, the Spanish had lost the will to fight. On July 3, Spain's Atlantic fleet tried to retreat from Santiago Harbor and was promptly destroyed by a U.S. fleet. The Spanish army in Santiago surrendered on July 16; on July 18, the Spanish government asked for peace. While negotiations for an armistice proceeded, U.S. forces overran the neighboring island of Puerto Rico. On August 12, the U.S. and Spanish governments agreed to an armistice; before this news reached the Philippines, the United States had captured Manila and had taken prisoner 13,000 Spanish soldiers.

The armistice required Spain to relinquish its claim to Cuba, cede Puerto Rico and the Pacific island of Guam to the United States, and tolerate the American occupation of Manila until a peace conference could be convened in Paris on October 1, 1898. At that conference, American diplomats startled their Spanish counterparts by demanding that Spain also cede the Philippines to the United States. After two months of stalling, the Spanish government agreed to relinquish its coveted Pacific colony for $20 million. The transaction was sealed by the Treaty of Paris on December 10, 1898.

THE UNITED STATES BECOMES A WORLD POWER

America's initial war aim had been to oust the Spanish from Cuba—an aim that both imperialists and anti-imperialists supported, but for different reasons. Imperialists hoped to incorporate Cuba into a new American empire; anti-imperialists hoped to see the Cubans gain their independence. But only the imperialists condoned the U.S. acquisition of Puerto Rico, Guam, and particularly the Philippines, which they viewed as integral to the extension of U.S. interests into Asia. Soon after the war began, President McKinley had cast his lot with the imperialists. First, he annexed Hawaii, giving the United States permanent control of Pearl Harbor. Next, he established a U.S. naval base at Manila. Never before had the United States sought such a large military presence outside the Western Hemisphere.

In a departure of equal importance, McKinley announced his intent to administer much of this newly acquired territory as U.S. colonies. Virtually all territory the United States had obtained in the 19th century had been part of the North American continent. These lands had been settled by Americans, who had eventually petitioned for statehood. Of these new territories, however, only Hawaii would be allowed to follow this traditional path toward statehood. There, the powerful U.S. sugar plantation owners prevailed on Congress to pass an act in 1900 extending U.S. citizenship to all Hawaiian citizens and putting Hawaii on the road to statehood. No such influential group of Americans resided in the Philippines. The

Leaders of the Cuban Struggle for Independence. *By 1898, Cubans had been fighting to free their country from Spain for 30 years. This lithograph, a souvenir of the Grand Cuban-American Fair held in New York in 1896, depicts five leaders of the Cuban struggle: Máximo Gómez (upper left), Antonio Maceo (upper right), Calixto García (bottom right), and Salvador Cisneros (bottom left). At the center is José Martí, the "Father of the Revolution," killed in battle in 1895.*

Library of Congress Prints and Photograph Division

country was made a U.S. colony and placed under a U.S. administration that took its orders from Washington rather than from the Filipino people. Such colonization was necessary, in the eyes of American imperialists, to prevent other powers, such as Japan and Germany, from gaining a foothold somewhere in the 400-island archipelago and launching attacks on the U.S. naval base in Manila.

The United States might have negotiated an arrangement with **Emilio Aguinaldo,** the leader of an anticolonial movement in the Philippines, that would have given the Philippines independence in exchange for a U.S. naval base at Manila. An American fleet stationed there would have been able to protect both American interests and the fledgling Philippine nation from assaults by Japan, Germany, or Britain. Alternatively, the United States might have annexed the Philippines outright and offered Filipinos U.S. citizenship as the first step toward statehood. McKinley and his supporters, however, believed that the "inferior" Filipino people lacked the capacity for self-government. The United States would undertake a solemn mission to "civilize" the Filipinos and thereby prepare them for independence, but until that mission was complete, the Philippines would submit to rule by presidentially appointed U.S. governors.

The Debate over the Treaty of Paris

The proposed acquisition of the Philippines aroused opposition both in the United States and in the Philippines. The Anti-Imperialist League, strong in the Northeast, enlisted the support of Carl Schurz, former senator from Missouri, and other elder statesmen in McKinley's own party, as well as the former Democratic president Grover Cleveland, the industrialist Andrew Carnegie, and the labor leader Samuel Gompers. William Jennings Bryan, meanwhile, marshaled a vigorous anti-imperialist protest among Democrats in the South and West, while Mark Twain, William James, William Dean Howells, and other men of letters lent the cause their prestige. Some anti-imperialists believed that subjugating the Filipinos would violate the nation's most precious principle: the right of all people to independence and self-government. Moreover, they feared that the military and diplomatic establishment needed to administer the colony would threaten political liberties at home.

Other anti-imperialists were motivated more by self-interest than by democratic ideals. U.S. sugar producers, for example, feared competition from Filipino producers. Trade unionists worried that poor Filipino workers would flood the U.S. labor market and depress wage rates. Still other anti-imperialists feared the contaminating effects of contact with "inferior" Asian races.

© Cengage Learning

MAP 22.1 Spanish-American War in Cuba, 1898

This map shows the following: the routes taken by U.S. ships transporting troops from Florida to Cuba; the concentration of troop landings and battles around Santiago, Cuba; and a U.S. naval blockade, stretching hundreds of miles from Puerto Rico to Cuba, that attempted to keep the Spanish troops in Cuba and Puerto Rico from being reinforced.

Despite their contrasting motivations, the anti-imperialists almost dealt McKinley and his fellow imperialists a defeat in the U.S. Senate. On February 6, 1899, the Senate voted 57 to 27 in favor of the Treaty of Paris, only one vote beyond the minimum two-thirds majority required for ratification.

The American-Filipino War

The acquisition of the Philippines embroiled the United States in a long, brutal war to subdue the Filipino rebels. In four years of fighting, more than 120,000 American soldiers served in the Philippines and more than 4,200 of them died. The war cost $160 million, or eight times what the United States had paid Spain to acquire the archipelago. The war brought Americans face-to-face with an unpleasant truth: American actions in the Philippines were virtually indistinguishable from Spain's actions in Cuba. Like Spain, the United States refused to acknowledge a people's aspiration for self-rule. Like "Butcher" Weyler, American generals permitted the use of savage tactics. Whole communities suspected of harboring guerrillas were driven into concentration camps, and their houses, farms, and livestock were destroyed. One New York infantryman wrote home that his unit had killed 1,000 Filipinos—men, women, and children—in retaliation for the murder of a single American soldier. A total of 15,000 Filipino soldiers died in the fighting. Estimates of total Filipino deaths from gunfire, starvation, and disease range from 50,000 to 200,000.

The United States finally gained the upper hand in the war after General Arthur MacArthur (father of Douglas) was appointed commander of the islands in 1900. MacArthur did not lessen the war's ferocity, but he understood that it could not be won by guns alone. He offered amnesty to Filipino guerrillas who agreed to surrender, and he cultivated close relations with the islands' economic elites. McKinley, meanwhile, sent William Howard Taft to the islands in 1900 to establish a civilian government. In 1901, Taft became the colony's first "governor-general" and declared that he intended to prepare the Filipinos for independence. He transferred many governmental functions to Filipino control and launched a program of public works (roads, bridges, schools) that would give the Philippines the infrastructure necessary for economic development and political independence. By 1902, this dual strategy of ruthless war against those who had taken up arms and concessions to those who were willing to live under benevolent American rule crushed the revolt. Though sporadic fighting continued until 1913, Americans had secured control of the Philippines. The explicit commitment of the United States to Philippine independence (a promise that was deferred until 1946), together with an extensive program of internal improvements, eased America's conscience.

Controlling Cuba and Puerto Rico

Helping the Cubans achieve independence had been a major rationale for the war against Spain. In 1900, the United States seemed to be delivering on this pledge when General Leonard Wood, commander of U.S. forces in Cuba, authorized a constitutional convention to write the laws for a Cuban republic. Yet, at the same time, the McKinley administration made clear it would not easily relinquish control of the island. At McKinley's urging, the U.S. Congress attached to a 1901 army appropriations bill the **Platt Amendment**, delineating three conditions for Cuban independence: (1) Cuba would not be permitted to make treaties with foreign powers; (2) the United States would have broad authority to intervene in Cuban political and economic affairs; and (3) Cuba would sell or lease land to the United States for naval stations. The delegates to Cuba's constitutional convention were outraged, but the dependence of Cuba's vital sugar industry on the U.S. market and the continuing presence of the U.S. Army on Cuban soil rendered resistance futile. In 1901, by a vote of 15 to 11, the delegates reluctantly wrote the Platt conditions into their constitution. "There is, of course, little or no independence left Cuba under the Platt Amendment," Wood candidly admitted to his friend Theodore Roosevelt, who had recently succeeded the assassinated McKinley as president.

Cuba's status, in truth, differed little from that of the Philippines. Both were colonies of the United States. In the case of Cuba, economic dependence closely followed political subjugation. Between 1898 and 1914, U.S. trade with Cuba increased more than tenfold (from $27 million to $300 million), while investments more than quadrupled (from $50 million to $220 million). In 1903, the United States compelled Cuba to lease it 45 square miles of land and water on the island nation's southeast coast. There the United States built the U.S. Naval Station at Guantanamo Bay, a facility that it maintains to this day. The United States also intervened in Cuban political affairs five times between 1906 and 1921 to protect its economic interests and those of the indigenous ruling class with whom it had become closely allied. The economic, political, and military control that the United States imposed on Cuba would fuel anti-American sentiment there for years to come.

Puerto Rico received somewhat different treatment. The United States annexed the island outright with the Foraker Act (1900). Unlike every previous annexation authorized by Congress since 1788, this act contained no provision for making the inhabitants of Puerto Rico citizens of the United States. Instead, Puerto Rico was designated an "unincorporated" territory, which meant that Congress would dictate the island's government and specify the rights of its inhabitants. Puerto Ricans were allowed no role in designing their government, nor was their consent to its establishment sought. With the Foraker Act, Congress had, in effect, invented a new imperial mechanism for ensuring sovereignty over lands deemed vital to U.S. economic and military security. The U.S. Supreme Court upheld the constitutionality of this mechanism in a series of historic decisions, known as the Insular Cases, in the years from 1901 to 1904.

In some respects, Puerto Rico fared better than "independent" Cuba. Puerto Ricans were granted U.S. citizenship in 1917 and won the right to elect their own governor in 1947. Still, Puerto Ricans enjoyed fewer political rights than Americans in the 48 states. Moreover, throughout the 20th century, they endured a poverty rate far exceeding that of the mainland. In its skewed distribution of wealth and its lack of industrial development, Puerto Rico resembled the poorly developed

Should America Become an Imperial Nation?

After the Spanish-American War of 1898, the McKinley administration proposed to make two of the territories it had taken from Spain, Puerto Rico and the Philippines, into American colonies. This proposal sparked furious debate both within Congress and in the country at large, for it marked the first time (outside of Indian affairs) that the United States was proposing to rule new territory indefinitely without the consent of the people who lived in those lands, and without intending to grant these people the rights and institutions of self-government as set forth in the Constitution. Was it legitimate for America to expand its rule in this way? The Democratic senator from Indiana, Albert Beveridge, believed it was. For Carl Schurz, former Republican senator from Missouri and a leading figure in the American Anti-Imperialist League, it was not.

Albert Beveridge, "The March of the Flag," September 1898

Have we no mission to perform, no duty to discharge to our fellow-man? Has God endowed us with gifts beyond our desserts and marked us as the people of His peculiar favor, merely to rot in our own selfishness .... [S]hall we reap the reward that waits on our discharge of our high duty; shall we occupy new markets for what our farmers raise, our factories make, our merchants sell—aye, and please God, new markets for what our ships shall carry?

Hawaii is ours; Porto Rico is to be ours; at the prayer of her people Cuba finally will be ours ... the flag of liberal government is to float over the Philippines ....

The Opposition tells us that we ought not to govern a people without their consent. I answer: The rule of liberty that all just government derives its authority from the consent of the governed, applies only to those who are capable of self-government. We govern the Indians without their consent, we govern our territories without their consent, we govern our children without their consent. How do they know what our government would be without their consent? Would not the people of the Philippines prefer the just, humane, civilizing government of the Republic to the savage, bloody rule of pillage and extortion from which we have rescued them? ... Shall we turn these peoples back to the reeking hands from which we have taken them? Shall we abandon them, with Germany, England, Japan, hungering for them? Shall we save them from those nations, to give them a self-rule of tragedy?

Carl Schurz, "American Imperialism," January 4, 1899

It is proposed to embark this Republic in a course of imperialistic policy by

nations of Central and South America more than it did the affluent country that took over its government in 1900.

The subjugation of Cuba and the annexation of Puerto Rico troubled Americans far less than the U.S. takeover in the Philippines. Since the first articulation of the Monroe Doctrine in 1823, the United States had, in effect, claimed the Western Hemisphere as its sphere of influence. Within that sphere, many Americans permanently annexing to it certain islands taken, from Spain in the late war .... If we adopt such a system, then we shall, for the first time since the abolition of slavery, again have two kinds of Americans: Americans of the first class, who enjoy the privilege of taking part in the government in accordance with our old constitutional principles, and Americans of the second class, who are to be ruled in a substantially arbitrary fashion by the Americans of the first class ....

This will be a difference no better—nay, rather somewhat worse—than that which a century and a quarter ago still existed between Englishmen of the first and Englishmen of the second class, the first represented by King George and the British Parliament, and the second by the American colonists. This difference called forth that great paean of human liberty, the American Declaration of Independence,—a document which, I regret to say, seems, owing to the intoxication of conquest, to have lost much of its charm among some of our fellow citizens. Its fundamental principle was that "governments derive their just powers from the consent of the governed." We are now told that we have never fully lived up to that principle, and that, therefore, in our new policy we may cast it aside altogether. But I say to you that, if we are true believers in democratic government, it is our duty to move in the direction toward the full realization of that principle and not in the direction away from it. If you tell me that we cannot govern the people of those new possessions in accordance with that principle, then I answer that this is a good reason why this democracy should not attempt to govern them at all.

Q *What are Beveridge's arguments for making Puerto Rico and the Philippines into colonies? What are Schurz's arguments against doing so?*

Q *Both men invoke self-government, or what Schurz calls democratic government, as a key American ideal, but they draw different lessons regarding its relevance to the territories acquired by the United States in its war against Spain. What are the different lessons the two men draw about democratic government in these territories?*

Sources: (first) Albert Beveridge, "The March of the Flag: Speech Opening the Indiana Republican Campaign at Tomlinson Hall, Indianapolis, September 16, 1898," in Albert J. Beveridge, *The Meaning of the Times, and Other Speeches (Indianapolis: Bobbs-Merrill, 1908)*, 47–57; (second) Carl Schurz, *American Imperialism: The Convocation Address Delivered on the Occasion of the Twenty-Seventh Convocation of the University of Chicago, January 4, 1899* (Boston: Dana Estes and Company, 1899), 3–31.

believed, the United States possessed the right to act unilaterally to protect its interests. Before 1900, most of its actions (with the exception of the Mexican War) had been designed to limit the influence of European powers—Britain, France, Russia, and Spain—on the countries of the hemisphere. After 1900, however, the United States assumed a more aggressive role, seizing land, overturning governments it did not like, and forcing its economic and political policies on weaker neighbors in

MAP 22.2 American South Pacific Empire, 1900

By 1900, the American South Pacific empire consisted of a series of strategically located islands with superior harbor facilities, stretching from the Hawaiian Islands and Samoa in the middle of the Pacific to the Philippines on the ocean's western edge.

order to turn the Caribbean Sea into what policymakers called (with the example of ancient Rome in mind) an American Mediterranean.

China and the "Open Door"

Except for Hawaii, the Philippines, and Guam, the United States made no effort to take control of Asian lands. Such a policy might well have triggered war with other world powers that were already well established in the area. The United States opted for a diplomatic rather than a military strategy to achieve its foreign policy objectives. For China, in 1899 and 1900, it proposed the policy of the "open door."

The United States was concerned that the actions of the other world powers in China would block its own efforts to open up China's markets to American goods. Britain, Germany, Japan, Russia, and France each coveted a chunk of China, where they could monopolize trade, exploit cheap labor, and establish military bases. By the 1890s, each of these powers was building a sphere of influence, either by wringing economic and territorial concessions from the weak Chinese government or by seizing outright the land and trading privileges it desired.

To prevent China's breakup and to preserve U.S. economic access to the whole of China, McKinley's secretary of state, John Hay, sent "open door" notes to the major world powers. The notes asked each power to open its Chinese sphere of influence to the merchants of other nations and to grant them reasonable harbor

New Americans? *The terms of Puerto Rico's 1900 annexation did not permit the island's inhabitants, such as those depicted in this 1900 photograph, to become citizens of the United States. Instead they became a colonized people.*

Library of Congress Prints and Photograph Division

fees and railroad rates. Hay also asked each power to respect China's sovereignty by enforcing Chinese tariff duties in the territory it controlled.

None of the world powers embraced either of Hay's requests, although Britain and Japan gave provisional assent. France, Germany, Russia, and Italy responded evasively, indicating their support for the **Open Door policy** in theory but insisting that they could not implement it until all of the other powers had done so. Hay put the best face on their responses by declaring that all of the powers had agreed to observe his Open Door principles and that he regarded their assent as "final and definitive." The rivals may have been impressed by Hay's diplomacy, but whether they intended to uphold the United States' Open Door policy was not at all clear.

The first challenge to Hay's policy came from the Chinese. In May 1900, a Chinese organization colloquially known as the "**Boxers**" sparked an uprising to rid China of all "foreign devils" and foreign influences. Hundreds of Europeans were killed, as were many Chinese men and women who had converted to Christianity. When the Boxers laid siege to the foreign legations in Beijing and cut off communication between that city and the outside world, the imperial powers raised an expeditionary force to rescue the diplomats and punish the Chinese rebels. The force, which included 5,000 U.S. soldiers, had put down the Boxer Rebellion by September.

Hay feared that other major powers would use the rebellion as a reason to demand greater control over Chinese territory. He sent out a second round of Open Door notes, now asking each power to respect China's political independence and territorial integrity, in addition to guaranteeing unrestricted access to its markets. Now, Britain, France, and Germany endorsed Hay's policy outright. With that support, Hay was able to check Russian and Japanese designs on Chinese territory. Significantly, when the powers decided that the Chinese government should pay them reparations for their property and personnel losses during the Boxer Rebellion, Hay convinced them to accept payment in cash rather than in territory. By keeping China intact and open to free trade, the United States had achieved a major foreign policy victory.

THEODORE ROOSEVELT, GEOPOLITICIAN

Roosevelt had been a driving force in the transformation of U.S. foreign policy during the McKinley administration. As assistant secretary of the navy, as a military hero, as a speaker and writer, and then as vice president, Roosevelt worked tirelessly to vault the country into the ranks of the world's great powers. He believed that Americans were a racially superior people destined for supremacy in economic and political affairs. He did not assume, however, that international supremacy would automatically accrue to the United States. A nation, like an individual, had to strive for greatness and cultivate physical and mental fitness; it had to build a military force that could convincingly project power overseas; and it had to be

The Granger Collection, NYC

Restoring Order in China. *This 1900 photograph depicts the international nature of the expeditionary force raised to defeat the Chinese rebels known as Boxers. The soldiers/ marines depicted in this photo represented these nations (left to right): Great Britain, the United States, Russia, India, Germany, France, Austria-Hungary, Italy, and Japan.*

prepared to fight. All great nations, Roosevelt declared, ultimately depended on the skill and dedication of their warriors.

Roosevelt's appetite for a good fight caused many people to rue the ascension of this "cowboy" to the White House after McKinley's assassination in 1901. But behind his blustery exterior lay a shrewd analyst of international relations. As much as he craved power for himself and the nation, he understood that the United States could not rule every portion of the globe through military or economic means. Consequently, he sought a balance of power among the industrial nations through negotiation rather than war. Such a balance would enable each imperial power to safeguard its key interests and contribute to world peace and progress.

Roosevelt had little patience with the claims to sovereignty of small countries or the human rights of weak peoples. In his eyes, the peoples of Latin America, Asia (with the exception of Japan), and Africa were racially inferior and thus incapable of self-government or industrial progress.

The Roosevelt Corollary

Ensuring U.S. dominance in the Western Hemisphere ranked high on Roosevelt's list of foreign policy objectives. In 1904, he issued a "corollary" to the Monroe Doctrine, which had asserted the right of the United States to keep European powers from meddling in hemispheric affairs. In his corollary, Roosevelt declared that the United States possessed a further right: to intervene in the domestic affairs of nations in the Western Hemisphere to quell disorder and forestall European intervention. The **Roosevelt Corollary** formalized a policy that the United States had already deployed against Cuba and Puerto Rico in 1900 and 1901. A few years later, the United States took over the Dominican Republic's customs collections and refinanced its national debt as a way of dissuading European powers from invading this island nation to collect on loans that Dominicans had not repaid.

The Panama Canal

Roosevelt had long believed, along with Alfred Mahan, that the nation needed a way of moving its ships swiftly between the Pacific and Atlantic oceans. Central America's narrow width, especially in its southern half, made it the logical place to build a canal. In fact, a French company had obtained land rights and had begun construction of a canal across the Colombian province of Panama in the 1880s. But even though a "mere" 40 miles of land separated the two oceans, the French were stymied by technological difficulties and by the financial costs of literally moving mountains. Moreover, French doctors found they were unable to check the spread of malaria and yellow fever among their workers. By the time Roosevelt entered the White House in 1901, the French Panama Company had gone bankrupt.

Roosevelt was not deterred by the French failure. He presided over the signing of the Hay-Pauncefote Treaty with Great Britain in 1901, releasing the United States from an 1850 agreement that prohibited either country from building a Central American canal without the other's participation. By threatening to build a canal from scratch across Nicaragua, Roosevelt persuaded the French company to lower the price on its half-finished Panamanian canal from $109 to $40 million. Secretary of State Hay quickly negotiated an agreement with Tomas Herran,

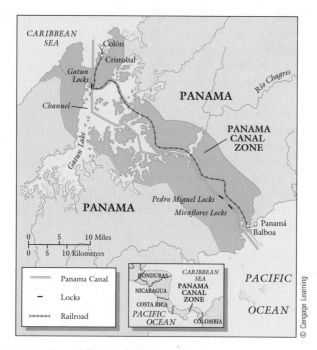

MAP 22.3   Panama Canal Zone, 1914

This map shows the route of the completed canal through Panama and the 10-mile-wide zone surrounding it that the United States controlled. The inset map locates the Canal Zone in the context of Central and South America.

the Colombian chargé d'affaires in Washington, which gave the United States a six-mile-wide strip across Panama on which to finish the canal started by the French. Colombia was to receive a one-time $10 million payment and annual rent of $250,000.

The Colombian legislature, however, rejected the proposed payment as insufficient and sent a new ambassador to the United States with instructions to ask for better terms. Roosevelt, in response, encouraged the Panamanians to revolt against Colombian rule. Panamanians had staged several rebellions in the previous 25 years, all of which had failed. The 1903 rebellion succeeded, mainly because a U.S. naval force prevented the Colombian government from landing troops in its Panama province. Meanwhile, the USS *Nashville* put U.S. troops ashore to help the new nation secure its independence. The United States formally recognized Panama as a sovereign state only two days after the rebellion against Colombia began.

Philippe Bunau-Varilla, a director of the French company from which the United States had bought the rights to the canal, declared himself Panama's diplomatic representative, even though he was a French citizen operating out of a Wall

Street law firm and hadn't set foot in Panama in 15 years. Before the true Panamanian delegation (appointed by the new Panamanian government) even reached the United States for negotiations over the canal, Bunau-Varilla and Secretary of State Hay signed the Hay–Bunau-Varilla Treaty (1903). The treaty granted the United States a 10-mile-wide canal zone in Panama in return for the package Colombia had rejected—$10 million down and $250,000 annually. Thus the United States secured its canal by dealing with Bunau-Varilla's French company rather than with the newly installed Panamanian government. The instrument through which the United States secured the Canal Zone is known in Panamanian history as "the treaty which no Panamanian signed," and it bedeviled relations between the two countries for much of the 20th century.

Roosevelt turned the building of the **Panama Canal** into a test of American ingenuity and willpower. The canal remains a testament to the labor of some 30,000 workers, imported mainly from the West Indies, who, over a 10-year period, labored 10 hours a day, six days a week, for 10 cents an hour. Roosevelt visited the canal site in 1906, the first American president to travel overseas while in office. When the canal was triumphantly opened to shipping in 1914, the British ambassador James Bryce described it as "the greatest liberty Man has ever taken with Nature." The canal shortened the voyage from San Francisco to New York by more than 8,000 miles and significantly enhanced the international prestige of the United States. The strategic importance of the canal, in turn, made the United States even more determined to preserve political order in Central America and the Caribbean.

In 1921, the United States paid the Colombian government $25 million as compensation for its loss of Panama. Panama waited more than 70 years, however, to regain control of the 10-mile-wide strip of land that Bunau-Varilla, in connivance with the U.S. government, had bargained away in 1903. President Jimmy Carter signed a treaty in 1977 providing for the reintegration of the Canal Zone into Panama, and the canal was transferred to Panama in 2000.

| Keeping the Peace in East Asia | Roosevelt strove to preserve the Open Door policy in China and the balance of power throughout the region. The chief threats came from Russia and Japan, both of whom wanted |

large chunks of China. At first, Russian expansion into Manchuria and Korea prompted Roosevelt to support Japan's 1904 attack on the Russian Pacific fleet anchored at Port Arthur, China. Once the ruinous effects of the war on Russia became clear, however, Roosevelt entered into secret negotiations to arrange a peace. He invited representatives of Japan and Russia to Portsmouth, New Hampshire, and prevailed on them to negotiate a compromise. The settlement favored Japan by perpetuating its control over most of the territories, including Korea, it had won during the brief **Russo-Japanese War**. Russia, however, avoided paying Japan a huge indemnity, and it retained Siberia, thus preserving its role as an East Asian power. Finally, Roosevelt protected China's territorial integrity by inducing the armies of both Russia and Japan to leave

© Cengage Learning

MAP 22.4 Colonial Possessions, 1900

In 1900, the British Empire was the largest in the world, followed by the French and Russian empires. The U.S. empire, if measured by the square miles of land held as colonial possessions, was small by comparison.

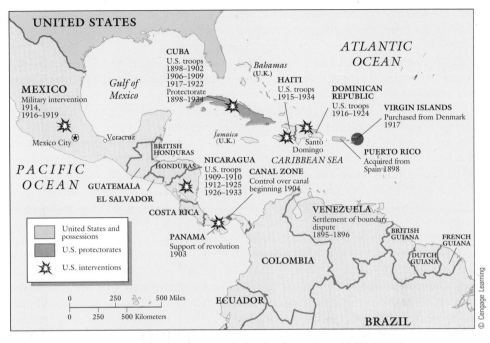

MAP 22.5   United States Presence in Latin America, 1895–1934

The United States possessed few colonies in Latin America but intervened (often repeatedly) in Mexico, Cuba, Nicaragua, Panama, Haiti, the Dominican Republic, and Venezuela to secure its economic and political interests.

Manchuria. Roosevelt's success in ending the Russo-Japanese War won him the Nobel Peace Prize in 1906; he was the first American to earn that award.

Although Roosevelt succeeded in negotiating a peace between these two world powers, he subsequently ignored, and sometimes encouraged, challenges to the sovereignty of weaker Asian nations. In a secret agreement with Japan (the Taft-Katsura Agreement of 1905), for example, the United States agreed that Japan could dominate Korea in return for a Japanese promise not to attack the Philippines. And in the Root-Takahira Agreement of 1908, the United States tacitly reversed its earlier stand on the inviolability of Chinese borders by recognizing Japanese expansion into southern Manchuria.

In Roosevelt's eyes, the overriding need to maintain peace with Japan justified ignoring the claims of Korea and, increasingly, of China. The task of American diplomacy, he believed, was first to allow the Japanese to build a secure sphere of influence in East Asia (much as the United States had done in Central America and the Caribbean), and second to encourage them to join the United States in pursuing peace rather than war. This was a delicate diplomatic task that required both sensitivity and strength, especially when anti-Japanese agitation broke out in California in 1906.

White Californians had long feared the presence of East Asian immigrants. They had pressured Congress into passing the Chinese Exclusion Act of 1882, which ended most Chinese immigration to the United States. They next turned their racism on Japanese immigrants, whose numbers in California had reached 24,000. In 1906, the San Francisco school board ordered the segregation of Asian schoolchildren so that they would not "contaminate" white children. In 1907, the California legislature debated a law to end Japanese immigration to the state. Anti-Asian riots erupted in San Francisco and Los Angeles, encouraged in part by hysterical stories in the press about the "Yellow Peril."

Outraged militarists in Japan began talking of a possible war with the United States. Roosevelt assured the Japanese government that he, too, was appalled by the Californians' behavior. In 1907, he reached a **gentlemen's agreement** with the Japanese, by which the Tokyo government promised to halt the immigration of Japanese adult male laborers to the United States in return for Roosevelt's pledge to end anti-Japanese discrimination in California. Roosevelt did his part by persuading the San Francisco school board to rescind its segregation ordinance.

At the same time, Roosevelt worried that the Tokyo government would interpret his sensitivity to Japanese honor as weakness. So he ordered the main part of the U.S. fleet, consisting of 16 battleships, to embark on a 45,000-mile world tour, including a splashy stop in Tokyo Bay. Many Americans deplored the cost of the tour and feared that the appearance of the U.S. Navy in a Japanese port would provoke military retaliation. Roosevelt brushed his critics aside, and, true to his prediction, the Japanese were impressed by the show of strength by the **Great White Fleet**. Their response seemed to lend validity to the African proverb Roosevelt often invoked: "Speak softly and carry a big stick."

Roosevelt's handling of Japan was arguably the most impressive aspect of his foreign policy. Unlike many other Americans, he refused to let racist attitudes cloud his thinking. He knew when to make concessions and when to stand firm. His policies lessened the prospect of a war with Japan while preserving a strong U.S. presence in East Asia.

WILLIAM HOWARD TAFT, DOLLAR DIPLOMAT

William Howard Taft brought impressive foreign policy credentials to the job of president. He had gained valuable experience in colonial administration as the first governor-general of the Philippines. As Roosevelt's secretary of war and chief negotiator for the Taft-Katsura agreement of 1905, he had learned a great deal about conducting diplomacy with imperialist rivals. Yet Taft lacked Roosevelt's grasp of balance-of-power politics and capacity for leadership in foreign affairs. Furthermore, Taft's secretary of state, Philander C. Knox, a corporation lawyer from Pittsburgh, was short on diplomatic expertise. Knox's conduct of foreign policy seemed directed almost entirely toward expanding opportunities for corporate investment overseas, a disposition that prompted critics to deride his policies as **"dollar diplomacy."**

Taft and Knox believed that U.S. investments would effectively substitute "dollars for bullets," and thus offer a more peaceful and less coercive way of maintaining stability and order. Taking a swipe at Roosevelt's "big stick" policy, Taft announced that "modern diplomacy is commercial."

North Wind/North Wind Picture Archives

Anti-Asian Hysteria in San Francisco. *In 1906, in the midst of a wave of anti-Asian prejudice in California, the San Francisco school board ordered the segregation of all Asian schoolchildren. Here, a nine-year-old Japanese student submits an application for admission to a public primary school and is refused by the principal, Miss M. E. Dean.*

The inability of Taft and Knox to grasp the complexities of power politics, however, led to a diplomatic reversal in East Asia. Prodded by banker associates, Knox sought to expand American economic activities in China—even in Manchuria, where they encroached on the Japanese sphere of influence. In 1911, Knox proposed that a syndicate of European and American bankers buy the Japanese-controlled South Manchurian Railroad to open up North China to international trade. Japan reacted by signing a friendship treaty with Russia, its former enemy, which signaled their joint determination to exclude American, British, and French goods from Manchurian markets. Knox's plan to purchase the railroad collapsed, and the United States' Open Door policy suffered a serious blow. Knox's further efforts to increase American trade with Central and South China triggered hostile responses from the Japanese and the Russians and contributed to the collapse of the Chinese government and the onset of the Chinese Revolution in 1911.

In the Caribbean, the United States did not hesitate to back up its dollar diplomacy with military might. When political turmoil threatened investments that American companies had made in the region, the United States simply sent in its troops. A force of marines toppled the regime of Nicaraguan dictator José Santos Zelaya after he reportedly began negotiating with a European country to build a second trans-Isthmian canal in 1910. Marines landed again in 1912 when Zelaya's successor, Adolfo Diaz, angered Nicaraguans with his pro-American policies. This time the marines were instructed to keep the Diaz regime in power, which they did by staying in Nicaragua almost continuously until 1933.

WOODROW WILSON, STRUGGLING IDEALIST

Woodrow Wilson's foreign policy in the Caribbean initially appeared no different from that of his Republican predecessors. In 1915, the United States sent troops to Haiti to put down a revolution; they remained as an army of occupation for 21 years. In 1916, when the people of the Dominican Republic (who shared the island of Hispaniola with the Haitians) refused to accept a treaty making them more or less a protectorate of the United States, Wilson forced a U.S. military government upon them. When German influence in the Danish West Indies began to expand, Wilson purchased the islands from Denmark, renamed them the Virgin Islands, and added them to the U.S. Caribbean empire. By the time Wilson left office in 1921, he had intervened militarily in the Caribbean more often than any American president before him.

Wilson's relationship with Mexico in the wake of its revolution, however, reveals that he was troubled by a foreign policy that ignored a less powerful nation's right to determine its own future. He deemed the Mexicans capable of making democracy work and, in general, showed a concern for morality and justice in foreign affairs—matters to which Roosevelt and Taft had paid scant attention. Wilson wanted U.S. foreign policy to advance democratic ideals and institutions in Mexico.

Another motivation in Wilson's Mexican dealings was a fear that political unrest in Mexico could lead to violence, social disorder, and a revolutionary government hostile to U.S. economic interests. With a U.S.-style democratic government in Mexico, Wilson believed, property rights would be respected and U.S. investments would remain secure. Wilson's desire both to encourage democracy and to limit the extent of social change made it difficult to devise a consistent foreign policy toward Mexico.

The Mexican Revolution broke out in 1910 when dictator Porfirio Diaz, who had ruled for 34 years, was overthrown by democratic forces led by Francisco Madero. Madero's talk of democratic reform frightened many foreign investors, especially those in the United States and Great Britain, who owned more than half of Mexico's real estate, 90 percent of the country's oil reserves, and practically all of its railroads. Thus, when Madero was overthrown early in 1913 by Victoriano Huerta, a conservative general who promised to protect foreign investments, the dollar diplomatists in the Taft administration and in Great Britain breathed a sigh of relief. Henry Lane Wilson, the U.S. ambassador to Mexico, had helped engineer Huerta's coup. Before close relations between the United States and Huerta could be worked out, however, Huerta's men murdered Madero.

Woodrow Wilson, who became president shortly after Madero's assassination in 1913, refused to recognize Huerta's "government of butchers" and demanded that Mexico hold democratic elections. Wilson favored Venustiano Carranza and **Francisco ("Pancho") Villa**, two enemies of Huerta who commanded rebel armies and who claimed to be democrats. In April 1914, Wilson used the arrest of several U.S. sailors by Huerta's troops as a reason to send a fleet into Mexican waters and to order the U.S. Marines to go ashore at the Mexican port city of Veracruz. In the resulting battle between U.S. and Mexican forces, 19 Americans and 126 Mexicans were killed. The battle brought the two countries dangerously close to war. American control over Veracruz weakened Huerta's regime to the point where Carranza was able to take power.

Carranza did not behave as Wilson had expected, however. Carranza proposed a bold land reform program that would redistribute property from the rich to the poor and that would transfer developmental rights on oil lands from foreign corporations, including U.S. petroleum companies, to the Mexican government. An angry Wilson now threw his support to Pancho Villa, who seemed more willing than Carranza to protect U.S. oil interests. When Carranza's forces defeated Villa's forces in 1915, Wilson reluctantly withdrew his support of Villa and prepared to recognize the Carranza government.

Furious that Wilson had abandoned him, Villa and his soldiers pulled 18 U.S. citizens from a train in northern Mexico and murdered them, along with another 17 in an attack on Columbus, New Mexico. Determined to punish Villa, Wilson received permission from Carranza to send a U.S. expeditionary force under General John J. Pershing into Mexico to hunt down Villa's "bandits." Pershing's troops pursued Villa's forces 300 miles into Mexico but failed to catch them. The U.S. troops did, however, clash twice with Mexican troops under Carranza's command, once again bringing the countries to the brink of war. The United States, about to enter the First World War, could not afford a fight with Mexico; in 1917, Wilson quietly ordered Pershing's troops home and grudgingly recognized the Carranza government.

Wilson's policies toward Mexico from 1913 to 1917 seemed to have produced few concrete results, except to reinforce an already deep antagonism among Mexicans toward the United States. His repeated changes in strategy, moreover, seemed to indicate a lack of skill and decisiveness in foreign affairs. Actually, however, Wilson recognized something that Roosevelt and Taft had not: that more and more peoples of the world were determined to control their own destinies. The United States, under Wilson, was looking for a way to support their democratic aspirations while also safeguarding its own economic interests. The First World War would make this quest for a balance between democratic principles and national self-interest all the more urgent.

CONCLUSION

We can assess the dramatic turn in U.S. foreign policy after 1898 either in relation to the foreign policies of rival world powers or against America's own democratic ideals. By the first standard, U.S. foreign policy looks impressive. The United States achieved its major objectives in world affairs: It tightened its control over the Western Hemisphere and projected its military and economic power into Asia. It did so while sacrificing relatively few American lives and while constraining the jingoistic appetite for truly extensive military adventure and conquest. The United States added only 125,000 square miles to its empire in the years from 1870 to

1900, while Great Britain, France, and Germany enlarged their empires by 4.7, 3.5, and 1.0 million square miles, respectively. Relatively few foreigners were subjected to U.S. colonial rule. By contrast, in 1900, the British Empire extended more than 12 million square miles and embraced one-fourth of the world's population. At times, American rule could be brutal, as it was to Filipino soldiers and civilians alike, but on the whole it was no more severe than British or French rule and significantly less severe than that of German, Belgian, or Japanese imperialists. McKinley, Roosevelt, Taft, and Wilson all placed limits on American expansion and avoided, until 1917, extensive foreign entanglements and wars.

If measured against the standard of America's own democratic ideals, however, U.S. foreign policy after 1898 must be judged more harshly. It demeaned the peoples of the Philippines, Puerto Rico, Guam, Cuba, and Colombia as inferior and primitive and denied them the right to govern themselves. In choosing to behave like the imperialist powers of Europe, the United States abandoned its longstanding claim to being a different kind of nation—one that valued liberty more than power.

Many Americans of the time judged their nation by both standards and thus faced a dilemma that would extend throughout the 20th century. On the one hand, they believed with Roosevelt that the size, economic strength, and honor of the United States required it to accept the role of world power and policeman. On the other hand, they continued to believe with Wilson that they had a mission to spread the democratic values of 1776 to the farthest reaches of the earth. The Mexico example demonstrates how hard it was for the United States to reconcile these two very different approaches to world affairs.

23

WAR AND SOCIETY, 1914–1920

T HE FIRST WORLD WAR broke out in Europe in August 1914. The **Triple Alliance**
of Germany, Austria-Hungary, and the Ottoman Empire squared off against
the **Triple Entente** of Great Britain, France, and Russia. The United States
entered the war on the side of the Entente (the Allies, or Allied Powers, as they
came to be called) in 1917. Over the next year and a half, the United States converted its large, sprawling economy into a disciplined war production machine,
raised a 5-million-man army, and provided both the war matériel and troops that
helped propel the Allies to victory.

The war also convulsed American society more deeply than any event since
the Civil War. This was the first "total" war, meaning that combatants
devoted virtually all of their resources to the fight. The U.S. government had
no choice but to pursue a degree of industrial control and social regimentation
that was unprecedented in American history. This level of government control
was controversial in a society that had long distrusted state power. Moreover,
significant numbers of Americans from a variety of constituencies opposed the
war. To overcome this opposition, Wilson couched American war aims in disinterested and idealistic terms: The United States, he claimed, wanted a **"peace
without victory,"** a "war for democracy," and liberty for the world's oppressed
peoples.

Although many people in the United States and abroad responded enthusiastically to Wilson's ideals, Wilson needed England and France's support to deliver
peace without victory, and this support never came. In America, protests spread
among groups who believed that war was undermining liberty, equality, and economic opportunity for the poor. Wilson supported repressive policies to silence
these rebels and to enforce unity and conformity on the American people. In the
process, he tarnished the ideals for which America had been fighting.

CHRONOLOGY

1914	First World War breaks out (July–August)
1915	German submarine sinks the *Lusitania* (May 7)
1916	Woodrow Wilson unveils peace initiative
	Wilson reelected as "peace president"
1917	Germany resumes unrestricted submarine warfare (February)
	Tsar Nicholas II overthrown in Russia (March)
	United States enters the war (April 6)
	Committee on Public Information established
	Congress passes Selective Service Act and Espionage Act
	War Industries Board established
	Lenin's Bolsheviks come to power in Russia (November)
1918	Lenin signs treaty with Germany, pulls Russia out of war (March)
	Germany launches offensive on western front (March–April)
	Congress passes Sabotage Act and Sedition Act
	Allied Powers and United States advance toward Germany (April–October)
	Eugene V. Debs jailed for antiwar speech
	Germany signs armistice (November 11)
1919	Treaty of Versailles signed (June 28)
	Chicago race riot (July)
	Wilson suffers stroke (October 2)
	Police strike in Boston
	Eighteenth Amendment (Prohibition) ratified
1919–1920	Steelworkers strike in Midwest
	Red Scare prompts "Palmer raids"
	Senate refuses to ratify Treaty of Versailles
	Universal Negro Improvement Association grows under Marcus Garvey's leadership
1920	Anarchists Sacco and Vanzetti convicted of murder

EUROPE'S DESCENT INTO WAR

Europe's descent into war began on June 28, 1914, in Sarajevo, Bosnia, when a Bosnian nationalist assassinated Archduke Franz Ferdinand, heir to the Austro-Hungarian throne. This act was meant to protest the Austro-Hungarian imperial presence in the Balkans and to encourage the Bosnians, Croatians, and other Balkan peoples to join the Serbs in establishing independent nations. Austria-Hungary responded to this provocation on July 28 by declaring war on Serbia, holding it responsible for the archduke's murder.

The conflict might have remained local if an intricate series of treaties had not divided Europe into two hostile camps. Germany, Austria-Hungary, and Italy, the so-called Triple Alliance, had promised to come to each other's aid if attacked. Italy would soon opt out of this alliance, to be replaced by the Ottoman Empire. Arrayed against the nations of the Triple Alliance were Britain, France, and Russia in the Triple Entente. Russia was obligated by another treaty to defend Serbia against Austria-Hungary, and consequently on July 30, it mobilized its armed forces to go to Serbia's aid. That brought Germany into the conflict to protect Austria-Hungary from Russian attack. On August 3, German troops struck not at Russia but at France, Russia's western ally. To reach France, German troops had marched through neutral Belgium. On August 4, Britain reacted by declaring war on Germany. Within the space of only a few weeks, Europe was engulfed in war.

Complicated alliances and defense treaties of the European nations undoubtedly hastened the rush toward war. But equally important was the competition among the European powers to build the strongest economies, the largest armies and navies, and the grandest colonial empires. Britain and Germany, in particular, were engaged in a bitter struggle for European and world supremacy. Few Europeans had any idea that these military buildups might lead to a terrible war that would kill millions and expose the barbarity lurking in their civilization. Historians now believe that several advisers close to the German emperor, Kaiser Wilhelm II, were eager to engage Russia and France in a fight for supremacy on the European continent. They expected that a European war would be swift and decisive—in Germany's favor.

Victory was not swift. The first wartime use of machine guns and barbed wire made defense against attack easier than staging an offensive. (Both tanks and airplanes had been invented, but military strategists were slow to put them to offensive use.) On the western front, after the initial German attack narrowly failed to take Paris in 1914, the two opposing armies confronted each other along a battle line stretching from Belgium in the north to the Swiss border in the south. Troops dug trenches to protect themselves from artillery bombardment and poison gas attacks. Commanders on both sides mounted suicidal ground assaults on the enemy by sending tens of thousands of infantry, armed only with rifles, bayonets, and grenades, out of the trenches and directly into enemy fire. Barbed wire further retarded forward progress, enabling enemy artillery and machine guns to cut down appalling numbers of men. Many of those who were not killed in combat succumbed to disease that spread rapidly in cold, wet, and rat-infested trenches. In eastern Europe, the armies of Germany and Austria-Hungary squared off against those of Russia and Serbia. Although that front did not employ trench warfare, the combat was no less lethal. By the time the First World War ended, an estimated 8.5 million soldiers had died, and more than twice that number had been wounded. Total casualties, both military and civilian, had reached 37 million.

American Neutrality

Soon after the fighting began, Woodrow Wilson told Americans that this was a European war; neither side was threatening a vital American interest. The United States would therefore proclaim its neutrality and maintain normal relations with both sides while seeking to secure peace. Normal relations meant that the United States would continue trading with both camps. Wilson's neutrality policy met with opposition, especially from Theodore Roosevelt, who was convinced that the United States should join the Entente to check German power and expansionism. A majority of Americans, however, applauded Wilson's determination to keep the country out of war.

Neutrality was easier to proclaim than to achieve, however. Many Americans, especially those with economic and political power, identified culturally more with Britain than with Germany. They shared with the English a language, a common ancestry, and a commitment to liberty. Meanwhile, Germany's acceptance of monarchical rule, the prominence of militarists in German politics, and its lack of democratic traditions inclined U.S. officials to judge Germany harshly.

The United States had strong economic ties to Great Britain as well. In 1914, the United States exported more than $800 million in goods to Britain and its allies, compared with $170 million to Germany and Austria-Hungary (which came to be known as the Central Powers). As soon as the war began, the British and then the French turned to the United States for food, clothing, munitions, and other war supplies. The U.S. economy, which had been languishing in 1914, enjoyed a boom as a result. Meanwhile, the British navy was blockading German ports, shrinking the United States' already limited trade with Germany. By 1916, U.S. exports to the Central Powers had plummeted to barely $1 million, a fall of more than 99 percent in two years.

The Wilson administration protested the British navy's search and occasional seizure of American merchant ships, but it never retaliated by suspending loans or exports to Great Britain. In failing to protect its right to trade with Germany, the United States compromised its neutrality and allowed itself to be drawn into war.

Submarine Warfare   To combat British control of the seas and to check the flow of U.S. goods to the Allies, Germany unveiled a terrifying new weapon, the *Unterseeboot*, or U-boat, the first militarily effective submarine. Early in 1915, Germany announced its intent to use its U-boats to sink on sight enemy ships en route to the British Isles. On May 7, 1915, without warning, a German U-boat torpedoed the British passenger liner *Lusitania*, en route

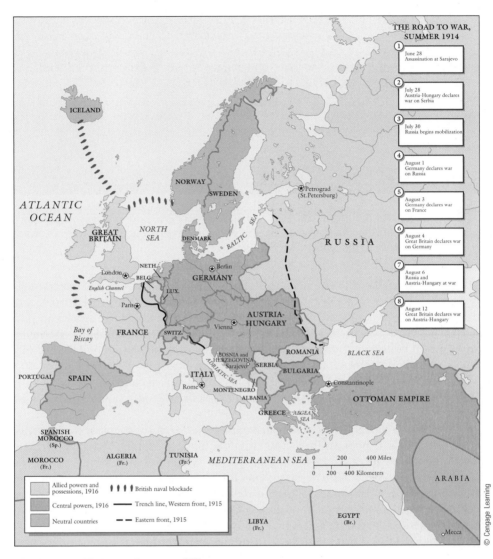

MAP 23.1 Europe Goes to War

In the First World War, Great Britain, France, and Russia squared off against Germany, Austria-Hungary, and the Ottoman Empire. Most of the fighting occurred in Europe along the western front in France (black line) or the eastern front in Russia (dotted line). This map also shows Britain's blockade of German ports. British armies based in Egypt (then a British colony) clashed with Ottoman armies in Arabia and other parts of the Ottoman Empire.

from New York to London. The ship sank in 22 minutes, killing 1,198 men, women, and children, 128 of them U.S. citizens. Shocked by the loss of life, the United States accused Germany of a barbaric act. The circumstances surrounding the sinking of the *Lusitania*, however, were more complicated than most Americans realized.

Gassed, by John Singer Sargent. *An artist renders the horror of a poison gas attack in the First World War. The Germans were the first to use this new and brutal weapon, which contributed greatly to the terror of war.*

Before its sailing, the Germans had alleged that the *Lusitania* was secretly carrying a large store of munitions to Great Britain (a charge that proved true), and that it therefore was subject to U-boat attack. Germany had warned American passengers not to travel on British passenger ships that carried munitions. Germany also claimed that the purpose of the U-boat attacks—the disruption of Allied supply lines—was no different from Britain's purpose in blockading German ports. If a submarine attack seemed more reprehensible than a conventional sea battle, the Germans argued, it was no more so than the British attempt to starve the German people into submission with a blockade.

American political leaders might have used the *Lusitania* incident to denounce both Germany's U-boat strategy and Britain's blockade. Only Secretary of State Bryan did so, however, and his stand proved so unpopular in Washington that he resigned from office; Wilson chose the pro-British Robert Lansing to take his place. Wilson denounced the sinking of the *Lusitania* and demanded that Germany pledge never to launch another attack on the citizens of neutral nations. Germany temporarily acquiesced to Wilson's demand.

In March 1916, however, a German submarine torpedoed the French passenger liner *Sussex*, causing a heavy loss of life and injuring several Americans. Such attacks strengthened the hand of Theodore Roosevelt and others who had been arguing that war with Germany was inevitable and that the United States must prepare to fight. Wilson in response sought and won congressional approval for bills to increase the size of the army and navy, tighten federal control over National Guard forces, and authorize the building of a merchant fleet. Still not ready to concede the inevitability of war, however, Wilson intensified his diplomatic initiatives to secure a peace, angering the British with his insistence on an impartial, negotiated settlement in which the claims of the Allies and Central Powers would be treated with respect.

The Peace Movement

Underlying Wilson's 1916 peace initiative was a vision of a new world order in which relations between nations would be governed by negotiation rather than war and in which justice would replace power as the fundamental principle of diplomacy. On May 27, 1916, Wilson formally declared his support for what he would later call the League of Nations, an international parliament dedicated to the pursuit of peace, security, and justice for all the world's peoples.

Many Americans supported Wilson's efforts to commit national prestige to the cause of international peace. Carrie Chapman Catt, president of the National American Woman Suffrage Association, and Jane Addams, founder of the Women's Peace Party, opposed the war. A substantial pacifist group emerged among the nation's Protestant clergy. Midwestern progressives such as Robert La Follette, William Jennings Bryan, and George Norris urged the United States to steer clear of this European conflict, as did leading socialists such as Eugene V. Debs. In April 1916, many of the country's most prominent progressives and socialists joined hands in the American Union Against Militarism, pressuring Wilson to continue pursuing the path of peace. The country's sizable Irish and German ethnic populations, who wanted to block a formal military alliance with Great Britain, also supported Wilson's peace campaign. Wilson embraced the portrait of himself as the "peace president" and rode the slogan "He kept us out of war" to victory over Republican Charles Evans Hughes in the 1916 presidential race.

On December 16, 1916, Wilson sent a peace note to the belligerent governments on both sides, entreating them to consider ending the conflict. Appearing before the Senate on January 22, 1917, Wilson reaffirmed his commitment to the League of Nations. For such a league to succeed, Wilson argued, it would have to be handed a sturdy peace settlement. This entailed a "peace without victory," one that refused to crown a victor or humiliate a loser. Only such a peace, Wilson argued, would last.

Wilson listed the crucial principles of a lasting peace: freedom of the seas; disarmament; and the right of every people to self-determination, democratic self-government, and security against aggression. Wilson was proposing to allow all of the world's peoples, regardless of their country's size or strength, to achieve political independence and to participate as equals in world affairs. These views, rarely expressed by the leader of a world power, stirred the masses of Europe and elsewhere caught in deadly conflict.

German Escalation   The German military responded to Wilson's entreaties for peace by preparing to throw its full military might at France and Britain. On February 25, 1917, the British intercepted and passed on to the president a telegram from Germany's foreign secretary, Arthur Zimmermann, to the German minister in Mexico. The infamous **Zimmermann telegram** instructed the minister to ask the Mexican government to attack the United States in the event of war between Germany and the United States. In return, Germany would pay the Mexicans a large fee and regain for them the "lost provinces" of Texas, New Mexico, and Arizona. Wilson, Congress, and the American public were outraged by this proposed deal.

In March, news arrived that Tsar Nicholas II's autocratic regime in Russia had collapsed and had been replaced by a liberal-democratic government under the leadership of Alexander Kerensky. As long as the tsar ruled Russia and stood to benefit from the Central Powers' defeat, Wilson could not honestly claim that America's going to war against Germany would bring democracy to Europe. The fall of the tsar and Russia's fledgling democratic government's need for assistance gave Wilson the rationale he needed to justify American intervention.

Appearing before a joint session of Congress on April 2, Wilson declared that the United States must enter the war because "the world must be made safe for democracy." He continued:

> We shall fight for the things which we have always carried nearest our hearts—for democracy, for the right of those who submit to authority to have a voice in their own Governments, for the rights and liberties of small nations, for a universal dominion of right by such a concert of free peoples as shall bring peace and safety to all nations and make the world itself at last free. To such a task we dedicate our lives and our fortunes.

After a few days of debate, Congress voted 373–50 in the House and 82–6 in the Senate to declare war on the Central Powers. Wilson understood all too well the risks of his undertaking. A few days before his speech to Congress, he had confided to a journalist his worry that the American people, once at war, will "forget there ever was such a thing as tolerance. To fight you must be brutal and ruthless, and the spirit of ruthless brutality will enter into the very fiber of our national life, infecting Congress, the courts, the policeman on the beat, the man in the street." Still, Wilson was hopeful that America could make this struggle "a war to end all wars" and use it as an occasion to strengthen liberty and democracy in countries where these principles were weak.

AMERICAN INTERVENTION

The entry of the United States into the war gave the Allies the muscle they needed to defeat the Central Powers, but it almost came too late. Germany's resumption of unrestricted submarine warfare took a frightful toll on Allied shipping. From February through July 1917, German subs sank almost 4 million tons of shipping, more than one-third of Britain's entire merchant fleet. One of every four large freighters departing Britain in those months never returned; at one point, the British Isles were down to a mere four weeks of provisions. American intervention ended Britain's vulnerability in dramatic fashion. U.S. and British naval commanders now grouped merchant ships into convoys and provided them with warship escorts through the most dangerous stretches of the North Atlantic. Destroyers armed with depth charges were particularly effective as escorts. Their shallow draft made them invulnerable to torpedoes, and their acceleration and speed allowed them to pursue slow-moving U-boats. The U.S. and British navies had begun to use sound waves (later called "sonar") to pinpoint the location of underwater craft, and this new technology increased the effectiveness of destroyer attacks. By the end of 1917, the tonnage of Allied shipping lost each month to U-boat attacks had declined by two-thirds, from almost 1 million tons in April to 350,000 tons in December.

The French and British armies had bled themselves white by taking the offensive in 1916 and 1917 and had scarcely budged the trench lines. The Germans had been content in those years simply to hold their trench position in the West until they defeated the Russians in the East. This they did in late 1917 when a second Russian revolution overthrew Kerensky's liberal-democratic government and brought to power a revolutionary socialist government under Vladimir Lenin and his Bolshevik Party. Lenin pulled Russia out of the war on the grounds that the war did not serve the best interests of the working classes, that it was a conflict between rival capitalist elites interested only in wealth and power (and indifferent to the slaughter of soldiers in the trenches).

Lenin also published the texts of secret Allied treaties showing that Britain and France, like Germany, had plotted to enlarge their nations and empires through war. The revelation that the Allies were fighting for land and riches rather than democratic principles outraged large numbers of people in France and Great Britain, demoralized Allied troops, and threw the French and British governments into disarray. The treaties also embarrassed Wilson, who had brought America into the war to fight for democracy, not territory. Wilson quickly moved to restore the Allies' credibility by unveiling, in January 1918, a concrete program for peace. His **Fourteen Points** reaffirmed America's commitment to an international system governed by laws rather than by might and renounced territorial aggrandizement as a legitimate war aim. This document provided the ideological cement that held the Allies together at a critical moment.

The Allies needed every bit of fortitude they could muster. In March and April 1918, Germany sent British and French troops reeling by launching a huge offensive against Allied positions. German troops advanced 10 miles a day—a faster pace than any on the western front since the earliest days of the war—until they reached the Marne River, within striking distance of Paris. The French government prepared to evacuate the city. At this perilous moment, a large American army—fresh, well equipped, and oblivious to the horrors of trench warfare—arrived to reinforce what remained of the French lines.

These American troops, part of the American Expeditionary Force (AEF) commanded by General **John J. Pershing**, had begun landing in France almost a year earlier. The United States had had to create a modern army from scratch, because its existing force was so small, ranking only 17th in the world. Men had to be drafted, trained, and supplied with food and equipment; ships for transporting them to Europe had to be found or built. In France, Pershing put his troops through additional training before committing them to battle. He was determined that the American soldiers—or "doughboys," as they were called—should acquit themselves well on the battlefield. The army he ordered into battle to counter the German spring offensive of 1918 fought well. Many American soldiers fell, but the German offensive ground to a halt. Paris was saved, and Germany's best chance for victory slipped from its grasp.

Buttressed by this show of AEF strength, the Allied troops staged a major offensive of their own in late September. Millions of Allied troops (including more than a million from the AEF) advanced across the 200-mile-wide Argonne Forest in

France, cutting German supply lines. By late October, they had reached the German border. Faced with an invasion of their homeland and with rapidly mounting popular dissatisfaction with the war, German leaders asked for an armistice, to be followed by peace negotiations based on Wilson's Fourteen Points. Having forced the Germans to agree to numerous concessions, the Allies ended the war on November 11, 1918.

MOBILIZING FOR "TOTAL" WAR

Compared to Europe, the United States suffered little from the war. The deaths of 112,000 American soldiers paled in comparison to European losses of 900,000 by Great Britain, 1.2 million by Austria-Hungary, 1.4 million by France, 1.7 million by Russia, and 2 million by Germany. The U.S. civilian population was spared most of the war's ravages—the destruction of homes and industries, the shortages of food and medicine, the spread of disease—that afflicted millions of Europeans. Only with the flu epidemic that swept across the Atlantic from Europe in 1919 to claim approximately 500,000 lives did Americans briefly experience wholesale suffering and death.

Still, the war had a profound effect on American society. Every military engagement the United States had fought since the Civil War—the Indian wars, the Spanish-American War, the American-Filipino War, the Boxer Rebellion, the Latin American interventions—had been limited in scope. Even the troop mobilizations that seemed large at the time—the more than 100,000 needed to fight the Spanish and then the Filipinos—did not overwhelm American resources.

The First World War was different. It was a "total" war for which every nation involved in the conflict had to mobilize virtually all its manpower and economic resources. The scale of the effort in the United States became apparent early in 1917 when Wilson asked Congress for a conscription law that would permit the federal government to raise a multimillion-man army. The United States would also have to devote much of its agricultural, transportation, industrial, and population resources to the war effort if it wished to end the European stalemate. Who would organize this massive effort? Who would pay for it? Would Americans accept the sacrifice and regimentation it would demand? These were vexing questions for a nation long committed to individual liberty, small government, and a weak military.

Organizing Industry   At first, Wilson pursued a decentralized approach to mobilization, delegating tasks to local defense councils throughout the country. When that effort failed, Wilson created centralized federal agencies, each charged with supervising nationwide activity in its assigned economic sector.

The success of these agencies varied. The Food Administration, headed by mining engineer and executive Herbert Hoover, substantially increased production of basic foodstuffs and put in place an efficient distribution system that delivered food to millions of troops and European civilians. Treasury Secretary William McAdoo, head of the U.S. Railroad Administration, also performed well in shifting the rail system from private to public control, coordinating dense train traffic, and making capital improvements that allowed goods to move rapidly to eastern ports, where they were loaded onto ships and sent to Europe. At the other extreme, the Aircraft Production Board and Emergency Fleet Corporation did a poor job of supplying the Allies with combat aircraft and merchant vessels. On balance, the U.S. economy performed wonders in supplying troops with uniforms, food, rifles, munitions, and other basic items; it did much less well in producing sophisticated weapons and machines such as artillery, aircraft, and ships.

Most of the new government agencies were more powerful on paper than in fact. Consider, for example, the **War Industries Board (WIB)**, an administrative body established by Wilson in July 1917 to harness manufacturing might to military needs. The WIB floundered for its first nine months, lacking the statutory authority to force manufacturers and the military to adopt its plans. Only the appointment of Wall Street investment banker Bernard Baruch as WIB chairman in March 1918 turned the agency around. Rather than force manufacturers to do the government's bidding, Baruch permitted industrialists to charge high prices for their products. He won exemptions from antitrust laws for corporations that complied with his requests. In general, he made war production too lucrative an activity to resist; however, he did not hesitate to unleash his wrath on corporations that resisted WIB enticements.

Baruch's forceful leadership worked reasonably well throughout his nine months in office. War production increased, and manufacturers discovered the financial benefits of cooperation between the public and private sectors. But Baruch's favoritism toward large corporations hurt smaller competitors. Moreover, the cozy relationship between government and corporations that he encouraged violated the progressive pledge to protect the people from the "interests." Achieving cooperation by boosting corporate profits, finally, was a costly way for the government to do business. The costs of the war soared to $33 billion, a figure more than three times expectations.

Securing Labor   War increased the demand for industrial labor while cutting the supply. European immigrants had long been the most important source of new labor for American industry, and during the war they stopped coming. Meanwhile, millions of workers already in America were conscripted into the military and thus lost to industry.

Manufacturers responded to the labor shortage by recruiting new sources of labor from the rural South; 500,000 African Americans migrated to northern cities between 1916 and 1920. Another half-million white southerners followed the same path during that period. Hundreds of thousands of Mexicans fled their revolution-ridden homeland for the American Southwest and Midwest. Approximately 40,000 northern women found work as streetcar conductors, railroad workers, metalworkers, munitions makers, and in other jobs customarily reserved for men. The number of female clerical workers doubled between 1910 and 1920, with many of these women finding work in government war bureaucracies. Altogether, a million women toiled in war-related industries.

These workers alleviated but did not eliminate the nation's labor shortage. Unemployment, which had hovered around 8.5 percent in 1915, plunged to 1.2 percent in 1918. Quick to recognize the benefits of the tight labor market, workers quit jobs they did not like and took part in strikes and other collective actions in large numbers. From 1916 to 1920, more than 1 million workers went on strike every year. Union membership almost doubled, from 2.6 million in 1915 to 5.1 million in 1920. Workers commonly sought higher wages and shorter hours through strikes and unionization. Wages rose an average of 137 percent from 1915 to 1920, although inflation largely negated these gains. The average workweek declined in that same period from 55 to 51 hours. Workers also struck in response to managerial attempts to speed up production and tighten discipline. As time passed, increasing numbers of workers began to wonder why the war for democracy in Europe had no counterpart in their factories at home. "Industrial democracy" became the battle cry of an awakened labor movement.

Wilson's willingness to include labor in his 1916 progressive coalition reflected his awareness of labor's potential power. In 1918, he bestowed prestige on the newly formed **National War Labor Board (NWLB)** by appointing former president William Howard Taft to be co-chair alongside Samuel Gompers, president of the American Federation of Labor. The NWLB brought together representatives of labor, industry, and the public to resolve labor disputes.

Raising an Army   To raise an army, the Wilson administration committed itself to conscription—the drafting of most men of a certain age, irrespective of their family's wealth, ethnic background, or social standing. The Selective Service Act of May 1917 empowered the administration to do just that. By war's end, local Selective Service boards had registered 24 million young men age 18 and older and had drafted nearly 3 million of them into the military; another 2 million volunteered for service.

Relatively few men resisted the draft, even among recently arrived immigrants. Foreign-born men constituted 18 percent of the armed forces—a percentage greater than their share of the total population. Almost 400,000 African Americans served, representing approximately 10 percent of the armed forces, the same as the percentage of African Americans in the total population.

The U.S. Army, under the command of Chief of Staff Peyton March and General John J. Pershing, faced the difficult task of fashioning these ethnically and racially diverse millions into a professional fighting force. Teaching raw recruits to fight was hard enough, Pershing and March observed; the generals refused the task of teaching them to put aside their racial prejudices. Rather than integrate the armed forces, they segregated black soldiers from white. Most African Americans were assigned to all-black units and barred from combat. Being stripped of a combat role was particularly galling to blacks, who, in previous wars, had proven to be among the best American fighters. Pershing was fully aware of the African American contribution. He had commanded African American troops in the Tenth Cavalry, the all-black regiment that had distinguished itself in the Spanish-American War. Pershing's military reputation had depended so heavily on the black troops who fought for him that he had acquired the nickname Black Jack.

For a time, the military justified its intensified discrimination against blacks by referring to the results of rudimentary IQ (intelligence quotient) tests administered by psychologists to 2 million AEF soldiers. These tests allegedly "proved" that native-born Americans and immigrants from the British Isles, Germany, and Scandinavia were well endowed with intelligence, whereas African Americans and immigrants from southern and eastern Europe were poorly endowed. The tests were scientifically so ill conceived, however, that their findings revealed nothing about the true distribution of intelligence in the soldier population. Their most sensational revelation was that more than half of the soldiers in the AEF—white and black—were "morons," men who had failed to reach the mental age of 13. After trying to absorb the apparent news that most U.S. soldiers were feebleminded, the military sensibly rejected the pseudoscience on which these intelligence findings were based. In 1919, it discontinued the IQ testing program.

Given the racial and ethnic differences among American troops and the short time Pershing and his staff had to train recruits, the AEF's performance was impressive. The United States increased the army from a mere 100,000 to 5 million in little more than a year. The Germans sank no troop ships, nor were any soldiers killed during the dangerous Atlantic crossing. In combat, U.S. troops became known for their sharp-shooting skills. The most decorated soldier in the AEF was Sergeant Alvin C. York of Tennessee, who captured 35 machine guns, took 132 prisoners, and killed 17 German soldiers with 17 bullets. One of the most decorated AEF units was **New York's 369th Regiment**, a black unit recruited in Harlem. Bowing to pressure from civil rights groups to allow some black troops to fight, Pershing had offered the 369th to the French army. The 369th served in forward Allied trenches along with French troops for 191 days (longer than any other U.S. regiment), and scored several major successes. In gratitude for its service, the French government decorated the unit with one of its highest honors—the *Croix de Guerre* (War Cross).

Paying the Bills   The government incurred large debts buying food, uniforms, munitions, weapons, vehicles, and sundry other items for the U.S. military. To help pay its bills, the government slapped the rich with a 67 percent income tax and a 25 percent inheritance tax. Corporations were ordered to pay an "excess profits" tax. Progressives wanted to make sure that all Americans would sacrifice something for the war and that monied interests would not be able to use the war to enrich themselves.

Tax revenues, however, provided only about one-third of the $33 billion that the government ultimately spent on the war. The rest came from the sale of **Liberty Bonds**. These 30-year government bonds offered individual purchasers a return of 3.5 percent in annual interest. The government offered five bond issues between 1917 and 1920 and all quickly sold out, thanks, in no small measure, to the high-powered sales pitch orchestrated by Treasury Secretary William G. McAdoo that equated bond purchases with patriotic duty.

The 369th Returns to New York. *Denied the opportunity to fight in the U.S. Army, this unit fought for the French. For the length and distinction of its service in the front lines, this entire unit was awarded the* Croix de Guerre *(War Cross) by the French government.*

**Arousing
Patriotic Ardor**   The Treasury's bond campaign was only one aspect of a wide-ranging government effort to arouse public support for the war. In 1917, Wilson set up a new agency, the **Committee on Public Information (CPI)**, to popularize the war. Under the chairmanship of George Creel, a midwestern progressive and a muckraker, the CPI distributed 75 million copies of pamphlets explaining U.S. war aims in several languages. It trained a force of 75,000 "Four-Minute Men" to deliver succinct, uplifting war speeches to numerous groups in their home cities and towns. It papered the walls of virtually every public institution (and many private ones) with posters, placed advertisements in mass-circulation magazines, sponsored exhibitions, and peppered newspaper editors with thousands of press releases on the progress of the war.

Faithful to his muckraking past, Creel wanted to give the people the facts of the war, believing that well-informed citizens would see the wisdom of Wilson's policies. He also saw his work as an opportunity to achieve the progressive goal of uniting all Americans into a single moral community. Americans everywhere

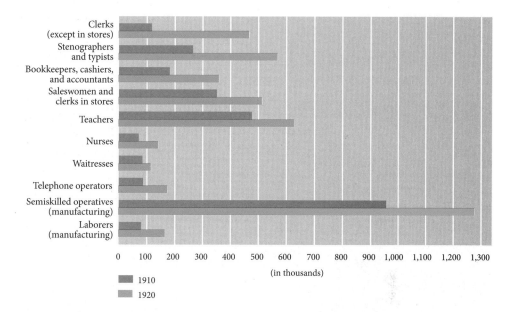

Occupations with Largest Increase in Women, 1910–1920

Source: Joseph A. Hill, *Women in Gainful Occupations*, 1870–1920, U.S. Bureau of the Census, Monograph no. 9 (Washington, D.C.: Government Printing Office, 1929), p. 33.

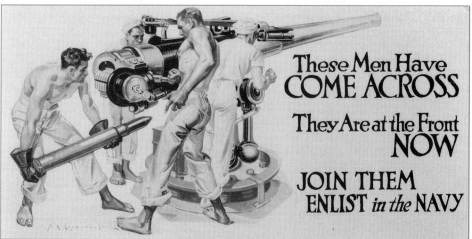

Recruiting Poster, First World War, 1917. *The government plastered public institutions with recruiting posters. This one represents navy work as glamorous, masculine, and brave.*

learned that the United States had entered the war "to make the world safe for democracy," to help the world's weaker peoples achieve self-determination, and to bring a measure of justice into the conduct of international affairs. Americans were asked to affirm those ideals by doing everything they could to support the war.

National Archives and Records Administration

Women Doing "Men's Work." *Labor shortages during the war allowed thousands of women to take industrial jobs customarily reserved for men. Here women operate pneumatic hammers at the Midvale Steel and Ordnance Company, Nicetown, Pennsylvania, 1918.*

This uplifting message affected the American people, although not necessarily in ways anticipated by CPI propagandists. Workers, women, European ethnics, and African Americans began demanding that America live up to its democratic ideals at home as well as abroad. Workers rallied to the cry of "industrial democracy." Women seized on the democratic fervor to bring their fight for suffrage to a successful conclusion. African Americans began to dream that the war might deliver them from second-class citizenship. European ethnics believed that Wilson's support of their countrymen's rights abroad would improve their own chances for success in the United States.

Although the CPI had helped to unleash it, this new democratic enthusiasm troubled Creel and others in the Wilson administration. The United States, after all, was still divided along class, ethnic, and racial lines. Workers and industrialists regarded each other with suspicion. Cultural differences compounded this class division: The working class was heavily ethnic in composition, and the industrial and political elites consisted mainly of the native-born whose families had been Americans for generations. Progressives had fought hard to overcome these divisions. They had tamed the power of capitalists, improved the condition of workers, encouraged the Americanization of immigrants, and articulated a new, more inclusive idea of who could belong to the American nation.

But their work was far from complete when the war broke out. German immigrants still formed the largest foreign-born population group at 2.3 million. Another 2.3 million immigrants came from some part of the Austro-Hungarian Empire, and more than 1 million Americans—native-born and immigrants— supported the Socialist Party and the Industrial Workers of the World (IWW), both of which opposed the war. The decision to authorize the CPI's comprehensive unity campaign indicates that the progressives understood how widespread the discord was. Still, they had not anticipated that the promotion of democratic ideals at home would exacerbate, rather than lessen, the nation's social and cultural divisions.

Wartime Repression   By early 1918, the CPI's campaign had developed a darker, more coercive side. Inflammatory advertisements called on patriots to report on neighbors, coworkers, and ethnics they suspected of subverting the war effort. Propagandists called on all immigrants, especially those from central, southern, and eastern Europe, to pledge themselves to "100 percent Americanism" and to repudiate all ties to their homeland, native language, and ethnic customs. The CPI aroused hostility toward Germans by spreading tales of German atrocities and encouraging the public to see movies such as *The Prussian Cur* and *The Beast of Berlin*. The Justice Department arrested thousands of German and Austrian immigrants suspected of subversive activities. Congress passed the Trading with the Enemy Act, which required foreign-language publications to submit all war-related stories to post office censors for approval.

RENAMED GERMAN AMERICAN WORDS

Original German Name	Renamed "Patriotic" Name
hamburger	salisbury steak, liberty steak, liberty sandwich
sauerkraut	liberty cabbage
Hamburg Avenue, Brooklyn, New York	Wilson Avenue, Brooklyn, New York
Germantown, Nebraska	Garland, Nebraska
East Germantown, Indiana	Pershing, Indiana
Berlin, Iowa	Lincoln, Iowa
Pinochle	Liberty
German shepherd	Alsatian shepherd
Deutsches Haus of Indianapolis	Athenaeum of Indiana
Germania Maennerchor of Chicago	Lincoln Club
Kaiser Street	Maine Way

Source: From La Vern J. Rippley, *The German Americans* (Boston: Twayne, 1976), p. 186; and Robert H. Ferrell, *Woodrow Wilson and World War I, 1917–1921* (New York: Harper and Row, 1985), pp. 205–6.

German Americans became the objects of popular hatred. In Boston, performances of Beethoven's symphonies were banned, and the German-born conductor of the Boston Symphony Orchestra was forced to resign. Although Americans would not give up the German foods they had grown to love, they would no longer call them by their German names. Libraries removed works of German literature from their shelves, and Theodore Roosevelt and others urged school districts to prohibit the teaching of the German language. Patriotic school boards in Lima, Ohio, and elsewhere burned the German books in their districts.

German Americans risked being fired from work, losing their businesses, and being assaulted on the street. A St. Louis mob lynched an innocent German immigrant they suspected of subversion. After only 25 minutes of deliberation, a St. Louis jury acquitted the mob leaders, who had brazenly defended their crime as an act of patriotism. German Americans began hiding their ethnic identity, changing their names, speaking German only in the privacy of their homes, and celebrating their holidays only with trusted friends.

The anti-German campaign escalated into a general anti-immigrant crusade. Congress passed the Immigration Restriction Act of 1917, over Wilson's veto, which declared that all adult immigrants who failed a reading test would be denied admission to the United States. The act also banned the immigration of laborers from India, Indochina, Afghanistan, Arabia, the East Indies, and other countries located within an "Asiatic Barred Zone."

Congress also passed the Eighteenth Amendment to the Constitution, which prohibited the manufacture and distribution of alcoholic beverages. The campaign for prohibition was not new, but anti-immigrant feelings generated by the war gave it added impetus. Prohibitionists pictured the nation's urban ethnic ghettos as scenes of drunkenness, immorality, and disloyalty. They also accused German American brewers of operating a "liquor trust" to sap people's will to fight. The states quickly ratified the Eighteenth Amendment, and in 1919, Prohibition became the law of the land.

In the **Espionage, Sabotage, and Sedition Acts** passed in 1917 and 1918, Congress gave the administration sweeping powers to silence and imprison dissenters. These acts went beyond outlawing behavior that no nation at war could be expected to tolerate, such as spying for the enemy, sabotaging war production, and calling for the enemy's victory. Now citizens could be prosecuted for writing or uttering any statement that could be construed as profaning the flag, the Constitution, or the military. These acts constituted the most drastic restrictions of free speech at the national level since the Alien and Sedition Acts of 1798.

Government repression fell most heavily on the IWW and the Socialist Party. Both groups had opposed intervention. Although they subsequently muted their opposition, they continued to insist that the true enemies of American workers were to be found in the ranks of American employers, not in Germany or Austria-Hungary. The government responded by banning many socialist materials from the mails and by disrupting socialist and IWW meetings. By spring 1918, government agents had raided countless IWW offices and had arrested 2,000 IWW members, including the organization's entire executive board. William Haywood, the IWW president, fled to Europe and then to the Soviet Union rather than go to jail. In summer 1918, Eugene V. Debs, the 62-year-old head of the Socialist Party, received a 10-year jail term for making an antiwar speech in Canton, Ohio.

This federal repression, carried out in an atmosphere of supercharged patriotism, encouraged local governments and private citizens to initiate their own anti-radical crusades. In the mining town of Bisbee, Arizona, a sheriff with a force of 2,000 deputized citizens kidnapped 1,200 IWW members, herded them into cattle cars, and dumped them in the New Mexico desert with little food or water. Vigilantes in Butte, Montana, chained an IWW organizer to a car and let his body scrape the pavement as they drove the vehicle through city streets. Next, they strung him up to a railroad trestle, castrated him, and left him to die. The 250,000 members of the American Protective League, most of them businessmen and professionals, routinely spied on fellow workers and neighbors. They opened mail and tapped phones and otherwise harassed those suspected of disloyalty. Attorney General Thomas Gregory publicly endorsed the group and sought federal funds to support its "police" work.

The spirit of coercion even infected institutions that had long prided themselves on tolerance. In July 1917, Columbia University fired two professors for speaking out against U.S. intervention in the war. The National Americanization Committee, which before 1917 had pioneered a humane approach to the problem of integrating immigrants into American life, now supported surveillance, internment, and deportation of aliens suspected of anti-American sentiments.

Wilson did attempt to block certain pieces of repressive legislation but did little to halt Attorney General Gregory's prosecution of radicals or Postmaster General Burleson's campaign to exclude Socialist Party publications from the mail. His acquiescence in these matters cost him support among progressives. Wilson believed, however, that once the Allies, with U.S. support, won the war and arranged a just peace in accordance with the Fourteen Points, his administration's wartime actions would be forgiven and the progressive coalition would be restored.

THE FAILURE OF THE INTERNATIONAL PEACE

In the month following Germany's surrender on November 11, 1918, Wilson was confident about the prospects of achieving a just peace. Both Germany and the Allies had publicly accepted the Fourteen Points as the basis for negotiations. Wilson's international prestige had grown. Poles, Lithuanians, and other eastern Europeans whose pursuit of nationhood had been frustrated for 100 years or more now believed that independence might be within their reach. Zionist Jews in Europe and the United States dared to dream of a Jewish homeland in Palestine within their lifetimes. Countless African and Asian peoples imagined achieving their freedom from colonial domination.

When Wilson arrived in France for the peace conference in January 1919, some 2 million French citizens—the largest throng ever assembled on French soil—lined the parade route in Paris to see him. In Rome, Milan, and La Scala, Italians acclaimed him "The Savior of Humanity" and "The Moses from Across the Atlantic."

New York Times

"The Savior of Humanity." *Wherever he went in Europe, Woodrow Wilson was greeted by huge crowds eager to thank him for ending Europe's terrible war and to endorse his vision of a peaceful, democratic world. Here millions of Italians greet Wilson's arrival in Milan.*

In the Fourteen Points, Wilson had translated his principles for a new world order into specific proposals for international peace and justice. The first group of points called for all nations to abide by a code of conduct that embraced free trade, freedom of the seas, open diplomacy, disarmament, and the resolution of disputes through mediation. A second group, based on the principle of self-determination, proposed redrawing the map of Europe to give the subjugated peoples of the Austro-Hungarian, Ottoman, and Russian empires national sovereignty. The last point called for establishing the League of Nations, an assembly in which all nations would be represented and in which international disputes would be given a fair hearing and an opportunity for peaceful solutions.

The Paris Peace Conference and the Treaty of Versailles   Although representatives of 27 nations began meeting in Paris on January 12, 1919, to discuss Wilson's Fourteen Points, negotiations were controlled by the "Big Four": Wilson, Prime Minister David Lloyd George of Great Britain, Premier Georges Clemenceau of France, and Prime Minister Vittorio Orlando of Italy. When Orlando quit the conference after a dispute with Wilson, the Big Four became the Big Three. Wilson quickly learned that his negotiating partners' support for the Fourteen Points was much weaker than he had believed. Clemenceau and Lloyd George refused to include most of Wilson's points in the peace treaty. The points having to do with freedom of the seas and free trade were omitted, as were the proposals for open diplomacy and Allied disarmament. Wilson won partial endorsement of the principle of self-determination: Belgian sovereignty was restored, Poland's status as a nation was affirmed, and the new nations of Czechoslovakia, Yugoslavia, Finland, Lithuania, Latvia, and Estonia were created. In addition, some lands of the former Ottoman Empire—Armenia, Palestine, Mesopotamia, and Syria—were to be placed under League of Nations' trusteeships with the understanding that they would someday gain their independence. Wilson failed in his efforts to block a British plan to transfer former German colonies in Asia to Japanese control, an Italian plan to annex territory inhabited by 200,000 Austrians, and a French plan to take from Germany its valuable Saar coal mines.

Nor could Wilson blunt the drive to punish Germany for its wartime aggression. In addition to awarding the Saar basin to France, the Allies gave portions of northern Germany to Denmark and portions of eastern Germany to Poland and Czechoslovakia. Germany was stripped of virtually its entire navy and air force, and forbidden to place soldiers or fortifications in western Germany along the Rhine. It was allowed to keep an army of only 100,000 men. In addition, Germany was forced to admit its responsibility for the war. In accepting this "war guilt," Germany was, in effect, agreeing to compensate the victors in cash (reparations) for the pain and suffering it had inflicted on them.

Lloyd George and Clemenceau brushed off the protests of those who viewed this desire to prostrate Germany as a cruel and vengeful act. That the German people, after their nation's 1918 defeat, had overthrown the monarch (Kaiser Wilhelm II) who had taken them to war, and had reconstituted their nation as a democratic republic—the first in their country's history—won them no leniency. On June 28, 1919, Great Britain, France, the United States, Germany, and other European nations signed the Treaty of Versailles. In 1921, an Allied commission notified the Germans that they were to pay the victors $33 billion, a sum well beyond the resources of a defeated and economically ruined Germany.

The League of Nations   The Allies' single-minded pursuit of self-interest disillusioned many liberals and socialists in the United States, but Wilson seemed undismayed. He had won approval of the most important of his Fourteen Points—that which called for the creation of the League of Nations. The League, whose structure and responsibilities were set forth in the Covenant attached to the peace treaty, would usher in Wilson's new world order. Drawing its membership from the signatories to the Treaty of Versailles (except, for the time being, Germany), the League would function as an international parliament and judiciary, establishing rules of international behavior and resolving disputes between nations through rational and peaceful means. A nine-member executive council—the United States, Britain, France, Italy, and Japan would have permanent seats on the council, while the other four seats would rotate among the smaller powers—was charged with administering decisions.

Wilson believed that the League would redeem the failures of the Paris Peace Conference. Under its auspices, free trade and freedom of the seas would be achieved, reparations against Germany would be reduced or eliminated, disarmament of the Allies would proceed, and the principle of self-determination would be extended to peoples outside Europe. Moreover, the **Article X of the Covenant** would endow the League with the power to punish aggressor nations through economic isolation and military retaliation.

Wilson versus Lodge: The Fight over Ratification   The League's success, however, depended on Wilson's ability to convince the U.S. Senate to ratify the Treaty of Versailles. Wilson knew that this would not be easy. The Republicans had gained a majority in the Senate in 1918, and two groups within their ranks were determined to frustrate Wilson's ambitions. One group was a caucus of 14 midwesterners and westerners known as the **irreconcilables**. Most of them were conservative isolationists who wanted the United States to preserve its separation from Europe, but a few were prominent progressives—Robert La Follette, William Borah, and Hiram Johnson—who had voted against the declaration of war in 1917. The self-interest displayed by England and France at the peace conference convinced this group that the Europeans were incapable of decent behavior in international matters.

Senator **Henry Cabot Lodge** of Massachusetts led the second opposition group. Its members subscribed to Theodore Roosevelt's vision of a world controlled by a few great nations, each militarily strong, secure in its sphere of influence, and determined to avoid war through a carefully negotiated balance of power. These Republicans preferred to let Europe return to the power politics that had prevailed before the war rather than experiment with a new world order that would recognize the rights of numerous new and weak nations and that might constrain and compromise U.S. power and autonomy.

This Republican critique was a cogent one that merited extended discussion. Particularly important were questions that Republicans raised about Article X, which gave the League the right to undertake military actions against aggressor nations. Did Americans want to authorize an international organization to decide when the United States would go to war? Was this not a violation of the Constitution, which vested war-making power solely in Congress? Even if the constitutional problem could be solved, how could the United States ensure that it would not be forced into a military action that might damage its national interest?

It soon became clear, however, that several Republicans, including Lodge, were as interested in humiliating Wilson as they were in developing an alternative approach to foreign policy. They accused Wilson of promoting socialism through his wartime expansion of government power. They were angry that he had failed to include any distinguished Republicans, such as Lodge, Elihu Root, or William Howard Taft, in the Paris peace delegation. And they were still bitter about the 1918 congressional elections, when Wilson had argued that a Republican victory would embarrass the nation abroad.

As chairman of the Senate Foreign Relations Committee, charged with considering the treaty before reporting it to the Senate floor, Lodge did everything

MAP 23.2 Europe and the Near East after the First World War

The First World War and the Treaty of Versailles changed the geography of Europe and the Near East. Nine nations in Europe, stretching from Yugoslavia in the south to Finland in the north, were created (or re-formed) out of the defeated Austro-Hungarian and Ottoman empires. In the Near East, meanwhile, Syria, Lebanon, Palestine, Transjordan, and Iraq were carved out of the Ottoman Empire, placed under British or French control, and promised eventual independence.

possible to obstruct ratification. He packed the committee with senators who were likely to oppose the treaty. He delayed action by reading every one of the treaty's 300 pages aloud and by subjecting it to endless criticism in six long weeks of public hearings. When his committee finally reported the treaty to the full Senate, it came encumbered with nearly 50 amendments whose adoption Lodge made a precondition of his support. Some of the amendments expressed reasonable concerns—namely, that participation in the League not diminish the role of Congress in determining foreign policy, compromise American sovereignty, or involve the United States in an unjust or ill-advised war—but many were meant only to complicate the task of ratification.

Despite Lodge's obstructionism, the treaty's chances for ratification by the required two-thirds majority of the Senate remained good. Many Republicans were prepared to vote for ratification if Wilson indicated his willingness to accept some of the proposed amendments. Wilson could have salvaged the treaty and, along with it, U.S. participation in the League of Nations, but he refused to compromise with the Republicans and announced that he would carry his case directly to the American people instead. In September 1919, Wilson undertook a whirlwind cross-country tour that covered more than 8,000 miles with 37 stops. He addressed as many crowds as he could reach, sometimes speaking for an hour at a time, four times a day.

On September 25, after giving a speech at Pueblo, Colorado, Wilson suffered excruciating headaches. His physician ordered him back to Washington, where on October 2 he suffered a near-fatal stroke. Wilson hovered near death for two weeks and remained seriously disabled for another six. His condition improved somewhat in November, but his left side remained paralyzed, his speech was slurred, his energy level low, and his emotions unstable. Wilson's wife, Edith Bolling Wilson, and his doctor isolated him from Congress and the press, withholding news they thought might upset him and preventing the public from learning how much his body and mind had deteriorated.

Many historians believe that the stroke impaired Wilson's political judgment. He refused to consider any of the Republican amendments to the treaty, even after it had become clear that compromise offered the only chance of winning U.S. participation in the League of Nations. When Lodge presented an amended treaty for a ratification vote on November 19, Wilson ordered Senate Democrats to vote against it; 42 of 47 Democratic senators complied, and with the aid of 13 Republican irreconcilables, the Lodge version was defeated. Only moments later, the unamended version of the treaty—Wilson's version—received only 38 votes.

The Treaty's Final Defeat   As the magnitude of the calamity became apparent, supporters of the League in Congress, the nation, and the world urged the Senate and the president to reconsider. Wilson would not budge. A last-ditch effort at ratification failed on March 8, 1920, by a margin of seven votes. Wilson's dream of a new world order died that day. The crumpled figure in the White House seemed to bear little resemblance to the hero who, barely 15 months before, had been greeted in Europe as the world's savior. Wilson filled out his remaining 12 months in office as an invalid, presiding over the interment of progressivism. He died in 1924.

The judgment of history lies heavily on these events, for many believe that the flawed treaty and the failure of the League contributed to Adolf Hitler's rise in Germany and the outbreak of a second world war more devastating than the first.

It is necessary to ask, then, whether American participation in the League would have significantly altered the course of world history.

The mere fact of U.S. membership in the League would not have magically solved Europe's postwar problems. The U.S. government was inexperienced in diplomacy and prone to mistakes. Its freedom to negotiate solutions to international disputes would have been limited by the large number of American voters who remained strongly opposed to U.S. entanglement in European affairs. Even if such opposition could have been overcome, the United States would still have confronted European countries determined to go their own way.

Nevertheless, one thing is clear: No stable international order could have arisen after the First World War without the full involvement of the United States. The League of Nations required American authority and prestige in order to operate effectively as an international parliament. We cannot know whether the League, with American involvement, would have offered the Germans a less humiliating peace, allowing them to rehabilitate their economy and salvage their national pride; nor whether an American-led League would have stopped Hitler's expansionism before it escalated into full-scale war in 1939. Still, it seems fair to suggest that American participation would have strengthened the League and improved its ability to bring a lasting peace to Europe.

POSTWAR: A SOCIETY IN CONVULSION

The end of the war brought no respite from the forces convulsing American society. Workers were determined to regain the purchasing power they had lost to inflation. Employers were determined to halt or reverse the wartime gains labor had made. Radicals saw in this conflict between capital and labor the possibility of a socialist revolution. Conservatives were certain that the revolution had already begun. Returning white servicemen were nervous about regaining their civilian jobs and looked suspiciously at black, Hispanic, and female workers recruited to take their places. Black veterans were in no mood to return to segregation and subordination. The federal government, meanwhile, uneasy over how much it had centralized power during the war, quickly dismantled much of its wartime bureaucratic infrastructure.

Labor-Capital Conflict   Nowhere was the escalation of conflict more evident than in the workplace. In 1919, 4 million workers—one-fifth of the nation's manufacturing workforce—went on strike. In January 1919, a general strike paralyzed the city of Seattle when 60,000 workers walked off their jobs. By August, walkouts had been staged by 400,000 eastern and midwestern coal miners, 120,000 New England textile workers, and 50,000 New York City garment workers. Then came two strikes that turned public opinion sharply against labor. In September, Boston policemen walked off their jobs after the police commissioner refused to negotiate with their newly formed union. Rioting and looting soon broke out. Massachusetts governor Calvin Coolidge, outraged by the policemen's betrayal of their sworn public duty, fired the entire police

Woodrow Wilson's Fourteen Points, 1918: Record of Implementation

1. Open covenants of peace openly arrived at	Not fulfilled
2. Absolute freedom of navigation upon the seas in peace and war	Not fulfilled
3. Removal of all economic barriers to the equality of trade among nations	Not fulfilled
4. Reduction of armaments to the level needed only for domestic safety	Not fulfilled
5. Impartial adjustments of colonial claims	Not fulfilled
6. Evacuation of all Russian territory; Russia to be welcomed into the society of free nations	Not fulfilled
7. Evacuation and restoration of Belgium	Fulfilled
8. Evacuation and restoration of all French lands; return of Alsace-Lorraine to France	Fulfilled
9. Readjustment of Italy's frontiers along lines of Italian nationality	Compromised
10. Self-determination for the former subjects of the Austro-Hungarian Empire	Compromised
11. Evacuation of Romania, Serbia, and Montenegro; free access to the sea for Serbia	Compromised
12. Self-determination for the former subjects of the Ottoman Empire; secure sovereignty for Turkish portion	Compromised
13. Establishment of an independent Poland with free and secure access to the sea	Fulfilled
14. Establishment of the League of Nations to secure mutual guarantees of independence and territorial integrity	Compromised

Source: From G. M. Gathorne-Hardy, *The Fourteen Points and the Treaty of Versailles*, Oxford Pamphlets on World *Affairs*, no. 6 (1939), pp. 8–34; and Thomas G. Paterson et al., *American Foreign Policy: A History*, 2nd ed. (Lexington, MA: Heath, 1983), vol. 2, pp. 282–93.

force. His tough stand would bring him national fame and the Republican vice presidential nomination in 1920.

Hard on the heels of the policemen's strike came a strike by more than 300,000 steelworkers in the Midwest. No union had established a footing in the steel industry since the 1890s, when Andrew Carnegie had ousted the ironworkers' union from his mills in Homestead, Pennsylvania. Most steelworkers labored long hours (the 12-hour shift was still standard) for low wages in dangerous workplaces. The organizers of the 1919 Steel Strike had persuaded steelworkers with varied skill levels and ethnic backgrounds to put aside their differences and demand an eight-hour day and union recognition. When the employers rejected those demands, the workers walked off their jobs. Employers responded by hiring nonunion labor to keep the plants running and by portraying strike leaders as dangerous radicals. In many areas, local and state police prohibited union meetings, ran strikers out of town, and opened fire on those who disobeyed orders. In these circumstances, public opinion turned against the steelworkers; their strike collapsed in January 1920.

Radicals and the Red Scare   The steel companies fanned the public's fear that revolutionary sentiment was spreading among workers. Radical sentiment was indeed on the rise. Mine workers and railroad workers had begun calling for the permanent nationalization of coal mines and railroads. Longshoremen in San Francisco and Seattle refused to load ships carrying supplies to the White Russians who had taken up arms against Lenin's Bolshevik government in Russia. Socialist trade unionists mounted the most serious challenge to Gompers's control of the AFL in 25 years. In 1920, nearly a million Americans voted for socialist presidential candidate Debs, who ran his campaign from the Atlanta Federal Penitentiary.

This radical surge did not mean, however, that leftists had fashioned themselves into a single movement or political party. On the contrary, the Russian Revolution had split the American Socialist Party. One faction, which would keep the "Socialist" name and would continue under Debs's leadership, insisted that radicals follow a democratic path to socialism. The other group, which would take the name "Communist," wanted to establish a Lenin-style "dictatorship of the proletariat." Small groups of anarchists, some of whom advocated campaigns of terror to speed the revolution, represented yet a third radical tendency.

Few Americans noticed the disarray in the radical camp. Most assumed that radicalism was a single, coordinated movement bent on establishing a communist government on American soil. They saw the nation's immigrant communities as breeding grounds for Bolshevism. Beginning in 1919, this perceived **Red Scare** prompted government officials and private citizens to embark on yet another campaign of repression.

The postwar repression of radicalism closely resembled the wartime repression of dissent. Thirty states passed sedition laws to punish those who advocated revolution. Numerous public and private groups intensified Americanization campaigns designed to strip foreigners of their subversive ways and remake them into loyal citizens. Universities fired radical professors, and vigilante groups broke into the offices of socialists and assaulted IWW agitators. A newly formed veterans' organization, the American Legion, took on the American Protective League's role of identifying seditious individuals and organizations and ensuring the public's devotion to "100 percent Americanism."

The Red Scare reached its climax on New Year's Day 1920, when federal agents broke into the homes and meeting places of thousands of suspected revolutionaries in 33 cities. Directed by Attorney General A. Mitchell Palmer, these widely publicized "Palmer raids" were meant to expose the extent of revolutionary activity. Palmer's agents uncovered three pistols, no rifles, and no explosives. Nevertheless, they arrested more than 4,000 people and kept many of them in jail for weeks

The 1919 Steel Strike Fails. *The steel corporations were united in their opposition to the steelworkers' union and skillful in their use of media to demoralize the strikers. This poster reveals another reason for the strike's failure: a workforce so diverse that strike announcements had to be communicated in eight languages.*

Library & Archives Division, Senator John Heinz History Center, Pittsburgh, PA.

without formally charging them with a crime. Finally, those who were not citizens (approximately 600) were deported and the rest were released.

Palmer's failure to expose a revolutionary plot blunted support for him in official circles. Undeterred, Palmer now alleged that revolutionaries were planning a series of assaults on government officials and government buildings for May 1, 1920. In this atmosphere, two Italian-born anarchists, Nicola Sacco and Bartolomeo Vanzetti, were arrested in Brockton, Massachusetts, and charged with armed robbery and murder. Both men proclaimed their innocence and insisted that they were being punished for their political beliefs. Their foreign accents and their defiant espousal of anarchist doctrines in the courtroom inclined many Americans, including the judge who presided at their trial, to view them harshly. Despite the weak case against them, they were convicted of first-degree murder and sentenced to death. Their lawyers attempted numerous appeals, all of which failed. Anger over the verdicts in the **Sacco-Vanzetti case** began to build among Italian Americans, radicals, and liberal intellectuals. Protests compelled the governor of Massachusetts to appoint a commission to review the case, but no new trial was ordered. On August 23, 1927, Sacco and Vanzetti were executed, still insisting they were innocent.

**Racial Conflict
and the Rise
of Black
Nationalism**

The more than 400,000 blacks who served in the armed forces believed that a victory for democracy abroad would help them achieve democracy for their people at home. At first, despite the discrimination they encountered in the military, they maintained their conviction that they would be treated as full-fledged citizens upon their return. Many began to talk about the birth of a New Negro—independent and proud. Thousands joined the National Association for the Advancement of Colored People (NAACP), an organization at the forefront of the fight for racial equality. By 1918, 100,000 African Americans subscribed to the NAACP's magazine, *The Crisis*, whose editor, W. E. B. Du Bois, had urged them to support the war.

This wartime optimism made the postwar discrimination and hatred African Americans encountered difficult to endure. Many black workers who had found jobs in the North were fired to make way for returning white veterans. Returning black servicemen, meanwhile, had to scrounge for poorly paid jobs as unskilled laborers. In the South, lynch mobs targeted black veterans who refused to tolerate the usual insults and indignities; 10 of the 70 blacks lynched in the South in 1919 were veterans.

The worst antiblack violence that year occurred in the North, however. Crowded city conditions during the war had forced black and ethnic white city dwellers into close proximity. Many white ethnics resented having to share neighborhoods, trolleys, parks, streets, and workplaces with blacks. Many also wanted African Americans barred from unions, seeing them as threats to their job security.

Racial tensions escalated into race riots. The deadliest explosion occurred in Chicago in July 1919, when a black teenager who had been swimming in Lake Michigan was killed by whites after coming too close to a whites-only beach. Rioting soon broke out, with white mobs invading black neighborhoods, torching homes and stores, and attacking innocent residents. Led by war veterans, some armed, blacks fought back, turning the border areas between white and black neighborhoods into battle zones. Fighting raged for five days, leaving 38 dead (23 black, 15 white) and more than 500 injured. Race riots in other cities pushed the death toll to 120 before summer's end.

The riots made it clear to blacks that the North was not the Promised Land. Confined to unskilled jobs and to segregated neighborhoods with substandard housing and exorbitant rents, black migrants in Chicago, New York, and other northern cities suffered economic hardship throughout the 1920s. The NAACP carried on its campaign for civil rights and racial equality, but many blacks no longer shared its belief that they would one day be accepted as first-class citizens. They turned instead to a leader from Jamaica, **Marcus Garvey**, who gave voice to their bitterness: "The first dying that is to be done by the black man in the future," Garvey declared in 1918, "will be done to make himself free. And then when we are finished, if we have any charity to bestow, we may die for the white man. But as for me, I think I have stopped dying for him."

Garvey called on blacks to give up their hopes for integration and to set about forging a separate black nation. He reminded blacks that they possessed a rich culture stretching back over the centuries that would enable them to achieve greatness as a nation. Garvey's ambition was to build a black nation in Africa that would bring together all of the world's people of African descent. In the short term, he wanted to help American and Caribbean blacks to achieve economic and cultural independence.

Garvey's call for black separatism and self-sufficiency—or black nationalism, as it came to be known—elicited a favorable response among African Americans. In the early 1920s, the Universal Negro Improvement Association (UNIA), which Garvey had founded, enrolled millions of members in 700 branches in 38 states. His newspaper, the *Negro World,* reached a circulation of 200,000. The New York chapter of UNIA undertook an economic development program that included the establishment of grocery stores, restaurants, and factories. Garvey's most visible economic venture was the Black Star Line, a shipping company with three ships flying the UNIA flag from their masts.

This black nationalist movement did not last long. Garvey entered into bitter disputes with other black leaders, including W. E. B. Du Bois, who regarded him as a flamboyant, self-serving demagogue. Garvey sometimes showed poor judgment, as when he expressed support for the Ku Klux Klan on the grounds that it shared his pessimism about the possibility of racial integration. Inexperienced in economic matters, Garvey squandered UNIA money on abortive business ventures. The U.S. government regarded his rhetoric as inflammatory and sought to silence him. In 1923, he was convicted of mail fraud involving the sale of Black Star stocks and was sentenced to five years in jail. In 1927, he was deported to Jamaica, and the UNIA folded. Garvey's philosophy of black nationalism, however, endured.

CONCLUSION

The resurgence of racism in 1919 was a sign that the high hopes of the war years had been dashed. Industrial workers, immigrants, and radicals also found their pursuit of liberty and equality interrupted by the fear, intolerance, and repression unleashed by the war. They came to understand as well that Wilson's commitment to these ideals counted for less than did his administration's and Congress's determination to discipline a people whom they regarded as dangerously heterogeneous and unstable. Of the reform groups, only woman suffragists made enduring gains—especially the right to vote. For feminists, however, these steps forward failed to compensate for the collapse of the progressive movement and with it, their program of achieving equal rights for women across the board.

A similar disappointment engulfed those who had embraced and fought for Wilson's dream of creating a new and democratic world order. The world in 1919 appeared as volatile as it had been in 1914. More and more Americans—perhaps even a majority—were coming to believe that U.S. intervention had been a mistake.

In other ways, the United States benefited a great deal from the war. By 1919, the American economy was by far the world's strongest. Many of the nation's leading corporations had flourished during the war. U.S. banks were poised to supplant those of London as the most influential in international finance. The nation's economic strength triggered impressive growth in the 1920s, and millions of Americans rushed to take advantage of the prosperity that a "people's capitalism" had put within their grasp. But even 1920s affluence would fail to dissolve the class, ethnic, and racial tensions that the war had exposed. And the failure of the peace process added to Europe's problems, delayed the emergence of the United States as a leader in world affairs, and created the preconditions for another world war.

24

THE 1920s

IN 1920, AMERICANS ELECTED AS PRESIDENT Warren G. Harding, a man who could not have been more different from his predecessor, Woodrow Wilson. A Republican, Harding presented himself as a common man with common desires. In his 1920 campaign, he called for a "return to normalcy." Although he died in office in 1923, his carefree spirit is thought to characterize the 1920s.

To many Americans, the decade was one of fun rather than reform, of good times rather than high ideals. It was, in the words of novelist F. Scott Fitzgerald, the "Jazz Age," a time when the search for personal gratification seemed to replace the quest for public welfare.

Despite Harding's call for a return to a familiar past, America seemed to be rushing headlong into the future. The word *modern* began appearing everywhere: modern times, modern women, modern technology, the modern home, modern marriage. Although the word was rarely defined, it connoted certain beliefs: that science was a better guide to life than religion; that people should be free to choose their own lifestyles; that sex should be a source of pleasure for women as well as men; that women and minorities should be equal to white men and enjoy the same rights.

Many other Americans, however, reaffirmed their belief that God's word transcended science; that people should obey the moral code set forth in the Bible; that women were not equal to men; and that blacks, Mexicans, and eastern European immigrants were inferior to Anglo-Saxon whites. They made their voices heard in a resurgent **Ku Klux Klan** and in the fundamentalist movement, and on issues such as evolution and immigration. In seeking to restore an older America, some in their ranks were prepared to deny individual Americans the liberty to choose their own ways of living and to insist that all people were not fundamentally equal.

CHRONOLOGY

1920	Prohibition goes into effect
	Warren G. Harding defeats James M. Cox for presidency
	Census reveals that a majority of Americans live in urban areas
	Eight million cars on roads
1921	Sheppard-Towner Act passed
1922	United States, Britain, Japan, France, and Italy sign Five-Power Treaty, agreeing to reduce size of their navies
1923	Teapot Dome scandal lands Secretary of the Interior Albert Fall in jail
	Harding dies in office
	Calvin Coolidge becomes president
1924	Dawes Plan to restructure Germany's war debt put into effect
	Coolidge defeats John W. Davis for presidency
	Ku Klux Klan membership approaches 4 million
	Johnson-Reed Immigration Restriction Act cuts immigration by 80 percent
1925	Scopes trial upholds right of Tennessee to ban teaching of evolution in public schools
	Survey Graphic publishes a special issue on the Harlem Renaissance
	F. Scott Fitzgerald publishes *The Great Gatsby*
	United States withdraws marines from Nicaragua
1926	Revenue Act cuts income and estate taxes
	United States sends marines back to Nicaragua to end civil war and protect U.S. property
1927	Coolidge vetoes high tariffs legislation (McNary-Haugen bill)
	Babe Ruth hits 60 home runs
	Charles Lindbergh flies across the Atlantic
1928	Fifteen nations sign Kellogg-Briand Pact, pledging to avoid war
	Coolidge vetoes McNary-Haugen bill again
	Herbert Hoover defeats Alfred E. Smith for presidency
1929	Union membership drops to 3 million
	Twenty-seven million cars on roads
	William Faulkner publishes *The Sound and the Fury*
	Josh Gibson joins the National Negro League
1930	Los Angeles's Mexican population reaches 100,000

Modernists and traditionalists confronted each other in party politics, in legislatures, in courtrooms, and in the press. Their battles belie the vision of the 1920s merely as a time for the pursuit of leisure.

PROSPERITY

On balance, the First World War had been good for the American economy. American industries had emerged intact from, even strengthened by, the war. Manufacturers and bankers had exported so many goods and extended so many loans to the Allies that, by war's end, the United States was the world's leading creditor nation. New York City challenged London as the hub of world finance.

From 1919 to 1921, the country struggled to redirect industry from wartime to civilian production, a process slowed by the government's hasty withdrawal from its wartime role as economic regulator and stabilizer. Workers went on strike to protest wage reductions or increases in the workweek. Farmers were hit by a depression as the overseas demand for American foodstuffs fell from its 1918–1919 peak. Disgruntled workers and farmers joined forces to form statewide farmer-labor parties, which for a time threatened to disrupt the country's two-party system in the upper Midwest. In 1924, the two groups formed a national Farmer-Labor Party. Robert La Follette, their presidential candidate, received an impressive 16 percent of the vote that year, but then the third-party movement fell apart.

Its collapse reflected a rising public awareness of how vigorous and productive the economy had become. From 1922 to 1929, the gross national product grew at an annual rate of 5.5 percent, rising from $149 billion to $227 billion. The unemployment rate never exceeded 5 percent, and real wages rose about 15 percent.

A Consumer Society   In the 19th century, economic growth had rested primarily on the production of capital goods, such as factory machinery and railroad tracks. In the 1920s, however, growth rested more on consumer goods. Some products, such as cars and telephones, had been available since the early 1900s, but in the 1920s their sales reached new levels. In 1920, just 12 years after Ford introduced the Model T, 8 million cars were on the road. By 1929, there were 27 million—one for every five Americans. Other consumer goods became available for the first time: tractors, washing machines, refrigerators, electric irons, radios, and vacuum cleaners. The term "consumer durable" was coined to describe such goods, which, unlike food, clothing, and other perishables, were meant to last. Even perishables took on new allure. Scientists had discovered the importance of vitamins in the diet and began urging Americans to consume more fresh fruits and vegetables. The agricultural economy of southern California grew rapidly as urban demand for its products skyrocketed. Improvements in refrigeration and in packaging, meanwhile, allowed fresh produce to travel long distances and extended its shelf life in grocery stores. And more stores were being operated by large grocery chains that could afford the latest refrigeration and packaging technology.

The public responded to these innovations with excitement. American industry had made fresh food and stylish clothes available to the masses. Refrigerators, vacuum cleaners, and washing machines would spare women the drudgery of housework. Radios would expand the public's cultural horizons. Cars, asphalt roads, service stations, hot dog stands, "tourist cabins" (the forerunners of motels), and traffic lights seemed to herald a wholly new automobile civilization. By the middle of the decade, the country possessed a network of paved roads. City dwellers now had easy access to rural areas and made a ritual of daylong excursions. Camping trips and long-distance vacations became routine. Farmers and their families could now hop into their cars and head for the nearest town to take advantage of its stores, movie theater, amusement park, and sporting events. Suburbs proliferated, billed as the perfect mix of urban and rural life. Young men and women everywhere discovered that cars were a place where they could "make out," and even make love, without fear of reproach by prudish parents or prying neighbors.

In the 1920s, some Americans also discovered the benefits of owning stocks. By 1929, as many as 7 million Americans owned stock, most of them people of middle-or upper-class means. The New York Stock Exchange, first organized in 1792, assisted in processing complicated transactions. Capitalists boasted that they had created a **"people's capitalism"** in which virtually all Americans could participate. Everyone could own a piece of corporate America and afford amenities. Poverty, capitalists claimed, was banished, and the gap between rich and poor would soon close.

Actually, although wages were rising, millions of Americans still earned too little to partake fully of the marketplace. The percentage of Americans owning stocks remained small. Social scientists Robert and Helen Lynd discovered, in their celebrated 1929 study of Muncie, Indiana, that working-class families who bought a car often lacked money for other goods. One housewife admitted: "We don't have no fancy clothes when we have the car to pay for …. The car is the only pleasure we have." Many industrialists resisted pressure to increase wages, and workers lacked the organizational strength to force them to pay more.

One solution came with the introduction of consumer credit. Car dealers, home appliance salesmen, and other merchants began to offer installment plans that enabled consumers to purchase a product by making a down payment and promising to pay the rest in installments. By 1930, 15 percent of all purchases were made on the installment plan.

Even so, many poor Americans benefited little from the consumer revolution. Middle-class Americans acquired a disproportionate share of consumer durables. They also could afford to purchase more fresh fruits and vegetables and stocks than most working-class Americans.

Middle-class consumers themselves had to be wooed. How could they be persuaded to buy another car only a few years after they had bought their first one? General Motors (GM) had the answer: the annual model change. Beginning in 1926, GM cars took on a different look every year as GM engineers modified headlights and chassis colors, streamlined bodies, and added new features. The strategy worked. GM leaped past Ford and became the world's largest car manufacturer.

Henry Ford reluctantly introduced his Model A in 1927 to provide customers with a colorful alternative to the drab Model T. Having spent his lifetime selling a product renowned for its utility and reliability, Ford rejected the idea that sales could be increased by appealing to the intangible hopes and fears of consumers. He was wrong. The desire to be beautiful, handsome, or sexually attractive; to exercise power and control; to demonstrate competence and success; to escape anonymity, loneliness, and boredom; to experience pleasure—all such desires, once activated, could motivate a consumer to buy a new car even when the old one was still serviceable, or to spend money on goods that might have once seemed frivolous.

Arousing such desires required more than bright colors, sleek lines, and attractive packaging. It called for advertising campaigns intended to make a product seem to be the answer to the consumer's desires. To create those campaigns, corporations turned to a new kind of company: professional advertising firms. Advertising entrepreneurs, people such as Edward Bernays, Doris Fleischmann, and Bruce Barton, tended to be well educated, sensitive to public taste, and knowledgeable about human psychology. In their campaigns, advertisers played on the emotions and vulnerabilities of their target audiences. A perfume manufacturer's ad pronounced: "The first duty of woman is to attract .... It does not matter how clever or independent you may be, if you fail to influence the men you meet, consciously or unconsciously, you are not fulfilling your fundamental duty as a woman." A tobacco ad matter-of-factly declared: "Men at the top are apt to be pipe-smokers .... It's no coincidence—pipe-smoking is a calm and deliberate habit—restful, stimulating. His pipe helps a man think straight. A pipe is back of most big ideas."

Advertising professionals believed they were helping people to manage their lives in ways that would increase their satisfaction and pleasure. American consumers responded enthusiastically. The most enthusiastic of all were middle-class Americans, who could afford to buy what the advertisers were selling. Many of them were newcomers to middle-class ranks, searching for ways to affirm—or even create—their new identity.

As male wage earners moved into the new middle class, their wives were freed from the necessity of working outside the home. Advertisers appealed to the new middle-class woman, too, as she refocused her attention toward dressing in the latest fashion, managing the household, and raising children. Vacuum cleaners and other consumer durables would make her more efficient, and books on child rearing, many imbued with a popularized Freudianism, would enable her to mold her children for future success in work and marriage. Cosmetics would aid women in their "first duty"—to be beautiful and sexual for their husbands and boyfriends.

Marriage,
Sexuality,
Celebrity

That husbands and wives were encouraged to pursue sexual satisfaction together was one sign of how prescriptions for married life had changed since the 19th century, when women were thought to lack sexual passion and men were tacitly expected to satisfy their drives through extramarital liaisons. Modern husbands and wives were expected to share other leisure activities as well—dining out, playing cards with friends, going to the movies, attending concerts, and

*The*NEW MORRIS-OXFORD SIX
FOR SPEED & COMFORT

MORRIS OXFORD

The Art of Selling Cars. *The creators of this dazzling advertisement mixed female sexuality, bold colors, and the power and speed of lightning bolts to generate consumer interest in the "New Morris-Oxford Six" automobile.*

discussing the latest selection from the newly formed Book-of-the-Month Club. Husbands and wives now aspired to a new ideal—to be best friends, full partners in the pursuit of happiness.

The public pursuit of pleasure was also noticeable among young and single middle-class women. The so-called **flappers** of the 1920s set out to break the informal rules governing young women's lives: They donned short dresses, rolled their stockings down, wore red lipstick, and smoked in public. Flappers were signaling their desire for independence and equality, but they had little thought of achieving those goals through politics as their middle-class predecessors had in the woman's suffrage movement. Rather, they aimed to create a new female personality endowed with self-reliance, outspokenness, and a new appreciation for the pleasures of life.

The pursuit of pleasure became both an individual and a group endeavor. Mass marketers began to understand that they could make money by staging mega-events, mostly connected to sports, that tens of thousands would attend and that radio announcers would broadcast to a virtual audience of millions. When Yankee Stadium opened in 1923, it set a new standard for the scale and magnificence of sports amphitheaters. Boxing matches began drawing audiences that would have been unimaginable 20 years earlier. To succeed on this scale, these sports required not just stirring athletic competitions but also individual athletes who seemed larger than life and whose exploits and character could be endlessly promoted.

No sports figure achieved greater fame than George Herman "Babe" Ruth, who overcame the hardships of a poor and orphaned youth in Baltimore to become the slugging star—the "Sultan of Swat"—of the New York Yankees. In the 1920s,

Ruth hit more home runs than baseball experts had thought humanly possible, culminating in 1927, when he hit a magical 60, a record that would last for 34 years and that would be surpassed only three times in the 20th century. A close second in popularity to Ruth was heavyweight prizefighter Jack Dempsey, whose combination of ruthlessness and efficiency in the ring with gentleness outside it enthralled millions.

Americans also drew their celebrities from the movies, where stars such as comedian Charlie Chaplin and the exotically handsome Rudolph Valentino stirred laughter and sexual longings, respectively, in audiences. These and other figures became so familiar on the silver screen that they created an insatiable appetite among movie fans for news about their private lives as well, an interest that the movie industry was only too eager to exploit.

Perhaps no one in the 1920s attracted as much adulation as was bestowed on **Charles A. Lindbergh,** the young airman who, in 1927, became the first individual to cross the Atlantic in a solo flight. Piloting his single-engine white monoplane, *The Spirit of St. Louis,* Lindbergh flew nonstop (and without sleep) for 34 hours from the time he took off from Long Island until he landed at Le Bourget Airport in Paris. Thousands of Parisians were waiting for him at the airfield and began charging his plane as soon as it landed. When Lindbergh returned to New York, an estimated 4 million fans lined the parade route. None of this fame could have happened without the new machinery of celebrity culture—aggressive journalists and radio commentators, promoters, and others who understood how fame could yield a profit. It mattered, too, that Lindbergh performed his feat in an airplane, one of the era's newest and most exciting innovations. But Lindbergh's celebrity involved more than hype and technology: He accomplished what others said could not be done, and he did it on his own in a time when corporations and other private institutions of power seemed to be shrinking the realm for individual initiative. Some of Lindbergh's popularity no doubt rested on his ability to demonstrate that an individual of conviction and skill could still make a difference in an increasingly industrialized and bureaucratized world.

Business Promises, Work Realities   Industrialists, advertisers, and merchandisers in the 1920s began to claim that their accomplishments lay at the heart of American civilization. Business, they argued, made America great, and businessmen provided the nation with its wisest, most vigorous leadership. In 1924, President Calvin Coolidge declared, "The business of America is business." Even religion became a business. Bruce Barton, in his best seller *The Man Nobody Knows* (1925), depicted Jesus as a business executive "who picked up twelve men from the bottom ranks of business and forged them into an organization that conquered the world." Elsewhere, Barton hailed Jesus as an early "national advertiser," and proclaimed that Peter and Paul were really not so different from Americans who sold vacuum cleaners.

Some corporate leaders adopted benevolent attitudes toward their employees. They set up workplace cafeterias, hired doctors and nurses to staff on-site medical clinics, and engaged psychologists to counsel troubled workers. They built ball fields and encouraged employees to join industry-sponsored leagues. They published employee newsletters and gave awards to employees who did their jobs well and with good spirit.

The real purpose of these measures—collectively known as welfare capitalism—was to encourage employees to be loyal to their firm and to convince them (contrary to what labor unions had been arguing) that industry did have the best interests of its employees at heart. As the decade proceeded and as prosperity rolled on, welfare capitalism reflected the confidence that capitalism had become more responsive to employee concerns and thus more humane.

Many industrial workers benefited from the nation's prosperity. A majority enjoyed rising wages and a reasonably steady income. Skilled craftsmen in the older industries of construction, railroad transportation, and printing fared especially well. Their real wages rose by 30 to 50 percent over the decade. The several million workers employed in the large mass-production industries (such as automobile and electrical equipment manufacture) also did well. Their wages were relatively high, and some of them enjoyed good benefits—paid sick leave, paid vacations, life insurance, stock options, and retirement pensions. Although all workers in companies with these programs were eligible for such benefits, skilled workers were in the best position to claim them.

Semiskilled and unskilled industrial workers had to contend with a labor surplus throughout the decade. As employers replaced workers with machines, the aggregate demand for industrial labor increased at a lower rate than it had in the preceding 20 years. Despite a weakening demand for labor, rural whites, rural blacks, and Mexicans continued their migration to the cities, stiffening the competition for factory jobs. Employers could hire and fire as they saw fit and could therefore keep wage increases lagging behind increases in productivity.

This softening demand for labor helps explain why many working-class families benefited little from the decade's prosperity or from its consumer revolution. An estimated 40 percent of workers remained poor, unable to afford a healthy diet or adequate housing, much less any of the more costly consumer goods.

The million or more workers who labored in the nation's two largest industries, coal and textiles, suffered the most during the 1920s. Throughout the decade, both industries experienced severe overcapacity. By 1926, only half of the coal mined each year was being sold. Many New England textile cities experienced levels of unemployment that sometimes approached 50 percent. One reason was that many textile industrialists had shifted their operations to the South, where taxes and wages were lower. But the southern textile industry also suffered from excess capacity. Plant managers North and South pressured their workers to speed up production. Workers loathed the frequent "speed-ups" of machines and the "stretch-outs" in the number of spinning or weaving machines each worker was expected to tend. By the late 1920s, labor strife and calls for unionization were rising among disgruntled workers.

Unionization of textiles and coal, and of more prosperous industries as well, would have brought workers a larger share of the decade's prosperity. Some labor leaders, such as Sidney Hillman of the Amalgamated Clothing Workers, argued that unionization would actually increase corporate profits by compelling employers to observe uniform wage and hour schedules that would restrain ruinous competition. Hillman pointed out—as Henry Ford had in the preceding decade—that rising wages would enable workers to purchase more consumer goods and thus increase corporate sales and revenues. Hillman's views, however, were largely ignored outside the garment industry.

In most industries, unions lost ground in the 1920s, as business and government, backed by middle-class opinion, remained hostile to labor organization. Employers attacked unions as un-American. A conservative Supreme Court whittled away at labor's legal protections, which made it more difficult to organize unions. Trade union membership fell from a high of 5 million in 1920 to less than 3 million in 1929, a mere 10 percent of the nation's industrial workforce. Other forces contributed to the decline, too. Many workers, especially those benefiting from welfare capitalist programs, decided they no longer needed unions. And the labor movement hurt itself by moving too slowly to open its ranks to semiskilled and unskilled factory workers.

Women workers experienced the same hardships as men in the industrial workforce and fewer of the benefits. They were largely excluded from the ranks of the skilled craftsmen and thus missed out on the substantial wage increases that the men in those positions enjoyed. Women also had trouble finding work in the automobile industry, the highest paying of the mass-production industries. They had better access to the electrical equipment and meatpacking industries, although they were often kept in departments given over to "women's work." Where women were allowed to compete for the same jobs as men, they usually earned less. Thus, a female trimmer in a meatpacking plant typically made only two-thirds of what a male trimmer earned. The textile industry had long been a major source of employment for women, but in the 1920s, women and men alike in this ailing manufacturing sector suffered high rates of unemployment and declining wages.

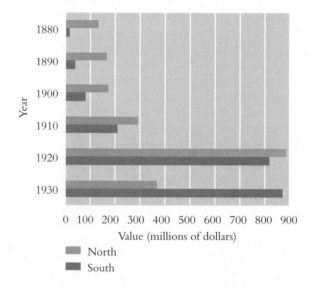

Value of Regional Cotton Textile Output, 1880–1930

Source: Data from Nancy F. Kane, *Textiles in Transition: Technology, Wages, and Industry Relocation in the U.S. Textile Industry, 1880–1939* (New York: Greenwood Press, 1988), p. 29.

Amelia Earhart, Aviation Pioneer. *Earhart strikes a flapper pose in front of the biplane that she was preparing to fly across the Atlantic.*

White-collar work established itself, in the 1920s, as a magnet for women. Discrimination generally prevented women from becoming managers, accountants, or supervisors, but they did dominate the lower-level ranks of secretaries, typists, filing clerks, bank tellers, and department store clerks. By the 1930s, 2 million women, or 20 percent of the female workforce, labored in these and related occupations. Initially, these positions had a glamour that factory work lacked. Work environments were cleaner and brighter, and women had the opportunity—indeed, were expected—to dress well. But wages were low and managerial authority was absolute. Unions had virtually no presence in white-collar places of employment, and workers had difficulty finding alternative ways of protesting unfair managers or difficult working conditions.

Women with ambitious work aspirations most often pursued the "female" professions, such as teaching, nursing, social work, and librarianship. Opportunities in several of these fields, especially teaching and social work, were growing, and women responded by enrolling in college in large numbers. The number of female college students increased by 50 percent during the 1920s. Some of these college graduates used their new skills in new fields, such as writing for women's magazines. A few, drawing strength from their feminist forebears during the

Progressive Era, managed to crack such male bastions of work as mainstream journalism and university research and teaching. In every field of endeavor, even such exotic ones as airplane flying, at least one woman arose to demonstrate that her sex had the necessary talent and drive to match or exceed what men had done.

Thus, in 1932, Amelia Earhart became the first woman to fly the Atlantic solo, matching Lindbergh's feat and inspiring women everywhere. Even so, Earhart's feat failed to improve substantially opportunities for women who wanted to work as pilots in the airline industry. In this industry, as in most lines of work, gender prejudices remained too entrenched, and the women who had broken the gender line remained, by and large, solitary figures.

The Women's Movement Adrift   Many supporters of the Nineteenth Amendment to the Constitution, which in 1920 gave women the right to vote, expected it to transform American politics. Women voters would reverse the decline in voter participation, cleanse politics of corruption, and launch a variety of reform initiatives that would improve the quality of life for women and men alike. This female-inspired transformation, however, failed to materialize. The women's movement, instead, seemed to succumb to the same exhaustion and frustration as had the more general progressive movement from which it had emerged 20 years earlier. Younger women searching for independence and equality (such as the flappers discussed earlier in this chapter) often turned away from reform altogether, preferring a lifestyle that emphasized private achievement and personal freedom to a political career devoted to improving the collective status of America's women. Those who continued to agitate for reform found progress more difficult to achieve once the conservative Republican administrations of Harding and Coolidge took office.

Nevertheless, some female reformers made significant strides in the 1920s. In 1921, one group succeeded in getting Congress to pass the **Sheppard-Towner Act**, a social welfare program that provided federal funds for prenatal and child health-care centers throughout the United States. It remained in effect until 1929. In 1923, Alice Paul, still head of the National Woman's Party, and her allies prevailed on Congress to consider an Equal Rights Amendment (ERA) to the Constitution, phrased as follows: "Men and women shall have equal rights throughout the United States and every place subject to its jurisdiction." And in 1920, the National American Woman Suffrage Association, the major force behind the struggle for suffrage, transformed into the **League of Women Voters (LWV)**. During the next decade, the LWV launched numerous initiatives to encourage women to run for elective office, to educate voters about the issues before them, and to improve the condition of those Americans—the poor, female and child laborers, the mentally ill—who needed assistance.

Sometimes the women's movement was stymied not just by external opposition but also by internal division—as it was over the ERA. The NWP and other supporters of the ERA insisted that there could be no compromise with the proposition that women were the equals of men in every respect. But, the LWV countered, child-rearing and mothering duties did render women different from men in key respects and thus, in some instances, in need of special treatment by Congress and other lawmaking bodies.

The question of female difference crystallized around the issue of protective labor legislation for women. Should women, on account of their sex, be given protections at the workplace—limitations on the hours of labor, prohibitions on overnight work, and other such measures—that men did not have? The League of Women Voters said yes; Alice Paul and supporters of the Equal Rights Amendment said no, arguing that women and men should be treated the same in all respects.

This issue of whether women should be treated somewhat differently than men was a genuinely complicated one, and women activists would continue to argue about it with each other for decades. In the 1920s, their inability to speak with a single voice on this matter weakened their cause in the eyes of their adversaries.

THE POLITICS OF BUSINESS

Republican presidents governed the country from 1921 to 1933. In the beginning, this transition engulfed national politics in scandal, as Warren Harding, the first of the decade's three Republican presidents, allowed high-ranking members of his administration to indulge in spectacular forms of corruption. But his successor, Calvin Coolidge, restored virtue and honor to the presidency while carrying out his 1924 campaign pledge to overturn the legacy of progressivism and reduce the role of the government in economic affairs. The most significant challenge to Coolidge's small-government program came from his own secretary of commerce and then his successor as president, Herbert Hoover, who sought to sustain the spirit of activist government that Theodore Roosevelt had introduced to Republican politics, albeit in a somewhat altered form.

Harding and the Politics of Personal Gain   Warren Gamaliel Harding defeated Democrat James M. Cox for the presidency in 1920. From modest origins as a newspaper editor in the small town of Marion, Ohio, Harding had risen to the U.S. Senate chiefly because the powerful Ohio Republican machine knew it could count on him to do its bidding. He gained the presidency for the same reason. The Republican Party bosses believed that almost anyone they nominated in 1920 could defeat the Democratic opponent. They chose Harding because they could control him. Harding's good looks and geniality made him a favorite with voters, and he swept into office with 61 percent of the popular vote, the greatest landslide since 1820.

To his credit, Harding released the aging Socialist Party leader Eugene V. Debs from jail and took other measures to cool the passions unleashed by the Red Scare. He also included talented men in his cabinet. His choices of Herbert Hoover as secretary of commerce, Charles Evans Hughes as secretary of state, and Andrew Mellon as secretary of the treasury were impressive. Still, Harding lacked the will to alter his ingrained political habits. He had built his political career on a willingness to please the lobbyists who came to his Senate office asking for favors and deals. He had long followed Ohio boss Harry M. Daugherty's advice and would continue to do so now that he had appointed Daugherty attorney general. Harding regarded Daugherty as his friend; they had been together since the beginning of Harding's career. Many a night Harding could be found drinking (despite **Prohibition**), gambling, and womanizing with Daugherty and other members of the "Ohio Gang" at its K Street hangout. Sometimes the gang even convened in the White House.

The K Street house was more than a place to carouse. It was a place of business where the Ohio Gang became rich selling government appointments, judicial pardons, and police protection to bootleggers. By 1923, the corruption could no longer be concealed. Journalists and senators began to focus attention on Secretary of the Interior Albert Fall, who had persuaded Harding to transfer control of large government oil reserves at **Teapot Dome**, Wyoming, and Elk Hills, California, from the navy to the Department of the Interior. Fall had immediately leased the deposits to two oil tycoons, Harry F. Sinclair and Edward L. Doheny, who pumped oil from the wells in exchange for providing the navy with a system of fuel tank reserves. Fall had issued the leases secretly, without allowing other oil corporations to compete for them, and he had accepted almost $400,000 from Sinclair and Doheny.

Fall would pay for this shady deal with a year in jail. Charles R. Forbes, head of the Veterans' Bureau, would go to Leavenworth Prison for swindling the government out of $200 million in hospital supplies. The exposure of Forbes's theft prompted his lawyer, Charles Cramer, to commit suicide; Jesse Smith, Attorney General Daugherty's close friend and housemate, also killed himself, apparently to avoid being indicted and brought to trial. Daugherty managed to escape conviction and incarceration for bribery by burning incriminating documents held by his brother's Ohio bank. Still, Daugherty left government service in disgrace.

Harding could only keep himself blind to this widespread use of public office for private gain for so long. In summer 1923, in poor spirits, he left Washington for a West Coast tour. He fell ill in Seattle and died from a heart attack in San Francisco. The train returning his body to Washington attracted crowds of grief-stricken mourners who little suspected the web of corruption and bribery in which Harding had been caught. Even as the revelations poured forth in 1924 and 1925, few Americans seemed to care. Some of this insouciance reflected the carefree atmosphere of the 1920s, but much of it had to do with the character of the man who succeeded Harding.

Coolidge and Laissez-Faire Politics

Calvin Coolidge rarely smiled. Silence was his public creed, much to the chagrin of Washington's socialites. He was never enticed into carousing with the "boys," nor did he ever stand by as liquor was being served. He believed that the best government was the government that governed least, and that the welfare of the country hinged not on politicians but on the people—their willingness to work hard, to be honest, and to live within their means.

Born in Vermont and raised in Massachusetts, Calvin Coolidge gained national visibility in September 1919, when as governor of Massachusetts he took a firm stand against Boston's striking policemen. His reputation as a man who battled labor radicals earned him a place on the 1920 national Republican ticket. His image as an ordinary man helped convince voters in 1920 that the Republican Party would return the country to its commonsensical ways after a decade or more of progressive reform. Coolidge won his party's presidential nomination handily in 1924 and easily defeated his Democratic opponent, John W. Davis. Coolidge's popularity remained strong throughout his first full term, and he probably would have been renominated and reelected in 1928, but he chose not to run.

Coolidge took greatest pride in those measures that reduced the government's control over the economy. The Revenue Act of 1926 slashed the high income and estate taxes that progressives had pushed through Congress during the First World War. Coolidge curtailed the power of the Federal Trade Commission to regulate business affairs and endorsed Supreme Court decisions invalidating Progressive Era laws that had strengthened organized labor and improved the conditions of children and women at workplaces.

Hoover and the Politics of Associationalism

Some Republicans in the 1920s conceived of government as having a more dynamic role than Coolidge favored. Their leader was Secretary of Commerce Herbert Hoover, who envisioned an economy built on the principle of association. Industrialists, wholesalers, retailers, operators of railroad and shipping lines, small businessmen, farmers, workers, doctors: Hoover wanted each of these groups to form a trade association whose members would share economic information, discuss problems of production and distribution, and seek ways of achieving greater efficiency and profit. Hoover believed that the very act of associating in this way—an approach that historian Ellis Hawley has called **"associationalism"**—would convince participants of the superiority of cooperation over competition, of negotiation over conflict, of public service over selfishness.

A graduate of Stanford University, Hoover had worked first as a mining engineer and then as an executive in multinational mining corporations. During the war, he had directed the government's Food Administration. From that experience, he had come to appreciate the role that government could play in coordinating the activities of thousands of producers and distributors scattered across the country. As commerce secretary, he persuaded farmers to join together in marketing cooperatives, steel executives to abandon the 12-hour day for their employees, and some groups of bankers in the South to organize their institutions into regional associations with adequate resources and expertise. Hoover's dynamic conception of government did not endear him to Coolidge, who declared in 1927: "That man has offered me unsolicited advice for six years, all of it bad."

The Politics of Business Abroad

Republican domestic policy disagreements over whether to pursue laissez-faire or associationalism spilled over into foreign policy as well. Hoover wanted the world's leading nations to meet regularly in conferences, to limit military buildups, and to foster an international environment in which

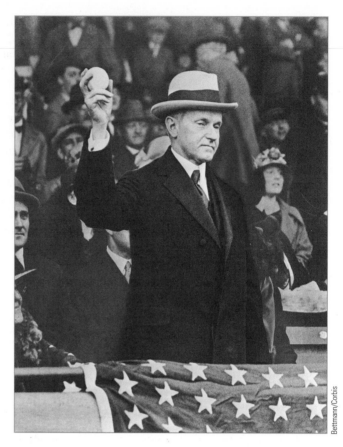

A Stern Yankee. *In contrast to Harding, President Calvin Coolidge did not enjoy informality, banter, or carousing. Here he seems to take little satisfaction in performing what most would have regarded as a pleasurable task: throwing out the first ball of the 1924 baseball season.*

Bettmann/Corbis

capitalism could flourish. Aware that the United States must help to create such an environment, Hoover hoped to persuade American bankers to adopt investment and loan policies that would aid European recovery. If they refused to do so, he was prepared to urge the government to take an activist, supervisory role in foreign investment.

In 1921 and 1922, Hoover helped design the Washington Conference on the Limitation of Armaments. Although he did not serve as a negotiator at the conference—Secretary of State Charles Evans Hughes reserved that role for himself and his subordinates—Hoover did supply Hughes's team with a wealth of economic information that became the basis for bold, detailed proposals for disarmament. Those proposals gave U.S. negotiators a decided advantage over their European and Asian counterparts and helped them win a stunning accord, the Five-Power Treaty, by which the United States, Britain, Japan, France, and Italy agreed to scrap more than 2 million tons of warships. Hughes also obtained pledges from all of the signatories that they would respect the "Open Door" in China, long a U.S. foreign policy objective.

These triumphs redounded to Hughes's credit but not to Hoover's, and Hughes used them to consolidate his control over foreign policy. He rebuffed Hoover's efforts to put international economic affairs under the direction of the Commerce

Department and rejected Hoover's suggestion to intervene in the international activities of U.S. banks.

Hughes's approach was not entirely laissez-faire, as he demonstrated in his 1923 reaction to a crisis in Franco-German relations. The victorious Allies had imposed on Germany an obligation to pay $33 billion in war reparations. When the impoverished German government suspended its payments in 1923, France sent troops to occupy the Ruhr Valley, whose industry was vital to the German economy. German workers retaliated by going on strike. The crisis threatened to undermine Europe's precarious economic recovery. Hughes responded by intensifying American financial pressure on the French and by compelling them to attend a U.S.-sponsored conference in 1924 to restructure Germany's debt obligation.

The conference produced the **Dawes Plan** (after the Chicago banker and chief negotiator, Charles G. Dawes), which reduced German reparations from $542 million to $250 million annually and called on U.S. and foreign banks to stimulate the German economy with a quick infusion of $200 million in loans. Within a matter of days, banker J. P. Morgan, Jr., raised more than $1 billion from American investors. Money poured into German financial markets, and the German economy appeared to stabilize.

The Dawes Plan won applause on both sides of the Atlantic, but soon the U.S. money flooding into Germany created its own problems. American investors were so eager to lend to Germany that their investments became speculative and unsound. At this point, a stronger U.S. government effort to direct loans to sound investments, a strategy that Hoover supported, might have helped. But neither Hughes nor his successor as secretary of state, Frank Kellogg, was interested in such initiatives, and neither was Secretary of the Treasury Mellon. The laissez-faire approach had reasserted itself, and Hoover's plan to involve the U.S. government directly in international economic matters had been rebuffed.

Republican initiatives to ensure world peace continued, however. Secretary of State Kellogg drew up a treaty with Aristide Briand, the French foreign minister, outlawing war as a tool of national policy. In 1928, representatives of the United States, France, and 13 other nations met in Paris to sign the Kellogg-Briand Pact, an agreement that soon attracted the support of 48 other nations. Coolidge viewed Kellogg-Briand as a way of reducing American military commitments abroad and thereby further shrinking the size of the U.S. government at home. With the threat of war removed, the United States could scale back its military forces and eliminate much of the bureaucracy needed to support a large standing army and navy. The celebrated pact contained no enforcement mechanism, however, rendering itself largely ineffective as a foreign policy tool.

Republican administrations did attempt to curtail American military involvement in the Caribbean and Central America as well. Thus, the Coolidge administration pulled U.S. troops out of the Dominican Republic in 1924 and Nicaragua in 1925. But U.S. investments in the region, which more than doubled from 1917 to 1929, proved too important for the U.S. government to ignore. Coolidge sent the marines back into Nicaragua in 1926 to end a war between liberals and conservatives there and to protect American property; this time they stayed until 1934. U.S. troops, meanwhile, occupied Haiti continuously between 1919 and 1934, keeping in power governments friendly to U.S. interests.

FARMERS, SMALL-TOWN PROTESTANTS, AND MORAL TRADITIONALISTS

Although many Americans benefited from the prosperity of the 1920s, others did not. Overproduction was impoverishing substantial numbers of farmers. Beyond these economic hardships, many white Protestants, especially those in rural areas and small towns, feared the new economy and new culture that were taking shape in the cities. Increasingly, these Americans made their voices heard in politics.

Agricultural Depression   During the war, domestic demand for farm products had risen steadily and foreign demand had exploded as the war disrupted agricultural production in France, Ukraine, and other European food-producing regions. Soon after the war, however, Europe's farmers quickly reestablished customary levels of production. Foreign demand for American foodstuffs fell precipitously, leaving U.S. farmers with an oversupply and depressed prices.

A rise in agricultural productivity made possible by the tractor also worsened the plight of farmers. The number of tractors in use almost quadrupled in the 1920s, and 35 million new acres came under cultivation. Produce flooded the market. Prices fell even further, as did farm incomes. By 1929, the annual per capita income of rural Americans was only $223, one-quarter that of the nonfarm population. Hundreds of thousands had to sell their farms and scrape together a living as tenants or abandon farming altogether. Many chose to abandon farm life and headed for the city.

Those who stayed on the land grew increasingly assertive in their demands. Early in the decade, radical farmers led the movement, working through such organizations as the Nonpartisan League of North Dakota and farmer-labor parties in Minnesota, Wisconsin, and other midwestern states. By the second half of the decade, however, leadership had passed from farming radicals to farming moderates, and from small farmers in danger of dispossession to larger farmers and agribusinesses seeking to extend their holdings. By lobbying through such organizations as the American Farm Bureau Federation, the more powerful agricultural interests pressured Congress to set up economic controls that would protect them from failure. Their proposals passed Congress twice, only to be vetoed by President Coolidge.

Cultural Dislocation   Added to the economic plight of the farmers was a sense of cultural dislocation among the majority who were white, Protestant, and of northern European descent. These farmers had long perceived themselves as the backbone of the nation—hardworking, honest, God-fearing yeomen, guardians of independence and liberty.

The 1920 census challenged the validity of that view. For the first time, a slight majority of Americans now lived in urban areas. That finding in itself signified little because the census classified as "urban" those towns with a population as small as

Price of Major Crops, 1914–1929

Source: Data from *Historical Statistics of the United States, Colonial Times to 1970* (White Plains, NY: Kraus International, 1989), pp. 511–12.

2,500. But the census figures did reinforce the widespread perception that both the economic and cultural vitality of the nation had shifted from the countryside to the city. Industry, the chief engine of prosperity, was an urban phenomenon. Commercialized leisure—the world of amusement parks, department stores, professional sports, movies, cabarets, and theaters—was to be enjoyed in cities; so too were flashy fashions and open sexuality. Catholics, Jews, and African Americans, who together outnumbered white Protestants in many cities, seemed to be the principal creators of this new world. They were also thought to be the purveyors of Bolshevism and other kinds of radicalism. Cities, finally, were the home of secular intellectuals who had scrapped their belief in scripture and in God and had embraced science as their new authority.

Throughout the Progressive Era, rural white Americans believed that the cities could be redeemed, that city dwellers could be reformed, and that the Protestant values of rural America would triumph. War had crushed that confidence and had replaced it with the fear that urban culture and urban people might swamp the "superior" values of rural America.

These fears grew more intense as consumer culture and its commodities entered the countryside. Even small towns now sported movie theaters and automobile dealerships. Radio waves carried news of city life into isolated farmhouses. The growth in the circulation of national magazines also broke down the wall separating country from city. Mail-order catalogs invited farmers to fantasize that they too could fill their homes with refrigerators, RCA Victrola phonographs, and Hoover vacuum cleaners.

Rural white Americans showed ambivalence toward this cultural invasion. On the one hand, most country dwellers were eager to participate in the consumer marketplace. On the other hand, many worried that doing so would expose the countryside to atheism, immorality, and radicalism. They expressed their determination to protect their imperiled way of life in their support for Prohibition, the Ku Klux Klan, immigration restriction, and religious fundamentalism.

Prohibition

The Eighteenth Amendment to the Constitution, which prohibited the manufacture and sale of alcohol, went into effect in January 1920. Initially it drew support from a large and varied constituency that included farmers, middle-class city dwellers, feminists, and progressive reformers who loathed the powerful "liquor trust" and who saw firsthand the deleterious effects of drink on the urban poor. It soon became apparent, however, that Prohibition was doing as much to encourage lawbreaking as abstinence. With only 1,500 federal agents to enforce the law, the government could not possibly police the drinking habits of 110 million people. With little fear of punishment, those who wanted to drink did so, either brewing liquor at home or buying it from speakeasies and bootleggers.

Because the law prevented legitimate businesses from manufacturing liquor, organized crime added alcohol to its portfolio. Mobsters procured much of their liquor from Canadian manufacturers, smuggled it across the border, protected it in warehouses, and distributed it to speakeasies. Al Capone's Chicago-based mob alone employed 1,000 men to protect its liquor trafficking, which was so lucrative that Capone became the richest (and most feared) gangster in America. Blood flowed in the streets of Chicago and other northern cities as rival mobs fought one another to enlarge their share of the market.

These unexpected consequences caused many early advocates of Prohibition, especially in the cities, to withdraw their support. Many rural white Protestants, however, became more, not less, determined to rid the country of liquor once and for all. The violence spawned by liquor trafficking confirmed their view of alcohol as evil. The high-profile participation of Italian, Irish, and Jewish gangsters in the bootleg trade caused many rural Protestant Americans to view Catholics and Jews as threats to law and morality.

Al Capone, Chicago Mob Leader. *Capone built a liquor distribution empire during Prohibition. In 1931, the government indicted him on tax evasion charges and sent him to jail in 1932. This 1920s photograph is a mug shot of Capone taken by police during one of his arrests.*

CHARLES PHELPS CUSHING/ClassicStock/Alamy

The Ku Klux Klan

The original Ku Klux Klan, formed in the South in the late 1860s, had died out with the defeat of Reconstruction and the reestablishment of white supremacy. A new Klan had been created in 1915 by William Simmons, a white southerner who had been inspired by D. W. Griffith's racist film, *Birth of a Nation*. By the 1920s, Hiram Evans, a Texas dentist, had replaced Simmons as head of the Klan, and the groups on its hate list had expanded to include Jews and Catholics, in addition to blacks. Evans's Klan propagated a nativist message that the country should contain—or better yet, eliminate—the influence of Jews and Catholics and restore "Anglo-Saxon" racial purity, Protestant supremacy, and traditional morality to national life.

By 1924, as many as 4 million Americans are thought to have belonged to the Klan, including the half million members of its female auxiliary, Women of the Ku Klux Klan. Not only was the Klan strong in states of the Old Confederacy, such as Louisiana and Texas, and in border states such as Oklahoma and Kansas, but it thrived, too, in such northern states as Indiana, Pennsylvania, Washington, and Oregon. It even drew significant membership from the cities of those states. Indiana, for example, was home to 500,000 Klansmen and women, many of them in

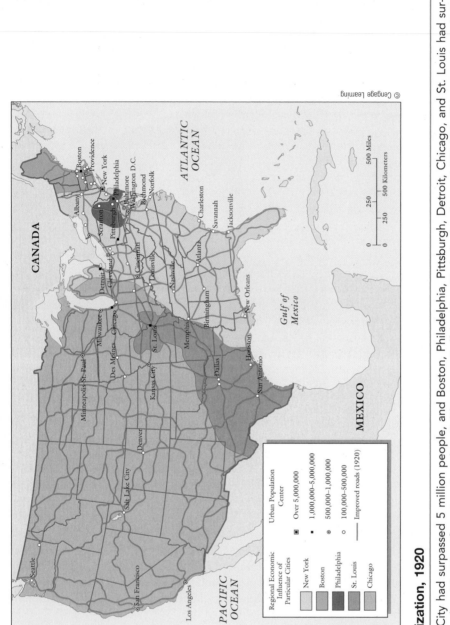

© Cengage Learning

MAP 24.1 Urbanization, 1920

By 1920, New York City had surpassed 5 million people, and Boston, Philadelphia, Pittsburgh, Detroit, Chicago, and St. Louis had surpassed 1 million. Another 10 cities, from Los Angeles, California, to Buffalo, New York, had surpassed 500,000. This map, through its color coding, also shows the regions in which the country's five largest cities exercised economic influence.

the Indianapolis area. In 1924, Indiana voters elected a Klansman to the governorship and sent several other Klan members to the statehouse.

The Klan offered its members friendship networks, social services, and conviviality. Its rituals, regalia, and mock-medieval language (the Imperial Wizard, Exalted Cyclops, Grand Dragons, and such) gave initiates a sense of superiority, valor, and mystery similar to what other fraternal societies—from the Masons to the Knights of Columbus—imparted to their members.

But the Klan also thrived on hate, much of it directed against blacks, Jews, and Catholics. The KKK saw itself as the enforcer of white supremacy, and was proud of its reputation for using force to punish blacks who dared to cross color lines or in other ways offend white sensibilities. Jews stood accused of international banking conspiracies on the one hand and of fomenting communist revolution on the other. And the presence of Catholics in America, the Klan alleged, would allow authoritarian popes to meddle in the affairs of American democracy.

Immigration Restriction   Although most white Protestants never joined the Klan, many of them did respond to the Klan's nativist argument that the country and its values would best be served by limiting the entry of outsiders who were thought to threaten America. That was the purpose of the **Johnson-Reed Immigration Restriction Act of 1924**.

By the early 1920s, most Americans believed that the country could no longer accommodate the million immigrants who had been arriving each year before the war and the more than 800,000 who arrived in 1921. Industrialists no longer needed unskilled European laborers to operate their factories, their places having been taken either by machines or by African American, Mexican, or Filipino workers. Most labor movement leaders were convinced that the influx of workers unfamiliar with English and with trade unions had weakened labor solidarity. Progressive reformers no longer believed that immigrants could be easily Americanized or that harmony between the native-born and the foreign-born could be readily achieved. Congress responded to constituents' concerns by passing an immigration restriction act in 1921. In 1924, the more comprehensive Johnson-Reed Act imposed a yearly quota of 165,000 immigrants from countries outside the Western Hemisphere, effectively reducing total immigration to only 20 percent of the prewar annual average.

The sponsors of the 1924 act believed that certain groups—British, Germans, and Scandinavians, in particular—were racially superior and that, consequently, these groups should be allowed to enter the United States in greater numbers; however, because the Constitution prohibited the enactment of explicitly racist laws, Congress had to achieve this racist aim through subterfuge. Lawmakers established a formula to determine the annual immigrant quota for each foreign country, which was to be computed at 2 percent of the total number of immigrants from that country already resident in the United States in the year 1890. In 1890, immigrant ranks had been dominated by the British, Germans, and Scandinavians, so the new quotas would thus allow for a relatively larger cohort of immigrants from those countries. Immigrant groups that were poorly represented in the 1890 population—Italians, Greeks, Poles, Slavs, and eastern European Jews—were effectively locked out.

ANNUAL IMMIGRANT QUOTAS UNDER THE JOHNSON-REED ACT, 1925–1927

Northwest Europe and Scandinavia		Eastern and Southern Europe		Other Countries	
Country	Quota	Country	Quota	Country	Quota
Germany	51,227	Poland	5,982	Africa (other than Egypt)	1,100
Great Britain and Northern Ireland	34,007	Italy	3,845	Armenia	124
Irish Free State (Ireland)	28,567	Czechoslovakia	3,073	Australia	121
Sweden	9,561	Russia	2,248	Palestine	100
Norway	6,453	Yugoslavia	671	Syria	100
France	3,954	Romania	603	Turkey	100
Denmark	2,789	Portugal	503	New Zealand and Pacific Islands	100
Switzerland	2,081	Hungary	473	All others	1,900
Netherlands	1,648	Lithuania	344		
Austria	785	Latvia	142		
Belgium	512	Spain	131		
Finland	471	Estonia	124		
Free City of Danzig	228	Albania	100		
Iceland	100	Bulgaria	100		
Luxembourg	100	Greece	100		
Total (number)	142,483	Total (number)	18,439	Total (number)	3,745
	86.5%	Total (%)	11.2%	Total (%)	2.3%

Note: Total annual immigrant quota was 164,667.

Source: From *Statistical Abstract of the United States* (Washington, D.C.: Government Printing Office, 1929), p. 100.

The Johnson-Reed Act also reaffirmed the long-standing policy of excluding Chinese immigrants, and it added Japanese and other groups of East and South Asians to the list of groups that were altogether barred from entry. The act did not officially limit immigration from nations in the Western Hemisphere, chiefly because agribusiness interests in Texas and California had convinced Congress that cheap Mexican labor was indispensable to their industry's prosperity. Still, the establishment of a Border Patrol along the U.S.-Mexican border and the imposition of a $10 head tax on all prospective Mexican immigrants made entry into the United States more difficult than it had been.

The Johnson-Reed Act accomplished Congress's underlying goal. Annual immigration from transoceanic nations fell by 80 percent. The large number of available

"Spoiling the Broth."
This anti-immigrant cartoon, appearing in 1921, shows America's fabled melting pot being forced to take in far more immigrants from Europe and Asia than it could possibly absorb. The result was hundreds of thousands, even millions, of immigrants being disgorged from the pot as "unassimilated aliens."

The Granger Collection, New York

slots for English and German immigrants regularly went unfilled, while the smaller number of available slots for Italians, Poles, Russian Jews, and others prevented hundreds of thousands of them from entering the country. A "national origins" system put in place in 1927 further reduced the total annual quota to 150,000 and reserved more than 120,000 of these slots for immigrants from northwestern Europe. Except for minor modifications in 1952, the Johnson-Reed Act would govern U.S. immigration policy until 1965.

Remarkably few Americans, outside of the ethnic groups being discriminated against, objected to these laws at the time they were passed—an indication of how broadly acceptable racism and nativism had become. In fact, racism and religious bigotry enjoyed resurgences during the Jazz Age. The pseudoscience of eugenics, based on the idea that a nation could improve the racial quality of its population by expanding its stronger racial strains and shrinking its weaker ones, found supporters not only in Congress but among the ranks of prestigious scientists as well.

Universities such as Harvard and Columbia set quotas similar to those of the Johnson-Reed Act to reduce the proportion of Jews among their undergraduates.

Fundamental-ism versus Liberal Protestantism   Of all the movements protesting against the modern elements of urban life in the 1920s, Protestant fundamentalism was perhaps the most enduring. **Fundamentalists** regarded the Bible as God's word and thus the source of all "fundamental" truth. They believed that every event depicted in the Bible, from the creation of the world in six days to the resurrection of Christ, happened exactly as the Bible described it. For fundamentalists, God was a deity who intervened directly in the lives of individuals and communities and who made known both his pleasure and his wrath to those who acknowledged his divinity. Sin had to be actively purged, and salvation actively sought.

The rise of the fundamentalist movement from the 1870s through the 1920s roughly paralleled the rise of urban-industrial society. Fundamentalists recoiled from the "evils" of the city—from what they perceived as its poverty, its moral degeneracy, its irreligion, and its crass materialism. Fundamentalism took shape in reaction against two additional aspects of urban society: the growth of liberal Protestantism and the revelations of science.

Liberal Protestants believed that religion had to be adapted to the skeptical and scientific temper of the modern age. The Bible was to be mined for its ethical values rather than for its literal truth. Liberal Protestants removed God from his active role in history and refashioned him into a distant and benign deity who watched over the world but did not intervene to punish or to redeem. They turned religion away from the quest for salvation and toward the pursuit of good deeds, social conscience, and love for one's neighbor. Although those with a liberal bent constituted only a minority of Protestants, they were articulate, visible, and influential in social reform movements. Fundamentalism arose in part to counter the "heretical" claims of the liberal Protestants.

Liberal Protestants and fundamentalists both understood that science was the source of most challenges to Christianity. Scientists believed that rational inquiry was a better guide to the past and to the future than prayer and revelation. Scientists even challenged the ideas that God had created the world and had fashioned humankind in his own image. These were assertions that many religious peoples, particularly fundamentalists, simply could not accept. Conflict was inevitable. It came in 1925, in Dayton, Tennessee.

The Scopes Trial   No aspect of science aroused more anger among fundamentalists than Charles Darwin's theory of evolution. There was no greater blasphemy than to suggest that man emerged from lower forms of life instead of being created by God. In Tennessee in 1925, fundamentalists succeeded in passing a law that forbade teaching "any theory that denies the story of the divine creation of man as taught in the Bible."

For Americans who accepted the authority of science, denying the truth of evolution was as ludicrous as insisting that the sun revolved around the earth. They

Darrow and Bryan Face Off at The Scopes Trial, 1925. *Clarence Darrow (left) was the lead defense attorney for John Scopes and William Jennings Bryan (right) was the chief prosecutor. They had known each other since the days when they had been allies in the progressive movement. The warmth emanating from both men's faces suggests that their respect for each other had endured.*

ridiculed the fundamentalists, but they worried that the passage of the Tennessee law might signal the onset of a campaign to undermine First Amendment guarantees of free speech. The American Civil Liberties Union (ACLU), founded by liberals during the Red Scare of 1919 and 1920, began searching for a teacher who would be willing to challenge the constitutionality of the Tennessee law. The ACLU found its man in John T. Scopes, a 24-year-old biology teacher in Dayton, Tennessee. After confessing that he had taught evolution to his students, Scopes was arrested. The case quickly attracted national attention. William Jennings Bryan, the former Populist, progressive, and secretary of state, announced that he would help prosecute Scopes, and the famous liberal trial lawyer Clarence Darrow rushed to Dayton to lead Scopes's defense. That Bryan and Darrow had once been allies in the progressive movement only heightened the drama. A small army of journalists descended on Dayton, led by H. L. Mencken, a Baltimore-based journalist famous for his savage critiques of the alleged stupidity and prudishness of small-town Americans.

Most observers expected Scopes to be convicted, and he was. But the hearing took an unexpected turn when Darrow persuaded the judge to let Bryan testify as an "expert on the Bible." Darrow knew that Bryan's testimony would have no bearing on the question of Scopes's innocence or guilt. The jury was not even allowed to hear it. His aim was to expose Bryan as a fool for believing that the Bible was a source of literal truth and thus to embarrass the fundamentalists. In a riveting confrontation, Darrow made Bryan's defense of the Bible look problematic and led Bryan to admit that the "truth" of the Bible was not always easy to determine. But Darrow could not shake Bryan's belief that the Bible was God's word and thus the source of all truth.

In his account of the trial, Mencken portrayed Bryan as a pathetic figure devastated by his humiliating experience on the witness stand, a view popularized in the 1960 movie *Inherit the Wind.* When Bryan died only a week after the trial ended, Mencken claimed that the trial had broken Bryan's heart. Bryan deserved a better epitaph than the one Mencken had given him. Diabetes caused his death, not a broken heart. Nor was Bryan the innocent fool that Mencken made him out to be. He remembered when social conservatives had used Darwin's phrase "survival of the fittest" to argue that the wealthy and politically powerful were racially superior to the poor and powerless. His rejection of Darwinism evidenced his democratic faith that all human beings were creatures of God and thus capable of striving for perfection and equality.

The public ridicule attendant on the Scopes trial took its toll on fundamentalists. Many of them retreated from politics and refocused their attention on purging sin from their own hearts rather than from the hearts of others. In the end, the fundamentalists prevailed on three more states to prohibit the teaching of evolution, but the controversy had even more far-reaching effects. Worried about losing sales, publishers quietly removed references to Darwin from their science textbooks, a policy that would remain in force until the 1960s. In this respect, the fundamentalists had scored a significant victory.

ETHNIC AND RACIAL COMMUNITIES

The 1920s were a decade of change for ethnic and racial minorities. Some minorities benefited from the prosperity of the decade; others created and sustained vibrant subcultures. All, however, experienced a surge in religious and racial discrimination that made them uneasy in Jazz Age America.

European Amer-ican Ethnics   European American ethnics—and especially the southern and eastern European majority among them—were concentrated in the cities of the Northeast and Midwest. Many were semi-skilled and unskilled industrial laborers who suffered economic insecurity. In addition, they faced cultural discrimination. Catholics and Jews were targets of the Klan. Catholics generally opposed Prohibition, viewing it as a crude attempt by Protestants to control their behavior. Southern and eastern Europeans, particularly Jews and Italians, resented immigration restriction and the implication that they were inferior to Anglo-Saxon whites. Many Italians were outraged by the execution of Nicola Sacco and Bartolomeo Vanzetti in 1927. If the two men had been native-born white Protestants, many Italian Americans argued, their lives would have been spared.

Southern and eastern Europeans everywhere endured intensive Americanization campaigns. State after state passed laws requiring public schools to instruct children in the essentials of citizenship. Several states, including Rhode Island, extended these laws to private schools as well, convinced that the children of immigrants who were attending Catholic parochial schools were spending too much time learning about their native religion, language, and country. An Oregon law tried to eliminate Catholic schools altogether by ordering all children aged 8 to 16 to enroll in public schools. But attending a public school was no guarantee of acceptance, either—a lesson learned by Jewish children who had excelled in urban public high schools only to be barred from Harvard, Columbia, and other elite universities.

Southern and eastern Europeans responded to these insults and attacks by strengthening the very institutions and customs Americanizers sought to undermine. Ethnic associations flourished in the 1920s—Catholic churches and Jewish synagogues, fraternal and mutual benefit societies, banks and charitable organizations, athletic leagues and youth groups. Children learned their native languages and customs at home and at church if not at school, and they joined with their parents to celebrate their ethnic heritage. Among Italians and French Canadians, saints' days were occasions for parades, speeches, band concerts, games, and feasts, all serving to solidify ethnic bonds and affirm ethnic identity.

Many of these immigrants and their children, however, also embraced the new consumer culture. They flocked to movies and amusement parks, to baseball games and boxing matches. Children usually entered more enthusiastically into the world of American mass culture than did their immigrant parents, a behavior that often set off family conflicts. For a time, however, many ethnics found it possible to reconcile their own culture with American culture.

European American ethnics also resolved to develop sufficient political muscle to defeat the forces of nativism and to turn government policy in a more favorable direction. One sign of this determination was a sharp rise in the number of immigrants who became U.S. citizens. The percentage of immigrant Poles, Slavs, Italians, Lithuanians, and Hungarians who became naturalized citizens nearly doubled during the decade; the percentage of naturalized Greeks almost tripled. Armed with the vote, ethnics turned out on election days to defeat unsympathetic city councilmen, mayors, state representatives, and even an occasional governor. Their growing national strength first became apparent at the Democratic National Convention of 1924, when urban-ethnic delegates almost won approval of planks calling for the repeal of Prohibition and condemnation of the Klan. After denying the presidential nomination to William G. McAdoo—Woodrow Wilson's treasury secretary, son-in-law, and heir apparent—they nearly secured it for their candidate, **Alfred E. Smith**, the Irish American governor of New York. McAdoo represented the rural and southern constituencies of the Democratic Party. His forces ended up battling Smith's urban-ethnic forces for 103 ballots, until both men gave up, and supporters from each camp switched their votes to a compromise candidate, the corporate lawyer John W. Davis.

The nomination fight damaged the Democratic Party in the short term, and popular Calvin Coolidge easily defeated the little-known Davis. The split between the party's rural Protestant and urban-ethnic constituencies would keep the Democrats from the White House for nearly a decade, but the convention upheaval

of 1924 also marked an important milestone in the bid by European American ethnics for political power. They would achieve a second milestone at the Democratic
National Convention of 1928 when, after another bitter nomination struggle, they
secured the presidential nomination for Al Smith. Never before had a major political party nominated a Catholic for president. Herbert Hoover crushed Smith in the
general election, as nativists stirred up anti-Catholic prejudice yet again and as large
numbers of southern Democrats either stayed home or voted Republican. Even so,
the campaign offered encouraging signs, not the least of which was Smith beating
Hoover in the nation's 12 largest cities.

African   Despite the urban race riots of 1919, African Americans
Americans   continued to leave their rural homes for the industrial cen-
                     ters of the South and the North. In the 1920s alone, nearly
a million blacks traveled north. In New York City and Chicago, their numbers
grew so large—300,000 in New York and 230,000 in Chicago—that they formed
cities unto themselves. When word of New York City's urban black enclave
reached the Caribbean, thousands of West Indian blacks set off for Harlem. Complex societies emerged within these black metropolises consisting of workers,
businessmen, professionals, intellectuals, artists, and entertainers. Social differenti-
ation intensified as various groups—long-resident northerners and newly arrived
southerners, religious conservatives and cultural radicals, African Americans and
African Caribbeans—found reason to disapprove of one another's ways. Still, the
diversity and complexity of urban black America were thrilling, nowhere more
so than in Harlem, the "Negro capital." Black writer James Weldon Johnson
described Harlem in the 1920s:

DEMOCRATIC PRESIDENTIAL VOTING IN CHICAGO
BY ETHNIC GROUPS, 1924 AND 1928

	Percent Democratic	
	1924	1928
Czechoslovaks	40%	73%
Poles	35	71
Lithuanians	48	77
Yugoslavs	20	54
Italians	31	63
Germans	14	58
Jews	19	60

Source: From John M. Allswang, A *House for All Peoples: Ethnic Politics in Chicago,
1890–1936* (Lexington: University Press of Kentucky), p. 42.

Throughout colored America Harlem is the recognized Negro capital. Indeed, it is Mecca for the sightseer, the pleasure-seeker, the curious, the adventurous, the enterprising, the ambitious, and the talented of the entire Negro world.... Not merely a colony or a community or a settlement—not at all a "quarter" or a slum or a fringe—[Harlem is] ... a black city, located in the heart of white Manhattan, and containing more Negroes to the square mile than any other spot on earth. It strikes the uninformed observer as a phenomenon, a miracle straight out of the skies.

Not even the glamour of Harlem could erase the reality of racial discrimination, however. Most African Americans could find work only in New York City's least-desired and lowest-paying jobs. Because they could rent apartments only in areas that real estate agents and banks had designated as "colored," African Americans suffered the highest rate of residential segregation of any minority group. Although Harlem had its fashionable districts where affluent blacks lived, much of the area's housing stock was poor and rents were high. Harlem became a black ghetto, an area set apart from the rest of the city by the skin color of its inhabitants, by its higher population density and poverty rate, by its higher incidence of infectious diseases, and by the lower life expectancy of its people.

Blacks did enjoy some important economic breakthroughs in the 1920s. Henry Ford, for example, hired large numbers of African Americans to work in his Detroit auto factories. Even here, however, a racist logic was operating, for Ford believed that automobile workers divided along racial lines would not challenge his authority. Until the 1940s, in fact, unions made less headway at Ford plants than at the plants of other major automobile manufacturers.

Racial divisions carried over from work to play. African Americans loved baseball as much as white Americans did, and Babe Ruth enjoyed a large black following, but black baseball players were barred from playing in the lily-white major leagues. In response, they formed their own Negro Leagues in the United States and also played professional ball in Mexico and the Caribbean, where they earned extra income and escaped some of the prejudice that met them everywhere in the United States.

The greatest black baseball player of the time was probably Josh Gibson, who joined the Homestead Grays of the National Negro League in 1929 at the age of 18. In his 17-year career, he compiled statistics that surpassed those of any professional ballplayer of his era, white or black, including those of the legendary Ruth. Gibson slugged 962 career home runs, hit 84 home runs in a single season, and compiled a .373 lifetime batting average. Because he died in 1947, at the age of 35, just months before the integration of major league baseball, Gibson rarely got the opportunity to test his skills against the best white ballplayers, and they rarely got a chance to play against him.

In the 1920s, African Americans grew pessimistic about achieving racial equality. After Marcus Garvey's black-nationalist movement collapsed in the mid-1920s, no comparable organization arose to take its place. The NAACP continued to fight racial discrimination, and the Urban League carried on quiet negotiations with industrial elites to secure jobs for African Americans. Black socialists led by A. Philip Randolph built a strong all-black union, the Brotherhood of Sleeping Car Porters, but the victories were small and white allies were scarce. The political

HISTORY THROUGH FILM

The Jazz Singer (1927)

Directed by Alan Crosland. Starring Al Jolson (Jake Rabinowitz/Jack Robin), May McAvoy (Mary Dale), and Warner Oland (Cantor Rabinowitz).

The Jazz Singer was a sensation when it opened because it was the first movie to use sound (although relatively few words of dialogue were actually spoken). It also starred Al Jolson, the era's most popular Broadway entertainer, and bravely explored an issue that the film industry usually avoided—the religious culture and generational dynamics of a "new immigrant" family.

The movie focuses on Jake Rabinowitz and his immigrant parents, who are Jewish and devout. Jake's father is a fifth-generation cantor whose job it is to fill his New York City synagogue with ancient and uplifting melodies on the Sabbath and Jewish holidays. Cantor Rabinowitz looks upon his work as sacred, and he expects Jake to take his place one day. But Jake has other ideas. He loves music but is drawn to the new rhythmic ragtime and sensual jazz melodies emerging from his American surroundings. In an early scene, we encounter Jake at a dance hall, absorbed in playing and singing ragtime tunes and forgetting that he should be at home preparing for Yom Kippur, the holiest day in the Jewish calendar. His distraught father finds him and whips him, and Jake, in anger and pain, runs away. These early scenes allow us to glimpse an important theme in the immigrant experience of the early 20th century: the deep attraction among the children of immigrants to the energy and vitality of American popular culture and the strains that this attraction often caused between these children and parents desperate to maintain the traditions they had brought with them from Europe.

Jake's estrangement from his family and community gives him the space to reinvent himself as Jack Robin, the jazz singer. His love relationship with a prominent (and non-Jewish) stage actress, Mary Dale, brings him the big break he needs, a starring role in a Broadway show. Jack hopes to use his return to New York to reconcile with his father. This eventually happens when Jake, on the eve of Yom Kippur once again, agrees to skip his show's premiere in order to take his ailing father's place as cantor in the synagogue. Jake's melodies soar and reach his bedridden father who, thinking that his son has succeeded him as cantor and thus fulfilled his (the father's) deepest wish, peacefully dies.

His father is deceived, for Jake returns to his Broadway show as soon as Yom Kippur ends to deliver an outstanding performance as the "Jazz Singer." His future lies with Broadway, rather than with a synagogue, and with the gentile Mary. The movie, however, makes it seem as though everything will work out: Jake's mother is in the audience for the Broadway show, enjoying her son's success and in effect blessing the career and woman he has chosen. That this resolution requires misleading the father reminds us, however, that the strains between immigrant parents and their American-born children could be deep and sometimes not resolvable.

initiatives emerging among European American ethnics had few counterparts in the African American community.

In terms of black culture, however, the 1920s were vigorous and productive. Black musicians coming north to Chicago and New York brought with

The movie also allows us to ask questions about the relationship between immigrants and African Americans. As part of his Broadway performance, Jake does a blackface routine, using burnt cork to turn his face and neck black and thus to appear to audiences as a "black" entertainer. From the early 19th to the early 20th centuries, "blacking up" was a performance style popular among white entertainers who wanted to appropriate and ridicule expressive aspects of black culture. What did it mean for a child of Jewish immigrants, himself vulnerable to being stigmatized as an outsider in America, to "black up"? Jake may have been expressing in part his desire to draw closer to rich elements in black musical culture. But Jake may also have been signaling his desire to distance himself from African Americans by participating in a tradition popular among white American entertainers. Ironically, "blacking up" may have been a way for an entertainer to embrace not black but white America, and for someone like Jake to be accepted by non-Jewish white Americans as one of them.

Bettmann/Corbis

A billboard in New York City advertising The Jazz Singer. *Al Jolson is shown in blackface.*

them their distinctive musical styles, most notably the blues and ragtime. Influenced by the harmonies and techniques of European classical music, which black musicians learned from European American ethnic counterparts, these southern styles metamorphosed into jazz. Urban audiences, first black and

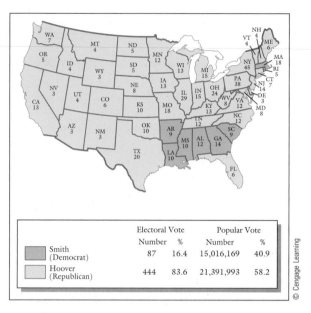

		Electoral Vote		Popular Vote	
		Number	%	Number	%
▓	Smith (Democrat)	87	16.4	15,016,169	40.9
☐	Hoover (Republican)	444	83.6	21,391,993	58.2

© Cengage Learning

MAP 24.2 Presidential Election, 1928

This map shows Hoover's landslide victory in 1928, as he carried all but eight states and won almost 84 percent of the electoral vote.

DEATH RATES FROM SELECTED CAUSES FOR NEW YORK CITY RESIDENTS, 1925

Cause of Death	Total Population	African American Population
General death rate (per 1,000 population)	11.4	16.5
Pneumonia	132.8	282.4
Pulmonary tuberculosis	75.5	258.4
Infant mortality (per 1,000 live births)	64.6	118.4
Maternal mortality (per 1,000 total births)	5.3	10.2
Stillbirths (per 1,000 births)	47.6	82.7
Homicide	5.3	19.5
Suicide	14.8	9.7

Note: Population rate is per 100,000, unless noted otherwise.

Source: Cheryl Lynn Greenberg, *"Or Does It Explode?" Black Harlem in the Great Depression* (New York: Oxford University Press, 1991), p. 32.

then white, found this new music alluring. They responded to its melodies, its sensuality, its creativity, its savvy. In Chicago, Detroit, New York, New Orleans, and elsewhere, jazz musicians came together in cramped apartments, cabarets, and nightclubs to jam, compete, and entertain. Willie Smith,

Charles P. Johnson, Count Basie, Fats Waller, Duke Ellington, and Louis Armstrong were among the most famous musicians of the day. By the late 1920s, they were being hailed in Europe as well.

Jazz seemed to express something quintessentially modern. Jazz musicians broke free of convention: They improvised and produced new sounds that created new sensations. Both blacks and whites found in jazz an escape from the routine, the predictable, and the conventions of their everyday lives.

The Harlem Renaissance   Paralleling the emergence of jazz was a black literary and artistic awakening known as the **Harlem Renaissance**. Black novelists, poets, painters, sculptors, and playwrights set about creating works rooted in their own culture instead of imitating the styles of white Europeans and Americans. The movement had begun during the war, when blacks sensed that they might at last be advancing to full equality. It was symbolized by the image of the "New Negro," a black man or woman who would no longer be deferential to whites and who would display his or her independence through talent and determination.

Langston Hughes, a young black poet, said of the Harlem Renaissance: "We younger Negro artists who create now intend to express our individual dark-skinned selves without fear or shame. If white people are pleased, we are glad. If they are not, it doesn't matter. We know we are beautiful. And ugly, too." Writers Claude McKay, Jean Toomer, and Zora Neale Hurston; poet Countee Cullen; painter Aaron Douglas; and philosopher and cultural critic Alain Locke were other prominent Renaissance participants. The appearance in 1925 of a special issue of *Survey Graphic,* a white liberal magazine, devoted entirely to "Harlem— the Mecca of the New Negro," announced the Renaissance's arrival.

Even these cultural advances, however, failed to escape white prejudice. The most popular jazz nightclubs in Harlem, most of which were owned and operated by whites, often refused to admit black customers; only African American jazz musicians, singers and dancers, prostitutes, and kitchen help were permitted inside. Moreover, the black musicians often had to perform what the white patrons wanted to hear. Some black entertainers, such as Josephine Baker, the legendary dancer, left America for Europe in the 1920s, in the hope that they would find in Paris and elsewhere greater artistic and personal freedom than they could attain in the land of their birth.

Black writers experienced similar pressures. Many depended for their sustenance on the support of white patrons, who often wanted a return on their investment. Charlotte Mason, the New York City matron who supported Hughes and Hurston, for example, expected them to entertain her friends by demonstrating "authentic Negritude" in their work. Hurston accepted this role, but for Hughes it became unbearable. Both Hughes and Hurston paid a price for their patron's support, including the collapse of their once-close friendship with each other.

Mexican Americans   After the Johnson-Reed Act passed Congress in 1924, Mexicans became the country's chief source of immigrant labor. A total of 500,000 Mexicans came to the United States in the 1920s. Some headed for the steel, auto, and meatpacking plants of the Midwest, but most settled in the Southwest, where they worked on railroads and in construction, agriculture, and manufacturing. In Texas, three of four construction workers and eight of every ten migrant farmworkers were Mexicans. In California, Mexican immigrants made up 75 percent of the state's agricultural workforce.

Mexican farm laborers in Texas worked long hours for little money. As a rule, they earned 50 cents to a dollar less per day than Anglo workers. Forced to follow the crops, they had little opportunity to develop settled homes and communities. They depended for shelter on whatever facilities farm owners offered. Because farm owners rarely required the services of Mexican workers for more than several days or weeks, few were willing to spend the money required to provide decent homes and schools. Houses typically lacked even wooden floors or indoor plumbing. Mexican laborers found it difficult to protest these conditions. Their knowledge of English was limited. Many were in debt to employers who had advanced them money and who threatened them with jail if they failed to fulfill the terms of their contract. Others feared deportation; they lacked visas, having slipped into the

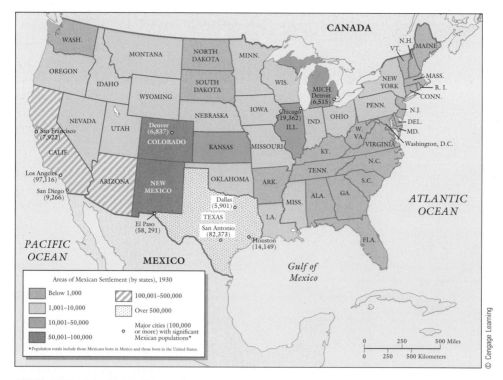

MAP 24.3 Mexican Population in the United States, 1930

By 1930, Mexican immigrants had established their pattern of settling primarily in the U.S. Southwest. Texas had the largest concentration of Mexican immigrants, followed by California and Arizona, and then by New Mexico and Colorado. In the 1920s, Los Angeles surpassed San Antonio as the city with the largest Mexican community in the United States.

United States illegally rather than pay the immigrant tax or endure harassment from the Border Patrol.

Increasing numbers of Mexican immigrants, however, found their way to California, where, on the whole, wages exceeded those in Texas. Some men escaped agricultural labor altogether for construction and manufacturing jobs. Others worked in the city's large railroad yards, at the city's numerous construction sites, and as unskilled workers in local factories. Mexican women labored in the city's garment shops, fish canneries, and food-processing plants. By 1930, Los Angeles had become the largest area of settlement for Mexicans in the United States.

By the mid-1920s, the Los Angeles Mexican American community included a sizable professional class, a proud group of **californios** (Spanish speakers who had been resident in California for generations), many musicians and entertainers, a small but energetic band of entrepreneurs and businessmen, conservative clerics and intellectuals who had fled or been expelled from revolutionary Mexico, and Mexican government officials who had been sent to counter the influence of the conservative exiles and to strengthen the ties of the immigrants to their homeland. This diverse mix created much internal conflict, but it also generated considerable cultural vitality. Los Angeles became the same kind of magnet for Mexican Americans that Harlem had become for African Americans.

Mexican musicians flocked to Los Angeles, as did Mexican playwrights. The city supported a vigorous Spanish-language theater. Mexican musicians performed on street corners, at ethnic festivals and weddings, at cabarets, and on the radio. Especially popular were folk ballads, called *corridos*, that spoke to the experiences of Mexican immigrants. Although different in form and melody from the African American blues, *corridos* resembled the blues in their emphasis on the suffering, hope, and frustrations of ordinary people.

This flowering of Mexican American culture in Los Angeles could not erase the low wages, high rates of infant mortality, racial discrimination, and other hardships Mexicans faced; nor did it encourage Mexicans, in Los Angeles or elsewhere, to mobilize as a political force. Unlike European immigrants, Mexican immigrants showed little interest in becoming American citizens and acquiring the vote. Yet, the cultural vibrancy of the Mexican immigrant community did sustain many individuals who were struggling to survive in a strange, often hostile, environment.

THE "LOST GENERATION" AND DISILLUSIONED INTELLECTUALS

Before the First World War, American intellectuals and artists had been deeply engaged with "the people." Although they were critical of many aspects of American society, they believed they could help bring about a new politics and improve social conditions. The war, however, shook their confidence in Americans' capacity for reform. The wartime push for consensus created intolerance of radicals, immigrants, and blacks. Intellectuals had been further dismayed by Prohibition, the rebirth of the Ku Klux Klan, the rise of fundamentalism, and the execution of Sacco and Vanzetti. To many it seemed as though ordinary middle-class Americans had embraced conformity for themselves and now sought to impose it on others. In 1921, the young critic Harold Stearns wrote that "the most moving and pathetic fact in the social life of America today is emotional and aesthetic starvation." Before these words were published, Stearns had sailed for France. So many alienated young men like Stearns showed up in Paris that Gertrude Stein, an American writer whose Paris apartment became a gathering place for them, took to calling them the "**Lost Generation.**"

Their indictment of America was harsh. Most of these white writers possessed little knowledge of how most Americans lived. Still, they managed to convert their disillusionment into a rich literary sensibility. The finest works of the decade focused on the psychological toll of living in what the poet T. S. Eliot referred to as *The Waste Land* (1922). F. Scott Fitzgerald's novel *The Great Gatsby* (1925) told of a man destroyed by his desire to be accepted into a world of wealth, fancy cars, and fast women. In the novel *A Farewell to Arms* (1929), Ernest Hemingway wrote of an American soldier overwhelmed by the senselessness and brutality of war who deserts the army for the company of a woman he loves. Playwright Eugene O'Neill created characters haunted by despair, loneliness, and unfulfilled longing. Writers innovated in style as well as in content. Sherwood Anderson, in his novel *Winesburg, Ohio* (1919), blended fiction and autobiography. John Dos Passos, in *Manhattan Transfer* (1925), mixed journalism with more traditional literary methods. Hemingway wrote in an understated, laconic prose that somehow drew attention to his characters' rage and vulnerability.

White southern writers found a tragic sensibility surviving from the South's defeat in the Civil War that spoke to their own loss of hope. One group of such writers, calling themselves the Agrarians, argued that the enduring agricultural character of their region offered a more hopeful path to the future than did the mass-production and mass-consumption regime that had overtaken the North. In 1929, William Faulkner published *The Sound and the Fury,* the first in a series of novels set in northern Mississippi's fictional Yoknapatawpha County. Faulkner explored the violence and terror that marked relationships among family members and townspeople, while maintaining compassion and understanding. Faulkner, Lewis, Hemingway, O'Neill, and Eliot would each receive the Nobel Prize for Literature.

Democracy on the Defensive   Disdain for the masses led many intellectuals to question democracy. Although few intellectuals were as frank as Mencken, who dismissed democracy as "the worship of jackals by jackasses," their distrust of democracy ran deep. Walter Lippmann, a former radical and progressive, declared that modern society had rendered democracy obsolete. In his view, average citizens, buffeted by propaganda emanating from powerful opinion makers, could no longer make the kind of informed, rational judgments needed to make democracy work. They were vulnerable to demagogues who played on their emotions and fears. Lippmann's solution, and that of many other political commentators, was to shift government power from the people to educated elites. Those elites, who would be appointed rather than elected, would conduct foreign and domestic policy in an informed, intelligent way. Only then, in Lippmann's view, could government be effective and just.

Mencken's and Lippmann's antidemocratic views did not go uncontested. The philosopher **John Dewey**, who taught at Columbia University but whose reputation and influence extended well beyond academia, was the most articulate spokesman for the "pro-democracy" position. He acknowledged that the concentration of power in giant organizations had eroded the authority of Congress, the presidency, and other democratic institutions, but democracy, he insisted, was not doomed. Government could use its power to democratize corporations and to regulate the communications industry to ensure that every citizen had access to the facts needed to make reasonable, informed political decisions.

Dewey's views attracted the support of a wide range of liberal intellectuals and reformers, including Robert and Helen Lynd; Rexford Tugwell, professor of economics at Columbia; and Felix Frankfurter, a rising star at Harvard's law school. Some of these activists had ties to labor leaders and to New York governor Franklin D. Roosevelt. They formed the vanguard of a new liberal movement committed to taking up the work the progressives had left unfinished.

These reformers were utterly without power, except in a few states, and they took little comfort in the presidential election of 1928. Hoover's smashing victory suggested that the trends of the 1920s—the dominance of the Republicans, the centrality of Prohibition to political debate, the paralysis of the Democrats, the growing economic might of capitalism, and the pervasive influence of consumer culture—would continue unabated.

CONCLUSION

Signs abounded in the 1920s that Americans were creating a new and bountiful society. The increased accessibility of cars, radios, vacuum cleaners, and other consumer durables; rising real wages, low unemployment, and installment buying; the widening circle of stock owners; the spread of welfare capitalism—all of these developments pointed to an economy that had become more prosperous, more consumer oriented, even somewhat more egalitarian. Moves to greater equality within marriage and to enhanced liberty for single women suggested that economic change was propelling social change as well.

Even so, many working-class and rural Americans benefited little from the decade's prosperity. Moreover, the decade's social changes aroused resistance, especially from white farmers and small-town Americans, who feared that the rapid growth of cities and the large urban settlements of European and Mexican Catholics, Jews, and African Americans were rendering their white Protestant America unrecognizable.

In the Democratic Party, farmers, small-town Americans, and moral traditionalists fought bitterly against the growing power of urban, ethnic constituencies. Elsewhere, the traditionalists battled hard to protect religion's authority against the inroads of science and to purge the nation of "inferior" population streams. In the process they arrayed themselves against American traditions of liberty and equality, even as they posed as the defenders of the best that America had to offer.

Their resistance to change caused many of the nation's most talented artists and writers to turn away from their fellow Americans. Meanwhile, although ethnic and racial minorities experienced high levels of discrimination, they nevertheless found enough freedom to create vibrant ethnic and racial communities and to launch projects—as in the case of African Americans in Harlem and Mexican Americans in Los Angeles—of cultural renaissance.

The Republican Party, having largely shed its reputation for reform, took credit for engineering the new economy of consumer plenty. It looked forward to years of political dominance. A steep and unexpected economic depression, however, would soon dash that expectation, revive the Democratic Party, and destroy Republican political power for a generation.

25

THE GREAT DEPRESSION AND THE NEW DEAL, 1929–1939

THE GREAT DEPRESSION began on October 29, 1929 (Black Tuesday), with a spectacular stock market crash. On that one day, stock values plummeted $14 billion. By the end of that year, stock prices had fallen 50 percent from their September highs. By 1932, the worst year of the Depression, they had fallen another 30 percent. In three years, $74 billion of wealth had simply vanished. Meanwhile, the unemployment rate had soared to 25 percent.

Many Americans who lived through the Great Depression could never forget the scenes of misery they saw everywhere. In cities, the poor meekly awaited their turn for a piece of stale bread and thin gruel at ill-funded soup kitchens. Scavengers poked through garbage cans for food, scoured railroad tracks for coal that had fallen from trains, and sometimes ripped up railroad ties for fuel. Hundreds of thousands of Americans built makeshift shelters out of cardboard, scrap metal, and whatever else they could find in the city dump. They called their towns "Hoovervilles," after the president they despised for his apparent refusal to help them.

The Great Depression brought cultural crisis as well as economic crisis. In the 1920s, American business leaders had successfully redefined the national culture in business terms, as Americans' values became synonymous with the values of business: economic growth, freedom of enterprise, and acquisitiveness. But the swagger of American businessmen during the 1920s made them vulnerable to attack in the 1930s, as jobs, incomes, and growth all disappeared. With the prestige of business and business values in decline, how could Americans regain their hope and recover

CHRONOLOGY

1929	Herbert Hoover assumes the presidency
	Stock market crashes on "Black Tuesday"
1930	Tariff Act (Hawley-Smoot) raises tariffs
1931	More than 2,000 U.S. banks fail
1932	Unemployment rate reaches 25 percent
	Reconstruction Finance Corporation established
	Bonus Army marches on Washington
	Roosevelt defeats Hoover for presidency
1933	Roosevelt assumes presidency
	Hundred Days legislation defines First New Deal (March–June)
	Roosevelt administration recognizes the Soviet Union
	Good Neighbor Policy toward Latin America launched
1934	Father Charles Coughlin and Huey Long challenge conservatism of First New Deal
	Two thousand strikes staged across country
	Democrats overwhelm Republicans in off-year election
	Radical political movements emerge in several states
	Indian Reorganization Act grants limited right of self-government to American Indians
	Reciprocal Trade Agreement lowers tariffs
1935	Committee for Industrial Organization (CIO) formed
	Supreme Court declares National Recovery Administration (NRA) unconstitutional
	Roosevelt unveils his Second New Deal
	Congress passes Social Security Act and National Labor Relations Act (Wagner Act)
	Holding Company Act breaks up utilities' near-monopoly
	Congress passes Wealth Tax Act
	Works Progress Administration established
	Rural Electrification Administration established
	Number of Mexican immigrants returning to Mexico reaches 500,000
1936	Roosevelt defeats Alf Landon for second term
	Supreme Court declares Agricultural Adjustment Act (AAA) unconstitutional
	Congress passes Soil Conservation and Domestic Allotment Act to replace AAA
	Farm Security Administration established

1937	United Auto Workers defeats General Motors in sit-down strike
	Roosevelt attempts to "pack" the Supreme Court
	Supreme Court upholds constitutionality of Social Security Act and National Labor Relations Act
	Severe recession hits
1938	Conservative opponents of New Deal do well in off-year election
	Superman comic debuts
1939	Crowd of 75,000 gathers to hear Marian Anderson sing at Lincoln Memorial

their confidence in the future? The first years of the 1930s held no convincing answers.

The gloom broke in early 1933 when **Franklin Delano Roosevelt** became president and unleashed the power of government to regulate capitalist enterprises, to restore the economy to health, and to guarantee the social welfare of Americans who were unable to help themselves. Roosevelt called his pro-government program a "new deal for the American people," and it would dominate national politics for the next 40 years. Hailed as a hero, Roosevelt became (and remains) the only president to be elected more than two times. In the short term, the New Deal failed to restore prosperity to America, but the **liberalism** it championed found acceptance among millions who agreed with Roosevelt that only a large and powerful government could guarantee Americans their liberty.

Causes of the Great Depression

America had experienced other depressions, or "panics," and no one would have been surprised if the boom of the 1920s had been followed by a one- or two-year economic downturn. No one was prepared, however, for the economic catastrophe of the 1930s.

Stock Market Speculation In 1928 and 1929, stock values had doubled. Money had poured into the market, but many investors were buying on 10 percent "margin," putting up only 10 percent of the price of a stock and borrowing the rest from brokers or banks. Few thought they would ever have to repay these loans with money out of their own pockets. Instead, investors expected to resell their shares within a few months at dramatically higher prices, pay back their loans from the proceeds, and still clear a handsome profit. And, for a while, that is exactly what they did.

The possibility of making a fortune by investing a few thousand dollars only intensified investors' greed. As speculation became rampant, money flowed indiscriminately into all kinds of risky enterprises. The stock market spiraled upward, out of control. When, in October 1929, confidence in future earnings faltered, creditors began demanding that investors who had bought stocks on margin repay their loans. The market crashed from its dizzying heights.

The crash by itself fails to explain why the Great Depression lasted as long as it did. Poor decision making by the Federal Reserve Board, an ill-advised tariff that took effect soon after the Depression hit, and excessive concentration of wealth in the hands of the rich deepened the economic collapse and made recovery more difficult.

Mistakes by the Federal Reserve Board   In 1930 and 1931, the Federal Reserve curtailed the amount of money in circulation and raised interest rates, thereby making credit more difficult for the public to secure. Employing a tight money policy during the boom years of 1928 and 1929 might have restrained the stock market and strengthened the economy. Deploying such a policy once the market had crashed was a disastrous decision. What the economy needed in 1930 and 1931 was an expanded money supply, lower interest rates, and easier credit. Such a course would have made it easier for debtors to pay their creditors. Instead, by choosing the opposite course, the Federal Reserve plunged an economy starved for credit deeper into depression. Higher interest rates also triggered an international crisis, as the banks of Germany and Austria, heavily dependent on U.S. loans, went bankrupt. The German-Austrian collapse, in turn, spread financial panic throughout Europe and hurt U.S. manufacturers and banks specializing in European trade and investment.

An Ill-Advised Tariff   The Tariff Act of 1930, also known as the Hawley-Smoot Tariff Act, accelerated economic decline abroad and at home. Throughout the 1920s, agricultural interests had sought higher tariffs to protect American farmers against foreign competition. But Hawley-Smoot not only raised tariffs on 75 agricultural goods from 32 to 40 percent (the highest rate in American history), it also raised tariffs by a similar percentage on 925 manufactured products. Angry foreign governments retaliated by raising their own tariff rates to keep out American goods. International trade, already weakened by the tight credit policies of the Federal Reserve, declined even further.

A Maldistribution of Wealth   A maldistribution in the nation's wealth that had developed in the 1920s also stymied economic recovery. Although average income rose in the 1920s, the incomes of the wealthiest families rose higher than the rest. Between 1918 and 1929, the share of the national income that went to the wealthiest 20 percent of the population rose by more than 10 percent, while the share that went to the poorest 60 percent fell by almost 13 percent. The Coolidge administration contributed to this maldistribution by lowering taxes on the wealthy, thereby allowing a higher proportion of national wealth to remain in their hands. The deepening inequality of income distribution slowed consumption and held back the growth of consumer-oriented industries (cars, household appliances, processed and packaged foods, recreation), the most dynamic elements of the U.S. economy. Even when the rich spent their money

Unemployed Men in New York City, 1931. *The thousands of men waiting to register at the Emergency Unemployment Relief office became so frustrated that they rioted. Police reserves arrived to restore order.*

Bettmann/Corbis

lavishly—building huge mansions, buying expensive cars, vacationing on the French Riviera—they still spent a smaller proportion of their total incomes on consumption than wage earners did. The average 1920s wage earner, for example, might spend one-quarter to one-half of his annual earnings to buy a car.

Putting more of the total increase in national income into the pockets of average Americans during the 1920s would have strengthened the newer consumer industries. Such an economy might have recovered relatively quickly from the stock market crash of 1929. Instead, recovery from the Great Depression lagged until 1941, more than a decade later.

CRISIS AND HOPE, 1929–1933

The magnitude of the economic collapse overwhelmed the newly elected Republican president, Herbert Hoover. Cultural gloom settled on the country as the Depression stretched into its third year.

The Fall of a Self-Made Man   In 1928, Herbert Hoover seemed to embody the American dream. From modest beginnings, Hoover had parlayed his intelligence and drive into gaining admission to Stanford University, becoming a mining engineer, and then rising rapidly to top management positions in globe-spanning mining companies. A talented and tireless administrator, Hoover won an international reputation in the First World War for his success, as head of the U.S. Food Administration, in feeding millions of European soldiers and civilians. Then, in the 1920s, he became an active and influential secretary of commerce. As the decade wound down, no American seemed better qualified to become president of the United States, an office that Hoover assumed in March 1929. Hoover was certain he could make prosperity a permanent feature of American life. "We in America today are nearer to the final triumph over poverty than ever before in the history of any land," he declared in August 1928. A little more than a year later, the Great Depression struck.

To cope with the crisis, Hoover encouraged organizations of farmers, industrialists, and bankers to share information, bolster one another's spirits, and devise policies to aid economic recovery. He urged farmers to restrict output, industrialists to hold wages at pre-depression levels, and bankers to help each other remain solvent. The federal government would provide them with information, strategies of mutual aid, occasional loans, and morale-boosting speeches.

Hoover also secured a one-year moratorium on loan payments that European governments owed American banks. He steered through Congress the Glass-Steagall Act of 1932, which was intended to help American banks meet the demands of European depositors who wished to convert their dollars to gold. And to ease the crisis at home, he created the Reconstruction Finance Corporation (RFC) to make $2 billion available in loans to ailing banks and to corporations willing to build low-cost housing, bridges, and other public works. The RFC was the biggest federal peacetime intervention in the economy up to that point in American history. The Home Loan Bank Board, set up that same year, offered funds to savings and loans, mortgage companies, and other financial institutions that lent money for home construction and mortgages.

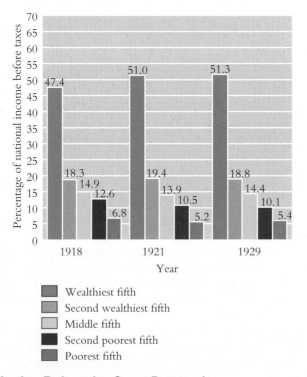

Income Distribution Before the Great Depression

Source: From Gabriel Kolko, *Wealth and Power in America: An Analysis of Social Class and Income Distribution* (New York: Praeger, 1962), p. 14.

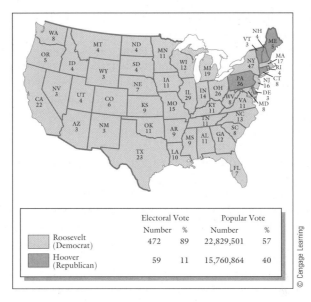

	Electoral Vote		Popular Vote	
	Number	%	Number	%
Roosevelt (Democrat)	472	89	22,829,501	57
Hoover (Republican)	59	11	15,760,864	40

© Cengage Learning

MAP 25.1   Presidential Election, 1932

The trauma of the Great Depression can be gauged by the shifting fortunes of President Herbert Hoover. In 1928, he had won 444 electoral votes and carried all but eight states (see Map 24.2). In 1932, by contrast, he won only 59 electoral votes and carried only seven states. His Democratic opponent, Franklin D. Roosevelt, was the big winner.

Despite this new government activism, Hoover was uncomfortable with the idea of high levels of government spending. When RFC expenditures, in 1932, created the largest peacetime deficit in U.S. history, Hoover tried to balance the federal budget. He also insisted that the RFC issue loans only to relatively healthy institutions that were capable of repaying them and that it favor public works, such as toll bridges, that were likely to become self-financing. Hoover was especially reluctant to engage the government in providing relief to unemployed and homeless Americans. To give money to the poor, he insisted, would destroy their desire to work and undermine their sense of self-worth.

Hoover saw no similar peril in extending government assistance to ailing banks and businesses. Critics pointed to the seeming hypocrisy of Hoover's policies. For example, in 1930, Hoover refused a request of $25 million to help feed Arkansas farmers and their families but approved $45 million to feed the same farmers' livestock. In 1932, shortly after rejecting an urgent request from the city of Chicago for aid to help pay its teachers and municipal workers, Hoover approved a $90 million loan to rescue that city's Central Republic Bank.

In spring 1932, a group of army veterans mounted a particularly emotional challenge to Hoover's policies. In 1924, Congress had authorized a $1,000 bonus for First World War veterans in the form of compensation certificates that would mature in 1945. Now the veterans were demanding that the government pay the bonus immediately. A group of Portland, Oregon, veterans, calling themselves the Bonus Expeditionary Force, hopped onto empty boxcars of freight trains heading east. As this "army" moved, its ranks multiplied, so that by the time it reached Washington its numbers had swelled to 20,000, including wives and children. The so-called **Bonus Army** set up camp in the Anacostia Flats, southeast of the Capitol, and petitioned Congress for early payment of the promised bonus. The House of Representatives agreed, but the Senate turned them down. Hoover refused to meet with the veterans. In July, federal troops led by Army Chief of Staff Douglas MacArthur and Third Cavalry Commander George Patton entered the veterans' Anacostia encampment, set the tents and shacks ablaze, and dispersed the protestors. In the process, more than 100 veterans were wounded and one infant died.

News that veterans and their families had been attacked in the nation's capital served only to harden anti-Hoover opinion. In the 1932 elections, the Republicans were voted out of office after having dominated national politics (excepting Woodrow Wilson's two terms) for 36 years. Hoover received only 39.6 percent of the popular vote and just 59 (of 531) electoral votes. He left the presidency in 1933 a bewildered man, reviled by Americans for his seeming indifference to suffering and his ineptitude in dealing with the economy's collapse.

Cultural Distress

The economic crisis of the early 1930s expressed itself not just in politics but also in the literature and cinema of the time. The journalist and literary critic Edmund Wilson found mostly economic misery and spiritual depression during his journey across America. A sense of aimlessness characterized one of the major literary works of the early 1930s, the Studs Lonigan trilogy (1932–1935) written by the Chicago-born writer James T. Farrell. Farrell's scrappy Irish American protagonist, Studs, lacks focus and is repeatedly overcome by the harshness of his environment. He dies poor and alone, not yet 30. Meanwhile, the popular writer Nathaniel West was publishing *Miss Lonelyhearts* (1933) and *A Cool Million* (1934), novels similarly built around central characters succumbing to failure, drift, even insanity.

One can detect parallel themes of despair in the period's cinema, especially in movies such as the Academy Award Winner *I Am a Fugitive from a Chain Gang* (1932), in which an industrious and honorable man, James Allen, is unfairly sentenced to 10 years on a Georgia chain gang. Allen escapes his penitentiary but is condemned to being a man on the run, unable to prove his innocence, earn a decent living, or build enduring relationships. Less grim but still sobering were the gangster movies of the early 1930s, especially *Little Caesar* (1930) and *The Public Enemy* (1931), which told stories of hard-nosed and violent men who became wealthy and influential by living outside the law and bending the people around them to their will.

Lawlessness also surfaced in the wild comedy of Groucho, Chico, Harpo, and Zeppo Marx, vaudevillians who, in the 1920s and 1930s, made the transition to the silver screen. The Marx Brothers ridiculed figures of authority, broke every rule of etiquette, smacked around their antagonists (and each other), and deliberately and delightfully mangled the English language. Anarchy ruled their world. While hilarious to watch, Marx Brothers movies sometimes carried serious political messages. *Duck Soup* (1933) made fun of the fictional nation of Fredonia, where leaders were pompous, the legal system a fraud, and clueless citizens easily misled. In this 90-minute movie, the Marx Brothers emptied politics of all meaning and honesty. This cinematic sentiment paralleled the conviction held by many Americans in 1932 and early 1933 that their own politicians had failed them in a time of need.

A Democratic Roosevelt   Franklin D. Roosevelt was born in 1882 into a patrician family descended, on his father's side, from Dutch gentry in New York. By the 1880s, the Hyde Park manor where Roosevelt grew up had been in the family for more than 200 years. His mother's family—the Delanos—traced its ancestry back to the *Mayflower*. Roosevelt's education at Groton, Harvard College, and Columbia Law School was typical of the path followed by the sons of America's northeastern elite.

Young Franklin at first found it hard to fill the shoes of his famous cousin, Theodore. Franklin distinguished himself neither at school nor at law. Prior to the 1920s, he could point to few significant political achievements. He was charming, gregarious, and fun loving, always eager to sail, party, and enjoy the company of women other than his wife, Eleanor. Then, in 1921, at the age of 39, Roosevelt was both stricken and transformed by a devastating illness, polio, which paralyzed him from the waist down for the rest of his life.

During the two years Roosevelt spent bedridden, he seemed to acquire a new determination and focus. He developed a compassion for those suffering misfortune that would later enable him to reach out to the millions caught in the Great Depression. Roosevelt's physical debilitation also transformed his relationship with Eleanor, whose dedication to nursing him back to health forged a new bond between them. More conscious of his dependence on others, he now welcomed her as a partner in his career. Eleanor soon displayed a talent for political organization and public speaking that surprised those who knew her only as a shy, awkward woman. She was an indispensable player in the revival of Franklin's political fortunes, which began in 1928 with his election to the governorship of New York State. Eleanor would also become an active, eloquent First Lady, her husband's trusted ally, and an architect of American liberalism.

As governor of New York for four years (1929–1933), Roosevelt had initiated various reform programs. He surrounded himself with men and women who embraced a reform movement that began to call itself "liberal." Frances Perkins, Harry Hopkins, Raymond Moley, Rexford Tugwell, Adolph Berle, Samuel Rosenman—all were interventionist in economic matters and libertarian on questions of personal behavior. In other words, they believed that the government had an active role to play in regulating the economy, but that the government should refrain from telling people how to live their lives. How much Roosevelt had himself embraced this liberalism before 1932 is not clear. But during his acceptance speech at the Democratic National Convention that year, he declared: "Ours must be the party of liberal thought, of planned action, of enlightened international outlook, and of the greatest good for the greatest number of citizens." He promised "a new deal for the American people."

THE FIRST NEW DEAL, 1933–1935

By the time Roosevelt assumed office in March 1933, the economy lay in shambles. From 1929 to 1932, industrial production had fallen by 50 percent, while new investment had declined from $16 billion to less than $1 billion. In those same years, more than 100,000 businesses went bankrupt. In early 1933, with the nation's banking system on the verge of collapse, 34 states had ordered all the banks in their jurisdictions to close their doors. No one seemed to be able to bring the unemployment rate under control. Some Americans feared that the opportunity for reform had already passed.

Not Roosevelt. "This nation asks for action, and action now," Roosevelt declared in his inaugural address. Roosevelt was true to his word. In his first Hundred Days, from early March through early June 1933, Roosevelt persuaded Congress to pass 15 major pieces of legislation to help bankers, farmers, industrialists, workers, homeowners, the unemployed, and the hungry. He also prevailed on Congress to repeal Prohibition. Not all of the new laws helped relieve distress and promote recovery, but in the short term that seemed to matter little. Roosevelt had brought excitement and hope to the nation. He was confident, decisive, and defiantly cheery. "The only thing we have to fear is fear itself," he declared.

On the second Sunday after his inauguration, he launched a series of radio addresses known as "fireside chats," speaking in a plain, direct voice to the forlorn and discouraged. In his first chat, he explained the banking crisis in simple terms but without condescension. "I want to take a few minutes to talk with the people of the United States about banking," he began. An estimated 20 million Americans listened.

To hear the president speaking as though he were actually there in the room was riveting. An estimated 500,000 Americans wrote letters to Roosevelt in the early weeks after he assumed office. Millions more would write to him and to

Connecting with Ordinary Americans.
In 1933, FDR began broadcasting "Fireside Chats," frank and accessible radio addresses about the problems confronting the nation and how Americans might solve them. Millions listened to these chats in their homes, gathered around the radio as though it were a hearth. This photograph captures FDR delivering a chat in 1937.

Underwood Archives/Archive Photos/Getty Images

Eleanor Roosevelt over the next few years. Many of the letters were simply addressed to "Mr. or Mrs. Roosevelt, Washington, D.C." Democrats began to hang portraits of Franklin Roosevelt in their homes, often next to a picture of Jesus or the Madonna.

**Saving
the Banks**

By Inauguration Day, many of the nation's banks had shut their doors. Roosevelt immediately ordered all the nation's banks closed—a bold move he brazenly called a "bank holiday." At his request, Congress rushed through the Emergency Banking Act, which made federal loans available to private bankers, and the Economy Act, which committed the government to balancing the budget. Both were fiscally conservative programs that Hoover had proposed.

After the financial crisis eased, Roosevelt turned to the structural reform of banking. A second Glass-Steagall Act (1933) separated commercial banking from investment banking. It also created the Federal Deposit Insurance Corporation (FDIC), which assured depositors that the government would protect up to $5,000 of their savings. The Securities Act (1933) and the Securities Exchange Act (1934) imposed long-overdue regulation on the New York Stock Exchange, both by reining in buying on the margin and by establishing the Securities and Exchange Commission (SEC) to enforce federal law.

Economic Relief

Roosevelt understood the need to temper financial prudence with compassion. Congress responded swiftly in 1933 to Roosevelt's request to establish the Federal Emergency Relief Administration (FERA), granting it $500 million for relief to the poor. To head FERA, Roosevelt appointed a brash young reformer, Harry Hopkins, who disbursed $2 million during his first two hours on the job. Roosevelt next won congressional approval for the Civilian Conservation Corps (CCC), which assembled more than 2 million single young men to plant trees, halt erosion, and otherwise improve the environment. The following winter, Roosevelt launched the Civil Works Administration (CWA), an ambitious work-relief program, also under the direction of Harry Hopkins, which hired 4 million unemployed people at $15 per week and put them to work on 400,000 small-scale government projects. For middle-class Americans threatened with the loss of their homes, Roosevelt won congressional approval for the Homeowners' Loan Corporation (1933) to refinance mortgages. These direct subsidies to millions of jobless and homeowning Americans lent credibility to Roosevelt's claim that the New Deal would set the country on a new course.

**Agricultural
Reform**

In 1933, Roosevelt expected economic recovery to come not from relief, but through agricultural and industrial cooperation. He regarded the Agricultural Adjustment Act, passed in May, and the National Industrial Recovery Act (NIRA), passed in June, as the most important legislation of his Hundred Days. Both were based on the idea that curtailing production would trigger economic recovery. By shrinking the supply of agricultural and manufactured goods, Roosevelt's economists reasoned, they could

Legislation Enacted During the "Hundred Days," March 9–June 16, 1933

Date	Legislation	Purpose
March 9	Emergency Banking Act	Provide federal loans to private bankers
March 20	Economy Act	Balance the federal budget
March 22	Beer-Wine Revenue Act	Repeal Prohibition
March 31	Unemployment Relief Act	Create the Civilian Conservation Corps
May 12	Agricultural Adjustment Act	Establish a national agricultural policy
May 12	Emergency Farm Mortgage Act	Provide refinancing of farm mortgages
May 12	Federal Emergency Relief Act	Establish a national relief system, including the Civil Works Administration
May 18	Tennessee Valley Authority Act	Promote economic development of the Tennessee Valley
May 27	Securities Act	Regulate the purchase and sale of new securities
June 5	Gold Repeal Joint Resolution	Cancel the gold clause in public and private contracts
June 13	Home Owners Loan Act	Provide refinancing of home mortgages
June 16	National Industrial Recovery Act	Set up a national system of industrial self-government and establish the Public Works Administration
June 16	Glass-Steagall Banking Act	Create Federal Deposit Insurance Corporation; separate commercial and investment banking
June 16	Farm Credit Act	Reorganize agricultural credit programs
June 16	Railroad Coordination Act	Appoint federal coordinator of transportation

Source: Arthur M. Schlesinger, Jr., *The Coming of the New Deal* (Boston: Houghton Mifflin, 1959), pp. 20–21.

restore the balance of normal market forces. As demand for scarce goods exceeded supply, prices would rise and revenues would climb. Farmers and industrialists, earning a profit once again, would increase their investment in new technology and hire more workers, and prosperity and full employment would be the final result.

To curtail farm production, the **Agricultural Adjustment Administration (AAA)**, which was set up by the Agricultural Adjustment Act, began paying farmers to keep a portion of their land out of cultivation and to reduce the size of their herds. The program was controversial. Many farmers were skeptical of a government offer to pay more money for working less land and husbanding fewer livestock, but few refused to accept payments. As one young Kansas farmer reported:

> There were mouthy individuals who seized every opportunity to run down the entire program ... condemning it as useless, crooked, revolutionary, or dictatorial; but ... when the first AAA payments were made available, shortly before Christmas, these same wordy critics made a beeline for the courthouse. They jostled and fell over each other in their mad scramble to be the first in line to receive allotment money.

The AAA had made no provision for the tenant farmers and farm laborers who would be thrown out of work by the reduction in acreage. In the South, the victims were disproportionately black. A Georgia sharecropper wrote Harry Hopkins of his misery: "I have Bin farming all my life But the man I live with Has Turned me loose taking my mule [and] all my feed .... I can't get a Job so Some one said Rite you." New Dealers within the Department of Agriculture, such as Rexford Tugwell and Jerome Frank, were sympathetic to the plight of sharecroppers, but they failed during the First New Deal to extend to them the government's helping hand.

The programs of the AAA also proved inadequate to Great Plains farmers, whose economic problems had been compounded by ecological crisis. Just as the Depression rolled in, the rain stopped falling on the plains, and the land, stripped of its native grasses by decades of excessive plowing, dried up and turned to dust. And then the dust began to blow, sometimes traveling 1,000 miles across open prairie. The worst dust storm occurred on April 14, 1935, when a great mass of dust, moving at speeds of 45 to 70 miles per hour, roared through Colorado, Kansas, and Oklahoma, blackening the sky, suffocating cattle, and dumping thousands of tons of topsoil and red clay on homes and streets.

The government responded to this calamity by establishing the Soil Conservation Service (SCS) in 1935, which assisted plains farmers in planting soil-conserving grasses and legumes in place of wheat. The SCS also taught farmers how to plow along contour lines and how to build terraces—techniques that had been proven effective in slowing the runoff of rainwater and improving its absorption into the soil. With this assistance, plains agriculture began to recover.

In 1936, the Supreme Court ruled that AAA-mandated limits on farm production constituted an illegal restraint of trade. Congress responded by passing the Soil Conservation and Domestic Allotment Act, which justified the removal of land from cultivation for reasons of conservation rather than economics. This new act also called on landowners to share their government subsidies with sharecroppers and tenant farmers, although many landowners managed to evade this requirement.

The use of subsidies, begun by the AAA, did eventually bring stability and prosperity to agriculture, but at high cost. Agriculture became the most heavily subsidized sector of the U.S. economy, and the Department of Agriculture grew into one of the government's largest bureaucracies. The rural poor, black and white, never received a fair share of federal benefits. Beginning in the 1930s, and continuing in the 1940s and 1950s, millions would be forced off the land and into the cities of the North and West.

Industrial
Reform

American industry was so vast that Roosevelt's administration never contemplated paying individual manufacturers direct subsidies to reduce, or even halt, production. Instead, the government decided to limit production through persuasion and association—techniques that Hoover had also favored. The first task of the **National Recovery Administration (NRA),** authorized under the National Industrial Recovery Act, was to persuade industrialists and businessmen to agree to raise employee wages to a minimum of 30 to 40 cents per hour and to limit employee hours to a maximum of 30 to 40 hours per week. The limitation on hours was meant to reduce the quantity of goods that any factory or business could produce.

The NRA undertook a high-powered publicity campaign, distributing pamphlets and pins throughout the country, promoting its goals on the radio, and urging employers to place a "blue eagle"—the logo of the NRA—on storefronts, at factory entrances, and on company stationery. Blue eagles began sprouting up everywhere, usually accompanied by the slogan "We Do Our Part." The NRA also brought together the largest producers in every sector of manufacturing and asked each group to limit production and to develop a code of fair competition to govern prices, wages, and hours in their industry.

In summer and fall 1933, the NRA codes drawn up for steel, textiles, coal mining, rubber, garment manufacture, and other industries seemed to be working. The economy improved, and hard times seemed to be easing. But in winter and spring 1934, economic indicators plunged downward once again, and manufacturers began to evade the code provisions. By fall 1934, it was clear that the NRA had failed. When the Supreme Court declared the NRA codes unconstitutional in May 1935, the Roosevelt administration allowed the agency to die.

Rebuilding the
Nation's
Infrastructure

In addition to establishing the NRA, the NIRA launched the Public Works Administration (PWA) to strengthen the nation's infrastructure of roads, bridges, sewage systems, hospitals, airports, and schools. The labor needed for these construction projects would shrink relief rolls and reduce unemployment, but the projects could be justified in terms that conservatives approved: economic investment rather than short-term relief.

The PWA authorized the building of three major dams in the West—Boulder, Grand Coulee, and Bonneville—that opened up large stretches of Arizona, California, and Washington to industrial and agricultural development. It funded the construction of the Triborough Bridge in New York City and the 100-mile causeway linking Florida to Key West. It also appropriated money for the construction of thousands of new schools.

The TVA
Alternative

One piece of legislation passed during Roosevelt's First New Deal specified a strategy for economic recovery significantly different from the one promoted by the NIRA. The Tennessee Valley Authority Act (1933) called for the government—rather than private corporations—to promote economic development throughout the Tennessee Valley, a vast river basin winding through parts of Kentucky,

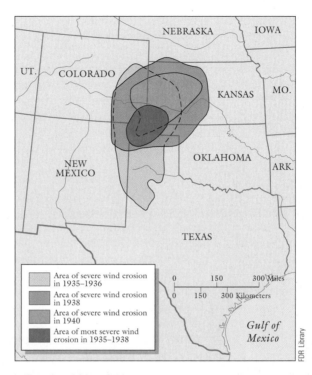

MAP 25.2   Dust Bowl, 1935–1940

This map shows the areas in six states—Texas, New Mexico, Oklahoma, Colorado, Kansas, and a bit of Nebraska—claimed by the Dust Bowl between 1935 and 1940. The dark gray color shows the area where the winds caused the worst damage.

Tennessee, Mississippi, Alabama, Georgia, and North Carolina. The act created the **Tennessee Valley Authority (TVA)** to control flooding on the Tennessee River, harness its waterpower to generate electricity, develop local industry (such as fertilizer production), improve river navigability, and ease the poverty and isolation of the area's inhabitants. In some respects, the TVA's mandate resembled that of the PWA, but the TVA enjoyed even greater authority. The extent of its control over economic development reflected the influence of Rexford Tugwell and other New Dealers who were committed to a government-planned and government-operated economy. Although they rarely said so, these reformers were drawn to socialism.

The accomplishments of the TVA were many. It built, completed, or improved more than 20 dams, including the huge Wheeler Dam near Muscle Shoals in Alabama. At several of the dam sites, the TVA built hydroelectric generators and soon became the nation's largest producer of electricity. Its low electric rates compelled private utility companies to reduce their rates. The TVA also constructed waterways to bypass nonnavigable stretches of the river, reduced the danger of flooding, and taught farmers how to prevent soil erosion and use fertilizers.

Although the TVA was one of the New Deal's most celebrated successes, it generated little support for more ambitious experiments in national planning. For the government to have assumed control of established industries and banks would have been quite a different matter from bringing prosperity to an impoverished region. Like Roosevelt, few members of Congress or the public favored the radical growth of governmental power that such programs would have entailed. Thus, the thought of replacing the NRA with a nationwide TVA, for instance, made little headway. The New Deal never embraced the idea of the federal government as a substitute for private enterprise.

The New Deal and Western Development   As the TVA showed, New Deal programs could powerfully influence a particular region's welfare. Other regional beneficiaries of the New Deal included the New York City area, which prospered from the close links of local politicians to the Roosevelt administration. The region that benefited most from the New Deal, however, was the West. Between 1933 and 1939, per capita payments for public works projects, welfare, and federal loans in the Rocky Mountain and Pacific Coast states outstripped those of any other region.

Dam building was central to this western focus. Western real estate and agricultural interests wanted to dam the West's major rivers to provide water and electricity for urban and agricultural development, but the costs were prohibitive, even to the largest capitalists, until the New Deal offered to defray the expenses with federal dollars. Western interests found a government ally in the Bureau of Reclamation, a hitherto small federal agency (in existence since 1902) that became, under the New Deal, a prime dispenser of funds for dam construction, reservoir creation, and the provision of water to western cities and farms. Drawing on PWA monies, the bureau oversaw the building of the Boulder Dam (later renamed the Hoover Dam), which provided drinking water for southern California, irrigation water for California's Imperial Valley, and electricity for Los Angeles and southern Arizona. It also authorized the Central Valley Project and the All-American Canal to provide irrigation, drinking water, and electricity to central and southern California farmers and towns. The greatest construction project of all was the Grand Coulee Dam on the Columbia River in Washington, which created a lake 150 miles long. Together with the Bonneville Dam (also on the Columbia), the Grand Coulee gave the Pacific Northwest the cheapest electricity in the country and created a new potential for economic and population growth. Not surprisingly, these two dams also made Washington State the largest per capita recipient of New Deal aid.

These developments attracted less attention in the 1930s than the TVA because their benefits did not fully materialize until after the Second World War. Also, dam building in the West was not seen as a radical experiment in government planning and management. Unlike the TVA, the Bureau of Reclamation hired private contractors to do the work. Moreover, the benefits of these dams were intended to flow first to large agricultural and real estate interests, not to the poor; they were intended to aid private enterprise, rather than bypass it. In political terms, dam building in the West was more conservative than it was in the Tennessee Valley.

MAP 25.3 Tennessee Valley Authority

This map shows the vast scale of the TVA and pinpoints the locations of 29 dams and 13 power plants that emerged from this project.

Even so, this activity made the federal government a key architect of the modern American West.

POLITICAL MOBILIZATION, POLITICAL UNREST, 1934–1935

Although Roosevelt and the New Dealers dismantled the NRA in 1935, they could not stop the political forces it had set in motion. Ordinary Americans now believed they could make a difference. If the New Dealers could not achieve economic recovery, then the people would find others who could.

Populist Critics of the New Deal   Some critics were disturbed by what they perceived as the conservative character of New Deal programs. Banking reforms, the AAA, and the NRA, they alleged, all seemed to favor large economic interests. Ordinary people had been ignored.

In the South and Midwest, millions listened regularly to the radio addresses of Louisiana senator **Huey Long**, a former governor of that state and an accomplished orator. In attacks on New Deal programs, he alleged that "not a single thin dime of concentrated, bloated, pompous wealth, massed in the hands of a few people has been raked down to relieve the masses." Long offered a simple alternative: "Break up the swollen fortunes of America and ... spread the wealth among all our people." He called for a redistribution of wealth that would guarantee each American family a $5,000 estate.

Long's rhetoric inspired hundreds of thousands of Americans to join the Share the Wealth clubs his supporters organized. Most came from middle-class ranks or from the ranks of skilled workers. By 1935, Roosevelt regarded Long as the man most likely to unseat him in the presidential election of 1936. Before that campaign began, however, Long was assassinated.

Meanwhile, in the Midwest, **Father Charles Coughlin**, the "radio priest," delivered a message similar to Long's. Like Long, Coughlin appealed to anxious middle-class Americans and to once-privileged groups of workers who believed that security and respectability were slipping from their grasp. A former Roosevelt supporter, Coughlin had become a critic. The New Deal was run by bankers, he claimed. The NRA was a program to resuscitate corporate profits. Coughlin called for a strong government to compel capital, labor, agriculture, professionals, and other interest groups to do its bidding. He founded the National Union of Social Justice (NUSJ) in 1934 as a precursor to a political party that would challenge the Democrats in 1936.

As Coughlin's disillusionment with the New Deal deepened, a strain of anti-Semitism became apparent in his radio talks, as in his accusation that Jewish bankers were masterminding a world conspiracy to dispossess the toiling masses. Although Coughlin was a compelling speaker, he failed to build the NUSJ into an effective political force. Its successor, the Union Party, attracted only a small percentage of voters in 1936. Embittered, Coughlin moved further to the political right. By 1939, his denunciations of democracy and Jews had become so extreme that some radio stations refused to carry his addresses. Still, millions of Americans continued to put their faith in the "radio priest."

Another popular figure was Francis E. Townsend, a California doctor who claimed that the way to end the Depression was to give every senior citizen $200 a month. The Townsend Plan briefly garnered the support of an estimated 20 million Americans.

Labor Protests   The attacks by Long, Coughlin, and Townsend on New Deal programs deepened popular discontent and helped to legitimate other insurgencies. The most important was the labor movement. Workers began joining unions in response to the NIRA, and especially its clause granting them the right to join labor organizations of their own choosing and obligating employers to bargain with them in good faith. Union members' demands were modest at first: They wanted to be treated fairly by their foremen, and they wanted employers to observe the provisions of the NRA codes and to recognize their unions. But few employers were willing to grant workers any say in their working conditions. Many ignored the NRA's wage and hour guidelines altogether and even used their influence with NRA code authorities to get worker requests for wage increases and union recognition rejected.

Workers flooded Washington with letters of protest and then began to take matters into their own hands. In 1934 they staged 2,000 strikes in virtually every

MAP 25.4 Federal Water Projects in California Built or Funded by the New Deal

This map demonstrates how much California cities and agriculture benefited from water projects—dams, canals, aqueducts, pumping stations, and power plants—begun under the New Deal. The projects extended from the Shasta Dam in the northern part of the state to the All-American Canal that traversed the Imperial Valley south of San Diego, and included the Colorado River Aqueduct that carried vital drinking water to Los Angeles.

industry and region of the country. A few of these strikes escalated into armed confrontations between workers and police that shocked the nation. In Toledo, Ohio, in May, 10,000 workers surrounded the Electric Auto-Lite plant, declaring that they would block all exits and entrances until the company agreed to shut down operations and negotiate a union contract. Two strikers were killed in an exchange of gunfire. In Minneapolis, unionized truck drivers and warehousemen fought police, private security forces, and the National Guard in a series of street battles from May through July that left four dead and hundreds wounded. In San

Francisco in July, skirmishes between longshoremen and employers killed two and wounded scores of strikers. This violence provoked a general strike in San Francisco that shut down the city's transportation, construction, and service industries for two weeks. In September, 400,000 textile workers at mills from Maine to Alabama walked off their jobs. Attempts by employers to bring in replacement workers triggered violent confrontations that caused several deaths, hundreds of injuries, and millions of dollars in property damages.

Anger at the Polls   In the fall of 1934, workers took their anger to the polls. In Rhode Island, they broke the Republican Party's 30-year domination of state politics. In the South Carolina gubernatorial race, working-class voters rejected a conservative Democrat, Coleman Blease, and chose instead Olin T. Johnston, a former mill worker and an ardent New Dealer. In the country as a whole, Democrats won 70 percent of the contested seats in the Senate and House. The Democrats increased their majority, from 310 to 319 (out of 432) in the House, and from 60 to 69 (out of 96) in the Senate. No sitting president's party had ever done so well in an off-year election.

The victory was not an unqualified one for Roosevelt and the First New Deal, however. The 74th Congress would include the largest contingent of radicals ever sent to Washington: Tom Amlie of Wisconsin, Ernest Lundeen of Minnesota, Maury Maverick of Texas, Vito Marcantonio of New York, and some 30 others. Their support for the New Deal depended on whether Roosevelt delivered more relief, more income security, and more political power to farmers, workers, the unemployed, and the poor.

Radical Third Parties   Radical critics of the New Deal also made an impressive showing in state politics in 1934 and 1936. In Wisconsin, Philip La Follette, the son of Robert La Follette was elected governor in 1934 and 1936 as the candidate of the radical Wisconsin Progressive Party. In Minnesota, discontented agrarians and urban workers organized the Minnesota Farmer-Labor (MFL) Party and elected their candidate to the governorship in 1930, 1932, 1934, and 1936. In Washington, yet another radical third party, the Commonwealth Builders, elected both senators and almost half the state legislators in 1932 and 1934. And in California, the socialist and novelist Upton Sinclair and his organization, End Poverty in California (EPIC), came close to winning the governorship.

A widespread movement to form local labor parties offered further evidence of voter volatility, as did the growing appeal of the **Communist Party**. The American Communist Party (CP) had emerged in the early 1920s with the support of radicals who wanted to adopt the Soviet Union's path to socialism. In the early 1930s, CP organizers spread out among the poorest and most vulnerable populations in America—homeless urban blacks in the North, black and white sharecroppers in the South, Chicano and Filipino agricultural workers in the West—and mobilized them into unions and unemployment leagues. CP members also played significant roles in strikes described earlier, and they were influential in the Minnesota Farmer-Labor Party and in Washington's Commonwealth Builders. Once they stopped preaching world revolution in 1935 and began calling instead for a "popular front" of democratic forces against fascism (a term used to describe the new kinds of dictatorships appearing in Hitler's Germany and Mussolini's Italy), their ranks grew even more. By 1938, approximately 80,000 Americans are thought to have been members of the Communist Party.

Although the Communist Party proclaimed its allegiance to democratic principles beginning in 1935, it nevertheless remained a dictatorial organization that took its orders from the Soviet Union. Many Americans feared the growing strength of the CP and began to call for its suppression. The CP, however, was never strong enough to gain power for itself. Its chief role in 1930s politics was to channel popular discontent into unions and political parties that would, in turn, force New Dealers to respond to the demands of the nation's poor.

THE SECOND NEW DEAL, 1935–1937

For a time, Roosevelt kept his distance from the masses mobilizing in his name, but in spring 1935, with the 1936 presidential election looming, he decided to place himself at their head. He called for the "abolition of evil holding companies," attacked the wealthy for their profligate ways, and called for new programs to aid the poor and downtrodden. Rather than becoming a socialist, as his critics charged, Roosevelt sought to reinvigorate his appeal among poorer Americans and turn them away from radical solutions.

Philosophical Underpinnings   To point the New Deal in a more populist direction, Roosevelt turned increasingly to a relatively new economic theory, **underconsumptionism**. Advocates of this theory held that a chronic weakness in consumer demand had caused the Great Depression. The path to recovery lay, therefore, not in restricting production, as the architects of the First New Deal had tried to do, but in boosting consumer expenditures through government support for strong labor unions (to force up wages), higher social welfare expenditures (to put more money in the hands of the poor), and ambitious public works projects (to create millions of new jobs).

Underconsumptionists did not worry that new welfare and public works programs might strain the federal budget. If the government found itself short of revenue, it could always borrow additional funds from private sources. These reformers, in fact, viewed government borrowing as a useful antidepression tool. Those who lent the government money would receive a return on their investment; those who received government assistance would have additional income to spend on consumer goods; and manufacturers would profit from increases in consumer spending. Government borrowing, in short, would stimulate the circulation of money through the economy, increase consumer demand, and end the Depression. This fiscal policy, a reversal of the conventional wisdom that government should always balance its budget, would in the 1940s come to be known as Keynesianism, after John Maynard Keynes, the British economist who had been its architect.

As the nation entered its sixth year of the Depression, Roosevelt was willing to give these new ideas a try. Reform-minded members of the 1934 Congress were eager for a new round of legislation directed more to the needs of ordinary Americans than to the needs of big business.

Legislation   Congress passed much of that legislation in January to June 1935, a period that came to be known as the Second New Deal. Two of the acts were of historic importance: the **Social Security Act** and the National Labor Relations Act. The Social Security Act, passed in May, required the states to set up welfare funds from which money would be disbursed to the elderly poor, the unemployed, unmarried mothers with dependent children, and the disabled. It also enrolled a majority of working Americans in a pension program that guaranteed them a steady income upon retirement. A federal system of employer and employee taxation was set up to fund the pensions. Despite limitations on coverage and inadequate pension levels, the Social Security Act of 1935 provided a foundation on which future presidents and congresses would erect the American welfare state.

Equally historic was the passage, in June, of the National Labor Relations Act (NLRA). This act delivered what the NRA had only promised: the right of every worker to join a union of his or her own choosing and the obligation of employers to bargain with that union in good faith. The **NLRA**, also called the **Wagner Act** after its Senate sponsor, Robert Wagner of New York, set up a National Labor Relations Board (NLRB) to supervise union elections and to investigate claims of unfair labor practices. The NLRB was to be staffed by federal appointees with power to impose fines on employers who violated the law. Union leaders hailed the act as their Magna Carta.

Congress also passed the Holding Company Act to break up the 13 utility companies that controlled 75 percent of the nation's electric power. It passed the Wealth Tax Act, which increased tax rates on the wealthy from 59 to 75 percent, and on corporations from 13.75 to 15 percent; and it passed the Banking Act, which strengthened the power of the Federal Reserve Board over its member banks. It created the Rural Electrification Administration (REA) to bring electric power to rural households. Finally, it passed the huge $5 billion Emergency Relief Appropriation Act. Roosevelt funneled part of this sum to the PWA, the CCC, and the newly created National Youth Administration (NYA), which provided work and guidance to the nation's youth.

Roosevelt directed most of the new relief money, however, to the **Works Progress Administration (WPA)** under the direction of Harry Hopkins, now known as the New Deal's "minister of relief." The WPA built or improved thousands of schools, playgrounds, airports, and hospitals. WPA crews raked leaves, cleaned streets, and landscaped cities. In the process, the WPA provided jobs to approximately 30 percent of the nation's jobless.

By the time the decade ended, the WPA, in association with an expanded Reconstruction Finance Corporation, the PWA, and other agencies, had built 500,000 miles of roads, 100,000 bridges, 100,000 public buildings, and 600 airports. The New Deal had transformed America's urban and rural landscapes. The awe generated by these public works projects helped Roosevelt retain popular support at a time when the success of the New Deal's economic policies was uncertain.

The WPA also funded a vast program of public art, supporting the work of thousands of painters, architects, writers, playwrights, actors, and intellectuals. Beyond extending relief to struggling artists, it fostered the creation of art that spoke to the concerns of ordinary Americans, adorned public buildings with colorful murals, and boosted public morale.

Victory in 1936: The New Democratic Coalition   In his 1936 reelection campaign, Roosevelt excoriated the corporations as "economic royalists" who had "concentrated into their own hands an almost complete control over other people's property, other people's money, other people's labor—other people's lives." He called on voters to strip the corporations of their power and "save a great and precious form of government for ourselves and the world." American voters responded by handing Roosevelt the greatest victory in the history of American presidential politics. He received 61 percent of the popular vote; Alf Landon of Kansas, his Republican opponent, received only 37 percent. Only two states, Maine and Vermont, representing a mere eight electoral votes, went for Landon.

The 1936 election won the Democratic Party its reputation as the party of reform and the party of the "forgotten American." Of the 6 million Americans who went to the polls for the first time, many of them European ethnics, 5 million voted for Roosevelt. Among the poorest Americans, Roosevelt received 80 percent of the vote. Black voters in the North left the Republican Party—the "Party of Lincoln"—calculating that their interests would be served better by the "Party of the Common Man." Roosevelt also did well among white middle-class voters, many of whom stood to benefit from the Social Security Act. These constituencies would constitute the "Roosevelt coalition" for most of the next 40 years, helping to solidify the Democratic Party as the new majority party in American politics.

Rhetoric versus Reality   Roosevelt's 1935–1936 anticorporate rhetoric was more radical than the laws he supported. The Wealth Tax Act took considerably less out of wealthy incomes and estates than was advertised, and the utility companies that the Holding Company Act was meant to break up remained largely intact. Moreover, Roosevelt promised more than he delivered to the nation's poor. Farmworkers, for example, were not covered by the Social Security Act or by the National Labor Relations Act. Consequently, thousands of African American sharecroppers in the South, along with substantial numbers of Mexican American and Filipino farmworkers in the Southwest and West, missed out on protections and benefits brought by these laws. The sharecroppers were shut out because southern Democrats would not have voted for an act that was seen as improving the economic or social condition of southern blacks. For the same reason, the New Deal made little effort to restore voting rights to southern blacks or to protect their basic civil rights. White supremacy lived on in New Deal democracy.

Roosevelt's 1935–1936 populist stance also obscured the support that some capitalists were giving the Second New Deal. In the West, Henry J. Kaiser headed a consortium of six companies that built the Hoover, Bonneville, and Grand Coulee dams. In Texas, building contractors Herman and George Brown were bankrolling a group of elected officials that included a young Democratic congressman named Lyndon Johnson. In the Midwest and the East, Roosevelt's corporate supporters included real estate developers, mass merchandisers (such as Bambergers and Sears, Roebuck), clothing manufacturers, and the like. These firms, in turn, had financial connections with recently established investment banks such as Lehman Brothers and Goldman Sachs, competitors of the House of Morgan and its allies in the Republican banking establishment, and with consumer-oriented banks such as the Bank of America and the Bowery Savings Bank. They tolerated strong labor unions, welfare programs, and high levels of government spending in the belief that these developments would strengthen consumer spending, but they had no intention of surrendering their own wealth or power. The Democratic Party had become, in effect, the party of the masses and one section of big business. The conflicting interests of these two constituencies would create tensions within the Democratic Party throughout the years of its political domination.

Men, Women, and Reform   The years 1936 and 1937 were exciting ones for academics, policymakers, and bureaucrats who designed and administered the rapidly growing roster of New Deal programs and agencies. Fueled by idealism and dedication, they were confident they could make the New Deal work. They planned and won congressional approval for the Farm Security Administration (FSA), an agency designed to improve the economic lot of tenant farmers, sharecroppers, and farm laborers. They drafted and passed legislation that outlawed child labor, set minimum wages and maximum hours for adult workers, and committed the federal government to building low-cost housing. They investigated and tried to regulate concentrations of corporate power.

Although they worked on behalf of "the people," the New Dealers constituted a new class of technocrats. The prospect of building a strong state committed to prosperity and justice fired their imaginations. They delighted in the intellectual challenge and the technical complexity of social policy.

Many of the male New Dealers had earned advanced degrees in law and economics at elite universities such as Harvard, Columbia, and Wisconsin. Not all had been raised among wealth and privilege, however. To his credit, Franklin Roosevelt was the first president since his cousin Theodore Roosevelt to welcome Jews and Catholics into his administration. Some became members of Roosevelt's inner circle of advisers—men such as Thomas "Tommy the Cork" Corcoran, Jim Farley, Ben Cohen, and Samuel Rosenman. These men had struggled to make their way, first on the streets and then in school and at work. They brought to the New Deal intellectual aggressiveness, quick minds, and mental toughness.

The profile of New Deal women was different. Although a few, notably Eleanor Roosevelt and Secretary of Labor Frances Perkins (the first woman to be appointed to the U.S. cabinet), were more visible than women in previous administrations had been, many of the female New Dealers worked in relative obscurity, in agencies such as the Women's Bureau or the Children's Bureau (both in the Department of Labor). Women who worked on major legislation, as did Mary Van Kleeck on the Social Security Act, or who directed major programs, as did Jane Hoey, chief of the Social Security's Bureau of Public Assistance, received less credit than men in

SELECTED WPA PROJECTS IN NEW YORK CITY, 1938

Construction and Renovation	Education, Health, and Art	Research and Records
East River Drive	Adult education: homemaking, trade and technical skills, and art and culture	Sewage treatment, community health, labor relations, and employment trends surveys
Henry Hudson Parkway	Children's education: remedial reading, lip reading, and field trips	Museum and library catalogs and exhibits
Bronx sewers	Prisoners' vocational training, recreation, and nutrition	Municipal office clerical support
Glendale and Queens public libraries	Dental clinics	Government forms standardization
King's County Hospital	Tuberculosis examination clinics	
Williamsburg housing project	Syphilis and gonorrhea treatment clinics	
School buildings, prisons, and firehouses	City hospital kitchen help, orderlies, laboratory technicians, nurses, doctors	
Coney Island and Brighton Beach boardwalks	Subsistence gardens	
Orchard Beach	Sewing rooms	
Swimming pools, playgrounds, parks, drinking fountains	Central Park sculpture shop	

Source: John David Millet, *The Works Progress Administration in New York City* (Chicago: Public Administration Service, 1938), pp. 95–126.

comparable positions. Moreover, female New Dealers tended to be a generation older than their male colleagues and were more likely to be Protestant than Catholic or Jewish. Many of them had known each other since the days of Progressive Era reform and women's suffrage.

The New Deal offered these female reformers little opportunity to advance the cause of women's equality. Demands for greater economic opportunity, sexual freedom, and full equality for women were put forward less often in the 1930s than they had been in the preceding two decades. One reason was that the women's movement had lost momentum after achieving the vote in 1920. Another was that prominent New Deal women, rather than vigorously pursuing a campaign for equal rights, chose to concentrate instead on

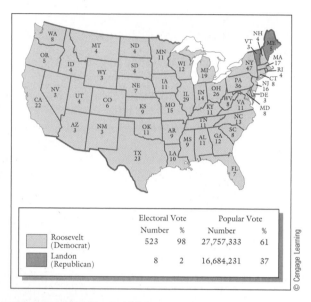

		Electoral Vote		Popular Vote	
		Number	%	Number	%
	Roosevelt (Democrat)	523	98	27,757,333	61
	Landon (Republican)	8	2	16,684,231	37

© Cengage Learning

MAP 25.5 Presidential Election, 1936

In 1936, Franklin D. Roosevelt's reelection numbers were overwhelming: 98 percent of the electoral vote, and more than 60 percent of the popular vote. No previous election in American history had been so one-sided.

"protective legislation"—laws that safeguarded female workers. Those who insisted that women needed special protections could not easily argue that women were equal to men in all respects.

Feminism was also hemmed in on all sides by a male hostility that the Depression had intensified. Many men had built their male identities on the value of hard work and the ability to provide economic security for their families. For them, the loss of work unleashed feelings of inadequacy. Male vulnerability increased as unemployment rates of men—most of whom labored in blue-collar industries—rose higher than those of women, many of whom worked in white-collar occupations less affected by job cutbacks. Many fathers and husbands resented wives and daughters who had taken over their breadwinning roles.

This male anxiety had political and social consequences. Several states passed laws outlawing the hiring of married women. New Deal relief agencies were reluctant to authorize aid for unemployed women. The labor movement made protection of the male wage earner one of its principal goals. The Social Security pension system left out waitresses, domestic servants, and other largely female occupations. Norman Cousins of the *Saturday Evening Post* suggested that the Depression could be ended simply by firing 10 million working women and giving their jobs to men. "Presto!" he declared. "No unemployment, no relief rolls. No Depression."

Many artists introduced a strident masculinism into their painting and sculpture. Mighty *Superman*, the new comic-strip hero of 1938, reflected the spirit of the times. Superman was depicted as a working-class hero, who on several occasions saved workers from coal mine explosions and other disasters caused by the greed and negligence of villainous employers.

Man of Steel. *The comic book Superman debuted in 1938, with the cover that appears in this reproduction. The character Superman partook of the New Deal's commitment to help ordinary Americans in need while offering men a fantasy about unconquerable male power.*

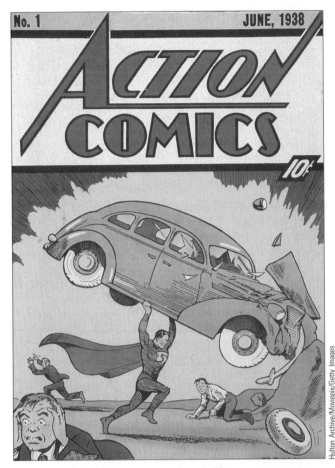

Hulton Archive/Moviepix/Getty Images

Superman's greatest vulnerability, however, other than kryptonite, was his attraction to the *working* woman Lois Lane. He could never resolve his dilemma by marrying Lois and tucking her away in a safe domestic sphere, because the continuation of the comic strip demanded that Superman be repeatedly exposed to kryptonite and female danger. But the producers of male and female images in other mass media, such as the movies, faced no such technical obstacles. Anxious men could take comfort from the conclusion of the movie *Woman of the Year,* in which Spencer Tracy persuades the ambitious Katharine Hepburn to exchange her successful newspaper career for the bliss of motherhood and homemaking. From a thousand different points, 1930s politics and culture made it clear that a woman's proper place was in the home. Faced with such obstacles, it is not surprising that women activists failed to make feminism a major part of New Deal reform.

Labor in Politics and Culture   In 1935, John L. Lewis of the United Mine Workers, Sidney Hillman of the Amalgamated Clothing Workers, and the leaders of six other unions that had seceded from the

American Federation of Labor (AFL) cobbled together a new labor organization. The Committee for Industrial Organization (**CIO**)—later renamed the Congress of Industrial Organizations—aspired to organize millions of unskilled and semi-skilled workers whom the AFL had largely ignored. In 1936, Lewis and Hillman created a second organization, Labor's Non-Partisan League (LNPL), to channel labor's money, energy, and talent into Roosevelt's reelection campaign. Roosevelt welcomed the league's help, and labor would become a key constituency of the new Democratic coalition. The passage of the Wagner Act and the creation of the NLRB in 1935 enhanced the labor movement's status and credibility. Membership in labor unions climbed steadily, and in short order union members began flexing their muscles.

In late 1936, the United Auto Workers (UAW) took on General Motors, widely regarded as the most powerful corporation in the world. Workers occupied key GM factories in Flint, Michigan, declaring that their **sit-down strike** would continue until GM agreed to recognize the UAW and negotiate a collective bargaining agreement. Frank Murphy, the pro-labor governor of Michigan, refused to use National Guard troops to evict the strikers, and Roosevelt declined to send federal troops. A 50-year-old practice of the government using soldiers to break strikes ended, and General Motors capitulated after a month of resistance. Soon, the U.S. Steel Corporation, which had defeated unionists in the bloody strike of 1919, announced that it was ready to negotiate a contract with the newly formed CIO steelworkers union.

RATES OF UNEMPLOYMENT IN SELECTED MALE AND FEMALE OCCUPATIONS, 1930

Male Occupations	Percentage Male	Percentage Unemployed
Iron and steel	96%	13%
Forestry and fishing	99	10
Mining	99	18
Heavy manufacturing	86	13
Carpentry	100	19
Laborers (road and street)	100	13
Female Occupations	**Percentage Female**	**Percentage Unemployed**
Stenographers and typists	96%	5%
Laundresses	99	3
Trained nurses	98	4
Housekeepers	92	3
Telephone operators	95	3
Dressmakers	100	4

Source: U.S. Department of Commerce, Bureau of the Census, *Fifteenth Census of the United States, 1930, Population* (Washington, D.C.: Government Printing Office, 1931).

An Activist First Lady. *No woman was more prominent or active in politics in Depression America than Eleanor Roosevelt. This 1935 photograph depicts Roosevelt meeting with miners and their supporters at the Willow Grove Mine in Bellaire Ohio. Roosevelt was seeking to learn about ways in which the New Deal could improve their conditions of work and family life.*

AP images

The labor movement's public stature grew along with its size. Many writers and artists, funded through the WPA, depicted the labor movement as the voice of the people and the embodiment of the nation's values. Murals sprang up in post offices and other public buildings featuring portraits of blue-collar Americans at work. Broadway's most celebrated play in 1935 was Clifford Odets's *Waiting for Lefty*, a raw drama about taxi drivers who confront their bosses and organize an honest union. *Pins and Needles,* a 1937 musical about the hopes and dreams of garment workers, performed by actual members of the International Ladies Garment Workers Union, became the longest-running play in Broadway history (until *Oklahoma!* broke its record of 1,108 performances in 1943).

Similarly, many of the most popular novels and movies of the 1930s celebrated the decency, honesty, and patriotism of ordinary Americans. In *Mr. Deeds Goes to Town* (1936) and *Mr. Smith Goes to Washington* (1939), Frank Capra delighted movie audiences with fables of simple, small-town heroes vanquishing the evil forces of wealth and decadence. Likewise, in *The Grapes of Wrath*, the best-selling novel of 1939, John Steinbeck told an epic tale of an Oklahoma family's fortitude in surviving eviction from their land, migrating westward, and suffering exploitation in the "promised land" of California. In 1940, John Ford turned Steinbeck's novel into one of that year's highest-grossing and most acclaimed movies. Movie-goers found special meaning in the declaration of one of the story's main characters, Ma Joad: "We'll go on forever ... cause we're the people."

The Okie migrants to California included a writer and musician named Woody Guthrie. Born in 1913 in Okemah, Oklahoma, Woody Guthrie grew up in nearby Pampa, Texas. He wasn't born poor—his father was a small businessman and a local politician—but by the time he reached his twenties, Guthrie had known a great deal of hardship: His father's business failed, three family homes burned down, one sister died from burns, and then the drought and dust storms struck. In the 1930s, Guthrie joined the migration of Okies to California. There, his musical gifts were discovered, chiefly because radio stations, in particular, were keen to put "singing cowboys" on the air. Guthrie had emerged from a country music tradition in Texas and Oklahoma and found an audience among the many people from those states who had gone to California.

Guthrie also developed a broader appeal as he cast himself as the bard of ordinary Americans everywhere. He loved America for the beauty of its landscape and its people, sentiments he expressed in one of his most popular songs, "This Land Is Your Land," which he wrote in 1940 in response to Irving Berlin's "God Bless America" (a song Guthrie did not like because of the false sense of complacency he thought it induced). Guthrie did not possess a refined singing voice, but his "hillbilly" lyrics, melodies, and humor were inventive and often inspiring. He would become a powerful influence on subsequent generations of musicians, including such major figures as Bob Dylan and Bruce Springsteen.

Guthrie traveled extensively in the 1930s. The more he learned about the hardships of individual Americans, the angrier and more politically active he became. He drew close to the labor movement and to the Communist Party, and increasingly, in his writings and songs, he criticized the industrialists, financiers, and their political agents who, he believed, had brought the Depression on America. But Guthrie always associated his criticism with the hope that the working people of America, if united, could take back their land—which is the message he meant to convey when he sang "This Land Is Your Land"—and restore its greatness. The optimism of his message underscored how much the cultural mood had changed since the early 1930s. In his focus on ordinary working Americans, in his hope for the future, and in his fusion of dissent and patriotism, Guthrie was emblematic of a major stream of culture and politics in the late 1930s.

AMERICA'S MINORITIES AND THE NEW DEAL

Reformers in the 1930s generally believed that issues of capitalism's viability, economic recovery, and the inequality of wealth and power outweighed problems of racial and ethnic discrimination; only in the case of American Indians did New Dealers pass legislation specifically designed to improve a minority's social and economic position. Because they were disproportionately poor, most minority groups did profit from the populist and pro-labor character of New Deal reforms, but the gains were distributed unevenly. Eastern and southern European ethnics benefited the most, and African Americans and Mexican Americans advanced the least.

Eastern and Southern European Ethnics   Eastern and southern European immigrants and their children had begun mobilizing politically in the 1920s in response to religious and racial discrimination. Roosevelt understood their political importance well, for he was a product of New York Democratic politics, where men such as Robert Wagner and Al Smith had begun to organize the ethnic vote even before 1920. He made sure that a significant portion of New Deal monies for welfare, building and road construction, and unemployment relief reached the urban areas where most European ethnics lived. As a result, Jewish and Catholic Americans, especially those descended from eastern and southern European immigrants, voted for Roosevelt in overwhelming numbers. The New Deal did not eliminate anti-Semitism and anti-Catholicism from American society, but it did allow millions of European ethnics to believe, for the first time, that they would overcome the second-class status they had long endured.

Eastern and southern European ethnics also benefited from their sizable presence in the mass-production industries of the Northeast, Midwest, and West Coast and in the new labor unions. Roosevelt understood and feared the power they wielded through their labor organizations.

African Americans   The New Deal did more to reproduce patterns of racial discrimination than to advance the cause of racial equality.

African Americans who belonged to CIO unions or who lived in northern cities benefited from New Deal programs, but most blacks lived in the rural South, where they were barred from voting, largely excluded from AAA programs, and denied federal protection in their efforts to form agricultural unions. The CCC ran separate camps for black and white youth. The TVA hired few blacks. Those enrolled in the CWA and other work-relief programs frequently

Marian Anderson and Abraham Lincoln. *The opera star Marian Anderson performs in 1939 at one of America's most sacred sites, the Lincoln Memorial, after having been denied the opportunity to sing at the Washington DC hall owned by the Daughters of the American Revolution.*

Hulton Archive/Archive Photos/Getty Images

received less pay than whites for doing the same jobs. Roosevelt consistently refused to support legislation to make lynching a federal crime.

This failure to push a strong civil rights agenda did not mean that New Dealers were oblivious to concerns about race. Eleanor Roosevelt spoke out frequently against racial injustice. In 1939, she resigned from the Daughters of the American Revolution when the organization refused to allow black opera singer **Marian Anderson** to perform in its concert hall. She then pressured the federal government into granting Anderson permission to sing from the steps of the Lincoln Memorial. On Easter Sunday, 75,000 people gathered to hear Anderson and to demonstrate their support for racial equality. The president did not attend.

Franklin Roosevelt did eliminate segregationist practices in the federal government that had been in place since Woodrow Wilson's presidency. He appointed Mary McLeod Bethune, Robert Weaver, William Hastie, and other African Americans to important second-level posts in his administration. Working closely with each other in what came to be known as the Black Cabinet, these officials fought hard to end discrimination in New Deal programs.

Roosevelt, however, refused to support the Black Cabinet if it meant alienating white southern senators who controlled key congressional committees. He believed that pushing for civil rights too much would cost him the support of the white South. Meanwhile, African Americans and their supporters were not yet strong enough as an electoral constituency or as a reform movement to compel Roosevelt to support a civil rights agenda.

Mexican Americans

The Mexican American experience in the Great Depression was particularly harsh. In 1931, Hoover's secretary of labor, William N. Doak, announced a plan for repatriating illegal aliens (returning them to their land of origin) and giving their jobs to American citizens. The federal campaign quickly focused on Mexican immigrants in California and the Southwest. The U.S. Immigration Service rounded up large numbers of Mexicans and Mexican Americans and demanded that each detainee prove his or her legal status. Those who failed to produce the necessary documentation were deported. Local and state governments pressured many more Mexicans into leaving. The combined efforts of federal, state, and local governments created a climate of fear in Mexican communities that prompted 500,000 to return to Mexico by 1935. This total equaled the number of Mexicans who had come to the United States in the 1920s. Los Angeles lost one-third of its Mexican population. Included in repatriate ranks were a significant number of legal immigrants who were unable to produce their immigration papers, the American-born children of illegals, and some Mexican Americans who had lived in the Southwest for generations.

The advent of the New Deal in 1933 eased but did not eliminate pressure on Mexican communities. New Deal agencies made money available for relief; Mexican Americans who worked in urban, blue-collar industries joined unions in large numbers. Most Mexicans, however, lived in rural areas and labored in agricultural jobs, and the New Deal offered them little help. The National Labor Relations Act did not protect their right to organize unions, and the Social Security Act excluded them from the new federal welfare system. Where Mexicans gained access to relief rolls, they often received payments lower than those given to "Anglos" (whites). New Dealers also did not do much to dissuade local officials from continuing their campaign to deport Mexican immigrants.

Life grew harder for immigrant Mexicans who stayed behind. The Mexican cultural renaissance that had emerged in 1920s Los Angeles stalled. Mexicans in the city retreated into the separate community of East Los Angeles. To many, they became the "invisible minority."

| **American Indians** | From the 1880s until the early 1930s, federal policy had contributed to the elimination of American Indians as a distinctive population. The Dawes Act of 1887 had called for |

tribal lands to be broken up and allotted to individual owners in the hope that Indians would adopt the work habits and lifestyles of white farmers. But American Indians had proved stubbornly loyal to their languages, religions, and cultures. Few of them succeeded as farmers, and many lost land to white speculators. By 1933, nearly half the American Indians living on reservations whose land had been allotted were landless, and many who retained allotments held largely desert or semidesert land.

The shrinking land base in combination with a growing population deepened American Indian poverty. The assimilationist pressures on American Indians, meanwhile, reached a climax in the 1920s, when the Bureau of Indian Affairs (BIA) outlawed Indian religious ceremonies, forced children from tribal communities into federal boarding schools, banned polygamy, and imposed limits on the length of men's hair.

Government officials working in the Hoover administration began to question this assimilationist policy, but its reversal had to await the New Deal and Roosevelt's appointment of **John Collier** as the commissioner of the BIA. Collier pressured the CCC, AAA, and other New Deal agencies to employ Indians on projects that improved reservation land and trained Indians in land conservation methods. He prevailed on Congress to pass the Pueblo Relief Act of 1933, which compensated Pueblos for land taken from them in the 1920s, and the Johnson-O'Malley Act of 1934, which provided funds to the states for Indian health care, welfare, and education. As part of his campaign to make the BIA more responsive to American Indian needs, Collier increased the number of Indian BIA employees from a few hundred in 1933 to 4,600 in 1940.

Collier also took steps to abolish federal boarding schools, encourage enrollment in local public schools, and establish community day schools. He insisted that American Indians be allowed to practice their traditional religions, and he created the Indian Arts and Crafts Board in 1935 to nurture traditional Indian artists and to help them market their work.

The centerpiece of Collier's reform strategy was the Indian Reorganization Act (IRA, also known as the Wheeler-Howard Act) of 1934, which revoked the allotment provisions of the Dawes Act. This landmark act recognized the rights of Native American tribes to chart their own political, cultural, and economic futures. It reflected Collier's commitment to "cultural pluralism," a doctrine that celebrated the diversity of peoples and cultures in American society and sought to protect that diversity against the pressures of assimilation. Specifically, the IRA restored land to tribes, granted Indians the right to establish constitutions and bylaws for self-government, and provided support for new tribal corporations that would regulate the use of communal lands.

Collier encountered opposition everywhere: from Protestant missionaries and cultural conservatives who wanted to continue an assimilationist policy; from white farmers and businessmen who feared that the new legislation would restrict their access to Native American land; and even from a sizable number of Indian groups, some of which had embraced assimilation and others that viewed the IRA cynically, as one more attempt by the federal government to impose "the white man's will" on the Indian peoples. This opposition made the IRA a more modest bill than the one Collier had originally championed.

A vocal minority of Indians continued to oppose the act even after its passage. The Navajo, the nation's largest tribe, voted to reject its terms, as did 76 other tribes. Still, 181 tribes, nearly 70 percent of the total, supported Collier's reform and began organizing new governments under the IRA. Although their quest for independence would suffer setbacks, these tribes gained significant measures of freedom and autonomy during the New Deal.

THE NEW DEAL ABROAD

When he first entered office, Roosevelt favored a nationalist approach to international relations. The United States, he believed, should pursue foreign policies to benefit its domestic affairs, without regard for the effects of those policies on world trade and international stability. Thus, in June 1933, Roosevelt pulled the United States out of the World Economic Conference in London, a meeting called by leading nations to strengthen the gold standard and thereby stabilize the value of their currencies. Roosevelt feared that the United States would be forced into an agreement designed to keep the gold content of the dollar high and U.S. commodity prices low, which would frustrate New Deal efforts to inflate the prices of agricultural and industrial goods.

Soon after his withdrawal from the London conference, however, Roosevelt put the United States on a more internationalist course. In November 1933, he became the first president to recognize the Soviet Union and to establish diplomatic ties with its communist rulers. In December 1933, he inaugurated a **Good Neighbor Policy** toward Latin America by formally renouncing U.S. rights to intervene in the affairs of Latin American nations. To back up his pledge, Roosevelt ordered home the U.S. Marines stationed in Haiti and Nicaragua; scuttled the Platt Amendment that had given the United States control over the Cuban government since 1901; and granted Panama more political autonomy and a greater administrative role in operating the Panama Canal.

None of this, however, meant that the United States had given up its influence over Latin America. When a 1934 revolution brought a radical government to power in Cuba, the U.S. ambassador there worked with conservative Cubans to replace the government with a regime more favorable to U.S. interests. The United States did refrain from sending troops to Cuba. It also kept its troops at home in 1936 when Mexico nationalized several U.S.-and British-owned petroleum companies. Instead, the United States demanded that Mexico compensate the oil companies for their lost property, which Mexico eventually did. In such ways, the United States exercised restraint while remaining the dominant force in hemispheric affairs.

The Roosevelt administration's internationalism also reflected its interest in stimulating trade. American businessmen wanted access to the Soviet Union's domestic market. Latin America was already a major market for the United States, but one in need of greater stability. To win the support of American traders and investors, Roosevelt stressed how the Good Neighbor Policy would improve the region's business climate.

Roosevelt further expressed his commitment to international trade through his support for the Reciprocal Trade Agreement, passed by Congress in 1934. This act allowed the United States to lower its tariffs by as much as 50 percent in exchange for similar reductions by other nations. By the end of 1935, the United States had negotiated reciprocal trade agreements with 14 countries. Roosevelt's emphasis on international trade—a move consonant with the Second New Deal's program of increasing the circulation of goods and money through the economy—further solidified support for the New Deal in parts of the business community, especially among those firms, such as United Fruit and Coca-Cola, with large overseas investments.

STALEMATE, 1937–1940

By 1937 and 1938, the New Deal had begun to lose momentum. One reason was an emerging split between working-class and middle-class Democrats. After the UAW's victory over General Motors in 1937, other workers began to imitate the successful tactics of the Flint, Michigan, militants. Sit-down strikes spread to many industries and regions, a development that worried many middle-class Americans.

The Court-Packing Fiasco   The president's proposal on February 5, 1937, to alter the makeup of the Supreme Court exacerbated middle-class fears. Roosevelt asked Congress to give him the power to appoint one new Supreme Court justice for every member of the Court who was older than age 70 and had served at least 10 years. His stated reason was that the current justices were too old and feeble to handle the large volume of cases coming before them, but his real purpose was to prevent the conservative justices on the court—most had been appointed by Republican presidents—from dismantling his New Deal. His proposal, if accepted, would have given him the authority to appoint six additional justices, thereby securing a pro–New Deal majority.

The president seemed genuinely surprised by the indignation that greeted his **"court-packing"** proposal. Although working-class support for Roosevelt remained strong, many middle-class voters turned away from the New Deal. In 1937 and 1938, a conservative opposition took shape, uniting Republicans and conservative Democrats (many of them southerners) who believed that the changes unleashed by the New Deal had gone too far.

Ironically, Roosevelt's court-packing scheme may have been unnecessary. In March 1937, just one month after he proposed his plan, Supreme Court Justice

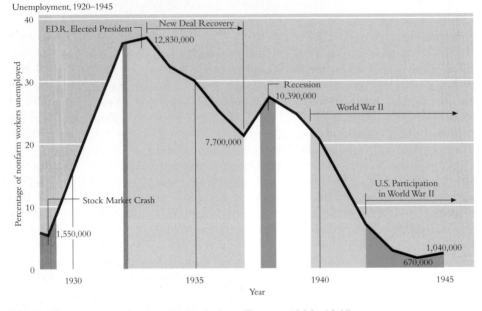

Unemployment, 1920–1945

Unemployment in the Nonfarm Labor Force, 1929–1945

Source: Data from *Historical Statistics of the United States, Colonial Times to 1970* (White Plains, NY: Kraus International, 1989), p. 126.

Owen J. Roberts, a former opponent of New Deal programs, decided to support them. In April and May, the Court upheld the constitutionality of the Wagner Act and Social Security Act, both by a 5-to-4 margin. The principal reforms of the New Deal would endure. Roosevelt allowed his court-reform proposal to die in Congress that summer. Within three years, five of the aging justices had retired, giving Roosevelt the opportunity to fashion a court more to his liking. Nonetheless, Roosevelt's reputation had suffered.

The Recession of 1937–1938   Whatever hope Roosevelt may have had for a quick recovery from his attempt at court-packing was dashed by a sharp recession that struck the country in late 1937 and 1938. The New Deal programs of 1935 had stimulated the economy, prompting Roosevelt to scale back relief programs. Meanwhile, new payroll taxes took $2 billion from wage earners' salaries to finance the Social Security pension fund even though the government did not intend to begin paying benefits until 1941. Thus, the government substantially shrank the volume of dollars it was putting into circulation. Starved for money, the economy and stock market crashed once again. Unemployment, which had fallen to 14 percent, shot back up to 20 percent. In the 1938 elections, voters vented their frustration by electing many conservative Democrats and Republicans who were opposed to the New Deal. These conservatives could not dismantle the New Deal reforms already in place, but they did block the passage of new programs.

CONCLUSION

Roosevelt first assumed the presidency in the same week that Adolf Hitler established a Nazi dictatorship in Germany. Some feared that Roosevelt, by accumulating more power into the hands of the federal government than had ever been held in peacetime, aspired to autocratic rule. Nothing of the sort happened. Roosevelt and the New Dealers not only strengthened democracy, they also inspired millions of Americans who had never before voted to go to the polls. Groups that had been marginalized—eastern and southern European ethnics, unskilled workers, American Indians—now believed that their political activism could make a difference.

Not everyone benefited to the same degree from the broadening of American democracy. Northern factory workers, farm owners, European American ethnics, and middle-class consumers (especially homeowners) were among the groups who benefited most. In contrast, the socialist and communist elements of the labor movement failed to achieve their radical aims. Unionization proceeded far more slowly among southern industrial workers, black and white. Sizable occupational groups, such as farm laborers and domestic servants, were denied Social Security benefits. Feminists made little headway. African Americans and Mexican Americans gained meager influence over public policy.

New Deal reforms might not have mattered to any group if the Second World War had not rescued the New Deal economic program. With government war orders flooding factories from 1941 on, the economy grew vigorously, unemployment vanished, and prosperity finally returned. The architects of the Second New Deal, who had argued that large government expenditures would stimulate consumer demand and trigger economic recovery, were vindicated.

The war also solidified the political reforms of the 1930s: an increased role for the government in regulating the economy and in ensuring the social welfare of those unable to help themselves; strong state support of unionization, agricultural subsidies, and progressive tax policies; and the use of government power and money to develop the West and Southwest. In contrast to progressivism, the reforms of the New Deal endured. Voters returned Roosevelt to office for unprecedented third and fourth terms, and these same voters remained wedded for the next 40 years to Roosevelt's central idea: that a powerful state would enhance the pursuit of liberty and equality.

26

AMERICA DURING THE SECOND WORLD WAR, 1939–1945

CHAPTER OUTLINE

• The Road to War: Aggression and Response • Fighting the War in Europe and the Pacific • The War at Home: The Economy • The War at Home: Social Issues • Shaping the Peace

---

THE SECOND WORLD WAR vastly changed American life. The United States abandoned isolationism, moved toward military engagement on the side of the Allies, and emerged triumphant in a global war. The nation's productive capacity—spurred by innovative technologies and by a new working relationship among government, business, labor, and scientific researchers—dwarfed that of all other nations and provided the economic basis for military victory. The mobilization for war finally lifted the economy out of the Great Depression.

The war also raised questions about the meanings of liberty and equality in America. How would the nation, while striving for victory, reorder its economy, its politics, and the cultural and social patterns that had shaped racial, ethnic, and gender relationships during the 1930s? What processes of reconstruction, at home and abroad, might be required to build a prosperous and lasting peace?

THE ROAD TO WAR: AGGRESSION AND RESPONSE

The road to the Second World War began at least a decade before U.S. entry in 1941. In Japan, Italy, and Germany, economic stagnation created political conditions that nurtured ultranationalist movements bent on territorial expansion. Elsewhere in Europe and in the United States, economic problems led governments to concentrate on domestic recovery and avoid foreign entanglements.

CHRONOLOGY

1931	Japanese forces seize Manchuria
1933	Hitler takes power in Germany
1936	Spanish Civil War begins
	Germany and Italy agree to cooperate as the Axis powers
1937	Neutrality Act broadens provisions of Neutrality Acts of 1935 and 1936
	Roosevelt makes "Quarantine" speech
	Japan invades China
1938	France and Britain appease Hitler at Munich
1939	Hitler invades Poland; war breaks out in Europe
	Congress amends Neutrality Act to assist Allies
1940	Paris falls after German *blitzkreig*
	Roosevelt makes "destroyers-for-bases" deal with Britain
	Selective Service Act passed
	Roosevelt wins third term
1941	Lend-Lease established
	Roosevelt creates Fair Employment Practices Commission
	Roosevelt and Churchill proclaim the Atlantic Charter
	Congress narrowly repeals Neutrality Act
	Japanese forces attack Pearl Harbor (December 7)
1942	President signs Executive Order 9066 for internment of Japanese Americans
	General MacArthur driven from Philippines
	United States victorious in Battle of Midway
	German army defeated at Battle of Stalingrad
	Operation TORCH begins
1943	Axis armies in North Africa surrender
	Allies invade Sicily and Italy
	"Zoot suit" incidents in Los Angeles; racial violence in Detroit
	Allies begin drive toward Japan through South Pacific islands
1944	Allies land at Normandy (D-Day, June 6)
	Roosevelt reelected to fourth term
	Bretton Woods Conference creates IMF and World Bank
	Dumbarton Oaks Conference establishes plan for United Nations

1945	United States firebombs Japan
	Yalta Conference
	Roosevelt dies; Truman becomes president
	Germany surrenders
	Hiroshima and Nagasaki hit with atomic bombs
	Japan surrenders
	United Nations established

The Rise of Aggressor States

On September 18, 1931, Japanese military forces seized Manchuria and created Manchukuo, a puppet state of Japan. This action violated the League of Nations charter, the Washington Naval Treaties, and the Kellogg-Briand Pact. Focused on domestic matters, the international community hesitated to oppose Japan's move. The Hoover-Stimson Doctrine (1931) announced a U.S. policy of "nonrecognition" toward Manchukuo, and the League of Nations condemned Japan's action. Japan simply ignored these rebukes.

Meanwhile, ultranationalist states in Europe also sought to alleviate domestic ills through military aggression. **Adolf Hitler's** National Socialist (Nazi) Party came to power in Germany in 1933 and instituted a fascist regime, a one-party dictatorial state. Hitler denounced the Versailles peace settlement of 1919, blamed Germany's problems on a Jewish conspiracy, claimed a genetic superiority for the "Aryan race" of German-speaking peoples, and promised a new Germanic empire, the **Third Reich**. His regime withdrew from the League of Nations in 1933 and, in a blatant violation of the Versailles Treaty, dramatically boosted Germany's military budget. Another fascist government, in Italy, headed by Benito Mussolini, also launched a military buildup and dreamed of empire. In October 1935, Mussolini's armies took over Ethiopia, an independent nation in Africa.

U.S. Neutrality

Many Americans wished to isolate their nation from these foreign troubles. Antiwar movies, such as *All Quiet on the Western Front* (1931), implicitly portrayed the First World War as a power game played by business and governmental elites, who used appeals to nationalism to dupe young soldiers into serving as cannon fodder. During the mid-1930s a Senate investigating committee headed by Republican Gerald P. Nye of North Dakota held well-publicized hearings and concluded that the United States had been maneuvered into the First World War to preserve the profits of bankers and munitions makers. By 1935, opinion polls suggested that Americans overwhelmingly opposed involvement in foreign conflicts.

To prevent a repetition of the circumstances that had supposedly drawn the United States into the First World War, Congress enacted neutrality legislation. The **Neutrality Acts** of 1935 and 1936 mandated an arms embargo against belligerents, prohibited loans to them, and curtailed travel by Americans on ships belonging to nations at war. The Neutrality Act of 1937 extended the embargo to include all trade with any belligerent, unless the nation paid in cash and carried the purchases away in its own ships.

Critics charged that foreswearing U.S. intervention actively aided expansionist powers. In March 1936, Nazi troops seized the Rhineland, a German area from which the 1919 peace settlement had barred military installations. A few months later, Hitler and Mussolini began assisting General Francisco Franco, a fellow fascist seeking to overthrow Spain's republican government. Republicans in Spain appealed to nonfascist nations for assistance, but only the Soviet Union responded. Britain, France, and the United States, fearing that the conflict would flare into world war if more nations took sides, remained uninvolved.

Although the United States remained officially aloof, the **Spanish Civil War** precipitated a major debate. Conservative groups generally hailed Franco as a staunch anticommunist who supported the Catholic Church and social traditionalism in Spain. In contrast, the political left championed republican Spain and denounced fascism. Cadres of Americans, including the famed "Abraham Lincoln Brigade," crossed the Atlantic to fight alongside republican forces in Spain. American peace groups splintered: Some continued to advocate neutrality and isolation, but others argued for intervention against the spread of fascism.

In October 1937, Franklin D. Roosevelt called for international cooperation to "quarantine" aggressor nations and suggested that Congress should modify its earlier neutrality measures. Still suspicious of foreign entanglements, a majority in Congress refused to budge, even when this meant a victory by Franco in Spain's civil war.

The Mounting Crisis   As Americans debated how to deal with foreign aggression, Japan invaded China. In summer 1937, after an exchange of gunfire between Japanese and Chinese troops at the Marco Polo Bridge near Beijing, Japanese armies captured Shanghai, Nanjing, Shandong, and Beijing. Japan demanded that China become subservient to Tokyo. It also proposed an **East Asian Co-Prosperity Sphere** that would supposedly liberate Asian nations from Western colonialism and create a self-sufficient economic zone under Japanese leadership. Later that year Japanese planes sank the American gunboat *Panay* as it evacuated Americans from Nanjing. Japan's quick apology defused a potential crisis, but the *Panay* incident and Japan's brutal occupation of Nanjing— where perhaps 300,000 Chinese civilians were killed—alarmed Roosevelt.

In Europe, Germany continued on the march. In March 1938, Hitler annexed Austria to the Third Reich and announced his intention to seize the Sudetenland, a portion of Czechoslovakia inhabited by 3.5 million people of German descent. In May, FDR began a program of naval rearmament. French and British leaders, still hoping to avoid war, met with Hitler at the **Munich Conference** in September. They acquiesced to Germany's seizure of the Sudetenland in return for Hitler's promise to seek no more territory. Hailed by Britain's prime minister as a guarantee of "peace in our time," the arrangement soon became a symbol of what interventionists called the "appeasement" of aggression.

In March 1939, Germans marched into Prague and, within a few months, annexed the rest of Czechoslovakia. In August, Hitler signed a nonaggression pact with the Soviet Union, previously his bitter enemy. In a secret protocol, Hitler and

Soviet leader Joseph Stalin agreed on a plan to divide up Poland and permit Soviet annexation of the Baltic states (Latvia, Lithuania, and Estonia).

The Outbreak of War in Europe   When Hitler's armies stormed into Poland on September 1, 1939, the Second World War officially began in Europe. Britain and France declared war against Germany, but these Allied powers could not mobilize in time to help Poland, which fell within weeks. Then an eerie calm settled over Europe during the winter.

In April 1940, a full-scale German *blitzkrieg,* or "lightning war," began moving swiftly, shocking Allied leaders and overrunning Denmark, Norway, the Netherlands, Belgium, Luxembourg, and France. Early in June, Italy and Germany—which had earlier formed the Axis powers—declared war on the Allies. Later in June, France fell, and Hitler installed a pro-Nazi government at Vichy in southern France. In only six weeks, Hitler's army had seized complete control of Europe's Atlantic coastline, from the North Sea south to Spain, where Franco remained officially neutral but decidedly pro-Axis. The Axis gained another member in September 1940, when Japan joined Germany and Italy in a Tripartite Pact.

The U.S. Response to War in Europe   Alarmed at the Nazi surge, Roosevelt pressured Congress to modify its neutrality legislation and called for other measures, "short of war," to help Britain and France. Late in 1939, Congress lifted the ban on selling military armaments to belligerents and substituted a cash-and-carry provision that permitted arms sales to belligerents who could pay cash and use their own ships for transport. This arrangement minimized risks to American exporters. Because its naval forces dominated the Atlantic sea-lanes, Britain primarily benefited from this policy change. Congress also boosted military funding and passed the Selective Training and Service Act of 1940, the first peacetime draft in U.S. history. Abandoning any pretense of neutrality, the United States also facilitated Britain's direct acquisition of U.S. "surplus" war materiel. In an attempt to broaden bipartisan support for these controversial measures, Roosevelt added pro-interventionist Republicans to his cabinet.

Meanwhile, from August through October 1940, Germany's *Luftwaffe* (air force) conducted daily raids on British air bases and nearly knocked out its Royal Air Force (RAF). On the verge of a knockout, however, Hitler suddenly changed strategy and ordered, instead, the bombing of London and other cities. The use of airpower against civilians in the Battle of Britain, as it was called, steeled Britain's resolve and aroused sympathy among Americans who heard of events during dramatic radio broadcasts from London. CBS's Edward R. Murrow, observed one American writer, "skillfully burned the city of London in our homes, and we felt the flames."

In September 1940, Roosevelt agreed to transfer 50 First World War–era naval destroyers to the British navy. In return, the United States gained the right to build eight naval bases in British territories in the Western Hemisphere. This "destroyers-for-bases" deal infuriated those who favored staying out of the war. The America First Committee, organized by General Robert E. Wood, head of Sears, Roebuck, and Company, launched a campaign to sway public opinion. The aviator hero

MAP 26.1 German Expansion at Its Height

This map shows the expansion of German power from 1938 through 1942. Which countries fell to German control? Why might Americans have differed over whether these moves by Germany represented a strategic threat to the United States?

Charles A. Lindbergh, America First's most famous member, flew around the country rallying opposition to aiding Britain.

Those who favored staying out of the war were generally lumped together as **"isolationists,"** but this single term obscures their diversity. Pacifists opposed all wars as immoral. Some political progressives detested fascism but feared even more the centralization of governmental power that conducting a war would require in the United States. And some conservatives sympathized with the anticommunism of fascist states.

An undercurrent of anti-Jewish sentiment also existed in the United States. In 1939, congressional leaders had quashed the Wagner-Rogers bill, which would have boosted immigration quotas in order to allow for the entry of 20,000 Jewish children otherwise slated for Hitler's concentration camps. Bowing to anti-Semitic prejudices, the United States adopted a restrictive refugee policy. The consequences of these policies became especially grave after June 1941, when Hitler established the death camps that would systematically exterminate millions of Jews, gypsies, homosexuals, communists, and anyone else whom the Nazis deemed unfit for life in the Third Reich. In September 1941, Senator Burton K. Wheeler created a Senate committee to investigate whether Jewish producers in Hollywood were using movies to promote pro-interventionist views. Some isolationists expressed blatantly anti-Semitic views.

Those who favored supporting the Allies also organized. The Committee to Defend America by Aiding the Allies, headed by a well-known Republican newspaper editor, organized more than 300 local chapters in just a few weeks. Similar to the isolationists, interventionist organizations mobilized a diverse group of supporters. All, however, sounded alarms that fascist aggressors might overrun Europe and thus threaten American security.

Electoral politics in 1940 forced Roosevelt, nominated for a third term, to tone down his pro-Allied rhetoric. He promised not to send American troops to fight in "foreign wars." Once he had won an unprecedented third term against Republican nominee Wendell Willkie, however, Roosevelt unveiled his most ambitious plan yet to support Britain's war effort.

An "Arsenal of Democracy"   Britain was nearly out of money, so the president proposed that the United States would now "lend-lease," or loan rather than sell, munitions to the Allies. Making the United States a "great arsenal of democracy," FDR claimed, would "keep war away from our country and our people." After bitter congressional debate, the **Lend-Lease Act** passed on March 11, 1941. When Germany turned away from Britain and suddenly attacked its recent ally, the Soviet Union, in June, Roosevelt extended Lend-Lease assistance to the communist regime of Joseph Stalin.

Roosevelt next began coordinating military strategy with Britain. He secretly pledged to follow a Europe-first approach if the United States were drawn into a two-front war against both Germany and Japan. Publicly, Roosevelt deployed U.S. Marines to Greenland and Iceland to free up the British forces. In August 1941, Roosevelt and British prime minister Winston Churchill met on the high seas off the coast of Newfoundland to forge a formal wartime alliance.

They agreed to an eight-point Atlantic Charter that disavowed territorial expansion, endorsed protection of human rights and self-determination, and pledged the postwar creation of a new world organization that would ensure "general security." Roosevelt also agreed to Churchill's request that the U.S. Navy convoy American goods as far as Iceland. Soon, in an undeclared naval war, Germany's formidable submarine packs began attacking U.S. ships.

By this time Roosevelt believed that defeating Hitler would require U.S. entry into the war, but public support still lagged. Privately, the president likely hoped that Germany would commit some provocative act in the North Atlantic that would jar public opinion. The October 1941 sinking of the U.S. destroyer *Reuben James* did just that. Congress repealed its earlier neutrality legislation, but the vote was so close and debate so bitter that Roosevelt could not yet seek a formal declaration of war.

Pearl Harbor   As it turned out, Japan, rather than Germany, sparked America's involvement. In response to Japan's 1937 invasion of China, the United States extended credit to China and curtailed sales of equipment to Japan. In 1939, the United States abrogated its Treaty of Commerce and Navigation with Japan, an action that further restricted U.S. exports to the island nation. A 1940 ban on the sale of aviation fuel and high-grade scrap iron was also intended to slow Japan's military advances.

These measures did not halt Japanese expansion, but made it seem even more imperative to Japan's leaders. As the European war sapped the strength of France, the Netherlands, and Great Britain, Japanese militarists hoped to grab Europe's Asian colonies and incorporate them into Japan's own East Asian Co-Prosperity Sphere. Japan therefore pushed deep into French Indochina, seeking the raw materials it could no longer buy from the United States, and prepared to launch attacks on Singapore, the Netherlands East Indies (Indonesia), and the Philippines.

Roosevelt expanded the trade embargo against Japan, promised further assistance to China, accelerated a U.S. military buildup in the Pacific, and in mid-1941 froze all Japanese assets in the United States. Faced with impending economic strangulation, Japanese leaders did not reassess their plan to create an East Asian empire. Instead, they began planning a preemptive attack on the United States. With limited supplies of raw materials, especially oil, Japan had little hope of winning a prolonged war. Japanese military strategists gambled that a surprise, crippling blow would force U.S. concessions. General Hideki Tojo, who became Japan's prime minister, knew the risks but remarked that "sometimes a man has to jump with his eyes closed."

On December 7, 1941, Japanese bombers swooped down on **Pearl Harbor**, Hawaii, and destroyed much of the U.S. Pacific Fleet. Altogether, 19 ships were sunk or severely damaged; nearly 200 aircraft were destroyed or disabled; and 2,200 Americans were killed. The attack could have been worse. U.S. aircraft carriers, out to sea at the time, were spared, as were the base's fuel storage tanks and repair facilities. In a dramatic message broadcast by radio on December 8, Roosevelt decried the attack and labeled December 7 as "a date which will live in infamy," a phrase that served as a battle cry throughout the war. Japan had rallied Americans, not brought them to terms.

A few Americans charged that Roosevelt had intentionally provoked Japan in order to open a "back door" to war. They asked why the fleet at Pearl Harbor lay vulnerable, not even in a state of full alert. The actions and inactions of leaders, however, were more confused than devious. Intelligence experts, who had broken Japanese diplomatic but not military code, expected Japan to move toward Singapore or other British or Dutch possessions in Asia. Intercepted messages, along with visual sightings of Japanese ships, seemed to confirm preparations for a strike in Southeast Asia (which did occur). American leaders doubted that Japan would risk a direct attack or that its military planners had the skill to mount an air assault of such distance.

On December 8, 1941, Congress declared war against Japan. Japan's allies, Germany and Italy, declared war on the United States three days later. Hitler mistakenly assumed that the fight against Japan would keep the United States preoccupied in the Pacific. The three Axis powers drastically underestimated America's ability to mobilize swiftly and effectively.

FIGHTING THE WAR IN EUROPE AND THE PACIFIC

Initially, the war went badly for the Allies. German forces controlled most of Europe, from Norway to Greece, and had pushed eastward into the Soviet Union. Now they rolled across North Africa, and German submarines endangered Allied supply lines in the Atlantic. Japan seemed unstoppable in the Pacific, overrunning Malaya, the Netherlands East Indies, and the Philippines and moving against the British in Burma and the Australians in New Guinea.

The United States had been unprepared for war, but new bureaucracies and technologies quickly guided a crash program for mobilization. The newly formed Joint Chiefs of Staff, consisting of representatives from each of the armed services, directed strategy. The War Department's **Pentagon** complex, a giant, five-story, five-sided building, was completed in January 1943 after 16 months of around-the-clock work. In 1942 aircraft equipped with radar, a new technology developed in collaboration with Britain, proved effective against submarines, and during 1943 Germany's U-boat threat faded "from menace to problem," in the words of one U.S. naval commander. Perhaps most critical, a massive Allied code-breaking operation perfected decryption techniques for use against Germany's supposedly inviolable encoding machine. Decrypted German messages, called "Ultra" for "ultrasecret," gave the Allies a crucial advantage. Throughout the war, the Germans never discovered that many of their decoded radio communications were being forwarded to Allied commanders—sometimes even before they had reached their German recipients. In the postwar world, the code-breaking effort would contribute to the development of computer technology.

Campaigns in North Africa and Italy   The Allies differed over military strategy. Stalin pleaded with Roosevelt and Churchill to open a second front in western Europe, by way of an invasion across the English Channel into France, to relieve pressure on the Soviet Union. Many of Roosevelt's advisers agreed: If German troops succeeded in knocking the Soviet Union out of the war, Hitler could turn his full attention toward Britain. Churchill urged instead the invasion of French North Africa, which German forces now controlled, in order to nibble away at the edges of enemy power.

At a meeting in Casablanca, Morocco, in January 1943, Roosevelt sided with Churchill. He argued that a cross-Channel invasion of France carried too many risks at that time. To assuage Stalin's fear that his allies might sign a separate peace with Hitler, however, Roosevelt and Churchill promised to remain in the fight until Germany agreed to an "unconditional surrender."

The North African operation, code-named TORCH, began with Anglo-American landings in Morocco and Algeria in November 1942. As TORCH progressed, the Soviets turned the tide of battle on the eastern front with a decisive victory at Stalingrad. The Battle of Stalingrad, which lasted nearly six months and killed over 1 million people, was perhaps the bloodiest in modern history.

Hitler poured reinforcements into North Africa but could stop neither TORCH nor the British drive westward from Egypt. In summer 1943, the Allies followed up their successful North African campaign by overrunning the island of Sicily and then fighting their way, slowly, northward through Italy's mountains.

Some U.S officials worried about the postwar implications of wartime strategy. Secretary of War Henry Stimson warned that the Allied campaigns through Africa and Italy might leave the Soviets dominant in most of Europe. Acting on this advice, Roosevelt finally agreed to set a date for the cross-Channel invasion that Stalin had long been promised.

Operation
OVERLORD

Operation **OVERLORD**, directed by General Dwight D. Eisenhower, began on June 6, 1944, D-Day. During the preceding months, probably the largest invasion force in history had assembled in England. Disinformation and diversionary tactics fooled the Germans into expecting a landing at the narrowest part of the English Channel rather than in the Normandy region. After several weather-related delays, nervous commanders finally ordered the daring plan to begin. The night before, as naval guns pounded the Normandy shore, three divisions of paratroopers dropped behind enemy lines to disrupt German communications. Then at dawn, more than 4,000 Allied ships landed troops and supplies on Normandy's beaches. The first American forces to come ashore at Omaha Beach took enormous casualties, but the waves of invading troops continued. Only three weeks after D-Day, more than a million Allied personnel controlled the French coast and opened the long-awaited Second Front.

Just as the 1943 Battle of Stalingrad had reversed the course of the war in the East, so OVERLORD changed the momentum in the West. Within three months, U.S., British, and Free French troops entered Paris. After repulsing a desperate German counteroffensive in Belgium, at the Battle of the Bulge in December and January, Allied armies swept eastward, crossing the Rhine, and headed toward Berlin to meet up with westward-advancing Soviet troops.

As the war in Europe drew to a close, the horrors perpetrated by the Third Reich became fully visible. Hitler's campaign of extermination, now called the Holocaust, killed more than 5 million Jews out of Europe's prewar population of 10 million. Hundreds of thousands more from various other groups were also murdered. Although only a military victory put an end to German death camps, the Allies might have saved thousands of Jews before and during the war by helping them escape and emigrate. Allied leaders, however, had worried about how to deal with large numbers of Jewish refugees, and they also claimed that, during the war, they could not spare scarce ships to transport refugees to sanctuary. The Allies would, in 1945 and 1946, bring 24 German high officials to trial at Nuremberg for "crimes against humanity." Large quantities of money, gold, and jewelry that Nazi leaders stole from victims of the Holocaust and deposited in Swiss banks, however, remained concealed for more than 50 years. Not until 1997 did Jewish groups and the U.S. government force an investigation of the Swiss banking industry's holdings of stolen "Nazi gold," an inquiry that finally prompted some monetary restitution for victims' families.

With Hitler's suicide in April and Germany's surrender on May 8, 1945, the military foundations for peace in Europe were complete. Soviet armies controlled

HISTORY THROUGH FILM

Saving Private Ryan (1998)

Directed by Steven Spielberg.
Starring Tom Hanks (Captain John Miller), Matt Damon (Private James Ryan), and Harve Presnell (General George Marshall).

Hollywood marked the 50th anniversary of the Allied effort in the Second World War with a series of films about "the good war." Although Saving Private Ryan invited comparison with The Longest Day (1962) because of its depiction of the D-Day invasion, Steven Spielberg's battlefield sequences represented a considerable advance in the art of waging war on film. His production team employed sophisticated computer graphics and nearly deafening Dolby sound to mount battle scenes so realistic that reviewers cautioned veterans susceptible to post–traumatic stress syndrome about watching the film.

The film also suggested the kind of family-centered melodrama that Spielberg had grafted onto the sci-fi genre in E.T.: The Extra-Terrestrial (1982). A heroic squad led by Captain John Miller is trying to locate a single U.S. soldier, Private James Ryan, whose mother has already lost her three other sons to the war. The film poses the question of whether such a family-related

mission legitimates and sanctifies the sacrifices of the Second World War. Private Ryan answers yes to this question.

The major body of the film carefully justifies the rescue mission. Although Captain Miller wonders if his dangerous assignment is simply a public relations stunt, he quickly drops this idea and pursues his mission with the gallantry required of a Hollywood-commissioned officer. Later, his platoon members debate the morality of risking eight lives to save one, but the cause of Ryan's mother always seems overriding. General George Marshall cuts off debate over the appropriateness of the Ryan mission by invoking an earlier war leader, Abraham Lincoln, who once faced a similar dilemma. When Miller's troops finally locate Private Ryan, the film's audience discovers that he is the kind of clean-cut Iowa farm boy who will stay with his would-be saviors rather than retreat to safety. Ryan survives, although most of his comrades perish. Captain Miller, dying, implores young Ryan to lead a "good" life to justify the sacrifice of so many others.

The film Saving Private Ryan, in contrast to its characters, takes few risks.

Eastern Europe; British and U.S. forces predominated in Italy and the rest of the Mediterranean; Germany and Austria fell under divided occupation. Governmental leaders now needed to work out a plan for transforming these military arrangements into a comprehensive political settlement for the postwar era.

Seizing the Offensive in the Pacific Meanwhile, the war in the Pacific was far from over. During the six months following Pearl Harbor, Japan's forces steadily advanced. Singapore fell. Japan overwhelmed U.S. naval garrisons in the Philippines and the islands of Guam and Wake. Filipino and American troops surrendered at Bataan and Corregidor in the Philippines. Other Japanese forces headed southward to menace Australia and New Zealand.

It secures its emotional investment in the rescue effort by bracketing the Second World War segments with two brief framing sequences in which an aging Ryan, along with his own family, returns to Normandy and visits the grave of Captain Miller. In the final segment, Ryan's wife provides the additional reassurance that the trauma of the Second World War served a good cause, because Private Ryan's own family life has justified Miller's sacrifice. "Tell me I've led a good life. Tell me I'm a good man," he implores his wife. After nearly three hours of this Spielberg epic, the question is rhetorical.

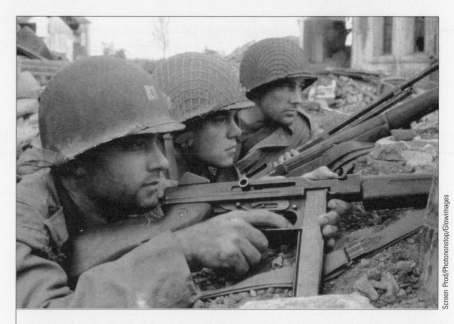

Screen Prod/Photononstop/Glowimages

Saving Private Ryan, *which garnered four Academy Award nominations, celebrated the heroism of what popular historians called America's "greatest generation."*

When Japan finally suffered its first naval setback at the Battle of the Coral Sea in May 1942, Japanese naval commanders decided to hit back hard. They amassed 200 ships and 600 planes to destroy what remained of the U.S. Pacific Fleet and to take Midway Island, from which they could assault Hawaii. U.S. naval intelligence, however, was monitoring Japanese codes and warned Admiral Chester W. Nimitz of the plan. Surprising the Japanese armada in the Battle of Midway, U.S. planes sank four Japanese carriers and destroyed a total of 322 planes.

Two months later, American forces splashed ashore at Guadalcanal in the Solomon Islands. The bloody engagements in the Solomons continued for months on both land and sea, but they accomplished one major objective: seizing the military initiative in the

MAP 26.2 Allied Advances and Collapse of German Power

This map depicts the final Allied advances and the end of the war in Germany. Through what countries did Soviet armies advance, and how might their advance have affected the postwar situation? How was Germany divided by occupying powers, and how might that division have affected postwar politics?

Pacific. According to prewar plans, the war in Europe was to have received highest priority, but by 1943 the two theaters were receiving roughly equal resources.

The bloody Pacific engagements reinforced racial prejudices and brutality on both sides. Japanese leaders hoped the war would confirm the superiority of their divine Yamato race. Prisoners taken by the Japanese, particularly on the Asian mainland, were brutalized in almost unimaginable ways. The Japanese Army's

Unit 731 tested bacteriological weapons in China and conducted horrifying medical experiments on live subjects. American propaganda images played on themes of racial superiority, portraying the Japanese people as animalistic subhumans. American troops often rivaled Japan's forces in their disrespect for the enemy dead and sometimes killed the enemy rather than take prisoners.

China Policy   U.S. policymakers hoped that China would fight effectively against Japan and emerge from the war as a strong, united nation. Neither hope seemed realistic. China was beset by civil war.

Jiang Jieshi's Nationalist government was incompetent and unpopular. It avoided engaging the Japanese invaders and still made extravagant demands for U.S. assistance. A growing communist movement led by Mao Zedong fought more effectively against the Japanese invaders, but U.S. policy continued to support Jiang as China's future leader. All the while, Japan's advance continued, and in 1944 its forces captured seven key U.S. air bases in China.

U.S. Strategy in the Pacific   In contrast to the European theater, no unified command guided the war in the Pacific, and military actions often emerged from compromise. General Douglas MacArthur, commander of the army in the South Pacific, favored an offensive launched from his headquarters in Australia through New Guinea and the Philippines and on to Japan. After Japan had driven him out of the Philippines in May 1942, he promised to return. Admiral Nimitz disagreed. He favored an advance across the smaller islands of the central Pacific, bypassing the Philippines. Unable to decide between the two strategies, the Joint Chiefs of Staff authorized both.

Both offensives moved forward, marked by heavy casualties. MacArthur took New Guinea. Nimitz's forces liberated the Marshall Islands and the Marianas in 1943 and 1944. An effective radio communication system conducted by a platoon of Navajo Indians, the Navajo Signal Corps, made a unique contribution to success. Navajo, a language unfamiliar to Japanese intelligence officers, provided a secure medium for sensitive communications.

In late 1944, the fall of Saipan in the Marianas brought American bombers within range of Japan. The capture of the islands of Iwo Jima and Okinawa during spring 1945 further shortened that distance. Okinawa illustrated the ferocity of the campaigns: An estimated 120,000 Japanese and 48,000 American soldiers died.

Given these numbers, U.S. military planners dreaded the prospect of invading Japan's home islands, and airpower looked more and more enticing. The results of the Allies' strategic bombing of Germany, including the destruction of such large cities as Hamburg and Dresden, were ambiguous, and military historians continue to debate whether the damage against military targets really offset the huge civilian casualties and the unsustainable losses of American pilots and aircraft. Nonetheless, U.S. strategists continued to claim that strategic bombing might provide the crucial advantage in the Pacific. In February 1944, General Henry Harley ("Hap") Arnold devised a plan for firebombing major Japanese cities. Bombers added to the horror of war and terrorized civilians, Arnold conceded, but when used "with the proper degree of understanding" could become "the most humane of all weapons" by

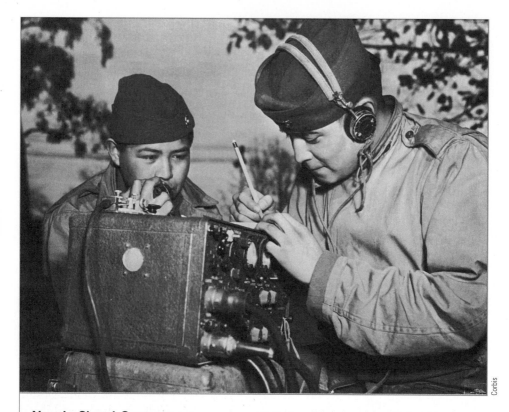

Corbis

Navajo Signal Corps. *Sending messages in their native language, which neither the Japanese nor the Germans could decipher, Navajo Indians in the Signal Corps made a unique contribution to preserving the secrecy of U.S. intelligence.*

shortening the war. Arnold's air campaign, operating from China, turned out to be cumbersome. It was replaced by a more effective and lethal operation run from Saipan by General Curtis LeMay.

LeMay summarized his strategy: "Bomb and burn them until they quit." The official position on the incendiary raids against Japanese cities was that they constituted "precision" rather than "area" bombing. In actuality, the success of a mission was measured by the number of square miles it left scorched. Air attacks on Tokyo during the night of March 9–10, 1945, leveled nearly a quarter of the city and incinerated more than 100,000 people.

By the winter of 1944–1945, a combined sea and air strategy had emerged: The United States sought "unconditional surrender" by blockading Japan's seaports, bombarding its cities from the air, and invading if necessary. Critics of the policy of unconditional surrender, which most Japanese assumed meant the death of their emperor, later suggested that it might have hardened Japan's determination to fight even after defeat had become inevitable. Defenders of the policy suggest that any softening of U.S. terms would have encouraged Japanese resistance. Whatever the case, American leaders decided that victory would only come through massive destruction.

A New President, the Atomic Bomb, and Japan's Surrender   On April 12, 1945, Franklin Roosevelt died of a cerebral hemorrhage. Sorrow and shock spread throughout a nation in which many young men and women had hardly known any other president. Through diplomatic conference halls, Roosevelt's personal magnetism had often brought unity, if not always clarity. To be sure, he had accumulated critics and enemies, and his support had waned. He had defeated Republican Thomas E. Dewey in the 1944 presidential election by the smallest popular-vote margin in nearly 30 years, and Republicans had further cut into the Democrat's majorities in the House and Senate. But among his supporters, he had symbolized optimism through depression and war.

Emerging from Roosevelt's shadow, Vice President Harry S Truman seemed an unimposing presence in the White House. Born on a farm near Independence, Missouri, Truman served in France during the First World War, became a U.S. senator in 1934, and was tabbed as Roosevelt's running mate in 1944. Roosevelt offered an upper-class image of well-practiced and worldly charm. In contrast, Truman came from a middle-class background, and he knew little about international affairs and virtually nothing about any informal understandings that Roosevelt may have had with foreign leaders.

Only after succeeding Roosevelt did Truman learn about events at Los Alamos, New Mexico. There, since the late 1930s, scientists from all across the world had been secretly working on a new weapon. Advances in theoretical physics had suggested that splitting the atom (fission) would release a tremendous amount of energy. Fearful that Germany was racing ahead of the United States in this research, Albert Einstein, a Jewish refugee from Germany, had urged Roosevelt to launch a secret program to build an atomic bomb. The government enlisted top scientists in the **Manhattan Project**, a huge, secret military operation. On July 16, 1945, the first atomic weapon was successfully tested at Trinity Site, near Alamogordo, New Mexico.

Truman and his top policymakers assumed that the weapon would be put to immediate use. They were eager to end the war, both because a possible land invasion of Japan might prove costly in American lives and because the Soviet Union was planning to enter the Pacific theater, where Truman wished to limit Soviet power. Churchill called the bomb a "miracle of deliverance." Truman later publicly claimed that he had never lost a night's sleep over its use.

Privately, there was disagreement over where and how the bomb should be deployed. A commission of atomic scientists recommended a "demonstration" that would impress Japan with the bomb's power, yet cause no loss of life. General George C. Marshall suggested using it on purely military installations or only on manufacturing sites, after first warning away Japanese workers. Ultimately, the Truman administration discarded these options. The bomb, Secretary of War Henry Stimson said, had to make "a profound psychological impression on as many inhabitants as possible."

In one sense, the atomic bombs dropped on the previously unbombed cities of **Hiroshima** and Nagasaki on August 6 and 9, 1945, could be regarded as merely bigger, more effective firebombs. In another sense, however, atomic weapons produced almost unimaginable destruction. Colonel Paul Tibbets, who piloted the

MAP 26.3   Pacific Theater Offensive Strategy and Final Assault against Japan

This map suggests the complicated nature of devising a war strategy in the vast Pacific region. What tactics did the United States use to advance upon and finally prevail over the island nation of Japan?

U.S. plane that dropped the first bomb, reported that "the shimmering city became an ugly smudge … a pot of bubbling hot tar." Teams of U.S. observers who entered Hiroshima and Nagasaki in the aftermath were stunned at the instantaneous incineration of both human beings and manmade structures and shocked to contemplate the longer-lasting horror of radiation disease.

The mushroom clouds over Hiroshima and Nagasaki inaugurated a new "atomic age" in which dreams of peace mingled with nightmares of global destruction. Shortly after the bombing, Stimson wrote to Truman that atomic weapons represented "a new control by man over the forces of nature too revolutionary and dangerous to fit into old concepts." But in those late summer days of 1945, most Americans sighed with relief. News reports of August 15 proclaimed Japan's surrender, V-J Day. All across the nation people spontaneously flooded into the streets to celebrate the end of the Second World War.

THE WAR AT HOME: THE ECONOMY

The success of the U.S. military effort depended on economic mobilization at home. Mobilization ultimately brought the Great Depression to an end and transformed the nation's government, its business and financial institutions, and its labor force.

Economic Mobilization

The federal bureaucracy nearly quadrupled in size during the war. New economic agencies proliferated. The most powerful of these, the War Production Board, oversaw the conversion and expansion of factories, allocated resources, and enforced production priorities and schedules. The War Labor Board adjudicated labor-management disputes. The Office of Price Administration regulated prices to control inflation and rationed such scarce commodities as gasoline, rubber, steel, shoes, coffee, sugar, and meat. Although most of the controls were abandoned after the war, the concept of greater governmental oversight of the economy survived, extending the New Deal's activist legacy that would begin to be called Keynesianism.

From 1940 to 1945, the U.S. economy expanded rapidly, and the gross national product (GNP) rose, year by year, by 15 percent or more. When Roosevelt called for the production of 60,000 planes shortly after Pearl Harbor, skeptics jeered. Yet within a few years, the nation had produced nearly 300,000 planes. The Maritime Commission oversaw the construction of millions of tons of new ships. The government's huge wartime spending provided a fiscal stimulus that eradicated the underconsumption of the Great Depression. The once-stagnant economy sprang to life and spewed out prodigious quantities of all kinds of supplies, including 2.5 million trucks and 50 million pairs of shoes.

Striving to increase production, industry entered into a close relationship with government to promote scientific and technological research and development (R&D). Government money subsidized new industries, such as electronics, and transformed others, such as rubber and chemicals. Eventually, an Office of Scientific Research and Development contracted with universities and scientists. Under this program, radar and penicillin (both British discoveries), rocket engines, and other new products were perfected for wartime use. The Manhattan Project, of course, provided the most dramatic example of the government's new involvement in military research. Refugees from Nazi tyranny contributed significantly to this scientific innovation.

Business and Finance

To finance the war effort, government spending rose from $9 billion in 1940 to $98 billion in 1944. In 1941, the national debt stood at $48 billion; by V-J Day, it was $280 billion.

As production shifted from autos to tanks, and from refrigerators to guns, consumer goods became scarce. With few goods to buy, Americans put money in their savings accounts and invested in war bonds. Essentials such as food, fabrics, and gasoline were rationed and, consequently, were shared more equitably than before the war. Higher taxes on wealthier Americans redistributed income and narrowed the gap in wealth between the well-to-do and other citizens. War bonds, rationing, and progressive taxation encouraged a sense of shared sacrifice.

The war fostered personal savings and lessened income inequality, but it also facilitated the dismantling of some New Deal agencies most concerned with the poor. A Republican surge in the midterm elections of 1942 helped strengthen an anti–New Deal coalition in Congress. In 1943, legislators abolished the job-creation programs of the Works Progress Administration (WPA), the Civilian Conservation Corps (CCC), and the National Youth Administration (NYA). They also shut down the Rural Electrification Administration (REA) and Farm Security Administration (FSA), agencies that had assisted rural areas.

As business executives flocked to Washington, D.C., to run the new wartime agencies, the Roosevelt administration adopted a cooperative stance toward big business, and corporations considered essential to wartime victory flourished under governmental subsidies. What was essential became a matter of definition. Coca-Cola and Wrigley's chewing gum won precious sugar allotments by arguing that GIs overseas "needed" to enjoy these products. The California-based Kaiser Corporation, whose spectacular growth during the 1930s had been spurred by federal dam contracts, now turned its attention to building ships, aircraft, and military vehicles. By 1943, Kaiser controlled nearly a third of the nation's military construction business and helped bring an economic boom to coastal California and Washington State. New manufacturing transformed cities particularly in the South and West, areas previously dominated mostly by agricultural production.

The war concentrated power in the largest corporations. Roosevelt ordered his justice department to postpone enforcement of antitrust laws.

Bettmann/Corbis

UPI-Bettmann/Corbis

Total War: Dresden and Hiroshima. *The effects of "total war" are graphically illustrated in these photographs. The top one shows the devastation of Dresden, Germany, by the British Bomber Command and the U.S. Eighth Air Force on February 13 and 14, 1945. The lower photo shows the destruction of Hiroshima, Japan, by the U.S. 509th Composite Group on August 6, 1945. During the initial attack on Dresden, 786 aircraft dropped 5,824,000 pounds (2,600 long tons) of bombs on the city, killing an estimated 60,000 people and injuring another 30,000. An area of more than 2.5 square miles in the city center was demolished, and some 37,000 buildings were destroyed. To critics, the bombing of Dresden, a target that seemed of little strategic value, exemplified the excessive use of airpower*

In sobering comparison, Hiroshima was devastated by a single bomb weighing only 10,000 pounds (4.4 long tons)—an atomic bomb—dropped from one aircraft. The U-235 bomb killed 68,000 people outright, injured another 30,000, and left 10,000 missing. (These figures do not include those who later developed diseases from deadly gamma rays.) The atomic bomb obliterated almost five square miles of the city's center and destroyed 40,653 buildings. Truman reported the strike as "an overwhelming success." Many hailed the atomic bomb as a necessary step toward military victory; others worried about what the dawn of the "nuclear age" portended.

Congressional efforts to investigate possible collusion in the awarding of large government contracts and to increase assistance to small businesses made little headway. The top 100 companies, which had provided 30 percent of the nation's total manufacturing output in 1940, provided 70 percent by 1943.

The Workforce   During the early years of the military buildup, people who had scrounged for jobs during the Great Depression found work. Employment in heavy industry invariably went to men, and most of the skilled jobs went to whites. But as military service depleted the ranks of white males, both private employers and public officials began encouraging women to join the paid labor force, southern African Americans to seek jobs in northern and western industrial cities, and Mexicans to enter the United States under the *bracero* guest farmworker program.

Hired for jobs never before open to them, women became welders, shipbuilders, lumberjacks, and miners. They won places in prestigious symphony orchestras, and one Major League Baseball owner financed the creation of a women's league to give new life to the national pastime. Many employers hired married women, who before the war would have been lucky to obtain a position even in traditionally female occupations such as teaching. Minority women moved into clerical and sales jobs, where they had not previously been welcome. Most workplaces, however, continued to be segregated by sex.

The scope of unpaid labor, long provided primarily by women, also expanded. Volunteer activities such as Red Cross projects, civil defense work, and recycling drives claimed the time of women, children, and older people. Government publications exhorted homemakers: "Wear it out, use it up, make it do, or do without." In both home and workplace, women's responsibilities and workloads increased.

The new labor market improved the general economic position of African Americans. By executive order in June 1942, Roosevelt created the Fair Employment Practices Commission (FEPC), which aimed to ban discrimination in hiring. In 1943 his administration announced that it would not recognize as collective bargaining agents any unions that discriminated on the basis of race. The War Labor Board outlawed the practice of paying different wages to whites and nonwhites doing the same job. Before the war, the African American population had been mainly southern, rural, and agricultural; within a few years, a substantial percentage of African Americans had become northern, urban, and industrial. Although employment discrimination was hardly eliminated, twice as many African Americans held skilled jobs at the end of the war as at the beginning.

For both men and women, the war brought higher wages and longer work hours. During the war, average weekly earnings for industrial workers rose nearly 70 percent. Farmers, who had suffered through many years of low prices and overproduction, doubled their income and then doubled it again.

The Labor Front   The scarcity of labor during the war strengthened the union movement. Union membership rose by 50 percent. Although women and workers of color joined unions in unprecedented numbers, the main beneficiaries of labor's new clout were the white males who still comprised the bulk of unionized workers.

Especially on the national level, the commitment of organized labor to female workers was weak. Not a single woman served on the executive boards of either the American Federation of Labor (AFL) or the Congress of Industrial Organizations

(CIO). The International Brotherhood of Teamsters even required women to sign a statement that their union membership could be revoked when the war was over. Unions did fight for contracts stipulating equal pay for men and women who worked in the same job, but these benefited women only as long as they held "male" jobs. The unions' primary purpose in advocating equal pay was to maintain wage levels for the men who would return to their jobs after the war. During the first year of peace, as employers trimmed their workforces, both businesses and unions gave special preference to returning veterans and eased women and minority workers out of their wartime positions. Unions based their policies on seniority and their wage demands on the goal of securing male workers a "family wage," one sufficient to support an entire family.

Some union leaders feared that hiring traditionally lower-paid workers (women and minorities) would jeopardize the wage gains and recognition that unions had won during the 1930s. As growing numbers of African Americans were hired, racial tensions in the workplace increased. At some plants white workers walked off the job to protest the hiring of African Americans, fearing that management might use the war as an excuse to erode union power.

The labor militancy of the 1930s, although muted by a wartime no-strike pledge, persisted into the 1940s. Wildcat strikes erupted among St. Louis bus drivers, Detroit assembly-line workers, and Philadelphia streetcar conductors. The

Library of Congress, Prints and Photographs Division

Children Enlist in the War Effort. *These children, flashing the "V-for-Victory" sign, stand atop a pile of scrap metal. Collecting scrap of all kinds for war production helped engage millions of Americans, young and old, on the home front.*

United Mine Workers called a walkout in the bituminous coal fields in 1943. When the War Labor Board took a hard line against the union's demands, the strike was prolonged. The increasingly conservative Congress responded with the Smith-Connally Act of 1943, which empowered the president to seize plants or mines if strikes interrupted war production. Even so, the war helped to strengthen organized labor's place in American life.

Enlarging the Role of Government   The growth of governmental power during the war years prompted debate over what the role of government should be in a postwar world. As military victory began to seem likely, President Roosevelt and his advisers talked of harnessing the national government's power behind expanded efforts to enhance personal security in everyday life. Some favored extending wartime health care and day-care programs into a more comprehensive social welfare system.

In 1944, Roosevelt introduced his ideas for a **"Second Bill of Rights,"** advocating measures to ensure that Americans could enjoy the "rights" to regular employment, adequate food and shelter, appropriate educational opportunities, and guaranteed health care. Translating this vision into reality, its proponents assumed, would require the government to continue playing a large role in economic and social planning.

Large insurance companies and some private businesses, recognizing the popularity of such proposals, advanced private alternatives to governmental programs. Insurers expanded their earlier efforts to market individual policies that would pay in cases of sickness, disability, and unexpected death. At the same time, insurance companies worked with large corporations to develop group insurance plans that would make expansion of government programs less attractive and provide supplements for existing New Deal–era programs such as Social Security. Questions about what should be the proper role for government in providing social safety nets would roil American life in the postwar era.

THE WAR AT HOME: SOCIAL ISSUES

The war demanded sacrifice from all, and most Americans willingly obliged. The war effort unsettled established patterns, and wartime ideals spotlighted everyday inequalities.

Selling the War   Hollywood answered the government's call to mobilize the country for war. The film factories produced both commercial movies with military themes, such as *Destination Tokyo* (1943), and documentaries, such as the *Why We Fight* series, directed by Frank Capra. Capra contrasted images of wholesome and diverse Americans with harrowing portrayals of the tightly regimented lifestyles in the dictatorships of Germany, Italy, and Japan. Walt Disney's animation teams produced war-themed cartoons. Hollywood personalities sold war bonds, entertained the troops, and worked on documentaries for the Army's Pictorial Division.

The advertising industry, lacking many consumer products to sell, also contributed. Roosevelt encouraged advertisers to sell the benefits of freedom. "Freedom" often appeared in the form of new washing machines, streamlined automobiles, a wider range of lipstick hues, and other consumer products. As soon as the fighting ended, wartime ads promised, technological know-how would transform the United States into a consumer's paradise.

In spring 1942, Roosevelt created the **Office of War Information (OWI)** to coordinate propaganda and censorship. Many New Deal Democrats viewed the OWI as catering more to advertisers who preferred imagery extolling the future joys of consumerism than to ones promoting broader visions of liberty and equality. Republicans, by contrast, blasted the agency for cranking out political appeals for causes favored by New Dealers. Despite criticism from both left and right, the OWI established branch offices throughout the world and produced hundreds of films, posters, and radio broadcasts.

Gender Issues

The changes sweeping American life became apparent in a range of social issues affecting women.

The wartime United States called on women to serve their country as more than wives and mothers. Some 350,000 women volunteered for military duty during the war, and more than a thousand became pilots for the Women Airforce Service Pilots (WASPs). Not everyone approved. One member of Congress asked: "What has become of the manhood of America?" Most in Congress, however, supported the creation of a women's corps in each branch of the military.

Even as the war brought larger numbers of women into the paid labor force, widespread imagery frequently portrayed this change as a short-term sacrifice intended, ultimately, to preserve and protect women's "natural" sphere in the home. Stereotypes abounded. A typical ad suggesting that women take on farmwork declared: "A woman can do anything if she knows she looks beautiful doing it."

An Equal Rights Amendment (ERA) to the Constitution continued to be debated both within Congress and around the country. Should the Constitution guarantee women "equal" status with men, or should the law continue to allow women some kind of "protected" status in view of their special vulnerability to exploitation? The war raised but did not settle this issue, over which even women's advocates were split.

In some ways, the war may have even widened the symbolic gap between notions of femininity and masculinity. Military culture fostered a "pinup" mentality toward women. Tanks and planes were decorated with images of female sexuality, and the home-front entertainment industry promoted its glamorous female stars as anxious to "please" their "boys" in the military.

Public policy-making sometimes worked to reinforce gender divisions. The military assigned most of the women who joined the armed services to stateside clerical and supply jobs. Day-care programs for mothers working outside their homes received reluctant and inadequate funding. The thousands of child-care centers set up during the conflict filled only a fraction of the need and were swiftly shut down after the war. Social scientists oftentimes blamed mothers for an apparent spike in rates of juvenile delinquency and divorce during the war years.

Racial Issues

Messages about race were as ambiguous as those related to gender. President Roosevelt refused to abandon the policy of segregation in the armed forces despite pressure from the NAACP and others.

Although the army integrated Latino and American Indian soldiers, along with those from various European ethnic groups, into its combat units, military leaders did not do the same for people of African and Japanese ancestry. Desegregation of the armed forces drew determined opposition from politically powerful white Democrats in the South, who feared it might lead to broader demands for desegregation at home. The army even adopted the scientifically absurd practice of segregating donated blood into separate stores of "white" and "black" plasma. African Americans were relegated to inferior, often highly dangerous, jobs and excluded from combat duty. Toward the end of the war, when troop shortages finally forced the administration to put African American units into combat, they performed with distinction.

On the home front, volatile social issues continued to simmer. As the wartime production system created more jobs, vast numbers of people from the rural South, including several hundred thousand African Americans, moved to cities such as Los Angles and Detroit. People already living in these areas often chafed at the influx of newcomers, who competed with them for jobs and housing and placed greater demands on public services such as transportation, education, and recreational facilities.

Social strains sometimes flared into violence. This escalation most often occurred in overcrowded urban spaces, where diverse populations and cultures already competed and clashed. In Detroit, in June 1943, conflict between white and black youth at an amusement park rapidly spiraled into a multiple-day riot. The violence left nearly 40 people, most of them African American, dead, injured hundreds, and inflicted millions of dollars worth of damage to property.

Racial disturbances were not restricted to confrontations between whites and blacks. In Los Angeles, complicated and long-standing ethnic tensions erupted in the "Zoot Suit Riots" of 1943. Soldiers and sailors from nearby military bases attacked young Mexican American and African American men wearing zoot suits—flamboyant outfits featuring oversized coats and trousers. Violence only escalated as the city's police force entered the fray, often beating and arresting Mexican Americans. A military order restricting servicemen to their bases finally helped quell the disorder.

Even when wartime tensions did not produce the level of violence seen in Detroit and Los Angeles, the Second World War highlighted long-standing social divisions. For many Native Americans, for instance, the wartime years increased the pressures associated with longer-term patterns of migration and assimilation. Approximately 25,000 Indian men and several hundred Indian women served in the armed forces. Tens of thousands of other American Indians, many leaving their reservations for the first time, found wartime work in urban areas such as Rapid City, Minneapolis, Flagstaff, and Billings. Many Indians moved back and forth between city and reservation, seeking to live in two significantly different worlds.

Internment of Japanese Americans   People of Japanese descent faced a unique situation. Shortly after the attack on Pearl Harbor, fear of sabotage by pro-Japanese residents engulfed West Coast communities. One military report claimed that a "large, unassimilated, tightly knit racial group, bound to an enemy nation by strong ties of race, culture, custom, and religion ... constituted a menace" that justified extraordinary action.

Buyenlarge/Archive Photos/Getty Images

Internment of Japanese Americans. *Taken by the famous photographer Ansel Adams, best known for his western landscapes, this image shows internees walking in the snow at a remote relocation camp in the West.*

Although lacking evidence of disloyalty, the president in February 1942 issued Executive Order 9066, directing the relocation and **internment** of first- and second-generation Japanese Americans (called Issei and Nisei, respectively) at inland camps. Nearly 130,000 people were affected. Significantly, in Hawaii, where the presumed danger of subversion might have seemed much greater, no internment took place. There, people of Japanese ancestry constituted nearly 40 percent of the population and were essential to the economy. The government also closely watched foreign-born Germans and Italians who lived in the United States and detained roughly 10,000 Germans and several hundred Italians.

Forced to abandon their possessions or sell them for a pittance, Japanese American evacuees were confined in flimsy barracks, enclosed by barbed wire and under armed guard. These camps, often in remote locations such as Heart Mountain, Wyoming, offered only the barest accommodations: cots for beds, a meager daily ration of food, overcrowded rooms. Two-thirds of the detainees were native-born U.S. citizens, and many gave up thriving agricultural enterprises that they had built in California over generations. Some evacuated so quickly that they arrived at their camps with little more than the clothes they wore.

Internment was controversial. In December 1944, a divided U.S. Supreme Court upheld the constitutionality of Japanese relocation in *Korematsu* v. *United States* (1944). In 1988, Congress officially apologized for the internment, revealed that military investigators at the time had reported no cases of subversion, and authorized a cash indemnity for anyone who had been confined in the camps.

Challenging The global fight against fascism proved helpful to movements
Racial working for greater racial equality in America. Nazism,
Inequality based on the idea of racial inequality, exposed the racist underpinnings of older social science research. The view that racial difference was not the result of biology gained wider acceptance during the war. "The Huns have wrecked the theory of the master race," stated an Alabama politician. The idea that a democracy could bridge cultural and social differences provided a basis for the postwar struggle against discrimination.

The *Amsterdam News*, a Harlem newspaper, called for a **"Double V" campaign**—victory at home as well as abroad. In January 1941, the labor leader A. Philip Randolph promised to lead tens of thousands of black workers in a march on Washington to demand more defense jobs and integration of the military forces. President Roosevelt feared the event would embarrass his administration and urged that it be canceled. Randolph's persistence ultimately forced Roosevelt to create the FEPC. Although this new agency gained little effective power, its very existence helped advance the ideal of nondiscrimination.

Northward migration of African Americans accelerated demands for equality. Drawn by the promise of wartime jobs, nearly 750,000 African Americans relocated to northern cities, where many sensed the possibility of political power for the first time in their lives. They found an outspoken advocate of civil rights in First Lady Eleanor Roosevelt, who antagonized southern white Democrats and members of her husband's administration by her advocacy of civil rights and her participation in integrated social functions.

Particularly in urban areas, civil rights groups emerged from the wartime years with a strong base from which to fight for jobs and political power. Founded in 1942, the interracial Committee (later, Congress) on Racial Equality (CORE) devised new ways of opposing discrimination. CORE activists staged sit-ins to integrate restaurants, theaters, and other public facilities, especially in Washington, D.C.

In California and throughout the Southwest during the war years, Latino organizations, too, highlighted the irony of fighting overseas for a nation that denied equality at home. They challenged the United States to live up to its democratic rhetoric. Approximately 500,000 Mexican Americans served, often with great distinction, in the military. Not wishing to anger this constituency, the Roosevelt administration also feared discrimination might harm the credibility of its Good Neighbor Policy in Latin America. The president's coordinator of Inter-American affairs allocated federal money to train Spanish-speaking workers for wartime employment, improve education in the *barrios*, and provide high school graduates with new opportunities to enter college.

Although legal precedents in California and other southwestern states classified Latinos as "white," actual practices, especially in public schools, usually discriminated against people of Mexican descent. Organizations such as the League of United Latin American Citizens (LULAC) mounted several drives against such discrimination during the war, and they prepared for greater challenges in the postwar period.

People of Japanese descent, despite their internment, also laid the basis for post-war campaigns for equality. The courage and sacrifice of Japanese American soldiers became legendary. The 100th Battalion and the 442nd Regimental Combat Team, segregated units, suffered stunning casualties, often while undertaking extremely dangerous combat missions in Europe. Moreover, in the Pacific theater, 6,000 Japanese American members of the Military Intelligence Service provided invaluable service.

In the face of divisive issues and calls for greater equality, wartime propaganda stressed national unity and contrasted America's "melting pot" ethos with German and Japanese obsessions about racial "purity." Movies, plays, radio dramas, and music fostered a sense of national community by celebrating cultural diversity. As members of each of America's racial and ethnic groups distinguished themselves in the military, the claim of equality—"Americans All," in the words of a wartime slogan—took on greater moral force. Imagery extolling social solidarity and freedom provided a foundation for the antidiscrimination movements of the decades ahead.

SHAPING THE PEACE

Even before the war ended, U.S. policymakers began considering postwar peace arrangements. The Truman administration built on Roosevelt's wartime conferences and agreements to shape the framework of international relations for the next half-century.

International Organizations   In the Atlantic Charter of 1941, and at a conference in Moscow in October 1943, the Allied powers had pledged to create a replacement for the defunct League of Nations. Internationalist-minded Americans hoped the new **United Nations (UN)** would offer a more realistic version of Woodrow Wilson's vision for a world body that could deter aggressor nations and promote peaceful political change. At the Dumbarton Oaks Conference in Washington in August 1944, and at a subsequent meeting in San Francisco in April 1945, the Allies worked out the UN's organizational structure. It included a General Assembly, in which each member nation would be represented and cast one vote. A smaller body, the Security Council, would include five permanent members from the Allied coalition—the United States, Great Britain, the Soviet Union, France, and Nationalist China—and six rotating members. The Security Council would have primary responsibility for maintaining peace, but permanent members could veto any council decision. A UN Secretariat, headed by a secretary general, would handle day-to-day business, and an Economic and Social Council would sponsor measures to improve living conditions throughout the world.

The U.S. Senate, with only two dissenting votes, approved joining the UN in July 1945. This victory for internationalism contrasted sharply with the Senate's 1919 rejection of membership in the League of Nations. Opponents of Wilson's dream had worried that internationalist policies might limit the ability of the United States to pursue its own interests, but following the Second World War a newly powerful United States appeared able to dominate international organizations such as the UN. In addition, most U.S. leaders recognized that the war had partly resulted from the lack of a coordinated, international response to aggression during the 1930s.

Eleanor Roosevelt played a prominent role in building the new postwar internationalist ethos. A delegate to the first meeting of the UN's General Assembly, she chaired its Commission on Human Rights and guided the drafting of a **Universal Declaration of Human Rights**, adopted by the UN in 1948. The document set forth "inalienable" human rights and freedoms as cornerstones of international law.

Economic agreements also illustrated a growing acceptance of international organizations. They sought to remedy some of the causes of international instability that had touched off the Great Depression and the war. At the Bretton Woods (New Hampshire) Conference of 1944, assembled nations created the International Monetary Fund (IMF), which was designed to maintain stable currency exchange rates by ensuring that each nation's currency could be converted into any other national currency at a fixed rate. The International Bank for Reconstruction and Development, later renamed the World Bank, was also created to provide loans to war-battered countries and promote the resumption of world trade. In 1948 the General Agreement on Tariffs and Trade (GATT) established the institutional groundwork for breaking up closed trading blocs and implementing free and fair trade agreements.

Spheres of Interest and Postwar Settlements   In wartime negotiations, Stalin, Churchill, and Roosevelt had assumed that powerful nations—their own—would enjoy special "spheres of influence" in the postwar world. As early as January 1942, the Soviet ambassador to the United States reported to Stalin that Roosevelt had tacitly assented to Soviet postwar control over the Baltic states of Lithuania, Latvia, and Estonia. In 1944 Stalin and Churchill agreed, informally and secretly, that Britain would continue its sway over Greece and that the Soviets could control Romania and Bulgaria. U.S. leaders assumed that Latin America would remain within their sphere of influence. Roosevelt expressed contradictory positions on the Soviet Union. He sometimes seemed to imply that he accepted Stalin's goal of having states friendly to the USSR on his vulnerable western border, but at the Tehran Conference of November 1943 he also told Stalin that U.S. voters of Eastern European descent expected their homelands to be independent after the war. After Roosevelt's death, the Soviets' powerful position in Eastern Europe became a focus of tensions with the United States.

Early in the war, both the United States and the Soviet Union had urged the dismemberment and deindustrialization of a defeated Nazi Germany. At a conference held at Yalta, in Ukraine, in February 1945, the three Allied powers agreed to divide Germany into four zones of occupation (with France as the fourth occupying force). Later, as relations among the victors worsened, this temporary division of Germany hardened into a Soviet-dominated zone in the east and the other three zones to its west. Berlin, the German capital, also was divided, even though the city itself lay totally within the Soviet zone.

The future of Poland also posed difficult issues. At Yalta, the Soviets agreed to permit free elections in postwar Poland, but Stalin believed that the other Allied leaders had tacitly accepted Soviet dominance over Poland's government. The agreement at Yalta was ambiguous at best; the war was still at a critical stage, and the western Allies chose to sacrifice clarity in order to encourage cooperation from the Soviets. After Yalta, the Soviets assumed that Poland would be in their sphere of influence, but many Americans charged the Soviets with bad faith for failing to hold free elections and for not relinquishing control.

In Asia, military realities likewise influenced postwar settlements. At Tehran and again at Yalta, Stalin pledged to send troops to fight Japan as soon as Germany surrendered. The first U.S. atomic bomb fell on Hiroshima, however, just one day before the Soviets were to enter the Pacific war, and the United States assumed total charge of the occupation and postwar reorganization of Japan. The Soviet Union and the United States divided Korea, which had been controlled by Japan, into separate zones of occupation. Here, as in Germany, these zones would later emerge as two antagonistic states.

The fate of the European colonies seized by Japan in Southeast Asia was another contentious issue. Most U.S. officials preferred to see the former British and French colonies become independent nations, but they also worried about the left-leaning politics of many anticolonial nationalist movements. As the United States developed an anticommunist foreign policy after the end of the war, it moved to support British and French efforts to reassemble their colonial empires.

In the Philippines, the United States honored its long-standing pledge to grant independence. A friendly government that agreed to respect American economic interests and military bases took power in 1946 and enlisted American advisers to help suppress leftist rebels. In 1947 the United Nations designated the Mariana, Caroline, and Marshall Islands as the "Trust Territories of the Pacific" and authorized the United States to administer their affairs.

Although the nations of Latin America had been only indirectly involved in military conflict and peace negotiations, the war directly affected U.S. relations with them. Roosevelt's Good Neighbor Policy and a new Office of Inter-American Affairs (OIAA), created in 1937, expanded cultural and economic ties, and Latin American leaders stood nearly united behind the Allies. After U.S. entry into the war, at a conference in Rio de Janeiro in January 1942, every Latin American country except Chile and Argentina broke diplomatic ties with the Axis governments. When naval warfare in the Atlantic severed commercial connections between Latin America and Europe, Latin American countries became critical suppliers of raw materials to the United States.

Wartime conferences avoided clear decisions about creating a Jewish homeland in the Middle East. The Second World War prompted survivors of the Holocaust and Jews from around the world to take direct action. Zionism, the movement to found a Jewish state in Palestine, which Jews claimed to be their ancient homeland, fuelled a mass migration of Jews. They began to carve out, against the resistance from Palestinians and other Arab people, the new nation of Israel.

CONCLUSION

The world changed dramatically during the Second World War. For the United States, wartime mobilization ended the Great Depression and focused attention on international concerns. A more powerful national government, concerned with preserving national security, assumed nearly complete control over the economy. Government, business, and scientific researchers worked together to provide the seemingly miraculous growth in productivity that ultimately won the war.

The 1940s also sharpened debates over liberty and equality. Many Americans saw the Second World War as a struggle to protect and preserve liberties they already enjoyed. Others, inspired by a struggle against racism and injustice abroad, insisted that a war for freedom overseas should help redress inequalities at home.

The war brought victory over dictatorial, expansionist regimes, and the United States emerged as the world's preeminent power. Still, Americans remained uncertain about postwar policies. As the dislocations of war gave way to the uncertainties of peace, they worried about the recovery of Europe and relations with their wartime ally, the Soviet Union. And the nation now faced the future without the charismatic leadership of Franklin D. Roosevelt.

27

THE AGE OF CONTAINMENT, 1946–1953

CHAPTER OUTLINE

• Creating a National Security State, 1945–1949 • The Era of the Korean War, 1949–1952 • Pursuing National Security at Home • Postwar Social and Economic Policy-Making • Signs of a Changing Culture • The Election of 1952

THE SECOND WORLD WAR, popularly portrayed as a struggle to preserve the "American way of life," ended up transforming it. The fight against fascism propelled foreign policy issues to the forefront of American politics, and postwar tensions kept them there. As combat operations gave way to friction between the United States and the Soviet Union, U.S. leaders overhauled military strategy. They claimed broad powers for the executive branch and called for a global stand against communism. The effort to shore up "national security" soon translated into an ever-larger military establishment and an economic system that could supply its needs.

At home, debate over increased governmental power generated immediate controversy. Wartime production, overseen by government bureaucracies in Washington, had finally ended the economic downturn of the 1930s. Should Washington help organize a postwar economy that satisfied household as well as military consumption? Should a more powerful and active government in Washington assist movements seeking greater equality? Could such a government limit security threats at home without endangering liberty? Questions such as these enlivened, and embittered, public debate in the aftermath of the Second World War.

CREATING A NATIONAL SECURITY STATE, 1945–1949

The wartime alliance between the United States and the Soviet Union proved little more than a brief marriage of convenience. Defeating the Axis had forced the two nations to cooperate, but collaboration began unraveling even before war's end.

CHRONOLOGY

1946	Employment Act passed
	Republicans gain control of Congress
1947	Truman Doctrine announced
	George Kennan's "Mr. X" article published
	National Security Act passed
	Marshall Plan proposed
	Taft-Hartley Act passed
1948	Marshall Plan adopted
	Berlin Airlift begins
	Truman wins reelection
1949	NATO established
	Soviet Union explodes atomic device
	Truman unveils his Fair Deal
1950	NSC-68 adopted
	Korean War begins
1951	Truman removes General MacArthur as commander in Korea
	Dennis decision in Supreme Court
1952	National Security Agency (NSA) created
	Republican Dwight Eisenhower elected president

Relations deteriorated into a **cold war** of mutual suspicions and massive military buildups but few direct confrontations between the superpowers.

Onset of the Cold War   Historians have dissected the onset of the cold war from different perspectives. A familiar view focuses on Soviet expansionism, stressing a historically rooted appetite for new territory, an ideological zeal to spread communism, or some interplay between the two. According to this interpretation, the United States needed to adopt firm anti-Soviet policies. Other historians—generally called revisionists—see the Soviet Union's desire to secure its borders as an understandable response to the invasion of its territory during both world wars. The United States, in this view, should have tried to reassure the Soviet Union (USSR), pursuing conciliatory measures instead of ones that intensified Soviet fears. Still other scholars maintain that assigning blame obscures how clashing interests and differing political cultures made postwar conflict between the two superpowers unavoidable.

In almost every view, President Harry Truman's role was central. Truman initially hoped to bargain productively with the Soviet Union and its premier, Joseph Stalin. As differences between the former allies sharpened, however, Truman came to distrust Stalin and to listen to hard-line anti-Soviet advisers.

The atomic bomb became an important source of friction. At the Potsdam Conference of July 1945, Truman had casually told Stalin, without mentioning the bomb, about a new U.S. weapon of "unusual destructive force." Well informed by Soviet intelligence operations about the Manhattan Project, Stalin calmly advised Truman to make "good use" of this weapon. Stalin also ordered Soviet scientists, with far less calm, to intensify their nuclear weapons program. Truman likely hoped that the bomb would scare the Soviets—and it did. Historians debate whether it frightened Moscow into more cautious behavior or made it a more aggressive cold war adversary.

As atomic warfare against Japan gave way to atomic diplomacy with the Soviet Union, U.S. leaders differed over how to proceed. One group, recognizing that the Soviets would soon possess atomic weapons, urged Truman to share technology with the USSR in hopes of forestalling a future arms race. Hard-liners, fearing Soviet intentions and underestimating their nuclear knowledge, rejected this approach.

In 1946, Truman authorized Bernard Baruch, his special representative at the United Nations, to explore ways of controlling atomic power. The Baruch Plan proposed that the United States abandon its atomic weapons if the USSR agreed to outside monitoring of its weapons program and surrendering its veto power in the UN on atomic issues. Soviet leaders counter-proposed that the United States destroy its atomic weapons as the first step toward any bargain. The United States rejected this idea. Both nations used the deadlock to justify a stepped-up arms race.

Other sources of friction involved U.S. loan policy and Soviet domination of Eastern Europe. Truman ended Lend-Lease assistance to the Soviet Union at the end of the war and linked any new loans for postwar reconstruction to Soviet cooperation with the United States over the future of Europe. This linkage strategy failed. Lack of capital and suspicions about the intentions of the United States and its allies provided the Soviets with excuses for their own hard-line stance. A repressive Soviet sphere of influence, which Stalin called defensive and Truman labeled expansionist, spread over Eastern Europe.

By 1946, the former allies seemed ready to become bitter adversaries. Early that year, Winston Churchill famously declared that an "Iron Curtain," with free nations on one side and communist ones on the other, had descended across Europe. The communist countries to the east, under the control of the Soviet Union, threatened the security of Western Europe, the British leader proclaimed. Truman agreed and pledged to stop any communist aggression. His anticommunist initiatives, in both foreign and domestic affairs, extended the power of the executive branch and laid the basis for a national security state.

The Truman Doctrine and Containment Abroad   In March 1947, the president announced what soon became known as the **Truman Doctrine** when speaking to Congress about a civil war in Greece, where communist-led insurgents threatened to topple a pro-Western government. In private, London had informed Washington that it lacked the economic and military resources to act in Greece, long within Great Britain's sphere of influence. Truman's advisers feared a leftist victory in Greece would expose Turkey, a nation critical to the U.S. strategic position, to Soviet expansionism. In publicly justifying U.S. aid to Greece and Turkey, Truman asserted that U.S. security interests now spanned the globe and that the fate of "free peoples" everywhere hung in the balance. Unless the United States aided people "resisting attempted subversion by armed minorities or by outside pressures," totalitarian communism would spread and ultimately threaten the United States.

The Truman Doctrine's global vision of national security encountered some skepticism. Henry A. Wallace, the most visible Democratic critic, chided Truman for exaggerating the Soviet threat and urged a more conciliatory approach toward Moscow. Conservative Republicans, though fervently anticommunist, feared the increase in presidential power and the vast expenditures that implementing the Truman Doctrine would seemingly entail. If Truman wanted broad support for his position, Republican senator Arthur Vandenberg had already advised, he should "scare hell" out of people, something Truman proved quite willing to do when justifying his new doctrine. With votes from Republicans and Democrats, the president gained congressional approval for $400 million in assistance to Greece and Turkey, most of it for military aid, in the spring of 1947. This vote signaled broad, bipartisan support for a national security policy that came to be called **containment**.

The term *containment* first appeared in a 1947 article in the journal *Foreign Affairs* by George Kennan, the State Department's leading Soviet expert. Writing under the pseudonym "X," Kennan argued that the "main element" in U.S. policy "must be that of a long-term, patient but firm and vigilant containment of Russian expansive tendencies." The measured and limited containment policy, which Kennan later claimed he had outlined in this article, soon became associated with the urgent tone and expansive approach of the Truman Doctrine.

Containment thus became a catchphrase for a global, anticommunist national security policy. As popularly articulated, containment linked all leftist insurgencies, wherever they occurred, to a totalitarian movement controlled from Moscow that directly threatened American security. Even a small gain for the Soviets in one part of the world could encourage communist aggression elsewhere. Although foreign policy debates included sharp disagreement over precisely how to pursue containment, most American leaders came to support an activist, anticommunist foreign policy that spanned the globe.

Truman's Loyalty Program and Containment at Home   Nine days after proclaiming the Truman Doctrine, the president issued Executive Order 9835. It authorized a system of government loyalty boards empowered to gather evidence in order to determine if there were "reasonable grounds" for concluding that a federal employee belonged to a subversive organization or espoused ideas that might endanger national security. Persons found to pose a "security risk" would lose their government jobs. The Truman administration also empowered the Justice Department to identify political organizations it deemed subversive and place them on a new Attorney General's List. The Loyalty Program, partly intended to show that Truman's administration considered communism a serious domestic threat, suggested that containing communist activities at home would require the type of aggressive measures being adopted overseas.

The Truman administration thus embarked on what became a controversial approach to containing communism, including Soviet espionage, at home. Although few people ever doubted that the Soviets were conducting spy operations inside the United States, there has long been sharp disagreement over their scope and effectiveness. Such debates now take place in light of declassified evidence from Soviet and U.S. surveillance files revealing that both nations conducted a wide range of intelligence activity. By 1943, the United States had begun intercepting transmissions between Moscow and certain American groups and individuals. The Collected as the VENONA files and finally released in 1995, these intercepted messages show that the Soviet Union had helped finance America's Communist Party, placed informants in governmental agencies, and obtained secret information about U.S. atomic work. Uncovering Soviet espionage, in short, was a legitimate objective. Historians remain divided, however, over the reliability and relevance of specific pieces of the evidence collected by the VENONA project—and also over how much of the intercepted information became immediately available to the Truman administration.

Truman's loyalty policy worried a diverse group of critics. The president claimed that the existence of even a few security risks demanded an unprecedented response. Truman's position, however, angered more fervent anticommunists, particularly Republicans, who accused the president of doing too little to fight subversion at home. Civil libertarians, in contrast, charged Truman with whipping up fear about communism that far exceeded any actual threat. They called for a carefully targeted approach. Internal security policy, for example, should treat an atomic scientist with links to the Soviet Union differently from an outspoken clerical worker in a nonsensitive governmental position.

The National Security Act, the Marshall Plan, and the Berlin Crisis   Shaking off criticism, the Truman administration continued to extend its containment initiative. It secured congressional approval of the **National Security Act of 1947**, which created several new government bureaucracies. The old Navy and War Departments, by 1949, would combine into the Department of Defense. An entirely new addition to the executive branch, the National Security Council, obtained broad authority over planning the new containment policy. The air force became a separate service equal to the army and navy. The National Security Act also created the Central Intelligence Agency (CIA) to gather information about communist threats and conduct covert activities outside the United States.

The CIA quickly became the most flexible arm of this new national security apparatus. A series of secret presidential directives expanded the CIA's role, while its activities and budget remained shrouded from public scrutiny. Soon, the CIA's covert operations crisscrossed the globe. CIA operatives cultivated ties with anti-Soviet groups in Eastern Europe and within the Soviet Union. The agency helped finance pro-U.S. labor unions in Western Europe to curtail the influence of leftist organizations. It orchestrated covert campaigns to prevent the Italian Communist Party from winning an electoral victory in 1948 and to bolster anticommunist political parties in France, Japan, and elsewhere.

The Truman administration also linked economic initiatives in Western Europe to its overall containment policy. Fearing that Europe's economic problems might create opportunities for local communist movements, Secretary of State General George C. Marshall sought to strengthen the region's economies. Under his 1947 proposal, known as the European Recovery Program or simply the Marshall Plan, U.S. funds would help postwar governments in Europe to coordinate programs of economic reconstruction. Although invited to participate, the Soviet Union quickly denounced the Marshall Plan as the economic component of a larger U.S. effort to dominate all of Europe.

The Marshall Plan, enacted by Congress in early 1948, ultimately achieved the hopes of its architects. It helped brighten the economic picture in Western Europe, where industrial production rebounded. Improved standards of living enhanced political stability and helped undercut the appeal of leftist movements. Between 1946 and 1951, the United States provided nearly $13 billion in assistance to 17 Western European nations. When critics in the United States condemned the Marshall Plan as an expensive "giveaway" scheme, supporters stressed how it would expand both overseas markets and investment opportunities for American businesses. They also hailed it for contributing to the larger containment strategy for safeguarding national security.

While lobbying for the Marshall Plan, the Truman administration also sought to expand U.S. military forces. The Soviet Union helped install a pro-Moscow government in Czechoslovakia in early 1948, and some U.S. officials warned of a Soviet military strike into Western Europe. Truman declared that "moral God-fearing peoples … must save the world from atheism" and Soviet totalitarianism. As a brief war scare gripped Washington, national security planners successfully implored Congress to increase defense spending, largely for new aircraft, and reinstate a military draft.

Policymakers in the United States viewed the future of Germany, initially divided into four zones of occupation, as crucial. In June 1948, the United States, Great Britain, and France announced currency reform as the first step toward integrating their separate sectors into a Federal Republic of Germany or West Germany. Having been invaded by German forces in both world wars, however, the Soviets feared a resurgent Germany. Hoping to sidetrack Western plans, the Soviets cut off all highways, railroads, and water routes into West Berlin, which was located within their zone of military occupation.

The Soviet's **Berlin Blockade** failed. American and British aircraft, in what became known as the **Berlin Airlift**, delivered the supplies West Berliners needed. Truman, hinting at a military response, dispatched to Great Britain two squadrons of B-29 bombers, reportedly able to deliver atomic bombs to Soviet territory. Unable to seal off West Berlin, Stalin abandoned his blockade in May 1949. The Soviets then created the German Democratic Republic, or East Germany, out of their military sector. West Berlin, which survived as an anticommunist enclave inside East Germany, would remain a focus of cold war tensions.

The Election of 1948

Meanwhile, national security issues helped Harry Truman win the 1948 presidential election. For several years, the president had been losing support among those Democrats—led by his secretary of commerce, Henry A. Wallace—who considered Truman's containment policies overly confrontational. When Wallace continued to criticize these initiatives, the president had ousted him from the cabinet. Two months later, in the midterm national elections of November 1946, voters had given the Republicans control of Congress for the first time since 1928. Although Truman's political fortunes had improved by late 1947, few political handicappers liked his chances in 1948.

Truman faced three other presidential hopefuls. Challenged from the left by a new Progressive Party, which nominated Wallace, and from the right by Thomas E. Dewey, the Republican nominee, and J. Strom Thurmond, the pro-segregationist candidate of the new States' Rights Party, or Dixiecrats, the president waged a vigorous campaign. Only months before Election Day, Truman called the GOP-controlled

Dewey Defeats Truman? *President Harry S Truman holds up an Election Day edition of the* Chicago Daily Tribune, *which embarrassingly announced "Dewey Defeats Truman" in the 1948 presidential election. The president told well-wishers, "That is one for the books!"*

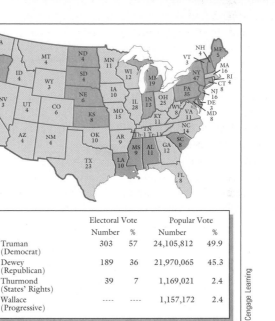

	Electoral Vote		Popular Vote	
	Number	%	Number	%
Truman (Democrat)	303	57	24,105,812	49.9
Dewey (Republican)	189	36	21,970,065	45.3
Thurmond (States' Rights)	39	7	1,169,021	2.4
Wallace (Progressive)	----	----	1,157,172	2.4

MAP 27.1 Presidential Election, 1948

This electoral map helps show how, in this close election, Truman won the presidency with less than 50 percent of the popular vote.

Congress into special session and presented it with a list of domestic programs, including a plan for national health care, abhorrent to most Republicans. Then he denounced "that do-nothing, good-for-nothing, worst Congress" for failing to enact his agenda.

Truman's victory now seems less surprising to historians than it did to analysts in 1948. Despite the GOP's electoral successes in 1946, the Democratic Party was hardly enfeebled. Loyalty to the memory of Roosevelt and his New Deal programs

Civil Rights Divide the Democratic Party, 1948

Although national party conventions have become scripted affairs designed for prime-time television viewing, earlier gatherings featured free-ranging, unpredictable debates. These included heated clashes over the "convention platforms," which were composed of the various "planks" or statements of the principles and programs for which the party stood—and on which its candidates would campaign. After particularly acrimonious debate, the 1948 Democratic National Convention voted a series of planks favoring national action to advance civil rights. This prompted some leading southern Democrats to form a rival States' Rights (or "Dixiecrat") Democratic Party with a platform offering very different civil rights planks.

1948 Democratic Party Platform

The Democratic Party is responsible for the great civil rights gains made in recent years in eliminating unfair and illegal discrimination based on race, creed or color.

The Democratic Party commits itself to continuing its efforts to eradicate all racial, religious and economic discrimination....

We highly commend President Harry S. Truman for his courageous stand on the issue of civil rights.

We call upon the Congress to support our President in guaranteeing these basic and fundamental American Principles: (1) the right of full and equal political participation; (2) the right to equal opportunity of employment; (3) the right of security of person; (4) and the right of equal treatment in the service and defense of our nation.

1948 Platform of the States' Rights Democratic (or "Dixiecrat") Party

We stand for the segregation of the races and the racial integrity of each race; the constitutional right to choose one's associates; to accept private employment without governmental interference, and to earn one's living in any lawful way. We oppose the elimination of segregation, the repeal of miscegenation statutes, the control of private employment by Federal bureaucrats called for by the

helped bring Truman's triumph. Moreover, although Thurmond's Dixiecrat movement portended a political shift among southern whites, who had voted overwhelmingly Democratic since the late 19th century, Truman carried all but four states of the old Confederacy in 1948. Finally, Truman's staunch anticommunism helped bury Henry Wallace's challenge. Hampered by his Progressive Party's refusal to reject support from the U.S. Communist Party, Wallace received less than 3 percent of the popular tally and no electoral votes. The 1948 election suggested a blueprint for winning elections to come: Successful presidential candidates must never appear "soft" on national security issues.

THE ERA OF THE KOREAN WAR, 1949–1952

A series of cold war crises in 1949 and the outbreak of war on the Korean peninsula in 1950, which heightened anticommunist fervor in the United States, boosted support for funding a vastly expanded national security state.

misnamed civil rights program. We favor home-rule, local self-government and a minimum interference with individual rights.

We oppose and condemn the action of the Democratic Convention in sponsoring a civil rights program calling for the elimination of segregation, social equality by Federal fiat, regulations of private employment practices, voting, and local law enforcement.

We affirm that the effective enforcement of such a program would be utterly destructive of the social, economic and political life of the Southern people, and of other localities in which there may be differences in race, creed or national origin in appreciable numbers. We demand that there be returned to the people to whom of right they belong, those powers needed for the preservation of human rights and the discharge of our responsibility as democrats for human welfare. We oppose a denial of those by political parties, a barter or sale of those rights by a political convention, as well as any invasion or violation of those rights by the Federal Government. We call upon all Democrats and upon all other loyal

Americans who are opposed to totalitarianism at home and abroad to unite with us in ignominiously defeating Harry S. Truman ... and every other candidate for public office who would establish a Police Nation in the United States of America.

Q *How do the 1948 civil rights planks of the Democratic Party link the cause of civil rights to that of advancing equality for all?*

Q *What are the different grounds on which the Dixiecrat platform opposed the civil rights planks of the Democratic Party? What rights claims do the southern Democrats invoke? Which of these rights claims, over time, largely disappeared from political rhetoric? Which ones continue to be invoked against using federal power to extend civil rights?*

Sources: (first) *1948 Democratic Party Platform*. Authors accessed at: http://www.presidency.ucsb.edu/ws/?pid=29599; (second) 1948 Platform of the States Rights Democratic (or "Dixiecrat") Party. Authors accessed at: http://www.presidency.ucsb.edu/ws/?pid=25851.

NATO, China, and Nuclear Weaponry

In April 1949, the United States, Canada, and 10 European nations formed the **North Atlantic Treaty Organization (NATO)**. They pledged that an attack against one nation would automatically be treated as a strike against all. Republican senator Robert Taft called NATO a provocation to the Soviet Union, an "entangling alliance" in violation of settled foreign policy principles, and a threat to Congress's constitutional power to declare war. Still, the NATO concept prevailed.

Events in China heightened cold war tensions. Although the United States had extended Jiang Jieshi's struggling Nationalist Party–led government billions in military aid and economic assistance, Jiang's forces had steadily lost ground to those of Mao Zedong's communist movement. Experienced U.S. diplomats privately predicted that incompetence and corruption would speed Jiang's downfall, but the Truman administration publicly portrayed Jiang as the respected leader of an embattled but "free" China. In 1949, Mao's armies forced Jiang off the mainland to the nearby island of Formosa (Taiwan).

Mao's triumph shocked most Americans. Financed by conservative business leaders, the powerful "China lobby" blamed Truman and his new secretary of state, Dean Acheson, for having "lost" China to communism. This domestic political pressure and new international tensions quickly convinced the Truman administration to embrace Jiang's fledgling government on Taiwan and to refuse diplomatic recognition for Mao's "Red China."

The communist challenge grew more alarming when, in 1949, the Soviets exploded a crude atomic device, marking the end of the U.S. monopoly. Besieged by critics who saw recent history marked by Soviet gains and U.S. losses, Truman authorized U.S. scientists to develop a deadly new weapon, the hydrogen bomb, or "superbomb."

NSC-68 and the Korean War   The Truman administration also reviewed its core assumptions about foreign policy. The task of coordinating this review fell to Paul Nitze, a hard-liner who shaped a top-secret policy paper, **NSC-68** (National Security Council Document 68). It opened with a dramatic account of a global clash between "freedom," spread by U.S. power, and "slavery," promoted by the Soviet Union, the center of an international communist movement. Despairing of fruitful negotiations with the Soviets, NSC-68 urged a dramatic upgrade of U.S. national security capabilities. The United States should "find every weak spot in the enemy's armor" and "hit him with anything that comes to hand," one of NSC-68's architects insisted. NSC-68 thus endorsed covert action, economic pressure, propaganda campaigns, and a massive military buildup. Because Americans might oppose larger military spending and budget deficits, the report cautioned, U.S. actions should be labeled as "defensive" and spending increases presented as a stimulus to the economy rather than as a drain on national resources. The details of NSC-68 remained secret until 1975, but the Truman administration immediately invoked its assumptions and rhetoric when framing specific policies and shaping public opinion.

The alarmist tone of NSC-68 seemed to be confirmed in June 1950 when communist North Korea invaded South Korea. Truman characterized the invasion, which U.S. intelligence agencies had failed to anticipate, as a simple case of Soviet-inspired aggression and invoked the rhetoric of containment: "If aggression is successful in Korea, we can expect it to spread through Asia and Europe to this hemisphere," the president declared.

The Korean situation, however, defied a one-dimensional analysis. Japanese military forces had occupied Korea between 1905 and 1945, and after Japan's defeat in the Second World War, Koreans had expected their country to reemerge as one independent nation. Instead, the Soviet and U.S. zones of occupation resulting from the war became the basis for two separate states, artificially divided at the 38th parallel. The Soviet Union backed a communist government in North Korea, headed by the dictatorial Kim Il-sung. The United States supported Syngman Rhee, the leader of an unsteady and autocratic, but anticommunist, government in South Korea.

On June 25, 1950, after receiving tacit approval from Soviet and Chinese leaders, Kim Il-sung moved troops across the 38th parallel in an attempt to reunify Korea. Rhee appealed to the United States for military assistance, and Truman responded without consulting Congress. Events quickly escalated into an

The Cold War split Europe into two opposing alliances. Germany was divided into two countries: The Federal Republic of Germany (West Germany) and the German Democratic Republic (East Germany). Berlin, the former capital of Germany, was also divided. In 1949 NATO was formed, and in 1955 the Warsaw Pact came into existence.

THE DIVISION OF BERLIN

American Zone
British Zone
French Zone
Soviet Zone

(The American, British, and French zones were consolidated as West Berlin)

NATO Countries
Warsaw Pact Countries
Nonaligned Countries

© Cengage Learning

MAP 27.2   Divided Germany and the NATO Alliance

This map shows the geopolitics of the Cold War. Which countries aligned with the United States through NATO? Which aligned with the Soviet Union through the Warsaw Pact? Note how Berlin became a divided city, even though it was located within East Germany.

international conflict, the **Korean War**. The Soviets, unaware of the details of Kim's plans, were boycotting the UN when North Korea's military action began and could not veto a U.S. proposal to send a UN peacekeeping force to Korea. Acting under UN auspices, the United States rushed assistance to Rhee, who moved to quell dissent in the South as well as to repel the armies of the North.

The United States confronted several options in Korea. It could simply contain communism by driving North Korea's forces back across the 38th parallel. It could

Time & Life Pictures/Getty Images

Devastation during Korean War. *In the wake of back-and-forth military campaigns by rival armies, Korean women and children search through the rubble of Seoul, South Korea's capital city, for anything that might be useful for survival.*

risk a wider war and seek to reunify Korea under Rhee's leadership. This option seemed somewhat fanciful when North Korean forces pushed rapidly southward. Within three months, they captured Seoul, the capital of South Korea, and approached the southern tip of the Korean Peninsula. UN troops, most of them from the United States, seemed initially unprepared. American firepower, however, gradually took its toll on North Korea's elite troops and on the ill-trained recruits sent to replace them.

General Douglas MacArthur, the U.S. Army commander who led UN forces in Korea, then devised a plan that most other strategists considered crazy: an amphibious landing behind enemy lines. Those stunned by his audacious proposal were even more astounded by its results. On September 15, 1950, General MacArthur's troops landed at Inchon, suffered minimal casualties, and quickly recaptured Seoul.

The shifting tide of battle devastated Korea. The Korean War is called a "limited" war because it never spread off the Korean Peninsula or involved nuclear weapons, but its impact was hardly narrow. Intense bombing preceded every military move, and neither side seemed particularly concerned about civilian casualties. The number of estimated dead and wounded reached perhaps one-tenth of North and South Korea's combined population. While rival armies battled for Seoul, the city became rubble, with only the capitol building and a train station left standing.

MAP 27.3 Korean War

This map shows the ebb and flow of military action and the armistice line that still divides the two Koreas. Note the advances made first by North Korean and then by UN (United States–led) troops.

As MacArthur's troops drove northward, Truman faced a crucial decision. Emboldened by success, MacArthur urged moving beyond containment to an all-out war of "liberation" and reunification. Other U.S. military strategists warned that China would retaliate if MacArthur's forces approached its border. Truman did allow the general to carry the war into the North but cautioned against provoking intervention by China or the Soviet Union.

When MacArthur pushed near to the Chinese–Korean border, however, China sent at least 400,000 troops into North Korea and forced MacArthur back across the 38th parallel. China's Mao Zedong envisioned helping unite Korea under communist control. With China now in the war and MacArthur seeking authority to use nuclear weapons, the Truman administration hastily reassessed U.S. priorities. "I could not bring myself to order the slaughter of 25,000,000 non-combatants" by using the atomic bomb, the president later claimed. Although Truman maintained a "limited" war, MacArthur's troops eventually regrouped and regained the initiative. As they moved back northward, Truman ordered the general to negotiate a truce at the 38th parallel. MacArthur, challenging the president, argued for a victory over North Korea—and over China, too. Truman thereupon relieved MacArthur of his command in April 1951. The Constitution made military officers subordinate to the president, the nation's commander in chief, Truman declared.

MacArthur returned to the United States a war hero. Yet, during Senate hearings on MacArthur's dismissal, strategists dismissed his scenario for Korea as the "wrong war in the wrong place." Expanding and securing American power elsewhere around the world, particularly in Europe, should remain the central objective of U.S. policy. This broader goal dictated merely the containment, not a rollback, of communism in Korea, they successfully argued. MacArthur's once luminous image, along with his political ambitions, soon faded.

As negotiations for a peace settlement for Korea stalled, another military hero, Dwight Eisenhower, became the 1952 Republican nominee for president. He promised to go to Korea if elected and accelerate the peace process. Harry Truman would leave office in 1953 without formally ending the Korean War.

Korea and Containment   The Korean War bolstered support for the global anticommunist vision of NSC-68. The United States formulated plans to rearm West Germany, scarcely five years after the defeat of the Third Reich, and to expand NATO's military forces throughout Western Europe. A proposal for direct military aid to Latin American governments, which had been rejected in the past, now slid through Congress. In the Philippines, the United States stepped up military and CIA assistance to the government of Ramón Magsaysay so it could suppress the leftist Hukbalahap (or Huk) movement. In 1951, Washington finally signed a formal peace treaty with Japan and secured a security pact that granted the United States a sprawling military base on the island of Okinawa. The United States acquired similar bases in the Middle East, bolstering its strategic position in that oil-rich area.

In addition, the Truman administration made important moves in French Indochina. It greatly expanded economic assistance for the effort to retain France's colonial possession against the challenge from communist Ho Chi Minh's Democratic Republic of Vietnam. Policymakers in Washington had hardly favored a communist-led government in Indochina but worries about identifying the United States too closely with French colonialism in Southeast Asia had initially limited U.S. support for France's military effort against Ho's forces. The outbreak of the Korean conflict, however, elevated preventing a communist victory in Indochina into a major policy goal.

Warning of potential communist gains, U.S. policymakers became increasingly insistent about opposing overseas movements that seemed to lean toward the political left. The U.S. occupation government in Japan, for example, restricted the activities of labor unions, suspended an antitrust program that American officials had earlier implemented, and barred communists from posts in Japan's government and universities. As in Germany, the United States tried to contain communism elsewhere by strengthening pro-U.S. elites and by promoting economic growth through marketplace rather than state-directed mechanisms.

Containment considerations also prompted the United States to ally with South Africa. In 1949, the all-white (and militantly anticommunist) Nationalist Party instituted a legal-social system called apartheid, based on elaborate rules of racial separation and subordination of blacks. Some State Department officials warned that a close relationship with South Africa, by implying support for apartheid, would damage America's international reputation, but the Truman administration nonetheless supported South Africa's white supremacist regime.

Most importantly, the elaboration of containment during the Korean War era featured the military buildup proposed in NSC-68. By early 1953, U.S. military production totaled seven times what it had been before the North Korean attack. The United States also continued to expand its worldwide system of military bases. And economic pressure, CIA covert activities, and propaganda campaigns helped further implement containment objectives. A global "Campaign of Truth," a sustained informational and psychological offensive, countered Soviet propaganda with mass media and cultural exchanges sponsored by Washington. A rhetoric organized around the concept of "national security" took hold: The Defense Department replaced the War Department, and the new phrase *national security* supplanted the older, more limited language of gauging the best *national interest*.

NSC-68 provided a master plan for using military, economic, and covert action to advance a worldwide national security policy. It also facilitated what the historian Michael Sherry has called "the militarization of American life." By 1951, two-thirds of the federal budget went for military-related spending, with continued bipartisan support. Congress granted a new Atomic Energy Commission broad authority to oversee development of a U.S. nuclear power industry. The prospect of creating military jobs in congressional districts muted opposition from cost-conscious members of Congress.

PURSUING NATIONAL SECURITY AT HOME

Although containment abroad generally gained bipartisan support, debate flared over programs for containing subversive influences at home. Civil libertarians complained about "witch hunts" against people who merely expressed dissent. Militant anticommunists leveled alarming allegations about internal communist subversion being left unchecked, while even firm anticommunists worried that exaggerated charges and wild goose chases after unlikely subversives harmed the effort to identify authentic Soviet agents. The search for supposed threats to national security eventually touched many areas of postwar life.

Anticommunism and the U.S. Labor Movement   The politics of anticommunism came to affect the U.S. labor movement. After the end of the Second World War, many workers struck for increased wages and benefits and for a greater voice in workplace routines and production decisions. Strikes brought both the auto and the electronics industries to a standstill. After President Truman threatened to seize mines and railroads that had been shut down by work stoppages and to order strikers back to work, labor militancy began to subside.

In 1947, a Republican-controlled Congress tapped anticommunist sentiment to help pass the Labor-Management Relations Act, popularly known as the **Taft-Hartley Act**. The law negated gains made by organized labor during the 1930s.

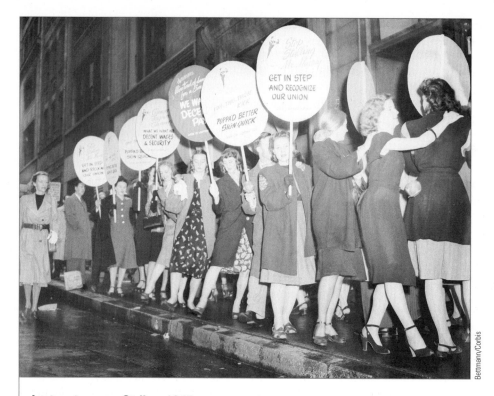

Bettmann/Corbis

Instructors on Strike, 1947. *Employees of an Arthur Murray Dance Studio in New York City demonstrate the conga, a popular Latin American dance—and their determination to form a union affiliated with the United Office and Professional Workers of America. In the immediate postwar period, in response to unionization campaigns, workers in a wide range of occupations used labor strikes to seek higher wages, better working conditions, and greater job security. After 1947 union gains met increased resistance.*

It limited a union's power to conduct boycotts, to compel employers to accept "closed shops" in which only union members could be hired, and to continue a strike that the president judged harmful to national security. In addition, the measure required union officials to pledge that they did not belong to the Communist Party or any other "subversive" organization. A union that refused to comply was denied protections under national labor laws. Congress overrode Truman's veto of Taft-Hartley, and by the end of his presidency a loyalty-security check had been conducted on about 20 percent of the U.S. workforce, more than 13 million people. The Congress of Industrial Organizations (CIO) expelled 13 unions—a full third of its membership—as anticommunism also influenced internal labor politics. Many workers found that their political commitments could put their own jobs at risk.

Containing Communism at Home   Anticommunists scrutinized workers in the entertainment industry with special zeal. In 1947, the House Un-American Activities Committee (HUAC) opened hearings into communist influences in Hollywood. Basking in the glare of newsreel cameras, members of this committee seized on the refusal of ten screenwriters, producers, and directors—all current or former members of the American Communist Party—to testify about political allegiances within the film community. "The Hollywood Ten" claimed that the First Amendment barred HUAC from scrutinizing their political activities. The federal courts upheld HUAC's investigative powers, however, and the Hollywood Ten eventually went to prison for contempt of Congress.

Hollywood studios as well as radio and television networks enforced their own internal "blacklists" of workers, allegedly subversives, whom they agreed not to hire. Blacklists affected not only prominent performers but many anonymous labor union members who worked behind the scenes in technical and support positions. Many entertainment workers were unable to find jobs unless they agreed to become "friendly witnesses" before HUAC or other investigative committees and to provide the names of people they had seen at some "communist meeting" in the past. Some of those called to testify, such as the screenwriter Lillian Hellman, refused to answer any questions. Others, such as the movie director Elia Kazan and the writer Budd Schulberg, cooperated. Decisions over whether or not to "name names" would divide people in the entertainment industry and the labor union movement for decades.

The search for subversives created anticommunist celebrities. Ronald Reagan, president of the Screen Actors Guild and a secret informant for the FBI (identified as "T-10"), testified about communist influence in Hollywood. Richard Nixon, an obscure member of Congress from California, began his political ascent in 1948 when Whittaker Chambers, a journalist formerly active in communist circles, came before HUAC. Chambers charged Alger Hiss, a prominent Democrat, with having been a party member and with passing classified information to Soviet agents during the late 1930s.

The Hiss–Chambers–Nixon affair still sparks controversy. Legal considerations barred an indictment of Hiss for espionage, but the government charged him with perjury for allegedly lying to Congress. Ultimately convicted on two counts, Hiss spent nearly four years in prison. To Nixon and his supporters, the case of Alger Hiss, who had advised Franklin Roosevelt during the Yalta Conference, demonstrated how deeply rooted communist subversion had become. To his supporters, Hiss appeared the victim of a frame-up. In the mid-1990s, newly declassified documents revived the Hiss controversy. A few scholars continued to defend Hiss. The vast majority, however, concluded that Hiss (along with several other high-ranking government officials) had likely passed information to the Soviets during the 1930s and 1940s. Historians continue to differ, however, over the precise nature of this material and its value to Moscow.

Meanwhile, the Truman administration pursued its own anticommunist course at home. It dismissed hundreds of federal employees under its loyalty program. Truman's attorney general, Tom Clark, secretly authorized J. Edgar Hoover, head of the FBI, to compile a list of alleged subversives the government could detain during any national emergency without any legal hearing.

Fear that subversives might immigrate to the United States helped shape several provisions of the **McCarran-Walter Act**. Also known as the Immigration and Nationality Act of 1952, this law authorized denial of immigrant status to anyone who might compromise national security by bringing dangerous ideas into the country. It also allowed the deportation of immigrants, even naturalized citizens, who belonged to organizations on the Attorney General's List. Calling these measures "un-American," Truman rejected McCarran-Walter, but Congress overrode his veto.

Hoover's FBI also undertook an extensive campaign of surveillance. It compiled confidential dossiers on artists and intellectuals suspected of radical views. Some of its targets, including the writers Ernest Hemingway and John Steinbeck, had no links to the Communist Party. The FBI often singled out prominent African Americans, including civil rights activist Bayard Rustin, Richard Wright (author of the acclaimed novel *Native Son*), and W. E. B. Du Bois (a celebrated African American historian). Paul Robeson (a well-known entertainer-activist) encountered trouble from the State Department and immigration officials. His association with the U.S. Communist Party and identification with anti-imperialist and antiracist organizations throughout the world curtailed his ability to travel overseas. In addition, suspicions of homosexuality could make people, including the nominally closeted Rustin, targets for governmental surveillance and discrimination.

Targeting Sexual Difference   Public focus on homosexual behavior increased. During the Second World War, very visible gay and lesbian subcultures had emerged, particularly in larger cities such as New York and San Francisco. After the war, Dr. Alfred Kinsey's research on sexual behavior—his first volume, on male sexuality, appeared in 1948—claimed to find homosexuality throughout American life and a wide range of sexual behaviors from exclusively heterosexual to exclusively homosexual. In 1952, transsexuality hit the headlines when the press revealed that, after a series of "sex-change" operations in Europe, George W. Jorgensen, Jr., had become a "blonde beauty," Christine Jorgensen.

By this time, a small "homophile" movement had emerged to challenge the most egregious forms of discrimination. Gay men formed the Mattachine Society (in 1950), and lesbians later founded the Daughters of Bilitis, organizations that sought legal protection for the basic constitutional rights of homosexuals. They condemned police departments for singling out businesses catering to gays and lesbians when making raids for "disorderly conduct" and the post office for banning homosexual publications on the basis of "decency" requirements.

The homophile movement of the 1950s, however, confronted a newly aggressive effort to restrict the visibility of homosexuality. The Kinsey Report's implicit claim that homosexuality was simply another form of sexuality, alongside the emergence of new gay and lesbian organizations, helped fuel this campaign. The fact that several founders of the Mattachine Society had also been members of the Communist Party, coupled with the claim that Soviet agents could blackmail homosexuals more easily than heterosexuals, helped link homosexuality with the communist threat to national security. "One homosexual can pollute a Government office," a U.S. Senate report claimed.

Today, historians of sexuality see a "Lavender Scare" about homosexuality accompanying the "Red Scare" about communism. Popular imagery portrayed both homosexuality and communism as subversive "diseases" that could spread throughout the body politic. Suspicion of "sexual deviance" became an acceptable basis for subjecting government employees to loyalty board hearings and, ultimately, denying them legal and constitutional protections enjoyed by heterosexuals.

The "Great Fear"   The postwar search for subversion unfolded within an atmosphere of anxiety that some cultural historians call the "Great Fear." Genuine threats, such as the atomic program of the Soviets, heightened the impact of spurious claims about communist agents roaming military bases or gay subversives shaping foreign policy. A growing sense of cultural and social insecurity, in turn, intensified efforts to safeguard national security.

As this atmosphere of fear was settling over American life, the Justice Department announced the arrests, in 1950, of several members of a spy ring alleged to have been channeling nuclear secrets to Moscow. Two of the arrested, Julius and Ethel Rosenberg, the parents of two young children and members of the Communist Party, became the central characters in a legal-cultural controversy.

The Rosenberg spy case became a cold war melodrama. The couple's trial, the guilty verdicts, the death sentences, the numerous legal appeals, the worldwide protests, and their 1953 executions for having committed atomic espionage captured media attention. To their supporters, the Rosenbergs (who died maintaining their innocence) had fallen victim to anticommunist hysteria. Federal officials, according to the couple's defenders, seemed primarily interested in finding scapegoats. To others, however, solid evidence pointed toward their involvement in an extensive operation, which included a confessed British spy. Documents released after the fall of the Soviet Union in 1989 now clearly confirm Julius Rosenberg's spying activities. Ethel Rosenberg likely knew about his work, but evidence of her direct involvement in passing information to the Soviets remains ambiguous.

The performance of the nation's criminal justice system in this cultural drama helps to complicate the historical picture. Federal prosecutors never moved, for example, against people who almost certainly were atomic spies. Theodore Hall, a physicist who worked on America's bomb and whose expertise about nuclear matters obviously exceeded that of Julius or Ethel Rosenberg, was among them. Officials likely feared revealing valuable counter-intelligence operations—or perhaps illegal surveillance activities. In any case, only the Rosenbergs, of all those who were identified or prosecuted, faced a charge that carried the death penalty.

The courts' response to the Great Fear has been a matter of sustained debate. During a 1949 prosecution of leaders of the American Communist Party, the trial judge accepted the Justice Department's plea that the 11 defendants be considered participants in an international conspiracy. Their Marxist ideas and publications, even without any proof of subversive acts, could justify convicting them of the crime of sedition. Civil libertarians insisted that the government never showed how Communist Party publications and speeches, by themselves, posed a "clear and present danger" to national security. In this view, *political expression* should enjoy the protection of the First Amendment and only *illegal activity* could be put on trial. In *Dennis* v. *U.S.* (1951), the Supreme Court upheld the convictions of the Communist Party leaders. The Soviet threat was so serious, the Court ruled, that pro-communist expression, in the absence of any overt criminal activity, could constitute sedition.

Meanwhile, the Truman administration continued to incur the ire of more zealous red-hunters. In Congress, Republicans and conservative Democrats denounced Truman's anticommunist initiatives as too limited and passed, over Truman's veto, the Subversive Activities Control Act of 1950. It created a Subversive Activities Control Board (SACB) to oversee the registration of groups allegedly controlled or infiltrated by communists. It barred communists from working in the defense industry, holding a labor union office, and acquiring a passport. Unaware of J. Edgar Hoover's secret detention program, Congress also authorized the confinement of alleged subversives during any national emergency.

Joseph McCarthy

Joseph McCarthy, a Republican senator from Wisconsin, became the Truman administration's prime accuser. An intelligence officer during the Second World War, McCarthy had entered politics as a battle-tested combat vet, "Tailgunner Joe." Elected to the U.S. Senate in 1946, McCarthy showed little interest in legislative matters, but he emerged as a two-fisted investigator of communist subversion during the Great Fear.

McCarthy became a celebrity when he claimed, during a 1950 speech in Wheeling, West Virginia, to have compiled a list of 205 communists then working in the State Department. Americans rightly feared the future, according to McCarthy, "not because our only powerful potential enemy has sent men to invade our shores, but rather because of the traitorous actions of those who have been treated so well by this Nation." Although McCarthy quickly shrank his number of subversives to 57, he also expanded his attacks. Secretary of State Dean Acheson and his predecessor, General George C. Marshall, soon came into range.

Adept at using political imagery and sexual innuendo, McCarthy linked the Lavender Scare and Red Scare. He portrayed key members of Truman's administration as both overly privileged and insufficiently manly. People like Acheson who had been "born with silver spoons in their mouths," represented effete "enemies from within." McCarthy derided the smartly dressed Acheson as the "Red Dean of fashion" and as the leader of the "lace handkerchief crowd."

Initially, McCarthy seemed unstoppable. He substantiated none of his more sensational claims but lacked neither imagination nor targets. In the summer of 1950 a Senate subcommittee, after examining government files, concluded that McCarthy's charges against the State Department amounted to "the most nefarious campaign of half-truths and untruths in the history of this republic." McCarthy responded that the files had been "raped," and he went after Millard Tydings, the Democratic senator who had chaired the subcommittee. In the November 1950 elections, Tydings went down to defeat, in part because of a fabricated photograph that linked him to communist activities.

Despite McCarthy's erratic course, influential people initially tolerated, even encouraged, him. Conservative anticommunist leaders of the Roman Catholic Church embraced McCarthy, himself a Catholic. Leading Republicans welcomed McCarthy's assaults on their Democratic rivals. Others insisted the senator's commitment to the cause of anticommunism outweighed complaints about his slapdash investigations and overzealous methods. In contrast, critics charged that the senator personified a reckless form of demagogic "attack politics," and they called his careless, flamboyant style "McCarthyism."

A National Security Constitution and the Structure of Governance

Focusing on the furor over McCarthyism, however, can obscure fundamental changes in constitutional governance that generated relatively little controversy. Except for the Twenty-Second Amendment, adopted in 1951, which barred presidents from following Franklin Roosevelt's example and being elected to more than two terms, there were no formal modifications to the written Constitution during the era of the Great Fear. But congressional legislation shaped a new national security constitutional framework during the early postwar years.

The view that the office of the president possessed only limited powers gave way to the idea that protecting national security justified extending the reach of the executive branch. Truman encountered no constitutional roadblocks to an undeclared war in Korea, and in 1952, he issued a secret executive order that created the super-secret **National Security Agency (NSA)**. Using sophisticated technology, the NSA began collecting any information, from communications networks around the globe, which might affect the nation's safety. Covert eavesdropping on a massive scale became part of a new, partially unwritten and secret, national security framework.

The specter of constitutional limitations on presidential power did arise in 1952, however, when Truman ordered his commerce secretary to seize control of the U.S. steel industry in order to prevent a threatened strike. Although Truman could have invoked a 60-day "cooling off" period under the Taft-Hartley Act, he sought to justify this action with a more fundamental, novel, and controversial constitutional claim: The president, as commander in chief, possessed extraordinary power whenever emergency action was required to safeguard national security.

The steel companies challenged this assertion in court. When *Youngstown Sheet & Tube Company* v. *Sawyer* (1952) reached the Supreme Court, three justices who had been nominated by Truman supported his claim of executive power. Six others, for differing reasons, rejected Truman's position in this particular instance, but all supported a broad view of presidential authority whenever national security seemed more clearly at stake. Constitutional scholars would come to see this case as a short-term defeat for Truman but a long-term victory for the idea of an expansive "National Security Constitution."

POSTWAR SOCIAL AND ECONOMIC POLICY-MAKING

Truman embraced Franklin Roosevelt's domestic agenda, and many supporters of FDR's New Deal still championed his Second Bill of Rights of 1944. But proposals for government planning and for new social welfare measures stalled during Truman's presidency. Any attempt to build on the New Deal and wartime arrangements, insisted most Republicans and some Democrats, would threaten unconstitutional intrusions into people's liberties and undermine individual initiative and responsibility. Dixiecrat Democrats from the South joined conservative Republicans to block any legislation that they believed might dismantle white supremacy in their region. The National Association of Manufacturers (NAM) denounced the Truman administration as a menace to the nation's free-enterprise system.

The Employment Act of 1946 and Economic Growth

The 1946 debate over the Full Employment Bill provided a new template for domestic policy-making. This measure, as conceived, would have empowered Washington to ensure employment for all citizens seeking work. To the bill's opponents, the emphasis on "full employment" implied a step toward a European-style welfare state, even socialism.

As the effort to enact this measure stalled, a scaled-back approach emerged. The law that Congress finally passed, the **Employment Act of 1946**, called for "maximum" (rather than full) employment and specifically declared that private enterprise, not government, bore primary responsibility for economic decision making. The measure nonetheless created a new executive branch body, the Council of Economic Advisers, to formulate long-range policy recommendations, and it signaled that government would assume considerable responsibility for the performance of the economy.

The Employment Act of 1946 underscored a growing faith that *advice* to public officials from economic experts, as an alternative to government *planning*, could guarantee a constantly expanding economy. An influential group of economists, disciples of Britain's John Maynard Keynes, insisted that their expertise could temper boom-and-bust cycles.

The promise of economic expansion dazzled postwar leaders. Using the relatively new measure of gross national product (GNP)—defined as the total dollar value of all goods and services produced in the nation during a given year—economists could calculate the nation's growing economic bounty. Corporate executives, who had feared that the end of the war would bring long-term labor unrest and trigger a deep recession, viewed a rising GNP as a guarantor of social stability. The Truman administration welcomed the prospect of an expanding economy, which would increase federal tax revenues and, in turn, finance governmental programs at home and abroad.

Truman and his advisers spread the gospel of economic growth. This new faith nicely dovetailed with their national security plans. Spending for the cold war could serve as a "pump primer" for the U.S. economy. Sharp increases in military rearmament signaled a tilt in economic policy that critical observers began calling "military Keynesianism." Moreover, cold war assistance programs such as the Marshall Plan could create markets and investment opportunities for Americans overseas. Economic growth at home was linked to development in the world at large—and to the all-pervasive concern with national security.

Truman's Fair Deal   In 1949, Truman unveiled his **"Fair Deal."** He proposed extending popular New Deal programs such as Social Security and minimum wage laws; enacting legislation dealing with civil rights, national health care, and federal aid for education; and repealing the Taft-Hartley Act. The Fair Deal also envisioned substantial spending on public housing projects and a complicated plan to support farm prices. The Fair Deal's faith that sustained economic growth could finance new government programs came to focus the Truman administration's policy planning.

Two prominent programs illustrate the background assumptions that shaped domestic social policy. The **GI Bill** (officially titled the Serviceman's Readjustment Act of 1944) had been passed during the war to provide comprehensive benefits for those who served in the armed forces. The bill offered veterans financial assistance for college and job-training programs. By 1947, the year of peak enrollment, roughly half of the students enrolled at colleges and universities were receiving aid under the GI Bill. Veterans also received preferential treatment when applying for government jobs; favorable financial terms when purchasing homes or businesses; and, eventually, comprehensive medical care in veterans' hospitals. The Veterans Readjustment Assistance Act of 1952, popularly known as the "GI Bill of Rights," extended these programs to veterans of the Korean War. Although the Truman administration never enacted FDR's Second Bill of Rights, the GI Bills did extend some of its key promises to veterans.

The Social Security program also expanded. Rebutting attacks from conservatives, Social Security's supporters defended its provisions for the disabled and the blind and argued that older people had earned its "income security" through years of work and monetary contributions withheld from their paychecks. Under the

Polio Scare. *Mary Kosloski, a young polio victim from Tennessee, was often pictured in posters for the March of Dimes, an organization that conducted fundraising throughout the country in an ultimately successful effort to find and distribute a vaccination against the often-crippling disease. In 1952 nearly 58,000 cases of polio were reported and nearly half of those afflicted either died or experienced disabling paralysis.*

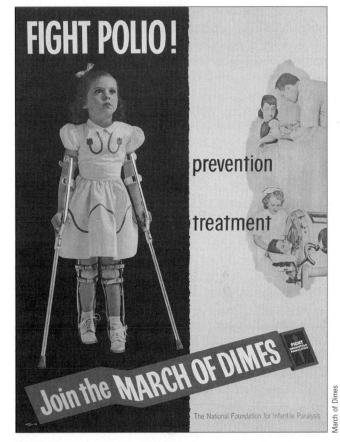

March of Dimes

Social Security Act of 1950, the level of benefits increased significantly; the retirement portions of the program expanded; and coverage was extended to more than 10 million people, including agricultural workers.

More expansive (and expensive) Fair Deal proposals, however, either failed or were scaled back. Truman's plan for a comprehensive national health insurance program faced opposition from several different quarters. Consumer groups and labor unions, intent on creating nonprofit community-run health plans, feared that a centralized system would unnecessarily bureaucratize medical care. The American Medical Association (AMA) and the American Hospital Association (AHA) opposed any governmental intervention in the traditional fee-for-service medical system. Large insurance companies, which were continuing to push their own private plans, also opposed the Truman initiative.

The Fair Deal's housing proposals made some headway. Continued shortage of affordable housing in urban areas stirred support for home-building programs. Even some conservatives supported the Housing Act of 1949. This law authorized construction of 810,000 public housing units and provided federal funds for "urban renewal" zones, areas to be cleared of run-down dwellings and rebuilt with new construction. The Housing Act proclaimed ambitious goals but provided relatively modest funding, especially for its public-housing component. Private construction firms and real estate agents welcomed funding for federal home loan guarantee programs—such as those established under the GI Bill—but they lobbied effectively against publicly financed housing projects.

Fair Deal policy-making thus ultimately focused on specific groups, such as veterans and older Americans, rather than on more extensive programs such as national health care or a national housing program. With opponents of the Fair Deal continually charging that it would move the United States toward a European-style "welfare state," the White House found it easier to defend more narrowly targeted programs that it could present as economic security measures for specific recipients who merited government assistance.

Civil Rights   The Truman administration also struggled to place the national government's power behind a growing civil rights movement. After returning home, veterans of African, Latino, and American Indian descent increasingly refused to remain passive bystanders when laws and discriminatory practices reduced them to second-class citizens. Moreover, the people of color who had moved to cities seeking wartime employment wanted to build on the gains they had made. Drives to translate their visions of liberty and equality into reality animated grassroots activists in the postwar period.

During his 1948 presidential campaign, Truman endorsed the proposals of his new civil rights committee. Its report, entitled "To Secure These Rights," called for federal legislation against lynching; a special civil rights division within the Department of Justice; antidiscrimination initiatives in employment, housing, and public facilities; and desegregation of the military. These proposals had helped prompt the Dixiecrat revolt of 1948, but they also gained Truman significant support from civil rights groups.

Civil rights became an increasingly important concern. After successive Congresses failed to enact any civil rights legislation—including a law against lynching and a ban on poll taxes—leaders of the movement turned to the White House and to the federal courts. A plan by labor leader A. Philip Randolph to organize a protest campaign prompted Truman to issue Executive Order 9981 (1948), which called for gradual desegregation of the armed forces. Truman understood how segregation tarnished America's image in a cold war world "which is 90 percent colored." Although cold war politics could help justify harassment of African American leaders allegedly linked to subversive causes, the crusade against communism on behalf of the "free world" also made racial discrimination into a foreign policy liability.

Truman's Justice Department thus appeared in court to support litigants who contested government-backed "restrictive covenants" (legal agreements that prevented racial or religious minorities from acquiring real estate) and segregated education. In 1946, the Supreme Court declared restrictive covenants unconstitutional and began chipping away at the "separate-but-equal" principle used since *Plessy v. Ferguson* (1896) to justify segregated schools. A federal court in California, ruling on a case brought the previous year in Orange County by a coalition of Mexican American and African American activists, held that segregating students of Mexican descent in separate, and unequal, schools violated their constitutional rights. In 1948, a second federal court—with the case now entitled *Westminster School District v. Mendez*—agreed with the first. In 1950, the Supreme Court ruled that, under the Fourteenth Amendment, racial segregation in state-financed graduate and law schools was unconstitutional. The familiar arguments used to legitimize racial segregation in public education seemed ripe for a successful challenge.

SIGNS OF A CHANGING CULTURE

The pace of cultural change accelerated during the postwar years. Encouraged by the advertising industry, Americans seemed, in one sense, to view anything new as "progress." Yet, in another, the speed and scope of change appeared to accentuate feelings of uneasiness and anxiety. As a result, the impulse toward containment affected postwar culture as well as foreign and domestic policy-making.

The "Color Line" and the National Pastime

The interplay between celebrating and containing change could be seen in the integration of organized baseball during the 1940s and early 1950s. In 1947, Jackie Robinson finally cracked Major League Baseball's policy of racial segregation. A graduate of UCLA who had battled segregation while serving in the U.S. Army during the Second World War, Robinson had also played semiprofessional football and in the Negro National Baseball League before joining the Brooklyn Dodgers. Some ballplayers opposed to integration, including several on Robinson's own team, considered a boycott. Baseball's leadership, seeking new sources of players and more African American fans coming through the turnstiles, threatened to suspend any player who would not play with or against Robinson.

Officially, organized baseball desegregated. The Cleveland Indians signed Larry Doby, and other stars began abandoning the Negro leagues for clubs in the American and National circuits. Eventually, the skills of Robinson—named Rookie of the Year in 1947 and the National League's Most Valuable Player in 1949—and other players of African descent carried the day. Although light-skinned Latinos had long passed through the racial barrier, Orestes ("Minnie") Minoso, a Cuban-born veteran of the Negro circuits, became the first Afro-Latino to break into the big leagues in 1949. Major League teams began fielding greater numbers of African American and Latino players, and some accelerated recruitment efforts in Mexico and the Caribbean.

Yet, baseball's leadership had unofficially limited its own desegregation effort. Several teams waited years before integrating their rosters, claiming that they could find no talented African American or Latino prospects. More commonly, clubs restricted the number of nonwhite players they would take on and hired only whites as managers, coaches, and front-office personnel.

African American and Latino players who followed in Robinson's footsteps confronted continuing obstacles. They encountered overt, off-the-field discrimination during spring training in the South and Southwest and in many small towns elsewhere when playing in the minor leagues. Spanish-speaking players struggled to convince managers, sportswriters, and teammates that they could "understand" the subtleties of either baseball or North American culture.

The New Suburbia

In suburbia, too, change was simultaneously celebrated and feared—and thus subject to various strategies for limiting the impact of the new.

Suburban living had long been a feature of the "American dream." The new Long Island town of Levittown, New York, which welcomed its first residents in October 1947, seemed to make that dream an affordable reality for middle-income families. Similar developments, such as Lakewood and Panorama City in California, soon began springing up in other parts of the country.

Nearly everything about Levittown and its counterparts seemed unprecedented. Levitt & Sons, a construction company that had mass-produced military barracks during the Second World War, claimed to be completing a five-room bungalow every 15 minutes. Architectural and cultural critics sneered at these "little boxes," but potential buyers stood in long lines for the chance to purchase one. By 1950, Levittown contained more than 10,000 homes and 40,000 residents. At the same time, bulldozers and construction crews were sweeping through other suburban developments across the country.

To assist potential buyers, the national government offered an extensive set of programs. The FHA underwrote an elaborate lending system through long-term, government-insured mortgages. Veterans enjoyed favorable terms under the GI loan program. These government programs made it cheaper to purchase a suburban house than to rent an apartment in most cities. Moreover, the law provided suburban homeowners with an additional subsidy: They could deduct the interest payments on their mortgages from their federal income tax.

The new suburbs quickly gained a reputation for being ideal places for nurturing a **baby boom generation**. Sheer numbers helped identify "baby boomers," people born between 1946 and 1964, as a unique social and cultural force. The Great Depression and the Second World War had deflated the U.S. birth rate, but it began to soar even before war's end. A number of factors, including earlier marriages and rising incomes, fueled a continuing boom in babies. More than 75 million babies were born in the United States during the baby boom era.

Although baby boomers lived everywhere, they became closely identified with the new suburbia. With houses occupying only about 15 percent of new suburban lots, large lawns served as private playgrounds. Suburban schools were as new as the homes, and their well-appointed facilities attracted both skilled and enthusiastic teachers. In many respects, suburbia symbolized new possibilities, confidence in the future, and embrace of change.

As contemporary observers noted, however, suburbia also appeared to offer a material and psychological refuge. Buying a suburban home seemed a way of containing the impact of the social and cultural changes of the cold war era. As African American families continued to migrate to northern and western cities in search of jobs and greater opportunity, for example, whites began to see a move to the new suburbs as a way to avoid living in racially integrated neighborhoods. Governmental policies contributed to this trend through the financial incentives provided to homebuyers. Even after the Supreme Court declared restrictive covenants unconstitutional, local officials often successfully undercut the ruling's immediate impact. Various informal and extralegal arrangements prevented, until well into the 1960s, any African American from buying a home in most new suburbs such as Levittown.

Other policies and practices helped to limit diversity. Local governments could veto public housing projects in their communities. Although land and building costs would have been cheaper in the suburbs, public housing remained concentrated on relatively expensive, high-density urban sites. At the same time, the lending industry channeled government-guaranteed loans away from most urban neighborhoods, and private lenders routinely denied credit to African Americans and Latinos seeking to buy new suburban housing.

Leaders of the postwar housing industry denied any discriminatory intent. William Levitt could identify his private housing projects with the public crusade

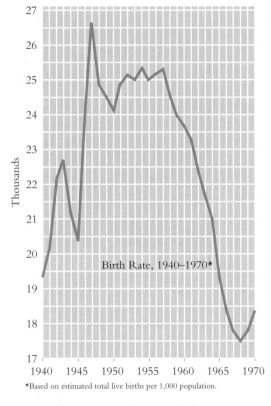

Birth Rate, 1940–1970*

*Based on estimated total live births per 1,000 population.

The Baby Boom

against communism. "No man who owns his house and lot can be a Communist," he remarked in 1948. "He has too much to do." Even as Levitt claimed he could help solve the problem of housing—and perhaps even that of communist subversion—he also resisted any suggestion that the private decisions of his construction business had anything to do with race. Architects of postwar suburbia similarly saw nothing problematic with postwar gender patterns. The private financial industry extended the vast majority of its loan guarantees to white men. Only rarely could single women obtain loans. The FHA, a governmental agency, justified a similar policy on the grounds that men were the family breadwinners and that women seldom qualified as good credit risks. Analogous justifications often kept men of non-European background from obtaining loans for housing in the new suburbs.

Postwar Hollywood   Hollywood turned out movies filled with powerful symbols of the cold war era's fascination with—and containment of—change. The motion picture industry still commanded the nation's entertainment dollars at the start of the postwar period. As overseas markets reopened and Hollywood's male stars returned from military service, the U.S. film industry expected to prosper and prepared to cheer the nation through the cold war much as it had through the Depression and the Second World War.

The New Suburbia: Levittown. *The success of Levittown, New York, during the late 1940s provided a pattern for mass-produced homes in new suburban developments elsewhere in the United States. Assistance from government financing programs, such as the GI Bill, and standardized production methods brought the cost of new suburban homes within the reach of millions of buyers.*

Hulton Archive/Archive Photos/Getty Images

The familiar musical genre, filled with lively stars, upbeat tunes, and flashy dance sequences, provided a ready formula for expressing postwar optimism. Attendance at movie theaters reached an all-time high in 1948.

Hollywood's fortunes, however, began changing. In 1948, the Supreme Court ruled that antitrust laws required the major studios to give up their highly profitable ownership of local movie theaters. This decision rocked Hollywood just as it faced labor strife, internal conflict over blacklisting, and soaring production costs. The challenge of television delivered yet another blow to an industry already reeling backward. Attendance figures—along with profits—began to plummet in 1949.

Hollywood had already begun to release a cycle of motion pictures that came to be called *film noir,* or "dark cinema." Almost always filmed in black and white and generally set in large cities, *film noir* peeked into the dark corners of postwar America and expressed the anxiety, even dread, associated with the Great Fear. *Noir* characters still pursued their dreams and hopes, but with little chance of fulfilling them. Failure and loss seemed to be the rule rather than the exception in these movies.

Film noir invariably featured alluring *femmes fatales.* These beautiful but dangerous female characters challenged the prevailing order, particularly its gender relationships. The *femme fatale* disdained the confinement that came with being a faithful, nurturing wife and mother. Usually unmarried and childless, her continual scheming to escape her containment threatened both men and women. The postwar era's leading female stars—including Barbara Stanwyck, Joan Crawford, Rita Hayworth, and Lana Turner—achieved both popular and critical acclaim playing *femmes fatales.*

THE ELECTION OF 1952

Harry Truman, his popular approval rating ultimately falling to near 20 percent, declined to run for another term in 1952. His presidency had put his Democratic Party on the defensive, while denunciations of communism and of Truman's outgoing administration animated Republicans.

| Continuing Containment | Both major political parties embraced the policy of containment in 1952. Adlai Stevenson of Illinois, the Democratic presidential candidate, warned that "Soviet secret agents and their dupes" |

had "burrowed like moles" into governments throughout the world. "We cannot let our guard drop for even a moment," he claimed. A solidly anticommunist stance, however, could not save Stevenson or his party. The Republicans linked Stevenson to the unpopular Truman presidency and highlighted several scandals that featured administration figures receiving kickbacks for granting government contracts. The GOP's vice presidential nominee, Senator Richard Nixon of California, called Stevenson "Adlai the appeaser." The Republican formula for electoral victory could be expressed in a simple equation, "K1C2": "Korea, corruption, and communism."

| A Soldier-Politician | For a presidential candidate, Republicans ultimately turned to a hero of the Second World War, General Dwight David Eisenhower, popularly known as "Ike." Eisenhower grew up in Kan- |

sas; graduated from West Point; ascended through the army ranks; and, as Supreme Allied Commander, directed the Normandy invasion of 1944. He served as Army Chief of Staff from 1945 to 1948 and, after an interim period as president of Columbia University, became the commander of NATO. Eisenhower had never before sought elective office, but a half-century of military service had honed his political instincts and administrative skills. Still vigorous at 62 years of age, Eisenhower seemed much younger than the departing Truman, only six years his senior.

Eisenhower's personal appeal dazzled political insiders, media commentators, and ordinary voters. Although his partisan affiliations seemed hazy enough that

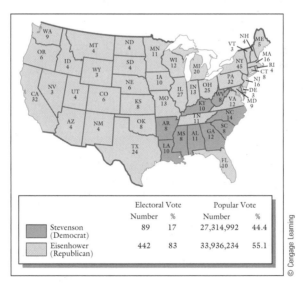

		Electoral Vote		Popular Vote	
		Number	%	Number	%
	Stevenson (Democrat)	89	17	27,314,992	44.4
	Eisenhower (Republican)	442	83	33,936,234	55.1

© Cengage Learning

MAP 27.4 Presidential Election, 1952

An overwhelming victory for Eisenhower, this election saw Stevenson carrying a handful of states. Note that the so-called Solid South, though, remained largely Democratic. The nation's political configuration, especially for presidential elections, would change substantially over the next two decades.

Democrats (as well as Republicans) had courted him as their presidential choice in 1948, Eisenhower eventually emerged as the standard-bearer of the GOP in 1952.

The crucial political battle of that year took place, before the general election, within Republican ranks. The more conservative of the party stalwarts rallied behind Senator Robert Taft of Ohio and his goals of reversing the New Deal and tempering Truman's global foreign policy. Marketed as a middle-of-the-road candidate, Eisenhower had broader appeal and appeared ready to direct the nation through a cold war as skillfully as he had led it through a hot one. The Republican campaign, the first to feature televised appeals, downplayed Eisenhower's uncertain grasp of complicated policy issues in favor of highlighting his winning personality. A special TV address helped Senator Richard M. Nixon of California, Ike's vice-presidential running mate, rescue his political career after allegations of having received illegal campaign funds threatened his place on the ticket.

The first military leader to gain the presidency since Ulysses S. Grant (1869–1877), Eisenhower could claim a great personal victory. The Eisenhower–Nixon ticket rolled up almost 7 million more popular votes than did the Democrats and carried the Electoral College ballots by a nearly five-to-one margin. The Republican Party, however, made only modest gains. It managed a single-vote majority in the Senate and an eight-vote edge in the House of Representatives. The New Deal political coalition still survived, even if it showed increasing signs of fraying in the South. There, some of the segregationist vote that had gone to the Dixiecrats in 1948 began moving toward the Republicans, and Eisenhower carried four states in the Democratic Party's once "Solid South" in 1952.

CONCLUSION

An emphasis on safeguarding national security reshaped national life during the immediate postwar years. As worsening relations between the United States and the Soviet Union produced a cold war, the Truman administration pursued anti-communist initiatives that expanded the power of the government, particularly the executive branch. The militarization of foreign policy intensified when the United States, after going to war in Korea in 1950, began implementing the assumptions laid out in NSC-68.

Americans also debated how best to safeguard security and calm cultural anxieties on the home front. The New Deal vision faded, but Truman's Fair Deal promised that new economic wisdom would guarantee economic growth and thereby provide tax revenues to expand domestic programs. The Truman administration also expressed support, even when it alienated many white southerners, for a civil rights agenda. Cultural change added to national security concerns in contributing to the Great Fear.

Although the 1952 election of Dwight Eisenhower gave the Republicans the presidency for the first time in two decades, Eisenhower's personal appeal did not signal an end to the Democratic coalition that had held sway since the 1930s.

28

AMERICA AT MIDCENTURY, 1953–1963

ONTAINMENT OF COMMUNISM continued to dominate American foreign policy between 1953 and 1963. Republican President Dwight David Eisenhower modulated the pitch of the anticommunist rhetoric, but both he and his Democratic successor, John F. Kennedy, pursued new ways to fight the cold war.

At home, Ike and JFK supported, with differing degrees of enthusiasm, social and economic programs that had been initiated during the 1930s and 1940s. Eisenhower's administration accepted the key elements of the New Deal: the economic regulatory structure, the safety net of Social Security, the ability of labor to bargain collectively, and the building of infrastructure projects. Calling Eisenhower's policies too cautious, Kennedy came to the presidency promising more vigorous governmental action at home and, especially, overseas.

Sustained economic growth encouraged talk about an age of "affluence." Economic data bolstered optimism. Between 1941 and 1950, the real income of the bottom 50 percent of the population grew by more than one-third. The bottom 20 percent saw its income rise by a higher percentage than the top 20 percent. Economic growth simultaneously generated discontent, particularly over conformity, restive young people, and commercial mass culture. At the same time, continued economic disparities and racial discrimination sparked debate over greater use of governmental power—and the meanings of liberty and equality.

CHRONOLOGY

1953	Eisenhower becomes president
	Korean War ends
1954	New Look in foreign policy unveiled
	Brown cases decided
	Geneva Peace Accords for Indochina signed
1955	Montgomery bus boycott begins
	National Review founded
1956	Federal Highway Act passed
	Eisenhower reelected
1957	Eisenhower sends troops to Little Rock
	Congress passes a Civil Rights Act
	Soviet Union sends *Sputniks* into orbit
1958	National Defense Education Act passes
1959	Khrushchev visits United States
	Castro overthrows Batista in Cuba
1960	Kennedy elected president
1961	Bay of Pigs invasion fails
	Berlin Wall goes up
1962	Cuban Missile Crisis endangers world
1963	Civil rights groups hold March on Washington
	Kennedy assassinated

REORIENTING CONTAINMENT, 1953–1960

The U.S. strategy for safeguarding national security by containing communism shifted emphasis during the 1950s. Bipolar confrontation between the United States and the Soviet Union over European issues gave way to greater reliance on nuclear weaponry and on power plays in the so-called Third World: the Middle East, Asia, Latin America, and Africa.

Eisenhower Takes Command   Eisenhower honored his campaign pledge to visit Korea and help end the military conflict there. Anxious to conclude matters, Eisenhower even began to hint about using nuclear weapons if diplomacy moved too slowly. In July 1953, the warring parties signed a truce, and a conflict that claimed the lives of more than 2 million Asians, mostly noncombatants, and 53,000 Americans finally ended. A formal peace treaty remained unsigned, however, and the heavily fortified 38th parallel divided the two Koreas.

At home, Ike patiently wrested control of the national security issue from more militant anticommunists. Congress exceeded the wishes of the Eisenhower administration when enacting the Communist Control Act of 1954, which barred the American Communist Party from running candidates in elections and extended the provisions of the Subversive Activities Control Act of 1950. With a GOP president in the White House, however, Republicans began turning away from the confrontational styles of anticommunist politics associated with Joe McCarthy.

McCarthy finally careened out of control. He railed against the Eisenhower administration and about supposed subversives in the U.S. Army. He denounced as "unfit to wear the uniform" a well-respected general who had denied his charges. A special Senate committee began investigating the sensational allegations, and these "Army-McCarthy Hearings" turned into a television miniseries that began in April of 1954. Under the glare of TV lights, McCarthy seemed a crude bully, hurling slanders in every direction. And his habit of interrupting the proceedings with a "point of order" made for tiresome television. In late 1954, McCarthy's colleagues in the Senate, including half of his fellow Republicans, voted to "condemn" him for "unbecoming" conduct. Three years later, McCarthy died, still in office but exiled from the national spotlight. Eisenhower's decision to allow McCarthy to self-destruct, rather than to confront him head-on, seemed vindicated.

Indeed, presidential historians now generally see Eisenhower as a skilled chief executive. By expanding the White House staff, he could employ the power of the presidency while seeming to do relatively little. Eisenhower, in the words of one scholar, conducted a "hidden hand presidency." Ike encouraged the idea that his aides directed domestic matters. Recognizing the importance of regular TV appearances, Ike honed his folksy image and became a capable television performer.

The New Look, Global Alliances, and Summitry

Working behind the scenes, Eisenhower collaborated with his national security advisers to reinforce executive branch leadership in foreign policy. He allowed Secretary of State John Foster Dulles to warn, repeatedly, that a new administration might seek to "roll back," rather than simply to contain, communism. The excesses of legislators like McCarthy helped the White House justify its claims for a constitutional privilege to withhold national security materials from Congress and to beat back a proposed constitutional amendment to limit presidential power in foreign affairs. Eisenhower also extended Harry Truman's earlier programs of domestic surveillance and continued a secret initiative to develop new aerial surveillance reconnaissance.

The Eisenhower administration also secretly reviewed overall military policy. It initially decided to rein in military spending by introducing a **New Look**, which emphasized nuclear weaponry and airpower as a way to halt spiraling expenditures. The former general and his allies in the military recognized that the cold war would not end any time soon and that they needed a national security policy that would be affordable over the long haul.

Eisenhower's New Look became associated with the doctrine of **massive retaliation**. In early 1954, John Foster Dulles announced that the United States reserved the right to respond to military aggression "with means of our own choosing." This thinly veiled threat to unleash U.S. nuclear weaponry was aimed at keeping the Soviets in check. To widen the U.S. nuclear umbrella, Eisenhower expanded NATO to include West Germany and added other mutual defense pacts with noncommunist nations in Central and Southeast Asia.

The Eisenhower administration soon began augmenting the New Look and massive retaliation by emphasizing more flexible approaches to national security policy. It embraced covert action and economic pressure as useful strategies. The administration also elevated psychological warfare and informational programs into additional weapons of the cold war. The government-run Voice of America extended its radio broadcasts globally. Washington secretly funded Radio Free Europe, Radio Liberty (beamed to the Soviet Union), and Radio Asia. In 1953, Eisenhower persuaded Congress to create the United States Information Agency (USIA) to coordinate anticommunist propaganda campaigns.

One piece of this cultural offensive fought the cold war with jazz. Beginning in 1955, Willis Conover hosted a program that hailed jazz as "music of freedom" and reached more than 100 million listeners around the globe. After Conover's death in 1996, an admiring obituary quipped that his show would "bombard Budapest with Billy Taylor, strafe Poland with Oscar Peterson and drop John Coltrane on Moscow." American mass culture in all its forms circled the globe.

The United States and the USSR, hoping to improve relations, began holding high-level "summit meetings" in 1955. In May, U.S. and Soviet leaders agreed to end the occupation of Austria and to transform it into a neutral nation. Two months later, the United States, the Soviet Union, Britain, and France met in Geneva, Switzerland, and inaugurated cultural exchanges. During fall 1959, hoping to heal a rift over the future of divided Berlin, Khrushchev travelled to the United States. He called on a farm family in Iowa, visited Hollywood, and toured Disneyland. Although a 1960 summit meeting in Paris fell apart after the Soviets shot down an American U-2 spy plane over their territory, the tone of cold war rhetoric became somewhat less strident during Eisenhower's two-term presidency.

The United States and the Soviet Union also began negotiations over their already vast stockpiles of nuclear weapons. Eisenhower's "Open Skies" initiative of 1955 proposed mutual reconnaissance flights over each other's territory to verify efforts at reduction. The Soviets balked, but some progress was made in limiting atomic testing. Responding to the health hazards of radioactive fallout, both nations slowed above-ground testing and discussed a broader test-ban agreement.

For some Americans, these efforts came too late. Documents finally declassified in the 1980s confirmed that people who had lived or worked downwind from nuclear test sites during the 1940s and 1950s suffered a number of atomic-related illnesses. More than one-third of the crew that worked on the Hollywood movie *The Conqueror* (1956), shot in a downwind area of Utah, contracted or died of cancer. Subsequent revelations also showed that the government had secretly experimented with radioactive materials on unsuspecting citizens.

Meanwhile, events in Eastern Europe tested the likelihood of the United States and the Soviet Union clashing militarily in this region. Dissidents within the Soviet-dominated "satellite" countries resented their badly managed communist economies and detested their police-state regimes. Insurgents in Poland, seizing on hints that the Soviet Union might relax its heavy hand, staged a rebellion in June 1956. They forced the Soviets to accept an old foe of Moscow as Poland's head of state.

Hungarians then rallied in support of Imre Nagy, a communist-nationalist who promised a multiparty political system for his country. Soviet military forces moved against the new government, and Hungarian insurgents appealed to the United States for assistance. Despite Secretary of State Dulles's rhetoric about "rolling back" Soviet power in Eastern Europe, strategists at the Pentagon recognized the danger of mounting any military operation so close to Soviet territory. Soviet armies brutally crushed the uprising in Hungary and killed thousands, including Nagy.

Covert Action and Economic Leverage   The U.S. campaign to contain communism increasingly shifted toward the Third World, with covert action and economic pressure as primary tools. These approaches, less visible and less expensive than military deployments, also seemed less likely to provoke political controversy at home or a showdown with the Soviets abroad.

The CIA, headed by Allen Dulles, brother of the secretary of state, played a key role. In 1953 the CIA helped engineer the election of the anticommunist Ramón Magsaysay as president of the Philippines. That same year, the CIA facilitated a coup in Iran, overthrowing Mohammed Mossadegh's constitutional (and left-leaning) government and restoring Shah (emperor) Reza Pahlavi to power. The increasingly dictatorial leader ensured that Iran would remain allied with Washington and supportive of American oil interests. In 1954 the CIA spearheaded a successful plot to topple President Jacobo Arbenz Guzmán's elected government in Guatemala. Officials in Washington and executives of the United Fruit Company desired the ouster of Arbenz, whose broad support included that of Guatemala's communist party. The CIA strategy included a full-scale propaganda offensive that helped undermine Arbenz's popular appeal among Guatemalans.

Impressed by these covert operations, the National Security Council widened the CIA's mandate. By 1961 the CIA deployed approximately 15,000 agents, as compared to about 6,000 only eight years earlier, around the world.

Eisenhower also employed economic strategies—trade and aid—to contain communism and win allies. Governmental initiatives sought to open new opportunities for American enterprises overseas, discourage other countries from adopting state-directed economic systems, and encourage expanded trade ties. Supporters of these efforts credited U.S. policy with promoting greater stability in recipient countries. U.S. military aid to the Third World nations also rose sharply between 1953 and 1963. This buildup of armaments provided the United States with stronger anticommunist allies but also contributed to the development of military dictatorships.

The Third World   In Latin America, the Eisenhower White House gravitated toward dictatorial regimes that welcomed U.S. economic investment and opposed leftist movements. Such policies encouraged anti-American sentiment, and events in Cuba dramatized the growing hostility. In late 1959, a revolutionary movement led by Fidel Castro toppled dictator Fulgencio Batista's pro-U.S. regime and pledged to reduce Cuba's dependence on the United States. The Eisenhower administration responded with an economic boycott. Castro turned to the Soviet Union, openly embraced communism, squashed dissent at home, and pledged to support Cuban-style insurgencies throughout Latin America. The CIA pondered how best to hamstring, and then eliminate, Castro.

In the Middle East, distrust of nationalism and neutralism shaped U.S. policy. In 1954, when Colonel Gamal Abdel Nasser led a successful military coup in Egypt against a corrupt monarchy, he promised to rescue other Arab nations from European domination and guide them toward "positive neutralism" in the cold war. Nasser denounced Israel; boosted Egypt's economic and military power; extended diplomatic recognition to the People's Republic of China; and purchased advanced weapons from communist Czechoslovakia.

The Eisenhower administration viewed Nasser's policies as neither positive nor neutral. It cancelled loans for building the Aswan Dam, a project designed to improve agriculture along the Nile River and provide power for new Egyptian industries. Nasser responded, in July 1956, by seizing the British-controlled Suez Canal. British forces, joined by those of France and Israel, attacked Egypt in October and took back the canal.

Eisenhower distrusted Nasser but also opposed Britain's attempt to retain its imperial position. Denouncing the Anglo-French-Israeli action, he threatened to destabilize Britain's currency unless the invasion ended. Eventually, a plan supported by the United States and the UN gave Egypt control over the Suez Canal, but U.S. influence in the area suffered as the Soviet Union underwrote construction of the Aswan Dam.

The Eisenhower administration feared the spread of "Nasserism" throughout the energy-rich Middle East. In spring 1957, the **Eisenhower Doctrine** pledged that the United States would defend Middle Eastern countries "against overt armed aggression from any nation controlled by international communism." When governments in Lebanon and Jordan faced revolts by domestic forces friendly to Nasser, Eisenhower dispatched U.S. Marines to Lebanon, and Britain helped Jordan's King Hussein retain his throne.

Eisenhower's effort to thwart communism and neutralism in the Third World set the stage for his most substantial commitment—in Indochina. During the Korean War, the Truman administration had increased economic aid for France's war to retain its colony in Indochina against a communist-nationalist movement led by Ho Chi Minh. Eisenhower continued Truman's policy.

During the early spring of 1954, Ho's forces surrounded French troops in the valley of Dien Bien Phu. France surrendered and abandoned the colony it had created in 1887. The **Geneva Peace Accords of 1954**, which the Eisenhower administration refused to sign, divided French Indochina into three new nations: Laos, Cambodia, and Vietnam. The accords temporarily split Vietnam, at the 17th parallel, into two jurisdictions—North Vietnam and South Vietnam—until a subsequent election could unify the country under a single government. Ho Chi Minh and his communist allies in China and the Soviet Union accepted this settlement, confident that Ho would win the election, scheduled for 1956.

Eisenhower's advisers feared that a communist electoral victory in Vietnam might set off a geopolitical chain reaction that could "endanger the stability and security" of noncommunist nations throughout Asia, a formulation known as the **"domino theory."** After Ho Chi Minh's communist government consolidated control over the Democratic Republic of Vietnam (North Vietnam), Eisenhower ordered covert operations and economic programs to forestall Ho from assuming control of a unified Vietnam. The CIA staged a rigged 1955 election that installed Ngo Dinh Diem as the first president of the Republic of Vietnam (South Vietnam).

An anticommunist Catholic, Ngo Dinh Diem renounced the Geneva Peace Accords and the election intended to create a unified government. He consolidated his political support, augmented his military forces, and cracked down on his opponents. Diem's policies cost him support inside South Vietnam, especially among the sizable Buddhist population, and he became increasingly dependent on the United States. Although Eisenhower feared that direct U.S. military involvement in South Vietnam would be a "tragedy," he increased aid, dispatched military advisers, and tied America's policy to Diem's shaky political fortunes.

The Eisenhower administration sent billions of dollars and hundreds of military advisers to prop up Diem's government. Meanwhile, in early 1959, North Vietnam finally decided to send troops as well as supplies into the South. They traveled along a shifting route of highways and roads that became known as the "Ho Chi Minh Trail." Any decision about whether Eisenhower's commitments would ever lead the United States to intervene with its own military forces would fall to his successors.

Affluence—A "People of Plenty"

In his farewell address of 1961, Dwight Eisenhower warned that the greatest danger to the United States was not communism but the nation's own **military-industrial complex**. This term signified an informal relationship among military, political, and economic elites committed to expanding national security capabilities. This complex, the former general warned, threatened to so accelerate the costs of cold war containment that the burden of military expenditures could eventually harm the U.S. domestic economy.

Eisenhower's speech masked certain ironies. Most obviously, his administration, while trying to contain costs, failed to prevent ever-larger sums of money from flowing to the military. Moreover, Ike's selection of corporate executives to head the Department of Defense seemingly dramatized the very same linkage his farewell address would later decry.

In 1940, the United States had still teetered on the brink of economic depression. Twenty years later, it could claim a GNP more than five times that of Great Britain and roughly 10 times that of Japan. National security policies facilitated U.S. access to raw materials and energy. Government spending for these same policies, what economists sometimes called "military Keynesianism," also pumped money into the economy. By 1955, military expenditures accounted for about 10 percent of the GNP.

Economic Growth   The post-1953 decade, despite three brief recessions, would mark the midpoint of a period of steady economic growth that would eventually stretch from the Second World War to the early 1970s. Corporations turned out vast quantities of consumer goods and enjoyed rising profits. The label "Made in America" announced both the quality of particular products and the economic power of the United States.

Newer American-based industries, such as those involving chemicals and electronics, dominated world markets. Corning Glass reported that most of its sales in the mid-1950s came from products that had been unknown in 1940. General Electric proclaimed, "Progress is our most important product."

The new suburbs highlighted the fruits of this booming economy. Because these outlying areas invariably lacked adequate mass transit, life revolved around the automobile. Car buying expanded during the 1950s as the two-car family and new suburban shopping malls, surrounded by acres of free parking, became tangible symbols of economic growth. Kitchen appliances, television sets, and automobiles supported the claim that Americans were, in the words of historian David Potter, a "people of plenty." *Fortune* magazine celebrated "The Rich Middle-Income Class." Harvard economist John Kenneth Galbraith reached the best-seller lists with a book entitled *The Affluent Society* (1958).

The term *affluence* nicely captured the dominant vision that celebrated constant economic growth and steady improvement of living standards as a uniquely American way of life. The gulf between rich and poor no longer seemed to be between people with cars and those without them, but between people with Cadillacs and Lincolns and those with Fords and Chevrolets. "Luxury has reached the masses," proclaimed *Fortune*.

Highways and Waterways   Eisenhower advocated the importance of a balanced federal budget but endorsed several costly new programs. He supported the **Highway Act of 1956**, citing national security considerations. Financed largely by a national tax on gasoline, the act funded a nationwide system of limited-access expressways. Touted as the largest public works project in world history, this program delighted the oil, concrete, and tire industries; provided steady work for construction firms and labor unions; and boosted the interstate trucking business. It confirmed the victory of the automobile over competing modes of surface transportation.

The White House also supported expensive water-diversion projects in the West. The Army Corps of Engineers and the Bureau of Reclamation, governmental agencies with powerful supporters in business and in Congress, spent billions of dollars on dams, irrigation canals, and reservoirs. Irrigation turned desert into cropland, and elaborate pumping systems even forced rivers to flow uphill. By 1960, much of the West enjoyed access to trillions of gallons of water per year, and governmental expenditures encouraged substantial economic growth in the "Sun Belt states" of Texas, California, and Arizona.

These water projects came at a price. Technologically complicated and costly to build, they spawned complex bureaucracies to operate them. Local communities lost power to government agencies and large-scale entrepreneurs, who pushed aside smaller farmers and ranchers. American Indian tribes found sections of their land being flooded for reservoirs or purchased by agribusinesses. These vast projects—which diverted surface waters, tapped into groundwater tables, and dotted the West with dams and reservoirs—also produced ecological problems. They degraded habitats and contributed to the buildup of salt by-products in the water and the soil. Some scientists began to warn about the overuse of toxic pesticides.

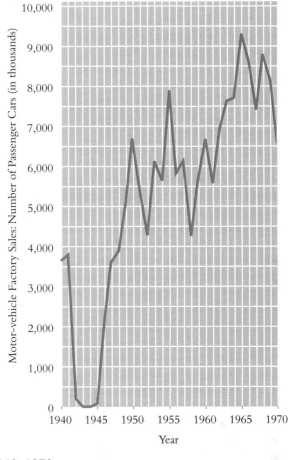

Auto Sales, 1940–1970

Eisenhower took a personal interest in agricultural policy. Although the number of farms plummeted during the 1950s, new machines, corporate-style operations, and hybrid seeds spurred greater production. As overproduction drove down commodity prices, government support programs propped up farm incomes. The idea that Washington should guarantee farmers "parity," or a fair price for their labor, remained the centerpiece of federal agricultural policy. The Eisenhower administration also tried to increase agricultural exports and began the "Soil Bank Program," which paid farmers for taking land out of production.

Labor-Management Accord

Labor leaders were coming to believe that cooperation with corporate management could promote union stability and political influence. Roughly 35 percent of nonagricultural workers belonged to a union during the 1950s. Taking its cue from the United Auto Workers (UAW), one of the most militant unions back in the 1930s, organized labor agreed to bargain aggressively on wages and fringe benefits but to defer to management on broader issues and to disavow militant tactics such as wildcat strikes. To oversee this new labor-management accord, both sides looked to the federal government's National Labor Relations Board (NLRB). Meanwhile, in 1955, the American Federation of Labor (AFL) and the Congress of Industrial Organizations (CIO), long at odds, merged. The 1950s thus seemed to signal an end to the kind of labor-capital conflict that had marked the 1930s and late 1940s.

Business leaders generally applauded the new direction. *Fortune* magazine noted that corporations paid a price in more costly employee benefits and higher wages, but that they "got a bargain" on the larger issues of labor peace and managerial power. The labor-management accord also divided the industrial workforce because workers in more profitable sectors could bargain more effectively than those in sectors with smaller profit margins.

Some nonunionized businesses voluntarily expanded benefits for their workers. Companies such as Sears and Eastman Kodak encouraged a cooperative corporate culture, which included health and pension plans, profit-sharing arrangements, and social programs. Some firms created private recreational parks for exclusive use by their employees. Satisfying workers, corporate executives reasoned, would reduce the appeal of both unionization and governmental regulatory measures.

During the 1950s and early 1960s real wages (what workers make after adjusting their paychecks for inflation) rose steadily, and jobs were plentiful. The frequency of industrial accidents dropped; fringe benefits (health insurance, paid vacation time, and retirement plans) improved; and job security was generally high. Still, most unionized workers lived in only 10 states and companies in some areas of union strength, such as the Northeast, were moving jobs to states in the South, where unions were weak.

Political Pluralism   Economic growth also gained credit for producing political stability. After the conflicts of the 1930s, the disruptions during the Second World War, and the Great Fear of the early cold war period, the 1950s seemed an era of relative tranquility. An increasingly prosperous nation, most observers agreed, would effectively mute social conflict and eventually help solve major problems. The future, according to one prominent sociologist, would see the end of clashing political ideologies.

According to this dominant viewpoint, which political scientists called "pluralism" (or "interest-group pluralism"), American politics featured a roughly equal bargaining process among well-organized interest groups. John Kenneth Galbraith coined the term *countervailing power* when claiming that labor unions, consumer lobbies, farm organizations, and other groups could check the desires of giant corporations. No single group could dictate terms to the others, celebrants of political pluralism claimed, because so many interests felt so securely empowered. Pluralists shrugged off signs of decline in political participation, clearly evident in how few people cast ballots on election days, by arguing that voter behavior showed widespread satisfaction with how well the process of political pluralism worked.

In addition to praising the process, pluralists praised the results. Short-term conflicts over specific issues would never disappear, but America's growing economy would continue to help moderate political passions and point warring interests toward agreement on fundamental arrangements. As a professor at Harvard Law School put it, constant economic growth meant that "in any conflict of interest," it was "always possible to work out a solution" because an expanding economy guaranteed that any settlement would leave all interests "better off than before."

A Religious People   Many observers professed an analogous faith in religious pluralism. Congress, as part of the crusade against "atheistic communism," constructed a nondenominational prayer room on Capitol Hill; added the phrase "under God" to the Pledge of Allegiance; and declared the phrase "In God We Trust" as the nation's official motto. In the view of pluralists, intense religious allegiances no longer divided people as much as in the past. President Eisenhower declared that "our government makes no sense unless it is founded in a deeply felt religious faith—and I don't care what it is."

Religious leaders echoed the theme of pluralism. Will Herberg's *Protestant-Catholic-Jew* (1955) argued that these three faiths were really "saying the same thing" in affirming the "spiritual ideals" and "moral values" of the American way of life. The rabbi who headed the Jewish Chaplain's Organization reassured Protestants and Catholics that they and their Jewish neighbors shared "the same rich heritage of the Old Testament ... the sanctity of the Ten Commandments, the wisdom of the prophets, and the brotherhood of man." A 1954 survey claimed that more than 95 percent of the population identified with one of the three major faiths, and religious commentators praised how the "Judeo-Christian tradition" enriched American life.

This tradition could also produce religious celebrities. The Baptist evangelist Billy Graham achieved superstar status during the 1950s. Norman Vincent Peale, a minister in the Reformed Church of America, sold millions of books which declared that belief in a higher power could bring "health, happiness, and goodness" to daily life. His most famous volume, *The Power of Positive Thinking* (1952), remained a best seller throughout the 1950s. The Catholic bishop Fulton J. Sheen moved from radio to TV during the 1950s, and won an Emmy Award for hosting a prime-time program entitled *Life Is Worth Living*.

Peale, Sheen, and Graham generally identified their religious ideals with conservative, anticommunist causes, but an emphasis on religious faith could be found all across the political spectrum. Dorothy Day, a Catholic who had been involved in community activism since the early 1930s, continued to crusade for world peace and for domestic programs aimed at redistributing wealth. Leaders from all three major religions supported civil rights efforts. Billy Graham, for example, refused to preach to racially segregated audiences.

DISCONTENTS OF AFFLUENCE

Alongside the celebration of economic growth, there were widely expressed fears about the impact of the new material bounty and about the celebration of economic growth, political pluralism, and religious faith. Much of the discontent revolved around several interrelated issues: the alleged threats posed by conformity, restive young people, and mass culture; the persistence of discrimination; and the effects of socioeconomic inequality.

Conformity in an Affluent Society

The least tangible concern involved "conformity." Affluence appeared to be undermining the nation's tradition of individualism, a peril most evident in the new suburbs. Suburbanites, according to a popular protest song, lived in "little boxes" that all "looked just the same." Working in the same satirical vein, the comedian Mort Sahl pioneered a form of stand-up comedy that lampooned people who were filling their "little boxes" with piles of consumer goods. Hi-fi speakers were becoming so large, according to one of his routines, that people might soon be living inside them and converting their house into part of their sound system.

Male social comics such as Mort Sahl implicitly identified their routines with other cultural critics. J. D. Salinger's iconic novel *Catcher in the Rye* (1951) takes a tragicomic look at Holden Caulfield, a rebellious high school student, who decries the conformists and "phonies" that he feels crush his spirit. *Rebel without a Cause* (1955) featured James Dean as another high school rebel who challenges a conformist adult world that is "trying to kill me," at least emotionally. The movie sympathetically portrays how growing up in the new suburbia of the 1950s could produce an understandable restiveness that adults too often mistook for "juvenile delinquency."

In *The Organization Man* (1956), the sociologist William H. Whyte, Jr., indicted corporate culture for also contributing to conformity. Whyte saw corporate employees deferring to the dictates of their bosses at the expense of their own wishes and values. Journalist Vance Packard's best-selling *The Hidden Persuaders* (1957) criticized the advertising industry's calculated appeals to the insecurities of consumers for encouraging conformist behavior. David Riesman, another sociologist, offered a broader critique of conformity in *The Lonely Crowd* (1950). This book envisioned a shift from an "inner-directed" culture, in which people looked to themselves and their immediate families for their sense of identity and self-worth, to an "other-directed" one, in which people looked to others for approval and increasingly measured their worth against mass cultural imagery. *The Lonely Crowd* claimed that *Tootle the Engine,* a popular children's book, was part of the mass culture that taught baby boomers conformist values. After Tootle shows a preference for jumping the rails and frolicking in the fields, intense pressure from his community gets him "back on the tracks." If he remains on the straight and narrow, following lines laid down by others, a bright future seems assured.

Critics such as Whyte, Packard, and Riesman highlighted signs of conformity among middle-class white men, but Betty Friedan warned about an analogous malaise among white women. Top business executives expected middle-class wives to help their husbands deal with the demands of corporate life, and many women found themselves trapped in a stultifying sphere of domestic obligations. A conformist "feminine mystique," Friedan wrote, stifled many women's individuality and power.

Other critics offered even harsher judgments. According to the sociologist C. Wright Mills, increasingly regimented work routines and meaningless leisure-time activities rarely produced genuine satisfaction. Mills also argued that a "power elite"—composed of corporate executives, military planners, political leaders, prominent academics, and media celebrities—set the agenda for public policy discussions. This undemocratic group dominated decisions about national security matters and domestic spending priorities.

Split-Level Living.
This 1960 cartoon, by the
Washington Post's
"Herblock" (Herbert
Block), illustrates the
growing critique of
Eisenhower era social
policy. While
suburbanites enjoy new
affluence in a split-level
home, public services
and distressed people
remain underfunded.

The "Beat movement," a loosely connected group of writers and poets, denied that either affluence or conventional spiritual ideals of the 1950s provided fulfillment. The Beats claimed that consumer goods and technology condemned most people to wander through alienated lives feeling oppressed, emotionally crippled, or just plain bored. Beat writers such as Jack Kerouac, author of *On the Road* (1957), praised nonconformists for challenging settled routines and seeking more instinctual and sensual ways of living. Beat poet Allen Ginsberg's *Howl* (1956) decried soulless materialism and puritanical moral codes. Ginsberg celebrated the kind of personal freedom that he found in drugs, mysticism, and same-sex love affairs.

Restive Youth   The restiveness among many young people drew attention. *Seduction of the Innocent* (1954), by the psychologist Frederick Wertham, blamed comic books featuring images of sex and violent crime for stimulating social unrest and juvenile delinquency. Responding to legislation by some U.S. cities and to calls for federal regulation, the comic book industry drafted its own self-censorship code. Publishers who followed the code's guidelines for portraying violence and deviant behavior could display a seal of approval. The "great comic book scare" soon faded away.

Other worrisome signs persisted, however. In 1954, Elvis Presley, a former truck driver from Memphis, enjoyed a string of "rock 'n' roll" hits on the tiny Sun record label. Presley's sensual, electric stage presence thrilled his young admirers and outraged critics. Presley and other youthful exponents of fifties rock—including Buddy Holly from West Texas, Richard Valenzuela (Richie Valens) from East Los Angeles, Frankie Lymon from Spanish Harlem, and "Little Richard" (Penniman) from Georgia—leaped over cultural and ethnic barriers. They reshaped older musical forms, especially African American rhythm and blues and the "hillbilly" music of southern whites, into new sounds. Rock 'n' rollers claimed to sing about the hopes and fears of the millions of their young fans. They celebrated the joy of "having a ball tonight"; decried the pain of the "summertime blues"; complained about the torment of being "a teenager in love"; and preached the promise of deliverance, through the power of rock, from "the days of old." Songs such as "Roll over Beethoven" by Chuck Berry became powerful teen anthems.

Guardians of more genteel cultural forms denounced rock 'n' roll as an assault on the very idea of music. Even its name, these critics complained, brazenly appealed to raging teenage hormones. Religious groups denounced rock as the "Devil's music"; anticommunists detected a covert Red strategy to corrupt youth; and segregationists saw rock as part of a plot to encourage "race-mixing." The dangers of rock 'n' roll seemed on display in *The Blackboard Jungle* (1955), a movie about a racially mixed group of sexually active students who defy adult authority and terrorize high school classrooms. Rock 'n' roll music spoke, however, to the concerns of its young fans. Chuck Berry's "School Days" challenged pieties about the benefits of schooling, as he sang of bored teenagers riding around "with no particular place to go." This kind of social criticism in songs anticipated the more overtly rebellious music of the 1960s.

At the same time, rock music and the larger youth culture of the 1950s merged into that era's general affluence. Sun Records, lacking sufficient capital to distribute Presley's hits and promote his image, sold his contract to RCA. Colonel Tom Parker, his personal promoter, soon had the Elvis brand affixed to everything from 45 rpm records to Hollywood musicals. Record companies and the new Top 40 radio stations saw teenagers, with their part-time jobs and their own allowances, as a market segment worth targeting. They promoted performers who exalted the pursuit of "fun, fun, fun," which apparently required the latest in "cool" clothes, late-model automobiles, and rock 'n' roll records.

The Critique of Mass Culture Concern about conformity and youth culture figured in the broader **mass-culture critique** of the 1950s. Anxiety about the decline of individualism and the rise of disruptive young people became linked to fears that the "hidden persuaders" of the commercial culture industry could reach millions of people with standardized imagery and messages. Critics worried that "bad" art—seemingly evident in comics and rock 'n' roll—would eventually purge anything "good" from the cultural marketplace. They further warned that the superficial imagery manufactured for a "mass" national audience could wipe out vibrant local and regional traditions.

Network television, dominated by three large corporations (NBC, CBS, and ABC) and sustained by advertising revenue, provided a prominent target for this mass-culture critique. Picturing millions of passive viewers gathered around "the boob tube," critics decried both the quality and the presumed impact of mass-produced TV programming. By the late 1950s, the television networks were stocking their prime-time hours with western-themed series (about a mythical Old West) and staged quiz programs (whose contestants had been supplied the answers that they pretended to be puzzling over). Independent stations without network ties programmed the cultural leftovers: ancient B movies from Hollywood's vaults, cheaply produced adventure series, and amateurish local programming. The head of the Federal Communications Commission (FCC) would soon denounce TV as a "vast wasteland."

Critics also disliked how the "boob tube" changed the fabric of everyday life. Architects rearranged living space so that the TV set could become the focal point of home life. New products—such as the frozen TV dinner, the TV tray, the recliner chair, and *TV Guide* magazine—became extensions of television culture.

The mass culture that critics decried, however, was embedded within the economic system and the pluralist political process they celebrated. If, for example, Congress legislated against "dangerous" comic books, its censorship might end up curtailing free expression. If local communities were to step in, the results might be even worse. The prospect of southern segregationists confiscating civil rights literature, or local censorship boards banning books by celebrated authors or "art films" from Europe, hardly appealed to the cosmopolitan critics of mass culture. Their extensive critique seemed short on solutions and offered nothing to halt the flood of consumer products and forms of entertainment aimed at an ever-expanding popular audience.

DEBATING THE ROLE OF GOVERNMENT

Although Eisenhower occasionally hinted that he favored rolling back the New and Fair Deals, he actually presided over a modest expansion of earlier initiatives: a broader Social Security system, a higher minimum wage, better unemployment benefits, and a new Department of Health, Education, and Welfare (HEW). Eisenhower liked to call his approach "modern Republicanism."

The New Conservatism   Eisenhower's brand of Republicanism angered members of a political movement eventually called the "new conservatism." It drew its energy from Republicans who conceded Eisenhower's popularity but questioned his commitment to core GOP principles. Eisenhower appeared to be allowing too many congressional Republicans to cross the aisle and support Democratic-backed spending programs.

Arizona's Senator Barry Goldwater emerged as the key political spokesperson for the new conservatism. After he won a second term in the U.S. Senate in 1958, a year when several other prominent GOP conservatives lost, a national magazine hailed him as "The Glittering Mr. Goldwater." A slim, ghostwritten book, *The Conscience of a Conservative* (1960), summarized Goldwater's critique. By refusing to take stronger military measures against the Soviet Union and by not making "victory the goal" of U.S. policy, Eisenhower was endangering the nation's security.

Goldwater portrayed most domestic programs, including those supported by Eisenhower, as threats to individual liberty and as steps toward national bankruptcy. The GOP needed a clean break from the Democratic Party's "New Deal antics" and Ike's "dime store New Deal," the senator charged.

For economic ideas, the new conservatism looked to Europeans, such as Friedrich von Hayek, and to their American disciples, particularly Milton Friedman. Once a Keynesian, the quick-witted, fast-talking Friedman had later reoriented his economic ideas in a libertarian direction. Governmental action, he argued, generally interfered with self-correcting marketplace forces and thus generated additional problems rather than genuine solutions. When government absolutely needed to act, as it should have done more forcefully during the Great Depression, its touch must be as light as possible. Friedman's impressive list of popular and scholarly publications showed that he could write as clearly, and as quickly, as he spoke. Headquartered at the University of Chicago, he helped symbolize a persistent pattern: Economists generally sympathetic to Keynesianism tended to migrate to institutions on either coast, while those embracing more free market approaches generally gravitated toward the heartland.

Meanwhile, Friedman's eventual ally, the author-publisher William F. Buckley, Jr., was framing a broad ideological platform for the new conservatism. In *God and Man at Yale* (1952), the devoutly Roman Catholic Buckley attacked what he saw as a "collectivist" and anti-religious tilt in higher education. A second book, *McCarthy and His Enemies* (1954), defended the controversial senator. Then, in 1955, Buckley began his most ambitious enterprise: a new conservative magazine, the **National Review**. This publication avoided the anti-Semitism of some old-line conservatives and adopted an organizational strategy for the long run. To this end, Buckley joined other conservatives in establishing Young Americans for Freedom (YAF) in 1960, several years before similar college-based political organizations emerged on the political left.

Buckley's group adopted another long-term approach to building a conservative movement, "fusionism." The *National Review* featured a creative tension that fused three broad constituencies: "traditionalist" conservatives, who insisted that social stability depended on the educated, talented few, such as themselves, dominating the nation's institutions; "libertarians," who favored drastically limiting the power of government; and staunch anticommunists who endorsed unleashing U.S. military power against the Soviets.

The *National Review* attracted an eclectic group of writers who collaborated on developing ideas that could shape the new conservatism. Any program for coexistence with communism, according to the magazine's manifesto, was "neither desirable nor possible, nor honorable." Excessive "bipartisanship" was robbing politics of necessary conflict, while "Big Brother government" and "union monopolies" were threatening economic freedom. The *National Review* also sought to cover cultural affairs from a conservative perspective that made "excellence (rather than 'newness')" and "honest intellectual combat (rather than conformity)" its watchwords.

A zest for cultural combat animated other conservative projects. The writer Ayn Rand's fierce brand of secular libertarianism and commitment to sexual experimentation made her unwelcome at the staid *National Review*. Her novel *Atlas Shrugged* (1957), however, confirmed Rand's iconic status among libertarians, who endorsed her call for ignoring any "public good" and for advancing, instead, one's own self-interest. A number of conservative groups spread the religious ideals that Rand ridiculed. The Campus Crusade for Christ urged college students to live according to traditional religious ideals and to preach this message among their peers. Clarence Manion, a prominent Catholic Democrat, developed a forceful conservative presence on the radio dial, *The Manion Forum,* and helped spearhead an effort to draft Barry Goldwater to run as Eisenhower's successor in 1960.

Goldwater's western brand of conservatism spread across the new suburbs of the Sun Belt states. Many suburban conservatives derived their family incomes from high-tech jobs in the military-related sector and called for increased federal spending on national defense. On domestic issues, however, these "suburban warriors" championed a vision of more limited government and denounced "outside" authorities, both state and national, for infringing on the liberty and power of their local communities.

The Case for a More Active Government   While a new conservatism argued for scaling back the domestic role of government, a diverse group urged expanding the national government's reach, at home as well as overseas. When unemployment shot up during an economic downturn in 1958–1959, Keynesian economists ridiculed Eisenhower's commitment to a balanced budget. They called for greater government spending, even a temporary deficit, to stimulate economic activity. Even after economic conditions improved, Keynesians such as John Kenneth Galbraith and Paul Samuelson urged significant deficit spending as a spur to greater growth. During the 1950s, Samuelson's textbook (or a less-demanding knockoff) became the standard choice for younger college professors who taught introductory economics.

Other members of this group also criticized Eisenhower's national security policies for their timidity. The **Gaither Report** urged an immediate increase of about 25 percent in the Pentagon's budget. Prepared by analysts with ties to the defense industry and links to NSC-68, the Gaither Report also endorsed building fallout shelters, developing intercontinental ballistic missiles (ICBMs), and expanding conventional military forces.

Eisenhower reacted cautiously. Keeping his defense budget well below the levels critics proposed, he even reduced the size of several army and air force units. As a consequence of super-secret U-2 surveillance flights over the Soviet Union, Eisenhower knew that the Soviets were lagging behind, rather than outpacing, the United States in military capability. Their missile program, he also learned, featured a few well-publicized successes but many unreported problems.

Concerns about national security and calls for greater government spending also affected U.S. educational policies. Throughout the 1950s critics complained about schools imparting "life-adjustment" skills instead of teaching traditional academic subjects. The best-selling *Why Johnny Can't Read* (1956) anticipated books that asked why Johnny and his classmates couldn't add or subtract very well either, and why they lagged behind their counterparts in the Soviet Union in science. These critics urged more funding for public schools. Simultaneously, the nation's leading research universities sought greater federal aid for higher education, and prominent scientists urged expanded government funding for basic scientific research. The case for increased spending suddenly became more compelling when, in October 1957, the Soviets launched the world's first artificial satellite—a 22-inch sphere called *Sputnik* (Russian for "satellite") that circled the earth, initially accompanied by a "beep beep" soundtrack, for nearly three months.

A *Sputnik* **crisis** gripped Washington when a second Soviet satellite, carrying a dog, went into orbit in early November. The missile technology that lifted up the *Sputniks*, argued Eisenhower's critics, could eventually rain down nuclear weapons on U.S cities. The United States needed, therefore, to expand its military arsenal, educational resources, and research capabilities.

After the *Sputniks*, new appeals to "national security" and "national defense" cleared the way for federal money to flow more freely to educational institutions. The National Defense Education Act of 1958 funneled financial aid to university programs in science, engineering, foreign languages, and the social sciences. This act marked a milestone in overcoming congressional opposition to federal funding of education, especially from southerners who feared that economic aid could increase pressure for racial integration. The Soviets' apparent superiority in satellite technology also fueled an ambitious R&D effort overseen by a new National Aeronautics and Space Administration (NASA).

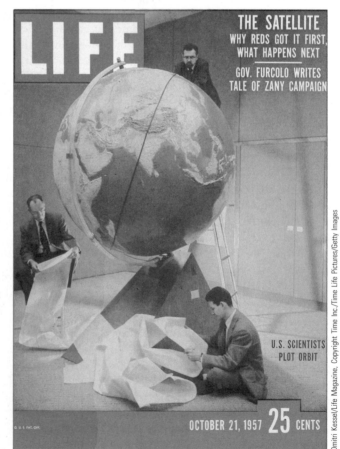

U.S. Scientists Plot Orbit. *In October 1957, the Soviets launched Sputnik, the first satellite to orbit the earth and a major achievement for the Soviet Union. U.S. scientists took measure of the achievement; popular magazines featured stories about how the "Reds got it first"; and Americans scanned the nighttime skies for a glimpse of the light refracted by the large Soviet rocket that had propelled Sputnik into space. A fear that the United States might lose the "space race" helped shape national politics in the 1950s and early 1960s.*

Dmitri Kessel/Life Magazine, Copyright Time Inc./Time Life Pictures/Getty Images

John Kenneth Galbraith spoke for those who hoped that domestic social welfare programs would become similar beneficiaries of increased federal spending. He saw a dangerous tilt in the "social balance" away from "public goods." Affluent families could vacation in their new automobiles, but they needed to pass through shabby cities along litter-filled roadsides. The researcher who improved automobile performance was well rewarded. But anyone "who dreams up a new public service" is accused of wasting tax dollars, Galbraith's book sardonically noted.

Galbraith's critique seemed mild when compared to that of the socialist writer Michael Harrington. His passionate writings about economic inequality, especially *The Other America* (1962), recalled the radical literature of the 1930s and his own apprenticeship at Dorothy Day's *Catholic Worker* during the early 1950s. At least one-third of the nation's people—living in rural areas, small towns, and cities—barely subsisted in a land of supposed abundance. Avoiding detached economic analysis, Harrington crafted dramatic stories about how poverty ravaged the health and spirit of people whose lives had been largely untouched by the economic growth of the post-Depression era. Americans and their politicians who celebrated affluence, Harrington charged, should be ashamed of ignoring such glaring economic inequalities. During the early 1960s, when addressing social and economic issues became a legislative priority, Galbraith and Harrington would become political celebrities. They had first entered the public arena, however, through the critical culture of the 1950s.

New Frontiers, 1960–1963

By 1960, the chance to revive the spirit of New Deal liberalism seemed at hand. The elections of 1958 had deposed some conservative Republican stalwarts and emboldened politicians sympathetic to more energetic government. One of these was John Fitzgerald Kennedy.

The Election of 1960   A wealthy, politically ambitious father had groomed John Fitzgerald Kennedy for the White House. The young Kennedy graduated from Harvard University, won military honors as a naval officer during the Second World War, became a representative from Massachusetts in 1946, and captured a Senate seat in 1952. Kennedy became better known for his social life than his command of legislative details, but he parlayed charm and youthful good looks into political stardom. His 1953 marriage to Jacqueline Bouvier added another dash of glamor. A favorite of the media herself, Jackie won plaudits for her cultural taste, stylish dress, and fluency in several languages.

Often accompanied by his family, John F. Kennedy (JFK) began barnstorming the country. His presidential campaigning, along with a talented staff and his family's vast wealth, helped Kennedy overwhelm two Democratic challengers, Senators Hubert Humphrey of Minnesota and Lyndon Johnson of Texas, two stalwarts of New Deal liberalism. By pledging to separate his Catholic religion from his politics and by directly confronting those who appealed to anti-Catholic prejudice, Kennedy defused the religious issue that had doomed the candidacy of Al Smith in 1928. Despite chronic and severe health problems, which his entourage concealed, Kennedy projected personal vigor and energy, if not much experience in directing affairs of state.

Vice President Richard Nixon, running for the Republicans, defied easy labeling. The new conservatives hardly needed to be reminded of Nixon's anticommunist credentials, but his record during the Eisenhower administration, particularly on civil rights, appeared that of a modern Republican. Indeed, Democrats with suspicions about Kennedy's priorities could arguably insist that Nixon's stand on policy issues hardly differed from that of JFK.

Nixon spent much of the 1960 presidential campaign on the defensive. Eisenhower would likely have run for a third term were it not for the Twenty-second Amendment, and he appeared unenthusiastic about Nixon's candidacy. Nixon himself seemed notably off-balance during the first of several televised debates in which a tanned, relaxed Kennedy emerged, according to surveys of TV viewers, with a clear victory over a pale, nervous Nixon. Radio listeners, in contrast, awarded Nixon no worse than a draw.

Kennedy's 1960 campaign highlighted issues from the 1950s that, taken together, became the agenda for his **New Frontier**. Although Senator Kennedy's civil rights record had been mixed, candidate Kennedy declared support for new legislation and, in an important symbolic act, dispatched aides to Georgia to assist the civil rights leader Martin Luther King, Jr., who was facing jail time for a minor traffic violation. Kennedy also endorsed new social programs to rebuild rural communities, increase educational opportunities, and improve urban conditions.

Kennedy's New Frontier included two other concerns rooted in the critical culture of the 1950s—promoting greater economic growth and conducting a more aggressive foreign policy. Kennedy suggested using tax cuts and deficit spending to juice the economy. He also criticized Eisenhower for failing to rid the hemisphere of Castro in Cuba and for allowing a "missile gap" to develop in the arms race with the Soviet Union. By spending more on national security, Kennedy claimed, he could create a more "flexible response" against communism, especially in the Third World. "Flexible response" became the umbrella term to cover a wide range of military and nonmilitary strategies for use overseas. The "American people are tired of the drift in our national course ... and ... they are ready to move again," Kennedy proclaimed.

Kennedy defeated Nixon by only about 100,000 popular votes, and his victory in the Electoral College rested on razor-thin margins in several states, including Illinois. Republicans urged their candidate to challenge Kennedy's suspicious vote total there, but Nixon chose to accept the disputed result. JFK's triumph owed a considerable debt to his vice presidential running mate, Lyndon Baines Johnson, whose regional appeal helped the Democratic ticket carry the Deep South and his home state of Texas. The Democratic Party, however, failed to duplicate its successes of 1958 and lost 20 seats in the House of Representatives and 1 in the Senate.

Supporters of the new president forgot about the closeness of his election, as JFK and Jackie, already first-name celebrities, riveted media attention on the White House. The couple hobnobbed with movie stars and hosted prominent intellectuals. Kennedy's inauguration featured designer clothing, a poignant appearance by the aged poet Robert Frost, and an oft-quoted speech in which JFK challenged people to "ask not what your country can do for you; ask what you can do for your country."

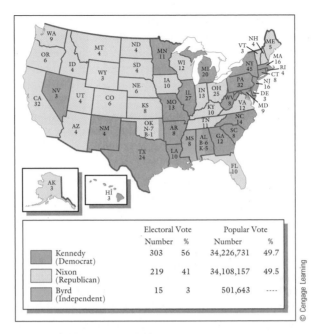

		Electoral Vote		Popular Vote	
		Number	%	Number	%
	Kennedy (Democrat)	303	56	34,226,731	49.7
	Nixon (Republican)	219	41	34,108,157	49.5
	Byrd (Independent)	15	3	501,643	----

© Cengage Learning

MAP 28.1 Presidential Election, 1960

In one of the closest elections in American history in terms of the popular vote, Kennedy only narrowly outpolled Nixon. Kennedy's more commanding victory in the electoral vote produced some discussion about the consequences of the Electoral College one day producing a president who had failed to carry the popular vote, a situation that the election of 2000 did produce.

Foreign Policy   Implementing flexible response gained Kennedy's immediate attention. Although Secretary of Defense Robert McNamara found that the missile gap never existed, the Kennedy administration boosted the defense budget anyway. It supported military assistance programs, propaganda agencies, and covert-action plans. In one of his most popular initiatives, the president created the Peace Corps, a volunteer program that sent Americans, especially young people, to nations around the world to work on development projects that might undercut communism's appeal.

Eisenhower's effort to reorient U.S.–Latin American policy away from dictators and toward socioeconomic programs was repackaged as Kennedy's "Alliance for Progress." Unveiled in spring 1961 in hopes of checking the spread of insurgencies that looked to Fidel Castro for inspiration, the Alliance promised $20 billion in loans over a 10-year period to Latin American countries that would undertake land reform and economic development.

Cuba and Berlin   The first misstep of the Kennedy presidency, an ill-conceived 1961 CIA mission against Cuba, also had its roots in the Eisenhower administration. The CIA had been secretly planning an invasion to oust Fidel Castro. Overriding the doubts of key advisers, Kennedy approved this Eisenhower-era plan. On April 17, 1961, however, when U.S.-trained forces (mainly anticommunist Cuban exiles) landed at the Bahia de Cochinas (Bay of Pigs) on the southern coast of Cuba, the expected popular uprising against Castro failed to materialize. Instead, forces loyal to the Cuban revolution quickly surrounded and captured members of the mission. Kennedy rejected any additional steps, including the air strikes that the Cuban exiles had expected, and initially denied any U.S. involvement in this **Bay of Pigs invasion**. The CIA's role quickly became public knowledge, however, and anti-U.S. sentiment swept across Latin America. Castro tightened his grip over Cuban life and strengthened his ties to the Soviet Union.

Kennedy responded by calling the Bay of Pigs invasion a mistake—and by devising a new, covert program called "Operation Mongoose." It abandoned the idea of an invasion in favor of destabilizing Cuba's economy and, in concert with organized crime figures, trying to assassinate the Cuban leader.

Tensions between the United States and the Soviet Union increased as well. In June 1961, Nikita Khrushchev and Kennedy met in Vienna, Austria, where the Soviets proposed ending the Western presence in Berlin and reuniting the city as part of East Germany. Kennedy refused to abandon West Berlin, but in August 1961 the communist regime began to erect a barbed wire fence and then a concrete barrier to separate East from West Berlin. This Berlin Wall became a symbol of communist repression. Kennedy's assertion in a 1963 speech, "*Ich bin ein Berliner* (I am a Berliner)," delivered in front of the wall to a cheering crowd of West Berliners, provided a memorable image of JFK's presidency.

Superpower confrontation, however, had already escalated to a potentially lethal level during the **Cuban Missile Crisis** of October 1962. The Soviet Union, responding to pleas from Castro, sent sophisticated armaments to Cuba. After U-2 spy planes revealed missile-launching sites in Cuba, the Kennedy administration declared it would never allow the Soviet Union to place nuclear warheads so close to U.S. soil. It demanded that the Soviets dismantle the missile silos and turn back supply ships heading for Cuba. After tense strategizing sessions with his top advisers, Kennedy rejected a military strike against Cuba, fearing it might lead to war with the Soviet Union. Instead, he ordered the navy to "quarantine" Cuba. The Strategic Air Command went on full alert for a possible nuclear conflict. Both sides also began frantic, secret diplomatic maneuvers to forestall such a catastrophe.

The showdown ended after 13 anxious days. On October 28, 1962, Khrushchev ordered the Soviet missiles in Cuba dismantled and the supply ships brought home; Kennedy promised not to invade Cuba and secretly assured Khrushchev that he would complete a previously planned withdrawal of U.S. missiles from Turkey. When Soviet archives were opened in the mid-1990s, people learned that the Cuban Missile Crisis had been even more dangerous than earlier imagined. Unknown to the Kennedy administration in 1962, the Soviets had already placed tactical nuclear weapons, which could have reached U.S. targets, inside Cuba. Some historical evidence suggests Castro favored atomic conflict over diplomatic concessions.

The Cuban Missile Crisis underscored the peril of nuclear conflict and made the two superpowers more cautious. To prevent a future confrontation or an accident, they established a direct telephone hot-line between Moscow and Washington, D.C.

Southeast Asia and Flexible Response   In Southeast Asia, Kennedy retained the goal of preserving a noncommunist state in South Vietnam. After the Bay of Pigs debacle, in which the overthrow of an already established communist government had failed, JFK became determined to prevent any communist-led "war of national liberation" from toppling a noncommunist regime.

Even so, the odds against nurturing a pro-U.S. government in South Vietnam seemed to grow longer as Kennedy's own presidency lengthened. Opposition to the regime of Ngo Dinh Diem, in power since the mid-1950s, had now coalesced in the National Liberation Front (NLF). Formed in December 1960, the NLF included noncommunist groups that resented Diem's dependence on the United States; communists who demanded more extensive land reform; an array of political leaders fed up with Diem's corruption and cronyism; and groups directly beholden to Ho Chi Minh's communist government in the North. North Vietnam continued sending supplies and troops to the South in support of the anti-Diem coalition.

The Kennedy administration saw Vietnam as the crucial test case for flexible response. It dispatched the Green Berets, elite U.S. troops who were trained in "counterinsurgency" tactics, to aid the South Vietnamese government. It also sent teams of social scientists, charged with "nation building," to consult on socioeconomic reforms and internal security. Finally, JFK dispatched U.S. combat troops. These forces, numbering nearly 24,000 by late 1963, would supposedly only advise, but were soon actively fighting alongside South Vietnam's forces.

South Vietnam still lacked a credible government. Diem's decision, in May 1963, to fire on Buddhist demonstrators in the city of Hue prompted confrontations between protestors and his government. In support of the anti-government effort, several Buddhist monks committed suicide by setting fire to their robes. The Kennedy administration recognized these self-immolations as a sign of the deep-seated opposition to Diem—and as a public relations disaster. The Kennedy administration signaled to South Vietnam's powerful military that U.S. support for Diem was nearing its end.

Domestic Policy   Kennedy's domestic agenda initially received far less attention than his foreign policy initiatives. Conservative Republicans and southern Democrats retained enough clout in Congress to stall or vote down proposals with which they disagreed. Despite his lengthy service in Congress, Kennedy seemed uncertain about how to deal with its old-line leadership and sided with advisers who urged a go-slow approach. This strategy meant that Kennedy did not press for the government-spending measures he had promised would speed economic growth. He feared any action that might unbalance the federal budget and thus alienate fiscal conservatives and business leaders.

In 1962, the White House finally asked Congress to lower tax rates as a means of stimulating economic growth. Kennedy argued that lower tax rates, along with special deductions for businesses that invested in new plants and equipment, would produce more jobs and greater growth. Despite opposition from fiscal conservatives and from Keynesians who thought Kennedy's proposal tilted toward corporations and the wealthy, the president's tax bill slowly moved through Congress.

On social welfare issues, the Kennedy administration proposed a higher minimum wage and new urban rebuilding programs. It also supported directing federal grants and loans to impoverished areas such as Appalachia, the 13-state region running along the Appalachian Mountain chain from southern New York to northern Mississippi.

THE POLITICS OF GENDER

The 1950s and early 1960s saw significant changes in how and where people lived and worked. This era produced especially important changes in the everyday politics of gender.

The New Suburbs and Gender Politics   In middle-class homes, especially in the new suburbs, women discovered the ambiguous impact of technological change. The time that women spent on domestic duties was not reduced so much as shifted to new activities requiring new household gadgets like automatic clothes washers and more powerful electric vacuum cleaners.

Life in the new suburbs, moreover, was structured by a broad pattern of "separate spheres": a public sphere of paid work and politics dominated by men, and a private one of unpaid housework and child care reserved for women. Because relatively few businesses initially located in the new suburbs, men commuted from home to work, while women found employment opportunities about as scarce as professional child-care facilities. Mothers thus spent considerable time tending to their baby boomer children. In contrast to the urban neighborhoods or small-town communities where many suburban housewives had grown up, newly constructed suburbs contained few older relatives or single women who could help with household and child-care duties.

Without mothers or grandmothers living close by, young suburban mothers often turned to child-care manuals for advice. The various editions of *Baby and Child Care* (1946), written by Dr. Benjamin Spock, sold millions of copies. Like earlier advice books, Spock's assigned virtually all child-care duties to women and implied that the family and the nation itself depended on how well mothers looked after the baby boom generation.

An alarmist tone in these books reflected—and helped generate—a widespread concern about juvenile delinquency. A problem teen, according to one study, sprang from a "family atmosphere not conducive to development of emotionally well-integrated, happy youngsters, conditioned to obey legitimate authority." The ideal mother devoted herself to rearing her children. Women who sought careers outside of the home and marriage risked being labeled as maladjusted and deviant—real-life versions of the *femme fatales* who populated *film noirs*.

Variations on this message appeared nearly everywhere. Even the nation's prestigious women's colleges assumed their graduates would pursue men and marriage. In a 1955 commencement address at Smith College, Adlai Stevenson, the Democratic Party's urbane presidential aspirant, reminded graduates of their "duty" to keep a husband "truly purposeful, to keep him whole." Popular magazines, psychological literature, and pop-culture imagery suggested that wives and mothers held the keys to social stability. This meant that women who desired alternative arrangements, either in their work or their sexual preferences, needed to be pressured, much as in *Tootle the Engine,* to return to the straight and narrow.

Competing portraits, however, painted a somewhat more complicated picture of gender arrangements. Most men told researchers that they preferred an "active partner" to a "submissive, stay-at-home" wife. Popular TV shows, such as *Father Knows Best* and *Leave It to Beaver,* suggested that fathers should be more engaged in family life than they seemed to be. Parenting literature, while envisioning suburban husbands earning their family's entire income, increasingly urged them to be "real fathers" at home and emphasized family togetherness. Institutions such as the Young Men's Christian Association (YMCA) offered courses on how to achieve it.

This call for family togetherness was partly in response to what cultural historians now see as an incipient "male revolt" against the "male breadwinner role." Hugh Hefner's *Playboy* magazine, which debuted in 1953, epitomized this trend. It ridiculed men who neglected their own happiness in order to support a wife and children as suckers rather than saints. *Playboy*'s first issue proclaimed: "We aren't a 'family magazine.'" In Hefner's version of the good life, a man rented a "pad" rather than owned a home, drove a sports car rather than a station wagon, and admired the Playmate of the Month rather than the Mother of the Year.

Signs of Women's Changing Roles   Meanwhile, greater numbers of women were working outside the house. Female employment, even among married women, rose steadily as jobs expanded in the clerical and service sectors. In 1948, about 25 percent of married mothers worked outside the home; at the end of the 1950s, nearly 40 percent did. With the 1960 introduction of a new method of oral contraception, the birth control pill, women could exercise greater control over family planning and career decisions—and over decisions about their own sexual behavior. By 1964, one-quarter of the couples that used contraception relied on "The Pill." At the same time, activists began to press for an end to state antiabortion laws that restricted the ability of women to find legal and relatively safe ways to terminate pregnancies.

Employment opportunities still remained circumscribed. Virtually all of the nation's nurses, telephone operators, secretaries, and elementary school teachers were women. Historically, pay scales in these areas lagged behind those for men in occupations that required comparable training. Jobs for women in the unionized job sectors remained rare. And chances for advancement in the corporate field were similarly limited. As the number of low-paying jobs for women expanded during the 1950s, better-paying professional opportunities actually narrowed. Medical, law, and other professional schools admitted lower percentages of women than in the past. When Sandra Day (who would later become U.S. Supreme Court Justice Sandra Day O'Connor) graduated with honors from a prestigious law school during the 1950s, not a single private firm offered her a job. She worked, without pay, in the public sector. The number of women on college faculties shrank even from the low levels of earlier decades.

Although employers still invoked the "family wage" ideal to justify higher pay for men, more women than ever before were trying to support a family on their own paychecks. This was especially true for women of color. Recognizing that images of domesticity hardly fit the lives of many African American women, *Ebony* magazine celebrated black women who combined success in parenting and at work.

Mass-circulation magazines aimed at women of European descent also carried increasingly mixed messages about gender roles. Although social commentators commonly labeled a woman's pursuit of activities outside the home as "unnatural," popular magazines increasingly featured stories about women in public life and in business. The 1950s, in short, saw growing diversity in both the social roles that women were assuming and the ways in which mass culture represented them.

A New Women's Movement   The seeds of a resurgent **women's movement** were also being sown between 1953 and 1963. All across the political spectrum, women began speaking out on contemporary issues. The energy of women such as Phyllis Schlafly, whose book *A Choice, Not an Echo* (1964) became a leading manifesto from the political right, helped fuel the new conservatism. African American activists such as Bernice Johnson Reagon (whose work with the Freedom Singers combined music and social activism) and Fannie Lou Hamer (who spearheaded the organization of a racially integrated Freedom Democratic Party in Mississippi) fought discrimination based on both race and gender. Women union leaders pushed for greater employment opportunities and more equitable work environments. Chicana farmworkers became key figures in union-organizing efforts in California. Women also played a central role in protests, through organizations such as the Committee for a Sane Nuclear Policy (SANE) and the Women's Strike for Peace, against the U.S.-Soviet arms race. During Kennedy's final year in office, Betty Friedan published *The Feminine Mystique*. Widely credited with helping to revive organized feminist activity in the United States, Friedan's book drew on her own social criticism from the late 1950s and articulated the dissatisfaction that many middle-class women felt about the narrow confines of domestic life and the lack of public roles available to them.

To address women's concerns, Kennedy appointed a Presidential Commission on the Status of Women, chaired by Eleanor Roosevelt. After negotiating differences between moderate and more militant members, the commission issued a report that documented discrimination against women in employment and wages. Kennedy responded with a presidential order to eliminate gender discrimination within the federal civil service. He also supported the Equal Pay Act of 1963, which made it a federal crime for employers to pay lower wages to women who did the same work as men.

THE EXPANDING CIVIL RIGHTS MOVEMENTS, 1953–1963

When Dwight Eisenhower took office in 1953, the U.S. Supreme Court was preparing to rehear a legal challenge to racially segregated educational systems. The NAACP and its chief legal strategist, Thurgood Marshall, spearheaded this effort. Before the rehearing took place, Eisenhower appointed Earl Warren, a former Republican governor of California, as chief justice. The Supreme Court, with Warren in its center chair, became a crucial force in the expanding civil rights struggle.

The Brown Cases, 1954–1955   The Supreme Court litigation popularly known as "the *Brown* decision" actually included a series of constitutional rulings, the **Brown cases**. In 1954, Chief Justice Warren wrote a unanimous opinion (in *Brown* v. *Board of Education of Topeka*) declaring that states could not segregate their public schools on the basis of race without violating the constitutional right of African American students to equal protection of the law. A companion case decided the same day (*Bolling* v. *Sharpe*) outlawed racially segregated schools in the District of Columbia. Although the *Brown* and *Bolling* decisions technically applied only to schools, they suggested that other segregated public facilities could no longer survive constitutional challenge. In 1955, though, a follow-up Supreme Court decision, known as "*Brown II*," decreed that the process of dismantling illegally segregated school systems should not go into effect immediately; desegregation could, instead, move forward "with all deliberate speed."

Implementing the *Brown* cases challenged the nation's political, social, and cultural institutions. The politics of civil rights sometimes seemed focused on the 16 states that the Census Bureau officially called "the South," but demographic changes helped make civil rights more than a regional phenomenon.

During the 1950s the South was becoming more like the rest of the country. Network television penetrated the region. Machines were displacing the region's fieldworkers, most of whom were black. The absence of strong labor unions and the presence of favorable tax laws encouraged northern-based businesses to move south. National chain stores, unaccustomed to state segregation laws elsewhere in the country, extended throughout the South.

Meanwhile, the racial composition of cities in the West, Midwest, and Northeast became more like that of the South. In 1940, more than three-quarters of the nation's African Americans lived in the South, many on farms and in small towns. During and after the Second World War, much of this population left the rural South and became important to political life in northern urban areas, where Republicans joined Democrats in generally supporting efforts to end racial discrimination. As more African Americans voted Democratic, however, the GOP gained ground among white voters in the South and in the new suburban neighborhoods, especially in the Middle and Far West.

The most familiar stories about civil rights activities during the 1950s have long concentrated on the South, but recent histories emphasize how the struggle increasingly became nationwide in scope. Efforts to end segregation and racial discrimination emerged in virtually every northern and western city. These urban-based movements employed a variety of tactics, such as "shop where you can work" campaigns, which urged black consumers to patronize only businesses that would employ them. They tried to bring more workers from non-European backgrounds into the union movement and the public-service sector, enlarging jobs in police and fire departments as well as in all of the agencies of state and local government. Increasingly, though, gaining legal-constitutional leverage seemed crucial to future successes.

As African Americans mounted new attacks on segregation and discrimination in the South, white segregationists pledged "massive resistance" to the *Brown* decisions and went to court with delaying tactics. One hundred members of Congress

Don Cravens/Time Life Pictures/Getty Images

Montgomery Bus Boycott. *The drive to desegregate municipal buses in Montgomery, Alabama, required an elaborately organized and skillfully coordinated effort. It primarily relied on the talents and commitment of volunteers, particularly women. African American residents of Montgomery shared automobile transportation, coordinated by the boycott movement, while avoiding city buses such as the one shown standing vacant across the street.*

signed a "Southern Manifesto" in 1956 that condemned the Supreme Court's desegregation rulings as a "clear abuse of judicial power" and pledged support for any state that intended "to resist forced integration by any lawful means."

Defiance went beyond the courtroom. White vigilantes unfurled the banners of the Ku Klux Klan and formed new racist organizations, such as the White Citizens Council. People who worked in the civil rights cause constantly risked injury and death. Racial tensions escalated. In August 1955, two white Mississippians murdered 14-year-old Emmett Till, a visitor from Chicago, because they thought he had been "disrespectful" toward a white woman. Mamie Till Bradley insisted that her son's death not remain a private incident. She demanded that his maimed corpse be displayed for "the whole world to see" and that his killers be punished. When their case came to trial, an all-white Mississippi jury quickly found the two men—who would subsequently confess their crime to a magazine reporter—not guilty.

The Montgom-
ery Bus Boycott   The southern civil rights movement increasingly supplemented legal maneuvering with direct action. Following an earlier, partially successful 1953 campaign to desegregate the transportation system in Baton Rouge, Louisiana, activists in Montgomery, Alabama, raised

their sights. After police arrested Rosa Parks for defying a segregation ordinance that required segregated seating on municipal buses, Montgomery's black community came to demand complete desegregation, boycotted public transportation, and organized carpools as alternative transit. Joining with Rosa Parks, a longtime bastion of the local NAACP chapter, many other black women in Montgomery helped coordinate the complicated, months-long boycott. Responding to events in Montgomery, the Supreme Court extended the premise of the *Brown* decisions on education and specifically declared segregation of public buses to be unconstitutional.

The year-long Montgomery bus boycott ended in victory. City officials, saddled with financial losses and legal defeats, agreed to end Montgomery's separatist transit policy. Events in Montgomery suggested that black activists, even in the segregated South, could effectively mobilize—and then organize—community resources to fight racial discrimination.

The bus boycott vaulted **Dr. Martin Luther King, Jr.**, one of its leaders, into the national spotlight. Born and educated in Atlanta, with a doctorate in theology from Boston University, King and other black ministers followed up the victory in Montgomery by forming the Southern Christian Leadership Conference (SCLC). In addition to demanding desegregated public facilities, the SCLC sought to organize an ongoing sociopolitical movement that would work for other changes.

The young, male ministers in the SCLC sought assistance across generational and gender divides. Tapping the strategic wisdom of Bayard Rustin, who had been involved in civil rights activism since the 1940s, and the tactical skills of Ella Baker, another veteran organizer, Dr. King led the SCLC's effort to register African American voters throughout the South.

King and the SCLC relied on civil disobedience to obtain change. Nonviolent direct action would dramatize, through both word and deed, the evil of racial discrimination. King's powerful presence and religiously rooted rhetoric carried the message of civil rights to most parts of the United States and the world.

The Politics of Civil Rights: From the Local to the Global

All across the country, civil rights activities went forward. Shortly after the conclusion of the Montgomery bus boycott, New York City passed the nation's first "open housing" ordinance, a model for other local and state measures aimed at ending racial discrimination in the sale and rental of homes and apartments. Efforts to change housing patterns faced tough going, however. Typically, white homeowners in those urban and older suburban neighborhoods where African Americans or Latinos might hope to buy or rent adopted the exclusionary strategies used so effectively by their counterparts in the new suburbs.

Outside the South, civil rights groups also sought legislation to outlaw racial discrimination in hiring. In 1958, for example, a labor union–civil rights coalition in California, joining under slogans such as "Fight Sharecropper Wages," defeated an anti-union right-to-work proposal it said threatened to drive down pay rates for all workers. Buoyed by this success, the same coalition began lobbying members of the California legislature to enact a statewide open housing measure.

Political institutions in Washington, D.C., felt similar pressure to act on civil rights. With southern segregationists, all members of the Democratic majority, holding key posts on Capitol Hill, antidiscrimination measures faced

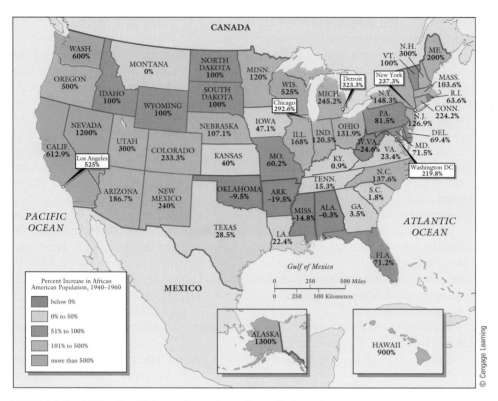

MAP 28.2   Shifts in African American Population Patterns, 1940–1960

During and after the Second World War, large numbers of African Americans left the rural South and migrated to new locations. Which states had the largest percentage of outmigration? Which saw the greatest percentage of population increase? How might this migration have affected American life?

formidable obstacles. Nevertheless, Congress did pass its first civil rights measures in more than 80 years. The **Civil Rights Act of 1957** expedited lawsuits by African Americans who claimed that southern states were systematically abridging their right to vote. The law also created a Commission on Civil Rights, an advisory body empowered to study alleged violations and recommend remedies. In 1960, with the crucial support of Lyndon Johnson of Texas, the Democratic leader in the Senate, a second civil rights act added more procedures to safeguard voting rights. These civil rights measures became law against fierce opposition from southern Democrats and conservative Republicans such as Barry Goldwater.

President Eisenhower initially hesitated to use his executive powers to aid civil rights efforts. He did support the Civil Rights Act of 1957 but held back when some Republicans urged a dramatic presidential step—such as barring racial discrimination on all construction projects financed by federal funds. Eisenhower saw ending racial segregation as a slow process, viewed desegregation as primarily a local matter, and doubted that federal power could change the attitudes of people opposed to integration.

In 1957, however, events in Little Rock, Arkansas, left Eisenhower no choice but to enforce a federal court decree ordering the desegregation of the city's Central High School. Orval Faubus, the state's segregationist governor, promised to prevent black students from entering the school building and deployed his state's National Guard to block them. Confronting this direct challenge to national authority, Eisenhower took command of the Arkansas National Guard and augmented it with members of the U.S. Army. Black students, protected by armed troops, finally entered Central High. The primary issue at stake, Eisenhower insisted, was a state's defiance of a federal court order rather than school desegregation.

The confrontation in Little Rock also underscored the international dimension of civil rights politics in the United States. Washington often found itself on the defensive when foreign critics pointed to the U.S. record on civil rights. The Soviet Union delighted in telling people, particularly in the Third World, how racial discrimination showed "the façade of the so-called 'American democracy.'" When the U.S. Supreme Court, in *Cooper* v. *Aaron* (1958), unanimously invalidated an Arkansas law intended to block school integration, the Eisenhower administration's global informational campaign stressed this decision as a good example of America's support for liberty and equality.

During the 1950s the State Department sent Dizzy Gillespie, Louis Armstrong, Duke Ellington, and many other African American jazz musicians as "goodwill ambassadors" to build more cordial relationships with new states in Africa and Asia. These tours presented jazz as a uniquely American art form that symbolized freedom, and sought to counter Soviet charges by highlighting the accomplishments of African Americans. America's cultural diplomacy, in fact, encouraged racially integrated musical acts to perform abroad—even though they might have been unwelcome in many venues at home. Racial discrimination and conflict, warned Secretary of State Dulles, was "not helpful to the influence of the United States abroad." The cold war's battle for hearts and minds throughout the world provided yet another kind of pressure on behalf of civil rights efforts.

The Politics of American Indian Policy

The Eisenhower administration also struggled with its policy toward American Indians. It attempted to implement two programs, **Termination and Relocation**, already under way before it took office. Termination called for an end to the status of Indians as "wards of the United States" and a grant of all the "rights and privileges pertaining to American citizenship." The goals of Termination, to be pursued on a tribe-by-tribe basis, were to abolish reservations, liquidate tribal assets, and curtail the social services offered by the Bureau of Indian Affairs (BIA).

Under the Relocation program, which had begun in 1951, Indians were encouraged to leave rural reservations and seek jobs in urban areas. In 1954, the BIA intensified its relocation efforts, with Minneapolis, St. Louis, Dallas, and several other cities joining Denver, Salt Lake City, and Los Angeles as relocation sites.

Proponents of Termination and Relocation insisted that American Indians could easily be assimilated into the mainstream of U.S. life.

These initiatives quickly failed. As several tribes were terminated during the 1950s, almost 12,000 people lost their status as tribal members, and the bonds of communal life for many Indians grew weaker. Land once held by tribes fell into the hands of commercial, non-Indian developers. Indians from terminated tribes also lost both their exemption from state taxation and social services provided by the BIA. They gained little in return. Relocation went no better. Most relocated Indians found only low-paying, dead-end jobs and discrimination from both public and private institutions.

American Indian activists and their allies mobilized against Termination and Relocation. By 1957, their efforts forced the Eisenhower administration to scale back the initial timetable, which had called for liquidating every tribe within five years. In 1960, the party platforms of both the Republican and Democratic parties repudiated Termination, and in 1962 the policy was ended. The Relocation program continued, however, and by 1967 almost half of the nation's Indians lived in relocation cities. This policy neither touched the deeply rooted problems that many Indians confronted, including a life expectancy only two-thirds that of whites, nor provided significantly better employment or educational opportunities.

Spanish-Speaking Communities and Civil Rights   Millions of Spanish-speaking people, many recently arrived in the United States, also began mobilizing in order to realize the nation's rhetorical commitment to liberty and equality. Puerto Ricans began moving in larger numbers than ever before from their island commonwealth to the mainland in the 1950s. By the early 1960s, New York City's Puerto Rican population was nearly 100 times greater than it had been before the Second World War. Large numbers of Puerto Ricans also settled in Chicago, Boston, and Hartford, Connecticut. Most of the newcomers spoke only Spanish; social and cultural clubs helped them connect with the Puerto Rican communities they had left behind. Officially U.S. citizens, Puerto Ricans organized against the discrimination they faced in housing and jobs. The Puerto Rican–Hispanic Leadership Forum, organized in 1957, presaged the emergence of groups that looked more to social and economic conditions—and, ultimately, greater political clout—in the United States than to cultural affinities with Puerto Rico.

Spanish-speaking people from Mexico were continuing to move to California and states in the Southwest, where they joined long-established Mexican American communities. In 1940, Mexican Americans had been the most rural of all the major ethnic groups; by 1950, in contrast, more than 65 percent of Mexican Americans were living in urban areas, a figure that would climb to 85 percent during the 1960s. Mexican Americans were becoming a political force in many southwestern cities and an important constituency for the national Democratic Party.

Beginning in 1942 and continuing until 1967, the U.S. government sponsored the *bracero* (or farmhand) program, which brought nearly 5 million Mexicans northward to fill agricultural jobs. Many *braceros* and their families remained in the United States after their work contracts expired. Legal immigrants from Mexico joined them, as did undocumented immigrants, who became targets of a government dragnet called "Operation Wetback." ("Wetback" was a term of derision, implying a person of Mexican descent had illegally crossed the Rio Grande River to reach the United States.) During a five-year period the government claimed to have rounded up and deported to Mexico nearly 4 million undocumented immigrants. This operation, critics charged, helped stigmatize U.S. citizens of Mexican heritage and justify further discriminatory treatment.

As a result, civil rights groups representing Mexican Americans intensified earlier mobilization efforts. Labor organizers sought higher wages and better working conditions in the factories, fields, and mines, even as the FBI labeled their efforts "communist inspired" and harassed unions with large Mexican American memberships, such as the United Cannery, Agricultural, Packing and Allied Workers of America (UCAPAWA). A lengthy mining strike in New Mexico became the subject of the independent motion picture *Salt of the Earth* (1954). Pressure from Washington, the film industry, and anticommunist labor unions throughout the 1950s prevented distribution of this collaboration among blacklisted filmmakers, striking miners (many of whom were Mexican American), and their families.

Civil rights organizations such as the League of United Latin American Citizens (LULAC) and the Unity League sought to desegregate schools and other public facilities throughout California and the Southwest. Lawyers for these groups faced a strategic dilemma, since most states classified persons whose ancestors came from Mexico as legally "white." As earlier cases such as *Westminster* had shown, school officials in states such as California and Texas cited language deficiencies, rather than race, as justification for segregating students of Mexican descent. The "other white" legal status of Mexican Americans, in other words, complicated the ability of organizations such as LULAC to frame court challenges that could rely on legal precedents involving white-against-black discrimination.

Urban-Suburban Issues   The growth of suburbia during the 1950s helped to highlight urban issues, many of them related to changing racial patterns. Throughout this period, both public and private institutions began shifting their financial resources away from cities, especially away from neighborhoods in which Latinos and African Americans lived. Adopting a policy called **redlining**, banks and other lending institutions generally denied loans for homebuyers and businesses in areas that were labeled "decaying" or "marginal" because they contained aging buildings, dense populations, and growing numbers of people of non-European descent. The Federal Housing Administration (FHA) and other governmental agencies channeled most of their lending activities toward the newer suburbs. In 1960, for example, the FHA failed to put up a single dollar for home loan guarantees in Camden or Paterson, New Jersey—cities in which minority populations were growing—while it poured millions of dollars into surrounding, largely all-white suburbs.

Urban renewal programs, authorized by the Housing Act of 1949, often seemed aimed at "urban removal." Although the law called for "a feasible method for the temporary relocation" of persons displaced, developers generally ignored the requirement. For several decades, the person who directed New York City's vast construction projects, Robert Moses, consistently understated the number of people dislocated by his urban renewal and highway building programs. Defenders of Robert Moses insisted that he pursued a progressive vision that ultimately benefited all New Yorkers, but the costs of progress—and perhaps its benefits—hardly seemed equally shared.

Plans for federally built public housing faltered. Although suburban areas, where land was abundant and inexpensive, seemed the obvious place to locate affordable housing, white homeowners used their political clout and local zoning laws to freeze out government-sponsored housing projects. Private housing interests lobbied to limit the number of public units actually constructed in urban areas and to ensure that they offered tenants fewer amenities, including closets with doors, than could be found in private units. Originally conceived as short-term alternatives for families who would soon move to their own homes, publicly built facilities became stigmatized as "the projects," permanent housing of last resort for people with chronically low incomes.

The urban-suburban policies came under bipartisan criticism. In 1960, both the Democratic and Republican parties pledged to create a new cabinet office for urban affairs and to reconsider how Washington could better address the cycle of continued suburban growth and onrushing urban decay.

New Forms of Direct Action, 1960–1963   Although John F. Kennedy had talked about new civil rights legislation, his administration initially tried to placate the segregationist wing of his Democratic Party. The president and his brother, Robert Kennedy, who had become attorney general, listened sympathetically when J. Edgar Hoover, director of the FBI, falsely warned of continuing ties between Martin Luther King, Jr., and members of the Communist Party. To monitor King's activities, the FBI illegally recorded many of his private conversations and clamped a tight web of surveillance around his every move. King's SCLC also faced another challenge: that from more militant civil rights organizations that favored new forms of direct action.

In early 1960, African American students at North Carolina A & T College in Greensboro sat down at a segregated lunch counter and politely asked to be served in the same manner as white customers. This was the beginning of the **sit-in movement**, a new phase of civil rights activism. In both the South and the North, young demonstrators staged nonviolent sit-ins at restaurants, bus and train stations, and other public facilities. Singing civil rights anthems such as "We Shall Overcome" to inspire solidarity, the sit-in movement encouraged further activism. In 1961, an interracial group from CORE and the Student Nonviolent Coordinating Committee (SNCC), a student-dominated organization that emerged from the sit-in movement, risked racist retaliation by reviving a form of direct action that CORE had first tried in the 1940s: "freedom rides" across the segregated South. The new **freedom riders** were challenging the Kennedy administration to enforce federal court decisions that had declared state laws requiring segregation on interstate buses (and in bus stations) to be unconstitutional.

The new grassroots activism forced the Kennedy administration into action of its own. It dispatched U.S. marshals and National Guard troops to protect the freedom riders. It also deployed federal power to help integrate educational institutions in the Deep South, including the University of Mississippi and University of Alabama. In November 1962, Kennedy issued a long-promised executive order that banned racial discrimination in federally financed housing. The following February he sent Congress a civil rights bill that called for speedier trials in cases involving challenges to racial discrimination in voting.

Nearly 1,500 civil rights demonstrations took place across the country the following spring. Protests in the urban Northeast and Midwest generally focused on improving educational opportunities. Most of these called for accelerating school integration plans, but a "Walk to Freedom March" in Detroit attracted more than 125,000 people on behalf of a broad agenda that included job creation and open housing legislation.

Events in the South, however, attracted the most attention. Beginning in the spring of 1963, violent conflict convulsed Birmingham, Alabama. Direct action in this Alabama industrial center, according to Dr. King, was to create a situation "so crisis packed that it will inevitably open the door to negotiation" over desegregation of public facilities. White police officers unleashed dogs and turned high-pressure water hoses on demonstrators, including children. Four young girls were later murdered (and 20 people injured) when white supremacists bombed Birmingham's Sixteenth Street Baptist Church, a center of the local civil rights campaign. After thousands of African Americans rallied in protest—and two more children were killed, this time by police officers—the Kennedy administration could no longer remain outside the struggle. It conceded that images from Birmingham played badly in the international media and among African American communities outside of Alabama.

The determination of Birmingham's civil rights activists created a real-life drama that played to the entire world on television. Kennedy had already used the same medium when pleading for a national commitment to the battle against discrimination. Recent events had raised "a moral issue ... as old as Scriptures and ... as clear as the Constitution." Racial violence was "weakening the respect with which the rest of the world regards us," the president insisted in a June televised address.

The White House still hoped to influence the direction and pace of change. It crafted additional civil rights legislation designed to dampen enthusiasm for demonstrations and other forms of direct action. It now called for a ban against racial discrimination in public facilities and housing and for new measures to protect the voting rights of African Americans in the South. The administration soon recognized that its legislative proposals would not derail a **March on Washington for Jobs and Freedom** scheduled for the late summer of 1963, modeled after the earlier march in Detroit and sponsored by a coalition of civil rights and labor organizations. It belatedly endorsed the demonstration.

On August 28, 1963, an integrated group of more than 200,000 people marched through the nation's capital to the Lincoln Memorial. There, Dr. Martin Luther King, Jr., delivered his famous "I Have a Dream" speech. Speakers on that day generally applauded Kennedy's latest initiatives but urged a far broader agenda, including a higher minimum wage and a federal program to guarantee new jobs. Well organized and smoothly run, the event received overwhelmingly favorable

Racial Conflict in Birmingham. *Images such as this 1963 photograph of a confrontation in Birmingham, Alabama, in which segregationists turned dogs on youthful demonstrators, helped rally popular support outside the white South for civil rights legislation. Events in Birmingham also presaged the increasingly violent clashes that would punctuate the efforts to end racial discrimination.*

coverage from the national media and put additional pressure on the White House and Congress to lend a hand to civil rights efforts.

NOVEMBER 1963

As fall turned to winter in 1963, the United States confronted major policy issues. They had deep historical roots but now carried special urgency.

Policy Choices   The Kennedy administration continued to puzzle over how to recast Eisenhower's containment policy and execute its own flexible-response approach in Vietnam. U.S. officials gave disgruntled South Vietnamese military officers the green light to orchestrate the overthrow of Diem's regime. On November 2, 1963, Diem was routed from his presidential palace and—despite assurances to the contrary from the coup's leaders—murdered. This coup, which brought a military regime to power in Saigon, bred even greater political instability throughout South Vietnam. The NLF and North Vietnam ratcheted up their military activities.

There were also domestic political dilemmas. Kennedy's tax bill was languishing in Congress. On the civil rights front, the administration renewed efforts to mobilize its political resources on behalf of long-promised congressional legislation. Recognizing that provisions to lessen discrimination in housing would never pass, White House strategists pondered how best to use federal power to eliminate state-sanctioned segregation in the South and to advance a "fair employment" agenda everywhere.

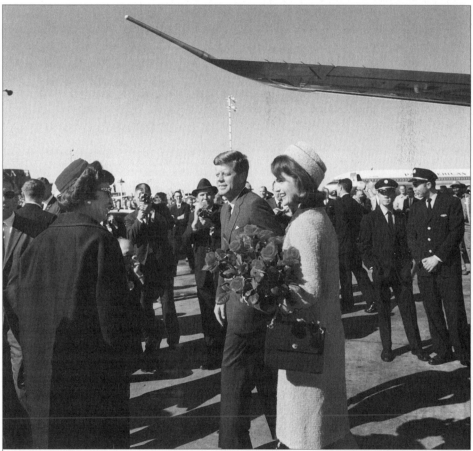

Photograph by Cecil Stoughton, White House, in the John F. Kennedy Presidential Library and Museum, Boston.

JFK and Jackie Arrive at Love Field, November 22, 1963. *President Kennedy and the First Lady, often treated in the manner of Hollywood movie stars, carefully orchestrated their public appearances. During Kennedy's final political trip to Texas, he and the First Lady traveled the short distance from Ft. Worth to Dallas by airplane, rather than automobile, as a way of making their arrival, marked by roses for the First Lady, appear more dramatic. Within hours, subsequent photographs of Jacqueline Kennedy would famously show her French-designed pink suit stained with the blood of the slain president, shot down while the presidential limousine passed through Dallas's Dealey Plaza.*

The Assassination of John F. Kennedy   On November 22, 1963, the president was shot dead as his presidential motorcade moved through Dallas, Texas. Vice President Lyndon Johnson, who had accompanied Kennedy to Texas, took the oath of office and rushed back to Washington. Equally quickly, the Dallas police arrested Lee Harvey Oswald and pegged him as JFK's assassin. Oswald had vague ties to organized crime; had once lived in the Soviet Union; and had a bizarre set of political affiliations, including shadowy ones with groups interested in Cuba. He declared his innocence but never faced trial. Jack Ruby, a Dallas nightclub owner, killed Oswald on national television, while the alleged gunman was in police custody. An investigation by a special commission headed by Chief Justice Earl Warren concluded that both Oswald and Ruby had acted alone.

Kennedy's life and presidency remain topics of historical debate and tabloid-style speculation. His assassination still provokes conspiracy theories and controversies. Researchers have provided new details about his poor health, reliance on exotic medications, and dalliances with women—all of which were kept from the public at the time. Historians continue to debate what JFK might have done in Vietnam and on the domestic front had he won the 1964 presidential election.

CONCLUSION

Tensions with the Soviet Union, which brought the superpowers to the brink of nuclear war during the Cuban Missile Crisis of 1962, dominated national security calculations between 1953 and 1963. The United States stockpiled nuclear weapons, employed new forms of economic pressure, and expanded covert activities. Left-leaning movements in the Third World, particularly in Cuba and Southeast Asia, became of growing concern to policymakers.

At home, the post-1953 decade brought economic growth. New consumer products encouraged talk about an age of affluence but also produced apprehension about conformity, unruly youth, and mass culture. At the same time, the millions of people whom economic prosperity bypassed, and those who faced racial and ethnic discrimination, worked to bring their causes to the center of public debate over the role of government. Critics charged the Eisenhower administration with failing to use governmental power to support civil rights and to promote faster, more equitably distributed economic growth. Although Kennedy also hesitated, the press of domestic events, particularly those associated with civil rights movements, forced him to consider how best to advance the issues of liberty and equality at home. More quietly, a new conservative movement with ideas different from those of Kennedy, and even Eisenhower, was also taking shape.

The years that immediately followed Kennedy's assassination would continue to highlight questions about liberty, equality, and power at home and abroad during an increasingly divisive war.

29

AMERICA DURING A DIVISIVE WAR, 1963–1974

CHAPTER OUTLINE

- The Great Society • Escalation in Vietnam • Activism at Home • 1968
- Continued Polarization, 1969–1974 • Foreign Policy in a Time of Turmoil, 1969–1974 • A Crisis of Governance, 1972–1974

What happened during the years between 1963 and 1974 profoundly affected how Americans viewed most public, and even personal, matters during the next half-century of U.S. history. This tumultuous era, often called "the Sixties," included a divisive, ultimately failed military intervention in Southeast Asia; a flood of social and regulatory legislation by Washington; sudden reversals in partisan political fortunes that included a Democratic and then a Republican president leaving office less than four years after both had gained overwhelming electoral victories; and new forms of citizen mobilization—including movements on behalf of Black Power, grassroots democracy, and conservatism—that changed the forms and meaning of political activism. Economic signals from this period suggested that the widely shared affluence of the immediate post–World War II era might not continue. Cultural disputes began expanding into heated clashes over the nation's core values. And rising levels of violence, including more assassinations of prominent public leaders, prompted anxiety and different responses.

By 1974, the nation's politics, social fabric, economic health, and culture looked very different from how they had appeared in 1963.

THE GREAT SOCIETY

Lyndon Johnson lacked John Kennedy's charisma, but during his long career in Congress he had learned to flatter, cajole, or threaten people until they lent him support. Johnson's skill in gaining congressional funding for building projects

CHRONOLOGY

1964	Civil Rights Act of 1964 passes
	Congress approves Gulf of Tonkin Resolution
	Johnson defeats Barry Goldwater
1965	Congress passes Voting Rights Act
	Violence hits Watts
	U.S. role in Vietnam dramatically expands
1966	Supreme Court decides *Miranda v. Arizona*
	United States begins massive air strikes in North Vietnam
1967	Large antiwar demonstrations begin
1968	Tet Offensive begins
	Martin Luther King, Jr., and Robert Kennedy assassinated
	Civil Rights Act passed
	Richard Nixon wins presidency
1969	Nixon announces "Vietnamization" policy
	My Lai massacre becomes public
1970	U.S. troops enter Cambodia
	Congress creates Environmental Protection Agency
1971	Stagflation upsets U.S. economy
	U.S. dollar begins to "float" on currency markets
1972	Watergate burglars caught inside Democratic headquarters
	Nixon crushes George McGovern in presidential election
1973	OPEC oil embargo begins
	Paris Peace Accords signed
	Supreme Court decides *Roe v. Wade*
	Special Senate committee begins hearings into "Watergate"
1974	House votes for impeachment and Nixon resigns
	Gerald Ford assumes presidency
1975	Saigon falls to North Vietnamese forces

boosted Texas cities such as Dallas and Houston, along with much of the Southwest. LBJ himself acquired a personal fortune.

Kennedy's death gave Johnson the opportunity to display his political skills on the presidential stage. Although eager to enact a bold social-economic program, Johnson began cautiously. He asked Congress to honor JFK's memory by addressing three legislative issues proposed by Kennedy's administration: tax cutting, economic inequality, and civil rights.

**Closing the
New Frontier**

Working behind the scenes, Johnson easily secured passage of the Kennedy tax cut. Although analysts still differ in their assessment of the contribution this legislation made to the economic boom of the mid-1960s, it appeared to work. GNP rose 7 percent in 1964 and 8 percent the following year, unemployment dropped, and inflation remained low.

In his January 1964 State of the Union address, Johnson upped the ante on Kennedy's cautious effort to address economic inequality by calling for "an unconditional war on poverty in America." Relentlessly prodded by the White House, Congress soon passed the Economic Opportunity Act of 1964. It created the Office of Economic Opportunity (OEO) to coordinate a multipart program for "eliminating the paradox of poverty in the midst of plenty." The act mandated loans for rural and small-business development; established a work-training program called the Jobs Corps; created Volunteers in Service to America (VISTA), a domestic version of the Peace Corps; provided low-wage, public service jobs for young people; began a "work-study program" to assist college students; and authorized the creation of federally funded social programs to be planned in concert with local community groups.

Johnson also helped push an expanded version of Kennedy's civil rights proposal through Congress. Although championing the measure as a memorial to JFK, LBJ knew that southerners in his own Democratic Party would try to block it. Consequently, he successfully sought Republican support to curtail a southern-led filibuster. Johnson also helped hammer out compromises on several key provisions and reconcile the differing bills enacted by the House and Senate.

The **Civil Rights Act of 1964**, passed in July, strengthened federal remedies, monitored by a new Equal Employment Opportunity Commission (EEOC), against racially inspired job discrimination. The act also prohibited racial discrimination in all public accommodations connected to interstate commerce, such as motels and restaurants. Moreover, Title VII, a provision added during congressional debate, barred discrimination based on sex and became an important legal tool for the reviving women's movement. Although opponents of the 1964 act argued that its extension of federal power violated the Constitution, the Supreme Court, effectively a political ally of Lyndon Johnson during his presidency, curtly rejected the claim.

That same summer, a coalition of civil rights groups recruited nearly a thousand young volunteers for **Freedom Summer**, an effort to register African American voters in Mississippi. During a tension-filled summer, at least six civil rights workers met violent deaths. In the most notorious incident, a conspiracy among Ku Klux Klan (KKK) leaders and law enforcement officers from Neshoba County, Mississippi, led to the brutal murders of three volunteers—James Chaney, Michael Schwerner, and Andrew Goodman. No one was convicted of any crime until 2005, when a Mississippi jury convicted a former KKK leader, by then in his 80s, of manslaughter for participating in the triple killing of 1964.

Meanwhile, supporters of Freedom Summer pressed forward, only to see the national Democratic Party reject their grassroots political work. Pressured by LBJ, the 1964 Democratic convention voted to seat Mississippi's "regular" all-white delegates rather than members of a new, racially diverse Mississippi Freedom Democratic Party (MFDP). The regulars had made clear their intention to support the

GOP's presidential candidate, but Johnson declined to support the MFDP in hopes of keeping some other southern states in the Democratic camp in the fall election. LBJ's rebuff of the MFDP prompted its leaders, such as Fannie Lou Hamer, to question the president's commitment to their cause.

The Election of 1964   After a bruising battle within GOP ranks, the Republicans nominated Senator **Barry Goldwater** of Arizona, hero of the new conservatism, to challenge Johnson. Goldwater's strategists claimed that a stoutly conservative GOP campaign would attract the vast number of voters who supposedly rejected both Democratic policies and Dwight Eisenhower's "modern Republicanism." Goldwater denounced Johnson's foreign policy for tolerating communist expansion and attacked his domestic agenda, including civil rights, for destroying individual liberties. One of only eight Republican senators who had opposed the 1964 Civil Rights Act, Goldwater condemned the measure as an unconstitutional extension of national power on behalf of the laudable goal of combating discrimination, a matter for state and local governments to address.

The Goldwater campaign quickly fizzled. The Democratic campaign savaged the candidate's policies, his grasp of issues, and even his mental stability. A tendency to make ill-considered remarks already haunted Goldwater. He had suggested that people who feared nuclear war were "silly and sissified." He had wondered out loud if participation in the Social Security program should become voluntary. And his proclamation at the 1964 Republican convention that "extremism in the pursuit of liberty is no vice" and "moderation in the pursuit of justice is no virtue" fed Democratic claims that "extremist" forces on the "radical right" would dominate a Goldwater presidency.

Many modern Republicans deserted Goldwater, who led the GOP to a spectacular defeat in November. Johnson carried 44 states and won more than 60 percent of the popular vote; Democrats also gained 38 seats in Congress.

Although the 1964 election boosted support for Johnson's agenda, it also foreshadowed significant political changes. Indeed, during the Democratic primaries of 1964, Alabama's segregationist governor, George Wallace, had run strongly against the president in several states by denouncing any "meddling" by Washington in local affairs. The 1964 election proved the last, until that of 2008, in which the Democratic Party would capture the White House by proposing an expansion in the power of the national government.

Goldwater's defeat invigorated rather than discouraged supporters of the new conservatism. His staff pioneered innovative campaign tactics, such as direct-mail fundraising. By refining these techniques during future campaigns, conservative strategists helped make 1964 the beginning, not the end, of their plan to push the Republican Party, and the country, to the right. Goldwater's continued criticism of the Civil Rights Act of 1964 helped him carry five southern states. These victories— along with Wallace's earlier appeal to "white backlash" voters—suggested that the new conservatism could woo southern whites away from the Democratic Party.

An important electoral issue in California gave conservatives further hope. The Democratic national ticket easily carried the state, but real-estate interests joined

LBJ's 1964 Campaign against Barry Goldwater.
In this controversial television ad from the 1964 campaign, Lyndon Johnson's supporters exploited Republican Barry Goldwater's image as a far-right "extremist" who might take the nation into a nuclear war.

Vote for
President Johnson
on November 3

with suburban conservatives to sponsor a referendum measure that repealed a recently enacted law prohibiting racial discrimination in the sale or rental of housing. Opponents of this "open housing" measure adopted a political strategy that conservatives would increasingly embrace: downplay racial issues and, instead, denounce governmental regulations for violating the principles of equal rights and individual liberties.

The Goldwater campaign also introduced a new corps of conservative celebrities, many of them from the Sunbelt, to national politics. Ronald Reagan championed the new conservatism so effectively that Goldwater Republicans in California began grooming the former movie and TV actor for a political career. Younger conservatives, such as William Rehnquist and Newt Gingrich, entered the national arena as supporters of Goldwater's vision. Goldwater also enlisted Milton Friedman, the staunchly conservative economist and a critic of Keynesian policies, as an adviser. Historians now credit the Goldwater effort of 1964 with helping to spearhead the overhaul of American conservatism—and the Republican Party.

Lyndon Johnson's Great Society

Lyndon Johnson rushed to capitalize on his electoral victory. Enjoying broad support in Congress, Johnson unveiled plans for a **Great Society**, an array of federal programs designed to "enrich and elevate our national life." Some of the programs fulfilled the dreams of his Democratic predecessors. Nationally funded medical coverage for the elderly (Medicare) and for low-income citizens (Medicaid) grew out of health-care proposals from the New Deal and Fair Deal eras. Similarly, a new cabinet office, the Department of Housing and Urban Development (HUD), built on earlier plans for coordinating urban revitalization programs.

The **Voting Rights Act of 1965**, which created mechanisms for national oversight of state and local elections in the South, capped the long-term effort to eliminate racial and ethnic discrimination, especially sham "literacy tests," from political life. The measure gave the Justice Department broad authority to monitor electoral procedures in jurisdictions with a history of discriminating against African American voters. Modified and extended over the years, the Voting Rights Act came to require ballots printed in languages other than English.

Congress also enacted another milestone measure that addressed matters long discussed—and long avoided. The **Immigration and Nationality Act of 1965** finally abolished the discriminatory "national origins" quota system established in 1924. Henceforth, roughly the same set of rules would apply to people wishing to immigrate to the United States from any part of the world. This change, in practice, would allow the entry of far more people from Asia and Africa than had previously been allowed.

Many of the Great Society's other proposals rested on the midcentury "affluence" that the Johnson administration expected to continue for years to come. Ongoing economic growth could provide the tax dollars to underwrite a bold expansion of national power without any overhaul of fundamental political and economic arrangements.

The array of Great Society initiatives that rolled through Congress during the mid-1960s heartened LBJ's supporters and appalled his critics. The Model Cities

Program (1966) offered smaller-scale alternatives to urban renewal efforts. Rent supplements and an expanded food stamp program went to help low-income families. The Head Start Program (1965) provided help for children considered educationally unprepared for kindergarten. Other new federal educational programs aimed to upgrade classroom instruction, especially in low-income neighborhoods, and a legal services initiative provided lawyers to clients who could not afford to hire an attorney. These measures aimed at providing low-income people with the kind of professional expertise, routinely available to the more affluent, that could help them fight their way out of social and economic distress. The Great Society's service-based approach, Johnson insisted, would give people a "hand up" rather than a "handout."

The Community Action Program (CAP) promised a different tack. It authorized local activists, working through neighborhood organizations, to design community-based projects that could gain funding from Washington. By promoting "maximum feasible participation" by ordinary citizens rather than relying on planning experts, the architects of CAP proposed to nurture a grassroots democracy that could revitalize American politics from the bottom up.

Evaluating the Great Society   How did the Great Society become so controversial? Most obviously, the extension of Washington's reach rekindled old debates about the proper use of the power of the national government. In addition, Johnson announced ambitious objectives, such as an "unconditional" victory over poverty, which failed to survive the short-term rhythms of partisan politics. Republicans picked up 47 seats in Congress in the midterm elections of 1966, and the Great Society ideal could never again gain the overwhelming congressional support that it had enjoyed when first announced.

The expectation that continued economic growth would generate tax revenues sufficient to finance new social programs faded. Uncertain economic conditions, exacerbated by the escalating cost of the war in Vietnam, made social welfare measures politically vulnerable. Facing financial worries of their own, people who had been initially supportive of the Great Society became receptive to the claim, first championed by George Wallace and the Goldwater campaign in 1964, that bureaucrats in Washington would waste their hard-earned tax dollars on flawed social experiments.

Historians disagree about the impact of Johnson's programs. Charles Murray's *Losing Ground* (1984) reframed the welfare policy debate by charging that the Great Society encouraged too many people, lured by welfare payments, to abandon the goals of marrying, settling down, and seeking jobs. Money spent on Johnson's programs, moreover, allegedly created government deficits that slowed economic growth. A central text of the new conservatism, Murray's book saw Johnson's Great Society as a cause of, not a solution for, economic distress.

Other analysts rejected this view, especially the claim that most people preferred welfare to meaningful work. Funds actually spent on Great Society programs neither matched Johnson's promises nor reached the lavish levels claimed by the new conservatism. The charge that government expenditures choked off growth ignored the systemic economic problems that emerged in the early 1970s. The data also point toward some successes for Great Society byitiatives. Poverty rates fell from 19 percent in 1962 to 10 percent by 1969.

Still, antipoverty activists complained that the Johnson administration failed to challenge the prevailing distribution of political and economic power and favored large-scale bureaucratic solutions forged by power brokers in Washington. The administration jettisoned the CAP model of grassroots empowerment when local politicians began complaining about having to compete for federal funding. The assumption that economic growth would fund the Great Society precluded any serious attempt, such as a revision of the tax code, to redistribute income and wealth.

Washington's financial outlay for domestic programs did increase more than 10 percent during every year of LBJ's presidency. In 1960, federal spending on social welfare constituted 28 percent of total governmental outlays; by 1970, this figure had risen to more than 40 percent. Moreover, Great Society programs such as Medicaid, legal assistance, and job training gave low-income families access to social services and slightly narrowed the disparity between rich and poor.

From the crucial perspective of political viability, though, the Great Society proved a failure. Opposition to the assumptions and goals of Johnson's Great Society gave new energy to the conservative movement. As support for domestic spending programs waned, even most Democrats hesitated to defend Lyndon Johnson's vision.

ESCALATION IN VIETNAM

Lyndon Johnson's divisive crusade to build a Great Society at home found its counterpart abroad. His pledge to protect South Vietnam from communism demanded ever more of the nation's resources, diminished the country's international standing, further polarized its domestic politics, and strained its economy.

The Gulf of Tonkin Resolution   Immediately after John Kennedy's assassination, Johnson resisted additional support for South Vietnam. His fears of appearing soft on communism, however, soon led him to side with advisers who recommended air strikes against North Vietnam as the necessary first step. Johnson prepared a congressional resolution authorizing this escalation of hostilities.

Events in the Gulf of Tonkin, off the coast of North Vietnam, provided the rationale for taking the resolution to Capitol Hill. On August 1, 1964, the U.S. destroyer *Maddox*, while on an intelligence-gathering mission, exchanged gunfire with North Vietnamese ships. Three days later, the *Maddox* returned with the *Turner Joy* and, during severe weather, reported what seemed to be signs of a failed torpedo attack. Although the *Maddox*'s commander advised that the episode needed further analysis, Johnson immediately denounced "unprovoked aggression" by North Vietnam against the United States. (A later study concluded that there had never been a North Vietnamese attack.) With only two dissenting votes in the Senate, Congress passed the **Gulf of Tonkin Resolution**, which authorized Johnson to take "all necessary measures to repel armed attack."

Johnson immediately began bombing strikes against North Vietnam and used the Gulf of Tonkin Resolution as tantamount to a congressional declaration of war. The congressional resolution also helped Johnson position himself as a tough but cautious moderate during the presidential campaign of 1964. Barry Goldwater demanded stronger measures against North Vietnam and even hinted at possible use of tactical nuclear weapons. Johnson's campaign managers portrayed Goldwater as a threat to the survival of civilization, and the president seemingly promised not to commit U.S. troops to any land war in Southeast Asia.

Soon after the November election of 1964, however, Johnson faced a complicated decision. More than a year after the 1963 coup against Diem, South Vietnam still faced political disarray, and South Vietnamese troops were deserting at an alarming rate. North Vietnam continued expanding its military aid to the National Liberation Front (NLF) and began sending more of its own troops into South Vietnam. By the beginning of 1965, the NLF controlled much of the countryside. In January, another government in Saigon collapsed, and factionalism stalled the emergence of any viable alternative.

National Security Adviser McGeorge Bundy predicted South Vietnam's collapse unless the United States greatly increased its military role. Another key aide, Walt W. Rostow, assured Johnson that North Vietnam would give up its aggressive plans if the United States clearly showed its determination to oppose them. Undersecretary of State George Ball, by contrast, warned that "no one has demonstrated that a white ground force of whatever size can win a guerrilla war—which is at the same time a civil war between Asians—in jungle terrain in the midst of a population that refuses cooperation to the white forces." Senate Majority Leader Mike Mansfield, an expert in Asian history, urged finding some way of reuniting Vietnam as a neutral country. Top military officials, beset by interservice rivalries, provided differing assessments and no clear guidance.

Although Johnson privately doubted the chances for a successful U.S. intervention, he seemed incapable of translating these doubts into a decision to alter the U.S. commitment to containing communism in Vietnam. Johnson became obsessed about the adverse political and diplomatic consequences of a U.S. pullout or compromise. He feared that domestic criticism of anything looking like a communist victory in Vietnam would endanger his Great Society programs and embolden the new conservatives.

Johnson also embraced the familiar domino theory, the claim that a U.S. withdrawal could lead to further communist aggression in Asia, encourage communist-leaning insurgencies in Latin America, increase Soviet pressure on West Berlin, and damage U.S. credibility around the world. Both Eisenhower and Kennedy had staked U.S. prestige on a noncommunist South Vietnam. Johnson either had to revise that commitment or chart an uncertain course by ordering the direct infusion of U.S. combat troops.

Ultimately, Johnson greatly expanded U.S. military involvement. A deadly attack on the U.S. military outpost at Pleiku in early 1965 prompted retaliatory bombing against North Vietnam. Within a month, the United States inaugurated a sustained campaign of bombing, code-named Rolling Thunder. Washington also began deploying U.S. ground forces to regain lost territory in the South, expanding covert operations, and boosting economic aid to the beleaguered South Vietnamese government. Only six months after the 1964 election, with his advisers still divided, Johnson had decisively committed the United States to a wider war.

The War Continues to Widen

Combat operations in Vietnam grew steadily more intense. Hoping to break the enemy's spirit, U.S. military commanders sought to inflict massive casualties. The Johnson administration authorized the use of napalm, an incendiary and toxic chemical that charred both foliage and people, and allowed the air force to bomb new targets. Additional U.S. combat troops arrived, but every escalation seemed to require a further one. After North Vietnam rejected a Johnson peace plan that Hanoi viewed as tantamount to its surrender, the United States again escalated. North Vietnam's leadership, pursuing a long-term strategy of attrition in South Vietnam, became convinced that Johnson would eventually lose public and congressional support for continuing the costly intervention.

In April 1965, Johnson applied his cold war, anticommunist principles in Latin America. Responding to exaggerated reports about a communist threat in the Dominican Republic, Johnson sent U.S. troops to unseat a left-leaning, elected president and to install a government supportive of U.S. interests. This incursion violated a long-standing "good neighbor" pledge not to intervene militarily in the Western Hemisphere. Although angering critics of the United States throughout Latin America, the overthrow of a leftist government in the Dominican Republic seemed to steel Johnson's determination to hold the line against communism in Vietnam.

Later that spring, as another South Vietnamese government was forming in Saigon, **General William Westmoreland**, who directed the U.S. effort, recommended using "search-and-destroy" missions against communist forces. By relying on helicopters to deploy U.S. forces quickly, Westmoreland envisioned that U.S. troops would engage enemy units, inflict as many casualties as possible, and withdraw without trying to secure the battleground. "Body count"—the number of enemy forces killed or disabled—became the key measure of success for these missions. In July 1965, Johnson publicly agreed to send 50,000 additional military personnel to Vietnam. Privately, he pledged to send another 50,000 and left open the possibility of deploying even more. LBJ also approved saturation bombing in the South Vietnamese countryside and intensified bombardment of the North.

Some advisers urged Johnson to inform the public candidly about the expanded U.S. military effort. They recommended seeking an outright declaration of war from Congress or at least legislation allowing the president to wield the economic and informational controls that previous administrations had used during wartime. Worried about provoking antiwar members of Congress and expanding a still-small antiwar movement, however, Johnson decided to stress the administration's willingness to negotiate and to act as if the war he was expanding was not really a war. The Johnson administration talked of seeing "light at the end of the tunnel" and apparently hoped that most people in the United States would remain largely in the dark about events in Vietnam.

Over the next three years, U.S. involvement steadily increased. The number of U.S. troops in Vietnam grew to 535,000. Operation Ranch Hand scorched South

MAP 29.1 Vietnam War

The war in Vietnam spread into neighboring countries as the United States sought to prevent North Vietnam from bringing supplies and troops southward along a network called the Ho Chi Minh Trail. Unlike the Korean War the guerrilla-style war in Indochina had few conventional battle "fronts."

Vietnam's croplands and defoliated half its forests in an effort to eliminate the natural cover for enemy troop movements. Operation Rolling Thunder, despite several brief pauses, continued until the Pentagon finally declared it a strategic failure in late 1968. Overall, U.S. planes dropped approximately 1.5 million tons of bombs—more than all the tonnage dropped during the Second World War—that pounded North Vietnamese cities and pummeled the villages and hamlets of the South.

Despite this level of violence, Vietnam remained a "limited" war. The United States avoided bombing close to the Chinese border. China had stationed more than 300,000 troops in North Vietnam, and Johnson feared provoking their entry, or possibly even that of the Soviet Union. The strategy remained one of containing the NLF and North Vietnam by steadily escalating the cost they would pay in lost lives and bombed-out infrastructure. Estimates that a kill ratio of 10 to 1 would force North Vietnam and the NLF to pull back encouraged the U.S. military command to unleash more firepower and further inflate enemy casualty figures. Whenever the number of enemy forces seemed to increase, the Pentagon requested more U.S. troops to maintain the desired kill ratio.

Johnson, whose notorious temper flared at the first hint of bad news, used body count numbers to justify public claims of victory being "just around the corner." Privately, though, a different picture began to emerge. Enjoying material assistance from the Soviet Union and China, North Vietnam could match every U.S. escalation. The North Vietnamese funneled troops and supplies into the South through the shifting network of roads and paths, primarily through Laos, called the Ho Chi Minh Trail. By the end of 1967, several of Johnson's key aides, most notably Secretary of Defense Robert McNamara, decided that the United States could not sustain its commitment to South Vietnam. The price for containing North Vietnam had become far too steep. The majority of Johnson's advisers, however, refused to accept McNamara's assessment.

Johnson continued to lack an effective ally in Saigon. The devastation of the countryside from the U.S. military strategy, the economic destabilization from the flood of U.S. dollars, and the political corruption of Saigon officials took their toll. The "pacification" and "strategic hamlet" programs, which gathered Vietnamese farmers into tightly guarded villages, sounded viable in Washington but created greater instability by uprooting many South Vietnamese from their villages and ancestral lands. Buddhist priests persistently demonstrated against foreign influence. In 1967, Generals Nguyen Van Thieu and Nguyen Cao Ky, having sustained a military regime in Saigon longer than any of their predecessors, tried to legitimate their rule by holding a new election. But a voting process shot through with corruption only highlighted their precarious political position and their dependence on aid from Washington.

The Media and the War   The destruction wreaked by U.S. forces was giving the NLF, North Vietnamese, Chinese, and Soviet leaders a propaganda advantage in what had become an international war of imagery. Pictures from Southeast Asia allowed critics around the world to condemn the U.S. bombardments and its search-and-destroy strategy. In Western Europe, demonstrations against the United States became prominent features of political life. Antiwar protesters at home constantly hounded the president and members of his administration, and Johnson eventually complained of being a prisoner in his own White House.

In previous wars, Washington had restricted media coverage. Hoping to avoid the controversy that overt censorship would surely cause, the Johnson administration tried to employ informal ways of managing information. With television making Vietnam a "living room war"—one that people could watch in their own homes—Johnson kept three TV sets playing in his office in order to monitor what viewers were seeing. Most of what he saw, early on, he liked. *Time* magazine initially praised General Westmoreland's leadership and named him its "Man of the Year" for 1965. In time, however, media coverage changed. Images of unrelenting destruction coming across TV screens undercut the optimistic words coming from the White House. After gazing at his TV sets, LBJ started telephoning network executives, castigating them for broadcasts to which he objected. More and more journalists, following the lead of Pulitzer Prize winning reporter David Halberstam, challenged reassuring claims by U.S. officials. Younger journalists who traveled alongside U.S. troops, such as Michael Herr, came to represent the American mission as a drug-drenched trip into the surreal.

As the conflict dragged on, the media began to talk about a "war at home." Initially, commentators generally adopted a stark, bipolar story frame. It pitted the "hawks," people who wanted to fight in Vietnam until the United States "won," against the "doves," those who desired to end U.S. involvement as quickly as possible. Johnson claimed to be following the time-tested policy of containment, and Secretary of State Dean Rusk warned of the dangers of "appeasement." But influential U.S. politicians—led by J. William Fulbright of Arkansas, chair of the Senate Foreign Relations Committee—complained of misplaced priorities in Vietnam and of an American "arrogance of power." Gradually, it seemed as if the fundamental structures of domestic politics, society, and culture might unravel.

ACTIVISM AT HOME

Even as Lyndon Johnson's policy in Southeast Asia was coming under attack from antiwar activists, a broader culture of dissent emerged. Growing tensions produced a political landscape marked by bitterness, confrontation, polarization, and violence on a scale not seen in the United States for many years.

The Movement of Movements   No single group can lay exclusive claim to "the Sixties," the period from roughly 1963 to 1974 that coincided with the war in Vietnam. Still, those on the political and cultural left, especially when gaining recruits from the huge baby boom generation, initially dominated media accounts and the earliest histories of the era. Iconic images from the 1960s provide a kaleidoscopic panorama of what can be called a "movement of movements" that generally rejected a dominant ideal of the 1950s and early 1960s: the faith that political pluralism would almost always unite the nation.

Activists increasingly questioned the existing political system. At the same time, disparate movements based on deeply held values—involving issues such as war and peace, race relations, gender politics, the environment, and sexuality—took shape. Many activists sought the media spotlight to attract support for their visions of change. Four of the earliest and most prominent of the movements involved a New Left, a counterculture, Black Power, and an antiwar insurgency.

A New Left   While relatively few college students actually joined left-leaning movements, the activities of a **New Left** dominated politics on many campuses, attracted media attention, and in time generated popular controversy.

In 1962, two years after the new conservatism had formed Young Americans for Freedom, the left-leaning Students for a Democratic Society (SDS) emerged on the opposite end of the political spectrum. Although SDS advocated familiar causes, especially civil rights, it also called for a new style of personal politics. SDS's *Port Huron Statement* (1962) pledged to fight the "loneliness, estrangement, isolation" that supposedly afflicted many people. Charging that the dominant political culture valued bureaucratic expertise over citizen engagement and economic growth over meaningful work, SDS spoke for alternative visions. In politics, it called for "participatory democracy"—grassroots activism and institutions responsive to local needs.

The 1964 Freedom Summer in Mississippi provided a tangible example of participatory democracy as volunteers from the North joined local activists in registering African American voters and organizing for political action. Some volunteers remained in the South, working for civil rights, but others joined neighborhood-based political projects elsewhere in the country. Small-scale movements promised young people and their older allies the chance to reenergize political life from the ground up.

New Left activists constantly expanded their view of what counted as "politics." Although voter registration drives remained important in the South, for example, local movements came to place greater emphasis on alternative political forms, such as sit-ins and demonstrations. Their generation's vast size and its educational attainments made these insurgents ideally suited to confront a political system dominated by powerful and entrenched interests.

On campus, discontent simmered. Many restive students chafed at classes that seemed irrelevant to the issues of the day and at college bureaucracies that imposed restrictions on their living arrangements and lifestyle choices. They challenged whether deans of students should be able to establish dress codes and restrict visiting hours in dorms for students who, while off campus, qualified as adults. Far worse, according to New Left activists, giant universities compromised their independence and integrity by welcoming funding from the military-industrial complex

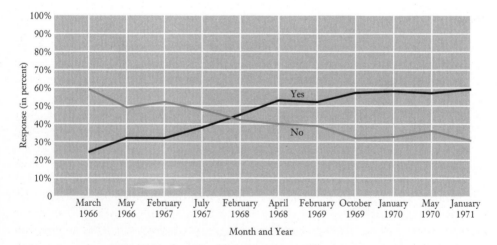

American Attitudes toward the Vietnam War

Responses to the question: "Do you think that the United States made a mistake in sending troops to fight there?"

and by seeming oblivious to the social and moral implications of war-related research.

During the "Berkeley Revolt" of 1964 and 1965, students and sympathetic faculty expanded their activism. They first protested how the University of California restricted political activity on campus and then began speaking out against its complicity in the Vietnam War and in racial discrimination. Protests rocked most other campuses during the Sixties, but the long-running drama at Berkeley, which disrupted classes and polarized one of the world's most prestigious universities, remained the preeminent symbol of the broader turmoil that the media began calling "the war on campus."

The Counterculture

Berkeley also hosted some of the earliest encounters between the political movements of the New Left and the freewheeling energies of a youth-dominated **counterculture**.

The counterculture of the mid-1960s remains a difficult "movement" to identify. Embracing the slogan "Do Your Own Thing," the counterculture elected no officers, held no formal meetings, and maintained no central office to issue manifestos. It burst into view in low-income neighborhoods, such as San Francisco's Haight-Ashbury area, and along the streets bordering college campuses, such as Berkeley's Telegraph Avenue. Its self-appointed spokespeople embraced values, lifestyles, and institutions hailed as alternatives to those of the dominant culture.

People drawn to this counterculture looked to earlier models, especially the Beats of the 1950s, but they eventually left their own imprint on a wide range of social and cultural movements, including the creation of cooperatives, radical feminism, environmentalism, and the fight against legal restrictions on lifestyle choices. The counterculture also affected mainstream consumer culture. The mass media, for example, invariably highlighted the flamboyant clothing, hairstyles, and uninhibited sexuality among younger devotees of the counterculture. They liked to portray countercultural "hippies" as being on the cutting edge of a massive, fun-filled "youth rebellion" and focused on use of drugs, such as marijuana and LSD, communal living arrangements, and new forms of music, such as the folk-rock of the Byrds and the acid rock of the Grateful Dead.

The counterculture developed its own soundtrack and created its own media. Music-oriented publications such as *Rolling Stone* magazine (founded in 1967) celebrated singer-songwriters, such as Bob Dylan and Joni Mitchell, as the counterculture's prophet laureates. Radio stations began featuring folk-rock and other sounds associated with the counterculture. In a pre-Internet age, these stations provided audio billboards for promoting musical and political events. Some stations joined print publications, such as the *Berkeley Barb*, in dispatching youthful journalists to report on—and participate in—the countercultural scene.

Images and products from the counterculture soon found a market among otherwise conventional consumers. The ad agency for Chrysler Motors urged car buyers to break from older patterns, purchase a youthful-looking 1965 model, and thereby join the "Dodge Rebellion." Recognizing the appeal of bands such as San Francisco's Jefferson Airplane, the music industry, too, saw profits to be made. An early countercultural happening, the "Human Be-In," organized by community activists from San Francisco in early 1967, provided a model for subsequent, commercially dominated music festivals such as Monterrey Pop (later in 1967) and Woodstock (in 1969).

Some of the students and faculty attracted to New Left politics worried that the counterculture would deflect young people from the hard work of political activism. The novelist Ken Kesey implicitly mocked a 1965 political demonstration at Berkeley with a style of politics indebted to the counterculture. Accompanied by veterans from the Beat movement and youthful members of his communal group, "the Merry Pranksters," Kesey alternated between singing choruses of "Home on the Range" and suggesting students ignore more traditional forms of politics and refashion, especially through drugs such as LSD, the personal politics of their own lives.

Civil Rights and Black Power	The media played an important and controversial role in efforts to achieve liberty and equality for African Americans. Civil rights leaders, of course, had long

recognized the value of media coverage. TV images of the violence in Selma, Alabama, in 1965 had helped Dr. King's Southern Christian Leadership Conference (SCLC) galvanize support for federal voting rights legislation. At one point, ABC television interrupted a special showing of the anti-Nazi film *Judgment at Nuremberg* to show white Alabama state troopers beating peaceful, mostly African American, voting rights marchers. Lyndon Johnson went on television to proclaim that "we shall overcome" the nation's "crippling legacy of bigotry and injustice."

The violence associated with the civil rights campaigns prompted different views. Segregationists and their allies insisted that media coverage of activism encouraged lawbreaking and violence and that only a renewed commitment to law and order would ease social tensions. Movement activists who looked to Dr. King replied that racism, lack of opportunity, and inadequate government remedies produced the frustration that spawned violence. Other more militant voices within the broad movement of movements argued that governments in the United States could not be relied upon to address race-related issues effectively and that aggrieved groups needed to mobilize themselves.

In 1965, this debate intensified in the wake of conflict in Los Angeles. An altercation between a white highway patrol officer and a black motorist escalated into six days of violence, centered in the largely African American community of Watts in the South-Central area of Los Angeles. Thirty-four people died; hundreds of businesses and homes were burned; heavily armed National Guard troops patrolled the streets; and television carried images of the destruction to the nation and the world. What provoked this conflagration? Had TV cameras and radio reports helped to fan the flames?

A stunned Lyndon Johnson called for new social welfare resources for Watts. "Let's move in—money, marbles, and chalk," LBJ reportedly ordered. The mayor and police chief of Los Angeles, conversely, blamed civil rights "agitators" and sought new resources for law enforcement. Local activist leaders created new organizations, such as the Watts Writers Workshop, and argued that only a determined strategy of local empowerment could produce access to more equitable policing practices, higher-paying jobs, and better housing.

The basic structure of the post-Watts debate would change relatively little as violence continued to move through, usually during the summer, other urban neighborhoods. According to one estimate, there were more than 300 cases of serious urban conflict between 1965 and 1969. Property damage reached into the billions of dollars, and hundreds of people lost their lives. Significant portions of major cities—but almost never the more affluent areas or nearby suburbs—became battlegrounds that would bear the scars of the Sixties for years to come. Commentators from different political camps applied their own value-soaked labels, including "riot," "rebellion," and "insurrection." The major outbreaks produced investigative commissions that debated these labels, parsed increasingly familiar arguments about causation, and pondered recommendations for change.

How do these "long, hot summers" fit into a history of the 1960s? The earliest narrative saw escalating violence and militant **Black Power** groups as splintering a previously united civil rights cause. A competing story about a movement of movements, however, suggests that there was never a single *movement* that could have been splintered. Long before Watts, a variety of black activist movements were advocating different ways to gain greater power for black communities.

Many Black Power efforts during the late 1950s and early 1960s looked to **Malcolm X**. He had initially gained attention as a minister in the Nation of Islam, a North American–based group popularly known as the "Black Muslims." Malcolm X oftentimes criticized Dr. King's gradual, nonviolent approach as largely irrelevant to the everyday problems of most African Americans and questioned the desirability or feasibility of racial integration. Malcolm X never advocated initiating confrontation, but he did endorse self-defense "by any means necessary."

Portrayed as a dangerous subversive by the FBI and most mainstream media, Malcolm X urged African Americans to "recapture our heritage and identity" and "launch a cultural revolution to unbrainwash an entire people." Seeking to extend his movement, Malcolm X eventually broke from the Black Muslims and established his own Organization of Afro-American Unity. Murdered in 1965 by enemies from the Nation of Islam, Malcolm X remained, especially after the posthumous publication of his *Autobiography* (1965), a powerful symbol for black-centered political and cultural visions of the future.

These visions increasingly diverged from those of LBJ's program for expanding civil rights legislation, and the president privately struggled to understand movements with goals that differed from his. During a "racial summit" at the White House in 1965, A. Philip Randolph, Bayard Rustin, and others lobbied for a Freedom Budget, an overt criticism of their host's spending priorities. They called for allocating $100 billion on infrastructure projects in low-income neighborhoods. Johnson privately denounced these veteran civil rights leaders and the Freedom Budget for "raising un-shirted hell" at *his* summit.

Events in the South highlighted other differences among the movements. In June 1966, a KKK gunman shot James Meredith, who had integrated the University

HISTORY THROUGH FILM

Malcolm X (1992)

Directed by Spike Lee. Starring Denzel Washington (Malcolm X), Angela Bassett (Betty Shabbaz), and Al Freeman, Jr. (Elijah Muhammad).

For more than 25 years, Hollywood tried to make a movie portraying Malcolm X, whose *Autobiography* (1965) is a literary classic. Problems always stymied production plans. Finally, in 1992, Spike Lee's independent production company (named Forty Acres and a Mule, after the land distribution program for former slaves advocated after the Civil War) released a movie that argues for Malcolm X's continuing relevance.

The montage sequences that begin and end the movie underscore the film director's outlook. Against the backdrop of the Warner Brothers logo, the soundtrack introduces the actual voice of Malcolm X decrying the nature of racial politics over the course of U.S. history. Malcolm X's accusations continue as a giant American flag appears on screen and is cut into pieces by jagged images from an amateur video of Los Angeles police officers beating Rodney

King, a notorious instance of police misconduct that took place in 1991. Next, the flag begins to burn until, revealed behind it, a giant "X," adorned with remnants of the flag, fills the frame. Some three hours later, the ending of the movie presents archival footage of Malcolm X, along with images of South African freedom fighter Nelson Mandela, while the voice of Ozzie Davis, the celebrated African American actor, gives a eulogy.

When first released, the film opened to packed movie houses. Despite a multimedia publicity blitz, box office revenues steadily declined. Viewers reported that the lengthy, episodic movie taxed their patience and attention spans.

Being able to watch a digital version of *Malcolm X* today, however, allows viewers to concentrate on its best sequences, speeding by ones that seem to drag, and returning to those that initially might seem muddled. *Malcolm X* offers a complex account of the early Black Power movement, its foremost spokesperson, and the social ferment that gripped the nation during the 1960s.

of Mississippi several years earlier and was now conducting a one-person March against Fear from Tennessee to Jackson, Mississippi. A coalition of civil rights groups quickly organized an expanded March against Fear that would complete Meredith's walk. This was the first large-scale movement project—in contrast to the 1963 March on Washington and the 1965 voting rights campaign in Alabama—that did not seek new civil rights legislation. It sought, instead, to demonstrate that movements for liberty and equality could advance everyday struggles for safety, dignity, pride, and empowerment. The march also tried to capitalize on the national media coverage that Meredith's shooting had already attracted.

During the march, Stokely Carmichael played to the omnipresent TV cameras. Carmichael's rise to prominence had begun the previous year, when he organized a third-party political movement, bearing the striking logo of a coiled black panther, in Lowndes County, Alabama. In Mississippi, he questioned an unwavering commitment to nonviolence and urged that the civil rights struggle not remain just one

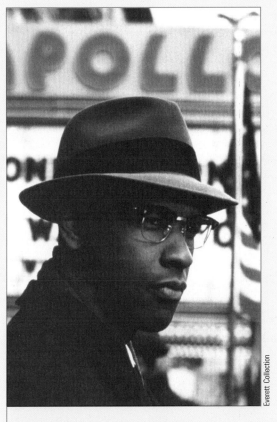

Everett Collection

Denzel Washington stars as Malcolm X

for "Freedom," the byword of the SCLC, but for "Black Power." As Carmichael later explained, Black Power was "a call for black people in this country to unite, to recognize their heritage, to build a sense of community." They should "define their own goals" and "lead their own organizations."

Black Power came to provide a sometimes inflammatory label for an often pragmatic set of claims that local civil rights groups had been making for some time. They sought greater on-the-ground power both in and for their own communities. Operating from this perspective, in 1966, several college students from Oakland announced a new Black Power organization that borrowed its name and logo from Carmichael's earlier movement in Lowndes County. This Black Panther Party's platform employed militant rhetoric on behalf of 10 objectives, including greater opportunities for housing, education, and employment; legal protections, especially against police misconduct; and improved health and nutrition initiatives in low-income black neighborhoods.

The Panther's trio of media-savvy young members—Huey Newton, Bobby Seale, and Eldridge Cleaver—adapted symbolism and rhetoric from Third World revolutionary movements. A 1967 rally in Sacramento, California, on behalf of the Second Amendment right to use firearms for self-defense attracted the notice of J. Edgar Hoover. He made destroying the Black Panther Party a key goal of his FBI.

Less flamboyant groups and movements were also invoking the Black Power approach. Fully embracing the word *black* and a political-cultural agenda based on racial identity, they sought the power to pursue separate, African American–directed routes not just toward liberty and equality but also toward "liberation" from the prevailing political culture. "Black Is Beautiful" became a watchword. James Brown, the "Godfather of Soul," captured this new spirit with his song, "Say It Loud, I'm Black and I'm Proud" (1968).

Within this volatile context, Congress passed the **Civil Rights Act of 1968**. One provision of this omnibus measure, popularly known as the "Fair Housing Act," followed in the wake of earlier state-level measures and aimed at eliminating racial discrimination in the national real estate market. The act, however, contained ambiguous language that eventually enfeebled its enforcement. Another section in the law declared it a crime to cross state lines in order to incite a "riot." Supporters hailed this provision as a victory for law and order, while critics countered that it targeted political activists, especially those in the Black Power movement.

The Antiwar Movement

Meanwhile, another of these multifaceted movements was coming to overshadow all others: the one to end the war in Vietnam.

The antiwar movement, like its counterparts, never fell into neat categories. Some of the strongest "antiwar" sentiment, for example, blamed LBJ for not prosecuting the war *aggressively enough*. At the other end of the spectrum, several small movements called for a North Vietnam–NLF victory. The chant, "Ho, Ho, Ho Chi Minh/NLF Is Gonna Win" enraged Johnson and distressed most others in the antiwar coalition.

The antiwar effort faced the same questions as the other movements of the Sixties. What kind of politics best expressed its ethical and spiritual values? How might it reach out to people not already in the movement? Could it mobilize enough support to change public policy?

The antiwar movement gradually expanded the scope of its activism. On college campuses, supporters and opponents of the war initially debated at "teach-ins," academic-style events that soon gave way to demonstrations and sit-ins. A draft-resistance effort emerged, often symbolized by the burning of draft cards, which urged young men to refuse to serve in the military. This effort gained its most celebrated member when the heavyweight boxing champion Muhammad Ali refused induction into the military. Campus protests passed into a new phase when a pitched, bloody battle broke out between antiwar demonstrators and police at the University of Wisconsin in Madison in 1967.

Dr. Martin Luther King, Jr., now faced pressure from other antiwar clergy to proclaim publicly his opposition to the war, connect this conflict overseas to the civil rights cause at home, and elaborate his vision of the moral-spiritual issues at stake. Speaking at New York's Riverside Church in April 1967, Dr. King highlighted a black-and-white truth. African American troops, mostly from low-income communities, served and died in numbers far greater than their proportion of the U.S. population "for a nation that has been unable to seat them together in the same schools." The immoral "madness" in Vietnam "must cease," Dr. King concluded. Voices from the political-media mainstream condemned his antiwar address, and as Dr. King continued to broaden his political agenda, criticism from onetime supporters commonly followed.

Meanwhile, a massive 1967 antiwar demonstration in Washington suggested how the politics of the New Left and the spirit of the counterculture could march together, at least when opposing LBJ's policies in Vietnam. Noting the visual media's voracious appetite for pictures of colorful dissenters, a small group of activists had invented a kind of "non-movement movement" that bypassed mobilization and organization in favor of making the media its primary constituency. Two members of this group, Abbie Hoffman and Jerry Rubin, proclaimed themselves leaders of a (nonexistent) Youth International Party (or YIPPIE!) and waited for media coverage to surround their activities, as they knew it would.

Hoffman and Rubin raised the curtain on a new style of countercultural-political performance. In one incident, they mocked the symbolic value of stocks on the New York Exchange by tossing real dollar bills onto the trading floor. Invoking the sit-in movement, they joked about staging department store "loot-ins." Their contribution to the 1967 antiwar march in Washington would be to lead a separate trek to the Pentagon, where marchers would chant mystical incantations and try to levitate the building.

Although the Pentagon remained firmly planted, the march against it did generate eye-catching media imagery. The event also gained the novelist and antiwar activist Norman Mailer a National Book Award for *Armies of the Night* (1968). Mailer's book, which wove together personal impressions and journalistic observation, helped to reinvent political reporting. Cultural observers identified accounts such as Mailer's as a "new journalism" and saw this form of reportage paralleling how political activists were creating a "new politics" that expanded ideas about what counted as political involvement.

1968

The relationship between this new politics and the media seemed uncertain. Might not images of colorful quipsters such as Hoffman and Rubin help fuel cultural polarization rather than political action? Was the media's taste for spectacular demonstrations trivializing underlying issues? Such questions became even more pressing during the tumultuous 12 months of 1968.

Turmoil in Vietnam, 1968   At the end of January 1968, during a supposed truce in observance of Tet, the Vietnamese lunar New Year celebration, NLF and North Vietnamese forces suddenly went on the attack throughout South Vietnam. A small NLF force even temporarily seized the grounds of the U.S. embassy in Saigon. Militarily, this **Tet Offensive** gained the NLF and the North relatively little territory at a very high cost. The NLF lost three-quarters of its military forces and much of its civilian support structure. But in the United States, the Tet Offensive was a turning point. It discredited General Westmoreland's pre-Tet forecasts about seeing "light at the end of the tunnel." Even after rolling back the communist onslaught, the U.S. military command appeared ill prepared to pursue the badly mauled enemy forces.

Most importantly, the mere fact of a Tet Offensive undercut the optimistic story that the Johnson administration had been spinning. After CBS-TV news anchor Walter Cronkite returned from a post-Tet trip to Vietnam, he told a national audience that the United States would never prevail militarily. Lyndon Johnson reportedly lamented that if he had lost "the most trusted person in America," as Cronkite was then known, he had lost the rest of the country.

Johnson received more bad news after summoning his most trusted advisers and a select group of senior outsiders, including Dean Acheson, for advice on General Westmoreland's request for an additional 206,000 U.S. troops. Most rejected Westmoreland's call and insisted that South Vietnamese troops shoulder more of the military burden. The views of the senior members, the so-called "Wise Men," proved especially sobering since they had formulated America's anti-communist containment policy following the Second World War. Dean Acheson now advised the president that the United States "could no longer do the job we set out to do" in Vietnam "in the time we have left, and we must begin to take steps to disengage."

Other factors weighed on Johnson as well. Any plan for using additional U.S. military power to crush North Vietnam carried an unthinkable risk: a larger conflict with China and/or the Soviet Union. Sobered by public opinion polls showing rapidly declining confidence in U.S. policy and pressured by his new secretary of defense, Clark Clifford, another early architect of cold war containment, Johnson changed his guiding assumption about Vietnam. The cost of continuing the U.S. intervention vastly outweighed whatever benefit might accrue. Johnson continued to prosecute the war but simultaneously moved toward negotiation.

Turmoil at Home   The Tet Offensive also destroyed Lyndon Johnson's political plans. The antiwar wing of the Democratic Party was already trying to do what seasoned political pundits had declared impossible: deny Johnson renomination. The dissidents backed **Senator Eugene McCarthy** of Minnesota, still the only prominent Democrat willing to challenge LBJ. The McCarthy movement's version of new politics relied on the wisdom of a few seasoned political strategists and the energy of thousands of college students. Young people packed away grubby campus attire, donned fresh clothing to "come clean for Gene," and stumped New Hampshire in the initial primary of 1968. Because Johnson refused to campaign personally, this "Dump Johnson" effort enjoyed unexpected media coverage. Johnson's forces actually won the New Hampshire primary, but McCarthy came close enough to claim a symbolic victory. Polls predicted he would easily beat Johnson, head-to-head, in the upcoming Wisconsin primary.

Even before the Wisconsin contest, Senator Robert Kennedy of New York, brother of the slain president, jumped into the race. He had refused earlier entreaties to challenge Johnson but now declared that the nation's "perilous course" impelled him to seek the presidency. Facing two Democratic challengers, President Johnson surprised all but his closest confidants when, during a live TV address in late March about Vietnam, he suddenly announced that he would not seek reelection. He also limited U.S. bombing of North Vietnam and signaled a readiness to begin peace negotiations in Paris.

Johnson's withdrawal created a three-way race for the Democratic nomination. McCarthy now faced Robert Kennedy and Johnson's ever-loyal vice president, Hubert H. Humphrey, who had entered the fray after LBJ's surprise announcement. Humphrey, however, steered clear of the remaining primaries, leaving the two senators to fight a series of brass-knuckled contests that pitted McCarthy's new politics against Kennedy's blend of the new and the old. Kennedy once quipped that the "'A' students may have already flocked to McCarthy," but that he was "locking up those receiving 'Bs.'" The Democratic Party's A-level celebrities generally divided their support between the two, while Humphrey courted the Democratic power brokers who had been allied with LBJ.

Martin Luther King, Jr., welcomed LBJ's withdrawal and hoped that an antiwar candidate, ideally Kennedy, would head the Democratic ticket in November. On April 4, 1968, however, Dr. King took a break from planning an upcoming "Poor People's March" on Washington and visited Memphis, Tennessee, in support of a strike by African American sanitation workers. There, he was assassinated while standing on the balcony of his motel. Law enforcement officials identified James Earl Ray, a career criminal, as the lone killer. Ray was eventually captured and charged with King's murder. He waived a jury trial, pleaded guilty, and received a 99-year prison sentence. Subsequently, Ray recanted and claimed to have been a pawn in a conspiracy directed by white supremacists. He died in prison still insisting on his innocence, but few people credit his claims.

As news of Dr. King's murder spread, violence swept through more than 100 cities and towns; 39 people died; 75,000 regular and National Guard troops were called to duty. When President Johnson proclaimed Sunday, April 7, as a day of national mourning for the slain civil rights leader, parts of the nation's capital city remained ablaze.

Following Dr. King's memorial service, Gene McCarthy and Robert Kennedy returned to campaigning. Kennedy sought to demonstrate that popular opinion favored his candidacy. He also hoped to convince the insiders now backing Humphrey that only a Democrat without ties to Lyndon Johnson, especially another Kennedy, could capture the White House in November.

On June 5, an ebullient Kennedy defeated McCarthy in California's Democratic primary. While preparing to leave the hotel that had hosted his victory celebration, Kennedy was slain by yet another political assassin. Bystanders grabbed Sirhan Sirhan, a Palestinian immigrant, who was later convicted of the killing. Nonstop network television coverage of Kennedy's body being returned by train to Washington

Bettmann/Corbis

The Funeral Procession of Dr. Martin Luther King, Jr., April 9, 1968. *A vast crowd of mourners, including ordinary people and dignitaries, accompanied the body of Dr. King through the streets of Atlanta, Georgia. The simple, horse-drawn wagon had become the symbol of one of his final efforts, a Poor People's Campaign, that was to include a march on the nation's capital. After Dr. King's assassination in Memphis, a wagon would bear his body through the streets of the city in which he had grown up and gone to college.*

and his state funeral were reminders of Dr. King's recent murder and of the 1963 assassination of RFK's own brother. Bowing to the reality of Humphrey's delegate total, McCarthy effectively closed down his campaign.

Questions abounded. Was some "sickness" plaguing American political culture? Did "government by gunplay," rather than political pluralism, best describe the current system? Could the presidential election of 1968 possibly produce a legitimate victor?

The violence of 1968 continued. That summer, thousands of antiwar demonstrators converged on Chicago, site of the Democratic Party's convention, to protest the nomination of Hubert Humphrey, still supporting Johnson's policy in Vietnam. Responding to provocative acts by some demonstrators, including Abbie Hoffman and Jerry Rubin, police officers attacked antiwar protestors and some nearby journalists. Opinion polls showed that most people supported the use of force against the demonstrators, a judgment subsequently challenged by a special commission, whose report assessed the violence in Chicago as a "police riot." Tensions from this "Siege of Chicago" filtered into the convention hall, as antiwar delegates and supporters of the vice president denounced one another. Humphrey easily captured the Democratic presidential nod, but bitter feelings over Johnson's Vietnam policy and the conduct of Chicago's police force left his party deeply divided.

The Election of 1968

Both Humphrey and the Republican nominee, former vice president Richard Nixon, worried about Alabama's George Wallace, who was running for president as a third-party candidate on the American Independent ticket. His opposition to civil rights well established, Wallace concentrated his fire on the counterculture and the antiwar movement. If any "hippie" protestor ever blocked his motorcade, he once announced, it would "be the last car he'll ever lay down in front of." Although Wallace had generally supported the Democratic Party's domestic spending programs, he now courted voters who saw themselves the captives of "tax-and-spend" bureaucracies in Washington.

Wallace never expected to gain the presidency. If a candidate from the two major parties failed to win a majority in the Electoral College vote, however, the Constitution required that the president be selected by the House of Representatives, where Wallace hoped to play the power-broker role by winning a sizable number of electoral votes.

Humphrey struggled with antiwar Democrats over his inability, until late in the campaign, to break from the Vietnam policies of Lyndon Johnson, his political patron. Conservative Republicans who favored Ronald Reagan as the GOP's 1968

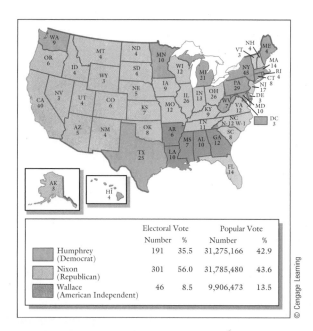

	Electoral Vote		Popular Vote	
	Number	%	Number	%
Humphrey (Democrat)	191	35.5	31,275,166	42.9
Nixon (Republican)	301	56.0	31,785,480	43.6
Wallace (American Independent)	46	8.5	9,906,473	13.5

© Cengage Learning

MAP 29.2 Presidential Election, 1968

George Wallace sought to throw the 1968 presidential election into the House of Representatives with his independent, third-party candidacy. What does this map suggest about the political changes already sweeping through the once solidly Democratic South?

nominee still suspected Nixon to be an Eisenhower moderate. They also recognized, however, that Nixon clearly stood to Humphrey's political right and that he appeared a safer guardian of conservative values than the mercurial Wallace. Nixon promised to restore order at home and hinted at a secret plan for ending U.S. involvement in Vietnam.

Nixon narrowly prevailed in November. Although he won 56 percent of the electoral vote, Nixon outpolled Humphrey in the popular vote by less than 1 percent. George Wallace's plan collapsed when he picked up only 46 electoral votes, all from the Deep South, and just 13.5 percent of the popular vote nationwide. Nixon won five crucial southern states and attracted, all across the country, votes from people he called "the forgotten Americans, the non-shouters, the non-demonstrators."

The results in several states, however, were so close that relatively small shifts could have produced a victory for Humphrey or the scenario that Wallace had envisioned playing out in the House of Representatives. Humphrey's campaign suddenly gained momentum when Lyndon Johnson temporarily halted all bombing of North Vietnam and sought to accelerate the peace talks in Paris. Nixon's forces responded with back-channel overtures to South Vietnamese leaders about getting a better deal if they stalled peace negotiations until a Nixon presidency. Illegal wiretaps informed Johnson of Nixon's maneuver, but LBJ never intervened on Humphrey's behalf.

Continued Polarization, 1969–1974

Raised a Quaker, **Richard Milhous Nixon** campaigned as someone able to restore the kind of tranquility he had known when growing up in Yorba Linda, California. His presidency, however, failed to calm the troubled waters.

Lawbreaking, Violence, and a New President   A handful of people on the leftist fringe embraced violence, generally through bomb attacks. There were nearly 200 actual and attempted bombings on college campuses during the 1969–1970 academic year; an explosion at the University of Wisconsin claimed the life of a graduate student. Nonlethal attacks rocked several large banks and the U.S. Capitol building. In 1970, three members of a small faction that had broken with SDS, "the Weather Underground," blew themselves apart when their bomb factory in New York City exploded.

At the same time, government officials stepped up their use of violent force. Fred Hampton of the Black Panthers and prison activist George Jackson died under circumstances their supporters called political assassination and public officials considered normal law enforcement. J. Edgar Hoover's FBI harassed activists, planted damaging rumors, and even dispatched *agent provocateurs* who incited protestors to undertake actions that officials could later prosecute as crimes.

State and local officials redoubled their efforts to bring order. During the fall of 1971, New York governor Nelson Rockefeller broke off negotiations with inmates at Attica State Prison, who had seized several cell blocks and taken guards hostage in a protest over living conditions. He then ordered heavily armed state troopers and National Guard forces into the complex. When this "Attica Uprising" finally ended, 29 prisoners and 11 guards lay dead. On college campuses, too, local officials were increasingly ready to employ force against demonstrators.

Richard Nixon insisted that his vast public experience made him the ideal leader for such turbulent times. After graduating from Whittier College in California, Nixon studied law at Duke University and served in the navy during the Second World War. He then began a political career that took him from a small-town law practice to the House of Representatives in 1946, the Senate in 1950, and the vice presidency in 1952.

Nixon claimed that he excelled at confronting personal and political challenges. He entitled an early memoir *Six Crises*. Nixon had announced his own retirement from politics in 1962, but campaigned loyally for Barry Goldwater in 1964 and for Republican candidates in 1966. The GOP's comeback that year boosted Nixon's stature, and supporters talked about a "New Nixon." Detractors complained of seeing "the same Old Nixon, now just a little older."

Social Policy   Although Nixon considered foreign policy his specialty, he initially crafted an ambitious domestic agenda. At the urging of Democrat Daniel Patrick Moynihan, a special presidential adviser, Nixon decided he could push through bolder programs than any Democratic president. Moynihan encouraged Nixon to think of himself as a conservative who could bring about progressive change. In 1969, Nixon thus proposed his **Family Assistance Plan (FAP)**, a dramatic overhaul of welfare policy. FAP proposed replacing most existing welfare measures, including the controversial Aid to Families with Dependent Children (AFDC). AFDC provided government payments to cover the basic costs of care for low-income children who had lost the support of a breadwinning parent.

Under the FAP proposal, *every* low-income family would be guaranteed an annual income of $1,600. Moynihan and Nixon touted FAP as advancing equality since it replaced existing arrangements that assisted only those with special circumstances. Nixon liked the measure because it promised to cut out the layers of bureaucracy needed to administer the requirements of a complicated program such as AFDC.

Nixon's FAP proposal debuted to tepid reviews. Conservatives complained about income supplements for families with regularly employed, albeit low-paid, wage earners. Proponents of more generous governmental assistance programs argued that FAP's income guarantee was too miserly. The House of Representatives approved a modified version of FAP in 1970, but a curious alliance of senators who opposed Nixon's proposal for very different reasons blocked its passage. Nixon quickly abandoned FAP, and the nation's welfare system would not be overhauled until the 1990s.

Congress did pass Nixon's revenue-sharing plan, part of his "new federalism," which returned a portion of federal tax dollars to state and local governments in the form of block grants. Instead of Washington specifying how these funds could be used, the block grant concept allowed state and local officials, within general guidelines, to spend the funds as they saw fit.

A Democratic-controlled Congress and a Republican White House also agreed to continue and even increase funding for many Great Society initiatives: Medicare, Medicaid, rent subsidies for low-income people, and Supplementary Security Insurance (SSI) payments to those who were elderly, blind, or disabled. In 1972, Social Security benefits were "indexed," which meant they would increase along with the inflation rate.

Nixon had adopted a complicated approach to civil rights during his campaign. He commonly criticized existing policies, such as the busing of children to advance school integration, but carefully distinguished his stance from that of George Wallace. The new Nixon administration included Republicans anxious to aid civil rights causes, and the White House allowed, and sometimes even urged, federal bureaucracies to extend the reach of civil rights measures passed during the Great Society. In line with candidate Nixon's call for supporting "black capitalism" through small-business loans, the new president helped extend the plan to other minority entrepreneurs, particularly Hispanics. His administration also helped implement the bilingual education programs that had been authorized in 1968 legislation. Indeed, many federal social welfare programs expanded during Nixon's first term, and the percentage of people living below the poverty line declined.

Environmentalism Nixon also worked with the new environmental movement that became a significant political force during his presidency. Landmark legislation of the 1960s—such as the Wilderness Act of 1964, the National Wild and Scenic Rivers Act of 1968, and the National Trails Act of 1968—had already protected large areas of the country from commercial development. In the 1970s, a broader environmental movement focused on people's health and on ecological balance. Accounts such as *The Silent Spring* (1962) by Rachel Carson raised concerns that the pesticides used in agriculture, especially DDT, threatened bird populations. Air pollution (smog) in cities such as Los Angeles had become so toxic that simply breathing became equivalent to smoking several packs of cigarettes per day. Industrial processes, atomic weapons testing, and nuclear power plants prompted fear of cancer-causing materials. The Environmental Defense Fund, a private organization formed in 1967, went to court to try to limit DDT and other dangerous toxins. Earth Day, a festival first held in 1970, aimed to raise awareness about the many newly publicized hazards of environmental degradation.

The Nixon administration, although remaining aloof from Earth Day, took environmental issues seriously. The president supported creation of the Environmental Protection Agency (EPA) and signed major pieces of congressional legislation: the Resources Recovery Act of 1970 (dealing with waste management), the Clean Air Act of 1970, the Water Pollution Control Act of 1972, the Pesticides Control Act of 1972, and the Endangered Species Act of 1973. National parks and wilderness areas were expanded, and a new law required that "environmental impact statements" be prepared in advance of any major government project.

The new environmental standards brought both unanticipated problems and significant improvements. The Clean Air Act's requirement for taller factory smokestacks, for example, moved pollutants higher into the atmosphere, where they produced a dangerous by-product, "acid rain." Still, the act's restrictions on auto and smokestack emissions cleared smog out of city skies and helped people with respiratory ailments. The law reduced six major airborne pollutants by one-third in a single decade. Lead emissions into the atmosphere declined by 95 percent.

| **Controversies over Rights** | Activism on social and environmental concerns accompanied fierce debate over the federal government's responsibility to protect the rights and liberties of citizens. The struggle to |

locate and define these rights soon embroiled the nation's constitutional culture in controversy.

A majority of the justices on the Supreme Court of the Sixties had supported the Great Society's political vision and sought to bring an expanding list of rights under constitutional protection. As this group charted the Court's path, two Eisenhower appointees, Chief Justice Earl Warren and Associate Justice William Brennan, often led the way. Although many of the Warren Court's decisions involving rights issues drew critical fire, the case that raised the most public controversy involved handling criminal suspects. *Miranda v. Arizona* (1966) famously held that the Constitution required police officers to advise persons suspected of having committed a felony offense of their constitutional right to remain silent and to consult an attorney, which would be provided to indigents by the government. Amid rising public concern over crime, political conservatives made decisions such as *Miranda* symbols of what they alleged were the judicial "coddling" of criminals and the Warren Court "inventing" rights not found in the Constitution.

Richard Nixon had campaigned for president as an opponent of the Warren Court and promised to appoint federal judges who would "apply" rather than "invent" the law on matters such as criminal rights and court-ordered school busing. As candidate Nixon continued to assail the Warren Court, the chief justice announced his retirement, and Lyndon Johnson's plan to anoint his close confidant, Associate Justice Abe Fortas, as Warren's successor stalled. Consequently, the victorious Nixon appointed a Republican loyalist, Warren Burger, as chief justice. Subsequent vacancies allowed Nixon to appoint three other Republicans to the High Court.

This new Burger Court immediately faced controversial rights-related cases. Lawyers sympathetic to the Great Society vision of social welfare advanced the argument that access to adequate economic assistance from the federal government was a constitutionally protected right. The Burger Court, however, narrowly rejected this claim in 1970 (*Dandridge v. Williams*), holding that payments to welfare recipients could vary from state to state without violating the constitutional requirement of equal protection of the law.

Other rights-related claims generally fared better. After vetoing two earlier versions, because of his opposition to funding levels, President Nixon signed the Rehabilitation Act of 1973. This civil rights law, pressed by a broadly based activist movement, not only helped people with disabilities fight against various forms of public and private discrimination but assisted them in gaining access to a wide range of governmental services. A vigorous consumer movement, which had initially drawn inspiration from Ralph Nader's exposé about auto safety (*Unsafe at Any Speed*, 1965), joined with environmentalists to bolster new rights claims in the context of workplace safety, consumer protection, and a nontoxic environment. Their efforts found expression in such legislation as the Occupational Safety Act of 1973 and stronger consumer and environmental protection laws. The Burger Court invariably supported the constitutionality of these measures.

At the same time, the newly energized women's rights movement pressed another set of issues. An **Equal Rights Amendment (ERA)**, initially proposed during the 1920s, would explicitly guarantee women the same legal rights as men. Easily passed by Congress in 1972 and quickly ratified by more than half the states, the ERA suddenly stalled. Conservative women's groups, such as Phyllis Schlafly's "Stop ERA," charged that this constitutional amendment would undermine traditional "family values" and expose women to new dangers such as military service. The ERA failed to attain approval from the three-quarters of states needed for ratification. Ultimately, women's groups abandoned the ERA effort in favor of using the courts to adjudicate equal rights claims on a case-by-case, issue-by-issue basis.

One of these issues, whether a woman possessed a constitutional right to terminate a pregnancy, became far more controversial than the ERA. The abortion issue, in contrast to controversies over busing and criminal procedure, had never played a prominent role in Nixon's 1968 campaign, and his administration thus paid little attention to this rights-related question when nominating federal judges. In *Roe v. Wade* **(1973)**, the Burger Supreme Court ruled, in a 7–2 decision, that a state law making abortion a criminal offense violated a woman's "right to privacy." Two of the three justices appointed by Nixon voted with the majority. The *Roe* decision outraged antiabortion groups, who rallied under the "Right-to-Life" banner on behalf of the unborn fetus and provided new support for the already expanding conservative wing of the Republican Party. On the other side, feminist groups made the issue of individual choice in reproductive decisions a central rallying point.

Meanwhile, with little controversy, President Nixon signed an extension of the Voting Rights Act of 1965, and in 1972 approved another civil rights measure popularly known as "Title IX." It banned sexual discrimination in higher education and became the legal basis for requiring colleges and universities to adopt "gender equity" in all areas, including intercollegiate athletics. The Nixon administration also refined the "affirmative action" concept, which had surfaced during Lyndon Johnson's presidency, and required that all hiring and contracting that depended on federal funding take "affirmative" steps to enroll greater numbers of people from underrepresented groups as union apprentices.

Economic Woes   The Nixon administration eventually confronted economic problems that had been unthinkable only a decade earlier. No single cause can account for them, but most analyses begin with the war in Vietnam. This expensive military commitment, along with increased domestic spending and a volatile international economy, began to curtail economic growth. Lyndon Johnson had been determined to contain communism in Indochina without cutting Great Society programs or raising taxes, and thus he had concealed the true costs of the war. Nixon inherited a deteriorating (although still favorable) balance of trade and rising rate of inflation. Nixon never expected to grapple with a faltering economy. One of his economic advisers conceded that the president had "an almost pathological block about considering economic issues."

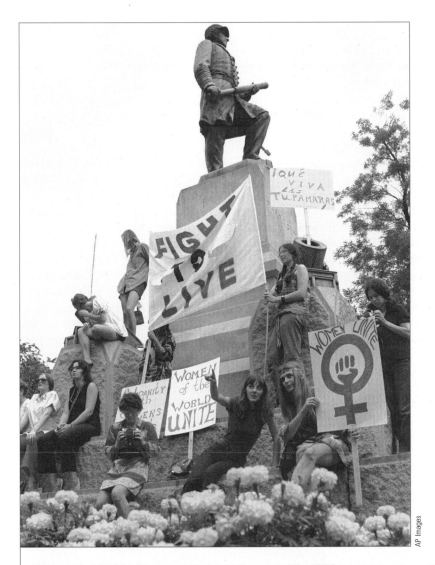

AP Images

Women's Rights Demonstrators, August 16, 1970. *Activists, who gathered in Washington, D.C. to demonstrate on behalf of women's rights, take time to rest. Why might they have chosen to "occupy" a statue erected in honor of a 19th-century military hero, Admiral David G. Farragut?*

By 1971, though, the unemployment rate topped 6 percent. According to conventional wisdom, expressed in an economic concept called "the Phillips curve," when unemployment rises, prices should remain constant or even decline. Yet *both* unemployment and inflation numbers were going up simultaneously. Economists coined the term **stagflation** to describe this puzzling convergence of economic stagnation and price inflation. Along with stagflation, U.S. exports were becoming less competitive in international markets and in 1971, for the first time in the 20th century, the United States ran a trade deficit, importing more products than it exported.

Although long critical of economic regulation, Nixon now needed a quick governmental cure for the nation's economic ills. His narrow victory in 1968 and GOP setbacks in the midterm elections of 1970 left him fearful of the political fallout from stagflation and trade imbalances. In January 1971 he suddenly, and surprisingly, announced, "I am now a Keynesian in economics" and began proclaiming his faith in governmental remedies. In August, he unveiled a "New Economic Policy" that included a 90-day freeze on any increases in wages and prices, to be followed by government monitoring to detect "excessive" increases in either.

Nixon simultaneously took an even more daring step. Dating from the 1944 Bretton Woods agreement, the value of the U.S. dollar had been tied to the value of gold—at $35 for every ounce. This meant that the United States would exchange its dollars for gold at that rate whenever any other nation's central bank requested it to do so. Other countries had fixed their own currency exchange rate in relation to the value of the U.S. dollar. But U.S. trade deficits were undermining the dollar and allowing foreign banks to exchange U.S. dollars for gold at rates far more favorable than $35 per ounce. In response, the Nixon administration abandoned the fixed gold-to-dollar ratio. Henceforth, the U.S. dollar would "float" in value against the prevailing market price for gold and against all other currencies in the world. This change would devalue the dollar and hopefully make American exports more competitive in the global marketplace. The strategy fundamentally altered the international economic order by allowing the value of all currencies to float and fluctuate.

In October 1973, oil-producing nations in the Middle East further changed international economic arrangements. Citing the declining U.S. dollar and falling oil revenues as justifications, petroleum producers began curtailing exports as a means of raising prices. About a week later, in response to U.S. military aid for Israel, then engaged in the Yom Kippur War with Egypt and Syria, Arab nations temporarily embargoed oil shipments to the United States. Nixon and Congress responded with a series of measures that included rationing, lower speed limits, and the naming of a new "energy czar." The days of "cheap oil" were coming to an end in the United States.

FOREIGN POLICY IN A TIME OF TURMOIL, 1969–1974

Even as it wrestled with divisive domestic concerns, the Nixon administration was far more interested in international affairs. Henry Kissinger, Nixon's national security adviser and later his secretary of state, laid out a grand strategy: **détente** with the Soviet Union, normalization of relations with China, and disengagement from direct military involvement in South Vietnam.

Détente   Although Nixon had built his early political career on hard-line anticommunism, he and Kissinger worked to ease tensions with the two major communist nations: the Soviet Union and China. The Nixon-Kissinger team expected that improved relations might lead these nations to reduce their support for North Vietnam, increasing chances for a successful pull-back of U.S. combat troops.

Arms control talks took top priority in U.S.-Soviet relations. In 1969, the two superpowers opened the Strategic Arms Limitation Talks (SALT); after several years of high-level diplomacy, they signed an agreement (SALT I) that limited further development of both antiballistic missiles (ABMs) and offensive intercontinental ballistic missiles (ICBMs). SALT I's impact on the arms race was limited because it said nothing about the number of nuclear warheads that a single missile might carry. Still, the ability to conclude any arms-control pact signaled improving relations.

Nixon's overtures toward the People's Republic of China brought an even more dramatic break with the cold war past. Secret negotiations, often conducted personally by Kissinger, led to a slight easing of U.S. trade restrictions and then to an invitation from China for Americans to compete in a table tennis match. This celebrated "Ping-Pong diplomacy" presaged more significant diplomatic exchanges. Most spectacularly, Nixon visited China in 1972, posing for photos with Mao Zedong and strolling along the Great Wall. A few months later, the UN admitted the People's Republic as the sole representative of China, and in 1973 the United States and China exchanged informal diplomatic missions.

Vietnamization and the Nixon Doctrine   In Vietnam, the Nixon administration decided to speed withdrawal of U.S. ground forces by embracing a policy called "Vietnamization," which had already informally begun during Lyndon Johnson's administration. Put simply, this meant that South Vietnamese, rather than U.S. troops, should bear the burden of ground combat operations. In July 1969, the **Nixon Doctrine** announced a broader version of this approach. It pledged that the United States would extend military assistance to anticommunist governments in Asia but would require them to supply their own combat forces. From the outset, the Nixon Doctrine for Vietnam envisioned the eventual removal of U.S. ground troops without accepting compromise or defeat. While officially adhering to Johnson's 1968 bombing halt over the North, Nixon and Kissinger accelerated both the ground and air wars by launching new offensives and by approving a military "incursion" into Cambodia, an ostensibly neutral country. The 1970 operation into Cambodia, which targeted North Vietnamese there, aimed at shortening U.S. military engagement in Southeast Asia by temporarily expanding it.

The invasion of Cambodia set off a new wave of protests in the United States and around the world. U.S. campuses exploded in angry demonstrations against this obvious widening of the war, and a number of institutions began the summer vacation early. White police officers fatally shot two students at the all-black Jackson State College in Mississippi, and National Guard troops at Kent State University in Ohio fired on unarmed protesters, killing four students. As antiwar demonstrators descended on Washington, D.C., Nixon seemed personally unnerved by the furor, especially during an unscheduled, late-night meeting with protesting students.

A continuing controversy over the **My Lai Incident** further polarized sentiment over the war. Shortly after the 1968 Tet Offensive, U.S. troops had entered the small South Vietnamese hamlet of My Lai and murdered more than 200 civilians, most of them women and children. This massacre only became public in 1969. Military courts convicted only one officer, Lieutenant William Calley, of any offense.

Library of Congress Prints & Photographs Division Washington, D.C. [LC-USZC2-486]

Henry Kissinger as a Hawk. *This 1973 caricature challenges Kissinger's reputation as a peacemaker by showing him as a foreign policy hawk, with planes flying overhead.*

Critics charged that the military was using Calley as a scapegoat for a failed strategy that emphasized body counts and lax rules of engagement. Injecting the White House into this controversy, Nixon ordered that the young lieutenant be confined to his officer's quarters, rather than prison, pending the results of his appeal. Ultimately, Calley was ordered released based on procedural irregularities. Controversy over the Calley case inflamed tensions between those Americans who backed and those who opposed the war.

Meanwhile, the Nixon administration widened military operations to include Laos as well as Cambodia. Although it denied waging any such campaign, large areas of those agricultural countries were ravaged. As the number of refugees inside Cambodia swelled and food supplies dwindled, the communist guerrilla force there—the Khmer Rouge—came to power and in a murderous attempt to eliminate dissent turned Cambodia into a "killing field." It slaughtered more than 1 million Cambodians. While Nixon continued to plan U.S. troop withdrawals and conduct peace negotiations with North Vietnam in Paris, the Vietnam War had become a conflict that destabilized all of Indochina.

Even greater violence was yet to come. During the spring of 1972, North Vietnam's "Easter Offensive" approached within 30 miles of Saigon before falling back. The surge showed the limits of Vietnamization and swelled South Vietnam's refugee population. Nixon responded with an escalation as great as that by Lyndon Johnson in 1965. He ordered the systematic bombing of North Vietnam, the mining of its harbors, and the institution of a naval blockade. Just weeks before the November 1972 elections in the United States, Henry Kissinger declared that "peace is at hand" and announced a cease-fire. After Nixon's reelection, however, the impending peace deal fell apart in Paris, and the United States unleashed even greater firepower over North Vietnam. During the "Christmas bombing" of December 1972, the heaviest bombardment in history, B-52 planes pounded military and civilian targets in North Vietnam around the clock. North Vietnam, which was also feeling diplomatic pressure from the Soviet Union and China, decided to conclude peace negotiations with Washington and Saigon.

The United States Leaves Vietnam   Much of the U.S. media, Congress, and the public were also calling for an end to the war. Many were tired of the violence in Asia and of the administration's effort to stem dissent at home. In addition, sagging morale among U.S. troops hindered the missions that the U.S. command was still conducting. Soldiers questioned the purpose of their sacrifices; some refused to engage the enemy; and a few openly defied their superiors. At home, Vietnam Veterans Against the War (VVAW), a new organization, joined the antiwar coalition. Running out of nonbombing options, Nixon proceeded with full-scale Vietnamization.

In January 1973, the warring parties signed peace accords in Paris that provided for the withdrawal of U.S. troops. The actual terms closely resembled those in the pre-election deal that Kissinger had celebrated but which had later fallen apart. By allowing North Vietnamese troops to remain in the South, the Paris accords left Nguyen Van Thieu's government in a precarious position, and Nixon may have anticipated preserving it by future bombing campaigns. As U.S. ground forces departed, the South Vietnamese army continued to fight. In spring 1975, nearly two years after the Paris accords, South Vietnam's army and Thieu's government collapsed as North Vietnamese armies entered the capital of Saigon. America's increasingly divisive war ended with its objective of maintaining a noncommunist South Vietnam unfulfilled.

Between 1960 and 1973, approximately 3.5 million American men and women served in Vietnam; 58,000 died, 150,000 were wounded, and 2,000 were classified as missing. War-related disabilities, both physical and mental, would continue to affect veterans and to challenge the nation's medical and social services. In this aftermath, Americans struggled to understand why their country failed to defeat a small, barely industrialized nation. Those still supporting the war argued that it had been lost on the home front. They blamed an irresponsible media, a disloyal antiwar movement, and a Congress afflicted by a "failure of will." The war, they insisted, had been for a laudable cause. Politicians, setting unrealistic limits on the Pentagon, had prevented strategists from attaining victory. By contrast, those who had come to oppose the war stressed the overextension of U.S. power, the misguided belief in national omnipotence, the dangers of touching off a wider war with China, and the strategic miscalculations of decision makers. For them, the United States had waged a war in the wrong place for the wrong reasons. The human costs in both the United States and Indochina outweighed any possible gain.

Regardless of their position on the war, most Americans seemed to agree on a single proposition: "no more Vietnams." The United States should never undertake another military operation unless it involved clear and compelling political objectives, sustained public support, and realistic means to accomplish its goals. Eventually, people who wanted to reassert U.S. power in the world dismissed this caution as "the Vietnam syndrome." The legacy of these divisions would continue far beyond the end of the war.

Expanding the Nixon Doctrine   Although the Nixon Doctrine initially only applied to the Vietnamization of the war in Indochina, Nixon and Kissinger extended its premise to the entire world. The White House made clear that the United States would not dispatch its troops to quash insurgencies but would generously aid anticommunist regimes or factions willing to fight their own battles.

During the early 1970s, U.S. cold war strategy came to rely on supporting staunchly anticommunist regional powers. These included nations such as Iran under Shah Reza Pahlavi, South Africa with its apartheid regime, and Brazil with its military dictatorship. All of these countries built large, U.S.-trained military establishments. U.S. military assistance, together with covert CIA operations, also incubated and protected anticommunist dictatorships in South Korea, the Philippines, and much of Latin America. U.S. arms sales to the rest of the world skyrocketed. In one of its most controversial foreign policies, the Nixon administration employed covert action against the elected socialist government of Salvador Allende Gossens in Chile in 1970. After Allende took office, Kissinger pressed for the destabilization of his government. On September 11, 1973, the Chilean military overthrew Allende, immediately suspended democratic rule, and announced that Allende had committed suicide.

Critics charged that the United States, in the name of anticommunism, too often linked its diplomatic fortunes to questionable covert actions and unpopular military governments. In 1973, Democratic senator Frank Church conducted Senate hearings into abuses of power by the executive branch, especially the CIA's actions in Chile. Supporters of Nixon and Kissinger, however, gave the pair high marks for a pragmatic foreign policy that combined détente toward the communist giants with containment directed against the spread of revolutionary regimes.

A CRISIS OF GOVERNANCE, 1972–1974

A political loner who ruminated about taking revenge against his enemies, Nixon often seemed his own greatest foe. He ordered the Internal Revenue Service (IRS) to harass prominent Democrats with expensive audits; placed antiwar and Black Power activists under surveillance; and conducted risky covert activities on the domestic front that even rattled the constitutional sensibilities of an old ally, J. Edgar Hoover. Isolated with a close-knit group of advisers, Nixon eventually created his own secret intelligence unit, "the Plumbers," which set up shop in the White House.

During the summer of 1971, Daniel Ellsberg, an antiwar activist who had once worked in the national security bureaucracy, leaked to the press a top-secret, highly critical history of U.S. involvement in the Vietnam War, subsequently known as the "Pentagon Papers." Nixon responded by seeking, unsuccessfully, a court injunction to stop publication and, more ominously, by unleashing his Plumbers unit to stop leaks to the media. Seeking something that might discredit Ellsberg, the Plumbers burglarized his psychiatrist's office. Thus began a series of secretive political "dirty tricks" and clear-cut crimes, sometimes financed by funds solicited for Nixon's 1972 reelection campaign.

The Election of 1972   Nixon's political strategists worried that domestic troubles and the war in Vietnam might deny the president another term. Creating a campaign organization separate from that of the Republican Party, with the ironic acronym of CREEP (Committee to Re-elect the President), they secretly raised millions of dollars, much of it from illegal contributions.

As the 1972 campaign took shape, Nixon's chances for reelection dramatically improved. An assassin's bullet crippled George Wallace and kept him from playing the spoiler's role in November. Senator Edmund Muskie of Maine, initially Nixon's leading Democratic challenger, made a series of blunders (some of them, perhaps, precipitated by Republican "dirty tricksters") that derailed his campaign. Eventually, Senator George McGovern of South Dakota, an outspoken opponent of the Vietnam War but a lackluster campaigner, won the Democratic nomination.

McGovern never seriously challenged Nixon. The Democratic candidate called for higher taxes on the wealthy, a guaranteed minimum income for all Americans, amnesty for Vietnam War draft resisters, and the decriminalization of marijuana. In foreign policy, he urged deep cuts in defense spending and peace in Vietnam—proposals that Nixon successfully portrayed as signs of "weakness." Nixon won an easy victory in November, receiving the Electoral College votes of all but one state and the District of Columbia. Although the Twenty-sixth Amendment, ratified one year before the election, had lowered the voting age to 18, relatively few of the newly enfranchised voters cast ballots.

While helping achieve this victory, the president's supporters left a trail of crime and corruption that eventually led to a crisis of governance. In June 1972, a surveillance team with links to both CREEP and the White House had been arrested while fine-tuning eavesdropping equipment in the Democratic Party's headquarters in Washington's Watergate office complex. In public, Nixon's spokespeople dismissed the Watergate break-in as a "third-rate burglary." In private, the president and his inner circle launched a cover-up. They paid hush money to the Watergate burglars and ordered CIA officials to misinform the FBI that any investigation into the episode would jeopardize national security. Nixon contained the political damage through the 1972 election, but events associated with **Watergate** soon overtook him.

The Watergate Investigations While reporters from the *Washington Post* pursued the taint of scandal coming from the election, Congress, the federal courts, and government prosecutors also sought evidence of lawbreaking. Federal District Judge John Sirica, a Republican appointee presiding over the trial of the Watergate burglars, suspected a cover-up and pressed the defendants before his court for additional information. In May 1973, U.S. Senate leaders convened a special, bipartisan Watergate Committee, headed by North Carolina's conservative Democratic senator Sam Ervin, to investigate. Federal prosecutors uncovered evidence that seemed to link key administration figures, including John Mitchell, Nixon's former attorney general and later the head of CREEP, to illegal activities.

The Ervin hearings, carried live on TV, eventually became a daily political drama that much of the country watched. Testimony from John Dean, who had been the president's chief legal counsel, linked Nixon himself to attempts to cover up Watergate and to other illegal activities. The president steadfastly denied Dean's charges.

Along the way, though, Senate investigators discovered that a voice-activated taping system had recorded conversations between Nixon and his aides in the Oval Office. These tapes made it possible to determine whether the president or Dean, Nixon's primary accuser, was lying. While contending he was not "a crook," Nixon also claimed an "executive privilege" to keep the tapes from being released, but Judge Sirica, Archibald Cox (a special, independent prosecutor in the Watergate case), and Congress all demanded access to them.

If Nixon's Watergate-related problems were not enough, his vice president, Spiro Agnew, suddenly resigned in October 1973 after pleading no contest to income tax evasion. Agnew agreed to a plea-bargain arrangement to avoid prosecution for having accepted illegal kickbacks while in Maryland politics. Acting under the Twenty-fifth Amendment (ratified in 1967), Nixon appointed—and both houses of Congress confirmed—Republican representative Gerald R. Ford of Michigan as the new vice president.

**Nixon's
Resignation**

Nixon's clumsy efforts to protect himself backfired. During the fall of 1973, Nixon had abruptly fired Archibald Cox, hoping to prevent him from gaining access to the tapes. Nixon's own release of edited transcripts of some Watergate-related conversations, including one key transcript containing an 18-minute gap in the tape, merely strengthened demand for the original recordings. Finally, by proclaiming that he would obey only a "definitive" Supreme Court decision, Nixon all but invited the justices to deliver a unanimous ruling against his withholding of the tapes in a criminal investigation. In July 1974, the Burger Court did just that in the case of *U.S. v. Nixon*. After televised deliberations, a bipartisan majority of the House Judiciary Committee voted three formal articles of impeachment against the president for obstruction of justice, violation of constitutional liberties, and refusal to produce evidence.

Nixon promised to rebut these accusations during a trial by the Senate, but his aides were already orchestrating his departure. One of his own attorneys had discovered that a tape Nixon had been withholding contained the long-sought "smoking gun," clear evidence of a criminal offense. It confirmed that during a 1972 conversation, Nixon had helped hatch a plan by which the CIA would advance the fraudulent claim of national security in order to stop the FBI from investigating the Watergate break-in. Nixon's own secretary of defense now ordered military

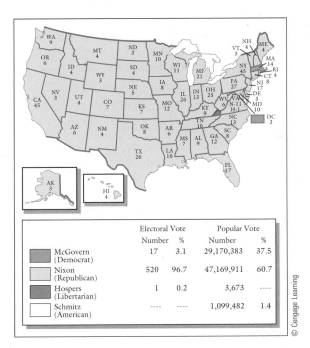

	Electoral Vote		Popular Vote	
	Number	%	Number	%
McGovern (Democrat)	17	3.1	29,170,383	37.5
Nixon (Republican)	520	96.7	47,169,911	60.7
Hospers (Libertarian)	1	0.2	3,673	----
Schmitz (American)	----	----	1,099,482	1.4

© Cengage Learning

MAP 29.3 Presidential Election, 1972

In contrast to the closely contested election of 1968, the 1972 election produced a landslide victory for Richard Nixon. What helps explain the stark difference between these two elections? What events would force Richard Nixon, in 1974, to leave an office to which he had been overwhelmingly returned?

commanders to ignore any order from the president, unless the secretary had countersigned it. Abandoned by most prominent Republicans and confronted by a Senate prepared to vote him guilty on the impeachment charges, Nixon went on television on August 8, 1974, to announce his resignation. On August 9, Gerald Ford became the nation's 38th chief executive. He assumed the post never having been elected president or vice president.

In 1974, most people told pollsters that the string of abuses collectively known as "Watergate" was one of the gravest crises in the history of the republic and that the Nixon administration had posed a serious threat to constitutional governance. Opinion polls conducted on the 20th anniversary of Nixon's resignation, however, suggested that Americans by then only dimly recalled the crisis of governance associated with the Nixon administration.

What might account for this change? First, nearly a dozen members of Nixon's administration—including its chief law enforcement officer, John Mitchell—were convicted of criminal activities, but the president avoided prosecution. Gerald Ford granted Nixon an unconditional pardon. The nation was spared the spectacle of a former president undergoing trial, but it was also denied an authoritative accounting, in a court of law, of Nixon's misdeeds.

Another reason for fading memories may be the media's habit of attaching the Watergate label to nearly every political scandal of the post-Nixon era. The suffix "gate" became affixed to grave constitutional episodes and to obviously trivial political events. Over time, then, "Watergate" became almost a synonym for "politics as usual." Finally, images of what the historian Stanley Kutler calls the "Wars of Watergate" have tended to blend into the broader picture of political, social, economic, and cultural turmoil that characterized the era.

Conclusion

The years from 1963 to 1974 brought fundamental changes to American life. At home, the first significant wave of domestic legislation since the New Deal stretched the reach of national programs (and that of the bureaucracies that administered them), thus igniting fierce debate over the proper power of Washington in American life. Legislative acts, court decisions, and administrative rulings aimed at addressing racial and gender discrimination helped produce the sectional realignment of the two major parties, as conservative white southerners dramatically accelerated their move from the Democratic into the Republican Party. The civil rights movements of the earlier post–World War II period broadened into an array of insurgencies that sought to mobilize and empower people according to group identities that included race, ethnicity, gender, sexual preference, and spiritual belief. These mobilizations sparked controversies over redefinitions of basic rights of citizenship.

Overseas, what began as a limited cold war era intervention against communism in Asia morphed into a brutal and divisive conflict that ended with the United States being forced to abandon its effort to maintain a noncommunist regime in South Vietnam. In trying to blunt domestic dissent against this Vietnam War and to shield foreign policy activities from public scrutiny, the executive branch, especially during Richard Nixon's administration, widened the gaze of surveillance bureaucracies. By 1974, most Americans, including a bipartisan majority of political leaders, judged the Nixon presidency so threatening to constitutional governance that they forced, through informal pressures as well as the impeachment process, the first presidential resignation in the nation's history.

During the rest of the 20th and the early years of the 21st centuries, debates over governance, fundamental rights, social-economic policy, and America's role in the world took place within frameworks constructed between 1963 and 1974. Decisions made and directions chosen, as one recent history puts it, initiated an important "realignment of American democracy."

30

UNCERTAIN TIMES, 1974–1992

CHAPTER OUTLINE

- Searching for Direction, 1974–1980 • The Reagan Revolution, 1981–1992
- Renewing and Ending the Cold War • The Politics of Social Movements

---

EVENTS OF THE 1960S AND EARLY 1970s, particularly Vietnam and Watergate, shook popular faith in government. Secrecy, corruption, and economic problems bred further disillusionment. During the 1970s and 1980s, Americans debated how to respond to an aging industrial economy, a growing federal deficit, and a beleaguered social welfare system. Did the country need new governmental programs, or might conditions improve if Washington reduced its role in daily life?

Disagreement extended to foreign policy. Should the United States minimize anticommunism to pursue other goals, as Democratic president Jimmy Carter (1977–1981) initially urged, or should it wage the cold war even more vigorously, as his successor, Republican Ronald Reagan (1981–1989), advocated? After 1989, when the cold war ended unexpectedly, the United States needed to find a foreign policy for a post–cold war world.

Meanwhile, the "movement of movements," a legacy of the 1960s, refused to fade away. Social movements associated with women's rights, gay rights, and racial and ethnic identities affected how Americans saw themselves and their nation's future. Some of the goals of these movements, however, met strident opposition from the New Right that had helped build Reagan's popularity. During these years, the polarization of American politics that had become so evident during the Vietnam War and Watergate eras deepened and broadened, sparking new controversies over issues such as abortion, taxation, affirmative action, and environmental regulations.

SEARCHING FOR DIRECTION, 1974–1980

When Richard Nixon resigned in August 1974, **Gerald R. Ford**, his vice president, moved from one office to which voters had never elected him to another, the presidency. Ford promised to "heal the land," but he achieved little success. A genial, unpretentious former college football star, Ford preferred that his public appearances be accompanied by the fight song of his alma mater, the University of

CHRONOLOGY

1974	Nixon resigns and Ford becomes president
	Ford soon pardons Nixon
1975	South Vietnam falls to North Vietnam
	Ford asserts U.S. power in *Mayaguez* incident
1976	Jimmy Carter elected president
	OPEC sharply raises oil prices
1978	Carter helps negotiate Camp David peace accords on Middle East
1979	Soviet Union invades Afghanistan
	Sandinistas come to power in Nicaragua
	U.S. hostages seized in Iran
1980	Reagan elected president
	U.S. hostages in Iran released
1981	Reagan tax cut passed
1983	U.S. troops removed from Lebanon
	Reagan announces SDI ("Star Wars") program
1984	Reagan defeats Walter Mondale
1986	Reagan administration rocked by revelation of Iran-contra affair
1988	George H. W. Bush defeats Michael Dukakis in presidential election
	Congress enacts Indian Gaming Regulation Act
1989	Communist regimes in Eastern Europe collapse
	Berlin Wall falls
	Cold war, in effect, ends
1990	Bush angers conservative Republicans by agreeing to a tax increase
1991	Bush orchestrates Persian Gulf War against Iraq
1992	Bill Clinton defeats Bush

Michigan, rather than "Hail to the Chief." His attempt to present his administration as an updated version of the "modern Republicanism" of the 1950s quickly foundered. His appointment of Nelson Rockefeller as vice president infuriated GOP conservatives, and his pardoning of former president Nixon, in September 1974, angered almost everyone. Ford's approval rating skidded downward, and he nearly lost the GOP's 1976 presidential nomination to Ronald Reagan, who campaigned as a "true conservative" owing nothing to Washington insiders.

The Democrats did turn to an outsider, **James Earl (Jimmy) Carter**. A retired naval officer, engineer, peanut farmer, and former governor of Georgia, Carter campaigned by stressing personal character. He highlighted his small-town roots and his Southern Baptist faith. To balance the ticket, he picked Senator Walter

Mondale of Minnesota as his running mate. In November of 1976 Carter won a narrow victory over Ford.

Carter's election rested on a transitory coalition. He carried every southern state except Virginia, running well among both whites who belonged to fundamentalist and evangelical churches and African Americans. Carter also courted former antiwar activists by promising to pardon most Vietnam-era draft resisters. Walter Mondale's appeal helped capture the Democratic strongholds of New York, Pennsylvania, and Ohio. The election was close, however, and voter turnout hit its lowest mark (54 percent) since the end of the Second World War.

Jimmy Carter's lack of a popular mandate and his outsider status proved serious handicaps. After leaving government, Carter reflected on his difficulties: "I had a different way of governing .... I was a southerner, a born-again Christian, a Baptist, a newcomer." Moreover, Carter was caught between advisers who, on the one hand, claimed that the national government exercised too much power and, on the other, argued that Washington did too little to address domestic and foreign problems.

The 865-day presidency of Ford and the one-term administration of Carter reflected the political uncertainties of post-Vietnam and post-Watergate America. The sense of national crisis seemed unrelenting, as politicians and citizens alike attempted to cope with a staggering economy, disruptive energy shortages, and sensationalized foreign challenges.

A Faltering Economy   Economic problems dominated the domestic side of Ford's caretaker presidency. Ford first touted a program called "Whip Inflation Now" (WIN), which included a temporary increase in income taxes and cuts in federal spending. WIN proved to be a loser. During 1975 unemployment reached 8.5 percent, and the inflation rate topped 9 percent. Ford also clashed with the Democratic-controlled Congress over how to deal with the ever-rising price of oil and with stagflation, which combined economic stagnation with price inflation. Democrats tended to favor programs that might stimulate employment and economic growth; most Republicans urged policies that cut government spending. Ford, who vetoed nearly 40 spending bills while in office, finally agreed to a congressional economic package forged from an uneasy compromise of diverse goals. It included a tax cut, an increase in unemployment benefits, an unbalanced federal budget, and limited controls on oil prices. Democrats charged that Ford could not implement coherent programs. Many Republicans complained that he could not stand up to congressional Democrats.

Although the rate of job creation during Jimmy Carter's presidency initially topped that of administrations that followed, economic problems persisted. Carter pushed for tax cuts, increased public works spending, and pro-growth Federal Reserve Board policies. These measures failed to bring the sustained economic recovery that had also eluded Carter's Republican predecessors. By 1980 the economy had virtually stopped expanding; unemployment was on the rise; and the rate of inflation reached double digits. Most voters told pollsters that their economic fortunes had deteriorated while Carter was in office.

Economic distress spread beyond individuals. Bankruptcy threatened New York City until private bankers and public officials secured congressional "bailout" legislation that granted special loan guarantees to America's largest city. Chicago lost 200,000 manufacturing jobs during the 1970s. Bricks from demolished buildings in St. Louis became one of that city's leading products. Rising unemployment, soaring crime rates, deteriorating downtowns, and shrinking tax revenues afflicted most urban areas, even as inflation further eroded the buying power of city budgets.

Conservative economists and business interests charged that domestic programs favored by most congressional Democrats contributed to economic distress. Increasing the minimum wage and enforcing stringent safety and antipollution regulations, they argued, drove up the cost of doing business and forced companies to raise prices to consumers. During his last two years in office, Carter seemed to tilt toward this analysis. Defying many Democrats in Congress, he cut spending for social programs, sought to reduce capital gains taxes to encourage investment, and inaugurated the process of "deregulating" key industries, beginning with the financial and transportation sectors. This policy of deregulation would become a major emphasis that Republican administrations would pursue after 1980.

Welfare and Energy Initiatives   Carter puzzled over how to respond to economic and social issues. His staff differed over whether to propose increasing monetary assistance to low-income families or to advocate increased federal spending to create several million public service jobs. A proposed compromise failed in Congress. Similarly, efforts to overhaul the nation's social welfare system went nowhere. Republicans tended to argue for reduced government spending on welfare programs; Democrats generally favored increasing federal assistance.

The president pushed the hardest on energy issues. The United States obtained 90 percent of its energy from fossil fuels, much of it from imported petroleum. In 1978, as in 1973, the Organization of Petroleum Exporting Countries (OPEC), a cartel dominated by oil-rich nations in the Middle East, dramatically raised the price of crude oil and precipitated acute worldwide shortages. As gasoline became expensive and scarce, drivers faced higher prices and long lines at the gas pumps around the country. Carter, in response, promised to make the United States less dependent on imported fossil fuel and charged James Schlesinger, head of a new Department of Energy, with developing a plan.

Neither Carter nor Schlesinger consulted Congress or even some key members of the president's own administration. Instead, in early 1977, Carter announced that the **energy crisis** represented "the moral equivalent of war," and he abruptly advanced a complex plan that included more than 100 interrelated provisions including increased taxation, deregulation, and promotion of coal and nuclear power. Congress quickly rejected it. Gas and oil interests opposed higher taxes. Consumer activists blocked deregulation. Environmentalists emphasized that greater use of coal would increase air pollution.

The nuclear option generated especially sharp controversy. In theory, nuclear reactors could provide inexpensive, almost limitless amounts of energy. The cost of building and maintaining them, however, far exceeded original estimates and posed safety risks. In 1979 a serious reactor malfunction at **Three Mile Island,**

Confronting Urban Decay in the 1970s.

Some of financially strapped New York City's most pressing problems during the 1970s were in the South Bronx area. Here, President Jimmy Carter (in the center) poses with his Housing and Urban Development secretary and New York's mayor in front of several of the thousands of buildings in the South Bronx that had fallen victim to decay, neglect, and arson. This widely circulated photo was intended to signal that national and local officials hoped to devise rebuilding programs for urban areas such as this.

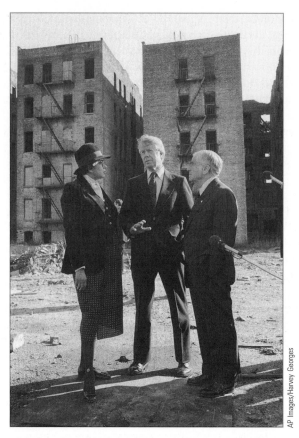

AP Images/Harvey Georges

Pennsylvania, along with a popular movie about a similar event *(The China Syndrome)* heightened fears of a nuclear reactor meltdown. Responding to growing concerns, power companies canceled orders for new reactors, and the nuclear power industry's expansion halted.

Meanwhile, OPEC oil prices continued to rise, from about $3.60 a barrel in 1971 to nearly $36 a decade later, at the end of Carter's presidency. Such dramatic price increases in a commodity that fueled the American economy helped drive the damaging stagflation of the 1970s. Although few Americans agreed on how to solve this oil crisis and America's broader energy problems, many lost confidence in Carter's domestic leadership.

Negotiation and Confrontation in Foreign Policy

Foreign policy lurched along a similarly uncertain course. Upon assuming office in late 1974, President Ford pledged renewal of U.S. military support to the government in South Vietnam, if North Vietnam ever directly threatened its survival. The antiwar mood in the United States and battlefield conditions in Vietnam, however, made fulfilling this commitment impossible. North Vietnam's armies stormed across the South in March 1975, and Congress, relieved that U.S. troops had finally been withdrawn after the 1973 Paris Peace Accords, refused to support any new American involvement. Conducting their last mission in Vietnam, U.S. helicopters scrambled to airlift U.S. officials and top-ranking South Vietnamese officers off the American embassy's rooftop.

Spring 1975 brought new communist victories in Indochina. In early April, Khmer Rouge forces in Cambodia drove a U.S.-backed government from the capital of Phnom Penh, and on April 30, 1975, North Vietnamese troops overran the South Vietnamese capital of Saigon, renaming it Ho Chi Minh City. Debate over U.S. policy in Indochina became especially heated in the months that followed.

Within this charged atmosphere, Ford tried to demonstrate U.S military power. In May 1975 a contingent of Khmer Rouge boarded a U.S. ship, the *Mayaguez*, taking its crew hostage. Secretary of State Henry Kissinger declared that it was time to "look ferocious" and convinced Ford to order bombing strikes against Cambodia and a rescue operation for the crew. This military response, coupled with Chinese pressure on the Khmer Rouge, secured the release of the *Mayaguez* and its crew. Although the *Mayaguez* rescue cost more lives than it saved, Ford's approval ratings briefly shot up. His other foreign policy initiatives, which included extending Nixon's policy of détente with the Soviet Union and pursuing peace negotiations in the Middle East, achieved little.

Carter promised new directions. On his first day in office, he granted amnesty to most Vietnam-era draft resisters. He soon declared that he would not display an "inordinate fear of Communism" and would endorse human-rights initiatives. After four years, however, Carter's foreign policy initiatives seemed in as much disarray as were his economic and energy policies.

Carter had little background in foreign policy, and his top aides advanced contradictory agendas. Secretary of State Cyrus Vance preferred quiet diplomacy and avoidance of confrontations, while National Security Adviser Zbigniew Brzezinski favored a hard-line anti-Soviet policy with an emphasis on military muscle. Pulled in divergent directions, Carter's foreign policy seemed to waffle.

Still, Carter's faith in his own skills as a facilitator and negotiator yielded some successes. On the issue of the Panama Canal, the object of diplomatic negotiations for 13 years, Carter secured treaties that granted Panama increasing authority over the waterway and full control in 2000. Carter convinced skeptical senators, whose votes he needed in order to ratify any treaty, that the canal was no longer an economic or strategic necessity.

Carter's personal touch also emerged during the **Camp David Peace Talks of 1978**. Relations between Egypt and Israel had been strained since the Yom Kippur War of 1973, when Israel repelled an Egyptian attack and seized the Sinai Peninsula and territory along the West Bank (of the Jordan River). Reviving earlier Republican efforts to broker a peace settlement, Carter brought Menachem Begin and Anwar Sadat, leaders of Israel and Egypt, respectively, to the presidential retreat at Camp David. After 13 days of difficult bargaining, the three leaders announced a framework for further negotiations and a peace treaty. Middle East tensions hardly vanished, but the accords reached at Camp David kept alive high-level discussions, lowered the level of acrimony between Egypt and Israel, and bound both nations to the United States through Carter's promises of economic aid.

In Asia, the Carter administration built on Nixon's initiative, expanding economic and cultural relations with the communist government in China. The United

States finally established formal diplomatic ties with the People's Republic on New Year's Day 1979.

Carter's foreign agenda emphasized a **human rights policy**. Carter argued that alliances with repressive dictatorships, even in the name of anticommunism, undermined U.S. influence in the world. The policy, however, proved difficult to orchestrate. His administration continued to support some harsh dictators, such as Ferdinand Marcos in the Philippines. Moreover, rhetoric about human rights helped justify uprisings against long-standing dictator-allies in Nicaragua and Iran. Revolutions in these countries, fueled by resentment against the United States, brought anti-American regimes to power and presented Carter with difficult choices.

In Nicaragua, the *Sandinista* movement toppled the dictatorship of Anastasio Somoza, which the United States had long supported. The Sandinistas, initially a coalition of moderate democrats and leftists, soon tilted toward a militant Marxism and began to expropriate private property. Republican critics charged that Carter's policies had given a green light to communism throughout Central America, and some pledged to oust the Sandinistas.

If events in Nicaragua brought dilemmas to Carter, those in Iran and Afghanistan all but shattered his presidency. The United States had steadfastly supported the dictatorial Shah Reza Pahlavi, who had reigned in oil-rich Iran since an American-supported coup in 1953. The shah's overthrow in the **Iranian Revolution of January 1979**, by a movement dominated by Islamic fundamentalists, signaled a massive repudiation of U.S. influence. When the White House allowed the deposed shah to enter the United States for medical treatment in November 1979, Iranians seized the U.S. embassy in Tehran and 66 American hostages. Iran demanded the return of the shah in exchange for the hostages' release.

In response, Carter turned to tough talk, levied economic sanctions against Iran, and—over the objections of Cyrus Vance (who subsequently resigned)—sent a combat team to rescue the hostages. This military effort ended in an embarrassing failure. Carter's critics cited this "hostage crisis" as conclusive proof of his incompetence and used the issue relentlessly in the next presidential campaign. After Carter's defeat in the 1980 election, diplomatic efforts finally freed the hostages, but the United States and Iran remained at odds.

Criticism of Carter also focused on the Soviet Union's 1979 invasion of Afghanistan, a move primarily sparked by Soviet leaders' fear of the growing influence of Islamic fundamentalists along their borders. Carter halted grain exports to the Soviet Union (angering American farmers), organized a boycott of the 1980 Summer Olympic Games in Moscow, withdrew a new Strategic Arms Limitation Treaty (SALT) from the Senate, and revived registration for the military draft. Still, Republicans (along with some Democrats) charged Carter with allowing U.S. power and prestige to decline while the Soviet Union was embarking on a new campaign of expanding communism.

For a time, after Senator Edward Kennedy of Massachusetts entered the 1980 presidential primaries, it seemed as if Carter's own Democratic Party might deny him a second term. Although Kennedy's challenge eventually fizzled, it popularized anti-Carter themes that Republicans would embrace in the election of 1980. "It's time to say no more hostages, no more high interest rates, no more high inflation, and no more Jimmy Carter," was Kennedy's standard stump speech.

The New Right   By 1976, the idea of preventing another Carter or another Kennedy presidency animated a diverse coalition of conservatives: a **New Right**. This broadly based movement succeeded in holding together several different constituencies. One was the already disparate group that had initially gathered around William F. Buckley's *National Review* during the 1950s. Buckley reached out to new converts through television. His long-running interview show, *Firing Line,* debuted on PBS in 1971 (and ran for another 28 years). The economist Milton Friedman—a frequent Buckley guest, 1976 Nobel laureate, and creator of a PBS series touting free-market economic principles—provided another important link between the conservatism of the 1950s and 1970s. In addition, many of the then-youthful conservatives who had energized Barry Goldwater's 1964 presidential campaign, such as Patrick Buchanan, came to the New Right after having worked in Richard Nixon's administration.

In contrast, the "neoconservative" (or "neocon") wing of the New Right of the 1970s had generally identified with Democrats, rather than Republicans, during the 1950s and the early 1960s. Anticommunist writers and academics such as Norman Podhoretz and Jeane Kirkpatrick feared that the Democratic Party might abandon a strong anticommunist stance, and neoconservatives viewed the movement of movements as threatening the social stability and intellectual values they admired. This initial generation of neoconservatives, many the offspring of European Jewish immigrants, also complained that U.S. foreign policy, even under Richard Nixon and Henry Kissinger, failed to support Israel strongly enough.

Bettmann / Corbis

American Hostages in Iran. *The Iranian government presents American hostages to the press under a banner protesting Carter's decision to admit the shah into the United States to obtain medical treatment.*

Conservative business leaders provided another important New Right constituency. In their view, new regulatory legislation accepted by the Nixon administration, especially measures dealing with workplace safety and environmental concerns, threatened "economic freedom" and "entrepreneurial liberty." Convinced that anticorporate faculties dominated most colleges and universities, conservative business leaders and their philanthropic foundations generously funded conservative-leaning research institutions, such as the American Enterprise Institute (founded in 1943), and created new ones, such as The Heritage Foundation (established in 1973) and the Cato Institute (founded in 1977).

Money from New Right businesspeople also financed lobbying efforts, such as those mounted by the Business Roundtable (created in 1973) and The Committee on the Present Danger (CPD), which argued that foreign policymakers, including the CIA, underestimated the threat that the Soviet Union still posed. In 1975, activists who had worked for Goldwater's 1964 campaign formed the National Conservative Political Action Committee (NCPAC), the first of many similar organizations aimed at grassroots organizing. The NCPAC backed conservative political candidates and supported a wide range of initiatives opposing feminism, legalized abortion, and LGBT (lesbian, gay, bisexual, and transgender) lifestyles.

The New Right of the 1970s also attracted support from Protestants in fundamentalist and evangelical churches. People from these religious groups had generally stayed clear of overtly partisan politics since the 1920s but continued to express concern about public issues that involved spiritual and social matters. Already angered by Supreme Court decisions that seemed to eliminate religious prayers from public schools, many expressed greater outrage over *Roe v. Wade* (1973), the landmark abortion ruling. Reaching out to antiabortion Catholics, people whom most members of southern Protestant congregations would have shunned a generation earlier, a "Religious Right" slowly took shape. The Reverend Jerry Falwell of the Thomas Road Baptist Church and *The Old Time Gospel Hour* television ministry declared that *Roe* showed the necessity of political action. Antireligious elites in Washington "have been imposing morality on us for the last 50 years," Falwell proclaimed.

Leaders of the Religious Right insisted that sacred values should actively shape political policy-making. They viewed a clear separation between church and state, a guiding principle of constitutionalism during the era of Earl Warren's Supreme Court, as a violation of a right specifically mentioned in the First Amendment: the "free exercise of religion." Particularly in the South, conservatives embarked on a lengthy legal struggle to prevent the Internal Revenue Service from denying tax-exempt status to the private Christian colleges and academies that opposed racial integration. They also urged that government should use tax dollars to help fund church-centered education and "faith-based" social programming. Most spokespeople for the Religious Right championed foreign policies that maximized the use of U.S. military power, especially on behalf of Israel. Protestants who embraced "dispensational premillennialism," the belief that the Second Coming of Christ would occur in their lifetimes, saw the survival of a Jewish state in the Middle East as crucial to the future they expected to unfold according to biblical prophesy.

In 1976, most evangelicals and fundamentalists from the South, including Falwell, supported Jimmy Carter. His religious values made him seem less committed to the *Roe* decision than Gerald Ford, whose spouse, Betty Ford, often identified herself with women's issues. Very soon, however, Falwell and others on the Religious Right began realigning their politics with those of the GOP's conservative bloc, placing their growing movement behind a refashioned Republican party under the leadership of Ronald Reagan.

THE REAGAN REVOLUTION, 1981–1992

Ronald Reagan courted the New Right on national security, economic, and social issues. He used the hostage crisis with Iran as a symbol of Carter's failures, while his militantly anticommunist rhetoric included calls for a stronger military posture and greater defense spending. A taxpayer revolt that had swept through California politics during the late 1970s provided a model for Reagan's attack on "tax-and-spend" policy-making at the federal level. (The situation was ironic, since California's tax revolt had emerged in response to tax increases adopted while Reagan was the state's governor.) Reagan also opposed abortion rights, advocated prayer in school, and extolled conservative "family values."

The Election of 1980   Easily capturing the Republican nomination, and anointing one of his defeated rivals, George H. W. Bush, as a running mate, Ronald Reagan advanced an optimistic vision of a rejuvenated America. Punctuating his speeches with quips inspired by Hollywood movies, he stressed his opposition to domestic social spending and high taxes while promising support for a stronger national defense. To underscore the nation's economic problems under Carter, Reagan asked repeatedly, "Are you better off now than you were four years ago?" Quickly offering his own answer, Reagan cited the "misery index," an economic measure that added the rate of inflation to the rate of unemployment and that Jimmy Carter had used during his 1976 presidential campaign against Gerald Ford.

Reagan also seized issues that the Democratic Party had long regarded its own: economic growth and increased personal consumption. In 1979, one of Jimmy Carter's advisers had gloomily portrayed the nation's economic and energy problems as so severe that there was "no way we can avoid a decline in our standard of living. All we can do is adapt to it." In contrast, Reagan promised that sharp tax cuts and policies to increase the supply of oil would restore robust economic expansion.

The Reagan-Bush team swept to victory. Although it gained only slightly more than 50 percent of the popular vote (John Anderson, a middle-of-the-road Republican who ran as an independent, won about 7 percent), the GOP ticket captured the Electoral College tally by a 489 to 49 margin. Republicans also took away 12 Democratic Senate seats, gaining control of the Senate, though not the House of Representatives.

The Reagan administration focused on three major priorities: cutting federal taxes, reorienting the national government's relationship to economic matters, and boosting national security capabilities.

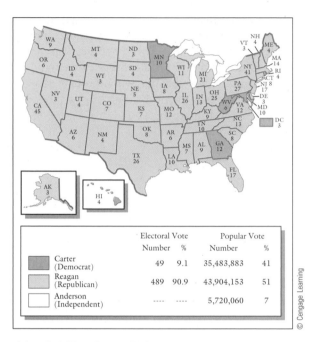

	Electoral Vote		Popular Vote	
	Number	%	Number	%
Carter (Democrat)	49	9.1	35,483,883	41
Reagan (Republican)	489	90.9	43,904,153	51
Anderson (Independent)	----	----	5,720,060	7

© Cengage Learning

MAP 30.1   Presidential Election, 1980

Supply-Side Economics

To justify cutting taxes, Reagan touted **supply-side econom-ics**. This economic theory held that tax reductions targeted toward investors and businesses would stimulate production, create jobs, and brighten the general economic picture. Reagan pushed a tax-reduction plan, endorsed by many Democrats, through Congress in 1981. At the same time, the Federal Reserve Board under Paul Volker, a Carter appointee, kept interest rates high to drive down inflation.

In the short run, high interest rates continued to choke off growth, and economic conditions deteriorated. A severe economic downturn in 1981 and 1982 sent Reagan's approval ratings diving below 40 percent, and the Republican Party experienced losses in the off-year election of 1982. Slowly, however, inflation moderated, and the economy rebounded to enter a period of noninflationary growth. According to one study, the economy added nearly 17 million new jobs and inflation dropped from double digits to around 2 percent. Although unemployment figures did not fall as sharply, Reagan's supporters hailed a "Reagan revolution" that had rescued the country from stagflation.

This revival and its causes remain controversial. Reagan had not matched tax cuts with sufficient spending reductions, and budget deficits soared. Reagan constantly inveighed against deficits and "big spenders," but his eight years in Washington, even after some of the early tax reductions were rolled back, saw annual deficits triple to nearly $300 billion. To finance such deficit spending, the United States borrowed abroad and piled up the largest foreign debt of any nation in the world at that time.

Although partisans of the Reagan revolution promised that its effects would ultimately "trickle down" and benefit everyone, its detractors countered that the country was developing a "Swiss-cheese" economy in which many groups were falling through the holes. The tax cuts of 1981 benefited the richest 1 percent and made little difference for everyone else. Farmers in the Midwest watched falling crop prices hamper their repayment of high-interest loans they had contracted during the inflation-ridden 1970s. Mortgage foreclosures, reminiscent of the 1930s, hit the farm states, and the ripple effect decimated the economies of small towns across the country. Urban areas saw a decline in federal spending for such things as public transit, housing, and job training, even as they tried to cope with growing unemployment, population loss, and falling tax revenues. One historian estimates that urban America bore two-thirds of the cost of Reagan-era budget cuts. The minimum wage, when adjusted for inflation, also declined in value during Reagan's presidency.

This mixed economic picture certainly applied to African Americans. The number of African American families earning a solid middle-class income, for example, more than doubled between 1970 and 1990. People with educational credentials and marketable skills made significant economic gains, and African American college graduates could expect incomes comparable to those of their white classmates. Partly as a result of affirmative action hiring plans put in place by the Nixon and Carter administrations, many could afford to leave problem-plagued inner-city neighborhoods. The situation looked different, however, for those who remained persistently unemployed, perhaps trapped in declining urban centers. At the end of the 1980s one-third of all African American families lived in poverty, and the number earning less than $15,000 per year had doubled since 1970. In inner cities, fewer than half of African American children were completing high school, and more than 60 percent were unemployed. The gap between the well off and the disadvantaged widened during the 1980s.

Curtailing Unions, Regulations, and Welfare   Meanwhile, Reagan pursued his second major goal: reorienting Washington's economic role. In 1981 Reagan fired the nation's air traffic controllers after their union refused to halt a nationwide strike. The action portended more aggressive anti-union strategies that both his administration and business interests would pursue during the 1980s. The percentage of unionized workers fell to just 16 percent by the end of Reagan's presidency. Recognizing the balance of power tilting against them, workers increasingly turned away from strikes as an economic weapon.

Reagan had entered office promising to tame OPEC by encouraging the development of new sources of oil. Rejecting environmentalists' calls to decrease U.S. dependence on fossil fuels by promotion of renewable sources, Reagan and his successor, George H. W. Bush, pursued a "cheap oil" policy. The tapping of new oil fields at home and abroad, together with rivalries among OPEC's members, weakened the cartel's hold on the world market and reduced energy prices worldwide. Lower energy costs, in turn, helped moderate the inflationary pressures.

To oversee environmental issues, Reagan appointed James Watt, an outspoken critic of governmental regulation, as secretary of the interior. Watt supported the so-called "sagebrush rebellion," in which western states demanded fewer federal restrictions on the use of natural resources from public lands within their borders. Reagan's first two appointees to the Department of Energy actually proposed eliminating the cabinet office they headed—an idea that Congress blocked. Both the Energy and Interior departments relaxed enforcement of federal safety and environmental regulations.

Reagan's agenda for **deregulation** singled out the financial system. His economic advisers insisted that financial markets were largely self-regulating and self-correcting. Minimal governmental interference in the marketplace, they argued, would bring greater economic efficiencies and therefore greater prosperity overall. The Carter administration had previously pursued programs of deregulation especially in the transportation sector, and many Democrats in Congress now joined Republicans in crafting a looser regulatory environment for financial institutions. Before the 1980s, state usury laws limited the interest rates that lending institutions could charge their clients, and "Savings and Loan" (S&L) institutions issued home mortgages under carefully controlled rules. Several pieces of legislation in the 1980s, however, wiped away these and other regulations. More credit became available to more people, as a new "sub-prime loan" industry boomed.

But there were hazards. During Reagan's second term, corruption and mismanagement in the financial industry increasingly appeared as toxic by-products of deregulation. S&L companies had ventured into risky loans, particularly in real estate. Regulators and politicians ignored forecasts of an impending meltdown until bankruptcies began to cascade through the S&L industry, eventually forcing the closure of 747 institutions. Finally, in 1989, Congress created a bailout plan designed to save some S&Ls and to transfer assets from already failed institutions to solvent ones. The plan proved astronomically expensive, and taxpayers footed costs that eventually reached around $125 billion. Meanwhile, the process by which large, well-connected commercial banks purchased the remaining assets of bankrupt S&Ls at bargain-basement prices reeked of corruption and scandal. As a result of the S&L debacle of the 1980s, the banking industry went through a sudden, unplanned consolidation. Many people lost savings.

The Reagan administration also sought to limit social welfare spending. It decreased funding for various public-benefit programs, particularly Aid to Families with Dependent Children (AFDC). The Family Support Act of 1988 pressured states to inaugurate work-training programs and to begin moving people, including mothers receiving AFDC payments, off the welfare rolls. Reductions in food stamps and other programs increased poverty rates and fell disproportionately on female-headed households and on children. By the end of the 1980s, one of every five children was growing up in a household where the income fell below the official poverty line.

The president nevertheless rejected calls for eliminating the basic set of New Deal–Great Society programs, such as Social Security and Medicare, which he called a "social safety net." During the 1970s Social Security payments had been "indexed" to automatically increase along with the rate of inflation. Larger Social Security checks, along with Medicare benefits, enabled millions of Americans over 65 to do relatively well during the Reagan years.

The Reagan administration also seized the opportunity to move the federal legal system in a more conservative direction. Reagan nominated a Supreme Court justice, Sandra Day O'Connor (the first woman to sit on the Court), who appeared to be a conservative. With the Republican Party controlling the Senate until 1986, he also named prominent conservative jurists, such as Robert Bork and Antonin Scalia, to lower federal courts. Conservatives who had decried the "rights revolution" of the Warren Supreme Court welcomed the influx of conservative judges, but civil libertarians complained that the federal courts were becoming less hospitable to the legal-constitutional arguments of criminal defendants, labor unions, and political dissenters.

In 1986, the resignation of Warren Burger allowed Reagan to elevate **William Rehnquist** to the position of chief justice and appoint Scalia to replace Rehnquist as an associate justice. In 1987, however, the Senate, now with a Democratic majority following the 1986 elections, rebuffed Reagan's attempt to place Bork, a particular favorite of the New Right, on the High Court. Bork's rejection enraged conservatives, some blaming Reagan for not working hard enough on Bork's behalf. Still, by 1990, a flood of retirements meant that about half of all federal judges had reached the bench during Ronald Reagan's presidency. Reagan also staffed the Justice Department with young attorneys, such as John Roberts and Samuel Alito, who expressed a desire to help conservative judges whittle back Warren-era judicial precedents.

No matter what problems beset his administration, criticism rarely stuck to Reagan, whom one frustrated Democrat dubbed the "Teflon president." His genial optimism seemed unshakable. His smile, jokes, and confident air disarmed and inspired many. He even appeared to rebound quickly—although close observers noted a clear decline in his energies—after being shot by a would-be assassin in March 1981.

Reagan to Bush   Democrats continually underestimated Reagan's appeal—a miscalculation that doomed their 1984 presidential effort. Walter Mondale, Jimmy Carter's vice president, ran on a platform calling for an expansion of social welfare programs. Mondale proposed higher taxes to fund this agenda and chose as his running mate Representative Geraldine Ferraro of New York, the first woman to run for president or vice president on a major party ticket.

Republican campaign ads—often framed by the slogan "It's Morning Again in America"—portrayed a glowing landscape of bustling small towns and lush farmlands. They attacked Mondale's support from labor unions and civil rights groups as a vestige of the "old politics" of "special interests" and his tax proposal as a return to the policies popularly associated with the stagflation of the 1970s. The 1984 presidential election ended with Mondale carrying only his home state of Minnesota and the District of Columbia.

The election suggested how the Reagan revolution had changed the nation's political vocabulary. Democrats had once invoked "liberalism" to stand for governmental initiatives to stimulate the economy, promote greater equality, and advance liberty for all. Republicans recast the term "liberal" as a code word for wasteful social programs devised by a bloated federal government that gouged hardworking people and squandered their tax dollars. The term "conservative," as used by New Right Republicans, came to stand for economic growth through the curtailment of governmental power and support for traditional sociocultural values. The once-dominant Democratic Party of the New Deal, Fair Deal, and Great Society seemingly confronted an uncertain future.

In the election of 1988, the Reagan legacy fell to the president's heir apparent, Vice President **George H. W. Bush**. Born into a wealthy Republican family and educated at Yale, Bush had prospered in the oil business, served in the House of Representatives, and headed the CIA. To court the New Right, decidedly lukewarm to his candidacy, he pledged "no new taxes" and chose Senator J. Danforth (Dan) Quayle, a youthful conservative from Indiana, as a running mate. Quayle would soon delight political comedians who highlighted his verbal blunders.

Governor Michael Dukakis of Massachusetts emerged as the Democratic presidential candidate. Dukakis avoided talk of new domestic programs and higher taxes. Instead, he pledged to bring competence and honesty to the White House.

Although Bush emerged the winner, Democrats retained control of both houses of Congress. The turnout was the lowest for any national election since 1924, and polls suggested that many voters remained unimpressed with either Bush or Dukakis.

Once in the White House, Bush began to lose crucial support. He angered New Right Republicans by agreeing to an increase in the minimum wage and by failing to veto a law that allowed for some affirmative action in the hiring of women and people of color into occupations where they were underrepresented. The Religious Right detected tepid support from the president in its campaigns against abortion and in favor of religious prayers in public schools. Most important, in 1990 Bush broke his "no new taxes" pledge in an attempt to curb the still-rising federal deficit. Taxation had emerged as one of the New Right's central issues, even though Reagan himself had raised taxes during his second term, and the New Right bitterly denounced Bush's tax policy. Worse for the president's political future, the economic growth of the Reagan years began slowing while the budget deficit continued to grow.

Millions of Americans remember Bush's presidency for its support for the last landmark civil rights act of the 20th century, the **Americans with Disabilities Act (ADA),** passed in 1990. Activists supportive of disability rights, who employed the strategies and tactics of other movements, provided the long-term impetus for this legislation. In addition, officials within the Bush administration and members of congress offered timely support. Building on earlier laws to assist people with disabilities, the ADA fully embraced the legal-constitutional framework of the Civil Rights Act of 1964. It banned discrimination against disabled persons—such as those with limitations of hearing, sight, and mobility—seeking educational advancement, gainful employment, housing, recreational opportunities, and access to other areas of daily life. The ADA empowered the Equal Employment Opportunities Commission (EEOC), the Civil Rights Division of the federal justice department, and the national judicial system to implement and enforce its guarantees.

RENEWING AND ENDING THE COLD WAR

In foreign policy, Reagan promised to reverse what he derided as Carter's passivity. He declared that the Vietnam War had been a "noble cause" that politicians had refused to win. Renewing the rhetoric of strident anticommunism, Reagan denounced the Soviet Union as an "evil empire" and promised a military buildup to confront communism. This renewal of the cold war, however, proved short lived. By the late 1980s, a variety of internal and external circumstances brought communist regimes under unsustainable pressure. Reagan had begun his presidency by renewing the cold war, but he and his successor, George H. W. Bush, also presided over its end.

The Defense Buildup   In response to his campaign promises, Reagan led off with dramatic increases in military spending, even as tax cuts reduced federal revenues. The Pentagon enlarged the navy and expanded strategic nuclear forces, deploying new missiles throughout Western Europe. At the height of Reagan's military buildup, which produced gaping budget deficits, the Pentagon was purchasing about 20 percent of the nation's manufacturing output.

In 1983 Reagan proposed the most expensive defense system in history: a space-based shield against incoming missiles. This **Strategic Defense Initiative (SDI)** soon had its own Pentagon agency, which sought $26 billion, over five years, for research costs alone. Controversy swirled around SDI. Skeptics dubbed it "Star Wars" and shuddered at its astronomical costs. Although most scientists dismissed the plan as too speculative, Congress voted appropriations for SDI. Reagan insisted that a defensive missile shield could work and also suggested that the Soviet Union might collapse under the economic strain of competing in an accelerating arms race.

Reagan's foreign policy agenda included numerous nonmilitary initiatives. A new "informational" offensive funded conservative media groups around the world and established Radio Martí, a Florida station beamed at Cuba and designed to discredit Fidel Castro's communist government. When the United Nations Educational, Scientific, and Cultural Organization (UNESCO) adopted an allegedly anti-American tone, Reagan cut off U.S. contributions to this agency. The White House also championed free markets, pressing other nations to minimize tariffs and restrictions on foreign investment. The Caribbean Basin Initiative, for example, rewarded with aid small nations in the Caribbean region that adhered to free-market principles.

The CIA, headed by William Casey, stepped up its covert activities. Some became so obvious they hardly qualified as covert. It was no secret, for instance, that the United States sent aid to anticommunist forces in Afghanistan, many of them radical Islamic fundamentalist groups. The CIA also helped train and support the *contras* in Nicaragua, a military force fighting to topple the Sandinista government. To contain the power of Iran, assistance went to its bitter enemy, Saddam Hussein in Iraq.

Deploying Military Power   In renewing the global cold war, Reagan promised military support to "democratic" revolutions anywhere, a move designed to contain the Soviet Union's sphere of influence. Reagan's UN ambassador, Jeane Kirkpatrick, wrote that "democratic" forces included almost any movement, no matter how autocratic, that was anticommunist. The United States thus funded opposition forces in countries aligned with the Soviet Union: Ethiopia, Angola, South Yemen, Cambodia, Guatemala, Grenada, Afghanistan, and Nicaragua. Reagan called the participants in such anticommunist insurgencies "freedom fighters," although few displayed any visible commitment to democratic values or institutions.

The Reagan administration also deployed U.S. military power, initially in southern Lebanon in 1982. Here, Israeli troops faced off against Islamic groups supported by Syria and Iran. Fearing loss of influence within Lebanon, the Reagan administration convinced Israel to withdraw and sent 1,600 U.S. Marines as part of an international "peacekeeping force." Islamic militias, however, turned against the U.S. forces. After a massive truck bomb attack against a military compound killed 241 U.S. troops, mostly marines, in April 1983, Reagan decided to end this ill-defined undertaking. In February 1984 he ordered the withdrawal of U.S. troops.

Another military intervention seemed more successful. In October 1983 Reagan sent 2,000 U.S. troops to the tiny Caribbean island of Grenada, whose socialist leader was forging ties with Castro's Cuba. U.S. troops swept aside Grenada's government and installed one friendlier to U.S. policies.

Buoyed by Grenada, the Reagan administration fixed its sights on Nicaragua, where the Marxist-leaning Sandinista government was trying to break Nicaragua's dependence on the United States. The administration responded with economic pressure, a propaganda campaign, and greater assistance to the contras—initiatives that stirred controversy because of mounting evidence of the contras' corruption and brutality. Finally, Democrats in Congress barred additional military aid to the contras.

Meanwhile, violence continued to escalate throughout the Middle East. Militant Islamic groups increased attacks against Israel and Western powers. Bombings and kidnappings of westerners became more frequent. Apparently, Libya's Muammar al-Qaddafi and Iranian leaders encouraged such activities. In the spring of 1986, the United States launched an air strike into Qaddafi's personal compound. It killed his young daughter, but Qaddafi and his government survived. Despite what looked like a long-range assassination attempt against a foreign leader —an action outlawed by Congress—Americans generally approved of using strong measures against sponsors of terrorism and hostage taking.

The Iran-Contra Controversy   In November 1986 a magazine in Lebanon reported that the Reagan administration was selling arms to Iran in order to secure the release of Americans being held hostage by Islamic militants. These alleged deals violated the Reagan administration's own pledges against selling arms to Iran or rewarding hostage taking by negotiating for the release of captives. During the 1980 campaign Reagan had made hostages in Iran a symbol of U.S. weakness under Carter. When Iranian-backed groups continued to kidnap Americans during Reagan's own presidency, it seemed that Reagan had sought clandestine ways to recover hostages and avoid such charges being leveled at him.

As Congress began to investigate, the story became more bizarre. It appeared that the Reagan administration had not only secretly sold arms to Iran but had funneled profits from these back-channel deals to the contra forces in Nicaragua, thereby circumventing the congressional ban on U.S. military aid. Oliver North, an aide to the national security adviser, had directed the effort, working with international arms dealers and private go-betweens. North's covert activities seemingly violated both the official policy of the White House and an act of Congress.

This **Iran-contra affair** never reached the proportions of the Watergate scandal. Ronald Reagan stepped forward and testified, through a deposition, that he could not recall any details about either the release of hostages or the funding of the contras. His management skills might deserve criticism, Reagan admitted, but he had never intended to break any laws or violate any presidential promise. Vice President George H. W. Bush also claimed ignorance. Several officials in the Reagan administration were convicted of felonies, including falsifying documents and lying to Congress, but appellate courts later overturned these verdicts. North destroyed so many documents and left so many false paper trails that congressional investigators struggled even to compile a simple narrative of his activities. Finally, in 1992, just a few days before the end of his presidency, George H. W. Bush pardoned six former Reagan-era officials connected to the Iran-contra controversy.

The Cold War Eases

After six years of renewed cold war confrontation, Reagan's last two years saw a sudden thaw in U.S.-Soviet relations. The economic cost of superpower rivalry was burdening both nations, and political changes sweeping the Soviet Union eliminated reasons for confrontation. **Mikhail Gorbachev**, who became general secretary of the Communist Party in 1985, understood that his nation faced economic stagnation and environmental problems brought on by decades of poorly planned industrial development. To redirect the Soviet Union's course, he withdrew troops from Afghanistan, reduced commitments to Cuba and Nicaragua, proclaimed a policy *of glasnost* ("openness"), and began to implement *perestroika* ("economic liberalization") at home.

Gorbachev's policies gained him acclaim throughout the West, and summit meetings with the United States yielded breakthroughs in arms control. At Reykjavik, Iceland, in October 1986, Reagan shocked both Gorbachev and his own advisers by proposing a wholesale ban on nuclear weapons. Although negotiations at Reykjavik stumbled over Soviet insistence that the United States abandon SDI, Gorbachev later dropped that condition. In December 1987, Reagan and Gorbachev signed a major arms treaty that reduced each nation's supply of intermediate-range missiles and allowed for on-site verification, which the Soviets had never before permitted. The next year, Gorbachev scrapped the policy that forbade nations under Soviet influence from renouncing communism. In effect, he declared an end to the cold war.

Within the next few years, communist states began to topple like dominoes. In 1989, the first year of George H. W. Bush's presidency, Poland's anticommunist labor movement, Solidarity, ousted a pro-Soviet regime. The pro-Moscow government in East Germany fell in November 1989. West and East Germans hacked down the Berlin Wall and then began the process of reunifying Germany as a single nation. Popular movements similarly forced out communist governments throughout Eastern Europe. Yugoslavia quickly disintegrated, and warfare ensued as rival ethnic groups recreated separate states in Slovenia, Serbia, Bosnia, and Croatia. Latvia, Lithuania, and Estonia, which had been under Soviet control since the Second World War, declared their independence. In December 1991 Boris Yeltsin, the president of the new state of Russia, brokered a plan to abolish the Soviet Union and replace it with 11 separate republics, loosely joined in a commonwealth arrangement.

Post–Cold War Policy and the Persian Gulf War

The Bush administration set about redefining U.S. national security in a post–cold war era. The collapse of the Soviet Union weakened support for the leftist insurgencies in Central America that had so preoccupied the Reagan administration. Nicaraguans voted out the Sandinistas, who became just another political party in a multiparty system. The Pentagon pondered new military missions, imagining rapid, sharply targeted strikes rather than lengthy, conventional campaigns. The armed forces assessed, for example, how they might serve in the "war against drugs," an effort that Bush had suggested during his 1988 presidential campaign.

General Manuel Noriega, the president of Panama, was deeply involved in the drug trade, and the Reagan administration had secured an indictment against him for international narcotics trafficking. Confronting Noriega posed a potentially embarrassing problem for Bush. The anticommunist general had been recruited as a CIA "asset" during the mid-1970s, when Bush had headed the agency. Nevertheless, the United States needed a friendly and stable government in Panama in order to complete the transfer of the Panama Canal to Panamanian sovereignty in 2000, and Bush decided to topple Noriega. During "Operation Just Cause," U.S. Marines landed in Panama in December 1989 and laid siege to the president's headquarters. Noriega soon surrendered, was extradited to Florida, and went to prison after a 1992 conviction for trafficking in cocaine.

Deposing the leader of a foreign government by unilateral military action raised questions of international law, but the Panamanian operation, which involved 25,000 U.S. troops and few casualties, provided a model for the post–cold war era. The Pentagon firmed up plans for creating highly mobile, rapid deployment forces. A test of its new strategy came during the Persian Gulf War of 1991.

On August 2, 1990, Iraq's Saddam Hussein ordered his troops to occupy the neighboring oil-rich emirate of Kuwait. U.S. intelligence analysts had been caught off guard, and they now warned that Iraq's next target might be Saudi Arabia, the largest oil exporter in the Middle East and a longtime U.S. ally.

Moving swiftly, Bush orchestrated a multilateral, international response. Four days after Iraq's invasion of Kuwait, he launched Operation Desert Shield by sending several hundred thousand U.S. troops to Saudi Arabia. Bush convinced the Saudi government, concerned about allowing Western troops on sacred Islamic soil, to accept a U.S. military presence in Saudi Arabia. After consulting with European leaders, Bush approached the UN, which denounced Iraqi aggression, ordered economic sanctions against Iraq, and authorized the United States to lead an international force into the Gulf region if Saddam Hussein's troops did not withdraw from Kuwait.

Bush assembled a massive coalition force, ultimately nearly 500,000 troops from the United States and some 200,000 from other countries. He claimed a moral obligation to rescue Kuwait, and his policymakers also spoke frankly about the economic threat that Hussein's aggression posed for the oil-dependent economies of the United States and its allies. These arguments persuaded Congress to approve a resolution backing the use of force.

In mid-January 1991 the United States launched an air war against Iraq and, after a period of devastating aerial bombardment, began a ground offensive in late February. Coalition forces, enjoying air supremacy, decimated Saddam Hussein's armies in a matter of days. U.S. casualties were relatively light (148 combat deaths). Estimates of Iraqi casualties ranged from 25,000 to 100,000 deaths. Although this **Persian Gulf War** lasted scarcely six weeks, it took an enormous toll on highways, bridges, communications, and other infrastructure facilities in both Iraq and Kuwait.

In a controversial decision, Bush stopped short of ousting Saddam Hussein, a goal that the UN had never approved and that U.S. military planners considered too costly and risky. Instead, the United States, backed by the UN, maintained its economic pressure, ordered the dismantling of Iraq's capability to produce nuclear and bacteriological weapons, and enforced "no-fly" zones over northern and southern Iraq to help protect the Kurds and Shi'a Muslims from Hussein's continued persecution. The Persian Gulf War temporarily boosted George H. W. Bush's popularity. An increasingly vocal and influential group of neoconservative critics, however, argued that Saddam Hussein should have been overthrown. Ten years later, with President Bush's son as president, they would get another chance.

Bush's economic foreign policy, although less visible than his leadership during the Persian Gulf War, comprised a key part of his post–cold war vision. It pressed a program of international economic integration. During the mid-1980s, huge debts that Third World nations owed to U.S. institutions had threatened the international banking system, but most of these obligations had been renegotiated by the early

MAP 30.2 Collapse of the Soviet Bloc

These contrasting maps show the Soviet Union and the countries it dominated before and after the fall of communist governments. What countries in Eastern Europe escaped Russian control after 1989? What new countries emerged out of the old Soviet Union?

1990s. Market economies, which replaced centrally planned ones, began to emerge in former communist states. Western Europe moved toward economic integration. Most nations of the Pacific Rim experienced steady economic growth. The president supported (but was unable to pass) a North American Free Trade Agreement (NAFTA), which proposed to eliminate tariff barriers and join Canada, the United States, and Mexico together in the largest free-market zone in the world.

Voters ultimately judged the president's record on foreign affairs as something of a muddle. He had organized an international coalition against Iraq, assisted a peaceful post–cold war transition in Russia and Eastern Europe, and embraced global economic integration. Despite this leadership, the president publicly projected indecisiveness. The United States remained on the sidelines as full-scale warfare erupted among the states of the former Yugoslavia, with Serbs launching a brutal campaign of territorial aggrandizement and "ethnic cleansing" against Bosnian Muslims. In Africa, when severe famine wracked Somalia, Bush ordered U.S. troops to secure supply lines for humanitarian aid, but the American public remained wary of this military mission. As the old objective of containing the Soviet Union became irrelevant, Bush failed to rally Americans around any new foreign policy goal.

The Election of 1992   The inability to project a coherent vision for either domestic or foreign policy threatened Bush's reelection and forced concessions to the New Right. Dan Quayle, although clearly a liability with voters outside his conservative constituency, returned as Bush's running mate. The president allowed New Right activists, who talked about "a religious war" for "the soul of America," to dominate the 1992 Republican National Convention. Conservative Democrats and independents, who had supported Reagan and Bush in the previous three presidential elections, found this rhetoric unsettling.

Bush's Democratic challenger, Governor William Jefferson Clinton of Arkansas, stressed economic issues. Campaigning as a "New Democrat," Bill Clinton promised job creation, deficit reduction, and an overhaul of the nation's health-care system. Sounding almost like a moderate Republican, Clinton pledged to shrink the size of government and to "end this [welfare] system as we know it." This platform made it difficult for Bush to label Clinton as a "big-government liberal."

Clinton's focus on the economy helped deflect attention from the sociocultural issues on which he was vulnerable. As a college student, Clinton had avoided service in Vietnam and, while in England as a Rhodes Scholar, had demonstrated against the Vietnam War. When Bush, a decorated veteran of the Second World War, challenged the patriotism of his Democratic challenger, Clinton emphasized, rather than repudiated, his roots in the 1960s. He appeared on MTV and touted his devotion to (relatively soft) rock music. In addition, he chose Senator Albert Gore of Tennessee, a Vietnam veteran, as his running mate.

The 1992 election brought Clinton a clear victory. The quixotic campaign of Ross Perot, a Texas billionaire who financed his own third-party run, took more votes from Bush than from Clinton. With Perot in the race, Clinton garnered only 43 percent of the popular vote but won 370 electoral votes by carrying 32 states and the District of Columbia. Bush won a majority only among white Protestants in the South. Clinton carried the Jewish, African American, and Latino vote by large margins and even gained a plurality among people who had served in the Vietnam War. He also ran well among independents who had supported Reagan and Bush during the 1980s. Perhaps most surprising, about 55 percent of eligible voters went to the polls, a turnout that reversed 32 years of steady decline in voter participation.

THE POLITICS OF SOCIAL MOVEMENTS

The activism associated with the 1960s became firmly embedded in most areas of American life during the decades that followed. Mass demonstrations reminiscent of those against the Vietnam War remained one tool of advocacy and protest. Both antiabortion and pro-choice forces, for example, regularly demonstrated in Washington, D.C. During the 1980s, the Clamshell Alliance conducted a campaign of civil disobedience against a nuclear reactor being built in Seabrook, New Hampshire, and a coalition of West Coast activists waged a lengthy, unsuccessful struggle to close the University of California's Lawrence Livermore National Laboratory, which was developing nuclear weapons. In nearly every major city and many smaller towns, women's groups staged annual Take Back the Night rallies to call attention to the issue of sexual assault.

The media increasingly ignored most mass demonstrations, however, unless they sparked violent conflict. In 1991, for example, 30,000 Korean Americans staged a march for racial peace in Los Angeles. Although it was the largest demonstration ever conducted by any Asian American group, even the local media failed to cover it. Only C-Span, a niche network devoted to public affairs programming, provided minimal coverage of events of social and political protest. Social activism from all parts of the political spectrum and all sections of the country, in short, did not go away during the 1980s, but it did become less reliant on media spectacles.

Women's Issues   In this political environment, women's groups adopted a range of methods to rally new supporters and reenergize their core constituencies. Struggles over gender-related issues had emerged within the labor movement and the civil rights and antiwar movements of the 1960s. Initially, many of the men involved in these causes complained that issues of gender equality interfered with broader fights to redirect labor, racial, or foreign policies. Women, however, insisted on calling attention to their second-class status in movements that claimed to be egalitarian. The spread of the birth control pill during the 1960s gave women greater control over reproductive choices but also complicated the meaning of "sexual freedom." Throughout the 1970s women promoted "consciousness-raising" sessions to discuss how *political* empowerment was inseparable from *personal* power relationships involving housework, child rearing, sexuality, and economic independence. "The personal is political" became a watchword for the new women's movement.

The number of groups addressing issues of concern to women continually expanded. The National Organization for Women (NOW) became generally identified with the rights-based agenda of the mainstream of the Democratic Party. African American women often formed separate organizations that emphasized issues of cultural and ethnic identity. Chicana groups coalesced within the United Farm Workers (UFW) movement and other Mexican American organizations. Lesbians organized their own groups, often allying with an emerging gay rights movement. Many U.S. feminist organizations joined with groups in other nations on behalf of international women's rights. Although never embracing the word "feminism," conservative women also played leadership roles in causes associated with the New Right.

With agendas often varying along lines of class, race, ethnicity, and religion, the women's movement remained highly diverse, but women from different backgrounds often cooperated to build new institutions and networks. Their efforts included battered-women's shelters; health and birthing clinics specializing in women's medicine; rape crisis centers; economic development counseling for women-owned businesses; union-organizing efforts led by women; organizations of women in specific businesses or professions; women's and gender studies programs in colleges and universities; and academic journals and popular magazines devoted to women's issues. Pressure for gender equity also affected existing institutions. Country clubs and service organizations began admitting women members. Many Protestant denominations came to accept women into the ministry, and Reform Judaism placed women in its pulpits. Educational institutions adopted "gender-fair" hiring practices and instructional material. American women by the beginning of the 21st century lived in an environment significantly different from that of their mothers.

Economic self-sufficiency became an especially pressing issue. Reagan-era budget cuts for social programs took their toll, especially in urban centers. Homeless shelters, which once catered almost exclusively to single men, began taking in growing numbers of women and children. As this feminization of poverty gained attention, proposals on the state and federal levels called for reshaping patterns of public support by limiting direct governmental payments and emphasizing strategies to move women, even those with young children, into the workforce.

The job market, however, remained laced with inequalities. Women constituted 30 percent of the labor force in 1950 and more than 45 percent in 2001. Although women increasingly entered the professions and gained unionized positions (by 2000 nearly 45 percent of union members were women, compared with 18 percent in 1960), the average female worker still earned around 75 cents for every dollar taken home by men. "Glass ceilings" limited women's chances for promotion, and childcare expenses often fell disproportionately on women who worked outside the home.

Sexual harassment in the workplace became a controversial issue. Most women's groups pressed government and private employers to curtail sexually charged behaviors that they saw as demeaning women and exploiting their lack of power vis-à-vis male supervisors and coworkers. In 1986, the U.S. Supreme Court ruled that sexual harassment constituted a form of discrimination covered by the Civil Rights Act of 1964.

In 1991, the issue gained national attention when Anita Hill, an African American law professor, accused Clarence Thomas, an African American nominee for the U.S. Supreme Court, of having sexually harassed her when both worked for the federal government. Feminists denounced the all-male Senate Judiciary Committee, which was responsible for considering Thomas's nomination, for failing even to understand, let alone investigate seriously, the issue of sexual harassment. Although the Senate narrowly approved Thomas for the High Court, women's groups mobilized female voters and elected four women as U.S. senators in 1992.

Sexual harassment also became of concern to the U.S. military, which began to recruit women more actively. The service academies accepted female cadets, and women found places within the military hierarchy. Soon, however, revelations about harassment and even sexual assaults against female naval officers by male comrades revealed problems. Attempts by navy officials to cover up sexual harassment during the 1991 Tailhook convention provoked outrage, and several high-ranking officers were forced to step down.

Sexual Politics   Issues involving gays and lesbians also became more public and political. In 1969, New York City police raided the Stonewall Inn, a bar in Greenwich Village with a largely homosexual clientele. Patrons resisted arrest, and the resultant confrontations pitted the neighborhood's gay and lesbian activists, who claimed to be the victims of police harassment, against law enforcement officials.

Historians of sexuality have come to criticize what they call "the Stonewall Narrative," in which events at a single Greenwich Village bar ignited what would become known as the LGBT (lesbian, gay, bisexual, and transgender) movement. Recent studies emphasize that LGBT activism did not suddenly emerge in 1969 but instead grew out of earlier movements, such as the Mattachine Society, and cultural communities such as the Beats.

Still, the 1969 events at the Stonewall Inn, because of the prominence they received in mainstream and alternative media, marked an important benchmark in sexual politics. Gay and lesbian activism became an important part of the larger movement of movements that continued during the 1970s and 1980s. Thousands of advocacy and support groups, such as New York City's Gay Activist Alliance (GAA), sprang up. As many individuals "came out of the closet," newspapers,

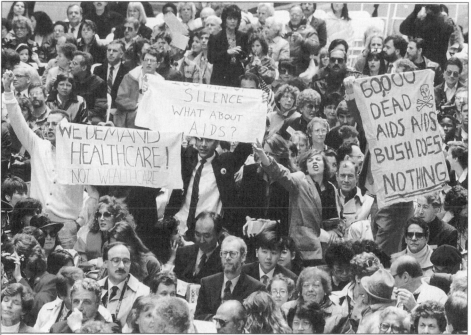

Aids "ACT UP" Campaign. *Health-care issues increasingly galvanized grassroots activists. In 1989, members of ACT UP, a group that embraced direct action, protested what they saw as the federal government's inattention to the issue of AIDS during the 1980s.*

theaters, nightspots, and religious groups proudly identified themselves as activists. LGBT communities emerged particularly in larger cities and benefited from a general relaxation of legal and cultural controls over the portrayal and practice of sexuality. They demanded that law enforcement officials treat attacks against them no less seriously than attacks against all other communities. They also asserted constitutional claims to equal access to housing, jobs, and benefits for domestic partners.

One issue, with international implications, was especially urgent. A human immunodeficiency virus produced an immune deficiency syndrome, HIV-AIDS, a contagious disease for which medical science offered virtually nothing in the way of cure. The disease could be transmitted through the careless use of intravenous drugs, tainted blood supplies, and unprotected sexual intercourse. At first, the incidence of HIV-AIDS in the United States was primarily limited to gay men, and activists charged that, as a consequence, cultural and religious conservatives placed a low priority on medical efforts to understand its causes, check its spread, or devise a cure. The resultant controversy over medical funding galvanized empowerment efforts among LGBT organizations, such as the Aids Coalition to Unleash Power, or ACT UP. With the development of prevention programs and drugs that could combat HIV-AIDS, however, most public figures came to support new efforts both at home and overseas, particularly in Africa, to address HIV-AIDS. It has remained a modern health threat in many parts of the world, but its specific identification with LGBT rights has faded.

Activism among African Americans   The emphasis on group identity as the fulcrum for social activism became especially strong among racial and ethnic communities. Extending the movement of movements of the 1960s, groups emphasized pride in their distinctive cultural traditions and insisted that differences should be affirmed rather than feared.

Having accomplished many of the legislative goals of the 1960s, African American activists, one observed, were "heading into a completely new era, and we don't know what to make of it." Mobilization to promote political and cultural change proceeded along many fronts.

African American leaders became increasingly prominent in national and local politics. One media spotlight fell on the Reverend Jesse Jackson. Jackson had spent the late 1960s in Chicago directing a local effort sponsored by Dr. Martin Luther King, Jr.'s, Southern Christian Leadership Conference (SCLC). After Dr. King's 1968 assassination, Jackson created his own Chicago-based organization, Operation PUSH, which pressured public officials and corporations to create jobs and promote community development projects. Abundant media coverage made Reverend Jackson best known for addressing a wide range of national and international issues, including the status of the Palestinians and apartheid in South Africa. During the 1980s, he formed the Rainbow Coalition to provide a national umbrella for his movement and to facilitate his campaigns for the Democratic Party's presidential nomination in 1984 and 1988. Jackson's efforts garnered several primary victories and helped shape Democratic Party politics.

Other types of political activism also left a significant imprint on electoral politics during the 1970s and 1980s. The civil rights movement of the 1960s provided the legal-constitutional basis for greater political participation by African Americans, and change came rapidly. In 1970, 13 African American members of Congress established the Congressional Black Caucus (CBC) to form a common front on a wide range of foreign and domestic issues. Picking up the mantle of A. Philip Randolph and Bayard Rustin's "Freedom Budget" of the 1960s, the CBC regularly issued a hypothetical "Alternative Budget," which proposed more money for social initiatives. The caucus also campaigned on behalf of better relations between the United States and African nations and took stands on issues that particularly affected African Americans, such as inequities in drug sentencing.

By the end of the 1980s, more than 7,000 African Americans (including nearly 1,500 women) held political office. The year the Voting Rights Act passed, 1965, there had been fewer than 200. Urban centers with significant African American populations, such as Gary and Detroit, elected black mayors, but so did cities such as Denver, where African American candidates successfully formed cross-ethnic alliances. The new direction pursued by the Republican Party during the 1970s and 1980s meant that virtually all of this political activity occurred within Democratic ranks.

This form of black political activism confronted clear limits. Few mayors, whatever their ethnic identity, could mobilize the economic resources that large cities required to deal with rising crime rates, decaying infrastructures, and galloping inflation. The stagnant economy under Carter and the urban budget cutting that characterized the Reagan years hit African Americans in inner cities with severity.

In addition to political activism, a diverse set of cultural movements emerged. The hyper-violent 1970s cycle of "Blaxploitation movies," such as *Shaft* (1971) and *Coffy* (1973), prompted heated debate over whether representing urban black life "like it [supposedly] was," rather than "like it [supposedly] should be," advanced African American interests. The 1980s movies of Spike Lee also created controversy by tackling issues such as the politics of gender and "light skin" in African American life. *Do the Right Thing* (1989), arguably an even more ambitious movie—though smaller budgeted—than the epic *Malcolm X* (1991), provided a complex meditation about African American heroes, multiculturalism, law enforcement patterns, and personal activism amidst the uncertainties of urban life.

Prominent academics such as **Henry Louis Gates, Jr.**, worked in another venue to expand the study of the African American experience and to challenge a movement that advocated creating an "Afrocentric" school curriculum. African American culture, in the view of Gates, was not "a thing apart, separate from the whole, having no influence on the shape and shaping of American culture." Gates insisted on viewing African American authors, such as Toni Morrison and Alice Walker, as writers who take "the blackness of the culture for granted" and use this as "a springboard to write about those human emotions that we share with everyone else." The cultural works of African Americans should simultaneously be seen as unique and different, *and also* be viewed in relationship to broader cultural traditions, he believed.

Activism among American Indians   American Indians, of course, had long-standing identities based on their tribal affiliation, and many issues, particularly those involving land and treaty disputes, turned on specific, tribal-based claims. Other questions, which seemed to require strategies that extended beyond a single tribe or band, became identified as "pan-Indian" in nature.

In 1969, people from several tribes began a two-year sit-in designed to dramatize a history of broken treaty promises, at the former federal prison on Alcatraz

Island in San Francisco harbor. Expanding on this tactic, the American Indian Movement (AIM), created in 1968 by young activists from several Northern Plains tribes, adopted even more confrontational approaches. Clashes with both federal officials and older American Indian leaders erupted in 1973 on the Pine Ridge Reservation in South Dakota. In response, federal officials targeted members of AIM with illegal surveillance and a series of controversial criminal prosecutions.

Meanwhile, important social and legal changes were taking place. In the Civil Rights Act of 1968, which contained several sections that became known as the "Indian Bill of Rights," Congress extended most of the provisions of the constitutional Bill of Rights to Native Americans living on reservations, while reconfirming the legitimacy of tribal laws. Federal legislation and several Supreme Court decisions in the 1970s subsequently reinforced the principle of "tribal self-determination." Tribal identification itself required legal action. By the early 21st century, the federal government officially recognized nearly 600 separate tribes and bands. After 1978 Congress also provided funds for educational institutions that would teach job skills and preserve tribal cultures.

Tapping the expertise of the Native American Rights Fund (NARF), tribes pressed demands that derived from old treaties with the U.S. government. Some

© Andre Jenny/The Image Works

Gaming at Potawatomi Casino. *During the 1980s, casino-style gaming became one of the nation's leading entertainment enterprises. Native Americans embraced casinos, such as this one located in Milwaukee, Wisconsin, as important sources of jobs and capital on Indian reservations. The Potawatomi complex, which opened in 1991, juxtaposes traditionally styled sculptures, an Indian heritage center and gift shop, an imaginatively designed building, more than 1,000 slot machines, and a cabaret-style dinner theater patterned after ones in Las Vegas.*

campaigns sought recognition of fishing and agricultural rights and often provoked resentment among non-Indians who argued that these claims, based on federal authority, should not take precedence over state and local laws. American Indians also sued to protect tribal water rights and traditional religious ceremonies, some of which included the ritualistic use of drugs such as peyote. In 1990, Congress passed the Native American Graves Protection and Repatriation Act, which required universities and museums to return human remains and sacred objects to tribes that requested them.

Claiming exemption from state gaming laws, Native Americans began to open bingo halls and then full-blown casinos. In 1988 the U.S. Supreme Court ruled that states could not prohibit gambling operations on tribal land, and Congress responded with the Indian Gaming Regulatory Act. Gambling emerged as one of the most lucrative sectors of the nation's entertainment business, and many Indian-owned casinos thrived. Ironically, the glitzy, tribal-owned casinos often financed tribal powwows and other efforts to nurture traditional cultural practices. Sometimes the competition to establish casinos in prime locations prompted intertribal political and legal conflicts.

To forestall the disappearance of native languages and cultures, American Indian activists urged bilingualism and renewed attention to tribal rituals. Indian groups also denounced the use of stereotypical nicknames, such as "Chiefs" and "Redskins," and Indian-related logos in sports. The federal government assisted this cultural-pride movement by funding two National Museums of the American Indian, one in New York and the other in Washington, D.C. The National Park Service changed the name of "Custer Battlefield" in Montana to "Little Bighorn Battlefield," redesigning its exhibits to honor American Indian culture.

Activism in Spanish-Speaking Communities

Spanish-speaking Americans, who constituted the fastest-growing ethnic group in the United States, highlighted the diversity and complexity of identity. Many Spanish-speaking people, especially in the Southwest, preferred the umbrella term "Latino," whereas others, particularly in Florida, used the term "Hispanic." At the same time, people the U.S. Census began (in 1980) labeling "Hispanic" most frequently identified themselves according to the specific Spanish-speaking country or commonwealth from which they or their ancestors had immigrated.

Mexican Americans, members of the oldest and most numerous Spanish-speaking group, could tap a long tradition of social activism. The late 1960s saw an emerging spirit of **Chicanismo**, a populist-style pride in a heritage that could be traced back to the ancient civilizations of Middle America. Young activists made the words *Chicano* and *Chicana*, terms of derision that most Mexican Americans had generally avoided in the past, into a rallying cry.

In cities in the Southwest during the 1970s, advocates of Chicanismo gained cultural influence. Members of La Raza Unida, a political party founded in 1967, began to win local elections. At the same time, Mexican American communities experienced a cultural flowering. New Spanish-language newspapers and journals reinforced a growing sense of pride, and many churches sponsored festivals with ethnic dancing, mural painting, poetry, and literature. Mexican Americans successfully pushed for programs in Chicano/a studies at colleges and universities.

Mexican Americans also organized politically. In San Antonio, Texas, in the 1970s Ernesto Cortes, Jr., took the lead in founding Communities Organized for Public Service (COPS), a group that brought the energy and talents of Mexican Americans, particularly women, into the city's public arena for the first time. Mexican American activists worked with Anglo business leaders and Democratic politicians such as Henry Cisneros, who became the city's mayor in 1981. Other locally based organizations formed on the model of COPS, such as United Neighborhood Organization (UNO) in Los Angeles, also worked on community concerns.

On the national level, the Mexican American Legal Defense and Education Fund (MALDEF), established in 1968, emerged as a highly visible advocacy group ready to lobby or litigate. Professional groups, such as the National Network of Hispanic Women, also proliferated. Mexican American activists, however, became especially well known for their labor-organizing efforts, particularly among farmworkers and in the rapidly expanding service sector.

Efforts to organize agricultural workers, who were largely of Mexican and Filipino descent, dramatized both the successes and the difficulties of expanding the union movement to largely immigrant workers. **Dolores Huerta and Cesar Chavez**, charismatic leaders who emulated the nonviolent tactics of Martin Luther King, Jr., vaulted the United Farm Workers (UFW) into public attention during the 1970s. Chavez undertook personal hunger strikes, and Huerta helped organize well-publicized consumer boycotts of lettuce and grapes to pressure growers into collective bargaining agreements with the UFW. Despite some successes, the UFW steadily lost ground

Ralf-Finn Hestoft/Encyclopedia/Corbis

Mural Art in Chicago. *Themes in Mexican history and culture, inspired by the great Mexican muralists, appeared in Mexican American communities throughout the country.*

during the later 1970s and the 1980s. Strong anti-union stands by growers and the continued influx of new immigrants eager for work undercut the UFW's efforts.

Social activism among Puerto Ricans in the United States emerged more slowly. Some stateside Puerto Ricans focused their political energy on the persistent "status" question—that is, whether Puerto Rico should seek independence, strive for state-hood, or retain a commonwealth connection to the mainland. New York City's Puerto Rican Day Parade became the city's largest ethnic celebration and an impor-tant focus of cultural pride. A 1976 report by the U.S. Commission on Civil Rights, however, concluded that Puerto Ricans remained "the last in line" for government-funded benefits and opportunity programs. Over time, the Puerto Rican Legal Defense and Education Fund and allied groups helped Puerto Ricans surmount obsta-cles to the ballot box, gain political office, and achieve social and economic gains.

Cuban Americans, who had begun immigrating in large numbers to south Flor-ida after Fidel Castro came to power, generally enjoyed greater access to education and higher incomes. They also tended to be politically conservative, generally voted Republican, and lobbied for a hard line toward Castro's communist government. Cuban Americans developed a dense network of institutions that leveraged them into positions of power in Florida politics and civic affairs.

Beneath a common Spanish language, then, lay great diversity in terms of eco-nomic status, national and cultural identification, political affiliation, and activist goals and organizations. Established communities that identified with Mexico, Puerto Rico, and Cuba developed a wide range of mobilizing and organizing styles. More recent immigrants from the Dominican Republic and Central America, who were among the most economically deprived and the least organized, also began to add their voices and concerns.

Activism among Asian Americans   Americans of Chinese, Japanese, Korean, Filipino, and other backgrounds began to create an Asian American movement in the 1970s. Organizations such as the Asian Pacific Planning Council (APPCON), founded in 1976, lobbied to obtain government funding for projects that benefited Asian American communi-ties. The Asian Law Caucus, founded during the early 1970s by opponents of U.S. intervention in Vietnam, and the Committee against Anti-Asian Violence, created a decade later in response to a wave of racially motivated attacks, mobilized for a wide range of legal battles. During the 1970s Asian American studies programs also took shape at colleges and universities, particularly on the West Coast. By the early 1980s, Asian American political activists enjoyed growing influence, especially within the Democratic Party, and began gaining public office.

Emphasizing a broad, Asian American identity raised questions of inclusion, exclusion, and rivalry. Filipino American activists, members of the second largest Asian American group in the United States in 2000, often resisted the Asian American label because they believed that Chinese Americans or Japanese Americans dominated groups such as APPCON. Many people of Filipino descent focused on specific goals, particularly an effort to obtain citizenship and veterans' benefits for former soldiers of the Second World War who had fought against Japan. Japanese American groups also lobbied on behalf of specific issues, and in 1988 Congress formally apologized and voted to approve a reparations payment of $20,000 to every living Japanese American who had been confined in internment camps during the Second World War. Similarly, Hmong and Vietnamese groups pursued their own concerns related to the aftermath of the struggles in Indochina.

Socioeconomic differences made it difficult to frame a single Asian American agenda. Although many groups showed remarkable upward educational and economic mobility during the late 1980s and early 1990s, immigrants who were especially recent or impoverished often struggled to find jobs that paid more than the minimum wage.

As a result of combined pressure from different ethnic groups, the federal government finally designated "Asian or Pacific Islanders" (API) as a single pan-ethnic category in the censuses from 1990 on. It also provided nine specifically enumerated subcategories (such as Native Hawaiian or Filipino) and allowed other API groups (such as Hmong or Samoan) to write in their respective ethnic identifications. Thus, the term "Asian American"—which by the second decade of the 21st century applied to more than 16 million people and dozens of different ethnicities—both reflected, and was challenged by, the new emphasis on ethnic identity.

Anti-Government Activism	Ronald Reagan's first inaugural address of 1981 declared that "government is not the solution to our problem; government is the problem." As president, Reagan exempted national security institutions from this principle and rarely applied it literally to

basic safety-net programs such as Social Security and Medicare. In the face of budget deficits, Reagan proved willing to raise taxes to support government's expenditures. His claim that government action was almost always harmful, however, did appeal to the increasingly important New Right segment of the larger Reagan coalition. During the 1980s, denunciations of federal power spread throughout the culture, propelled especially by controversies over affirmative action and various regulatory rules.

Affirmative action programs had grown from bipartisan roots in the administrations of Lyndon Johnson and Richard Nixon. Public officials, proponents argued, should act affirmatively to help people who belonged to groups with a shared history of discrimination—especially African Americans, Latinos, and women—obtain an equitable share of the nation's jobs, public spending, and educational programs. Affirmative action would help compensate for past discrimination and for continued, sometimes hidden, prejudice that laws merely guaranteeing formal equality failed to rectify. Advocates of affirmative action emphasized that *any* process of selection inevitably "affirmed" some qualities, such as family or old school lineages, at the expense of others. Efforts at undoing years of discrimination against entire groups of people, in this view, required a complicated, seemingly paradoxical view of what counted as "equal" treatment by government.

Critics of affirmative action began to identify it as one of the most dangerous examples of increased governmental power. They noted that until the mid-1960s even supporters of civil rights had opposed government officials categorizing individuals according to group identities based on race or ethnicity. They often quoted Dr. King's words about judging people by the "content of their character" rather than the "color of their skin" and argued that government should remain "blind" to color and gender. They rejected the claim that policymakers needed to craft special rules or programs in order to eliminate discriminatory barriers to individual opportunity. Even some beneficiaries of these programs, such as Supreme Court Justice Clarence Thomas, charged that the derogatory label of "affirmative action applicant" threw into question the talents and capabilities of individuals. More broadly, critics of affirmative action programs denounced "set-aside" job programs and special educational admission procedures for previously disadvantaged groups as examples of illegal quotas, violations of constitutional guarantees, and even harbingers of totalitarianism. Did not affirmative action *on behalf of* people in some groups always constitute "reverse discrimination" *against* those in others?

In the midst of this controversy, federal courts initially managed to square affirmative action programs with older antidiscrimination precedents. They struck down affirmative action plans that contained inflexible quotas but upheld ones that made group identity only one of several criteria for making hiring or educational decisions. In the celebrated Supreme Court decision popularly known as the *Bakke* case (1978), a majority of justices ruled that affirmative action programs in educational settings could pass constitutional muster because they aimed at redressing past discrimination *and* because they contributed to "diversity," an intangible social and psychological quality important in any social, educational, or business environment. Many leaders of corporations, educational establishments, and the military came to endorse this *Bakke* principle: Diversity benefited not just applicants from historically discriminated groups but *all* people who worked within those environments as well as *all* those who relied on their services and expertise.

Opposition to affirmative action programs mobilized anti-government activists who found a close ally in New Right radio. During the 1970s, the FM dial had become dominated by musical programming, and many AM radio stations switched to an all-talk format. One of the personalities who made the switch was Rush Hudson Limbaugh III. Raised in a staunchly conservative Republican family, Limbaugh broke into AM as a radio host in several different markets under (as was the custom) several different names. Then, in 1984, Limbaugh took over an already-prominent New Right talk show in California. Limbaugh's ability to galvanize anti-government listeners gained him a spot in New York City and propelled him to the top ranks of a rapidly expanding, informal radio network that fueled anti-government activism.

New Right radio also thrived by attacking federal environmental regulations in the name of defending property rights. During the 1970s, western entrepreneurs associated with the sagebrush rebellion advocated transferring to state and private hands some of the vast amount of land held by the federal government for recreational parks and environmental purposes. Freed of restrictions from Washington, the rebels argued, westerners could make productive use of lands that lay within their states. A parallel effort, the "property rights movement," emerged across much of the country, particularly in areas of scenic beauty and where plans of suburban developers encountered environmental restrictions. Private builders denounced government for insisting on environmental impact assessments that might limit the ability of property owners to use land as they wished. In this movement, anti-government activists fought not only regulations from Washington but from any governmental body that claimed the power to regulate the use of private property in the name of some larger public purpose.

Denunciations of government regulations also flourished within a freshly deregulated communications industry. Beginning in 1949, the Federal Communications Commission (FCC), the government agency that regulated broadcasting, had required stations to represent a diversity of viewpoints. This "Fairness Doctrine" had survived constitutional challenge in the courts. Anti-government activists in the legal community, however, worked to overturn the doctrine, and in 1986, two conservative jurists, Atonin Scalia and Robert Bork, issued a federal court opinion ruling that Congress had never given the FCC any authority to mandate fairness. One year later, this decision prompted an FCC dominated by members appointed by Ronald Reagan to eliminate the Fairness Doctrine. New Right radio now enjoyed freedom to further ramp up its rhetoric against governmental power.

The overturning of the Fairness Doctrine dovetailed with the central tenet of the new anti-government activism: "Free markets," not government, provided the best structures for enhancing individual freedom and ensuring social-economic progress. The faith that markets served people better than governments, an idea older than the U.S. Constitution, had taken a considerable hit during the economic disarray of the 1930s. As a consequence, New Dealers had built on a very different conviction popularized under the label of Keynesianism: that government regulation must tame market excesses and prevent them from unleashing irrational and self-destructive forces into the larger political economy. In the 1950s and 1960s, conservative academics such as Milton Friedman had fired away at the Keynesian underpinnings of the New Deal–Great Society governmental structure, but during the 1970s and 1980s, conservatives rolled out much heavier weaponry.

Academics in the fields of law and economics at the University of Chicago took the lead. The economists crafted highly technical, mathematically complex arguments for ideas that soon became the new economic orthodoxy. Government regulators could never understand the risks from economic activities such as trading stocks or lending money as well as the people who actually worked in the marketplace. Markets almost always got things right, at least in the long run, while government regulators invariably got them wrong. Moreover, governmental bureaucracies such as the Securities and Exchange Commission (SEC) and the Federal Reserve Board were not really regulating markets in the public interest. Government bureaucrats were just another "special interest" looking out for themselves or for some other interest groups. They seldom acted as honest brokers between contending interests, as the interest-group pluralist model of the 1950s had claimed. Most importantly, the argument went, bureaucrats armed with the power of government invariably interfered with the most magical quality of free markets—their ability to provide self-correcting mechanisms.

A widening circle of academic and legal proponents of these anti-government ideas pressed this case. New economic textbooks challenged the Keynesian-oriented ones that had once dominated college and university classrooms. A new legal field, called "law and economics," attracted lawyers and judges (including Bork and Scalia) who crafted doctrines that accorded with free-market assumptions rather than the pro-regulatory ones that had guided New Deal–Great Society jurisprudence. Economist-activists carried the case against government regulation into the conservative think tanks, such as the Heritage Foundation, which were helping to shape public policy discussions. Taking advantage of loosened regulations, the business and financial world began to test the theories of self-regulating markets on Wall Street by devising new investment and creative financial instruments.

By the end of the 1980s, opposition to government had become a prominent feature of American political culture. Although the left-leaning movements still argued for an activist government to promote social equality and economic fairness, they found a significant challenge in those who claimed that reducing the power of government would be the best way to solve social-economic problems and preserve liberty. Within this debate, anti-government activists, like other activists, hardly moved in lockstep. Some cared deeply about opposing new rules for affirmative action; others placed greater priority on economic or environmental deregulation. While remaining a coalition of disparate parts, however, anti-government activism (always linked to antitax sentiment) became a powerful force. It drew populist strength from the expertly crafted speeches of Ronald Reagan, the bombast of New Right radio, and the political mobilization of the religious right. It found justification within the mathematically informed papers of Nobel Prize winners and top-rung law professors. Successfully challenging the once-dominant political agendas of the Democratic Party, it propelled the mainstream of the Republican Party decidedly rightward, established a strong foothold in public policy and media discussions, and succeeded in remapping the nation's cultural and informational landscape.

Conclusion

The "Reagan revolution" of the 1980s rested on a conservative movement that had been taking shape for several decades. New Right Republicans distrusted extending federal government power, advocated sharp tax cuts with deregulation, and stressed a sociocultural agenda emphasizing "traditional" values. The dozen years of Republican dominance of the White House, from 1980 to 1992, helped shift the terms of political debate in the United States. The "liberal" label became one that most Democrats sought to avoid. In the international realm, the Reagan and Bush presidencies facilitated the end of the cold war, a struggle that had defined U.S. foreign policy since the end of the Second World War.

Meanwhile, American society seemed to fragment into specialized identifications. Social activism increasingly organized around sexual, racial, ethnic, and ideological identities. The New Right's stress on limiting the power of government and promoting conservative values reconfigured discussions about how government power could best promote liberty and equality.

31

ECONOMIC, SOCIAL, AND CULTURAL
CHANGE IN THE LATE 20TH CENTURY

CHAPTER OUTLINE

• A Changing People • Economic Transformations • Culture and Media

---

THE FINAL DECADES of the 20th century brought sweeping change to American life. A dramatic increase in immigration, along with movements of people throughout metropolitan areas and into states in the West and South, altered the demographic landscape. The continuing decline of employment in the manufacturing sector changed the workplace. A digital revolution re-arranged how people communicated. The entertainment-informational complex, with an emphasis on professional sports, steadily expanded. At the same time, religious life became more diverse and more closely intertwined with the nation's politics.

A CHANGING PEOPLE

America's population became older, more metropolitan, and more ethnically and racially diverse. Moreover, the nation's centers of power continued shifting away from the Northeast and toward the South and West.

An Aging, Shift-ing Population During the 1950s, the height of the baby boom, the population had grown by 1.8 percent per year; after 1970, even with new waves of immigration and longer life expectancies, the growth rate slowed to about 1 percent per year. Younger people often delayed marriage until well into their 20s; most raised smaller families than had their parents; and many adults remained unmarried for much of their lives. The number of households with at least one child under 18 continually shrank. In 1960, nearly half fell into this category; by 1999, only about a third of U.S. households contained even one person under the age of 18. Consequently, by the mid-1980s, people in the 25 to 44 age category constituted a larger slice of the U.S. population than any other, and the number in their teens to early 20s was relatively small.

CHRONOLOGY

1971	Starbucks Coffee opens first store
1972	Congress passes Title IX (Patsy Mink Equal Opportunity in Education Act)
1973	Federal Express opens for business
1977	Congress passes Community Reinvestment Act
1978	Supreme Court decision frees banks to relocate credit-card operations
1979	ESPN joins the cable TV lineup
1981	MTV and CNN debut on cable TV
1982	Congress relaxes regulations on S&Ls
1986	Congress passes Immigration Reform and Control Act
1987	Prices crash on New York Stock Exchange and then rebound
1988	Fox television network begins
1989	Congress enacts bailout plan for S&L industry
1990	Congress passes another Immigration Act
1991	First McDonald's opens in Moscow
1995	Amazon.com begins selling books online
1996	Fox News Network debuts
2000	Human Genome Project issues preliminary draft

The steady rise of the median age of the population brought public policy, as well as personal, dilemmas. As aging baby boomers pondered retirement, policy-makers began debating how to cover projected Social Security and Medicare pay-outs. Trend watchers of the 1960s had talked of a "youth revolt." By the end of the 20th century, their counterparts pondered the "graying of America."

The changing geographical distribution of population restructured political and economic life. After 1970, most of the population growth occurred in the South and the West. Nevada, California, Florida, and Arizona became the fastest-growing states, and by 2000 more than 1 in 10 Americans lived in California. Western and southern states gained seats in the U.S. House of Representatives, while northeastern states shed them. Many reasons helped account for this demographic shift: affordable air-conditioning; the expansion of tourism and new retirement communities; and for businesses, the attraction of lower labor costs and the absence of strong unions.

The development of high-tech industries connected to military spending and the computer revolution also played important roles. California's Santa Clara County, a once rural area near San Francisco, benefited from spectacular growth in its semiconductor industry and its network of computer-related enterprises and became known as "Silicon Valley" during the 1970s. It spawned companies such as Google and Yahoo!

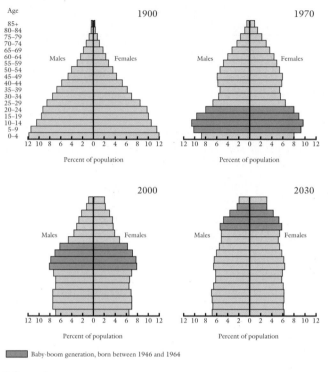

The Aging of America

Source: U.S. Census Bureau. Adapted from C. L. Himes, "Elderly Americans," *Population Bulletin*, 2002, 56(4), p. 4.

The governmentally financed space program, directed by the National Aeronautics and Space Administration (NASA) from installations in Texas and Florida, propelled the shift of research and technology to the Sun Belt. In 1961, President Kennedy had announced plans for the manned Apollo program, and in July 1969, astronaut Neil Armstrong had walked on the lunar surface. Apollo flights continued until 1972, when NASA began to develop a space station. In the 1980s, NASA started operating space shuttles, manned craft that served as scientific laboratories in outer space and could be flown back to earth for reuse. In early 1986, the program suffered a tragic setback when the *Challenger* shuttle exploded shortly after liftoff. After a hiatus of more than two years, the program resumed its operations, with new safety procedures in place.

Individual entrepreneurs and giant corporations also migrated to the Sun Belt and crafted multiple versions of a single product: *entertainment*. The Sun Belt featured a host of "magical" places such as Disneyland and Las Vegas. These tourist destinations predated the 1970s, but they boomed during the final decades of the 20th century as they constantly expanded their offerings in search of ever-larger crowds and ever-greater profits. An enlarged version of Disneyland in Florida, Walt Disney World, opened in 1971. Las Vegas morphed from an underworld-controlled outpost for sin, a jungle with green felt gaming tables, into an

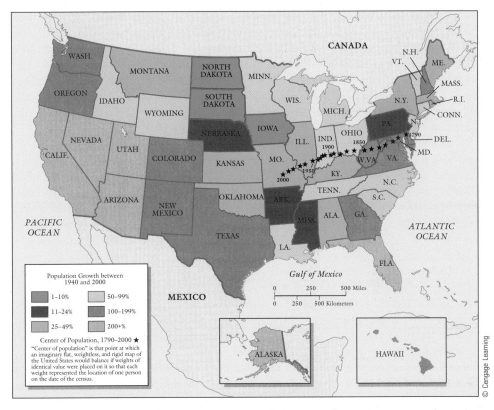

MAP 31.1   Population Shifts Toward the Sun Belt

In the era after the Second World War, Americans gravitated toward the South and West. Which states grew the fastest? What might be some of the causes and consequences of such population shifts?

entertainment magnet that added family-oriented attractions to the mix. A spectacle itself, Las Vegas hosted other spectacles: architecture that replicated the world's greatest cities, past and present; performers from every area of show business; art collections that rivaled those in museums; and luxurious resort-hotels that could house and feed thousands of guests. The Las Vegas "strip," retrofitted with mass transit, remained a round-the-clock entertainment venue.

The New Immigration   A dramatic increase in immigration from countries mostly to the south and west of the United States accounted for much of the U.S. population growth in the late 20th century. The vast bulk of post-1970 immigration came from Asia, Oceania, Latin America, and Africa rather than from Europe, which had previously been the primary source of immigrants. In 2000, roughly 12 percent of the U.S. population had been born outside the United States, compared to the all-time high of 15 percent in 1890.

The largest number of non-European immigrants came from Mexico. Responding to labor shortages in the United States and poor economic prospects at home, immigration from Mexico rose substantially in every decade. Ninety percent of all Mexican Americans lived in the Southwest, primarily Texas and California.

Most people moving from Puerto Rico to the mainland settled around New York City, but sizable Puerto Rican communities developed in Chicago and in cities in New England and Ohio as well. The economic problems of the 1970s prompted some to return to the island, but the flow reversed again after about 1980. By 2000, the Puerto Rican population on the U.S. mainland totaled about 3 million, compared to a population of nearly 4 million in Puerto Rico.

Cubans had begun immigrating in large numbers in response to Fidel Castro's revolution. In 1962, Congress had designated people fleeing from Castro's Cuba as refugees eligible for admittance, and during the next 20 years, more than 800,000 Cubans from every strata of society came to the United States. They gradually moved northward into many major American cities, but the greatest impact was in south Florida. An agreement with Castro in 1995 brought the first U.S. restrictions on the flow of immigrants from Cuba, but about half of all Miamians were of Cuban descent by 2000.

The number of Spanish-speaking people in the United States at the end of the 20th century exceeded that of all but four countries of Latin America. Los Angeles became the second largest "Mexican city" in the world, trailing only Mexico City, and its Salvadoran population just about equaled that of San Salvador. More Puerto Ricans lived in New York City than in San Juan, and the Big Apple's Dominican population rivaled that of Santo Domingo.

These changes in immigration patterns began with the landmark **Immigration and Nationality Act of 1965**, which abolished quotas based on national origin. Instead, it placed a ceiling of 20,000 immigrants for every country, gave preference to people with close family ties in the United States, and accorded priority to those with special skills and those classified as "refugees." Although largely unforeseen at the time, this legislation laid the basis for not only a resumption of high-volume immigration but also a substantial shift in region of origin.

International events also affected U.S. immigration policy. Following the American withdrawal from Vietnam, for example, U.S. officials facilitated the admittance of many Vietnamese, Cambodians, Laotians, and Hmong (an ethnically distinct people who inhabited lands extending across the borders of these three Asian countries). The goal was to resettle some of the people who had allied with the United States during the Vietnam War and whose families were consequently in peril.

In response to the growing number of people seeking admission to the United States, Congress passed the Refugee Act of 1980. It favored political refugees, "those fleeing overt persecution," over people seeking simply to improve their economic circumstances. In practice, U.S. officials interpreted the terms "political" and "economic" so that people leaving communist regimes were generally admitted but those fleeing right-wing dictatorships were usually turned away or deported. For example, Cubans and Soviet Jews were admitted, but most Guatemalans and Salvadorans, hoping to escape repressive military governments backed by the United States during the 1980s, stood little chance of being admitted.

Immigration policy remained a political puzzle. The **Immigration Reform and Control Act of 1986 (or the Simpson-Mazzoli Act)** imposed stricter penalties on businesses employing undocumented workers, increased border security, and granted permanent residency to people with proof they had been living in the United States since 1982. Immigration continued to soar as the economic upturn during the 1990s acted as a magnet for newcomers. Another Immigration Act in 1990 raised the number of people who could be admitted on the basis of special job skills or the investment capital they could bring into the United States. Those favoring continued high levels of immigration saw potential benefits for the entire nation, but proponents of greater restrictions decried the economic, social, and cultural burdens that newcomers supposedly posed. Starkly conflicting perspectives stalemated new congressional legislation on immigration policy.

The Metropolitan Nation   Relationships between urban centers and outlying areas, too, were in a state of flux. At the end of the 20th century, more than 80 percent of Americans lived in sprawling metropolitan corridors, strips of suburbs that ran between older cities such as Seattle and Tacoma or Washington D.C. and Baltimore. In some cases, "edge cities" such as Irvine in California or Boca Raton in Florida sprouted up in these corridors and competed with older urban centers for businesses, job opportunities, retail shopping outlets, cultural institutions, and people. Residents of these edge cities rarely found it necessary to visit the nearby center cities such as Los Angeles or Miami.

Demographic patterns within urban and suburban areas were also changing. Especially during the last decade of the century, minority groups began moving to suburbs, just as more affluent white suburbanites were relocating in cities. As a result, the percentage of African Americans residing in urban centers steadily declined, and the percentage living in suburbia increased. With some new immigrants settling outside central cites, some suburbs—in metropolitan areas such as Chicago and Minneapolis—came to contain more foreign-born residents than the central cities they surrounded.

Moreover, the newest suburbs sprouted up farther and farther away from either core or edge cities. A frenzy of new construction, financed by innovative lending arrangements, transformed farmland and small towns into a series of sprawling housing developments, which demographers called "**exurbs.**" Built on relatively inexpensive land, exurbs offered homebuyers more space for less money. When commuting to work, however, exurbanites could easily spend several hours every day trapped inside a car, inching in and out of places where the transportation infrastructure seldom kept pace with home construction.

Meanwhile, core cities were transformed. During the 1970s and 1980s, as manufacturing jobs left and retail shopping shifted to suburban malls, cities became primarily financial, administrative, and entertainment centers. Many faced rising rates of homelessness and crime and deterioration in schools and infrastructure, especially sewage and water systems. Big-city mayors complained that Washington did little to address urban problems. Federal funding for urban projects decreased from $64 per urban resident in 1980 to less than $30 by the early 1990s.

In time, though, certain areas within most central cities underwent stunning revivals. Building booms brought new office towers, residential buildings, arts complexes, and sports facilities to many downtowns across the country. People with

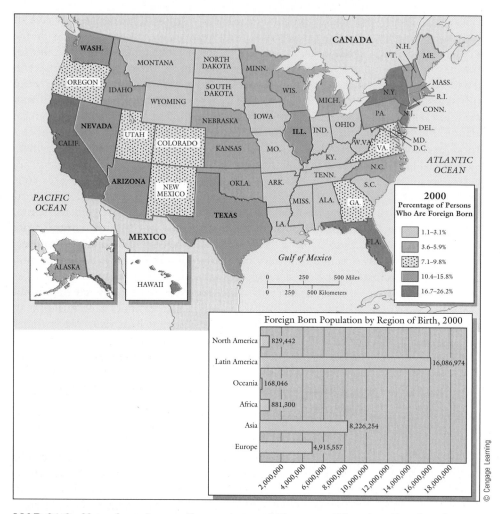

MAP 31.2 New Americans: Percentage of Persons Who Are Foreign Born and Foreign-Born Population by Region of Birth, 2000

This map and chart illustrate the wave of new immigration into the United States. Which regions of the world contributed the most immigrants? Which states received the most, and the least, immigration?

cash or credit to spend on housing, restaurants, and entertainment began flocking to select areas, which became labeled as "gentrified."

This urban renaissance, which gained momentum throughout the 1990s, sprang from many sources. A brighter economic picture and improvements in air quality helped. Innovations in urban design integrated diverse architectural styles with new green spaces and revitalized riverbanks and lakefronts. Community development corporations (CDCs), grassroots efforts indebted to movement cultures of the 1960s, supported initiatives for affordable housing, better child-care facilities, and expanded employment opportunities. The **Community Reinvestment Act of 1977**, which obliged banks to finance more home buying in low-income neighborhoods, provided a stimulus. Community policing, a trend toward harsher sentencing, and an aging population lowered urban crime rates. Affluent suburban commuters realized that they could save both time and money by moving to the revitalizing downtowns. In addition, some new immigrants repopulated once-declining neighborhoods, refurbishing the housing stock and reviving the commercial zones. By 2000, many U.S. cities featured vibrant, transnational spaces.

These transformed urban areas especially appealed to college-educated professionals who had benefited from the dramatic expansion of higher education. During the 1960s, colleges and universities had doubled their enrollment. The boom continued as the federal government's Pell Grant program (which provides financial assistance to students from low-income families) and various loan arrangements softened the immediate economic burden of attending college. More students of non-European ancestry and increasing numbers of women enrolled. Gaining a college degree could produce a costly debt burden but would generally increase a person's income and occupational mobility.

The ability to live and play in the new metropolitan spaces, of course, ultimately depended on household income. During the two decades after 1980, households in the top 10 percent of the income pyramid saw a substantial increase. The incomes of those at the *very* top, the superwealthy 1 percent, fared even better. The vast majority of individuals and families, by contrast, saw far more modest, if any, gains. An important part of this story of widening income inequality involved the transformations that were occurring throughout the U.S. and international economies.

Economic Transformations

A latter-day Rip van Winkle, awakening from a 30-year sleep in 1999, would have marveled at the consumer products in daily use. People could awaken to sounds from a digital device; glance at the morning news on a personal computer; use the same PC or Mac to work from home; and later watch a daytime soap opera they had recorded earlier. They could also enter a fantasy world through a video game or catch up with the world and friends via the Internet or mobile phone. If one looked past large pockets of persistent poverty, it could seem as if new technologies and innovative businesses were transforming America into a consumer paradise.

New Technologies The computer revolution, which had begun during the 1940s, entered a new phase after 1970. Microchips increased hardware capacity and reduced the size and cost of computers. Microsoft and Apple, two companies founded during the 1970s, challenged mighty IBM for supremacy in the personal computer market and introduced competing operating systems and Web browsers. Their celebrity CEOs, Bill Gates and Steve Jobs, became two of the wealthiest and most influential people in the world—and came to symbolize key differences between these cyber-era giants. Although Microsoft quickly beat out Apple for domination in the war over lucrative operating systems, the companies continued to battle over virtually every-thing else, including that all-important intangible: the loyalty of customers who saw their computers, especially if they owned a Mac, as part of their personal identity.

Changes in the speed and accessibility of informational systems rearranged how people interacted with the larger economy and lived their daily lives. Enhanced mem-ory capacity and parallel processors, which allow many computer operations to run simultaneously, rapidly transformed the handling of words and images. Enhanced by new communications technologies, such as fiber-optic networks and then satellite transmission, successive generations of computers fueled an **information revolution**. Libraries replaced card catalogs with networked computer databases; screens replaced paper. Voicemail, fax transmissions, e-mail, and text messaging came to sup-plement or substitute for posted mail and telephone conversations. The use of cellular phones spread rapidly during the 1990s and, along with improved computer access, made telecommuting from home to work an attractive option.

Innovation in other fields such as biotechnology promised to produce similarly dramatic effects. Beginning in 1990, for example, the **Human Genome Project** sought to map the genetic code. This international effort, which unveiled a prelimi-nary draft of the human genome in 2000, sought to provide techniques for gene transfer, embryo manipulation, tissue regeneration, and even cloning. Other biotech-nological research portended new approaches to the treatment of cancer and other diseases. Breakthroughs in genetic manipulation promised to revolutionize waste con-version and toxic cleanup. Large food producers heralded the use of genetically mod-ified crops as an extension of the earlier "green revolution," which had boosted agricultural yields. Foods that had been modified, beginning with those derived from soybeans and corn, first reached consumers during the early 1990s. A geneti-cally modified tomato, which would ripen without softening, debuted in 1994.

These new technologies raised legal and ethical questions. How would the com-puter revolution, for example, affect traditional ideas and laws about privacy? Bio-technological research also generated controversial questions. Almost immediately after the Supreme Court decided the abortion case of *Roe v. Wade*, for instance, Con-gress banned federal funding for research involving fetal tissue. Fears that experimen-tation with embryonic stem cells would increase abortions blocked federal support for research, but scientific work with other kinds of stem cells began to show benefits in regenerating human tissue. Controversy, more gradually, came to swirl around geneti-cally modified (GM) foods. Critics asked how GM foods might affect individuals with allergies and, more ominously, harm biodiversity across the entire planet.

Changes in the Structure and Operations of Business

Computerization encouraged businesses to change their modes of operation. Computer networks helped lower costs and boost productivity (the output of goods per labor hour). Companies increasingly abandoned paperwork in favor of computerized tracking systems. The resulting improvement in information processing helped businesses more accurately calculate the relation-ship between what they produced (or ordered from suppliers) and sales projections. Computers thus enabled "just in time production," or JIT. This streamlined process eliminated waste throughout the production-consumption loop and permitted the downscaling of warehousing operations for unsold products and unused supplies.

The computer revolution also speeded the continued expansion of chain and franchise businesses. McDonald's and Holiday Inn had pioneered nationwide standardization in the fast-food and travel industries during the late 1950s. Other businesses adapted this model. Starbucks Coffee Company began as a local operation in 1971, rapidly expanded beyond Seattle during the 1980s, and opened a new store somewhere in the world every day during the 1990s. Starbucks helped to add a new term to the labor lexicon, *barista*, and to elevate a once-simple beverage into a pricey designer commodity.

The Wal-Mart chain prospered by moving in the opposite direction: The company promised customers it was constantly rolling back prices. Wal-Mart initially avoided the upscale metropolitan areas where Starbucks was thriving, focusing instead on small towns and exurban areas, places where someone other than a *barista* was likely serving coffee. Here, the company could find workers, called "associates," willing to work part-time at relatively low pay. Wal-Mart's labor force thus contained many married women and retirees who could not find or did not desire full-time employment. Wal-Mart became the largest private employer in the United States; by the end of the century, nearly 1 of every 120 workers, and 1 of every 20 in the retail sector, worked for the company. Communities were often divided over the arrival of a Wal-Mart. The retailing giant did offer consumers a wide array of merchandise at lower prices, but it also crushed local, independent businesses in thousands of midsized and small towns.

U.S.-owned chain and franchise businesses also expanded overseas, especially after the end of the cold war. In 1991, McDonald's opened to great fanfare in Moscow, and its Pushkin Square restaurant immediately claimed the title of the world's busiest "Mickey D's." U.S.-based hotel chains opened competing, luxury facilities in the former Soviet Union and throughout Eastern Europe. The demise of the Soviet Union also allowed Pepsi and Coke to carry their ongoing "cola wars" into new territory. During the 1970s, Pepsi had struck a special deal with the Kremlin that allowed its cola to be the first American product sold in the Soviet Union. During the 1990s, Coca-Cola debuted and quickly challenged its rival for cola supremacy in Russia's newly competitive soft-drink market.

Launched in 1995, Amazon.com led a different kind of retailing revolution— e-commerce, or the practice of selling over the Internet. It began with books and soon added other products. Toward the very end of the 1990s, a wave of new "dot-com" businesses flooded the Internet and set off a short-term bubble in dot-com stocks that Amazon.com managed to survive. Buying and selling over the Internet quickly became a regular feature of consumer culture. Amazon and the online auction site eBay became models for doing business in cyberspace.

Changes in the transportation of products, when joined to the computer revolution, transformed the global economic marketplace—and America's place within it. Air cargo service improved dramatically, and the Federal Express Corporation (or FedEx) could claim annual revenues of $1 billion only a decade after its debut in 1973. The greatly expanded use of **steel cargo containers**, which dramatically lowered the cost of transporting finished goods and raw materials over long distances, similarly facilitated national and international commerce. Containers could be easily stacked, refrigerated, unloaded from a cargo ship or plane, and trucked to their final destination.

David Paul Morris/Bloomberg/Getty Images

Cyber-assembly line. *The Internet transformed retailing, distribution, and labor arrangements. In this massive center in Phoenix, workers assembled for shipment the computerized orders that consumers had placed on Amazon.com.*

As suppliers and markets increasingly gave businesses worldwide scope, commercial publications began to refer to the process as **globalization**. U.S. automakers, for example, increasingly looked outside the United States to procure parts and even to assemble automobiles and trucks. The trend toward privatization (the sale of government-owned industries to private business) in many overseas economies provided firms based in the United States with new opportunities for acquisitions. Conversely, foreign buyers purchased companies and real estate holdings inside the United States. So many industrial giants had become globalized that it became difficult to define what constituted a U.S. company or a foreign one.

New technologies and globalization interacted to change the basic structure of American businesses and their workforces. Citing pressure from declining profits and international competitors, which often paid workers a fraction of the U.S. wage rate, many industrial companies cut back their labor pools and trimmed their management staffs. This process became known as "**downsizing**." The U.S. auto industry, for example, began to lay off thousands of workers.

Business restructuring, encouraged by globalization and generous interpretations of antitrust laws by both Republican and Democratic administrations, touched off a merger boom. During the late 1990s, huge mergers, with acquisitions totaling more than $1.6 trillion per year, brought a concentration in production unseen since the 1890s.

As employment in traditional manufacturing and extractive sectors (such as mining) declined, jobs in service, high-tech, and information and entertainment sectors increased. Positions in financial services, computing, and other high-tech industries offered high salaries—astronomical ones for top management—but most jobs in the rapidly expanding service sector, such as clerical and janitorial jobs, remained low paying, part-time, and nonunionized. Wal-Mart's enormous non-union workforce, for example, earned an average of $7 to $8 per hour and had limited, or no, health benefits. U.S. manufacturers wanting to lower costs moved plants to countries with cheap labor environments, further contributing to the decline of relatively better-paid manufacturing jobs in the United States.

The impact of these changes became a matter of bitter debate. Celebrants of change insisted that globalization and corporate downsizing would temporarily mean lost jobs, but that gains in productivity would soon translate into lower consumer prices and a rise in living standards for everyone. They also highlighted the success stories, especially in high-tech industries, where constant technological innovation paved a broad avenue of upward economic mobility for people with skills in post-industrial areas such as computing. Real wages did rise slightly for a brief period during the late 1990s, especially for women.

Critics worried that this shift toward a service economy could permanently change the wage structure, "de-skill" the American labor force, and erode the standard of living in the United States. They warned that the widening gulf between highly paid skilled positions and minimum-wage jobs with few benefits was undermining the middle-class nature of American society.

The labor market changed in other ways. Skilled workers during the middle of the 20th century, for example, had generally stuck to one profession and even the same place of employment throughout their working life. By the end of the century, however, both blue- and white-collar workers were likely to switch employers several times before retiring. The need for training and retraining programs that served people of all ages transformed ideas about the relationship between education and work.

There was also a dramatic drop in labor union membership. During the 1950s, more than 30 percent of American workers belonged to a union. By the end of the 20th century, the figure stood at only 13 percent. Although the labor movement mounted organizing drives among clerical, restaurant, and hotel workers, it struggled to make significant inroads into these sectors of the economy. The major growth for organized labor came among government employees and health-care workers.

Most businesses adamantly fought unionization, and the health and retirement benefits that American companies had once proudly offered began to disappear. During the 1940s and 1950s, a generous benefit package had helped employers attract workers without having to pay dramatically high wages and salaries. Moreover, the amount of money a company paid toward its share of a health plan did not count, under federal law, as part of an employee's taxable compensation. Labor and management both stood to gain, it had seemed, from generous benefit programs.

Things began to change as U.S. companies claimed the need to meet increasing foreign competition and manage the rising costs for health care. In 1960, only about 7 percent of the entire U.S. gross domestic product (GDP) went for health care; some 40 years later, the comparable figure neared 15 percent, a greater percentage than people paid for food. (In Canada, by contrast, health care totaled less than 10 percent of GDP.) The annual cost of providing health care for a family, according to most estimates, came to about what a full-time, minimum-wage worker would earn over a year and twice the pay of the average Wal-Mart employee. U.S. companies facing foreign competition complained about extensive benefit packages that included health care for their aging workforces.

Individuals and families increasingly maintained their lifestyles by incurring rising levels of debt. Economists began to analyze this **household deficit**—the difference between what U.S. households earned and what they spent. As late as 1980, the rate of household indebtedness, though higher than that during the 1950s, still remained lower than it had been during the 1920s. The 1980s, however, inaugurated a trend that would accelerate into the next century. As more people shouldered greater debt, the number of personal bankruptcies increased, and the rate of personal savings in the United States fell to the lowest level in the industrialized world.

The Financial Sector   The household deficit became intertwined with one of the most dramatic post-1970 economic changes: the expansion of a vast, constantly innovating financial industry. A wide range of financial institutions—from international superbanks such as Citigroup, to payday loan institutions like Moneytree, to pawnshop chains such as Pawn America, right on down to illegal loan-sharking operations—profited from people unable to balance their personal books. By the end of the century, loans to home-buyers who lacked the resources to repay them were helping to sustain the financial industry. The industry also thrived, however, on wealthy investors who appeared awash in assets to invest. By 2000, according to one estimate, more than 40 percent of U.S. corporate profits came from the financial services sector while only about 10 percent derived from manufacturing.

The computer revolution helped the financial industry expand and changed its relationship to customers. Use of bank-issued credit cards, monitored through computerized systems, vastly expanded, and extending credit via "plastic" became a highly lucrative enterprise, especially after a 1978 U.S. Supreme Court decision declared that national banks headquartered in one state could move their card operations to any other. This ruling effectively eliminated anti-usury laws, which had traditionally limited interest rates, as states competed to attract the credit-card operations of giant banks. These institutions deluged potential cardholders, particularly college students, with competing enticements. "Free" credit cards, once interest and service charges began piling up, proved anything but free to most people who used them. Other innovations—automated teller machines (ATMs), automatic deposits, debit cards, and electronic bill payment—moved Americans ever closer to a cashless economy.

The financial system increasingly shed the regulatory restrictions crafted earlier in the century, particularly during the New Deal. Free-market economists and the financial industry argued that deregulation would speed the flow of investment capital, and Congress initially responded by lifting many of the restrictions on the operation of Savings and Loan institutions (S&Ls) in 1982. The S&L industry boomed, but too many institutions enjoyed deregulation far too much. They made risky loans, speculated in real estate, or simply cooked their books. The entire industry eventually required a massively expensive governmental bailout but problems elsewhere in the financial sector seemed limited to individual firms and to specific times, such as the meltdown on the New York Stock Market in October 1987. A rapid rebound of stock prices seemingly confirmed claims that all markets, including the larger financial ones, were self-correcting, even self-regulating. The S&L debacle, from this perspective, did not signal any serious structural problems within the larger financial industry.

During the last two decades of the 20th century, some celebrants of the financial sector presented it as a model for how deregulation led to dynamic growth. Wall Street investment firms, such as Lehman Brothers, and large banks, such as Chase Manhattan, did well. Newer types of financial ventures, such as the "hedge fund" operations, which managed complicated investment portfolios for a limited number of affluent clients, performed *very* well. These funds, which took in vast pools of money and paid out sizable profits to their investors, came to make up a "shadow banking system"—one whose financial dealings were not covered by the regulatory system that oversaw more traditional banking institutions. Financial investments—whether in real estate, individual stocks, corporate bonds, or hedge funds—still risked losing money, but a new generation of managers claimed the ability to forecast and thus *manage* risk.

The financial sector could also create, and then trade, new forms of investment that carried the generic name of "derivatives," because they had been "derived" from other financial transactions. Entrepreneurs in the financial sector, for example, began purchasing individual home-loan contracts. Combining those of dubious value with sounder ones, they would market the resultant package of loan contracts as a new form of investment called a "collateralized debt obligation" (CDO). Complex mathematical calculations, which relatively few people in the financial industry fully understood, supposedly proved that a CDO carried little risk to the financial firm that had created it or to investors who purchased it. Financial analysts argued that the chance of so many different loan contracts defaulting at the same time was so slim that a CDO was comparatively safe.

CDOs based on home loans were only one of many different types of new securities derived from other kinds of financial transactions. This part of the larger financial system produced huge profits. It also provided similarly outsized payouts, in bonuses and stock options, to the people who worked in this largely unregulated, little-understood enterprise. Economists and public officials, including those at the Treasury Department and the Federal Reserve System, cheered the creation of new types of securities. Governmental regulation of them, according to Alan Greenspan, chairman of the Federal Reserve Board from 1987 to 2006, would discourage innovation and prevent the financial system from delivering an ever-increasing array of secure investments to clients all over the world. The deregulation and globalization of the financial industry echoed other economic transformations that began during the last three decades of the 20th century. The hazards would become all too apparent in 2008, when a massive financial crisis would hit.

The Sports-Entertainment Industry

The sports-entertainment industry also grew exponentially during this era. Metropolitan areas competed to obtain—or retain—professional teams. TV contracts and tax write-offs tempted tycoons such as George Steinbrenner of the New York Yankees to run a sporting empire.

Baseball led off this expansionist era. Seeking a better fit with emerging economic, demographic, and social forces, the leadership of Major League Baseball (MLB) realigned the "national pastime." During a single decade, the 1970s, MLB shuffled teams in and out of Milwaukee, Seattle, and Washington, D.C. By relocating franchises from struggling to thriving metropolitan areas, MLB acquired new ticket buyers, advantageous TV deals, and stadiums financed by public money. If moving existing franchises made sense, creating new ones seemed an even shrewder option. During the mid-1950s, there had been only 16 Big League teams, none located west of Chicago; by 2000, 30 MLB franchises stretched across the United States and into Canada.

Other sports followed baseball's lead. The National Football League (NFL), noting how surveys showed fans shifting their allegiances from baseball to faster-paced sports, also expanded into new metropolitan areas. Just in time for the 1970 season, the NFL merged with the rival American Football League (AFL), with which it had been playing a "Super Bowl" since 1967. In contrast to the economic philosophy of MLB, that of the revamped NFL helped small-market teams such as the Green Bay Packers remain competitive with larger-market franchises. During the 1970s, ABC began televising an NFL game during primetime hours, and the success of *Monday Night Football* signaled the growing importance of football to TV and to the nation's popular culture.

Basketball's small court made National Basketball Association (NBA) games extremely TV-friendly, and entrepreneurs easily gained television contracts to underwrite new professional franchises. As a result, the NBA faced a lengthy off-the-court rivalry with the upstart American Basketball Association (ABA). When the two leagues finally merged in 1976, the NBA jettisoned the ABA's garish, multicolored basketball but retained its three-point shot and emphasis on marketing African American stars like Julius ("Dr. J") Irving. After joining the league in 1984, Michael Jordan soon became the preeminent symbol for marketing the NBA and anchored the "Dream Team" of professionals that captured basketball's Gold Medal at the 1992 Olympic Games. The NBA also elevated African Americans into coaching and management positions far more quickly than did the NFL and MLB.

Several efforts to make soccer a major attraction in the United States faltered, but most other sports-entertainment operations flourished. By the end of the 20th century, the National Hockey League (NHL) supported 28 franchises. Professional play in tennis, aided by TV coverage, featured tours for both men and women. Professional golf for men—tightly controlled by the Professional Golfing Association (PGA)—continually grew in popularity, especially after it found its own version of Michael Jordan, Eldrick (Tiger) Woods. During the early 1990s, Woods became *the* brand name for a sports business that attracted corporate sponsors, sold a vast array of high-end products, and sustained a media presence that included a separate Golf Channel (1995–) on cable TV. The economic and cultural impact of the Ladies Professional Golf Association (LPGA) lagged behind that of the men's, but the women's tour still prospered and added a number of players from outside the United States to its ranks.

The national romance with automobiles helped to speed the growth of auto racing. The Indianapolis 500 initially vied with the Super Bowl for recognition as the most spectacular one-day event in sports, but events sponsored by the National

Association for Stock Car Racing (NASCAR) eventually overtook those of Indy-style racing. As new technologies brought TV viewers onto the track and even into the cars, NASCAR moved beyond its traditional base in the South. Its signature event, the Daytona 500, replaced the Indy 500 as the nation's premier automobile race.

College sports grew in similar fashion. Television coverage mushroomed, especially after TV entrepreneurs created **ESPN** (1979–), a cable network devoted entirely to sports. ESPN initially helped so-called minor collegiate sports, such as gymnastics and lacrosse, gain TV time, but college football and basketball, with their highly popular postseason contests, ultimately benefited the most. The vast revenues from television allowed the National Collegiate Athletic Association (NCAA) to create more lucrative bowl games and build the playoff arrangement in basketball into an extended extravaganza that became marketed as "March Madness." University administrators insisted that success on their playing fields and in their arenas, which became ever larger and more luxurious, translated into visibility and prestige, and into increased donations that helped support the educational mission of their institutions.

The glamour and excitement generated by the sports-entertainment industry increasingly merged with political culture. Candidates competed to sign up prominent athletes for their campaign squads, and some retired players, including football's Jack Kemp and Hall of Fame baseball hurler Jim Bunning, made the transition from the sports to the political field. In addition to tapping his family connections, George W. Bush parlayed his family name and partial ownership of the Texas Rangers baseball team into an entrée into electoral politics, first as governor of Texas and then as the first president of the 21st century.

With the business of sports booming, its legal foundations inevitably shifted. MLB's star players, armed with union advisers and their own attorneys, successfully spearheaded new legal challenges to old doctrines that contractually bound them to a single franchise year after year. Court rulings eventually brought differing versions of "free agency" to the major team sports. These systems soon produced powerful new players in the sporting world: sports agents who could help professional athletes auction their athletic talents and celebrity status to the highest bidder. Although some fans and sportswriters grumbled when highly paid players seemed to underperform, owners discovered that steadily rising TV revenues, tax breaks, and favorable stadium deals allowed them to adjust to the new salary structures and strong union movements. The truly knowledgeable sports fan became as conversant in contract law and labor-management relations as in more traditional matters such as batting averages and yards-per-carry statistics.

Sports and legal disputes also became intertwined with social issues. Women's rights advocates saw big-time sports promoting gender stereotypes—pointing, for example, to *Sports Illustrated*'s swimsuit issue and to NFL cheerleading squads that resembled Las Vegas chorus lines—and urged equality for women athletes. One result of this pressure was **Title IX** of a 1972 congressional measure, which was later retitled the **Patsy Mink Equal Opportunity in Education Act.** By mandating gender equity in intercollegiate sports activities, Title IX required colleges and universities to upgrade the financing and promotion of women's sports. A much-hyped 1973 exhibition tennis match between Billy Jean King, the leading women's player of the day, and an aging male star from the 1940s, Bobby Riggs, helped dramatize the gender-equity issues that Title IX addressed. (Billy Jean King won the match.) Over time, professional tennis surpassed every other sport in narrowing the gender gap in prize money, endorsement contracts, and media coverage. And it also was the first major sport to feature LGBT stars.

While the sports-entertainment complex was growing in visibility and profitability, traditionalists detected signs of corruption. The familiar complaint about intercollegiate athletics debasing educational standards gained new force. Critics also found too many sporting enterprises awash in hypercommercialism, financial double-dealing, and on-field cheating. The success of MLB, for example, seemingly owed much to the prodigious feats of home run hitters who, it ultimately became apparent, were using performance-enhancing drugs—and perhaps also benefiting from souped-up baseballs.

CULTURE AND MEDIA

New technologies significantly altered how people received and used books, movies, TV, music, and other sources of information and entertainment. By the end of the 20th century, virtually every home or apartment had at least one television and an accompanying recording device. About 80 percent had a personal computer. People began looking to the Internet for access to print publications, music, television programming, and movies. E-mail became, before the popularity of text messaging, the first choice for contacting friends. The omnipresent video screen seemed the preeminent symbol of American popular culture.

The Video Revolution   At the beginning of the 1970s, three broadcast networks could promise advertisers that a rough cross section of the American public would be watching their nighttime programs and the accompanying commercials. During that decade, however, changes in the viewing habits of Americans increasingly led the networks to embrace the strategy called "**narrowcasting**," in which TV programmers acknowledged that the viewing audience was fragmenting into different demographic segments. CBS replaced several highly watched programs, such as *The Beverly Hillbillies*, with "edgier" shows aimed at viewers under the age of 40, who were coveted by advertisers because they were most likely to purchase products and services. *All in the Family*, a sitcom about intergenerational conflict within a blue-collar family, made its proudly bigoted protagonist, "Archie Bunker," a lightning rod for issues involving race and gender. Although *The Mary Tyler Moore Show* rarely took overtly feminist positions, it did address the personal politics of working women. In 1980, 9 of every 10 television sets were still tuned to a network program during primetime viewing hours.

The narrowcasting strategy helped the entire TV industry prosper until the 1990s, when programmers began to struggle as viewers began deserting network offerings. The networks responded by slashing budgets and staff, especially in their news divisions. Local stations without any network affiliation, which had been limping along, began picking up viewers by carrying older Hollywood movies, sporting events, and reruns of canceled primetime shows now being syndicated to individual stations. Several hundred of these independent television stations debuted during the 1980s.

Capitalizing on this trend, the media mogul Rupert Murdoch introduced the first new network in decades, Fox TV, in 1988. Using a pattern later adopted by far less-successful imitators, Fox's operation began by offering a limited schedule to previously nonaffiliated stations. Fox's first big hit, *The Simpsons* (1989–), an animated send-up of the standard family sitcom, became a pop culture phenomenon and mass-marketing bonanza. In 1993 Fox outbid CBS for the TV rights to carry NFL games. Throughout the 1990s, Fox and the other fledgling networks introduced programs—such as *In Living Color* and *Buffy the Vampire Slayer*—for audiences that contained more minority, young, and urban viewers than those of the three older networks.

New technologies, which promised viewers greater choice, challenged all of the broadcast networks. The remote control, an innovation introduced during the 1960s that finally clicked during the 1980s, created a television aesthetic called "channel surfing," in which viewers flip rapidly from program to program. Videocassette recorders (VCRs), introduced during the 1970s, became the first of the record-and-view-later technologies that allowed viewers to create their own TV schedules.

The primary threat to the broadcast networks came from cable television, which had wired nearly three-quarters of the nation's homes by 2000. The expansion of cable accentuated audience fragmentation and narrowcasting. Atlanta's Ted Turner led the way by introducing the Cable News Network (CNN), several movie channels, and an all-cartoon network before his communication empire merged with that of Time-Warner in 1996. Challenging both the networks and cable, companies selling direct satellite transmission began gaining an important share of the increasingly fragmented viewing audience. By the end of the 20th century, the share of viewers watching primetime network programs had fallen to less than 60 percent, and cable shows were beginning to compete with those carried on the networks for the industry's annual Emmy Awards.

Hollywood

Hollywood also adapted to changing business arrangements and new technologies. With movie attendance in 1970 about the same as it had been in 1960, the movie industry began raising ticket prices, betting on a few blockbuster films such as the highly profitable *Star Wars* series (1977–2005), and hoping for a surprise hit such as *The Blair Witch Project* (1999). Although Hollywood endured super-expensive flops such as *Heaven's Gate* (1980) or *Eyes Wide Shut* (1999), motion pictures survived and even thrived through adaptation.

Volatility in the movie market encouraged most filmmakers to play it safe, recycling many titles and special effects that had made money in the past. They transferred popular stories, such as *How the Grinch Stole Christmas* (2000), and TV shows, such as *The Brady Bunch* (1995), to the big screen and produced sequels for any movie, such as *Speed* (1992), that had even approached blockbuster status. In addition, Hollywood expanded the older practice of targeting younger viewers with movies such as *Ferris Bueller's Day Off* (1986). Meanwhile, dramatic stories that tapped themes in popular history, such as *Braveheart* (1995) and *Titanic* (1997), impressed both ticket buyers and industry insiders.

The Sports Construction Boom: Who Pays, Who Gains?

During the 1990s, the growing importance of the sports-entertainment industry brought a boom in the construction of expensive facilities in which baseball, football, and basketball teams competed. New sports complexes appeared in Baltimore, Charlotte, Chicago, Cincinnati, Cleveland, Milwaukee, Nashville, San Francisco, St. Louis, Seattle, Tampa, and Washington, D.C. Other cities, including New York and Dallas, began planning for new construction.

Funding almost always came from public sources as well as from the privately owned teams and leagues that benefited most directly. Some localities used their own taxing authority to help foot the bill, but the national government played an important role as well. The Tax Reform Act of 1986 supposedly barred the federal government from the game, but sports attorneys still found a loophole that enabled state and local governments to help finance new complexes by issuing revenue bonds that enjoyed the same exemption from federal taxation as did bonds issued for school construction and other public projects. Tax experts differed on how much potential revenue this loophole cost the federal government but agreed it was considerable. Critics such as Senator Daniel Patrick Moynihan of New York argued that the bulk of the economic benefits from this subsidy accrued to the wealthy owners of sports franchises and to the relatively small group of similarly well-heeled investors who purchased the tax-exempt bonds.

Senator Moynihan made several attempts during the 1990s to pass new legislation that would end this federal tax subsidy for the construction of sports facilities. All of his efforts failed. Meanwhile, proponents of public financing continued to extoll the benefits that flowed from constructing new sports facilities.

Senator Daniel Patrick Moynihan (June 6 and September 20, 1996) explains his bill entitled "The Stop Tax Exempt Arena Debt Issuance Act"

This legislation will close a big loophole, a loophole that ultimately injures State and local governments and other issuers of tax-exempt bonds, that provides an unintended Federal subsidy (in fact, contravenes congressional intent), and that contributes to the enrichment of persons who need no Federal assistance whatsoever.

I refer to the large number of professional sports facilities subsidized in recent years through the issuance of tax-exempt bonds. It seems that nearly every day, another professional sports franchise owner demands a new stadium, one subsidized by Federal, State and local taxpayers.

Why do owners want new stadiums? Our existing stock of stadiums is not functionally obsolete. Many stadiums are new, and our older ones generally can and will continue to serve, and serve well, for the exhibition of professional sports for years to come. In fact many older, historic stadiums are beloved by fans. The reason for new stadiums is economics—the team owners' bottom line. The owner can generate more revenues with a new stadium replete with luxury skyboxes and other amenities.

Building new professional sports facilities is fine by me. Let the new stadiums be built. But, please, do not ask the American taxpayer to pay for them.

In the last 6 years alone, over $4 billion has been spent to build 30 new professional sports stadiums. According to Prof. Robert Baade, an economist at Lake Forest College in Illinois and an expert in stadium financing, that amount could "completely refurbish the physical plants of the Nation's public elementary and secondary schools." An additional $7 billion of stadiums are in the planning stages, and there is no end in sight. This is why I recently introduced S. 1880—the Stop Tax-exempt Arena Debt Issuance Act—or STADIA for short—to end the Federal tax subsidy for these stadium deals. Only the team owners and players profit, while taxpayers and fans pick up the tab.

Rick Horrow, president of a Miami-based sports consulting firm, makes the case for public financing in a U.S. Senate committee hearing held on June 22, 1999.

There are a number of quantifiable and intangible benefits that have been accepted by over 100 regions that have successfully implemented major and minor league sports and entertainment facilities during this decade.

First, the facilities have been perceived to generate substantial economic impact during construction....

Second, successful projects have also generated substantial retail sales and development activities surrounding these facilities. As Jacobs Field opened in Cleveland in 1995, more than 20 restaurants or retail establishments have opened after that. And more than 85 store fronts have been renovated, at a cost of $1.2 million. The downtown development-oriented Gateway Project has created 6,200 permanent jobs since 1994, generating $6.5 million in payroll taxes.

The third major impact involves the major and special events that will occasionally be attracted to a new facility. Recent Super Bowls in San Diego, Arizona, New Orleans and Miami have each generated over $250 million of new spending to their respective local economies.

Fourth, many communities will identify the intangible impact of a sports franchise and corresponding facility on its marketability and potential to attract new business. The Jacksonville Chamber of Commerce spoke about the Jacksonville Jaguars and Alltel Stadium as being indirectly responsible for creation of upwards of 50,000 new jobs by virtue of companies expanding or relocating to Jacksonville as a consequence of a successful marketing campaign.

And, finally, although more difficult to quantify, many community leaders have advocated a franchise facility as a critical component of image enhancement and community pride.

Once these facilities are developed, they provide substantial economic, tangible and psychological benefits for the entire region for years to come.

Q *What were the major arguments for and against public tax subsidies (federal or state) for sports facilities during the 1990s? Have these arguments changed during the years since then?*

Q *How do these arguments flow from differing views about how to build strong, vibrant communities?*

Q *How might the boom in the construction of expensive sports facilities be related to the development of metropolitan corridors?*

Sources: (first) Senator Daniel Patrick Moynihan statement (June 6 and September 20, 1996), accessed at: http://capitolwords.org/date/1996/09/20/S11103_s-1880-the-stop-tax-exempt-arena-debt-issuance-act/http://capitolwords.org/date/1996/06/14/S6305-3_statements-on-introduced-bills-and-joint-resolutio/; (second) Rick Horrow statement (June 22, 1999), accessed at: http://www.gpo.gov/fdsys/pkg/CHRG-106shrg63000/pdf/CHRG-106shrg63000.pdf

At the same time, a cultural complex that nurtured "independent" films emerged. Woody Allen became one of the first U.S. filmmakers to specialize in movies, such as *Annie Hall* (1977), which borrowed techniques and themes from European cinema. In 1981, Robert Redford launched the Sundance Film Institute in hopes of encouraging innovative screenwriting and direction. Its annual Sundance Festival, held in Park City, Utah, began attracting Hollywood moguls. They sought the next small movie, such as *The Brothers McMullan* (1995), that might find a large audience. Sundance supported the work of African American, Latino, and Asian American directors by showcasing movies like *Hoop Dreams* (1994), *El Mariachi* (1993), and *Picture Bride* (1995). It also celebrated women directors such as Lizzie Borden (*Working Girls*, 1986) and Barbara Kopple (*American Dream*, 1990). The Landmark movie chain led the way in screening independent films unlikely to find space in any of the growing number of suburban multiplexes. Major studios even created special divisions, such as Fox Searchlight Pictures, which specialized in so-called independent films.

Hollywood became increasingly intertwined with the changing television establishment, once its feared rival, and with the emerging home-viewing industries. Hollywood gained badly needed revenue by licensing its offerings to TV and for VCR and DVD distribution. For a brief time during the early 1990s, the United States could claim more video rental outlets than movie theaters. Advances in DVD technology provided improved visual imagery, bonus attractions (such as footage cut from the theatrical release), widescreen prints, and expert commentary by a movie's director. As Hollywood discovered that DVD sales could match theatrical receipts, it came to favor action movies with elaborate special effects that promised to sell well in the home-viewing and international markets. Filmmakers also confronted new "pirating" technologies that meant their movies might appear in bootlegged editions at virtually the same time they debuted in theaters.

The Changing Media Environment for Pop Music

New business ventures and technologies also transformed the relationship between the media and the lucrative pop music industry. A Music Television channel (MTV) debuted in 1981 and subsequently adjusted to changes in the cable TV and music industries. Initially offering a 24-hour supply of rock videos, MTV came under fire for portraying women as sex objects and excluding artists of color. The network eventually defused complaints, especially after featuring Michael Jackson's 29-minute video based on his hit single "Thriller" (1983). By the end of the 20th century, MTV and other cable channels programmed videos that represented the increasingly multiethnic nature of the music industry.

MTV also seemed on the cutting edge of changes in media programming. Its stars of the 1980s such as Jackson and Madonna used MTV to forge a new relationship between music and visual imagery: the "**MTV aesthetic**." This fast-paced visual style played with traditional ideas about time and space, recycled images from earlier movies and TV programs, and often carried a sharply satirical edge. During the 1990s, MTV introduced a wide range of youth-oriented programming such as *The Real World* (1992–). MTV's longest-running program, *The Real World*, popularized the "reality TV" genre that spread to other cable channels and the broadcast networks.

Entertainment conglomerates began marketing music in ever-newer formats. The 45-rpm record and the long-play album (LP), associated with the musical revolutions of the 1950s and 1960s, all but disappeared. Analog cassette tapes, which could be played through a variety of portable stereo devices including Sony's Walkman, arrived during the 1970s. The compact discs (CDs) of the early 1980s changed not only the technology for delivering pop music but also, eventually, the nature of the product and the listening experience. The now-classic rock LPs of the 1960s and early 1970s, such as The Beatles' *Magical Mystery Tour* (1967), had featured 10 to 12 songs, split between the two sides and often organized around a core concept. By the late 1990s, however, CD offerings were coming to mirror those that MP3 technology was just beginning to provide by offering unusual musical mixes that generally lacked any unifying theme.

Changing formats enabled listeners to obtain, preserve, and exchange music in entirely new ways. FM radio stations began to stream their programs over the Internet during the early 1990s, and one of rock's most venerable bands, The Rolling Stones, was the first to simulcast a live concert in 1994. After several years in which Internet users experimented with exchanging musical files, in 1999 a college student introduced Napster. This short-lived venture provided a technology by which users could freely share music gleaned from commercially produced CDs. Artists as well as corporate executives confronted a serious threat to CD sales—and the future of their industry. They charged Internet technologies with facilitating the "pirating" of copyrighted material. Their legal actions prompted a prolonged battle—which extended into the new century—over how music was made, stored, and distributed.

New Mass Culture Debates   New trends in mass commercial culture generated other controversies. In 1975, the Federal Communications Commission (FCC) ordered the television networks to dedicate the first 60 minutes of primetime each evening to "family" programming free of violence and "mature" themes. Federal courts struck down this family-hour requirement as a violation of the First Amendment. Demands that Congress regulate rock lyrics and album covers soon ran afoul of predictions that this kind of legislation would be unconstitutional. TV programmers, record producers, and new Internet gaming ventures responded by following the example of the Hollywood film industry and using "warning labels" that supposedly informed parents about products with violent and sexually explicit imagery.

Commercial pop culture also produced new aesthetic disputes. Unlike the cultural critics of the 1950s, who had dismissed mass fare as trivial and degenerate, analysts from the new academic field of "cultural studies" often seemed unabashed fans of the commercial products they studied. They jettisoned any bright-line distinction between lowbrow and highbrow as untenable. The music of The Beatles could be studied along with that of Beethoven, the lyrics of Bob Dylan alongside classic poetry. Rejecting the elitist-themed criticism of the 1950s, which had seen consumers as cultural dupes who passively soaked up junk, cultural studies stressed people's creative interaction with commercial culture. Scholarly accounts of *Star Trek*, for example, examined how, through self-produced magazines (called "fanzines"), conventions, and the Internet, Trekkies created a grassroots subculture that used the original TV series and its spinoffs to launch serious discussions about social and political issues. The cultural studies approach also tended to embrace multiculturalism, highlighting works produced by women, political outsiders, and non-Western writers and artists. It encouraged students to see traditional texts within their political and historical contexts rather than as timeless works. Traditionalists condemned this "cultural turn" as a legacy of the counterculture of the 1960s and blamed it for eroding settled ideas about the quality and value of artistic expression.

Some of the fiercest debates over popular culture involved the impact of an "infotainment" complex. An imprecise cultural category, infotainment signaled that the always-delicate balance between actually informing and merely amusing audiences had tilted decisively toward the latter.

Cable TV's news operations embraced infotainment in ways that the major broadcast networks had long avoided. While maintaining a 24/7 schedule, CNN initially followed the networks in pursuing a "hard-news" agenda from camera crews and correspondents stationed around the globe, claiming "News is the star." It also introduced, however, programs such as *Crossfire*, which featured the in-studio pyrotechnics of verbally dueling pundits. CNN's eventual rival, the Fox News Channel (FNC), which debuted in 1996, retrofitted the *Crossfire* model to much of its programming. FNC featured verbally nimble personalities who covered the news from studio sets and emphasized, despite labels such as "fair and balanced," opinions that tilted toward those of political conservatives and the Republican Party.

Public affairs broadcasting on cable TV increasingly adopted a narrowcasting strategy. FNC made clear, for example, that its idea of "balance" would attract viewers who saw the major networks and CNN as "biased." CNN and MSNBC, in response, began positioning their coverage toward people uncomfortable with FNC. This approach, critics charged, featured news programming that reinforced rather than broadened the perspectives of core constituencies. A fake news program, *The Daily Show*, satirized the narrowness of its cable TV counterparts. It also arguably produced—or simply attracted—viewers who were more broadly informed about issues than were the aficionados of "real" newscasts. After Jon Stewart assumed the "anchor desk" in January 1999, *The Daily Show* quickly became a favorite news source for college students.

The Religious Landscape

A pervasive religiosity differentiated the United States from most European nations. Attention commonly focused on Americans drawn to the Religious Right, but a propensity to see daily life and world events through religious teachings spanned the political and cultural spectrums. Polls taken at the end of the 20th century suggested that more than three-quarters of Americans believed in a divine being that performed miracles on earth.

The nation's religious landscape showed greater diversity than ever before. During the 1950s, Will Herberg could see his book entitled *Protestant-Catholic-Jew* (1955) as adequately covering the religious dimension of the "American way of life." A half-century later, however, these three faiths represented only some of the religious denominations in the United States.

After about 1970, cultural and social change helped produce this religious diversity. Movements such as the Jesus People loosely affiliated with the counterculture.

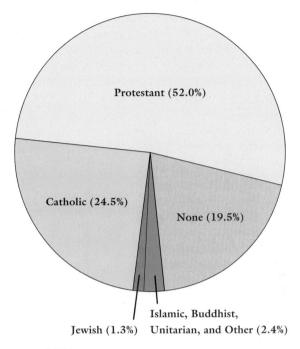

Religion in America, 2001

This chart shows the self-described religious affiliations of the American people compiled through sampling techniques.

Source: Data adapted from *The American Religious Identification Survey*, Graduate Center, City University of New York.

A few other countercultural groups withdrew to communal retreats structured by religious teachings. Many people drawn to alternative cultures also embraced spiritual impulses outside the Protestant-Catholic-Jewish triad. Asian-inspired traditions, such as Transcendental Meditation and Buddhism, proved particularly appealing. New Age spiritual movements, which stressed individual insights over group doctrines, also traced their most immediate origins back to the early 1970s.

Immigration swelled the numbers in various faiths, especially Islam, which had held a minimal presence in the United States prior to 1970. The Black Power movement had attracted new converts to the homegrown Nation of Islam (NOI) during the 1960s, and post-1970 immigration from countries with large Islamic populations brought millions of people who practiced more orthodox versions to the United States. The dynamic and outspoken Louis Farrakhan, once a rival to Malcolm X, revived the NOI during the 1980s, but it attracted far fewer members than other versions of Islam. According to some estimates (the official U.S. Census does not track religious affiliations), the number of residents practicing Islam by the year 2000 surpassed the number practicing Judaism—and even the number identifying with several mainline Protestant denominations, including Presbyterian and Episcopalian. Adapting to American cultural practices, mosques began making Sunday, rather than the traditional Friday, the week's major Islamic holy day.

The Islamic Center of America, Dearborn, Michigan. *This 70,000-square-foot facility dramatizes the growing presence of Islam in the United States. It features building materials imported from all over the world, a gold dome, twin minarets, and a prayer hall that accommodates a thousand worshipers.*

The faith's leading institutions, such as the Islamic Center of Southern California, provided a variety of religious and nonreligious services for their congregations. They also sought to inform non-Muslims about Islam, which claimed more followers worldwide than any other religion.

Other religions experienced similar growth. The number of Protestant evangelicals, for a time, grew faster than the U.S. population. Between 1970 and the late 1990s, the Southern Baptist Convention expanded beyond its traditional regional base and added 6 million new members. The Church of Jesus Christ of Latter-day Saints (the Mormon faith) gained more than half that many. Along with augmenting their membership rolls at home, many of these groups greatly expanded their international missionary activities.

Religious faith did not determine political belief. Most fundamentalists and evangelicals favored the politics of the New Right, but there were evangelical groups, such as the Sojourners, that espoused political-social positions identified with the political left. Moreover, some evangelicals joined mainline religious movements in espousing environmental causes opposed by conservatives. In 1991, the United States Conference of Catholic Bishops issued a lengthy document focused on the relationship between Church teachings and environmental movements for the "planetary common good."

Most organized religious groups also struggled with the relationship between their spiritual faiths and other social and cultural causes. Religious communities offered very different responses, for example, to the emergence of lesbian, gay, bisexual, and transgender (LGBT) movements. Most leaders of the Religious Right, such as Jerry Falwell and Pat Robertson, mobilized against what they saw as the "moral decay" posed by LGBT activism. Orthodox Judaism, Islam, and Catholicism, without mobilizing on the scale of the Religious Right, still labeled same-sex relationships as sinful. In stark contrast, a minority of churches, synagogues, and temples—especially in larger cities—welcomed LGBT members. A few denominations accepted gays and lesbians as ministers and rabbis, and recognizable bodies of "gay theology," grounded in specific biblical passages and on more general principles of tolerance, began to emerge. Churches also faced, along with the nation at large, growing pressure to address the legality of gay marriages.

Religious divisions emerged over foreign policy questions. The movement to contain the spread of nuclear weaponry attracted a number of religious groups. After prolonged internal debate, the Conference of Catholic Bishops issued a pastoral letter entitled "The Challenge of Peace" (1983). It joined statements by several Protestant groups and, in effect, declared U.S. nuclear policy in conflict with religious teachings. At about the same time, some Catholic priests joined dissident Protestant congregations in offering sanctuary to undocumented refugees from Latin America, particularly El Salvador and Guatemala, who were fleeing U.S.-supported military regimes and, once they reached the United States, American immigration authorities. On the other hand, many spiritual leaders and laypeople, particularly those associated with evangelical churches, gravitated toward the fervent anticommunist initiatives supported by the New Right and the Reagan administration.

Three prominent religious figures who entered the partisan arena exemplified the diversity of organized religion's relationship to political action. Father Robert F. Drinan, a member of the U.S. House of Representatives from 1971 to 1981, often embraced positions on issues, such as abortion, contrary to the pronouncements of his own Roman Catholic Church. Eventually, the Church hierarchy decreed that no priest should hold a political office, and Father Drinan resigned from the House. The presidential bids, in 1984 and 1988, of the Reverend Jesse Jackson, a Baptist, recalled movement-style politics that looked back to the religious fervor of the civil rights crusade but also moved in step with the largely secular multiculturalism of the 1980s. Pat Robertson, in contrast, used his firm identification with the Religious Right to unsuccessfully challenge Vice President George H. W. Bush for the 1988 GOP presidential nomination.

Although his presidential bid failed, Robertson did shore up his religious empire at a time when several other media-enabled religious movements were being swamped by controversy. Jim and Tammy Faye Bakker of the "Praise the Lord" (PTL) movement and Jimmy Lee Swaggart saw their multimillion-dollar operations collapse when they violated the moral values their ministries preached. After being convicted on multiple counts of fraud, Jim Bakker landed in jail. Swaggart's dalliances with prostitutes left his ministry, which had once claimed a worldwide media audience of more than 500 million people, relegated to cable TV's public access channels.

Others religious ministries, however, prospered in the manner of Pat Robertson's. The Billy Graham Evangelistic Association's crusade (created in 1950) avoided even the hint of financial or moral malfeasance, and Graham himself remained one of the nation's most admired—and officially nonpartisan—citizens. Another charismatic Baptist minister, Rick Warren, gradually established a thriving "mega-church" in

Southern California; by 2000, his Saddleback Church ranked among the 10 largest congregations in the country.

Successful movements on the Religious Right, such as Falwell's and Warren's, became cultural conglomerates. They included publishing enterprises, bookstores, radio and TV outlets, Christian academies and other "charter" schools, religiously affiliated colleges and seminaries, and even schools of law and of public policy. Apocalyptic novels from this religious milieu, including the *Left Behind* series by Tim LaHaye and Jerry Jenkins, and Christian-themed movies, including *A Thief in the Night* (1972), found large audiences. The Christian music industry easily surpassed the classical and jazz genres in sales by the end of the 20th century.

The Religious Right also advanced several influential cultural narratives about the nation's past and the role that people of faith should play in shaping its future. The influential historian-theologian Francis Schaeffer, a committed evangelical, argued that the "secularist humanist" ideas on which the United States had been founded bequeathed an insufficiently solid religious base. According to an alternative history that slowly gained ascendancy over that of Schaeffer, however, the original intent of the Founding Fathers was to create a Christian nation. The subsequent movement toward secularism, grounded in claims about a "separation between church and state," lacked both historical and legal-constitutional grounding. Both of these historical narratives pointed toward forging a new politics devoted to joining the sacred with the secular.

The Republican Party remained the primary political vehicle for this project. The Religious Right, in addition to gravitating to the post-Reagan GOP at the national level, became a vital force in state and local politics, steadily pressing Republican organizations toward its perspective on issues such as school curricula and textbook selection. It also placed supporters on officially nonpartisan bodies such as local school boards.

CONCLUSION

Sweeping changes occurred in demographics, economics, culture, and society during the last quarter of the 20th century. The nation aged, and more of its people gravitated to the Sun Belt. Sprawling urban corridors challenged older central cities as sites for development. Technological change fueled the growth of globalized industries and the restructuring of the American labor force.

The most prominent development in American popular culture was the proliferation of the video screen. Television, motion pictures, the Internet, and even services for phones increasingly targeted specific audiences, and the fragmentation of cultural reception—exemplified by the rise of new, particularistic media ventures—affected entertainment, politics, and religion.

32

A TIME OF HOPE AND FEAR, 1993–2014

THE DECADES that directly preceded and followed the turn of the 21st century featured a tension between hope and fear. With the collapse of the Soviet Union in 1991, America's military and economic institutions seemed to have emerged triumphant from the cold war challenge of communism. The Pentagon operated nearly 1000 military installations around the globe; American consumers enjoyed an expanding array of products and services; and stock markets reached record highs in early 2000 and again in 2007 and 2014.

Hopes for the future, however, found their match in new fears. Was the nation's economy strong enough to withstand new challenges? Was its political structure flexible enough to meet the demands of governance? Could America's vast military power deal with threats from terrorist networks? The attacks in New York City and Washington on September 11, 2001, brought a new urgency to fears about the future. How could Americans best protect national security? Might new powers for fighting terrorism endanger liberty and equality?

The two-term administrations of Democrat **William Jefferson (Bill) Clinton** and Republican George W. Bush tried, in different ways, to redesign the political landscape, yet the nation 's politics became increasingly polarized. The economic meltdown of 2008 helped bring Democrat Barack Obama, the first African American president and the second youngest in U.S. history, to the White House. Obama campaigned on what he called "the audacity of hope" in a time of war and economic uncertainty.

CHRONOLOGY

1993	Congress approves North American Free Trade Agreement (NAFTA)
1994	Republicans gain control of Congress
	O. J. Simpson saga begins
1996	Congress overhauls national welfare system
	Clinton reelected president
	FOX News debuts
1997	Congress and White House agree on deficit reduction plan
1998	House of Representatives impeaches Clinton
1999	Senate trial ends with Clinton's acquittal
2000	*Bush v. Gore* decision clears way for George W. Bush to become president
2001	Congress passes Bush tax cut
	Terrorists from al-Qaeda destroy World Trade Center and attack Pentagon
	Congress passes Patriot Act
	U.S. forces invade Afghanistan
2002	*National Security Strategy of 2002* reasserts the Bush Doctrine
2003	Bush secures another tax cut
	U.S. invades Iraq to topple Saddam Hussein government
2004	Bush defeats Kerry in the presidential race
	Facebook debuts at Harvard
2005	Hurricane Katrina hits Gulf Coast
	YouTube goes online
	Insurgency in Iraq continues as permanent Iraqi government debuts
2006	Democrats gain control of Congress
	Housing "bubble" reaches its peak
2007	New U.S. strategy adopted in Iraq
	Housing "bubble" bursts
2008	Bush administration and Federal Reserve Board respond to financial meltdown
	Great Recession, worst since 1930s, begins
	Barack Obama wins presidential race
2009	Obama administration passes economic stimulus plan
	U.S. devotes more resources to war in Afghanistan while withdrawing from Iraq
2010	Republicans surge at national, state, and local levels in elections of 2010

2011	A White House–ordered, CIA-directed raid into Pakistan by U.S. Navy SEALs kills Osama bin Laden in early May
2012	Facebook begins offering stock shares to the public
	Barack Obama reelected president
2014	Midterm elections

THE POLITICS OF POLARIZATION, 1993–2008

Bill Clinton—the first Democratic president since another southerner, Jimmy Carter—brought images of youth, vitality, and cultural diversity to Washington. Events at his inauguration included separate parties for different musical tastes, including one broadcast on MTV. His initial cabinet included three African Americans and two Latinos; three cabinet posts went to women. Ruth Bader Ginsburg, his first nominee to the Supreme Court, became only the second woman to sit on the High Court. As ambassador to the United Nations, Clinton named Madeleine Albright, who, during his second term, would become the country's first female secretary of state.

A New Democrat

The Clinton administration achieved several of its domestic goals. It steered through Congress the Family Medical Leave Act, which allowed most working parents to take unpaid leaves in times of emergency; helped establish AmeriCorps, a program that allowed students to repay college loans through community service; and secured passage of the Brady Bill, which instituted restrictions on handgun purchases that the Supreme Court subsequently declared unconstitutional. An executive order ended, for the duration of Clinton's presidency, the Reagan era's ban on federal funding for abortion counseling.

Vice President Al Gore's tiebreaking vote in the Senate allowed passage of Clinton's 1993 economic package. It featured a modest tax increase and cuts in spending aimed at reducing the federal deficit and lowering interest rates to stimulate economic growth. The plan also expanded an existing governmental program, the **Earned Income Tax Credit (EITC)**, for low- and moderate-income households with children. This measure, which lowered tax bills and increased refunds for those who qualified, provided millions of people with another safety-net program.

Identifying himself as a **"New Democrat,"** Clinton broke with his party's recent stance on criminal justice issues. He backed a 1994 law that provided funding for more police officers and more prisons. Its controversial "three strikes" provision required a life sentence for a third felony conviction in federal courts. Clinton later supported limiting appeals by prisoners on death row and a 1996 antiterrorist bill opposed by civil libertarian groups.

The Clinton administration carefully calculated its positions on social-cultural issues. While endorsing a woman's right to a safe and legal abortion, the president also stressed that the procedure should be a "rare" occurrence. Clinton arrived in Washington as a supporter of ending the military's prohibition against gay men and lesbians being open about their sexuality, but he implicitly accepted the argument that ending this ban would spark "discomfort" among heterosexual service personnel and possibly harm morale within military ranks. His administration's compromise policy based on silence and denial—popularly known as "don't ask, don't tell"—had little effect on discrimination against gays and lesbians in the military.

The administration's effort to revamp the nation's health-care system ended in failure. A task force chaired by Hillary Rodham Clinton, the First Lady, began with two basic goals: extend coverage to the tens of millions who lacked insurance and contain the rising cost of care. The plan that emerged contained complex mechanisms for financing and delivering health care. Republicans denounced it, extolled the existing system, and assailed Clinton as a proponent of "big government." Sick on arrival, the health-care proposal died in Congress during early 1994.

The November 1994 elections proved a stunning triumph for the GOP. An aggressive campaign spearheaded by Representative Newt Gingrich of Georgia produced Republican majorities in both houses of Congress for the first time in 40 years. Republicans also won several new governorships, gained ground in most state legislatures, and made significant headway in many city and county elections, particularly across the South. There, for the first time since the 19th century, the number of Republicans sitting in Congress topped the number of Democrats. Gingrich claimed a mandate for what he labeled a **Contract with America**. It drew from Ronald Reagan's 1985 State of the Union address and included calls for overhauling the welfare system, enacting additional anticrime legislation, streamlining federal legal procedures, requiring a three-fifths majority for any increase in taxation, and reducing the nation's role in the UN.

Gingrich downplayed polls that showed few voters knew much about the contract and overplayed his new role as Speaker of the House by continually challenging Clinton's policies. A deadlock between a Democratic president and a GOP Congress over federal spending produced two brief shutdowns of federal agencies in late 1995 and early 1996. Most people blamed Gingrich and the Republicans rather than the White House for interrupting the delivery of government services.

A continually improving economy sustained Clinton's approval ratings. Economic growth spurred millions of new jobs, decreased the federal deficit, boosted corporate profits, propelled stock and bond markets to new heights, and enabled an astronomical boom in the financial industry. The fruits of economic expansion, however, were distributed unequally, as the income gulf between the wealthiest 1 percent of households and the other 99 percent deepened. Still, most people did see their economic fortunes improve, however slightly. Unemployment fell, averaging less than 2 percent a year during the 1990s, and real income inched upward for the first time in nearly 15 years.

Clinton's 1996 State of the Union address declared that the era of "big government" was at an end. The president suggested a willingness to work with congressional Republicans in reducing social welfare costs. The Personal Responsibility and Work Opportunity Reconciliation Act of 1996 did incorporate a series of accommodations between the Republican-dominated Congress and Clinton, who had vetoed two earlier welfare-related measures. The new law replaced the controversial AFDC program, which provided funds and services to poor families headed by single, unemployed women, with **Temporary Assistance to Needy Families (TANF)**. This measure allowed individual states to design, under general federal guidelines, programs aimed at getting people off welfare and into paying jobs.

TANF worried many Democrats. Provisions limiting governmental assistance over a person's lifetime to five years and authorizing states to suspend benefits if recipients failed to find employment within two years ignored the difficulties faced by people without job skills. TANF's opponents also feared its impact on children, particularly in states with already minimal child-care, nutrition, and medical care programs. Senator Daniel Patrick Moynihan, who had earlier devised Richard Nixon's FAP program, denounced TANF as "the most brutal act of social policy" since the 19th century.

New Democrats such as Clinton, however, saw a necessary merger of policy innovation with electoral reality. TANF could assuage conservatives by embracing their call for a smaller federal government; acknowledging critiques of the existing system of social support; and affirming the idea that wages, rather than welfare, should provide the primary source of personal income. TANF's Democratic supporters echoed Republicans who predicted the new arrangement would encourage states to devise programs that both reduced welfare costs and created jobs. TANF immediately assisted Clinton's reelection prospects by eliminating the welfare issue from partisan debate and bolstering the president's claim that he was reducing the size and cost of government.

In the 1996 election, the Clinton-Gore team defeated Republicans Robert Dole and Jack Kemp by about the same margin as it had beaten George H. W. Bush and Dan Quayle four years earlier. Although another presidential run by Ross Perot again denied the Democratic ticket a popular majority, a low-key campaign effort gained Perot's third-party candidacy less than 10 percent of the vote. Clinton became the first Democratic president since Franklin D. Roosevelt to win back-to-back terms. A reelected president and a Congress still controlled by Republicans then agreed on a timetable for eradicating the federal deficit, which the president accurately predicted would soon disappear. But any hope for further accommodations disappeared as the nation's political culture began revolving around a legal-constitutional debate over the future of Bill Clinton's presidency rather than his policy initiatives.

The Investigation and Trial of a President

Intensive legal inquiries into Clinton's public and private life capped a decade of popular fascination with investigations and trials. Americans, of course, had long been drawn to legal spectacles, such as the Scopes trial of the 1920s. During the 1990s, however, investigative and courtroom dramas inundated popular culture. Coverage of real trials, a staple of media culture, entered a new phase when Court TV (renamed truTV in 2008) arrived in 1991. The legal thrillers of John Grisham made this author-attorney the best-selling fiction writer of the 1990s, and six of his novels became feature motion pictures. Tom Cruise, perhaps Hollywood's most celebrated male star of the decade, played a lawyer in two Oscar-nominated legal dramas, *A Few Good Men* (1992) and *The Firm* (1993). The year 1990 marked the debut of what would become one of TV's longest-running drama series, *Law & Order* (1990–2010). And the much-anticipated final episode of *Seinfeld*

(1989–1998) featured a satirical trial sequence that revolved around fictional crimes allegedly committed by the leading characters over the life of this hit comedy series.

Long before the end of *Seinfeld*, groups on the New Right started bankrolling private inquiries into supposed crimes in Bill Clinton's past. One investigation concerned a scandal-plagued real estate venture called "Whitewater," to which Hillary and Bill Clinton had been financially connected. Confident of rebutting all allegations, the Clinton administration asked for the appointment of a special independent prosecutor to investigate Whitewater. The president also faced a seemingly frivolous civil suit for monetary damages by Paula Jones, who claimed that Clinton, while governor of Arkansas, had sexually harassed her. The U.S. Supreme Court ruled that this private lawsuit could proceed while Clinton still held public office, and it became entangled with the Whitewater inquiry when Kenneth Starr replaced the initial special prosecutor. A conservative attorney with Supreme Court ambitions and scant background in criminal work, Starr allowed his staff to extend the Whitewater investigation into allegations that Clinton was concealing a series of sexually charged encounters.

Clinton's denials crumbled in early 1998 after conservative activists helped Starr obtain irrefutable evidence of White House trysts between Clinton and a young intern, Monica Lewinsky. Republican leaders in the House of Representatives claimed that Clinton's conduct justified his removal from office. Democrats condemned Clinton's behavior but insisted that private failings did not qualify as the kind of "high crimes and misdemeanors" the Constitution required for impeachment, let alone conviction, of a president.

At Newt Gingrich's insistence, Republicans made Clinton's character their major issue during the midterm elections of 1998, but the president won this electoral trial. Republicans, surprisingly, lost five seats in the House of Representatives. Even worse for Gingrich, public revelation of a long-term extramarital affair forced him to resign from the House. Kenneth Starr conceded that the original Whitewater charges lacked merit, but his official report detailed Clinton's dalliances with Monica Lewinsky and the president's effort to conceal them when testifying under oath. Using evidence gathered by Starr's investigators, the Republican majority in the lame-duck House of Representatives mobilized enough votes, in mid-December 1998, for two articles of impeachment (one for perjury and another for obstruction of justice) against Clinton. The subsequent Senate trial generated surprisingly little drama and concluded (on February 12, 1999) with both articles of impeachment gaining nowhere near the 67 votes that the Constitution required for conviction.

Although Clinton remained president, he hardly escaped unscathed. His presidency remained under sustained GOP attack, and the evolution of Fox News on cable TV added a spicy new ingredient to the media recipe book. Initially, Fox's partisan Republican slant was less important than its popularization of an adversarial format for political coverage on cable TV. Fox perfected a cost-cutting technique by which its camera crews gathered eye-catching imagery and brief interviews that its producers could, employing new digital technologies, archive, quickly retrieve, and re-edit for endless recycling. On-air commentators became ever more skillful in using fleeting imagery and brief sound bites as the basis for trading opinions and speculation without leaving the studio or doing any actual reporting.

A medium newer and even more adversarial than cable TV—political sites on the Internet—came online at a critical point during the Clinton presidency. Other outlets eventually might have reported rumors about the president's personal life, but there was a long tradition (most evident for John F. Kennedy) of burying such stories as purely private matters. In any event, the first news of the Clinton-Lewinsky relationship surfaced on *The Drudge Report*, a conservative opinion-gossip site that other media had previously disdained. Over the course of the 1990s, in short, discussions of public affairs increasingly took on an investigative format that helped to slow—indeed, almost paralyze—the Clinton administration's effort to do the actual work of governance.

The Long Election and Trials of 2000   The lengthy presidential election of 2000 eventually featured a legal drama that attracted this sound-bite style of coverage, especially on cable TV news. Al Gore, Clinton's vice president for eight years, ran as the Democratic presidential nominee and selected Senator Joseph Lieberman of Connecticut as his running mate. The Republican ballot, for the fifth time in the last six elections, bore the name of Bush. **George W. Bush** chose **Richard (Dick) Cheney**—a conservative Republican stalwart who had served in the administration of George H. W. Bush (1989–1993)—to be his vice presidential running mate.

The campaign of 2000 energized the Republican Party's base but stirred less passion elsewhere. Bush claimed his record as governor of Texas showed he could work with Democrats, appeal to African Americans and Hispanics, and pursue a "compassionate conservatism." Gore's disorganized campaign struggled to articulate coherent themes. By distancing himself from Clinton, the vice president likely squandered his primary asset—eight years of relative prosperity with a Democratic administration in the White House. Barely 50 percent of eligible voters went to the polls in 2000. Following recent patterns, the vote highlighted the gender, racial, and ethnic differences between the two major parties. Bush attracted 54 percent of the ballots cast by men but only 43 percent of those from women. He received 38 percent of the votes from Latinos, 37 percent from Asian Americans, and 9 percent from African Americans.

The election ended in a near dead heat. Republicans narrowly maintained control of the House of Representatives, and the Senate ended up evenly split between the two parties. Al Gore carried the popular vote by about 500,000 ballots, but the only tally that mattered, the one in the Electoral College, turned on the 25 electoral votes from Florida. Only about 1,000 popular votes from the Sunshine State initially separated the two candidates. As other media outlets held back, Fox News declared that the Republican ticket had carried Florida—and thus had secured its electoral votes and the presidency.

When it became evident that no clear winner had emerged, cable TV news shifted to an "All Election, All the Time" focus on Florida, where Bush's brother Jeb was governor and the GOP dominated the state legislature. Republican officials declared Bush the victor in Florida by a margin of 930 votes. Democrats charged that numerous irregularities—including antiquated voting machines, deliberately confusing ballots, and an apparent effort to suppress the African

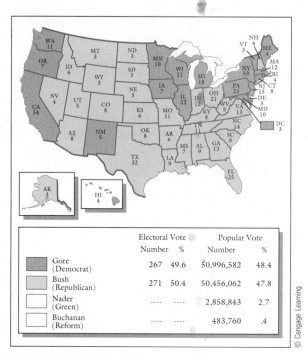

		Electoral Vote		Popular Vote	
		Number	%	Number	%
	Gore (Democrat)	267	49.6	50,996,582	48.4
	Bush (Republican)	271	50.4	50,456,062	47.8
	Nader (Green)	----	----	2,858,843	2.7
	Buchanan (Reform)	----	----	483,760	.4

© Cengage Learning

MAP 32.1 Presidential Election, 2000

Although Gore won the popular vote, Bush won the electoral vote after a bitter fight over disputed ballots in Florida.

American vote—had distorted the count. A torrent of lawsuits, by Democrats and Republicans alike, quickly ensued. Both parties, especially the GOP, flooded Florida with cadres of lawyers and party activists who performed for the benefit of TV cameras. Florida's highest court finally ordered hand recounts in several counties where Gore's totals seemed suspiciously low. When early results began reducing Bush's slim lead, Republicans charged Democrats with "stealing" his victory and appealed to the U.S. Supreme Court.

With media coverage approaching a near-frenzied state, the Supreme Court handed down its final decision during the evening of December 12, 2000, in **Bush v. Gore**. Five conservative Republicans (over the dissents of two other Republicans and two Democrats) ruled that no more Florida ballots could be recounted. Outvoted in court, Gore conceded political defeat, and George W. Bush became the 43rd president of the United States.

A Conservative Washington, 2001–2008   The Bush presidency's program for tax cuts, educational reform, and expanding oil drilling got off to a fast start. Conservative think tanks had already assembled thousands of policy proposals and a similar number of resumes from reliably conservative job seekers. In contrast to Clinton, who preferred lengthy, loosely structured, intellectual give-and-take sessions, Bush favored brief, tightly controlled meetings that moved toward clearly delineated decisions. According to dissident members of his administration, Bush rarely seemed interested in exploring, or some-times even hearing or reading, ideas in conflict with his instincts. He initially allowed Vice President Cheney and Donald Rumsfeld, the secretary of defense, wide latitude to set policy directions. Bush also proclaimed that religious faith directly shaped his political outlook.

Several divisive issues immediately emerged. An economic downturn accompa-nied by an early 2001 plunge in U.S stock markets—a consequence of a bubble in high-tech stocks and fraudulent activities by several large corporations—signaled trouble ahead. Revenue surpluses at the national and state levels began dwindling and then turning to deficits. Consumer confidence slumped. The Bush administra-tion responded by urging a tax cut to provide an economic stimulus.

The White House pressed two other proposals. First, Cheney put together an ambitious energy plan, focused on easing restrictions on oil drilling and regulations on pricing. Critics complained that it primarily benefited large oil and gas firms—many headquartered in Texas—and did little to develop alternative sources of energy. Second, the president personally championed an educational initiative called "No Child Left Behind" that would employ nationwide testing to determine which schools were teaching students effectively.

Bush's proposals seemed bolder than either his campaign rhetoric or his loss of the popular vote might have suggested. A revised tax plan, which phased in the sub-stantial cuts that tilted toward the wealthiest 1 percent of Americans, became law in June 2001. "No Child Left Behind" also passed. Opponents of the pro-oil and pro-gas energy bill blocked its passage, but only until 2005. In 2003 the administration narrowly passed a costly addition (the first in 35 years) to the Medicare system. **The Medicare Prescription Drug Improvement and Modernization Act** created complex arrangements by which federal funds would pay for some, but not all, of the drug costs of Medicare recipients. Benefiting drug companies as well as patients, this measure helped further increase the federal deficit.

The president's approval ratings, which had hovered under 50 percent, soared after the attacks on the World Trade Center and the Pentagon on September 11, 2001. The midterm elections of 2002 left the GOP with secure control of the U.S. Senate and an even larger margin in the House of Representatives.

Downplaying the rapidly growing federal deficit, largely the result of Bush's earlier tax reductions, the White House secured yet another tax cut in 2003. It again insisted that this measure would spur economic growth. Democrats con-demned these cuts for tilting toward the already wealthy in an economy that had shed nearly 3 million jobs and had shown a widening income gap.

The White House's political strategy for the 2004 elections, fine-tuned by con-sultant Karl Rove, stressed Bush's role in combating terrorism. The Democratic nominee, Senator John Kerry of Massachusetts, had served in Vietnam during the 1960s before becoming an antiwar activist. Kerry endorsed the rationale for the Bush administration's national security initiatives, while criticizing its strategy and tactics for combating the terrorist threat and keeping his distance from a small anti-war movement.

A fiercely partisan campaign ensued. Some Bush supporters falsely disparaged Kerry's Vietnam War record, and the GOP campaign team portrayed a Kerry presi-dency as a danger to national security. Democrats charged Bush with bumbling

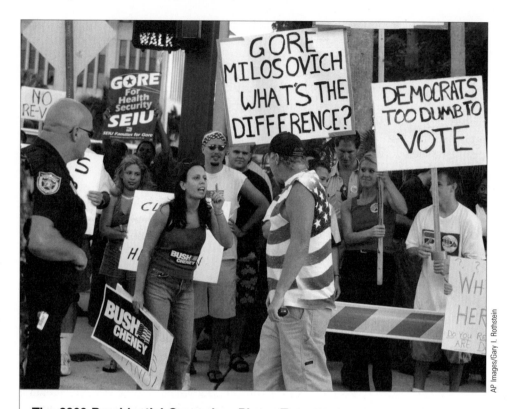

The 2000 Presidential Campaign, Phase Two. *The inconclusive popular vote in Florida extended the 2000 presidential election process. Partisan activists, especially on the Republican side, rushed to Florida and onto TV. GOP demonstrators insisted that George W. Bush had carried the Sunshine State and that the hand counting of ballots was meant to steal his victory.*

leadership, an escalating burden of debt, and a tax policy favoring the wealthiest Americans. The GOP's mobilization effort produced a large Republican turnout and charges of voter fraud, especially in Ohio. Bush defeated Kerry by about 3 percent of the popular vote and 15 electoral ballots. As in 2000, Bush did best in suburbia and small towns, among men, and with people who attended church regularly. Kerry failed to do as well as had Al Gore in 2000 among white voters—still more than three-quarters of the electorate—or to win enough middle-income voters, people whom Democrats claimed were suffering from Bush's economic policies.

Bush claimed an electoral mandate and announced an ambitious second-term agenda that featured substantial overhauls of the Social Security system and the tax code. He barnstormed the country on behalf of these initiatives, but most people appeared wary in light of a shaky economy, a yawning federal deficit, and warfare overseas. Moreover, a Republican-controlled Congress became a depreciating asset to the White House after revelations of illegal contributions from lobbyists and personal misconduct forced the resignation of several GOP legislators. Congress's approval rating skidded below that of President Bush.

Politics and Social-Cultural Issues

With the major political parties locked in partisan stalemate, a variety of movement groups tried to seize the initiative on specific issues. Immigration policy emerged as one of the most contentious. Entering the United States in near-record numbers, immigrants were now seeking jobs throughout the country, particularly in the South. Organizations opposed to immigration demanded new legislative restrictions, tighter border security, and stronger penalties for employers of undocumented immigrants. A few formed militia-like patrols and threatened to turn back people trying to enter the United States along the southwestern border.

Pro-immigration organizations responded, particularly in California and other states with large Mexican American populations. Tapping the power of Spanish-language radio and TV, they staged temporary work stoppages and street demonstrations intended to show the economic importance of immigrant workers and the political clout of their movement. They cited economic studies that challenged claims that undocumented immigrants "took away" jobs from American citizens and depressed wage levels.

Political leaders moved cautiously. House Republicans from districts with strong anti-immigration sentiment favored new restrictions, but enough Republicans in the Senate joined Democrats to block any such measure. The Bush administration promised a more vigorous effort to police the U.S.-Mexican border but angered congressional Republicans by endorsing a "guest worker" arrangement, an option favored by most business interests. Uncertain about how immigration legislation might affect electoral results in 2008, Republicans backed off taking action at the national level.

Differences also sharpened over the role the government should play in regulating businesses in order to address possible public health risks. Business interests joined prominent Republicans in supporting continued deregulation and opposing new governmental restrictions. The free market, they contended, would self-correct to protect the public, and regulators would stifle business growth. In response to this position, environmentalist groups increasingly merged social justice concerns with quality of life issues. They argued that hazardous wastes, though a potential threat to everyone, most directly affected people with low incomes who lacked the political power to keep toxic by-products out of their neighborhoods and off their lands. Activists further charged that the relatively few corporations that dominated the global production and sale of food brutalized animals, overused antibiotics, depleted soil quality and vital rain forests, and polluted the environment with toxic waste. New governmental regulations, they argued, were needed to safeguard the health of people—and of the entire planet. "Good food" advocates who were also environmentalists spearheaded a "buy local" movement that sparked a growing consumer demand for organic products, farmers' markets, and well-prepared "slow food."

The issue of gay rights also emerged as a major political-cultural flashpoint, as LGBT movements sought legal recognition of long-term partnerships that they viewed to be as legitimate as heterosexual marriages. When the U.S. Supreme Court struck down state anti-sodomy laws (in *Lawrence v. Texas,* 2003), the constitutional rationale for this decision seemingly suggested that bans against same-sex marriage could not withstand legal scrutiny either. In several states, courts held that the bedrock principle of legal-constitutional equality guaranteed gays and lesbians a "right to marry," a liberty that some state legislatures also began to affirm.

Conservative activists joined the Bush administration in seeking an amendment to the U.S. Constitution that specifically declared marriage as a "union between a man and a woman." Opponents of the amendment narrowly turned back a congressional effort to send such a measure to the states for ratification in 2006. In response, conservatives mobilized to overturn, by constitutional amendment or referendum, legislative and court actions that legalized gay marriage in a number of states.

Mobilization on the political right also highlighted conflict between the religious beliefs held by some and scientific research and medical practice. In July 2006, after Congress passed a law in support of stem cell research, President Bush responded by issuing, on live television, the first veto of his presidency, rejecting this measure on "culture-of-life" grounds.

Many of these religious-cultural issues became entangled in judicial politics.. The conservative legal movement continued its successful campaign to staff the lower federal courts with rightward-tilting judges and even blocked a Bush nominee for the Supreme Court, Harriet Myers, because of her seemingly moderate stance on abortion and gay rights. The White House easily obtained Senate confirmations for two staunchly conservative Supreme Court nominees: John Roberts to replace William Rehnquist as Chief Justice of the United States, and Samuel Alito (rather than Harriet Myers) to succeed the retiring Sandra Day O'Connor as an associate justice.

The **Roberts Court** generally converted the arguments of the conservative legal movement into constitutional law. In one of several key decisions breaking 5–4— with Justice Anthony Kennedy replacing Justice O'Connor as the swing vote—the Supreme Court limited women's access to abortion. It rebuffed traditional civil rights groups with a similarly restrictive view of the ability of local school districts to use racial identification in pursuit of desegregation strategies. In another 5–4 decision that Second Amendment activists applauded, the Roberts Court ruled that the right to bear arms included that of individual citizens to possess firearms and thus struck down an ordinance regulating gun ownership in Washington, D.C. Moreover, the logic of this 2008 decision pointed toward the subsequent invalidation of similar regulations at the state and local levels. The Court also invariably upheld claims made by corporations that were fighting government regulations.

FOREIGN POLICIES OF HOPE AND TERROR: 1993–2008

For nearly half a century, the goal of containing Soviet communism had shaped U.S. foreign policy. After the collapse of the Soviet Union, George H. W. Bush's attempt to fashion new goals for a post–cold war world had failed to impress either his Democratic or Republican critics. Thus, Bill Clinton came to the White House with a more ambitious foreign policy agenda. A committed internationalist, he assigned top priority to devising guidelines for military intervention, improving relations with the UN, promoting free-market policies that supported globalization, addressing environmental concerns that were both global and local in nature, and reducing threats from nuclear materials. After Clinton's internationalist approach, his successor, George W. Bush, assumed a more unilateralist tone, especially after the terrorist attacks of September 11, 2001.

Clinton's Internationalist Agenda   One of the most perplexing foreign policy issues involved decisions about when to employ U.S. military power in localized conflicts that no longer could be traced back to the now-defunct Soviet Union. No consistent guidelines for intervention ever emerged. In Somalia, U.S. troops, under the umbrella of a UN mission since May 1992, had been assisting a humanitarian effort to provide food and relief supplies. After a battle in Mogadishu (subsequently portrayed in the book and movie *Black Hawk Down*) took the lives of 18 U.S. service personnel in the fall of 1993, however, domestic criticism mounted. Clinton ordered a pullout the following spring. Recalling the criticism of involvement in Somalia, Clinton withheld support from a UN peacekeeping effort in Rwanda, where 500,000 Tutsis died during a genocidal civil war. In Haiti, though, Clinton dispatched U.S. troops, in cooperation with the UN, to reinstall an elected president who had been ousted in a coup. The White House, in cooperation with NATO, also deployed 20,000 U.S. troops in the former Yugoslavia to prevent Bosnian Serbs from massacring Bosnian Muslims. U.S. forces remained in Bosnia to oversee a ceasefire and peace-building process that resulted from the U.S.-brokered Dayton (Ohio) Peace Accords of 1995.

In March 1999 Clinton supported a NATO bombing campaign to protect Muslims from Serbia's "ethnic cleansing" program in its province of Kosovo. After heavy bombardment, the Serbian government withdrew its forces from Kosovo; Serbs soon elected a new president supportive of multiethnic democracy and the West, and former Serbian officials faced trial before an international human rights court in the Netherlands. U.S. and NATO troops remained in Kosovo as peacekeepers.

Clinton's military moves in Haiti, Bosnia, and Kosovo provoked controversy. Republican critics accused the president of lacking clear guidelines about when, where, and how to employ U.S. force. Suspicious of cooperating with the UN, they denounced peacekeeping and "nation-building" programs, and demanded clear-cut exit strategies to prevent the United States from getting bogged down in lengthy occupations. Defenders of intervention insisted that Clinton's flexibility and willingness to work with NATO and the UN were strengths, not weaknesses, in a post–cold war world. Such debates about when and where to intervene in trouble spots would increase over the coming years.

Globalization   In addition, the Clinton administration placed great emphasis on lowering barriers to trade and expanding global markets to advance the international economic process called "globalization." His stance angered many labor leaders, who claimed that globalization was contributing to the loss of industrial jobs in the United States. It also sparked a highly visible anti-globalization movement that emerged in most nations to challenge corporate elites.

In pursuit of globalization, Clinton pushed the stalled North American Free Trade Agreement (NAFTA) among the United States, Canada, and Mexico through Congress in a close vote that depended on Republican support and faced fierce opposition from labor unions. Then, in early 1995, a severe debt crisis and currency devaluation in Mexico prompted the Clinton administration to extend a $20 billion loan. Unprecedented and controversial, the loan stabilized the Mexican economy and, within a few years, had been repaid with $1 billion in interest. When Asian economies later faltered, Clinton lobbied the International Monetary Fund (IMF) to provide emergency credits to shore up financial systems from Korea to Indonesia.

Promising that expanded trade ties would benefit all nations, the Clinton administration supported creation of the **World Trade Organization (WTO)** in 1995. It also signed more than 300 bilateral trade agreements with other nations. Anxious to move China toward a market economy, Clinton backed China's entry into the WTO, in exchange for its promise to relax trade restrictions. Similarly, the United States ended its 19-year-old trade embargo against Vietnam. Clinton continually extolled the coming of a "New Century" in which freer trade would expand prosperity, and "liberty will spread by cell phone and cable modem."

Protecting the Planet   International environmental issues were another area of major concern. Clinton's secretary of the interior set aside 16 new national monuments and blocked road construction and logging in nearly 60 million acres of wild areas in national forests. Building on decisions by his Republican predecessors, Clinton placed almost 6 million new surface and underwater acres under federal protection.

The Clinton administration also revealed how, during the cold war past, actions by the U.S. government had contributed to environmental degradation. Governmental nuclear facilities had spewed toxic wastes, and workers had been inadequately warned about the dangers of radiation. In 1993 Clinton's energy secretary released long-secret medical records relating to radiation and promised programs to inform and compensate victims. The legacy of other military-related pollutants also became evident after many of the nation's military bases were shut down during the post–cold war 1990s.

Most importantly, Clinton supported the environmental movement's increasing focus on international ecological dangers. Environmentalists warned of holes in the ozone layer caused by chlorofluorocarbons (CFCs), potentially catastrophic climate change associated with deforestation and desertification, pollution of the world's oceans, and the decline of biodiversity in plant and animal species. Solutions to global environmental problems seemingly required worldwide cooperation toward "sustainable development." An "Earth Summit" was held in Brazil in 1992. International conventions signed in Kyoto in 1997 and at The Hague in 2000 pointed toward establishing international standards on emissions of CFCs and gases that contributed to global climate changes.

Clinton's post–cold war agenda also included nonproliferation of nuclear weapons. His administration dismantled some of the U.S. nuclear arsenal and increased economic aid to Ukraine, then the third greatest nuclear power in the world, in exchange for a pledge to disarm its 1,600 Soviet-era warheads. The White House successfully pressed for a new Nuclear Nonproliferation Treaty in the spring of 1995, and three years later neared the brink of war with Iraq to maintain international inspections of Saddam Hussein's weapons programs. After enduring punishing air strikes, Iraq still expelled the investigators and left analysts wondering if Saddam had resumed building weapons of mass destruction (WMDs).

September 11, 2001, and the Bush Doctrine   During the 1990s, intelligence experts highlighted a growing concern about attacks by a foreign terrorist network called al-Qaeda. Its operatives bombed the World Trade Center in New York City in 1993; U.S. embassies in Kenya and Tanzania in 1998; and a U.S. battleship, the *Cole*, in 2000. These bombings prompted heightened security efforts and special efforts to track al-Qaeda's leaders. As the Clinton administration left office, national security officers feared what al-Qaeda's Osama bin Laden, an Islamic fundamentalist from Saudi Arabia, might be plotting. The Bush administration rejected their sense of urgency.

On September 11, 2001, 19 suicide terrorists, organized in separate squads, seized four jetliners, already airborne and loaded with flammable jet fuel, for use as high-octane, human-guided missiles. Two planes toppled the Twin Towers of New York's World Trade Center; another ripped into the Pentagon building; and only the courageous action of passengers on a fourth plane, which crashed in Pennsylvania, prevented an attack against the United States Capitol in Washington, D.C. Nearly 3,000 people, including several hundred plane passengers and an even larger number of police officers and firefighters in New York City, perished.

George W. Bush, donning the mantle of a wartime president, declared a war on terrorism. Tracing the attacks to Osama bin Laden and al-Qaeda operating out of Afghanistan, the Bush administration organized a multinational invasion force. In December 2001, U.S.-led troops toppled the Taliban regime that had been dominating Afghanistan with bin Laden's help and installed a pro-U.S. government in Afghanistan's capital city of Kabul. The effort failed, however, to secure that nation's countryside or to capture bin Laden and his top aides.

Meanwhile, the president proclaimed what became known as the **Bush Doctrine**. As fully expressed in the **National Security Strategy of 2002**, it denounced not only terrorist networks but any nation sponsoring terrorism or accumulating WMDs that terrorists might use. The Bush Doctrine additionally proclaimed that the United States possessed the unilateral authority to wage preemptive war against any force, including any foreign nation, threatening American security.

Congressional legislation bolstered the Bush Doctrine. Many Democrats joined Republicans in passing the USA Patriot Act, which gave the executive branch broad latitude to watch over and detain people it considered threats to national security. A newly created agency, the Department of Homeland Security, launched an array of new measures including screenings for all airline passengers. Fear of more terrorist attacks, heightened by mysterious mailings of deadly anthrax bacteria to several public officials, strengthened the case for extending the power of the executive branch.

Unilateralism and the Iraq War

After Osama bin Laden dropped from sight, the White House invoked the Bush Doctrine against Iraq and Saddam Hussein, the old nemesis of the president's father, who controlled some of the richest oil reserves in the world. The Bush administration contended that Iraq posed a clear and immediate danger to the United States. Claiming that intelligence reports showed that Saddam Hussein possessed WMDs and had ties to al-Qaeda, the Bush administration asked the UN and other nations to support a military strike to remove Saddam from power.

The Bush administration, which preferred taking unilateral action rather than working with international bodies, included a group of **neoconservatives** who had been calling for such an approach to foreign affairs since the 1990s. According to neoconservative advisers to Vice President Dick Cheney and Secretary of Defense Donald Rumsfeld, the United States should use its enormous military power to go on the offensive and clear away threatening, repressive regimes, beginning with that in Iraq. International organizations and agreements should not hamper efforts to spread liberty and enhance U.S. influence, especially in the Middle East. In contrast to his father, an internationalist who had carefully courted UN backing for the Persian Gulf War in 1991, George W. Bush endorsed a policy of overthrowing Saddam regardless of the UN's position.

Acting without UN support, in early 2003 the Bush administration assembled its own "coalition of the willing"—troops from the United States and Great Britain, plus smaller contingents from several other countries. On March 20, this coalition launched an air and ground assault against Iraq. Overriding military planners who recommended at least 300,000 U.S. troops, the White House's Operation Iraqi Freedom deployed only one-third that many. Saddam Hussein's regime did fall in less than two months, and on May 1 President Bush proclaimed, during a celebration staged on the deck of the aircraft carrier *Abraham Lincoln*, that "significant combat" had ended in Iraq.

This carefully crafted media event quickly rebounded against the president, however, as resistance flared against the ill-planned, American-led occupation of Iraq, which aimed at creating a pro-U.S. government and a new economic order closely tied to U.S. companies. Terrorist groups from outside Iraq, particularly those claiming connections to al-Qaeda, joined the fight, while internal divisions among religious, ethnic, and political factions inside Iraq fueled an insurgency that soon overlapped with a civil war. The Joint Chiefs of Staff warned that the Iraq War was stretching military resources so thin that the United States might not be able to respond in other areas of the globe. As U.S. casualties in Iraq mounted, so did the monetary costs. The lack of international support for U.S. action meant that, unlike in the 1991 Persian Gulf War, U.S. taxpayers directly bore the costs, and the Bush administration repeatedly asked Congress for billions of dollars, but no increase in taxes, to fund the lengthening engagement in Iraq. Meanwhile, the war in Afghanistan stalled, the Taliban regrouped, and the al-Qaeda leaders who had attacked on September 11, 2001, retreated into mountainous safe havens and into Pakistan.

As the Iraqi operation faltered, the Bush administration's public rationale for having undertaken it fell apart. The White House could never document any connection between al-Qaeda and Saddam Hussein, and an exhaustive official report concluded that Iraq had possessed no biological or nuclear WMDs at the time of the invasion. Later evidence suggested that the Bush administration had used bogus intelligence information to bolster its justification for war. In response, Congress in December 2004 placed existing intelligence-gathering and assessment efforts under a new umbrella agency, headed by a new coordinating official, the director of national intelligence.

As the initial case for war came under fire, so did its conduct. Photographs showing abuse of detained Iraqis, especially at Baghdad's Abu Ghraib prison, and stories of a few U.S. troops deliberately killing civilians cast doubt on the wisdom of U.S. forces occupying a country about which they knew relatively little. Controversy also developed over whether what the Bush administration called "enhanced interrogation" of prisoners was largely a euphemism for what others called "torture."

Contrary to the premise of the Bush Doctrine and neoconservative claims, regime change in Iraq produced neither a stable nor a pro-American Middle East. Ever-growing Iranian influence within Iraq especially irked neoconservatives who had hoped the Iraqi invasion would be the first step toward a similar operation

Baghdad, Iraq, 2006. *Bombings aimed at both Iraqis and U.S. personnel followed the fall of Saddam Hussein. In May 2006, a bomb attack hit a news crew from CBS, underscoring the danger that journalists, as well as troops, confronted whenever they left the relative safety of the U.S.-controlled "Green Zone" in central Baghdad.*

against Iran. In addition, the backlash against U.S. interventionism inflamed passions across the Middle East and made the policy of Israel, a U.S. ally, toward Palestinians more complicated than ever.

National Security and Presidential Power

Hurricane Katrina, slamming into the U.S. Gulf Coast region in late August 2005, prompted an intense, if short-lived, controversy over national security on the home front. Local and state officials bumbled through the first serious post–9/11 emergency when the area around New Orleans experienced severe flooding and devastation. The Department of Homeland Security, presumably created to deal efficiently with threats, seemed unprepared. Although the White House would claim no one had "anticipated the breach of levees" intended to protect New Orleans from floodwaters churned up by hurricanes, videotapes later showed the president receiving precisely such a warning. Katrina exacted an especially heavy toll, including several thousand deaths, on the Gulf Coast's oldest, poorest, primarily African American residents.

The Bush administration's limited response to Katrina departed from its usual preference for expanding the reach of the executive branch. Vice President Cheney and Secretary of Defense Rumsfeld, who had served in Republican administrations during the immediate post-Watergate era of the 1970s, pressed Bush to challenge congressional and judicial restrictions put in place in response to executive-branch

WHAT THEY SAID

Debating Torture

In the wake of the 9/11 attacks by operatives of al-Qaeda, attorneys working in President George W. Bush's Department of Justice issued a series of advisory opinions that supported the legality of certain antiterrorist measures. One of the most controversial issues involved whether the use of various tactics for interrogating terrorists, especially "waterboarding," would violate a specific U.S. criminal statute that prohibited "torture." The Bush Justice Department, relying on a memorandum of March 14, 2003, drafted by John Yoo, a law professor at the University of California, Berkeley, offered a very narrow definition of what constituted torture.

March 14, 2003

Memorandum from John Yoo for William J. Haynes, General Counsel of the Department of Defense

Re: Military Interrogation of Alien Unlawful Combatants Held Outside the United States

[According to this legal analysis, torture] is not the mere infliction of pain or suffering on another, but is instead a step well removed. The victim must experience intense pain or suffering of the kind that is equivalent to the pain that would be associated with serious physical injury so severe that death, organ failure, or permanent damage resulting in a loss of significant body function will likely result …. In addition, these acts must cause long-term mental harm.

Indeed, this view of the criminal act of torture is consistent with the term's common meaning. Torture is generally understood to involve "intense pain" or "excruciating pain," or put another way, "extreme anguish of body or mind." *Black's Law Dictionary* at 1498 (7th Ed. 1999); *Random House Webster's Unabridged Dictionary* 1999 (1999); *Webster's New International Dictionary* 2674 (2d ed. 1935). In short, reading the definition of torture as a whole, it is plain that the term encompasses only extreme acts.

In April 2005, Professor Yoo engaged in a debate over his views at Columbia University Law School. There, law professor Jeremy Waldron of Columbia directly challenged Yoo's position.

[T]he restriction on torture is absolute, even in times of emergency. To sneakily mess with the definition seems to me a terrible mistake, and flies directly in the face of the absoluteness of the prohibition. There is a danger of turning the word torture into a technical, legalistic term. If someone is being half drowned, and we say it is not torture, torture becomes a legal term like "certiorari." The ordinary [U.S.] soldiers understand that they benefit from a convention framed in ordinary language terms. When we laid down an absolute prohibition on torture in human rights instruments, we didn't do so as an academic exercise. We laid down this law specifically to constrain us in the circumstances where torture would be a temptation, not in peacetime academia. Apart from the disgraceful discussion in Yoo's memo, you undermine the legal and military culture by changing the meaning of torture.

Professor Yoo stuck to the basic position he had outlined in his memorandum.

---

overreach by Richard Nixon. Initially, when dealing with alleged terrorists captured overseas, especially in Afghanistan, the Bush administration chose to operate outside both domestic and international precedents and detain captives at a new facility in the U.S. enclave at Guantanamo Bay, Cuba. Later, it devised special legal

The federal criminal statute prohibits torture abroad, but not cruel, unusual inhuman treatment. In a traditional war, we may not need intelligence information from captures because we can survey troop movements, but when we're fighting a non-state actor, probably the only way to pre-emptively stop an attack is to gain intelligence from captured operatives.

Professor Waldron, again, disputed such a view, especially in response to a question from the debate's moderator about the legitimacy of using any means necessary to obtain information from someone who knows about the whereabouts of a "ticking time bomb," the explosion of which would cause extensive loss of life. This often-used hypothetical question, Professor Waldron argued, was

... corrupt [as a matter of fact because it] supposes that torture is capable of getting accurate information. The war on terror is a war of information and intelligence. To think primarily in terms of TV scenarios of massively important pieces of information that we know are there is not realistic. The nature of the relationship between torturer and victim means that the victim will tell the torturer what the torturer thinks he wants to know.

Also, the question assumes that somehow we have the people who are trained to torture, yet who will do it only in this one case. There will be a cadre of torturers sitting around looking for work. There will be a culture of torture developed, changing the politics, training and discipline of the CIA and FBI. Everything we know about torture from the 20th century is that it grows out of control. We unleash everything depraved and sadistic in human affairs. We need to think about the trauma to the legal system, of having it be known that we have concocted room for torture. Everything that's had its reference on respect for human dignity begins to totter and crumble under this response.

Q What strategy does the Justice Department memorandum, as framed by Professor Yoo, employ to claim it is not endorsing torture?

Q How does Professor Waldron counter this strategy?

Q In the debate at Columbia Law School, how does Professor Yoo invoke the "realities" of the war on terror to defend the position outlined in his memorandum?

Q What, according to Professor Waldron, will be the real-world consequences of using interrogation methods that, by any use of ordinary language, amount to "torture"?

Sources: (first) From March 14, 2003 Memorandum by John Yoo for William J. Haynes, General Counsel of the Department of Defense Re: Military Interrogation of Alien Unlawful Combatants Held Outside the United States. This is a public document, accessed at: https://www.aclu.org/sites/default/files /pdfs/ safefree/yoo_army_torture_memo.pdf (pp. 44–45); (second) From April 2005 debate at Columbia University between law professor Jeremy Waldron of Columbia and law professor John Yoo of the University of California, Berkeley on the definition of torture. Accessed at: http://expost.blogspot.com/2005 /04/waldron-yoo-debate-on-torture.html.

procedures for trying detainees, which the U.S. Supreme Court, on three separate occasions, declared unconstitutional. The Bush administration bypassed the Foreign Intelligence Surveillance Act of 1978 (FISA), which mandated special procedures before undertaking domestic wiretaps, until it and Congress agreed on revisions to

FISA that granted surveillance agencies broader power to monitor communication networks in the name of safeguarding national security. The Bush administration also convinced Congress to renew the Patriot Act, which otherwise would have automatically expired in 2006.

Personnel changes in Washington drained some of the discord from the issues of war and presidential power during the final years of the Bush presidency. In late 2006, Bush named Robert Gates, a resourceful bureaucratic manager, to replace the mercurial Donald Rumsfeld as head of the Department of Defense. Gates helped design a new strategy for Iraq: **the surge**. It temporarily increased U.S. troop levels and placed in command General David Petraeus, an expert on counterinsurgency warfare. Deploying U.S. troops more selectively, General Petraeus also stepped up training for Iraqi forces and ramped up payments to tribal leaders in exchange for their political cooperation. The surge strategy reduced the level of civil violence and decreased political tension within Iraq as Bush prepared to leave office and began drawing down U.S. troop levels.

Divisions over Foreign Policy Direction   By the end of Bush's presidency, the wars in Afghanistan and Iraq had claimed the lives of nearly 5,000 U.S. troops. Iraqi civilian casualties numbered, by the most conservative estimates, in the tens of thousands. The war against terrorism also took a toll on the physical and mental health of U.S. service personnel who survived. (By the end of 2013, roughly half of those who had served in Iraq and Afghanistan had filed for permanent disability status.) By 2008, the ongoing occupation of Iraq was costing the United States $6 billion per month. George W. Bush, once a critic of "nation-building" projects, had embarked in Iraq on just such an effort, the largest in the history of the United States. With Americans deeply divided over the justification for the invasion and the conduct of the occupation, popular support for Bush dropped below 30 percent. This backlash against Bush helped the Democratic Party capture control of Congress in the midterm elections of November 2006.

Democratic critics, looking toward the election of 2008, articulated a foreign policy agenda that repudiated the Bush administration's neoconservative blueprint in favor of new approaches. They advocated a timetable for removing U.S. combat troops from Iraq, a renewed military and diplomatic effort to stabilize Afghanistan, and a clearer focus on al-Qaeda, which seemed increasingly entrenched in remote areas of Pakistan and Yemen. Critics also urged moving away from the military emphasis of the Bush years. In their view, Bush's unilateralism had neglected threats to national security that required international cooperation, such as securing loose stockpiles of nuclear material before they fell into the hands of terrorists.

Another threat, according to most scientists, involved human-made climate change. Republican neoconservatives opposed the Kyoto Protocol, under which nations would agree to curb emissions that contributed to global warming. Members of the Bush administration joined most other Republicans in rejecting the scientific case for climate change, and they objected to emission-reduction targets that did not apply evenhandedly to developed and developing nations. After a Republican-dominated Senate rejected the Kyoto Protocol, prominent Democrats, such as the former vice president, Al Gore, continued to highlight the dangers of climate change and advocate rejoining the international forums working on the issue. They also pressed for development of "green energy" sources that would both lessen U.S. reliance on supplies of oil from the Middle East and help reduce carbon output.

AN ECONOMY OF BUBBLE AND BUST, 1993–2008

In 2003, the Nobel Prize–winning economist Robert Lucas credited his generation with effectively mastering the "central problem of depression-prevention." He spoke for those who believed that the U.S. economy was enjoying "The Great Moderation," a term that signified a faith that the economy, increasingly free from the burdens of government regulation, would no longer face the extremes of boom and bust. At times, the economy might not perform to its optimum level, but downturns would be temporary— and moderate. This conviction dominated economic thought and policy-making during the 1990s and the first years of the 21st century. Then, beginning in 2006, the American economy reached the high point of what, in retrospect, was an economic-financial bubble that helped conceal other, dismal economic trends. During the Bush presidency, for example, the economy gained only about 3 million new jobs, a fraction of the total added during the 1990s. Economic trouble loomed on the horizon.

Deregulation of the Financial Sector during the 1990s   The financial sector had remained the most dynamic and exciting part of the economy throughout the 1990s. Its leaders could take credit for generating roughly 30 percent of all domestic profits by the mid-1990s. The financial industry produced profits and wealth—and the people who worked in it gained a special aura. Talented college graduates, primarily but not exclusively men, began abandoning plans to become physicians or engineers in favor of seeking the rewards and excitement associated with a financial career.

Robert Rubin, who accepted a huge pay cut when leaving Wall Street, assumed responsibility for coordinating the Clinton administration's economic policy-making. To execute this demanding and delicate task, Rubin recruited talented theorists and technicians from academia and the financial industry. In 1995, he became secretary of the treasury. Clinton's economic brain trust concluded that the late-20th-century economy had outgrown the New Deal regulatory structure, but it still saw a limited economic role for government. If the economy were to continue growing, these New Democrats argued, Washington occasionally needed to mount activist rescue efforts both at home and abroad to ensure that problems remained moderate in nature. They touted the 1995 effort that restored Mexico's financial and economic stability and one in 1998 that bailed out a shoddily run financial venture at home known as Long-Term Capital Management as textbook examples of their preference for government rescuing rather than regulating. For the most part, though, government needed to stand clear and continue removing regulations.

The Clinton administration and the Federal Reserve Board under Republican Alan Greenspan thus showed scant reverence for financial regulations from the New Deal era. In 1999, Rubin supported Republican senator Phil Gramm's successful effort to repeal the Glass-Steagall Act. "We have learned government is not the answer," said Gramm. "We have learned that freedom and competition are the answers" in the financial world.

The Clinton administration also resisted regulation of new financial products for fear of hampering innovation. Using regulatory ideas of the 1930s, a Clinton adviser once quipped, would be akin to forcing modern tennis pros to play with outmoded wooden rackets. Advocates of "Rubinomics" thus sided with financial interests outside the administration that wanted to translate the dominant faith in minimal regulation into congressional legislation. The Commodities Futures Modernization Act of 2000 prohibited Washington from regulating the new financial inventions called "derivatives."

Economics for a New Century, 2000–2006   The administration of Republican George W. Bush surpassed that of New Democrat Bill Clinton in its enthusiasm for supporting deregulation and promoting financial innovation. Henry (Hank) Paulson, who became secretary of the treasury in 2006, was another alumnus of Wall Street. Just before joining the Bush administration, Paulson had successfully pressed federal regulators to exempt the five largest investment houses, including his own Goldman Sachs, from a rule that required investment firms to reserve a specific amount of capital to cover their debt obligations. This move dramatically increased the capacity of these five firms to borrow money and, consequently, to speculate in risky investments.

Critics of deregulation noted early signs of trouble. During 2002, several fraud-plagued firms fell into bankruptcy. The most spectacular case involved Enron, a Texas-based energy firm with close ties to members of the Bush administration. The absence of effective regulation had allowed the company to engage in legally suspect speculation in the trading of energy-related contracts and in clearly illegal bookkeeping that lifted its profits to fictional heights. Congress responded with legislation (the Sarbanes-Oxley Act of 2002) designed to prevent publicly traded companies from fraudulently reporting their financial condition as Enron and others had done.

The financial and political impact of the scandals of the early 2000s paled in comparison to larger systemic problems in the real estate sector. The Bush administration had quickly abandoned its predecessor's commitment to balanced budgets and a small federal deficit, but it retained its goal of promoting homeownership. Owning a home, according to conventional wisdom, increased people's ties to their communities and provided a rock-solid financial investment. Bush touted the importance of an "ownership society," and his administration encouraged financial institutions to help low- and moderate-income homebuyers. By 2006, nearly 70 percent of households lived in their own homes, an all-time high.

The nation, however, became increasingly caught up in an unsustainable **housing bubble**. Why? First, as more buyers entered the housing market, prices for new and existing homes moved upward and then skyrocketed toward the stratosphere. Many people who desired—and were being urged—to become homeowners simply lacked household incomes that could handle a conventional mortgage.

Second, the home lending industry devised an array of "nonconventional" mortgages for people whose incomes or credit histories disqualified them from obtaining a fixed rate loan. By 2006, far too many new loans involved **subprime mortgages**, meaning that they, unlike those of better quality, carried a high risk of default. In 2001, less than 10 percent of home mortgages had qualified as less than prime quality. In contrast, 40 percent of the new loans processed between 2001 and 2006 fell into this category.

Third, problems extended beyond subprime mortgages. People with houses whose market value had dramatically increased could refinance their existing mortgage at a lower interest rate. As if by magic, refinancing on the basis of the higher valuation gave them more money to spend. Mortgage refinancing helped stimulate overall economic activity but at the risk of creating mortgage holders who would, if the economy seriously faltered, be unable to meet their payments.

Fourth, people at the commanding heights of the financial system worked overtime to boost the residential housing market. They recognized that the home-buying and home-building industries were the primary engines driving the U.S., and even much of the world, economy. The Federal Reserve Board, under Alan Greenspan (who began a fifth term in 2002) and his successor Ben Bernanke (who took over in 2006), pegged interest rates at historic lows. This kept relatively "cheap money" flowing through the financial sector—and kept the residential housing market bubbling. Greenspan and Bernanke insisted, however, that economic "fundamentals" remained sound.

Finally, the giant firms at the top of the financial structure kept their optimistic risk assessments in place. Compliant investing services such as Moody's provided "low-risk" ratings for the mortgage-backed collateralized debt obligations (CDOs) that investment firms such as Goldman Sachs and Lehman Brothers were marketing as top-grade securities.

By 2006, knowledgeable observers all along the line detected a bubble about to burst. At the grassroots level, perceptive lenders privately joked about offering "pick-a-payment loans" and dealing with "zombie buyers," whose newly minted mortgages were virtually certain to go into default. The fabled investor Warren Buffett of Berkshire Hathaway called mortgage-backed CDOs "financial weapons of mass destruction" and forecast trouble for the home loan industry: "Dumb lending always has its consequences."

The Bubble Bursts, 2006–2008   Buffett, long-hailed as "the Oracle of Omaha," proved prophetic. Beginning in late 2006, the rise in housing prices first slowed and, then, home prices headed rapidly downward. The financial industry soon fell victim to the housing bubble it had helped inflate. As loans went into default, the ripple effect cascaded into financial institutions overloaded with mortgage-derived securities. Credit stopped flowing, and economies throughout the world began to contract. As economic growth halted in most places in the world, future factory orders declined, and unemployment figures rose.

The Bush administration and the Federal Reserve's Bernanke sought to respond. First, the Fed extended massive financial assistance to the banking industry. Then, during spring 2008, Bernanke's Federal Reserve and the Treasury Department's Hank Paulson helped J. P. Morgan Chase acquire a rival Wall Street firm headed for bankruptcy, but later allowed Lehman Brothers, another Wall Street stalwart, to collapse. The Bush administration and the Fed appeared to be signaling that a short-lived era of governmental rescue was over.

Almost instantaneously, a complete global financial meltdown loomed. In a massive sell-off, the Dow Jones stock average plummeted nearly 20 percent during a single week in early October 2008. People began draining cash from their savings and money market accounts. The world's financial system seized up, as it had done at the start of the Great Depression of the 1930s. The economy began to slip into what would later be known as the "Great Recession."

Bush's Treasury Department, the Federal Reserve, and governments around the world recognized the need for a coordinated response to the immediate financial crisis. Paulson hastily designed a rescue plan and Congress passed a revised version as the Emergency Economic Stabilization Act of 2008, enacted with greater support from Democrats than from Republicans. It included the **Troubled Assets Relief Program (TARP)**. Implicitly based on the principle that giant financial institutions were "too big to fail" or to go through normal bankruptcy procedures, TARP empowered the Treasury Department, guided only by loosely defined rules, to spread $700 billion throughout the financial system.

The Election of 2008   Differences over how to respond to this Great Recession dominated the 2008 political season. The presidential contest featured septuagenarian Republican senator John McCain of Arizona and his much-younger senatorial colleague, Democrat **Barack Obama**. The Democratic effort capitalized on a media-savvy campaign staff, an innovative fundraising operation, Obama's skills at oratory, and the unpopularity of the outgoing Bush administration. The Obama campaign also energized many of the movements, such as those opposing immigration restriction and favoring gay rights, which had become active during the early years of the 21st century. Many voters blamed Bush for the economic morass and viewed McCain, who admitted to knowing little about the economy, as lagging behind Obama in economic sagacity. Obama's campaign featured two words: "hope" and "change."

McCain's zigzag effort undercut his always-slim chances for victory. He distanced his own campaign from the false claims that Obama had not been born in the United States (and therefore was ineligible for the presidency) and secretly practiced Islam. McCain's gamble in selecting Alaska's half-term governor, Sarah Palin, as a running mate mollified some of the most conservative Republicans but dismayed independents and crossover Democrats.

Veteran pundits who personally admired McCain expected a very close finish, but younger, Internet-based forecasters correctly predicted a fairly substantial Obama victory. Young voters turned out in record numbers. Voting by Latinos and Asian Americans also reached all-time highs. In contrast, the percentage of white Americans casting ballots fell slightly from that of 2004. Forty-three percent of this vote, a slight increase from what Kerry had gained four years prior, went to Obama. In addition to the presidency, the Democratic Party picked up seats in both branches of Congress and in many state and local races, especially outside the South.

CHANGING TIMES, 2009–

Barack Obama's administrative team displayed even greater diversity—and more star power—than had those of Clinton and Bush. The key position of secretary of state went to Hillary Clinton. Steven Chu, a Nobel Prize winner, became secretary of energy. Perhaps most crucially, Robert Gates, a Republican who had been a calming presence toward the end of Bush's presidency, agreed to remain as secretary of defense. The president's inaugural address urged the nation to tackle the current crises with "hope and virtue."

Political Polarization   The appointment of Gates signaled Obama's inclination to reach out to Republicans and thus disappointed Democrats hoping for fundamental changes. The new administration's stance on counterterrorism, for instance, initially resembled that employed during the final years of the Bush presidency. It set aside, after fierce opposition from Republicans in Congress, Obama's earlier pledge to close the detention facility at Guantanamo and try terrorist suspects in U.S. courts. Civil libertarians found only minor differences between the broad legal-constitutional claims for executive power made by the Bush and Obama administrations. On the crucial economic front, Timothy Geithner, a Federal Reserve official who had helped devise the Bush administration's financial bailout of 2008, became Obama's treasury secretary, and the new president reappointed Ben Bernanke to lead the Federal Reserve Board.

In the Middle East, the Obama administration brought modest changes of emphasis. In Afghanistan and along that nation's border with Pakistan, it upped troop levels, placed increased reliance on air attacks by unmanned drones, and budgeted additional financial resources. It authorized an ambitious counterinsurgency

Shawn Thew-Pool/Getty Images

The First Family, 2013. *President Barack Obama walks with his wife, Michelle (right), and two daughters, Malia (left) and Sasha (second from right), through Lafayette Park to St. John's Church in Washington, D.C.*

effort against the Taliban modeled on the surge in Iraq, pressed the Afghani government to rein in corruption, and pressured Pakistani officials to move more determinedly against Taliban supporters in their own country. The administration, however, promised to withdraw troops by 2014 and continued Bush's troop withdrawal from Iraq.

Most domestic initiatives, however, produced steadily escalating Republican opposition. The Obama administration could claim some victories—Senate confirmation of two Supreme Court nominees (Sonia Sotomayor and Elena Kagan), a law regulating tobacco products, an expansion of Bush's effort to bail out auto manufacturers, another measure extending land conservation policies, and yet another creating a "bill of rights" for credit card holders. Only three Republican senators (and no Republican representatives in the House), however, supported its plan to stimulate the economy. The American Recovery and Reinvestment Act of 2009, popularly known as "the Stimulus," provided $212 billion in tax cuts and $575 billion in new federal spending. A congressional measure to re-regulate parts of the financial industry passed in the face of Republican criticism.

Months of negotiation between the White House and congressional Democrats finally yielded the **Affordable Health Care for America Act** of 2010 (also known as the Affordable Care Act or ACA). Republicans revived the strategy used to derail the Clinton health-care plan 16 years earlier and unanimously opposed the measure. ACA's proponents, however, rounded up just enough Democratic votes to pass the law designed to extend, over time, coverage to some 30 million people. The ACA also expanded the Medicaid system, created mechanisms (called "exchanges") for increasing competition among insurance companies, and prohibited insurers from denying coverage to people with preexisting health conditions. Its most controversial provision required every American to carry health insurance. Critics charged that the ACA would surely cost much more than official estimates, endanger the Medicare program, kill off jobs, and create uncertainty throughout the health-care system. The administration countered with studies that showed it saving money and making health care available to all Americans.

The GOP's most conservative factions rebranded themselves as part of a "Tea Party" movement and threatened primary challenges to any Republican incumbent tempted to support White House initiatives. Pressed by Tea Party activists, the GOP increasingly portrayed Obama as a danger to fundamental liberties and accelerated the party's decades-long movement toward the political right. To the horror of economists supportive of Keynesian policies, Republicans rejected any hint of additional federal spending to stimulate a still-sputtering economy and insisted that cutting governmental programs and lowering the federal deficit should take precedence over programs for creating jobs and assisting unemployed workers. A familiar question resurfaced: Was government action the core cause of economic problems or a necessary part of their solutions?

An explosion in April 2010, of a BP (formerly British Petroleum) pumping rig in the Gulf of Mexico—which took 11 lives and sent 62,000 barrels of oil a day spilling into the water and fragile coastal habitats—focused further debate about this contentious question. The White House immediately joined BP in devising a response effort, but environmental groups criticized Obama for having failed to change the regulatory approach of his predecessor quickly enough and for permitting BP to direct the cleanup. Republicans simultaneously criticized the president for overmanaging the federal government's response and for pressuring BP and the oil industry to change their drilling practices.

The GOP ran squarely against Obama and his domestic policies in the midterm elections of 2010. The party's most conservative Tea Party activists denounced Democrats as well as Republican "RINOS" (Republicans In Name Only), whom they considered insufficiently oppositional. GOP primary contests eliminated a number of Republican stalwarts in favor of Tea Party activists. Democratic candidates, especially those who had benefited in 2006 and 2008 from economic turmoil and an unpopular Republican president, found themselves burdened by a jobless economic recovery and their own embattled president. In contrast to 2008, many younger voters stayed home in 2010 while older ones, who tended to favor Republican candidates, turned out in higher numbers. Republicans linked Obama to continued high unemployment and federal budget deficits, legacies of the Great Recession that began before his presidency. As a result, the 2010 midterm elections followed a long-familiar pattern: The party controlling the White House and Congress almost always loses legislative seats.

The results of the GOP's well-funded electoral effort, however, exceeded the historical averages and the early projections of most analysts. Republicans took control of the House of Representatives, cut into the Democrats' majority in the Senate, and gained more than 600 legislative seats and 20 gubernatorial offices in states throughout the country. A national political culture marked by extreme partisanship, dramatically shifting electoral outcomes, and new communication technologies would surely continue into a new decade.

The Digital Domain of Liberty, Equality, Power

Life during the early 21st century increasingly unfolded within a digitized environment. Any institution, movement, or individual hoping to make a mark on the world did so by leaving digital footprints. The Internet, for example, increasingly influenced post-2000 elections, along with the fundraising and campaigning that accompanied them. One of the creators of the **social networking** service Facebook joined the Obama team early on and helped build the Internet-assisted operations that outperformed the digital campaigns of John McCain and Mitt Romney in 2008 and 2012. Similarly, the blueprint for health-care reform rested on a vision of creating a series of Web sites, headed by healthcare.gov, for enrolling people in new insurance plans; of digitizing all patient records; and of monitoring and sharing these records to facilitate greater efficiency and better patient care. A 2014 memoir by a professor of medicine with 60 years of teaching experience but hardly any as a hospital patient discovered that his team of much younger physicians "spent most of their time outside my room, studying and discussing the data on their mobile computers."

Celebrants of a digital future proclaimed that new technologies could forge networks that transcended the boundaries of time and space far more quickly and effectively than the best machinery from the old analog world. Only four years into the 21st century, undergraduates at Harvard University created Facebook to facilitate "linking up" with other students. The venture quickly attracted wealthy investors from Silicon Valley and tapped sufficient advertising revenue to make its operations profitable by 2009. YouTube, developed by Silicon Valley entrepreneurs in 2005, offered a different kind of social networking model. People could post footage derived from motion picture and TV sources; music from just about anywhere; and, most importantly, original material they had created. Its rate of growth, a measure of the popular desire to produce as well as consume visual imagery, surpassed even that of Facebook, and YouTube eventually became part of Google's digital empire. *Time* magazine, seeing the handwriting (or imagery) on the wall, selected You—all of the millions of people using networking sites—as its Person of the Year for 2008. By this time, well over a billion people were using the Internet to facilitate both their social and workplace lives.

The specter of a digitized world worried some observers. They feared that Internet news and commentary only expanded the adversarial framework that had come to dominate cable TV news. They saw Internet "bloggers" preying on the legwork of journalists from print publications rather than doing original reporting. At the same time, online sites were luring readers from print publications and thus diminishing their value to potential advertisers. Losing readership and revenue, magazines and newspapers began to cease publication. Frequent Internet postings, moreover, seemed to be accelerating the already frenetic 24/7 news cycle. American politics was becoming "an almost minute-by-minute spectacle," growled an editor at one embattled newspaper. While voicing analogous concerns about the cultural impact of social networking sites, critics also feared that linking up digitally would obliterate traditional notions of privacy and threaten the safety of the young and vulnerable.

Champions of the Internet, however, praised it—and the larger digital environment—for creating new networks that could help people reimagine liberty, equality, and power. Freely shared and communally developed software might help liberate communication from corporate control. Interactive Internet sites might empower people and challenge hierarchical arrangements. Political activists as well as ordinary users might employ Web sites and networking services such as Facebook to evade traditional media gatekeepers. Internet journalists, especially those adept at using digitized data, effectively took on, and oftentimes took down, media commentators and spinmeisters for special interests. Networking sites helped reconfigure restaurant, TV, and motion picture reviews by aggregating responses from diners and audiences without special expertise in culinary or cultural artistry, a form of populist criticism that bypassed reviewing elites. Wikipedia supplanted hard-copy encyclopedias with a collaboratively written, ever-changing, and controversial source on virtually everything. Even history textbooks began to devise more participatory digital formats.

The most ebullient of digital enthusiasts heralded the arrival of a new epoch in human history, one in which older institutions and routines, especially of governance, seemed outdated. In the wake of the earthquake that devastated large parts of Haiti (in 2010) and the massive storm that devastated a Philippines (in 2013), for instance, "computer geeks" mobilized their browsers, pointed them toward digital imagery of disaster scenes, and used the power of "crowdsourcing" to pinpoint especially hard-hit areas more rapidly than governmental and private relief bureaucracies. And the collapse—and extraordinarily expensive rescue—of much of the world's banking system in 2008–2009 encouraged digital visionaries to introduce "bitcoin." This digitized monetary system, based on open-source software and operated independently of governmental regulators, brought concern and ridicule from financial experts who saw the theoretical and practical pitfalls of this peer-to-peer medium of exchange as insolvable. Bitcoin's libertarian-leaning supporters, though, argued that virtually every earlier digital enterprise, including Amazon and Facebook, had once faced similar scorn.

For almost everyone, online connectivity through increasingly smaller devices and screens became ever more integral to daily life. Most people, especially those who had grown up in the digital world, seemed inclined to accept the collection, storage, and dissemination of digitized data on a massive scale as inevitable. What some called "Big Data" seemed a new source of immense power. Might the result foster tighter forms of centralized control—and new ideas about the meaning of liberty and equality?

The Election of 2012

Intense partisanship shaped the 2012 election season. The Republican leader of the U.S. Senate announced a simple priority: managing the GOP minority so that Obama would be a one-term president. When Chief Justice John Roberts, a conservative Republican, voted to uphold the constitutionality of the Obama-sponsored Affordable Care Act of 2010, many other GOP conservatives denounced his breaking ranks as tantamount to political treason.

As the center of the Republican Party continued to move rightward, W. Mitt Romney struggled to gain its presidential nomination. The GOP's conservative stalwarts had long distrusted Romney's commitment to their views on issues such as abortion, taxes, immigration, and health care. Romney—a wealthy venture capitalist from a devout Mormon family with a long record of governmental service—sought to win them over by pledging a presidency that would scale back government regulations, slash taxes, expand the military, and erase the federal budget deficit through spending cuts. Seeking to mobilize the Republican base, Romney also advocated the immediate repeal of what the Republicans derisively called "Obamacare," termination of federal funding for Planned Parenthood, and elimination or reduction of the disaster relief programs of the Federal Emergency Management Agency (FEMA). He also selected U.S. Representative Paul Ryan of Wisconsin, a conservative favorite, as his running mate. The broader Republican campaign of 2012 denounced Obama's presidency as "socialistic," and its fiercest anti-Obama spokespeople fueled suspicions grounded in the president's racial heritage and spread misinformation about his religious faith.

As the general election neared, however, the Romney campaign tried to hit the reset button. The candidate cautiously endorsed most of Obama's foreign policy moves, praised popular provisions of the Affordable Care Act, and promised to work with congressional Democrats on taxes and spending. The Romney camp enjoyed lavish funding as a consequence of the Supreme Court's decision to strike down previous limits on political contributions in its *Citizens United v. Federal Election Commission* decision (2010).

The Obama campaign, which also garnered sizable donations, focused on several central themes. It touted Obama's first term for achieving health-care legislation, for stabilizing financial institutions and saving the auto industry, improving broader economic conditions, killing Osama bin Laden, and winding down the unpopular wars in Iraq and Afghanistan. More often, though, Democrats were on the attack, assailing Romney as beholden to ultraconservatives on social issues, such as abortion and contraception, and to the very wealthy on tax policy. They also charged the Romney-Ryan ticket with failing to show a clear link between its vague economic proposals and its promise of "millions of new jobs." Moreover, Democrats firmly backed immigration reform.

Supporters of the Republican candidate ridiculed statistical data that showed Obama was maintaining a solid lead and apparently expected a Romney victory, but the president dominated the Electoral College vote and captured the popular one as well. The Romney campaign did best among white voters, especially men, over the age of 50, while Obama won overwhelming majorities among African Americans, Hispanics, and Asian Americans. About 55 percent of women voters broke for Obama, and people between the ages of 18 and 29, who voted in record numbers, strongly supported the president.

The post-electoral cycle of partisan spin, 140-character "tweets," and lengthy data-rich analyses quickly began. While some Republican strategists were debating fears that their party faced an inevitably shrinking demographic base, those from the Democratic side were hoping the nation's changing demography offered the opportunity to forge a new Democratic-dominated political era. But with Democrats solidifying their hold over the Senate and Republicans maintaining their majority in the House, the safest prediction remained that national governance would stay polarized along partisan lines.

Contentious Times   Political polarization affected a wide range of issues. When matters such as climate change, gun laws, or even personal sexuality entered the political arena, differences over both underlying values and specific policies tracked "blue" (Democratic) versus "red" (Republican) divisions at the state, county, city, and even neighborhood levels. Increasingly, Republicans tended to live near other Republicans and Democrats near other Democrats, and people seemed inclined to discuss public issues with only those whose partisan preferences and sources of information approximated their own. Not surprisingly, the elections of 2012 saw about 90 percent of voters casting either a straight Republican or Democratic ballot rather than selecting candidates from both major parties.

Similarly, Congress became more polarized than at any time since the 19th century. The GOP's commitment to scuttling the ACA, for example, prompted the Republican-controlled House of Representatives to take more than 50 votes on bills to repeal it, even though there was no chance the Senate would have concurred. Republicans in the Senate made the filibuster, once a relatively rare parliamentary maneuver, central to a larger strategy of blocking Democratic legislative initiatives and presidential appointments. House Speaker John Boehner, who sometimes seemed willing to bargain with the Democrats over various issues, including immigration policy, struggled to control the Tea Party wing of his own Republican caucus. Even solidly conservative Republican senators and representatives came to fear primary challenges from their political right more than general-election contests

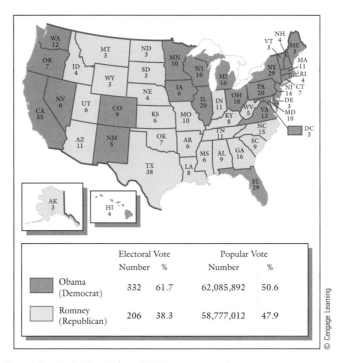

	Electoral Vote		Popular Vote	
	Number	%	Number	%
Obama (Democrat)	332	61.7	62,085,892	50.6
Romney (Republican)	206	38.3	58,777,012	47.9

© Cengage Learning

MAP 32.2 Presidential Election, 2012

President Barack Obama won a second term by dominating the Electoral College vote. He also captured the popular vote.

against Democrats. For their part, Democratic congressional candidates generally saw little to be gained from appealing to voters unlikely to vote a crossover ticket, a situation that only ratcheted up the polarization.

Partisan conflict spread even to issues on which there had long been grounds for bipartisan votes. Republicans in the House, for example, revolted against the long-standing, across-the-aisle practice of preserving the nation's credit rating by raising the debt ceiling unless the White House backtracked on implementing the ACA. In the fall of 2013 they orchestrated a 16-day shutdown of many federal government operations in an effort to delay or suspend the heath-care program. The parties did reach an agreement on budget deficit reduction through "sequestration"—a mandate for across-the-board spending reductions—but hopes for a "grand bargain" involving both selective spending cuts and revenue enhancements failed to materialize. Republicans claimed that the great-est threat to America came from Washington—and from a president hostile to basic lib-erties. Democrats, highlighting the country's growing economic inequality, decried cutting domestic programs that helped the poor and unemployed and favored tax increases on the very wealthy. The legislative machinery in Washington slowed down and, then, ground to a virtual halt. The 113th Congress passed fewer than 60 bills during 2013, and many Republicans hailed this record-low number as a positive sign.

Decisions in the federal court system also followed broader patterns of polari-zation. A 2013 Supreme Court decision (that broke 5–4 along partisan lines) declared a key provision of an iconic civil rights law, the Voting Rights Act of

1965, to be unconstitutional. This decision meant that nine states, eight of them in the now Republican-dominated South and all with a pre-1965 history of overtly discriminating against non-Caucasian voters, could now revise their electoral procedures without prior approval from the Justice Department. Chief Justice John Roberts argued that the forms of racial discrimination against which Congress had legislated in 1965 no longer existed, and Republican activists promoted the idea that states needed wider authority to enact laws that would prevent people who were ineligible to vote from casting ballots. Democrats, by contrast, warned that racial discrimination could reemerge in new and less visible ways, and they challenged claims that voter fraud had become a serious problem.

Debate over social and economic policies became another partisan flashpoint, especially after studies conclusively showed that the economic recovery, which had done little to help the long-term unemployed, had been far more beneficial to stock prices on Wall Street and to the wealthiest 1 percent of the population than to the 99 percent of Americans below the super-rich category. Claims that such inequality represented the consequences of post-1970 economic policy and merited redress, however, sparked emotional, polarized debates that recalled—and also went beyond—those over the war on poverty of the 1960s. Were governmental policies the cause or the cure for some people falling behind economically? Were people without work or stuck in low-paying jobs deserving of taxpayer assistance, or were their own failings the primary cause of their situation?

Such general questions prompted highly partisan controversy on a range of specific policy issues such as unemployment insurance and the minimum wage rate. In 2014, for example, when Democrats in the Senate finally found enough Republican votes to break a filibuster against a bill extending payments to the long-term unemployed, the Republican leadership in the House declared it would not even consider such a measure. Similarly, calls for raising the federal minimum wage to $10.10 (the current rate of $7.25 had declined to less than $5 per hour when measured in constant dollars) won widespread support from Democrats but virtually none from Republicans. Neo-Keynesian economists cited models showing that a hike in the minimum wage would both benefit low-paid workers and, by boosting demand for goods and services, stimulate economic growth. Free-market economists countered with models depicting how a higher minimum wage would increase unemployment and generate renewed inflation; they continued to call for new tax cuts and reduction of the federal deficit as the path toward improving both workers' pay and the economy's overall health. Economists from both of these warring camps found fault with a nuanced study by the nonpartisan Congressional Budget Office that forecast both gains and losses from raising the federal minimum wage.

The dynamics of hyperpolarization continued to revolve around the Affordable Care Act. It had passed both houses of Congress without a single Republican vote, the only sign of bipartisanship being the 30-plus House Democrats who had voted against it, and had remained the object of constant legislative wrangling. During the fall of 2013, however, the Obama administration mishandled the rollout of the Web site for the new program. Republicans envisioned this bumpy beginning as a harbinger of future failures, but actual enrollments eventually came to roughly match those predicted, passing the 8 million mark in early 2014. The ACA's opponents took out major attack ads charging that "Obamacare" was harming

A Revolution in Warfare. *A remotely controlled Predator drone takes off from Balad Air Base, Iraq.*

health-care consumers, even as the president and the law's supporters used every possible venue—including an Internet comedy show—to encourage participation and tout the overall benefits they saw the ACA ultimately providing. Polls during spring 2014 showed a slim majority of respondents either approving of the ACA or favoring an even more extensive overhaul of existing health-care arrangements.

Controversies over the ACA both reflected and stoked regionally based partisan configurations. Although the Supreme Court had upheld the constitutionality of the act's requirement that everyone be required to purchase insurance, the justices also ruled that the national government lacked the constitutional power to require states to participate in the ACA's expansion of Medicaid. Consequently, solidly Republican states, particularly in the South, refused to expand their Medicaid rolls. Some red state activists tried to leverage the broader constitutional logic of this ruling against federal power into claims that states could openly nullify federal mandates, especially those related to Second Amendment rights, gay marriage, and access to federal land. In addition, conservative constitutional lawyers pressed arguments that the First Amendment's free exercise of religion clause should bar Washington from enforcing provisions of the ACA, such as requirements for covering birth control and abortions, on groups and corporations who asserted religiously based objections.

Foreign policy issues added to controversy during Obama's second term. Obama had rejected the Bush administration's controversial methods of "enhanced interrogation" that were tantamount to torture, but his national security team enhanced other Bush-era developments such as broad data sweeps to gather information about potential terrorism and remotely controlled drones or unmanned aerial vehicles (UAVs) to kill people designated as enemies.

The post-9/11 increase in data collection by the CIA and the National Security Agency (NSA) became especially contested after Edward Snowden, a former NSA civilian-contract employee, revealed a massive surveillance operation that extended from collecting the phone call data of ordinary American citizens to monitoring the communications of foreign leaders. In the wake of Snowden's 2013 release of classified documents, which recalled but dwarfed that by Daniel Ellsberg in the 1970s, investigators uncovered controversial practices of data collection and data mining. The Obama administration rejected arguments that Snowden merited protection as a whistleblower, indicted him for espionage, and convened a presidential task force to recommend new rules for safeguarding privacy while still collecting massive amounts of information on the grounds of national security. Senators, however, learned that secretive CIA surveillance even extended into the halls of government; they discovered that the CIA had covertly monitored a Senate investigation into possible CIA involvement in the torture of suspected terrorists between 2002 and 2006.

Although the Obama administration stepped up its commitment to withdrawing military forces from Afghanistan, it also greatly expanded the use of drones, often directed from computer terminals in the United States, against suspected terrorists overseas. Very quickly, these UAVs became favored weapons, and a special group within the Obama White House approved which people, including American citizens living abroad who were deemed terrorists, merited inclusion on a "kill list." Although the administration defended drone operations as carefully targeted, critics charged they could produce casualties among innocent people near a drone strike and therefore might actually create more enemies. Moreover, the secrecy surrounding the selection of victims, civil libertarians charged, violated the most elementary legal and constitutional protections, such as a public indictment and a trial in open court prior to punishment. Opinion polls, however, showed overwhelming popular support in the United States for the use of drones as a substitute for American "boots on the ground."

Obama's foreign policy faced growing challenges as the midterm elections of 2014 approached. Republicans, especially those on the party's far right had been charging the Obama administration, particularly the president and Hilary Clinton, with serious misconduct surrounding two September 11, 2012 attacks by Islamic terrorists in Benghazi, Libya, that took the lives of 4 Americans. Libya, however, was not the only country descending into chaos. A civil war raged in Syria, and as religious rivalries among different Islamic groups spread throughout the region, Iraq fell apart. A militant Sunni group gained control of Iraq's western regions even as regional Kurdish leaders assumed greater sovereignty in its northeast. Meanwhile, civil strife surged in Ukraine, where factions allied with Western Europe and with Russia faced off against each other and threatened to re-ignite the rivalries of the cold war. While some people called for greater assertion of U.S. power in such troubled regions, others argued that the complexities of multipolar alliances necessitated a measured assessment and response.

Debate over domestic and foreign policies, especially the U.S. role in the Middle East, escalated during the summer and fall of 2014. A group calling itself the Islamic State, a violent fundamentalist Sunni group, declared formation of a new Islamic "caliphate" based in eastern Syria and parts of Northern Iraq. While the Islamic State seized more and more Iraqi territory, the Shia-dominated armies of the central government proved ineffective. Moreover, the Islamic State released videos showing the gruesome beheadings of two western journalists. In response, President Obama announced in early September a "comprehensive strategy": an expanded air war led by the United States, more arms and additional training to local groups fighting against the Islamic State, and mobilization of international allies including those in the Arab world. Although the President ruled out any reintroduction of U.S. ground forces into Iraq, he dispatched several hundred troops to "advise and assist" the Iraqi military and the Kurdish peshmerga forces who were engaging fighters from the Islamic State.

Uncertainty over the international situation rippled through an already bitterly partisan political season, one in which billions of dollars financed especially nasty campaigns. The mid-term election of November 2014 suggested that a majority of voters were confused about contested issues or simply disgruntled by politics in general. The turnout fell under 40 percent, the lowest since 1940. People inclined to vote Democratic, especially younger people, sat out the election in far greater numbers than older, Republican stalwarts, reinforcing the longstanding pattern in which any party holding the White House stood to lose seats in mid-term balloting. A wave of Republican victories resulted. The GOP took control of the U.S. Senate and padded its majority in the House of Representatives. The nation faced its future with a sharper-than-ever partisan division between executive and congressional branches of the national government.

CONCLUSION

Three presidents, two of them Democrats and one a Republican, dominated national politics at the end of the 20th and the beginning of the 21st centuries. Bill Clinton's administration pressed a modest domestic agenda that moved the Democratic Party away from its "big government" image. It worked with Republicans to pare back the welfare system and supported economic policies that eliminated the federal deficit. As partisan polarization escalated during the late 1990s, however, Clinton's personal behavior ensnared him in legal investigations that led to an impeachment trial in 1999. The Bush administration's conservative agenda featured tax cuts, deregulation, overhaul of education practices, and an expensive prescription drug subsidy. It also converted the budget surplus left by Clinton into a rising federal deficit.

The U.S. economy enjoyed a lengthy period of sustained growth during the 1990s, but the early years of the 21st century produced a mixed picture. The financial industry continued to reap phenomenal profits, aided by a spectacular bubble in the residential housing market. In 2007, declining home prices and a wave of mortgage foreclosures rocked the financial sector, and the impact rippled quickly throughout the entire global economy. Although the Bush administration and the Federal Reserve Board, with more Democratic than Republican support, rescued the financial industry, the larger economy slid into the Great Recession, the worst since the 1930s.

Both Clinton and Bush tried to chart foreign policies for a post–cold war world. Clinton's internationalist policy deployed military power selectively and concentrated on measures fostering the globalization of economic relationships. After the terrorist attacks of 9/11, the Bush administration focused its unilateralist foreign policy on fighting a global "war on terror." The United States first invaded

Afghanistan and then attacked Iraq, where it began the kind of expensive "nation-building" project that Republicans had once opposed.

The country's expanding economic distress and the growing unpopularity of the war in Iraq helped the Democratic Party regain control of Congress in 2006 and lifted its standard-bearer, Barack Obama, to the presidency in 2008 and again in 2012. While seeking to help end the Great Recession, the Obama administration began a phased withdrawal of U.S. forces from Iraq and then Afghanistan, revamped the domestic health-care system, and returned some greater degree of regulation to the financial system. Discussions of social policy, international relations, and economic recovery continued against a polarized backdrop of hope and fear that increasingly circulated within rapidly changing forms of digitized networks.

Appendix A

The Declaration of Independence

The Unanimous Declaration of the Thirteen United States of America

When in the Course of human events it becomes necessary for one people to dissolve the political bands which have connected them with another, and to assume among the Powers of the earth, the separate and equal station to which the Laws of Nature and of Nature's God entitle them, a decent respect to the opinions of mankind requires that they should declare the causes which impel them to the separation.

We hold these truths to be self-evident, that all men are created equal, that they are endowed by their Creator with certain unalienable Rights, that among these are Life, Liberty and the pursuit of Happiness. That to secure these rights, Governments are instituted among Men, deriving their just Powers from the consent of the governed. That whenever any Form of Government becomes destructive of these ends, it is the Right of the People to alter or to abolish it, and to institute new Government, laying its foundation on such principles and organizing its Powers in such form, as to them shall seem most likely to effect their Safety and Happiness. Prudence, indeed, will dictate that Governments long established should not be changed for light and transient causes; and accordingly all experience hath shewn, that mankind are more disposed to suffer, while evils are sufferable, than to right themselves by abolishing the forms to which they are accustomed. But when a long train of abuses and usurpations, pursuing invariably the same Object evinces a design to reduce them under absolute Despotism, it is their right, it is their duty, to throw off such Government, and to provide new Guards for their future security. Such has been the patient sufferance of these Colonies; and such is now the necessity which constrains them to alter their former Systems of Government. The history of the present King of Great Britain is a history of repeated injuries and usurpations, all having in direct object the establishment of an absolute Tyranny over these States. To prove this, let Facts be submitted to a candid world.

He has refused his Assent to Laws, the most wholesome and necessary for the public good.

He has forbidden his Governors to pass Laws of immediate and pressing importance, unless suspended in their operation till his Assent should be obtained; and when so suspended, he has utterly neglected to attend to them.

He has refused to pass other Laws for the accommodation of large districts of people, unless those people would relinquish the right of Representation in the Legislature, a right inestimable to them and formidable to tyrants only.

He has called together legislative bodies at places unusual, uncomfortable, and distant from the depository of their Public Records, for the sole Purpose of fatiguing them into compliance with his measures.

He has dissolved Representative Houses repeatedly, for opposing with manly firmness his invasions on the rights of the People.

Text is reprinted from the facsimile of the engrossed copy in the National Archives. The original spelling, capitalization, and punctuation have been retained. Paragraphing has been added.

He has refused for a long time, after such dissolutions, to cause others to be elected; whereby the Legislative Powers, incapable of Annihilation, have returned to the People at large for their exercise; the State remaining in the mean time exposed to all the dangers of invasion from without, and convulsions within.

He has endeavoured to prevent the Population of these States; for that purpose obstructing the Laws for Naturalization of Foreigners; refusing to pass others to encourage their migrations hither, and raising the conditions of new Appropriations of Lands.

He has obstructed the Administration of Justice, by refusing his Assent to Laws for establishing Judiciary Powers.

He has made Judges dependent on his Will alone, for the tenure of their offices, and the amount and payment of their salaries.

He has erected a multitude of New Offices, and sent hither swarms of Officers to harass our People, and eat out their substance.

He has kept among us, in times of peace, Standing Armies without the Consent of our legislatures.

He has affected to render the Military independent of and superior to the Civil Power.

He has combined with others to subject us to a jurisdiction foreign to our constitution, and unacknowledged by our laws; giving his Assent to their Acts of pretended Legislation: For Quartering large bodies of armed troops among us: For protecting them, by a mock Trial, from Punishment for any Murders which they should commit on the Inhabitants of these States: For cutting off our Trade with all parts of the world: For imposing Taxes on us without our Consent: For depriving us in many cases, of the benefits of Trial by Jury: For transporting us beyond Seas to be tried for pretended offences: For abolishing the free System of English Laws in a neighbouring Province, establishing therein an Arbitrary government, and enlarging its Boundaries so as to render it at once an example and fit instrument for introducing the same absolute rule into these Colonies: For taking away our Charters, abolishing our most valuable Laws, and altering fundamentally the Forms of our Governments: For suspending our own Legislatures, and declaring themselves invested with Power to legislate for us in all cases whatsoever.

He has abdicated Government here, by declaring us out of his Protection, and waging War against us.

He has plundered our seas, ravaged our Coasts, burnt our towns, and destroyed the lives of our people.

He is at this time transporting large Armies of foreign Mercenaries to compleat the works of death, desolation and tyranny, already begun with circumstances of Cruelty and perfidy scarcely paralleled in the most barbarous ages, and totally unworthy the Head of a civilized nation.

He has constrained our fellow Citizens taken Captive on the high Seas to bear Arms against their Country, to become the executioners of their friends and Brethren, or to fall themselves by their Hands.

He has excited domestic insurrections amongst us, and has endeavoured to bring on the inhabitants of our frontiers, the merciless Indian Savages, whose known rule of warfare, is an undistinguished destruction of all ages, sexes and conditions.

In every stage of these Oppressions We have Petitioned for Redress in the most humble terms: Our repeated Petitions have been answered only by repeated injury. A Prince, whose character is thus marked by every act which may define a Tyrant, is unfit to be the ruler of a free People.

Nor have We been wanting in attentions to our British brethren. We have warned them from time to time of attempts by their legislature to extend an unwarrantable jurisdiction over us. We have reminded them of the circumstances of our emigration and settlement here. We have appealed to their native justice and magnanimity, and we have conjured them by the ties of our common kindred to disavow these usurpations, which, would inevitably interrupt our connections and correspondence. They too have been deaf to the voice of justice and of consanguinity. We must, therefore, acquiesce in the necessity, which denounces our Separation, and hold them, as we hold the rest of mankind, Enemies in War, in Peace Friends.

We, therefore, the Representatives of the United States of America, in General Congress, Assembled, appealing to the Supreme Judge of the world for the rectitude of our intentions, do, in the Name, and by Authority of the good People of these Colonies, solemnly publish and declare, That these United Colonies are, and of Right ought to be Free and Independent States;

that they are Absolved from all Allegiance to the British Crown, and that all political connection between them and the State of Great Britain, is and ought to be totally dissolved; and that, as Free and Independent States, they have full Power to levy War, conclude Peace, contract Alliances, establish Commerce, and to do all other Acts and Things which Independent States may of right do. And for the support of this Declaration, with a firm reliance on the protection of divine Providence, we mutually pledge to each other our Lives, our Fortunes and our sacred Honor.

Appendix B

THE CONSTITUTION OF THE UNITED STATES OF AMERICA

We the People of the United States, in Order to form a more perfect Union, establish Justice, insure domestic Tranquility, provide for the common defence, promote the general Welfare, and secure the Blessings of Liberty to ourselves and our Posterity, do ordain and establish this Constitution for the United States of America.

Article I

Section 1 All legislative Powers herein granted shall be vested in a Congress of the United States, which shall consist of a Senate and House of Representatives.

Section 2 The House of Representatives shall be composed of Members chosen every second Year by the People of the several States, and the Electors in each State shall have the Qualifications requisite for Electors of the most numerous Branch of the State Legislature.

No Person shall be a Representative who shall not have attained to the Age of twenty five Years, and been seven Years a Citizen of the United States, and who shall not, when elected, be an Inhabitant of that State in which he shall be chosen.

Representatives and direct Taxes[1] shall be apportioned among the several States which may be included within this Union, according to their respective Numbers, which shall be determined by adding to the whole Number of free Persons, including those bound to Service for a Term of Years, and excluding Indians not taxed, three fifths of all other Persons.[2]

The actual Enumeration shall be made within three Years after the first Meeting of the Congress of the United States, and within every subsequent Term of ten Years, in such Manner as they shall by Law direct. The Number of Representatives shall not exceed one for every thirty Thousand, but each State shall have at Least one Representative; and until such enumeration shall be made, the State of New Hampshire shall be entitled to chuse three; Massachusetts eight; Rhode Island and Providence Plantations one; Connecticut five; New York six; New Jersey four; Pennsylvania eight; Delaware one; Maryland six; Virginia ten; North Carolina five; South Carolina five; and Georgia three.

When vacancies happen in the Representation from any State, the Executive Authority thereof shall issue Writs of Election to fill such Vacancies.

The House of Representatives shall chuse their Speaker and other Officers; and shall have the sole Power of Impeachment.

Section 3 The Senate of the United States shall be composed of two Senators from each State, chosen by the Legislature thereof, for six Years; and each Senator shall have one Vote.[3]

Text is from the engrossed copy in the National Archives. Original spelling, capitalization, and punctuation have been retained.

Immediately after they shall be assembled in Consequence of the first Election, they shall be divided as equally as may be into three Classes. The Seats of the Senators of the first Class shall be vacated at the Expiration of the second Year, of the second Class at the Expiration of the fourth Year, and of the third Class at the Expiration of the sixth Year, so that one third may be chosen every second Year; and if Vacancies happen by Resignation, or otherwise, during the Recess of the Legislature of any State, the Executive thereof may make temporary Appointments until the next Meeting of the Legislature, which shall then fill such Vacancies.[4]

No Person shall be a Senator who shall not have attained to the Age of thirty Years, and been nine Years a Citizen of the United States, and who shall not, when elected, be an Inhabitant of that State for which he shall be chosen.

The Vice President of the United States shall be President of the Senate, but shall have no Vote, unless they be equally divided.

The Senate shall chuse their other Officers, and also a President pro tempore, in the Absence of the Vice President, or when he shall exercise the Office of President of the United States.

The Senate shall have the sole Power to try all Impeachments. When sitting for that Purpose, they shall be on Oath or Affirmation. When the President of the United States is tried, the Chief Justice shall preside: And no Person shall be convicted without the Concurrence of two thirds of the Members present.

Judgment in Cases of Impeachment shall not extend further than to removal from Office, and disqualification to hold and enjoy any Office of honor, Trust or Profit under the United States: but the Party convicted shall nevertheless be liable and subject to Indictment, Trial, Judgment and Punishment, according to Law.

Section 4   The Times, Places and Manner of holding Elections for Senators and Representatives, shall be prescribed in each State by the Legislature thereof, but the Congress may at any time by Law make or alter such Regulation, except as to the Places of chusing Senators.

The Congress shall assemble at least once in every Year, and such Meeting shall be on the first Monday in December, unless they shall by Law appoint a different Day.[5]

Section 5   Each House shall be the Judge of the Elections, Returns and Qualifications of its own Members, and a Majority of each shall constitute a Quorum to do Business; but a smaller Number may adjourn from day to day, and may be authorized to compel the Attendance of absent Members, in such Manner, and under such Penalties as each House may provide.

Each House may determine the Rules of its Proceedings, punish its Members for disorderly Behaviour, and, with the Concurrence of two thirds, expel a Member.

Each House shall keep a Journal of its Proceedings, and from time to time publish the same, excepting such Parts as may in their Judgment require Secrecy; and the Yeas and Nays of the Members of either House on any question shall, at the Desire of one fifth of those Present, be entered on the Journal.

Neither House, during the Session of Congress, shall, without the Consent of the other, adjourn for more than three days, nor to any other Place than that in which the two Houses shall be sitting.

Section 6   The Senators and Representatives shall receive a Compensation for their Services, to be ascertained by Law, and paid out of the Treasury of the United States. They shall in all Cases, except Treason, Felony and Breach of the Peace, be privileged from Arrest during their Attendance at the Session of their respective Houses, and in going to and returning from the same; and for any Speech or Debate in either House, they shall not be questioned in any other Place.

No Senator or Representative shall, during the Time for which he was elected, be appointed to any civil Office under the Authority of the United States, which shall have been created, or the Emoluments whereof shall have been encreased during such time; and no Person holding any Office under the United States, shall be a Member of either House during his Continuance in Office.

Section 7   All Bills for raising Revenue shall originate in the House of Representatives; but the Senate may propose or concur with Amendments as on other Bills.

Every Bill which shall have passed the House of Representatives and the Senate shall, before it become a Law, be presented to the President of the United States; If he approve he shall sign it, but if not he shall return it, with his Objections to that House in which it shall have originated, who shall enter the Objections at large on their Journal, and proceed to reconsider it. If after such Reconsideration two thirds of that House shall agree to pass the Bill, it shall be sent, together with the Objections, to the other House, by which it shall likewise be reconsidered, and if approved by two thirds of that House, it shall become a Law. But in all such Cases the Votes of both Houses shall be determined by yeas and Nays, and the Names of the Persons voting for and against the Bill shall be entered on the Journal of each House respectively. If any Bill shall not be returned by the President within ten Days (Sundays excepted) after it shall have been presented to him, the Same shall be a Law, in like Manner as if he had signed it, unless the Congress by their Adjournment prevent its Return, in which Case it shall not be a Law.

Every Order, Resolution, or Vote to which the Concurrence of the Senate and House of Representatives may be necessary (except on a question of Adjournment) shall be presented to the President of the United States; and before the Same shall take Effect, shall be approved by him, or being disapproved by him shall be repassed by two thirds of the Senate and House of Representatives, according to the Rules and Limitations prescribed in the Case of a Bill.

Section 8   The Congress shall have power To lay and collect Taxes, Duties, Imposts and Excises, to pay the Debts and provide for the common Defence and general Welfare of the United States; but all Duties, Imposts and Excises shall be uniform throughout the United States; To borrow Money on the credit of the United States; To regulate Commerce with foreign Nations, and among the several States, and with the Indian Tribes; To establish an uniform Rule of Naturalization, and uniform Laws on the subject of Bankruptcies throughout the United States; To coin Money, regulate the Value thereof, and of foreign Coin, and fix the Standard of Weights and Measures; To provide for the Punishment of counterfeiting the Securities and current Coin of the United States; To establish Post Offices and post Roads; To promote the Progress of Science and useful Arts, by securing for limited Times to Authors and Inventors the exclusive Right to their respective Writings and Discoveries; To constitute Tribunals inferior to the supreme Court; To define and punish Piracies and Felonies committed on the high Seas, and Offences against the Law of Nations;

To declare War, grant Letters of Marque and Reprisal, and make Rules concerning Captures on Land and Water; To raise and support Armies, but no Appropriation of Money to that Use shall be for a longer Term than two Years; To provide and maintain a Navy; To make Rules for the Government and Regulation of the land and naval Forces; To provide for calling forth the Militia to execute the Laws of the Union, suppress Insurrections and repel Invasions; To provide for organizing, arming, and disciplining, the Militia, and for governing such Part of them as may be employed in the Service of the United States, reserving to the States respectively, the Appointment of the Officers, and the Authority of training the Militia according to the discipline prescribed by Congress; To exercise exclusive Legislation in all Cases whatsoever, over such District (not exceeding ten Miles square) as may, by Cession of particular States, and the Acceptance of Congress, become the Seat of the Government of the United States, and to exercise like Authority over all Places purchased by the Consent of the Legislature of the State in which the Same shall be, for the Erection of Forts, Magazines, Arsenals, dock-Yards, and other needful Buildings;—And To make all Laws which shall be necessary and proper for carrying into Execution the foregoing Powers, and all other Powers vested by this Constitution in the Government of the United States, or in any Department or Officer thereof.

Section 9   The Migration or Importation of such Persons as any of the States now existing shall think proper to admit, shall not be prohibited by the Congress prior to the Year one thousand eight hundred and eight, but a Tax or duty may be imposed on such Importation, not exceeding ten dollars for each Person.

The Privilege of the Writ of Habeas Corpus shall not be suspended, unless when in Cases of Rebellion or Invasion the public Safety may require it.

No Bill of Attainder or ex post facto Law shall be passed.

No Capitation, or other direct, Tax shall be laid, unless in Proportion to the Census or Enumeration herein before directed to be taken.

No Tax or Duty shall be laid on Articles exported from any State.

No Preference shall be given by any Regulation of Commerce or Revenue to the Ports of one State over those of another: nor shall Vessels bound to, or from, one State, be obliged to enter, clear, or pay Duties in another.

No Money shall be drawn from the Treasury, but in Consequence of Appropriations made by Law, and a regular Statement and Account of the Receipts and Expenditures of all public Money shall be published from time to time.

No Title of Nobility shall be granted by the United States: And no Person holding any Office of Profit or Trust under them, shall, without the Consent of the Congress, accept of any present, Emolument, Office, or Title, of any kind whatever, from any King, Prince, or foreign State.

Section 10 No State shall enter into any Treaty, Alliance, or Confederation; grant Letters of Marque and Reprisal; coin Money; emit Bills of Credit; make any Thing but gold and silver Coin a Tender in Payment of Debts; pass any Bill of Attainder, ex post facto Law, or Law impairing the Obligation of Contracts, or grant any Title of Nobility.

No State shall, without the Consent of the Congress, lay any Imposts or Duties on Imports or Exports, except what may be absolutely necessary for executing its inspection Laws: and the net Produce of all Duties and Imposts, laid by any State on Imports or Exports, shall be for the Use of the Treasury of the United States; and all such Laws shall be subject to the Revision and Controul of the Congress.

No State shall, without the Consent of Congress, lay any Duty of Tonnage, keep Troops, or Ships of War in time of Peace, enter into any Agreement or Compact with another State, or with a foreign Power, or engage in War, unless actually invaded, or in such imminent Danger as will not admit of delay.

Article II

Section 1 The executive Power shall be vested in a President of the United States of America. He shall hold his Office during the Term of four Years, and, together with the Vice President, chosen for the same Term, be elected, as follows: Each State shall appoint, in such Manner as the Legislature thereof may direct, a Number of Electors, equal to the whole Number of Senators and Representatives to which the State may be entitled in the Congress: but no Senator or Representative, or Person holding an Office of Trust or Profit under the United States, shall be appointed an Elector.

The Electors shall meet in their respective States, and vote by Ballot for two Persons, of whom one at least shall not be an Inhabitant of the same State with themselves. And they shall make a List of all the Persons voted for, and of the Number of Votes for each; which List they shall sign and certify, and transmit sealed to the Seat of the Government of the United States, directed to the President of the Senate. The President of the Senate shall, in the Presence of the Senate and House of Representatives, open all the Certificates, and the Votes shall then be counted. The Person having the greatest Number of Votes shall be the President, if such Number be a Majority of the whole Number of Electors appointed; and if there be more than one who have such Majority, and have an equal Number of Votes, then the House of Representatives shall immediately chuse by Ballot one of them for President; and if no Person have a Majority, then from the five highest on the List the said House shall in like Manner chuse the President. But in chusing the President, the Votes shall be taken by States, the Representation from each State having one Vote; A quorum for this Purpose shall consist of a Member or Members from two thirds of the States, and a Majority of all the States shall be necessary to a Choice. In every Case, after the Choice of the President, the Person having the greatest Number of Votes of the Electors shall be the Vice President. But if there should remain two or more who have equal Votes, the Senate shall chuse from them by Ballot the Vice President.[6]

The Congress may determine the Time of chusing the Electors, and the Day on which they shall give their Votes; which Day shall be the same throughout the United States.

No Person except a natural born Citizen, or a Citizen of the United States, at the time of the Adoption of this Constitution, shall be eligible to the Office of President, neither shall any Person be eligible to that Office who shall not have attained to the Age of thirty five Years, and been fourteen Years a Resident within the United States.

In Case of the Removal of the President from Office, or of his Death, Resignation, or Inability to discharge the Powers and Duties of the said Office, the Same shall devolve on the Vice President, and the Congress may by Law provide for the Case of Removal, Death, Resignation or Inability, both of the President and Vice President, declaring what Officer shall then act as President, and such Officer shall act accordingly, until the Disability be removed, or a President shall be elected.[7]

The President shall, at stated Times, receive for his Services, a Compensation, which shall neither be encreased nor diminished during the Period for which he shall have been elected, and he shall not receive within that Period any other Emolument from the United States, or any of them.

Before he enter on the Execution of his Office, he shall take the following Oath or Affirmation:—"I do solemnly swear (or affirm) that I will faithfully execute the Office of President of the United States, and will to the best of my Ability, preserve, protect and defend the Constitution of the United States."

Section 2   The President shall be Commander in Chief of the Army and Navy of the United States, and of the Militia of the several States, when called into the actual Service of the United States; he may require the Opinion, in writing, of the principal Officer in each of the executive Departments, upon any Subject relating to the Duties of their respective Offices, and he shall have Power to grant Reprieves and Pardons for Offences against the United States, except in Cases of Impeachment.

He shall have Power, by and with the Advice and Consent of the Senate, to make Treaties, provided two thirds of the Senators present concur; and he shall nominate, and by and with the Advice and Consent of the Senate, shall appoint Ambassadors, other public Ministers and Consuls, Judges of the supreme Court, and all other Officers of the United States, whose Appointments are not herein otherwise provided for, and which shall be established by Law; but the Congress may by Law vest the Appointment of such inferior Officers, as they think proper, in the President alone, in the Courts of Law, or in the Heads of Departments.

The President shall have Power to fill up all Vacancies that may happen during the Recess of the Senate, by granting Commissions which shall expire at the End of their next Session.

Section 3   He shall from time to time give the Congress Information of the State of the Union, and recommend to their Consideration such Measures as he shall judge necessary and expedient; he may, on extraordinary Occasions, convene both Houses, or either of them, and in Case of Disagreement between them, with Respect to the Time of Adjournment, he may adjourn them to such Time as he shall think proper; he shall receive Ambassadors and other public Ministers; he shall take Care that the Laws be faithfully executed, and shall Commission all the Officers of the United States.

Section 4   The President, Vice President and all civil Officers of the United States, shall be removed from Office on Impeachment for, and Conviction of, Treason, Bribery, or other high Crimes and Misdemeanors.

Article III

Section 1   The judicial Power of the United States, shall be vested in one supreme Court, and in such inferior Courts as the Congress may from time to time ordain and establish.

The Judges, both of the supreme and inferior Courts, shall hold their Offices during good Behaviour, and shall, at stated Times, receive for their Services, a Compensation, which shall not be diminished during their Continuance in Office.

Section 2   The judicial Power shall extend to all Cases, in Law and Equity, arising under this Constitution, the Laws of the United States, and Treaties made, or which shall be made, under their Authority;—to all Cases affecting Ambassadors, other public Ministers and Consuls;—to all Cases of admiralty and maritime Jurisdiction;—to Controversies to which the United States shall be a Party;—to Controversies between two or more States;—between a State and Citizens of another State;[8]—between Citizens of different States,—between Citizens of the same State claiming Lands under Grants of different States, and between a State, or the Citizens thereof, and foreign States, Citizens or Subjects.

In all Cases affecting Ambassadors, other public Ministers and Consuls, and those in which a State shall be Party, the supreme Court shall have original Jurisdiction. In all the other Cases before mentioned, the supreme Court shall have appellate Jurisdiction, both as to Law and Fact, with such Exceptions, and under such Regulations as the Congress shall make.

The Trial of all Crimes, except in Cases of Impeachment, shall be by Jury; and such Trial shall be held in the State where the said Crimes shall have been committed; but when not committed within any State, the Trial shall be at such Place or Places as the Congress may by Law have directed.

Section 3 Treason against the United States, shall consist only in levying War against them, or in adhering to their Enemies, giving them Aid and Comfort. No Person shall be convicted of Treason unless on the Testimony of two Witnesses to the same overt Act, or on Confession in open Court.

The Congress shall have Power to declare the Punishment of Treason, but no Attainder of Treason shall work Corruption of Blood, or Forfeiture except during the Life of the Person attainted.

Article IV

Section 1 Full Faith and Credit shall be given in each State to the public Acts, Records, and judicial Proceedings of every other State. And the Congress may by general Laws prescribe the Manner in which such Acts, Records and Proceedings shall be proved, and the Effect thereof.

Section 2 The Citizens of each State shall be entitled to all Privileges and Immunities of Citizens in the several States.

A Person charged in any State with Treason, Felony, or other Crime, who shall flee from Justice, and be found in another State, shall on Demand of the executive Authority of the State from which he fled, be delivered up, to be removed to the State having Jurisdiction of the Crime.

No Person held to Service or Labour in one State, under the Laws thereof, escaping into another, shall, in Consequence of any Law or Regulation therein, be discharged from such Service or Labour, but shall be delivered up on Claim of the Party to whom such Service or Labour may be due.

Section 3 New States may be admitted by the Congress into this Union; but no new State shall be formed or erected within the Jurisdiction of any other State, nor any State be formed by the Junction of two or more States, or Parts of States, without the Consent of the Legislatures of the States concerned as well as of the Congress.

The Congress shall have Power to dispose of and make all needful Rules and Regulations respecting the Territory or other Property belonging to the United States; and nothing in this Constitution shall be so construed as to Prejudice any Claims of the United States, or of any particular State.

Section 4 The United States shall guarantee to every State in this Union a Republican Form of Government, and shall protect each of them against Invasion; and on Application of the Legislature, or of the Executive (when the Legislature cannot be convened) against domestic Violence.

Article V

The Congress, whenever two thirds of both Houses shall deem it necessary, shall propose Amendments to this Constitution, or, on the Application of the Legislatures of two thirds of the several

States, shall call a Convention for proposing Amendments, which, in either Case, shall be valid to all Intents and Purposes, as Part of this Constitution, when ratified by the Legislatures of three fourths of the several States, or by Conventions in three fourths thereof, as the one or the other Mode of Ratification may be proposed by the Congress; Provided that no Amendment which may be made prior to the Year One thousand eight hundred and eight shall in any Manner affect the first and fourth Clauses in the Ninth Section of the first Article; and that no State, without its Consent, shall be deprived of its equal Suffrage in the Senate.

Article VI

All Debts contracted and Engagements entered into, before the Adoption of this Constitution, shall be as valid against the United States under this Constitution, as under the Confederation.

This Constitution, and the Laws of the United States which shall be made in Pursuance thereof; and all Treaties made, or which shall be made, under the Authority of the United States, shall be the supreme Law of the Land; and the Judges in every State shall be bound thereby, any Thing in the Constitution or Laws of any State to the Contrary notwithstanding.

The Senators and Representatives before mentioned, and the Members of the several State Legislatures, and all executive and judicial Officers, both of the United States and of the several States, shall be bound by Oath or Affirmation, to support this Constitution; but no religious Test shall ever be required as a Qualification to any Office or public Trust under the United States.

Article VII

The Ratification of the Conventions of nine States, shall be sufficient for the Establishment of this Constitution between the States so ratifying the Same.

Done in Convention by the Unanimous Consent of the States present the Seventeenth Day of September in the Year of our Lord one thousand seven hundred and Eighty seven and of the Independence of the United States of America the Twelfth. In witness whereof We have hereunto subscribed our Names,

Articles in Addition to, and Amendment of, the Constitution of the United States of America, Proposed by Congress, and Ratified by the Legislatures of the Several States, Pursuant to the Fifth Article of the Original Constitution.

Amendment I[9]

Congress shall make no law respecting an establishment of religion, or prohibiting the free exercise thereof; or abridging the freedom of speech, or of the press; or the right of the people peaceably to assemble, and to petition the Government for a redress of grievances.

Amendment II

A well regulated Militia, being necessary to the security of a free State, the right of the people to keep and bear Arms shall not be infringed.

Amendment III

No Soldier shall, in time of peace, be quartered in any house, without the consent of the Owner, nor in time of war, but in a manner to be prescribed by law.

Amendment IV

The right of the people to be secure in their persons, houses, papers, and effects, against unreasonable searches and seizures, shall not be violated, and no Warrants shall issue, but upon probable cause, supported by Oath or affirmation, and particularly describing the place to be searched, and the persons or things to be seized.

Amendment V

No person shall be held to answer for a capital or otherwise infamous crime, unless on a present-ment or indictment of a Grand Jury, except in cases arising in the land or naval forces, or in the Militia, when in actual service in time of War or public danger; nor shall any person be subject for the same offence to be twice put in jeopardy of life or limb; nor shall be compelled in any criminal case to be a witness against himself, nor be deprived of life, liberty, or property, without due process of law; nor shall private property be taken for public use, without just compensation.

Amendment VI

In all criminal prosecutions, the accused shall enjoy the right to a speedy and public trial, by an impartial jury of the State and district wherein the crime shall have been committed, which dis-trict shall have been previously ascertained by law, and to be informed of the nature and cause of the accusation; to be confronted with the witnesses against him; to have compulsory process for obtaining witnesses in his favor, and to have the Assistance of Counsel for his defence.

Amendment VII

In suits at common law, where the value in controversy shall exceed twenty dollars, the right of trial by jury shall be preserved, and no fact tried by a jury, shall be otherwise reexamined in any Court of the United States, than according to the rules of the common law.

Amendment VIII

Excessive bail shall not be required, nor excessive fines imposed, nor cruel and unusual punish-ments inflicted.

Amendment IX

The enumeration in the Constitution, of certain rights, shall not be construed to deny or dispar-age others retained by the people.

Amendment X

The powers not delegated to the United States by the Constitution; nor prohibited by it to the States, are reserved to the States respectively, or to the people.

Amendment XI[10]

The Judicial power of the United States shall not be construed to extend to any suit in law or equity, commenced or prosecuted against one of the United States by Citizens of another State, or by Citizens or Subjects of any Foreign State.

Amendment XII[11]

The Electors shall meet in their respective States and vote by ballot for President and Vice-President, one of whom, at least, shall not be an inhabitant of the same State with themselves; they shall name in their ballots the person voted for as President, and in distinct ballots the person voted for as Vice-President, and they shall make distinct lists of all persons voted for as President, and of all persons voted for as Vice-President, and of the number of votes for each, which lists they shall sign and cer-tify, and transmit sealed to the seat of the government of the United States, directed to the President of the Senate;—The President of the Senate shall, in the presence of the Senate and House of Representatives, open all the certificates and the votes shall then be counted;—The person having the greatest number of votes for President, shall be the President, if such number be a majority of the whole number of Electors appointed; and if no person have such majority, then from the persons having the highest numbers not exceeding three on the list of those voted for as President, the House of Representatives shall choose immediately, by ballot, the President.

But in choosing the President, the votes shall be taken by states, the representation from each state having one vote; a quorum for this purpose shall consist of a member or members from two-thirds of the states, and a majority of all the states shall be necessary to a choice. And if the House of Representatives shall not choose a President whenever the right of choice shall devolve upon them, before the fourth day of March next following, then the Vice-President shall act as President, as in the case of the death or other constitutional disability of the President.—The person having the greatest number of votes as Vice-President, shall be the Vice-President, if such number be a majority of the whole number of Electors appointed, and if no person have a majority, then from the two highest numbers on the list, the Senate shall choose the Vice-President; a quorum for the purpose shall consist of two-thirds of the whole number of Senators, and a majority of the whole number shall be necessary to a choice. But no person constitutionally ineligible to the office of President shall be eligible to that of Vice-President of the United States.

Amendment XIII[12]

Section 1   Neither slavery nor involuntary servitude, except as a punishment for crime whereof the party shall have been duly convicted, shall exist within the United States, or any place subject to their jurisdiction.

Section 2   Congress shall have power to enforce this article by appropriate legislation.

Amendment XIV[13]

Section 1   All persons born or naturalized in the United States, and subject to the jurisdiction thereof, are citizens of the United States and of the State wherein they reside. No State shall make or enforce any law which shall abridge the privileges or immunities of citizens of the United States; nor shall any State deprive any person of life, liberty, or property, without due process of law; nor deny to any person within its jurisdiction the equal protection of the laws.

Section 2   Representatives shall be apportioned among the several States according to their respective numbers, counting the whole number of persons in each State, excluding Indians not taxed. But when the right to vote at any election for the choice of electors for President and Vice-President of the United States, Representatives in Congress, the Executive and Judicial officers of a State, or the members of the Legislature thereof, is denied to any of the male inhabitants of such State, being twenty-one years of age, and citizens of the United States, or in any way abridged, except for participation in rebellion, or other crime, the basis of representation therein shall be reduced in the proportion which the number of such male citizens shall bear to the whole number of male citizens twenty-one years of age in such State.

Section 3   No person shall be a Senator or Representative in Congress, or elector of President and Vice-President, or hold any office, civil or military, under the United States, or under any State, who, having previously taken an oath, as a member of Congress, or as an officer of the United States, or as a member of any State legislature, or as an executive or judicial officer of any State, to support the Constitution of the United States, shall have engaged in insurrection or rebellion against the same, or given aid or comfort to the enemies thereof. But Congress may by a vote of two-thirds of each House, remove such disability.

Section 4   The validity of the public debt of the United States, authorized by law, including debts incurred for payment of pensions and bounties for services in suppressing insurrection or rebellion, shall not be questioned. But neither the United States nor any State shall assume or pay any debt or obligation incurred in aid of insurrection or rebellion against the United States, or any claim for the loss or emancipation of any slave; but all such debts, obligations, and claims shall be held illegal and void.

Section 5   The Congress shall have the power to enforce, by appropriate legislation, the provisions of this article.

Amendment XV[14]

Section 1   The right of citizens of the United States to vote shall not be denied or abridged by the United States or by any State on account of race, color, or previous conditions of servitude—

Section 2   The Congress shall have power to enforce this article by appropriate legislation.

Amendment XVI[15]

The Congress shall have power to lay and collect taxes on incomes, from whatever source derived, without apportionment among the several States, and without regard to any census or enumeration.

Amendment XVII[16]

The Senate of the United States shall be composed of two Senators from each State, elected by the people thereof, for six years; and each Senator shall have one vote. The electors in each State shall have the qualifications requisite for electors of the most numerous branch of the State legislatures.

When vacancies happen in the representation of any State in the Senate, the executive authority of such State shall issue writs of election to fill such vacancies: Provided, That the legislature of any State may empower the executive thereof to make temporary appointments until the people fill the vacancies by election as the legislature may direct.

This amendment shall not be so construed as to affect the election or term of any Senator chosen before it becomes valid as part of the Constitution.

Amendment XVIII[17]

Section 1   After one year from the ratification of this article the manufacture, sale, or transportation of intoxicating liquors within, the importation thereof into, or the exportation thereof from the United States and all territory subject to the jurisdiction thereof for beverage purposes is hereby prohibited.

Section 2   The Congress and the several States shall have concurrent power to enforce this article by appropriate legislation.

Section 3   This article shall be inoperative unless it shall have been ratified as an amendment to the Constitution by the legislatures of the several States, as provided in the Constitution, within seven years from the date of the submission hereof to the States by the Congress.

Amendment XIX[18]

The right of citizens of the United States to vote shall not be denied or abridged by the United States or by any State on account of sex.

Congress shall have power to enforce this article by appropriate legislation.

Amendment XX[19]

Section 1   The terms of the President and Vice-President shall end at noon on the 20th day of January, and the terms of Senators and Representatives at noon on the 3d day of January, of the years in which such terms would have ended if this article had not been ratified; and the terms of their successors shall then begin.

Section 2   The Congress shall assemble at least once in every year, and such meeting shall begin at noon on the 3d day of January, unless they shall by law appoint a different day.

Section 3   If, at the time fixed for the beginning of the term of the President, the President elect shall have died, the Vice-President elect shall become President. If a President shall not have been chosen before the time fixed for the beginning of his term, or if the President elect shall have failed to qualify, then the Vice-President elect shall act as President until a President shall have qualified; and the Congress may by law provide for the case wherein neither a President elect nor a Vice-President elect shall have qualified, declaring who shall then act as President, or the manner in which one who is to act shall be selected, and such person shall act accordingly until a President or Vice-President shall have qualified.

Section 4   The Congress may by law provide for the case of the death of any of the persons from whom the House of Representatives may choose a President whenever the right of choice shall have devolved upon them, and for the case of the death of any of the persons from whom the Senate may choose a Vice-President whenever the right of choice shall have devolved upon them.

Section 5   Sections 1 and 2 shall take effect on the 15th day of October following the ratification of this article.

Section 6   This article shall be inoperative unless it shall have been ratified as an amendment to the Constitution by the legislatures of three-fourths of the several States within seven years from the date of its submission.

Amendment XXI[20]

Section 1   The eighteenth article of amendment to the Constitution of the United States is hereby repealed.

Section 2   The transportation or importation into any State, Territory, or possession of the United States for delivery or use therein of intoxicating liquors, in violation of the laws thereof, is hereby prohibited.

Section 3   This article shall be inoperative unless it shall have been ratified as an amendment to the Constitution by conventions in the several States, as provided in the Constitution, within seven years from the date of the submission hereof to the States by the Congress.

Amendment XXII[21]

No person shall be elected to the office of the President more than twice, and no person who has held the office of President, or acted as President, for more than two years of a term to which some other person was elected President shall be elected to the office of the President more than once.

But this Article shall not apply to any person holding the office of President when this Article was proposed by the Congress, and shall not prevent any person who may be holding the office of President, or acting as President, during the term within which this Article becomes operative from holding the office of President or acting as President during the remainder of such term.

Amendment XXIII[22]

Section 1   The District constituting the seat of Government of the United States shall appoint in such manner as the Congress may direct: A number of electors of President and Vice President equal to the whole number of Senators and Representatives in Congress to which the District would be entitled if it were a State, but in no event more than the least populous State; they shall be in addition to those appointed by the States, but they shall be considered, for the purposes of the election of President and Vice President, to be electors appointed by the State; and they shall meet in the District and perform such duties as provided by the twelfth article of amendment.

Section 2   The Congress shall have power to enforce this article by appropriate legislation.

Amendment XXIV[23]

Section 1   The right of citizens of the United States to vote in any primary or other election for President or Vice President, or for Senator or Representative in Congress, shall not be denied or abridged by the United States or any State by reason of failure to pay any poll tax or other tax.

Section 2   The Congress shall have power to enforce this article by appropriate legislation.

Amendment XXV[24]

Section 1   In case of the removal of the President from office or of his death or resignation, the Vice President shall become President.

Section 2   Whenever there is a vacancy in the office of the Vice President, the President shall nominate a Vice President who shall take office upon confirmation by a majority vote of both Houses of Congress.

Section 3   Whenever the President transmits to the President pro tempore of the Senate and the Speaker of the House of Representatives his written declaration that he is unable to discharge the powers and duties of his office, and until he transmits them a written declaration to the contrary, such powers and duties shall be discharged by the Vice President as Acting President.

Section 4   Whenever the Vice President and a majority of either the principal officers of the executive department or of such other body as Congress may by law provide, transmit to the President pro tempore of the Senate and the Speaker of the House of Representatives their written declaration that the President is unable to discharge the powers and duties of his office, the Vice President shall immediately assume the powers and duties of the office of Acting President.

Thereafter, when the President transmits to the President pro tempore of the Senate and the Speaker of the House of Representatives his written declaration that no inability exists, he shall resume the powers and duties of his office unless the Vice President and a majority of either the principal officers of the executive department or of such other body as Congress may by law provide, transmit within four days to the President pro tempore of the Senate and the Speaker of the House of Representatives their written declaration that the President is unable to discharge the powers and duties of his office. Thereupon Congress shall decide the issue, assembling within forty-eight hours for that purpose if not in session. If the Congress, within twenty-one days after receipt of the latter written declaration, or, if Congress is not in session, within twenty-one days after Congress is required to assemble, determines by two-thirds vote of both Houses that the President is unable to discharge the powers and duties of his office, the Vice President shall continue to discharge the same as Acting President; otherwise, the President shall resume the powers and duties of his office.

Amendment XXVI[25]

Section 1   The right of citizens of the United States, who are eighteen years of age or older, to vote shall not be denied or abridged by the United States or by any State on account of age.

Section 2   The Congress shall have power to enforce this article by appropriate legislation.

Amendment XXVII[26]

No law, varying the compensation for the service of the Senators and Representatives, shall take effect, until an election of Representatives shall have intervened.

NOTES

1. Modified by the Sixteenth Amendment.
2. Replaced by the Fourteenth Amendment.
3. Superseded by the Seventeenth Amendment.
4. Modified by the Seventeenth Amendment.
5. Superseded by the Twentieth Amendment.
6. Superseded by the Twelfth Amendment.
7. Modified by the Twenty-fifth Amendment.
8. Modified by the Eleventh Amendment.
9. The first ten amendments were passed by Congress September 25, 1789. They were ratified by three-fourths of the states December 15, 1791.
10. Passed March 4, 1794. Ratified January 23, 1795.
11. Passed December 9, 1803. Ratified June 15, 1804.
12. Passed January 31, 1865. Ratified December 6, 1865.
13. Passed June 13, 1866. Ratified July 9, 1868.
14. Passed February 26, 1869. Ratified February 2, 1870.
15. Passed July 12, 1909. Ratified February 3, 1913.
16. Passed May 13, 1912. Ratified April 8, 1913.
17. Passed December 18, 1917. Ratified January 16, 1919.
18. Passed June 4, 1919. Ratified August 18, 1920.
19. Passed March 2, 1932. Ratified January 23, 1933.
20. Passed February 20, 1933. Ratified December 5, 1933.
21. Passed March 12, 1947. Ratified March 1, 1951.
22. Passed June 16, 1960. Ratified April 3, 1961.
23. Passed August 27, 1962. Ratified January 23, 1964.
24. Passed July 6, 1965. Ratified February 11, 1967.
25. Passed March 23, 1971. Ratified July 5, 1971.
26. Passed September 25, 1789. Ratified May 7, 1992.

Index

AAA (Agricultural Adjustment Administration), 826–827

ABA (American Basketball Association), 1040

Abbott, Edith, 689

ABC television, 927, 966

Abell, Mary, 605

Abortion rights, 980

Abu Ghraib prison, 1068

ACA (Affordable Health Care for America Act of 2010), 1078, 1082, 1083–1085

AC (alternating current), 628

Acheson, Dean, 892, 902, 972

Acid rain, 979

ACLU (American Civil Liberties Union), 801

Activism: African American, 1016–1017; American Indian, 1017–1019; anti-government, 1022–1025; Asian American, 1021–1022; grassroots, 946, 953, 957, 964, 1000, 1032; LGBT, 1015–1016; in Spanish-speaking communities, 1019–1021; Vietnam War and, 965, 971, 983–985. *See also* Civil rights movement; Women's movement; *specific issues and movements*

ACT UP (Aids Coalition to Unleash Power), 1016

ADA (Americans with Disabilities Act of 1990), 1006

Addams, Jane, 683, 688–690, 696, 751

Advertising: consumer culture and, 633–634, 780. *See also* Propaganda

AERA (American Equal Rights Association), 575

AFDC (Aid to Families with Dependent Children), 977, 1004

Affirmative action, 980, 1022–1023, 1025

The Affluent Society (Galbraith), 920

Affordable Health Care for America Act of 2010 (ACA), 1078, 1082, 1083–1085

Afghanistan: Soviet invasion of, 998; U.S. war in, 1067, 1072, 1077

AFL (American Federation of Labor), 643–645, 872, 922

African Americans: activism among, 1016–1017; clubwomen and, 691; cultural advances of, 806–809; emigration of, 561, 615; in First World War, 756–757; in Harlem, 804; literacy of, 569; literary and

artistic awakening among, 809; lynching of, 616; in middle class, 617–618, 674; migration to northern cities, 755, 757 (map), 803, 878; New Deal and, 844; in political office during Reconstruction, 578; population patterns, 942(map); Reagan economics benefiting, 1002–1003; in Spanish-American War, 724; in suburbs, 908; in workforce, 673–674, 872; Zoot Suit Riots and, 876. *See also* Civil rights movement

Africanization of southern government myth, 579

Agnew, Spiro, 988

Agrarians, 812

Agricultural Adjustment Act of 1933, 825, 826

Agricultural Adjustment Administration (AAA), 826–827

Agriculture: depression in, 792; New Deal reforms and, 825–827; in New South, 614–615. *See also* Farms and farming

Aguinaldo, Emilio, 726

AHA (American Hospital Association), 905

Aids Coalition to Unleash Power (ACT UP), 1016

AIDS/HIV, 1016

Aid to Families with Dependent Children (AFDC), 977, 1004

AIM (American Indian Movement), 1018

Airline industry, 786

Alabama (ship), 578

Albany & Susquehanna Railroad, 629

Albright, Madeleine, 1055

Alcott, Louis May, 637

Ali, Muhammad, 970

Alien Land Law of 1913, 670

Alito, Samuel, 1005, 1064

Allen, Woody, 1046

Allende Gossens, Salvador, 986

Alliance for Progress, 933

Allies (First World War), 745, 748, 752, 753–755. *See also* First World War

Allies (Second World War): advances by, 864 (map); code-breaking operations of, 860; North Africa and Italy campaigns, 860–861; Operation OVERLORD, 861–862; on organizational structure of United Nations, 879–880; Pacific campaign, 862–865,